THE HP PHENOMENON

THE HP PHENOMENON

INNOVATION AND BUSINESS TRANSFORMATION

Charles H. House and Raymond L. Price

STANFORD BUSINESS BOOKS
An Imprint of Stanford University Press
Stanford, California

Stanford University Press
Stanford, California

Printed in the United States of America on acid-free, archival-quality paper

Library of Congress Cataloging-in-Publication Data
House, Charles H.
The HP phenomenon : innovation and business transformation / Charles H. House and Raymond L. Price.
p. cm.
Includes bibliographical references and index.
ISBN 978-0-8047-5286-2 (cloth : alk. paper)
1. Hewlett-Packard Company—History. 2. Hewlett-Packard Company—Management. 3. Electronic industries—United States—Management—Case studies. 4. Computer industry—United States—Management—Case studies. I. Price, Raymond L. (Raymond Lewis) II. Title.
HD9696.A3U5588 2009
338.7'610040973—dc22
2009011576

Typeset by Bruce Lundquist in 10/15 Sabon

We dedicate this book to the men and women, past and present, of the Hewlett-Packard Company—who made it what it became, who nurtured it into greatness, and who persevered through six transformations to keep the HP Way alive and well for generations.

Contents

CONTENTS

Figures

FIGURES

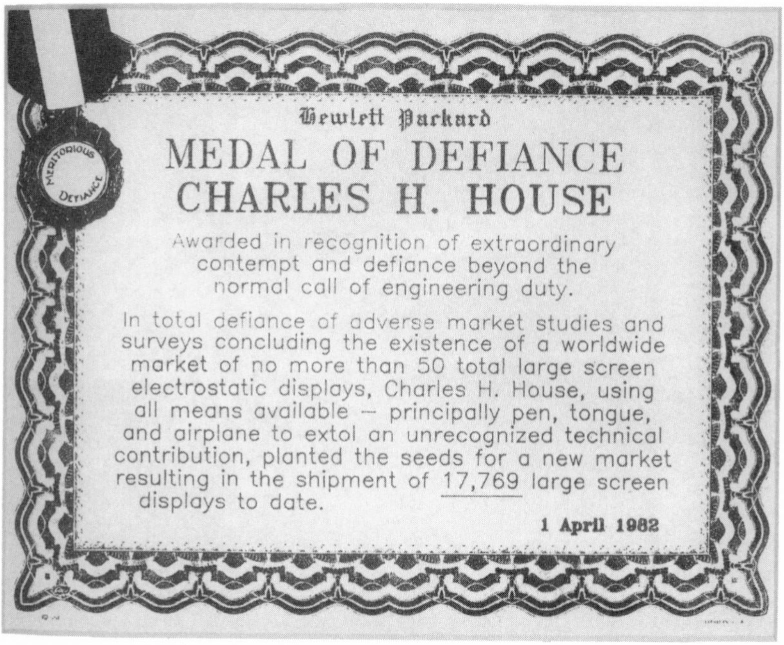
Hewlett Packard

MEDAL OF DEFIANCE
CHARLES H. HOUSE

Awarded in recognition of extraordinary contempt and defiance beyond the normal call of engineering duty.

In total defiance of adverse market studies and surveys concluding the existence of a worldwide market of no more than 50 total large screen electrostatic displays, Charles H. House, using all means available – principally pen, tongue, and airplane to extol an unrecognized technical contribution, planted the seeds for a new market resulting in the shipment of 17,769 large screen displays to date.

1 April 1982

Foreword

You might think twice about reading a book by the only person in the history of Hewlett-Packard to win the company's Award for Meritorious Defiance.

But it turns out Chuck House is an intriguing storyteller with a very important topic and tons of inside information.

Chuck was given the "Hewlett-Packard Award for Meritorious Defiance" in 1982 to honor his indefatigable (some might call it bull-headed) pursuit of a large-screen electrostatic monitor—a product that the initial target customer had declined ("The display is too fuzzy"); his boss had killed ("Does not meet spec"); his division's marketing department had roundly rejected ("There are too few customers"); and the company's CEO, Dave Packard, had unequivocally deep-sixed while reviewing the product ("When I come back in a year, I don't want to see that product in the lab!").

When Chuck heard that the CEO had killed his product, his response was typically entrepreneurial: "If we have it in production before he returns, he won't find it in the lab!" His courageous boss, Dar Howard, funded the project for another year, and, indeed, when Packard came back a year later, he did not see it in the lab: the monitor had already gone through accelerated testing and into production, and was on its way to earning over $10 million a year in sales.

Chuck and Dar were honored for this disobedience—which tells us that Hewlett-Packard was very different from the typical company of the day. It is this difference, and Chuck's total immersion as the HP story evolved, that makes this book so fascinating.

Chuck started at HP in Palo Alto, California, in 1962 as an oscilloscope designer. By then, Bill Hewlett and Dave Packard had already moved well beyond the small engineering job shop they had founded in a garage in 1939 and become leaders in measuring equipment for electronics, communication systems, and computers. The high-tech field was still young; products as well as corporate cultures were rapidly evolving; and Bill and Dave were essentially making it up as they went along, trusting their smarts and intuition to guide them as they pursued new products and new ways of managing their company. They had no idea that the freedoms they gave their teams; their combination of trust, fairness, and uncompromising honesty; and their willingness to change direction and embrace the new would become a model for their industry. Nor could they know that the culture they were inventing would spread to thousands of other companies and become so integral to the success of the American high-tech industry.

The HP culture was built on contribution, profitability, fairness, and trust. It was an exacting culture. At the same time that it respected and encouraged innovation and intrapreneuring, it was committed to the highest standards of honesty and technical excellence. The culture was not planned, or even envisioned, from the start. Rather, two great leaders—men of integrity, fairness, and great technical gifts—conducted a continuous, dynamic experiment. In the process, they discovered the genes of one of America's greatest institutions.

Chuck's story at HP reflects the development of that culture. He moved with the Oscilloscope Division to Colorado Springs in 1964, where he developed the display system a year later. When the first widescreen electrostatic display failed to meet the specifications of its intended customer, Chuck didn't see failure; instead he saw potential. "The monitor isn't right for that customer," he said, "but it will be right for someone." And with his boss's permission, he took vacation time, removed the front seat of his VW, loaded the monitor into the empty space, and set off for Arizona and California to find customers. At another company, such intrapreneurialism would have been unthinkable—but HP gave that kind of discretion to its managers. And the freedom paid off. Chuck did indeed find customers, and those customers encouraged his boss to continue funding the project. Years later, Dave Packard acknowledged how right Chuck and his boss had been.

Over the next twenty-nine years, Chuck had a major role in the development of many of HP's products—an output that the company formally recognized in 1988 with the creation and presentation of the "Chuck

House Productivity Award." By that time, Chuck had risen to the position of corporate engineering director and had witnessed a hundred-fold growth of the company, from $98 million in mid-1962 to $9.8 billion. In *The HP Phenomenon* he chronicles that growth with an engineer's eye on the products and a manager's attention to the people.

I've long thought that someone who lived that culture from its early days should write a book about how it happened and teach us the recipe for the secret sauce. Someone has finally done it, and done a superb job.

This is an important book for the same reason that Hewlett-Packard is an important company—because the growth and learning curve described are not just those of a single company, but of all of Silicon Valley. HP's evolution mirrors the evolution of the Valley—its technology, its leadership style, its business and culture. And even for an old-timer like myself, who considers himself something of a student of Silicon Valley, Chuck's account contains innumerable "aha's" as well as lessons on leadership ready to apply. For people who live in the high-tech culture and want to understand it, this book is required reading.

Gifford Pinchot
April 2009

THE HP PHENOMENON

INTRODUCTION

Shards in the Glass Ceiling

The experiment ended, suddenly and ignobly. It caught most industry watchers by surprise, even though they all claimed soon enough that they'd have done the same thing. Carly Fiorina, Hewlett-Packard's forceful CEO, saw the storm brewing; in mid-January at the prestigious Davos, Switzerland, World Economic Forum she broached the question with several CEOS of how to "retire" gracefully. The denouement was swift, the judgment merciless. On Monday, February 7, 2005, HP's board chairperson, Pattie Dunn, fired Fiorina for poor performance, for arrogance, for self-aggrandizement, for all manner of ills.

A late January *Fortune* story anticipated her departure (ironically, the issue dateline was February 7). *BusinessWeek* rushed an article to print: "Can Anyone Save HP?" *The Wall Street Journal* carried pages of analysis and interpretation. *Fortune* hurried a self-congratulatory second story, hinting that they perhaps had stimulated the action.[1]

HP's business record, in aggregate, wasn't that bad. Moreover, it was getting better. Compared to a group of six other large American technology vendors—IBM, Dell, Intel, Microsoft, Sun, and Cisco—HP was above median on revenue growth after the consolidation of Compaq, and at median for profits. Sure, the stock price had languished, but no worse than that of Intel, Microsoft, or Oracle. Sun's capitalization had nearly evaporated, along with any notion of profits. HP had nearly driven IBM out of the personal computer (PC) business as it tried to master the cost-cutting requirements imposed by Dell's sales model. Also important, HP seemed to have rebuffed Dell's energetic efforts to make inroads into desktop printing.

Hewlett-Packard had missed Fiorina's plans, forecasts, and possibilities once again. Moreover, the photogenic CEO seemed too proud, or too insecure, to accept help. The board wanted her to bring in a senior chief operating officer, a steady COO to hold down the fort and manage day-to-day operations while Carly traveled, exhorting and charming customers, conferences, workshops, and the press. An astute board would already have lined up COO candidates. But Fiorina—sore from the bruising merger fight over Compaq—chose to fight again, only to be summarily guillotined, a classic Robespierre in the high-tech field.

Reactions to Fiorina's dismissal were mixed. Board members opined that Fiorina was great, even spectacular, at what she did well, but that HP needed a lot more of what she didn't do well. Director Tom Perkins would say a year later, "She'd still be in place, with a winning strategy, if she'd just accepted a strong helper COO."[2] Many professional women were anguished—Carly was their inspiration, not only surmounting the glass ceiling but taking on and besting the strongest in the land, garnering admiring press and acclaim. Many long-term HPites were overjoyed—their vaunted HP Way could now be resurrected, after the Huns had stormed the castle. Other CEOs—fellow travelers in the most lonely of seats—were more pensive, more measured, and perhaps a little worried. Who knew when their turn might come?

What had happened at this proud company? How had it come to this? Many thought back to 1999. Hewlett-Packard had missed the dot-com boom. CEO Lew Platt, voted "class plugger" in high school, had a decidedly low-key leadership style that lost the confidence of the board. From consistent top-ten rankings in lists of best-managed, highest-quality, and most-admired companies for decades, Hewlett-Packard fell in peoples' perceptions markedly, for example to 43rd in *Fortune*'s 2000 list of best companies to work for.[3]

Fiorina, flamboyant where all previous leadership was subdued, had brought star quality to the job. She had proclaimed that the new, streamlined HP would remain true to the culture of integrity and respect known as the HP Way. For a honeymoon period, enthusiasm soared. And then reality set in with a visibly failed acquisition attempt. Disillusionment followed, and then the contested Compaq plan caused a public schism with the Hewlett and Packard families. Fiorina had polarized the HP community in ways foreign to its history. The business world took notice. Again, ratings plummeted—HP was 173rd of 611 companies in the February 2006 *Fortune* "Most Admired" listing.[4] When revenue and earnings projections fell short in third quarter fiscal 2004, Fiorina's game essentially was over.

Mark Hurd was named to replace Fiorina. He was a strange choice by some standards, certainly for business pundits and market analysts who sought a big-name replacement. Hurd was low-key, conservative, and operational where Carly was high-profile, bold, and strategic. A few noted that Hurd was more like Dave Packard, the more well-known of the two founders. Today many might even compare his public reticence more to Hewlett's. Hurd fits the HP image, if not the culture, in a way that Carly never did.

The business press proffered Hurd advice aplenty: "Sell off the imaging and printing lines," said some, picking up Walter Hewlett's proposal during the merger battle. "Abandon low-margin PCs, where Dell has HP beat," said others. Some clamored for a services acquisition, akin to the PricewaterhouseCoopers deal that Fiorina almost accomplished. Some despaired: "HP will never regain its spot in the sun." Hurd did nothing flashy, held few press conferences, and, much like Gerstner at IBM a decade earlier,[5] eschewed describing his vision of "where next."

A year later, the critics had moved on. A few analysts noted that Hurd seemed to be righting things. After the robust third-quarter 2006 earnings statement was compared to the earnings shortfall at Dell, a growing minority began to comment that maybe Fiorina's strategy wasn't so bad after all:

> While analysts praise Hurd's low-key style, many are quick to credit Fiorina for laying the groundwork. HP desperately needed someone like her, said Roger L. Kay, president of Endpoint Technologies Associates. "Carly did a lot of the shaking up, which was necessary to get the hidebound organization liquefied again—and that left the field open for Mark Hurd to reorganize. The ironic postscript here is that Carly deserves far more credit than she got," Kay said.[6]

And then, unbelievably, a second bombshell hit.

Challenges to the HP Way

SEPTEMBER 28, 2006, WASHINGTON, D.C.: Grim-faced, CEO Mark Hurd strode to the hotseat in front of the House Investigative Committee that Patricia Dunn had just vacated. Dunn, the recently defrocked board chairperson of the legendary Hewlett-Packard Company, was defensive rather than contrite about the use of "pretexting"—using private investigators to sleuth personal telephone records to locate the source of "leaks" from HP board members to the press. She seemed to condone widespread spying to contain boardroom leaks—leaks felt critical enough to occasion illegal surveillance of twenty citizens, arguing that it was just something to be expected in this day and age. Hurd took a different tack, intoning that Hewlett-Packard employees didn't deserve either the spying or the associated scandal. Unable to explain his own oversight of the actions, he solemnly pledged to correct this blot on the integrity of the company—historically the icon of trust and fair dealing in corporate America. A blog, repeated in *BusinessWeek,* captured the mood: "Our boardroom lighting system is powered solely by Hewlett and Packard spinning in their graves."[7]

In the grand sweep of history, the pretexting issue at Hewlett-Packard may well be but a journalistic footnote. But it did highlight two significant facts—first, that electronic snooping, the Orwellian Big Brother concern in the book *1984,* has become far more the norm in our society than we might care to recognize; second, even the Silicon Valley company revered for decades for its leadership and ethics proved susceptible.

Some of the old guard railed, "The HP Way is dead, dead, dead." Many alumni stated that the only company with a shred of the HP Way today is Agilent Technologies, which should have kept the HP name in the divestiture in 1999. To most outsiders, though, HP history has been veiled and obscure, even if the HP Way is legendary.

The HP story is unique in American business, with fundamental leadership lessons at many junctures. The evolution of a successful company with strong allegiances to its employees and its communities is compelling enough. When that evolution is coupled with consistent profitability and revenue growth comparable to the most powerful global corporations, it becomes imperative to understand HP history, strategies, and approaches.

HP, known primarily for its employee-centric "HP Way," has always been a high-tech electronics equipment manufacturer. Many may be aware that HP borrowed the General Electric organizational model of quasi-autonomous divisions, but HP atomized its divisions by an order of magnitude, creating unusual renewal strengths previously unknown in large enterprise and fueling a consistent growth rate far longer than in any other high-tech company. Moreover, HP cannibalized its roots repeatedly, replacing established products with bold new ideas. Focusing on contribution rather than endeavor, HP morphed six times into something else, changing its leading products each decade. Such transformation is unparalleled in modern business. Even more stunning is the discovery that Hewlett resisted three transformations, and Packard is on record at some point opposed to each of the six. So much for today's conventional leadership wisdom!

In HP history, transformative change always left its mark, as well as casualties along the way; each time people said that HP had lost its way, never to be regained. By the time the founders died (Packard in 1996, Hewlett in 2001), the company was yet again in transition. In a company four hundred times the size of HP when Packard was last CEO, the mythic origins could seem ancient and irrelevant, if not antithetical. Indeed, as Hewlett-Packard morphs into something else for the sixth time in the sixth decade after going public, it feels different. To be sure, it is different: the Compaq acquisition brought a huge contingent of new employees who didn't share the cultural DNA; pretexting was an enormous challenge to a company whose very foundations epitomized the purest business ethics; and the EDS acquisition, announced in 2008, augurs to push the envelope still further, nearly doubling the number of employees while adding just 20 percent to revenues.

But companies, like people, cannot change their stripes easily. Their style gets baked in, perpetuated, and inculcated so deeply that it becomes ingrained, patterned, and virtually innate. Indeed, if culture is something that becomes intrinsic and deep, it should be able to resist and repel even substantial challenges, to reassert its imprint and impact.

We believe that HP's core values, approach, attitude, culture, and philosophy are built solidly into the fiber of its employees and practices, broadly determining its overall capability. The future can be inferred from the past. Not, of course, in a lineal revenue or even product sector projection, but absolutely in terms of competitive response and opportunity recognition. The legacy of the founders and the cultural imprint of the HP Way are not passing historical phenomena. They are deeply embedded. Rather than becoming anachronistic, even impediments to coping with today's world, they are more relevant than ever to provide a compass for innovative and differential contribution, as this huge corporation—the largest high-tech firm on the globe—becomes ever more virtual and diffuse.

The Evolution of HP

Hewlett-Packard's origins, in a simple one-car garage in downtown Palo Alto, were memorialized fifty years later as "The Birthplace of Silicon Valley" in a 1989 California State dedication.[8] The garage is so modest in appearance, one would hardly suspect that the Hewlett-Packard Company started there, let alone the Electronic Age, as the world has come to know it. Two-and-a-half miles away at 3000 Hanover Street, just off Page Mill Road, is global headquarters for Hewlett-Packard—the world's largest electronics manufacturer, California's second largest industrial corporation, America's eighth largest, eighteenth in the world. HP's headquarters is an unpretentious building for a company with such a large impact on our society.[9]

The story began with two self-effacing, shy Stanford engineers. Bill Hewlett, addressed by a new hire as "Mr. Hewlett," turned to him, stuck out his hand, and said, "That was my father's name. Mine's Bill." At Packard's funeral services, a poignant picture graced the pamphlet: an elderly man driving a tractor, the gaze from his tanned, wrinkled face looking backward with a big smile. The simple epitaph read, "Dave Packard: rancher, etc." No pomp and circumstance surrounded Bill 'n' Dave. Bigger than life, destined to build one of America's greatest corporations, amassing huge fortunes along the way, they seldom lost sight of their humanity, their dignity, or their indebtedness to their colleagues. The reverence with which HP alumni and the business world have viewed these two men is extraordinary. But the HP story is far more than a Bill 'n' Dave tale, and their own leadership was more complicated and clouded with darker moments than most accounts portray. The evolution of HP is a remarkably under-reported story, revealing a strategic approach to innovation that merits much wider understanding and emulation.

Inside the hushed lobby of Hewlett-Packard's Palo Alto headquarters sits just one person—a guard at the front desk, who will politely ask your purpose for visiting and then discreetly call your contact. While you wait in the cavernous room, your attention might wander to the picture of Bill Hewlett and David Packard at the far end. Until Mark Hurd decided not to have his portrait hung, pictures of the two founders and the current CEO had usually adorned this lobby. When the building opened in 1981, it had a portrait of Hewlett and Packard and John Young. Then, Lew Platt joined Hewlett and Packard in a team photo. Later, individual photos of Hewlett and Packard flanked Carleton Fiorina.[10] Two founders, two insider CEOs, two outsider CEOs—seventy years.

Four other men, not pictured, also mattered enormously to HP's success. Two preeminent scientists, Barney Oliver and Joel Birnbaum, ran research for five decades. Oliver, one of very few Americans elected to two National Academies, placed HP firmly in the scientific instrumentation arena—a legacy carried on today at spin-out Agilent Technologies.[11] Joel Birnbaum, arriving in 1981 when Oliver retired, brought a deep understanding of computing technologies to the corporation as it embarked on a remarkable quest. Paul Ely, a microwave engineer when he joined HP, became the redoubtable leader who put HP firmly into the computing business. Richard Hackborn, HP's "master gamesman," would put an enduring stamp on HP as well, first by helping lead the computer entrée, and then by building and leading a highly effective peripherals strategy.[12]

Hewlett-Packard—HP—the company built by these leaders plus another half-million dedicated employees, was unique. It had enormous impact on the scientific underpinnings of our age—medicine, biology, chemistry, physics, civil engineering, electronics, space exploration, and astronomy. Its products have radically altered the business underpinnings of our society—industrial automation, machine control, satellite communications, color graphics, desktop printers, scalable computing, and handheld calculators, to name a few. Yet these impacts are scarcely recognized as HP contributions.

A leader in product sector after product sector, the company became better known for its cultural practices than its products. Profit sharing, flexible work hours, extended medical coverage, and "Management by Wandering Around"—and especially belief in the dignity of the individual employee—were all part of the HP Way long before these concepts were embraced by other companies.

Fifteen years after HP unexpectedly entered the computing field, new leadership challenged the aging, reticent, retired founders to embrace the next wave of computing—whereupon Packard said, "If you do, we need to become *the* leading computer company, which will take twenty-five years," a seemingly preposterous goal. Despite false starts for another decade, however, HP surpassed the behemoth IBM to become the largest computer equipment provider in the world twenty-two years later (2003). It took another four years for journalists at *The Wall Street Journal* to notice.

Notwithstanding these contributions, critics have consistently argued for decades that Hewlett-Packard lacks energy, stardom, leadership, will, and direction. HP itself has always resisted fast growth, while taking pride in moderate, steady results. Almost no one realized, or could even believe when told, that HP was the fastest-growing New York Stock Exchange company over the last forty years of the 20th century, and by 2007 had become the largest electronics equipment vendor in the world.[13]

Events of the past decade have been tumultuous. So, although HP is one of the more remarkable corporate success stories of the 20th century, some questions haunt: Was HP's success a function just of its founders, Dave Packard and Bill Hewlett, never to be recaptured once they were off the scene, or was it more than that? Will the renewal factor, fundamental to revenue and profit growth over the years, continue to drive the company? What may we learn from the successes and failures of this company?

CHAPTER 1

Creating the HP Way

It was so hard to really comprehend the greatness of HP because one of the great features was that they wouldn't talk about their virtues. They weren't going to sell you on their virtues. You had to see for yourself.

DON HAMMOND[1]

The *Forbes* issue reached local mailboxes on March 1, 2007, with a stunning cover story: "HP: Tech's New King."[2] How satisfying the coronation was for Hewlett-Packard employees and leadership alike. Weeks before, a *BusinessWeek* story led with the words "Hewlett-Packard has taken a big step toward laying official claim to the title of world's biggest tech company. . . . 'This has been a defining year for HP,' a buoyant Chief Executive Mark Hurd told reporters during a conference call. And no, he wasn't referring to the pretexting scandal that dominated headlines earlier this fall."[3] The story was hardly new—HP had passed IBM in equipment revenues four years earlier, in 2002, before the Compaq merger. But this modest company never made the claim, even with flamboyant Carly Fiorina at its helm. One has to wonder—why did people fail to notice this company for so long?

The HP saga began with a clever but simple idea: to insert a small lightbulb into one side of a circuit as the resistance element, rather than a standard resistor. Whether Bill Hewlett understood the probable effect ahead of time is unimportant—he instantly recognized the result when he turned it on. He had constructed an automatically controlled amplitude limiter for a resistance-capacitance signal generator. His innovation was adequate for a fifteen-page engineer's thesis from Stanford University in 1939; it was also good enough for U.S. patent number 2,268,872.[4] And it led to the Model 200A Oscillator, a brand-new product from a brand-new company named Hewlett-Packard after Hewlett won the coin toss for the right to put his name first. The first big order—$517.50 for nine units—was garnered from Walt Disney Studios in 1939, intended for use in creating and balancing stereo soundtrack music for the cartoon "Fantasia." The movie was a pioneering effort, with six individual soundtracks, two mixing tracks, and a metronome track to capture Leopold Stokowski's orchestra in very high-fidelity sound. One oscillator per track was required; HP's new machine, offered at $54.50 versus the General Radio machines at $400 each, was an exciting find for Disney's chief engineer Johnny (Bud) Hawkins. But as it turned out, the HP 200A didn't have quite the frequency range desired. So Hewlett changed the capacitor and charged $3.00 more per unit, and Disney actually bought the company's second product, the 200B. Over time, at least twenty-four variations of the lamp-stabilized oscillator would be offered for sale.[5]

From that auspicious beginning, the company quietly set about doing business in a most unorthodox manner. Contribution, more than profit or growth, was the watchword. Years later, Packard told a biographer, "I never really thought about how much money we might make. The question was, 'What contribution can we make?'" The company began in the single-car garage behind the house that Dave and his bride, Lucile, rented at 367 Addison Avenue in Palo Alto, California, now graced with a granite monument plaque denoting it as the origin of fabled Silicon Valley.

Legendary even in their lifetimes, each founder of the Hewlett-Packard Company—William Hewlett and David Packard—had a giant intellect with uncommon integrity and character. Their business approach from the earliest days became known as the HP Way. Each could have stood alone, and did, on occasion, but the most remarkable fact was that they stood together for a lifetime, building a resolute partnership founded on core values of honesty in dealings, faith in people, and excellence in performance.

David Packard was an imposing figure. He stood six-foot-five-inches tall, with a hawkish nose and deep-set eyes that seemed to not miss a thing. Once, while touring Russia in the glasnost aftermath of the Reagan years, he mused to companions about the tire marks on the tarmac, "Look how close together they are; their pilots must get far better training than ours," an observation missed by everyone else.[6]

Another time, Packard took the floor at the end of an HP general managers meeting and announced that the Berlin Wall would be falling soon. He exhorted the group to ponder the significance for each of their divisional product lines.[7] At coffee break, chief operating officer Dean Morton could scarcely contain his dismay: "The damn Berlin Wall? We've got problems with Spectrum, we've got problems in computing, we've got problems with managing this place—he wants us to worry about the market in East Berlin?"[8] The wall fell less than ten months later. One attendee at the meeting opined to an external group that Packard had predicted this when the entire U.S. State Department missed it—the dismissive reply was that his role as Deputy Secretary of Defense must have given him special insight that was lacking at State.[9] When Packard was asked, the stunningly simple answer was that "I was in our Vienna office, and I was reading the telephone log book. I noticed that the number of calls in 1988 from the East Bloc had gone up by nearly a factor of ten from the year before, and I figured something must be changing for so many phone calls to be coming our way."[10] Again sensitive to the nuances of what he was seeing—intuitive, clear, and insightful, with decisiveness about what to do with the data thus collected. Such a combination has seldom come together in one person.

Al Bagley, a key early inventor and HP's first division manager, noted that Packard was an engineer at heart, as well as a business guy: "He had a great big heart and sense of integrity. He really had a belief in people, that if you give them an opportunity, they can surprise you with how well they can perform."[11] Self-deprecating, he jocularly answered questions about his height by saying he was five-foot-seventeen. He was a regular at the Friday night beer busts, singing and telling jokes with guys from the machine shop and production lines—the same folks he often invited fishing or hunting.

Carl Cottrell, a thirty-nine-year Hewlett-Packard employee, bluntly said, "There's not been anything that really expresses what a giant he was in so many ways. He was a born leader and an unusual leader, and he had tremendous business sense. He looked at things in a very logical way, but he also had a keen intuition about business decisions, and he believed in making decisions. There was nothing wishy-washy about Dave."[12] CEO Lew Platt expressed the mood of many at Packard's public memorial: "Our closest personal experience to greatness."[13]

Michael Malone, Silicon Valley's chronicler, was rhapsodic in "The Packard Way" chapter of his book *The Valley of Heart's Delight:* "David Packard is the greatest figure of the electronics age, its most admired entrepreneur, and, history may well record, the most important businessman of the twentieth century. . . . Most of all, David Packard exhibited a trait once synonymous with Americans: an absolute, rock-hard integrity."[14]

If Packard was a giant, the five-foot-seven-inch Hewlett by contrast was an elfin figure—with an otherworldly demeanor and a fine sense of good-natured mischievousness. Curiosity defined Bill quite as much as his taste for a simple approach. Lew Platt succinctly summed it up: "He was one of the most inquisitive people I ever met. . . . When I look out the window, I'd see a tree. But he'd want to know what kind of tree it was, how it worked, what was its genesis—and he was that way whether it was art or music or botany or electronics. That was the seed that was planted inside HP. Hewlett was the guy who gave the invention DNA to HP."[15]

Hewlett was a consummate engineer—practical, ingenious, with an easy air. Diffident about how much he knew, at times he seemed not to understand why the things he saw clearly were so obscure to others. He used such insight to coax the best from others. As David Pierpont Gardner, ex-chancellor of the University of California and a past president of the Hewlett Foundation, wrote for the American Philosophical Society:

> Bill was not fond of looking backward. Instead, he looked steadily forward, beyond most people's more limited perspectives or the natural limits of their imaginations, searching for the nuances and subtleties of the problems encountered, discovering how, by redefining a problem, the solution was made clearer or even self-evident, challenging when complacency became confused with contentedness, and asking, always asking, if there was not a better way or a more fundamental question to ask. Bill's character, honesty, generosity, and quiet, self-effacing ways, to his great credit, have come to be as much respected as his company. These personal traits were the markers of one whose life should be a source of inspiration to the young and a cause of admiration and respect for the rest of us.[16]

A grandchild's parting thoughts:

> In the end, his greatest gift to future generations was not the compass he could build with his hands, but his moral compass. Its cardinal points were knowledge,

modesty, justice and hard work. His life was guided by what seem to me innate principles of rectitude. He never wavered at home or at work. He was true to himself and an example to us all.[17]

Beginnings

Frederick Hewlett, Bill's paternal grandfather, was born in London in 1846. Arriving in California as an adult, he met and married Cleora Melissa Whitney in Marin County. The couple had six children; the oldest was Albion Walter, born in August 1874, named for his maternal grandfather. Tragedy dogged the family—four of the children would not survive past three years of age, which compelled Albion to become a doctor. While in residency at Ann Arbor, he met his future wife, Louise Redington. William Redington was born May 20, 1913, four years after sister Louise. Dr. Hewlett, appointed in 1916 to the Stanford Medical School based in San Francisco, became prominent in West Coast medical circles. The family traveled frequently, especially to Stanford's Sierra Nevada mountain retreat at Fallen Leaf Lake. Bill developed a love for wilderness; he met his future wife Flora during these summer excursions. Tragically, Dr. Hewlett, fifty, suffered an untimely death from a brain tumor in 1925, after which Louise, the senior, took her mother and two children to Paris for fifteen months. For Bill, aged twelve, the trip abroad was very formative.[18]

Dyslexia and lack of interest combined to cause difficulties in some school subjects, but Bill's interest in math and science was easily piqued. Bill took to scaling buildings for sport and eventually became a pretty fair mountaineer. A grand tinkerer in high school, he graduated just before his seventeenth birthday and headed off to Stanford, thanks to intervention by a relative who spoke to his poor grades from dyslexia and connected the boy with his famous father. At Stanford, he earned recognition for his quirky sense of humor, usually at professor expense.

David Packard was a true westerner, born September 7, 1912, in Pueblo, Colorado—a western frontier city, even a border town, as he would describe it later. He grew up outdoors, learning to ride horses as a boy and becoming accustomed to catching the daily limit of fifty trout in the Gunnison River. He also became a proficient radio operator, involved both in the high school club and at the state convention. Pueblo, with forty thousand people, a steel mill, and several foundries smelting ore from high mountain towns in Colorado, was a locus of bustling activity—tough and violent in Packard's view. Colorado in 1912 was remote—not far from Pueblo, Colorado Springs was an upscale resort community of thirty thousand, where Packard's parents met at Colorado College. Denver was sizable, with two hundred thousand people, but aside from it, there was only one town as large as Pueblo within six hundred miles, and only ten more within a thousand miles. A century later, Pueblo isn't as isolated, or prominent—there are sixteen larger cities within six hundred miles, and another forty-eight within a thousand miles. In 1912, six hundred miles was a long distance.

San Francisco, on the other hand, was twice Denver's size, with nearby Stanford University already billing itself as the "Harvard of the West." In summer 1929, Dave traveled by car to California with his mother, Ella, and sister, Ann Louise. Louise Neff, Ella's best friend from Colorado College, lived near Stanford in Palo Alto; her daughter Alice had just completed her freshman year there. Alice took Dave, about to become a high school senior, around campus. Dave's book, *The HP Way,* opened by noting that certain events, seemingly unimportant at the time, have a "profound effect in shaping our business or professional careers"—visiting Stanford that summer was one of only two events he cited for his own life. It changed his mind from attending the University of Colorado at Boulder to applying to Stanford. In the throes of the Depression, September 1930, he enrolled.

The new president of the United States, Herbert Hoover, was a Stanford alumnus, conferring a certain cachet on the school. The current university president, Ray Lyman Wilbur, was well-known in both business and academic circles. David Starr Jordan, the founding president (1891–1913), was still an active chancellor, with both national and international fame. And Lewis Madison Terman, a faculty psychologist, was gaining notice for popularizing the Stanford-Binet IQ Test under their tutelage.

Packard met Bill Hewlett the week he enrolled; over four years, especially in their senior year, they became fast friends. Dave would be busy at Stanford—he lettered in three sports freshman year, and he worked as well. He later dropped track and basketball, but played football for four years, including on the 1934 Rose Bowl team. Packard also worked every summer—even though his father was fully employed during the Depression as a bankruptcy judge in Pueblo, every spare dollar mattered.

Packard's second serendipitous career-altering event in his life occurred through his love of the ham radio club. He met Dr. Frederick Terman, Lewis's son, who was well launched on a teaching career in radio engineering at Stanford University. Although it is widely acknowledged that Terman became the inspiration and stimulus for Packard and Hewlett to start a company, the depth of guidance and perspective that Terman provided for the duo cannot be overstated. He mentored the pair for nearly five decades, even as their fame grew to match his own.

Terman, interviewed about how prescient it had been to start Silicon Valley, said,

> The Depression years were more difficult than you can imagine. We had nothing, literally nothing, to work with. An accident that burned out a few vacuum tubes or damaged a meter would produce a crisis in the laboratory budget for a month. . . . The prewar electronics laboratory was in an attic under the eaves, over the electrical machinery laboratory. The roof of the attic leaked; at times these leaks became quite bad. There was no money to repair the roofs, so they built big wooden trays, lined with tar-paper and tar. As the trays filled, we walked around them. One winter Bill Hewlett added a homey touch, stocking the trays with goldfish.[19]

For the young Packard, Terman stood out like a beacon. He served as an inspiration for the interests Dave was developing in a way that Dave's own father couldn't.

> I spent a spare hour now and then in the radio shack in the Engineering Building attic. Professor Terman's laboratories were next door. Sometimes he would stop to chat for a minute or two. I was amazed to find that he knew a great deal about me. He knew my interests and abilities in athletics; he knew what courses I had taken and my grades. He had even looked up my high school record and my scores on the entrance exams.
>
> The highlight of his course for me was the opportunity to visit some of the laboratories and factories in this area. Here, for the first time, I saw young

entrepreneurs working on new devices in firms that they had established. One day Professor Terman remarked that many of the firms we visited had been founded by men with little or no formal education. He suggested that someone with a formal engineering education, and perhaps a little business training, might be even more successful.[20]

The overriding characteristic that drew Hewlett and Packard together was a belief that they could build a company with friends, a place with high integrity, close associations, and solid expectations. They both knew and respected two classmates, Noel Porter and Barney Oliver, and the four talked at length about the possibilities of starting a company together. Noel Edmund (Ed) Porter was Bill Hewlett's closest boyhood friend. The two had enrolled at Stanford together.[21] Ed, a ham radio zealot, had call letters W6BOA that earned him the handle "Frisco Snake." Adept enough with radio equipment to partially earn his way through Stanford repairing it, Ed helped to cement the relationship between Hewlett and Packard.[22] Ed joined HP after World War II, to run manufacturing operations, a job he would do well for thirty years.

Bernard (Barney) More Oliver was younger than Hewlett or Packard, born in 1916 on the family farm near Soquel in Santa Cruz County. His paternal grandfather bought the property in 1858—the oldest continuously owned ranch in Santa Cruz County some 130 years later. His father, William H. Oliver, graduated as a civil engineer from Berkeley in 1905 and worked much of his life in the county surveyor's office. His mother, a liberal bombshell, earned two history degrees at UC Berkeley and taught school for much of her life. She taught him about both education and politics. Oliver skipped three grades early, entering Caltech at just barely age fifteen. By seventeen, more interested in radio than physics, he had transferred to Stanford to study under Terman.

Barney found Hewlett much easier to engage than Packard:

I rather soon got to know Bill and Ed Porter. I didn't get to know Dave very well. He played football, he was a member of a fraternity, and the group he went with was just a different stratum than ours. Bill, on the other hand, was interested in gadgetry. He got me involved in synchronizing the speed of an air turbine magnetically-controlled centrifuge he was working on. Bill always had an interest in biological sciences and medical sciences because his father was in medicine. I knew Ed because Ed was working his way through Stanford by repairing radios. I'd give him a hand and repair a few for him.[23]

Although the four classmates had many discussions about starting a company together, the Depression dictated that their plans be set aside. Nonetheless, Dave later noted, "It is not a coincidence that a few years later this group would become the management team of Hewlett-Packard."[24]

Two others would matter greatly. Both Packard and Hewlett had met women who would bring much satisfaction and balance to their lives. While he was slinging hash at a Stanford sorority dining room, Dave met Lucile Laura Salter, a San Francisco native. She was a Delta Gamma girl available for a dance. Dave was smitten. Even as he went to work for GE in Schenectady, New York, they maintained a long-distance relationship; he returned to see her in 1937 in courtship. It was during this time that he and Bill sat down, along with Ed Porter, for their first official company meeting, on August 23. The minutes: "tentative organization plans and a tentative work program for a proposed business venture."[25]

Lucile and Dave married in April 1938 in Schenectady after she resigned her job at the Stanford registrar's offices and hopped a train alone to New York. After sending a telegram from Chicago to her parents, she married Dave the day she arrived, then they took a two-day honeymoon. The East Coast was not to her liking, and she sent a note home saying that "I'm afraid most of these serious discussions are just a lot of playing around. Maybe I'm wrong, and someday the world will beat a pathway to our door, to see that great engineer who did this or that with this or that."[26]

Hewlett finally felt the time was right, and he implored Packard with a memorable note that "there will never be a better time, and I feel that we must act."[27] Lucile watched her new husband struggle with the decision, writing, "Dave won't get out of bed. Sometimes he gets to the edge of the bed and sits there in deep contemplation of the floor or his feet for ten minutes, but eventually he will get up."[28] Fred Terman found a fellowship for Dave in mid-1938, enabling the cautious Packard to take a leave of absence from his job at GE, put his one major asset—a drill press—into his convertible, and drive west with his California bride Lucile into an unknown future.[29] Lucile got her job at Stanford back; evenings she helped out at HP, even after David Woodley Packard, oldest of their four children, was born in October 1940.

Bill Hewlett met his love, Flora Lamson, at Stanford's Fallen Leaf Lake while still in high school. Flora, a Northern California native, followed in her father's footsteps to graduate from UC Berkeley. In the Kappa Alpha Theta sorority, she loved the arts, music, and the campus ferment. Her sorority sisters were truly concerned when she fell in love with a young engineer from across the Bay. He "wanted to start his own company" in the depths of the Depression, which dismayed her friends. She always had been prone to dreaming, but they felt this was the height of insanity. Notwithstanding her friends' advice, she married Bill in late 1939.[30]

Flora, while seldom involved in the affairs of the company, did provide help on occasion. At Packard's request, she asked her father for legal and accounting advice. He recommended F. W. LeFrentz, a San Francisco public accounting firm, through which Edwin van Bronkhorst, later a company CFO, was introduced. Flora's chief contribution was via the wonderful nurturing home that she created for the family, and the support and delight that this afforded Bill, whose need for public acclaim and activity was modest indeed.[31]

The Genesis of the HP Way

Folklore has it that the Walt Disney order started the company. The facts are more pedestrian. The duo essentially ran a job shop, designing many things for clients, with some interesting breadth but not much depth in any direction. They made bowling foul-line checkers, automated urinal flushers, a harmonica tuner, and even an automated lettuce crop thinner.[32] While the first name they selected, the Engineering Services Company, was prosaic, the results were not. Bill and Dave built a very large, very successful job shop, with their own names on the building. It focused on producing tools for its customers that helped them do their jobs faster or more accurately. They called it the next-bench syndrome: build something to solve the problems of the person seated next to you, and the odds are good that others have that same problem, and hence will buy your product.[33]

Hewlett and Packard resonated with Fred Terman's peculiar brand of business philosophy. In some sense, the HP Way was an evolved Terman Way.[34] Just how unusual Terman's business attitudes were would be brought home to the idealistic young Packard in a talk that he gave at Stanford in 1942: Packard got into a fairly heated discussion with Stanford professor Paul Holden and a small group when he stated that management's responsibility is not just to shareholders, but also to "its employees . . . its customers . . . and to the community at large." He said, "They almost laughed me out of the room."[35] Packard persisted; he and Hewlett instituted a variety of policies buttressing these views—respect and autonomy for all workers, from the lowest to the highest; emphasis on innovation and contribution with a high standard of excellence; camaraderie and informality, including using first names. They lived by a creed of contribution, profitability, fairness, and trust, and they built a company from the start on these principles. There was an ineffable quality about the two and their manner of dealing with situations and people that, even today, maybe especially today, seems surrealistic. It is antithetical to most modern business conduct, even as many Silicon Valley companies claim it as their heritage. This HP Way is elusive, hard to capture, and yet vital to understand.

Profit sharing for all workers, not just professionals, was first instituted at HP, and the pair followed it in due course with an equally innovative catastrophic health insurance plan. Events from these early years are the stuff of legends, and these legends became the folklore and cultural backdrop of the company for years. In time, especially as HP became recognized for its remarkable growth and unique company approach, anecdotal stories filled chapters of innumerable management books. Said marketing manager Joe Schoendorf: "People think it's all schmaltz, but it really happened."[36]

Hewlett and Packard were dedicated, passionate, articulate leaders. One didn't have to wonder where they stood on various issues, or who was in charge. Given their engineering backgrounds, perhaps their most surprising characteristic was the breadth of their knowledge. But their leadership difference was also striking. Ralph Lee, eventually HP's manufacturing vice president, had been at the MIT Rad Lab, and in the summer of 1945 he interviewed with a number of West Coast firms seeking employment.

When asked what attracted him to HP, he was animated:

> You'd talk to Packard, and he knew what the hell the score was. He was running the show and he could tell flat out where the money was going. These other places weaseled around. Nobody knew what was going on, and they didn't have any plans. He definitely knew what he wanted to do; he told me how he was going to run this company and what kind of people he wanted on board.[37]

The ethos was built in a hands-on manner. Bill and Dave were deeply and intimately involved in the operations. Both had an extremely broad range of knowledge, curiosity, and self-assurance. Neither brooked fools. Each demanded utmost integrity. Both men put enormous responsibility in the hands of their employees, and they made sure that this was understood and exercised. And they had no problem with honest mistakes; people really could learn from miscues rather than shrink from risk-taking endeavors. Both were untroubled by what they didn't know, and they did things in a commonsense way rather than use a textbook approach. They learned by doing and practiced what worked. And they were understated—Frank Cavier, HP's first CFO, said, "Mary and I drove by the plant. Boy! It was less than impressive. It had a little dinky sign saying Hewlett-Packard. You really had to look around to find it."[38]

Al Bagley heard about the company in 1946 from his wife's sister's husband:

> He told of two fellows in the San Francisco Engineer's Club "who have got a little company and I think they are really going places." I asked what they were making, and he said, "measuring test equipment." That didn't sound very exciting, and I asked if they would try something different, anything new. And he said, "Will they ever! They're trying to make a lettuce picker." And he described the lettuce picker that had photocells over each row, and it looked at the ground and stored in memory the size of leaf it saw for each row and it would thin out the crop and leave just the right size of leaf to germinate [*sic*] into a full head of lettuce.

Bagley won an HP Fellowship at Stanford for a master's degree in 1948; he said Hewlett told him,

> Spend the first quarter in the library. Study from all the magazines about nuclear physics today—what is it they are trying to do and what are some of the prob-

lems they have making measurements. Then in the second quarter, draw up some proposals of what you would do, and if those proposals are good, in the last quarter you can come out to the company in some spare time and work on those things.[39]

The proposal turned out to be a good one. Bagley invented a nuclear counter, which presaged the highly successful HP 524A Electronic Counter. After leading the Frequency and Time (later Santa Clara) Division for two decades, he became R&D director for all of HP's test equipment families.

At HP, as with virtually all companies of the day, projects were developed in the lab and then handed off to a production engineering group that readied them for manufacture. Notoriously, animosity develops between such groups; it was no different at HP. Bruce Wholey, HP's first Microwave Division manager, observed,

It was a major hurdle because once the lab got done with the projects . . . the attitude about production engineering was, "If they can't build them, they're a bunch of idiots!" I found that an hour spent on the test line with those guys was worth about ten hours of hard work. An hour spent in the machine shop . . . was worth a couple of days of hard thinking. That's one thing that a lot of engineers still have to learn.[40]

Enter the HP Way. The team felt empowered to change things that didn't make sense. Practices that came out of the resultant changes were uniquely tuned to company needs. No product sold in high volume, and the small company produced a bewildering array of products. Techniques for managing the change process—the development of new products and learning how to document and manufacture them to high-quality standards, as well as how to juggle myriad small production runs for assembly and test—were specially developed at HP. Bagley called the company "a high-level special-handling outfit," and noted, "You don't learn much about these techniques in business schools."[41] Thus HP created novel methodologies: project-based organization for the development labs, designer responsibility for the project even after it shipped to customers, customer feature research by the design team, project-based reviews and accounting, and development engineers having hiring responsibility.

Barney Oliver, arriving in 1952, had some trenchant observations on this evolution:

Production engineering would take our lab design and make it manufacturable. The production engineering people often would screw it up in the interest of doing something right but do something else wrong. They hadn't been with the thing from the beginning so they didn't know what degrees of freedom they had. So there was a lot of bickering back and forth. About the time that we came up here [to 1501 Page Mill Road, in 1957], we rearranged things and started operating on an entirely different scheme. We decided to disband the production engineering group and distribute the production engineering among the electronic engineers and let them work on the product from the very beginning, from the very outset, as a kind of task force. That team would start on the project and the same person would follow it through from the very beginning fully to the end. If there was any problem, he had access to the people who had been on his team to come help fix it. And he didn't lose responsibility for that product until it was out in the field and running trouble-free. So, by identification of a team with a product, we achieved a coherence that hadn't been present before.[42]

To handle the transition into production, the group created a different kind of production engineering group. It was a validation team primarily—handling documentation, quality audit, and preferred parts verification. Bill Myers, a Princeton graduate engineer, led the team, working for Ralph Lee. Al Bagley commented to Lee years later,

Boy, did we resent that in the lab. In fact, we called it the lead balloon. . . . "Have we got to go through that thing again!" But we finally got instruments that would hit production and it didn't take forever to understand what they were supposed to do. . . . We had to have everything supported by drawings. You could turn the drawings over to the pilot run guys. You couldn't talk to them, but they could make what you said it was. Before, you just went out and said, "That's not where I want the hole drilled. Put it here." It slowly became more formal. This would sardonically be called the Myers' Filter.[43]

Today, most R&D books preach the value of project-based management, extolling the virtues of tighter focus, better motivation, and clearer communications, even as virtual teams—spread across multiple geographies, cultures, and time zones—are challenging such structures.

At HP these insights, coupled with the freedom to pioneer new practices, were the more valuable (and less visible) aspect of the HP Way. Such innovative practices were found throughout the company. Market research serves as a good example. When asked where the ideas came from for new instrument features, Wholey described a method:

Noel Eldred (HP's first marketing vice president) figured if he could pull an engineer into the field to see, that you got a lot of feedback from the field. I really don't know how that started, but it's where a lot of ideas came from. I went down to Hughes with Lyle Jevons once with a whole pack of waveguide equipment. I spent two days showing them how to run it and showing them that we knew better than Narda and FXR [competitors]. I got a lot of feedback from Hughes on what was wrong with our equipment and what was good about it. Engineers were allowed a lot of freedom.[44]

Don Hammond, who pioneered much of HP's leadership work in crystals and later managed a critical section of HP Laboratories, shared some strong views:

A lot of the stimulus came from questions from Packard or Hewlett, or from Barney or Bagley, or from a lot of different people. We were encouraged to probe, to think, and we were encouraged to do it the right way. We were always encouraged to do it the best way possible. We often did invent a better way, but they worked very hard to try to free us from feeling that we had to invent it all. Go for the best ultimate solution. That is one of the great dimensions of genius of HP. Bill and Dave would review it and say, "Why didn't you do that? Or that? Well, I think you'd better take it back and work on it a bit longer." Also, there was . . . Hewlett asking questions and Packard asking questions. A lot of times you could just see that they knew where they wanted to go, but they weren't going to tell you where to go. And they didn't care who got the credit.

Hammond, a soft-spoken archetypal scientist, spoke of the strong role that Eldred established for new products—this after the market failure of the lettuce thinner:

I remember Noel Eldred's three-legged milk stool. If you enter a new business, you'll be using different facets (e.g. manufacturing, R&D and the technology, and marketing). Each one of those is a leg . . . If you try to do that with all three new, you'll fall flat on your face. But you can probably get by with one new leg of the three, and if you try two, you're really in a precarious position.[45]

Oliver thought that the principal sources of ideas for new products were "new concepts, face-lifted old products, and simply requests from the field to do something to fill in our line." Asked about new concepts, Barney commented,

This was done by reading the literature, keeping up with new developments, and asking ourselves what can they be used for. Fundamental things like lasers came along, and we decided we ought to be working with them, getting to understand them because there undoubtedly were going to be applications for them. So we did. We learned about optical modulators, and how to do heterodyne detection at optical frequencies, things like that.[46]

With project-based management and Packard's strong sense of profit requirements, it became very important to understand the potential returns of the new product development program. Both Packard and Hewlett were self-taught accountants, quite adept as it turned out. Asked how much Packard knew about accounting and finance, Frank Cavier replied,

Well, he seemed to know a hell of a lot. . . . We'd have an accounting problem which seemed to me pretty sophisticated and complicated and I'd start to explain it to him. He'd let me know in no uncertain terms that he knew what I was talking about and understood it. When someone would send him a memo and underline certain sections, he'd say, "You don't have to underline anything for me. I understand what I'm reading."[47]

Hewlett and Packard had rules of thumb that they used for overview accounting. For the company to be self-financing, it had to earn enough profit to pay for new investment at an adequate rate. Packard worked out a relatively simple formula—(capital turnover) × (profitability) = self-funding growth rate—which he presented to a disbelieving audience in 1957. His speech became legendary within HP for its simplicity and its tenets.[48] Hewlett in turn had a belief that every project had to earn a healthy return. He aptly dubbed this the return factor, and set it at six. Every project had to earn in profit six times the amount that it required for the original investment. Derived from Packard's article, this number put a premium on each project review. The project team had to demonstrate that the project had a high likelihood of earning enough money to make it worthwhile to finish development.

This same willingness to experiment led to a nontraditional October 31 fiscal year end. Ed van Bronkhorst began work for HP in 1947 when Hewlett and Packard incorporated:

> The date of incorporation was August 17, 1947; the first fiscal year closing was October 31, 1947. We agreed on an October 31 fiscal year for two reasons. One, the outside accountants weren't going to be very busy at that time of year, whereas if you picked a December 31 date, the calendar year, you just got thrown in with all the rest of them. The other reason was in those days you could accrue for expense purposes anything paid within two and one-half months after the fiscal year close. That made it possible to accrue salaries and bonuses and deduct in October 31 and not pay them until January—the person receiving that money didn't have to report it until the following year.[49]

Hewlett and Packard held a strong view that personnel departments just got in the way, and that engineering managers ought to be interviewing and hiring their own people. Other companies would send a phalanx of professional recruiters to college campuses in the 1970s and 1980s; HP sent engineering project leaders seeking prospective designers on behalf of themselves or their colleagues. This technique worked extraordinarily well, as faculty members usually knew the HP recruiters because they had been their students some years earlier, and they tended to encourage their better students to interview with HP. In addition, students found the recruiters credible—they could speak authoritatively about what kind of work the student would do and what type of environment he or she would encounter at HP.

In earlier days, it was even simpler. Bruce Wholey worked on signal generators and spectrum analyzers at MIT's Rad Lab during World War II. At the end of the war, he spent two weeks in Palo Alto readying the company to understand the specifics of the Navy "A" project that was being transferred to HP. At the end of the two weeks, Wholey recalled,

> Dave and Lu said they would take me back to the airport. [We went] to dinner first; the service was slow, and Packard was getting upset. Finally we got fed,

sped up to the airport, and he dropped me off, saying, "Do you want a job out here?" I said, "I don't know, but I'll think about it." He said, "Well, think about it." That's all that was said.

About a week later we had one of those early vicious snowstorms in Boston. I got home and the first thing I did after I got my feet dry was phone Dave and ask, "Is that job still available?" He said, "Yup." I said, "Okay, I'll take it." The 15th of the month, a guy named Traxler said, "Here's your paycheck." That was the first time I knew what I was making.[50]

John Cage, earlier Packard's boss at GE, was an electrical engineering professor at Purdue; in 1952, he urged his student Bob Grimm to consider HP:

We had an oscillator or voltmeter in the lab made by HP at that time, and that's all I knew about the company. I wrote a two-page letter to Bill Hewlett outlining how I'd gotten into the Navy electronics course and then I told them about what I'd taken in college and I described several of the projects I'd built with this Campus Electronics Service. There was never a phone call between us, and they never invited me out to interview, but I got this letter back saying, "We'd like to offer you a job, and if you'll show up in Palo Alto, you've got a job." They didn't offer to pay my way out or anything. I had all these other offers, and HP's was not the highest offer. It was pretty close to the lowest, but it had a nice appeal. I wrote back and accepted it.[51]

Whether it was in project-based development, hiring, or accounting, the company put its own stamp on things. This was perhaps most obvious in manufacturing. HP produced an incredible array of low-volume products for such a small company. At its twentieth-year anniversary, the company had 373 products in the catalog, with sales of $48 million. At an average selling price of $600, median sales were just eighteen units per month per product.[52] The standard production run was twenty-five units. High-volume products might have two or three runs per month—for low-volume products, some were built before being sold, and these went into finished goods inventory, although both Packard and Ralph Lee abhorred such a use of funds. Competition was modest enough that HP could essentially build to order, often quoting twelve to sixteen weeks for deliveries. Their strategy conserved cash and smoothed out episodic order rates—customers waited because the products were of such high quality.

Scheduling such a mélange of products was a monumental chore. Cort Van Rensselaer began with the company in 1942, while attending Stanford. Drafted upon graduation in 1944, he returned to HP on January 1, 1948, after getting an MBA. His first assignment was to make inventory control and production planning more manageable:

> We really had to build instruments in anticipation of orders. Otherwise, we would have had unsatisfactorily long deliveries. So we were building these instruments in production runs of twenty-five at a time. To do that, you had to figure out how many resistors, capacitors, and tubes to buy. My job was to make a sales forecast. I had to figure out how many of each product we were going to sell every week and then how to build the different runs. I would forecast out for a few months and then calculate the materials required. I introduced a Kardex system with a card file for each part. The card described the part, where we purchased it, how many we had on order and how many we had in stock. We posted all that information constantly. Then we had what was called "the bible." It is now called a material requirements planning (MRP) system, done on computers. The bible was a huge multi-sheet document that had the products along the top, the parts along the side, and it had squares that showed how many of each part were used in a product. Then we used a Friden calculator to add up—based on the sales forecast—everything and determine what our requirements were.[53]

Cort recalled that everyone concerned with production would go off to a restaurant once a month, have lunch, and then "have a production meeting. Packard and Porter and Eldred were always there. . . . Eldred would talk about the sales forecast. We didn't have any auditorium in those days, so we had to use a restaurant." Van Rensselaer was impressed with how much Packard wanted to know.

> Packard called one Sunday morning, and he said, "I'm concerned about our production schedule and I would like to review this and wondered if you could come in today and we could go over it." I came in and Eldred was there. Eldred and Packard and I spent six hours going through every detail of the sales forecasts of all these Gantt charts we're talking about, the whole business. Packard was basically auditing every single detail.[54]

Packard's drive for excellence was legendary. Robert Grimm described a situation when the Navy wanted urgent delivery of the HP 618B Sweeper:

We were having a great time at Adobe Creek [picnic spot] late Friday evening on our own time, and Packard came up and was irate. The very idea that anybody on a project with such high priority would be spending any time on anything except that project infuriated him. They could be pretty outspoken about their priorities.[55]

Bruce Wholey reminisced about how it worked among the hundred employees:

People didn't have any clearly defined jobs. [In 1949], Packard was running the place. Cavier was finance, but he had the switchboard and the office functions under him. Eldred had balked over the traces a little bit, and said if he was going to be marketing manager he was going to be marketing manager! So Packard had let back on that one a little bit. Glenn Zieber had manufacturing—Packard told him what size screws to use.[56]

Working or traveling with Packard could be tiring, even exhausting. Cavier said, "He'll run you ragged. One of the reps came out to check our books to see if they were getting the proper amount of commission from us. We worked on that until three in the morning. He'd just go like that with the stamina and energy to do it." Dave Kirby, HP's first public relations director, rejoined, "I recall walking with him in a city like Chicago or Washington or New York and walking maybe three blocks. It was just incredible. You had to run to keep up with him." Cavier replied, "That's right. He's just so energetic. And he's really anti-wasting time. . . . if somebody is running off at the mouth, boy, he just can't stand that."[57]

A clerical story tells of "Packard coming around when things were pretty tough, giving secretaries hell for throwing away paper clips."[58] The quintessential Packard, though, was the man who refused to accept the ruling of the War Resources Board in 1942 when they felt the company was making excessive profits and paying extraordinary wages via the unique profit-sharing plan. Packard described it quite succinctly in *The HP Way:* "I felt very strongly about this issue . . . and they said I would have to take my case to Washington. I did so and worked out an agreement with the government that gave our company virtually everything we asked for."[59] His autobiography omitted the facts that (a) he was twenty-nine years old; (b) his company had eight full-time employees; (c) Washington was besieged in a wartime bureaucratic snarl; (d) no other electronics company had a profit-sharing plan; and (e) as CEO, his salary was $110 per month to match his partner Bill Hewlett's while Hewlett was in the Army. In short, the case was nearly preposterous on the surface of it. So the phrase "I worked out an agreement that gave us virtually everything we asked for" left a lot of emotional undercurrent unspoken. Dave got things done.

Hewlett loved to develop people. Bagley related an event from the early 1950s:

> For a while, every Friday Hewlett would come in and say we're going to hear somebody talk about his project. He wanted us to learn to express ourselves better. So on coffee break every Friday morning somebody would have to talk about his project to the rest of the guys in the lab. Hewlett said this was another good way to get the feedback from more than one engineer. They might have a good suggestion for you. He said it would make us a lot better for standing up in an IRE [Institute of Radio Engineers] meeting.[60]

Packard described Hewlett as unusually able to wear three successive hats when he'd talk to engineers about new ideas. The first was enthusiasm, expressing excitement where appropriate and appreciation in general without too many questions. The second was inquisition about a week later, with a "thorough probing of the idea, lots of give-and-take." The third, his decision hat, came into view the next week, "with appropriate logic and sensitivity." The net result, wrote Dave, was that "this process provided the inventor with a sense of satisfaction, even when the decision went against the product."[61]

Al Bagley, proudly independent, outlined the experience for a new engineer at HP:

> An engineer, assigned a project area, did his own market research, tried some product ideas on paper, then demonstrated a prototype. At the demonstration, he usually estimated the cost and the sales volume and proposed a reasonable price. If the boss said, "Go," the estimates were firmed up with manufacturing and

marketing, and a more finished prototype was sent to pilot run with manufacturing drawings. The engineer then put together a proposed operating manual and drafted the specs and story for the catalog. In other words, delegation and accountability in the extreme, as the HP Way made the development engineer into a business manager. In the early days, most development projects were one-man shows, but as products became more complicated, projects became team efforts, with many more checks and balances.[62]

Both Hewlett and Packard had a bias for action. They were not given to studying a problem for very long before making a decision and moving on to implementation. As executive vice president Bill Terry said, they had "a pretty strong attitude that the management was going to be people who had grown up in the company—who knew how to get things done, understood the objectives. And [they] weren't going to go out and hire some big-time expensive, razzle-dazzle character to run [any] business."[63] This attitude was baked into the culture, explaining part of the visceral reaction of many employees to the board decision down the road to hire outsider CEOs—first Carleton Fiorina and then Mark Hurd: What happened to home-grown?

How did it work? Bill Terry described a typical monthly executive committee meeting when the founding pair was active (the annual general manager meetings were similar):

> It was technology and business—it was not visiting speakers talking about interesting things. It was kind of hardcore: How are we doing and what are we going to do next? People would get up and give reports for thirty minutes and say, "Here's how things are going in the analytical group. And we're behind on our profit, but we've got some ideas here: A, B, and C on how to get from here to there. And I need the help of you, you, and you." It was a chance to get your face out in front of other people. And van Bronkhorst would give a report on overall company progress or lack thereof.[64]

Both Hewlett and Packard abhorred paperwork, including annual performance appraisals, a bit of an HP management hallmark. Ed van Bronkhorst noted that Packard "absolutely hated it, and I don't think he ever wrote a performance evaluation. He gave me an evaluation only once and it took about thirty seconds. 'Just keep doing what you're doing and that's fine!'"[65] John Doyle, for years the VP of personnel (and personnel policies), observed,

> The only place I noticed where they absolutely never practiced what they preached was performance evaluations. I never had one from either one of them. Hewlett was once bullied into giving me one. And he just took the form and wrote one word diagonally across it in capital letters and said, "Give this to Ray" [Wilbur, then VP of personnel].[66]

A phrase that became quite common around HP was that these two men ran their business in a "hard-headed, soft-hearted way." Both Hewlett and Packard had a compassion and a concern for people that was quite remarkable—it was often hard to say whose idea it was to do some charitable act, because they thought so much alike on such matters. Packard, simply because he was the more visible externally, tended to get the credit for many of the company innovations, including the comprehensive health insurance program that HP put in place early. Although Packard was supportive, it was actually Hewlett who took up that particular cause. Cort Van Rensselaer recalled,

> In the early '50s, it was not customary for companies to have health insurance. A number of HP employees had gotten sick and had had to take substantial time off, and they'd had very high medical bills. Bill Hewlett sent a questionnaire out to all the employees in the company asking them about their medical bills, and it turned out that Jean and I had . . . medical bills that were above average. He called all the people into his office who had medical bills that were out of the ordinary to inquire about it, to try to get some understanding of how much of a burden this was for people. I was very impressed that he showed this personal interest. Shortly after that, HP started a health insurance program, years before other companies did.[67]

Fred Terman knew the pair extremely well; in the late 1970s, he said,

> Hewlett and Packard are interesting. Commonly you get two people together, and they're complementary, but actually these people are not. Either of them can do all of the things that the other does and at times has done them. Hewlett's been

running the company; Packard's really gone. Hewlett, for instance, for a number of years concentrated on the new product development. Then they started their international operation and Hewlett took that on. On the domestic operations, back in the 1930s through most of the 1950s, if you talked to Hewlett about what was going on in the marketing, the accounting problem—the cost factors, and so on—you found that Hewlett knew just as much about them as Packard did, and if you'd talk to him about some of these things alone, you could get just as quick and clear and quantitative answers as Packard was giving.[68]

Roger Heyns, ex-chancellor of the University of California system, while serving as president of the Hewlett Foundation, leaned over at a UC Davis Advisory Board dinner in 1985 to ask, "Do you know the problem with the Hewlett-Packard Company today?" The startled reply was "No, not really," to which he smiled and said, "The company is being run by seven Packard clones, but they haven't sought to replace Hewlett. It was the combined genius that made it click."[69] Twenty years later, retired HP executive vice president John Doyle agreed, noting that "Dave and Bill were remarkable individuals, but as a pair, there's never been anything like them."[70]

Contribution

Both Hewlett and Packard insisted on pragmatic contribution, disdaining innovation for its own sake. They were crystal-clear that the purpose of the company was to create products and services for which customers would pay more than they cost to make. Profit was the metric of contribution. Growth was also a metric, absolutely required so that the company could provide opportunity for employees to progress in their careers. But it was slow, steady growth—eschewing big government contracts, concentrating always on contribution, refusing to chase fads. Emerging out of the Depression era, a few other precepts arose: (1) absolute integrity, where the company's words and actions were totally trustworthy; (2) the view that a company had obligations to the community in which it operated, rather than just to the shareholders of the corporation; (3) a belief in pay-as-you-go management; and (4) an incredible sense of fairness and ethical behavior.

In contrast to conventional wisdom from America's business schools and business press, Hewlett and Packard largely shunned visions and mission statements. They preferred instead contributions from individuals at all levels of the organization—certainly in products and services, but also in policies, processes, and infrastructure. One result was that the company was seldom identified by a central product segment as its defining theme. Indeed, HP has morphed its main product line six times in six decades—unheard of in American industry at this level (see Appendix A). What stands out, though, is that David Packard resisted all six business shifts, while Hewlett actively drove only one. How, then, did the company transform so often? The secret is that they backed people—often mavericks—and gave them enormous power to succeed if they could demonstrate positive results. This unusual approach built an immensely loyal, dedicated, energized cadre of people, alert to new, paradigm-shifting opportunity. And, for a remarkably long time, the corporate structure allowed such creativity to get to the marketplace.

Hewlett-Packard quickly became known by engineers for its sophisticated tools. Over time, HP also became known as an innovative company, one with a unique approach to business. Consider the first acquisition, some twenty years after the company began. After receiving a bid from the owner, Packard intoned that HP valued his company 33 percent higher than the owner did, and that they'd pay it if he'd stay with the firm when acquired. Or consider the faith that was shown to a project manager in a remote division who had failed twice over eight long years on a project once valued highly by Hewlett—when he came back a third time, saying "I think I can do it this time," he led the LaserJet project, HP's most successful product of all time.

Processes and technologies were improved by this penchant for contribution. Fred Schröder, HP's first German hire, obtained a license from Siemens in 1965 for light-emitting diodes (LEDs) for more effective display readouts for HP counters and voltmeters at Al Bagley's instigation. HP's LED business became huge in calculator readouts and automotive taillights, while white-light capabilities perfected at HP thirty years later augur to change indoor and outdoor lighting globally by 2020.[71]

HP built one of the first integrated circuit (IC) facilities in the industry to develop higher-performance chips not yet available in the commercial markets so that HP instruments could remain leaders. Esoteric requirements for instrument needs proliferated IC capabilities, enabling some astonishing breakthroughs. The Frequency and Time Division installed HP's first silicon processing capability, to miniaturize electronic counters. Buzzword acronyms—N-MOS, C-MOS, and SOS capabilities—emerged at HP for semiconductors, well ahead of commercial vendors. HP microprocessors led Intel designs for both density and speed-power product by a two- to three-year margin for twenty years, a remarkable, yet scarcely noted achievement. C-MOS breakthroughs led to long-lasting battery-operated calculators, and SOS pioneering enabled the development of radiation-hardened chips for space designs. HP gallium-arsenide devices powered a high percentage of America's defense communication system transceivers for thirty years. By the early 1980s, HP had twice as many semiconductor processes in production as any other company on the planet, yet few except those within the industry seemed to know that HP even produced these devices; those that did know, including Bell Labs and IBM, calibrated their sophisticated IC fabrication techniques against HP.[72]

HP's *élan* differed significantly from other companies in manner, approach, organization, and values, not to mention strategies, tactics, products, and services. HP today is primarily thought of in brand awareness studies as producing printers and ink or personal computers. Instrumentation origins may seem both archaic and irrelevant. Indeed, the HP Way itself has been largely dismissed with the same disdain—outmoded, anachronistic. But the HP Way captures a pervasive spirit, deeply embedded in both why and how problems are tackled. The approach that put HP into printers and into computing was so different from conventional morés that it enabled the company to create entirely orthogonal products and services, a very unique recipe for success time and again. Ironically, the HP Way written about in most business texts focuses only on superficial elements regarding people management—the soft, fuzzy side of business—while completely missing the vibrant, visceral elements that drove the strategies and tactics that account for the bulk of HP's differentiated success.

The lessons learned slowly and painfully at HP are strangely absent from traditional business literature, analogous to the low profile of the overall company. Even within HP, the lessons are muted, carried as lore rather than explicit knowledge. Printing and imaging systems today generate 25 percent of HP revenue, and fully half of the profits. While an internal HP article once titled the printing business as an "Eight-Year Overnight Success Story,"[73] an incredible three-decade learning curve had elapsed before the overnight success occurred. But analysts, MBA students, and consultants are loath to consider culture, history, and lore. So such factoids, even if discovered and verified, are often dismissed as ancient history, irrelevant to the task at hand. To offer the serious business student some significant alternative lessons for today's leadership challenges requires revealing the secrets of the HP odyssey, hidden so long behind a cloak of anonymity.

The significant story about HP's success is not concerned so much with leadership at the top as it is with leadership at all levels of the company. Wide-ranging contributions, from every job function, in all departments and divisions, characterize this company; they are the true basis of the HP Way. What lessons from the HP experience may today's reader take away and use most advantageously? Six fundamental points stand out:

1. Focus on significant contribution, followed by continual rapid refinement
2. Create a corporate structure to allow, stimulate, and nurture new ideas—in sharp contrast to the typical audit-and-control approach in corporate headquarters
3. Move decision making as low in the organization as possible
4. "Stay the course" on new ideas in the marketplace
5. Centralize crucial infrastructure, and decentralize everything else
6. Take the time to get the right people—don't settle for second-best

Hewlett and Packard each encouraged dissent and independent action. They were more impressed by the thinking than the answer, more inclined to celebrate the effort than the result, and more apt to reward passion than careful planning. The belief that small work groups offered motivation, team building, and tolerance of individual idiosyncratic behaviors led them to support radical divisionalizing. A happy by-product was the discovery or affirmation that new ideas were more apt to emanate from such groups than from larger, more impersonal structures. This rarified atmosphere allowed a slow and steady growth mechanism to arise, nurtured by the autonomy of small divisions, coordinated by a corporate staff that believed in contribution as well as staying the course for the evolution of new innovative arenas while betting heavily on key individuals. This latter point, often overlooked, showed up in the hiring approaches toward Barney Oliver, Don Hammond, and Joel Birnbaum. Each was identified early as the key person for new initiatives for the company—and each spurned HP's initial offers. Persistence paid off, as HP waited a year or more for each of them to make the significant decision to leave a prestigious situation and throw their lot in with a company that, on the surface, seemed like a long-shot bet. The contributions of each would help propel HP to the next level, reducing the bet to a sure thing.

Summing up the HP Way is difficult—it was a constellation of practices of how to invent, develop, and produce products of value. It placed the responsibility for the success of the program primarily with the design team and expected every employee to do the right thing for the company and, especially, for the customer. It permeated the company: line workers mingled with engineers at coffee breaks, told them they were wasting money, and urged them not to do so, because it "comes out of our profit sharing." Unheard of at the time, it was unusually able to tap the enthusiasm, drive, and dedication of key technologists of the day. It set the tone for a company going places.

CHAPTER 2

Lord Kelvin's Imperative

When you can measure what you are speaking about, and express it in numbers, you know something about it; but when you cannot measure it, when you cannot express it in numbers, your knowledge is of a meager and unsatisfactory kind: It may be the beginning of knowledge, but you have scarcely, in your thoughts, advanced to the stage of science.

WILLIAM THOMSON, LORD KELVIN

(1824–1907)[1]

Terman's Protégés

Prewar America was still a rural nation, unified for the first time by a Great Depression and a president who used radio to communicate to a dispirited nation. Franklin Roosevelt's fireside chats struck a resonant chord even as radio signals faded and crackled with static. They still faded in the 1940s and 1950s—not unlike cell phone signal drops today. For example, if you were listening to a Pacific Coast League Los Angeles Angels baseball or Rams football game on a Saturday afternoon in the Los Angeles basin, it was exasperating—just as the crucial play started, the signal would fade or drift, or fill with static noise. A scramble to re-tune the dial would ensue, usually just in time to hear the aftermath rather than the event itself. Television was even more problematic—this newfangled invention required numerous knobs to fiddle with for contrast and it suffered frequent loss of synchronization.

The popularity of these communications and entertainment mediums was unmistakable, however, signaling a huge appetite for nationwide broadcasts. Long-distance broadcast had even more difficult technical issues to solve. A key invention originating in Professor Fred Terman's electrical engineering labs at Stanford in 1937 would provide the breakthrough needed. The klystron tube, a high-frequency (microwave) amplifying vacuum tube, would prove as powerful for analog communications as the microprocessor would later for computers.

Terman's work in communications and microwave electronics was so impressive that he was recruited right after Pearl Harbor to head the nation's premier defense research lab, the Radio Research Laboratory at Harvard. This lab and its sister MIT laboratory, the Radiation Laboratory, were phenomenally creative places during World War II. Alumni from both labs would lead a new field, electronics, a superset of radio. Whereas prewar electrical engineering departments focused on radio and telephony, microwave communications and television promised to change the national communication capability after the war. Terman seized upon this new field to train his students. Long resenting the fact that his best students had to seek work back east after graduation, Terman felt that the leadership of East Coast companies didn't fully appreciate the magnitude of this national communications opportunity.

It is hard to overstate how nurturing the Stanford campus had already been for nascent electronic businesses. Lee de Forest, inventor of the vacuum tube in 1906, moved to Palo Alto in 1910 to build a radio transmitter for the newly formed Federal Telegraph and Radio company, started by Cyril Elwell of Stanford University in Palo Alto, just after the nation's first broadcast station launched in San Jose. David Starr Jordan, Stanford's first president, was the first venture capitalist of Silicon Valley, investing $500 with twenty-four-year-old Elwell. By the 1930s, the Peninsula, a fifty-mile-long corridor between San Francisco and San Jose, with Palo Alto in the middle, was the place to be for students interested in radio and television. The Depression was a tremendously hard time for most companies, so many students stayed at the relatively well-endowed university.

Terman delighted in seeding small companies. He helped William Eitel and Jack McCullough establish Eitel-McCullough to build beam power tubes in 1934. He encouraged the Varian brothers, Sigurd and Russell, who invented the klystron and a decade later launched Varian Associates.[2] He aided Norman Moore, who started Electrodynamic Corporation in San Carlos to build microwave tubes. Charlie Litton built glass tubes for all of them on a special lathe, starting Litton Industries, which later merged with Electrodynamic.

Terman was especially fond of two remarkable young men in his 1934 graduate course—William Hewlett and David Packard.[3] Although Hewlett and Packard had discussed starting a business in the early 1930s, the Depression was in full swing when they graduated. Packard joined General Electric, and Hewlett continued studies at MIT. Packard's work group, led by John Cage, both built its own test gear and modified acquired tools to suit GE requirements. John Fluke, rooming with Packard, was in the group. Hewlett met Howard Vollum in a wartime Army lab, and urged Packard to interview Vollum in 1944 for a possible job at HP. Vollum, Fluke, and Hewlett and Packard all went on to found electronic test equipment companies—HP, Fluke, and Tektronix—which became the largest three in the world within thirty years.[4]

Practicing electrical engineers in 1940 used oscillators to simulate a radio signal, and voltmeters to measure the output signal level. Specialty test units, such as an amplitude distortion meter, could reveal specific problems. The Hewlett oscillator, derived from Hewlett's thesis under Terman's tutelage, gave the young company an interesting product much cheaper than competitive units from General Radio Company (GR). They dubbed it the HP 200A Audio Oscillator, because, as Hewlett said, "We didn't want a low number for the model, as people might think we were a small company."[5] The technology was straightforward—simple sheet metal fabrication assembled with standard radio parts—capacitors, vacuum tubes, resistors.

Fred Terman noted, "You could see how business was by just driving past it in the evenings, and seeing where the car was. If the car was in the driveway, you knew they had a good backlog."[6] Products were built to order; even standard products were modified for individual needs. Hewlett's venerable oscillator eventually had twenty-four standard variations, plus hundreds of unique versions. Years after retirement, Packard heard someone describing the early oscillator that Disney Studios bought as a marvelous technical contribution. The septuagenarian was apoplectic: "All we did was build a cheaper unit than General Radio. . . . Stop propagating the myth." While an adulating biographer called it rock-hard integrity, naysayers decried it as myopic marketing savvy. Steve Jobs at Apple Computer mocked HP's LaserJet marketing efforts years later, saying, "HP would market sushi as cold, dead fish."

The design for a second electronic test product category, voltmeters, was done by Packard—it emerged as the HP 400A AC Voltmeter, on the pricelist by September 1941. By including rectifier diodes in the feedback of the high-gain amplifier to stabilize calibration drift as the vacuum tubes aged, and using a linear AC scale, Dave's design virtually eliminated Ballantine Labs, the leading vendor at the time.[7]

The HP 300A Wave Analyzer in late 1941 was Hewlett's next major product contribution, aside from variations of the original oscillator. John Minck, an early HP marketing manager, noted that it "was a remarkable instrument, in a huge wooden cabinet, almost 3 feet high. It was . . . *very* sophisticated for 1941, when feedback theory was [new]. This product led the field for nearly two decades."[8]

As the success of HP products grew, the organization began to take shape with an employee base of strong talent. Both Hewlett and Packard were part-time HP employees the first year; Harvey Zieber became the first full-time employee. Packard didn't resign his GE job officially until the end of the year. In 1940, they hired Harvey's brother Glenn and Bill Girdner.[9] HP ended fiscal 1941 with six full-time employees. Hewlett rejoined the Army, as a liaison officer for the Signal Corps, when World War II began, leaving Packard to run the company. In 1942, four more full-time employees were added, including designers Brunton Bauer and Norm Schrock, and operations manager Frank Cavier. The company's manufacturing activities grew with a contingent of women working as part-time assemblers. Taking manufacturing contracts for products designed on the East Coast, the company thrived. It grew to nearly two hundred people, with sales of $1,538,902 and $288,543 in profits for fiscal 1944, the peak for both profits and employees for another seven years.[10] Noel Eldred, an earlier prized Terman student, joined in 1944 from local radio manufacturer Heintz and Kaufman, providing engineering and, later, marketing strength.[11] Ralph Lee joined in 1945, as did their Stanford friend, Ed Porter; the two teamed up to run manufacturing. When Hewlett rejoined in late 1945, he again became leader of the lab.

Packard was often in Washington, D.C., competing for government contracts. Fifty-hour work weeks were normal for employees; Packard devoted eighty hours, frequently sleeping on the premises. HP, more nimble than the much larger General Radio, won a lot of business during the war. Professor Terman helped steer several engineering jobs to HP; they produced finished products from the working prototypes developed at either MIT or Harvard Labs. Thus HP was able to move from the audio range—20 cycles to 20 kilocycles—into the UHF (ultra high frequency) radio frequency range with the Model A, designed by the U.S. Navy labs.[12] HP contributions were mechanical only—machine lapping and honing surfaces, which improved electrical noise performance.

Frank Cavier said, "The word was all around the [Stanford] labs that HP put out excellent equipment and that Dave Packard was a wonderful fellow to work with. All that reputation was established that early."[13] Cort Van Rensselaer, as an undergraduate Stanford engineering student, worked on an RF-frequency meter that tuned over a wide frequency range, for which HP had a production contract for a hundred units: "It was designed by General Radio, but apparently they couldn't fill the needs of the buyer."[14] Van Rensselaer was very impressed by the design team. He cited the time when Brunton Bauer, HP's lead designer, saw a GR wave analyzer prototype and, with HP techniques, got an equivalent HP product done within three months, beating GR to market handily.[15]

When World War II ended, the requirement to produce microwave products designed by others stopped. HP found itself reduced to building its original low-frequency audio-video test equipment. Many HP employees, most of them women, quit working of their own volition. Nevertheless, Packard had to lay off workers, resizing HP from nearly two hundred to about seventy employees. It was a traumatic time, one that he vowed they'd never repeat if possible.

But the new communications boom would play in their favor. It is difficult today to appreciate how isolated the cities of America were at midcentury. There was neither a nationwide communications network nor a national road system. Cities and states were local, parochial, and nearly autonomous in administration and activities. Some national radio programming such as FDR's fireside chats reached everyone, but radio even today is primarily local content. Television was barely accessible to most citizens. Though the technology had been available for a dozen years, televisions were rare because of Depression wages and lack of programming.

Only nine commercial television stations existed on V-J Day in 1945, in but eight cities. In 1950, television was just debuting in cities as large as St. Louis and Denver. President Harry Truman opened the Japanese Peace Conference in San Francisco on September 4, 1951, a historic event for the nation, television, and AT&T, because it was the first live transcontinental television program. Bobby Thomson's dramatic home run for the New York Giants over the Brooklyn Dodgers on October 3, 1951, made the first nationally televised sporting event memorable.[16]

When *I Love Lucy* debuted on October 15, 1951, it promptly became America's top-rated TV show: "From that minute forward, *I Love Lucy* has never been off the air since."[17] Americans bought televisions as never before, in order to watch the zany couple—Lucille Ball and Desi Arnaz—in improbable weekly escapades that broke numerous cultural barriers in mid-century America. Only 2,000 television sets had been sold in America by January 1940; some 3.6 million sets were in use by the end of the next decade. From 1950 through 1953, an amazing 6 million sets per year were purchased. Watching television became the national pastime, and on Monday night, all sets seemed tuned to *I Love Lucy.*[18]

The popularity of *I Love Lucy* underscored the nation's desire for nationwide broadcast signals. Fortunately, behind the scenes, AT&T was already deploying a vast network of microwave repeater stations so that signals (radio, TV, and telephone) could be easily beamed from anywhere in the country to anywhere else with relative ease. It became the information highway for a nation building a national identity, in essence, the Internet of its day. The basis for this national infrastructure was a grid of radio towers, all with line-of-sight connectivity. Repeater stations, no more than thirty miles apart, received the signal and then re-amplified it to overcome transmission losses. A broadcast from the East Coast to Chicago might involve forty repeater stations.[19] If any tower had transmission difficulty, the TV signal or telephone circuit could fail. Reliability was of paramount concern.[20] With this enormous backbone in place, nationally syndicated stations (ABC, CBS, NBC) could provide America a new taste of homogeneity in television content, in national news, idiomatic expressions, and fads. This grid enabled *I Love Lucy* to become a national phenomenon.

Most Hewlett-Packard products provided little value for this infrastructure. The grid, a many-thousand-node backbone of high-strength industrial equipment running with heavy power loads at microwave frequencies, required help at frequency ranges a million times higher than the audio sound waves for a radio and thousands of times higher than carrier signals for the local radio station broadcaster. Amplitude and frequency stability mattered; distortion introduced anywhere along the line was not easily removed; and the volume and importance of the national feeds meant that outages and interruptions were critical.

A phenomenal consumer electronics growth curve began. Although Bell Laboratories had invented the transistor in 1946, it only arrived in the consumer world during the Christmas shopping season of 1954, when Texas Instruments (TI) transistors powered the first battery-operated transistor radio. By 1960 there were 440 commercial VHF and 75 UHF stations; 85 percent of U.S. homes had a TV. Today, cell phones are ubiquitous, and iPods and personal DVD players are commonplace, but such things were Dick Tracy fantasies fifty years ago. Just as Ferdinand Porsche and Henry Ford were the only two in the world of several hundred automotive manufacturers to see the value of the personal automobile, one man—Akio Morita—would foretell the value of this revolution. In 1957, Morita bet his small Tokyo-based company, Toksuko Electronics, on it, creating Sony Electronics.[21] Its pocket radio in 1958 was the first electronics product to sell a half-million units in a year.

Against this backdrop, designers in myriad companies began developing televisions, stereos, radios, and other devices for an eager public. HP's audio-video oscillators and voltmeters were indispensable for designers and electronics technicians. These products presaged a broad line of test equipment, featuring high reliability, good accuracy, and moderate cost.

Packard wavered, though, about making investments in the much more difficult high-frequency microwave radio opportunities that Terman so fervently espoused. Because of what Hewlett had learned in his unique World War II service role as liaison between Army radio research and the Office of Scientific Research and Development (OSRD), he enthusiastically supported an investment in the microwave test business. To that end, Bill hired Bruce Wholey and Howard Zeidler from the Harvard Radio Research Lab, and Art Fong and Ralph Lee from the MIT Radiation Labs even as HP was laying off nearly 70 percent of its employees.[22] Key designer Norm Schrock had used an RCA version of Varian's klystron tube in the company's contracted microwave signal generators during the war; he had also built a distributed microwave amplifier.[23] Packard was persuaded that these new employees gave HP adequate background to buy the rights to the Harvard Naval Research program.

Ironically, the market had been incubating for so long that the prime movers in the first wave—General Radio and Varian—had both given up on its further development, and were actively pursuing other avenues.

This investment quickly paid off. Revenues in 1948 nearly tripled to $2 million, taking the company to a new plateau. HP sustained this level of business for three years. Then, in 1951, a second wave of investments, along with the Korean War need for microwave equipment, paid off with another doubling of revenue. Revenues doubled again the following year. The 1952 Hewlett-Packard catalog listed fifty-seven instruments, thirty-four of them audio-video, twelve in communication test, and eleven in RF or microwave. Average revenue per product in 1951 was $90,000 per year, producing a very modest median of sixteen units per month per instrument.

Suddenly, the little Palo Alto–based instrument company had joined the big leagues, exceeding $10 million in annual revenue in 1952. The company had expanded during the war, contracting for the Redwood Building two blocks north at Ash and Page Mill in late 1942. Subsequent growth fueled further buildings. A true headquarters, two blocks north at 395 Page Mill Road, was completed in early 1954. Packard, ever cautious, had the headquarters designed so that it could be reconfigured as a grocery store—just in case. He feared another layoff when the Korean War ceased and the television fad slowed.[24]

The first twenty-five years were good for Hewlett, Packard, and their company. They focused on electronic test equipment, a small niche in the grand panoply of electronics, where the emphasis was on reliable and accurate performance. When an engineer uses a piece of test equipment to measure a circuit, there is no room for questioning whether the test equipment is wrong rather than the circuit. When a doctor takes the temperature of a patient, for example, if the answer is 103 degrees, the doctor never asks, "I wonder if the thermometer is wrong." If confidence in the measuring tool is impaired, the measurement is compromised. HP products had to be three to five times as fast as the system being tested so that the measurement data represented the system under test rather than the test equipment. These constraints set high expectations for HP design engineers, demanding tools more advanced than the "state of the art" in order to measure "the state of the art" accurately. Hewlett-Packard's name became synonymous with high performance, quality, and reliability. Hewlett insisted that products had to exceed published specifications by an average 30 percent, a performance level often verified by customers.[25] An uncompromising integrity in technical accuracy, in advertising copy, in conduct with suppliers and customers, and with employees, became a hallmark of the company.

The nation's radio frequency spectrum was starting to be used. And for every category of usage, an opportunity arose to build or operate equipment, or to build test tools for those who build or operate equipment. Both founders seldom wavered with respect to their focus on test equipment during this period, as opposed to user or operator equipment. Building a radio was out of the question, but building a test tool suite to verify radio performance was approved. Although test was a somewhat less competitive portion of the food chain, it demanded skills well advanced from typical designer requirements for the operational equipment itself.[26]

Hewlett and Packard had strong beliefs about how to run a company. They believed in the dignity of each employee, that people like to do a good job, and that the employee usually knows best the needs and problems of his or her job. So the goal became how to give people the responsibility for performing that job. Their attitude built enormous goodwill and sense of pride, in addition to getting the jobs performed to a high standard. They liked the informality of calling people by first names; they were called Bill and Dave by everyone at the company. As the company grew, their desire for keeping informality was a large factor in deciding to organize the company by divisions. Hewlett said, "You can keep track of five hundred names, but not a thousand."[27]

Neither Hewlett nor Packard sought growth for growth's sake. They always concluded that growth was a reflection of other more important values. They strongly held that the company should be self-financed. Because no growth could occur without profits, profits were the most significant objective. Their stance, though, was that profits should be appropriate—if too high, competitors as well as scrutiny are attracted.[28] The two founders decided that they would never again take government contracts, because they wanted to avoid downsizing their workforce if possible.[29] Both were cautious, avoiding the limelight, fads, or quick profits. Hewlett strongly felt that the company should avoid competing with fortified hills, areas where strong competitors were entrenched. Packard echoed those sentiments often.[30] Caution, though, didn't keep them from curiosity or risk-taking.

Five years after Hewlett returned from military service, Terman's protégés were off to a good start.

A Paradigm Shift in Communications Electronics

Both Hewlett and Packard were adept at attracting and retaining talented, self-assured people. Art Fong, a Berkeley graduate who joined the MIT Radiation Lab in 1943 and HP in 1946, was the lead designer with Bruce Wholey for a series of microwave signal generators, which were essentially Hewlett's audio oscillator for very high frequencies, coupled with an automatic frequency changer that swept across a band of frequencies. The Hewlett oscillator produced a signal at any audio frequency, just as hitting a piano key would do for middle C. A sweeper is akin to running your hand quickly up or down the piano keyboard to hit all the discrete key frequencies in order. Fong became known as Mr. Microwave at HP, as he designed multiple versions of signal generators as well as spectrum analyzers.[31]

Barney Oliver was another key hire destined to make a profound mark on both the research capability and the product portfolio of HP. Oliver, Hewlett, and Packard had talked in the early 1930s about building a business together, and Oliver had stayed in touch with Bill. Oliver had become a respected scientist at Bell Laboratories, working on space telemetry and space satellite communications, the technology successor to the terrestrial microwave grid infrastructure just being constructed. Barney turned Bill down at first, saying, "I just can't leave this." Bill rejoined, "Okay, I understand, but you're not off the hook." A year later, Hewlett returned, saying, "How about it?" Barney agreed to come in early 1952.[32] Bill Hewlett, delighted, recalled that Barney had petitioned Fred Terman to let him take a graduate course at age seventeen. "Fred let him take it on the stipulation that if Barney didn't pass the first midterm examination, he'd have to drop out. Well, Barney got the highest grade not only on the midterm, but on every exam for the rest of the year!"[33]

When Oliver arrived in 1952, much of what he found was stimulating, enjoyable, and rewarding, but his opinion of the team was variable:

> It was a spotty organization when I first came. I felt a great need to conduct a course in modern circuit theory and the mathematics pertaining to functions of a complex variable. . . . I ran that course every week for a year, preparing a lecture for it, giving tests and grading problem sets. In the mature atmosphere of Bell Labs I became quite used to a very high, uniform technical level. The lab at HP was assembled catch-as-catch-can, out of people who happened by. So there was quite a disparity in the technical sophistication of the group. There were some caustic comments about it, too. "Who does this &#$&* think he is?" Those things were minor. [HP had] a spirited, enthusiastic group that really believed that they had the best outfit on earth. There was a very high morale and a very high determination to build quality into things. There was much more daily dedication to progress for each individual's work than there was at Bell. The pace was much slower at Bell, things were more relaxed. . . . You didn't feel the blowtorch on you to get the job finished to nearly the extent I felt it when I first came to HP.[34]

Oliver strengthened both the design capability and the research leadership perspective. He focused the lab team of twenty designers on the communications sector. A stream of products emerged, and the company expanded by another 250 percent in the next five years.

It was a tough five years emotionally. The lab's direction was still set by the strong-willed Packard and the zesty Hewlett, but now with a new ingredient: the stern, brilliant, iconoclastic Oliver, who brooked no fools. Project reviews became ordeals. "Somebody comes up with an idea that doesn't make a whole lot of sense to [Barney], and boy, he blasts them out of there," said Cavier.[35] Oliver soon meshed with the more informal ways of Hewlett and Packard. Oliver's recollections are telling:

> I was very pleased with the spirit of HP when I first came. In those early years, we'd always collect at the end of the week at the Heidelberg and drink a few beers and review the week. It was very much a family atmosphere and a very positive attitude that pervaded the company in those days. Everybody felt part of the act. Everybody expected you to produce and by God, you'd get up early to do it.[36]

Oliver shared another story he relished. He met Packard when he was in on a Saturday to check the progress of some projects that were "a bit behind schedule." Packard asked, "When are we going to get some products out of this lab?" Oliver began by saying, "Well, I know there are some things lagging . . ." when Packard cut him off to say, "Are you going to give me a lot of excuses or are you going to get something done?"

Asked about product strategies, Oliver had a disarmingly simple answer: "There were certain obvious places where we needed projects, and we arrived at them almost automatically, it seems to me. It was usually obvious what we should be doing."

Barney was candid about the major projects and programs of HP:

> The RC Oscillator (HP 200A) was a very good product because it was the product that started the company and was big enough in itself that, together with its cousins and its variations, it sustained the company . . . until additional products could be added. . . . It was a helluva contribution. . . . Generically, the microwave signal generators were quite important. The HP 608 was developed before I came out here . . . the whole concept of filling in the line up to twenty gigahertz took a big part of our time in the '50s.[37]

Barney arrived in the midst of the Korean War years, years that had seen the company grow at a torrid pace, increasing revenue by more than five times in three years, as microwave test equipment was sorely needed for new military communications. And Barney got something done. His leadership fueled Hewlett-Packard's first business transformation, from radio test equipment to microwave gear. HP was now recognized as the leading signal generator company in the world, from low-end audio frequency ranges up through microwave frequencies. Competition in this space was limited, both because few engineers in the country understood the technology at this frequency, and because the market had been too small to be tempting. Heeding Terman's prompts, Hewlett-Packard found itself well ahead of competitors. The company stayed ahead, eventually becoming the predominant test equipment supplier to the microwave communications industry.

The partners had experienced more success by the end of 1953 than either might have imagined. They enjoyed the business and their colleagues, they had made a difference in the industry, and they had developed a solid reputation within the wider electronics community. Both founders sought broader fields, the reason that they had persuaded Oliver to join the firm. Packard especially envisioned this as an opportunity to acquire some technology or other companies. Because of his youthful experience abroad and his wartime service, Hewlett wanted to move the company to a more international stance. Nonetheless, when they tried in early 1954 to persuade the management team to broaden their goals—to view the future as an unlimited horizon that could take them in untold directions—they received a tepid response. The management team was dispirited. Tired from the pace, they were not at all certain that they wanted to take on even more challenges. Although they were not mutinous, they were recalcitrant.

Packard and Hewlett acquiesced, unexpectedly choosing to focus considerable time and energy outside the company; the management team was granted more overall responsibility for operating and maintaining the business. Dave and Bill bought a large working cattle ranch with company funds in San Felipé, forty-five miles south of their Palo Alto homes. Cavier, writing a $350,000 check, lamented that the money could have been put to better use within the company. In his autobiography, Packard noted with pride that he personally helped build twenty miles of road on the ranch with his D8 Caterpillar, something hard to imagine being completed during a few weekends.[38] The duo had already donated a wing for the new Electronics Research Laboratory on the Stanford campus. Packard, deeply involved on the Palo Alto School Board since 1948, became a Stanford

University trustee in mid-1954. In late 1953, Hewlett was elected president of the Institute of Radio Engineers (IRE), the largest electrical engineering professional society. They were now "men of society."[39]

A Paradigm Shift in Digital Electronics

I think there is a world market for about five computers.

THOMAS J. WATSON JR., 1953[40]

APRIL 1954, PALO ALTO, CALIFORNIA: Norman Neely was upset. Waving his arms, his voice booming, he implored both Hewlett and Packard to pay attention. Tektronix was beating HP with their new oscilloscopes, time after time, and he was tired of it. Norm Neely was the leading sales agent for the Hewlett-Packard Company. He had founded Neely Enterprises in North Hollywood, California, in the mid-1930s, arguably the most successful electronics test equipment manufacturer's representative in the world. But Hewlett and Packard had their hands full. The microwave business was consuming their company. Growth had been tumultuous, the team nearly mutinous. The two men listened with impatience as Neely ranted about this missed opportunity. DuMont Laboratories in New Jersey had long been the leading oscilloscope manufacturer, just as General Radio was the signal generator leader. But a small company in Beaverton, Oregon—Tektronix—was serving notice that it would be a serious contender for providing excellent and valuable test equipment.

Founded by Howard Vollum after the war, Tektronix by 1954 matched DuMont in a nicely growing market. Packard replied that he had sent Vollum to Norm's sales company in the first place. Norm said that he sold for both companies, and he knew the sales magnitude for Tektronix much better than Packard or Hewlett. Within seven years, with only one product, Tektronix was half the size of the entire Hewlett-Packard Company. Vollum's company grew nicely during the aftermath of the Korean War wind-down, whereas HP's heady growth rate abruptly stopped. In addition, Tektronix began to establish its own sales group in 1953, leaving Neely without an oscilloscope product.[41]

Packard strongly believed that HP's objective should be to dominate any market it entered. He and Hewlett were clear that true contributions would lead to superior recognition by customers, and that such products could fuel HP with sufficient profit to self-fund its growth. HP history showed that contributions could win loyal support from customers. Hewlett's oscillator was very successful against General Radio; HP's microwave test equipment quickly outdistanced the former test equipment leader; and Packard's HP 400A vacuum tube voltmeter was likewise able to thwart Ballantine early in World War II.[42]

Beckman Instruments also loomed as a competitor, moving strongly into electronics from a chemistry instrumentation base with the purchase of Berkeley Labs in 1950. Berkeley Labs had a frequency counter useful for radio stations to stabilize their signals. Here again, when Al Bagley reconfigured his nuclear counter into the HP 524A Frequency Counter, HP's new product proved far superior in performance for a roughly equivalent price. Beckman quickly shifted focus elsewhere, and HP held a commanding position in this space as well.[43]

To Neely, HP's founders seemed a bit smug. After failing to budge them, Neely persuaded, cajoled, and berated fellow distributors, "who clamored for a scope to sell to flesh out their catalogs," to get the message to the partners, who by now were busy cattle ranching.[44] In truth, Tektronix wasn't beating HP head-to-head. Discretionary dollars for test equipment were being diverted to this new oscilloscope; indirectly, HP's representatives were being beaten in the competition for capital funds. Doug Strain, lead designer for Beckman Instruments, and later founder of Electro-Scientific Industries in Portland, described the value of the tool: "We tried it out on some pulse circuitry. Suddenly we could see what we were doing and we didn't let it go. We wouldn't let him out the door with it."[45] Vollum's "best guess was the entire world market for his sophisticated oscilloscope was . . . about 500 to 600."[46] Tektronix sold 5 units in 1947, 50 in 1948, 150 the next year, and over 240 in fiscal 1950, three weeks before the Korean War broke out. The next year, a surprising 800 units sold.[47]

Ernst Guillemin, a professor as noteworthy at MIT as Terman was at Stanford, changed the balance. Guillemin, Hewlett's major professor for his MIT master's degree, was at the Radiation Labs during the war, adapting Fourier Analysis mathematics to reconcile the continuous wave technologies of radio with radar switching techniques—called the frequency domain and the time domain. After the war, Guillemin returned to MIT and wrote *Introductory Circuit Theory* to add pulse circuit design to the radio engineering curriculum. Guillemin's work provided quantitative support for the replacement of signal generators and voltmeters with oscilloscope analysis methods as a preferred stimulus-response test system. Guillemin's book swept the universities in 1953; senior and graduate laboratories sought Tektronix scopes, as did industry.[48]

Grudgingly, Hewlett and Packard approved a modest oscilloscope development at HP to appease Neely. They commissioned two products, a high-performance HP 150A and a low-frequency HP 130A. Veteran designer Norm Schrock headed the HP 150A team; young recruits were assigned to the HP 130A. The recipe learned against GR—build something much cheaper than leading competitive products, and aim it at the low end of the market—defined the HP 130A.[49] It filled a low-end niche that Tektronix had overlooked, selling well to radio and TV manufacturers such as Magnavox, Collins Radio, and Zenith, who were traditional HP customers. Fast iteration kept it in front. Four more models soon followed, giving HP very successful audio-video scope products.[50]

Alas, the high-performance HP 150A oscilloscope carried a flawed trigger circuit and unexpected reliability problems, dooming the product.[51] Within HP, unaccustomed to market failure, scapegoating began almost immediately, a dirge sung by naysayers for a full decade as the scope division struggled. Tektronix surged from 45 percent of HP's total revenue in 1953 to 80 percent by 1956—Tektronix profits were 150 percent of the entire Hewlett-Packard company, whose founders had been preoccupied on their ranch. Tektronix now had a ten-to-one lead on HP in oscilloscopes, much more commanding even than the position that HP built vis-à-vis General Radio in microwave. Such leads are hard to overcome. Bill Webber, in charge of Tektronix's patent management, noted,

> When HP went in the [oscilloscope] business, they had no choice really but to use our patents. We had several discussions . . . with Dave Packard, who said, "If we're using your patents, we'll pay you." . . . [Hewlett] said, "No, Howard [Vollum], we're not going to pay you. Barney Oliver says he can design around

your patents and we're not going to pay you.' Finally . . . Hewlett said, "Howard, I don't know how you guys did it, but every decision your guys made was right. We can't design around your patents."[52]

With Oliver's direct involvement, Rod Carlson and Kay Magleby led a team that developed the first successful sampling oscilloscope, enabling high-frequency observation of repetitive waveforms. Lumatron, a little company in upstate New York, had pioneered the concept under contract to IBM in the mid-1950s but was unable to produce quality equipment.[53] IBM took the idea to Tektronix, which declined the proposal. Barney leapt at it, and HP designers came through in dramatic fashion. Oliver proudly said, "It sold like hotcakes"—perhaps by comparison with other HP scopes, but not in any economic sense. Although forty-one units were sold in the peak month, typical unit volumes were twenty per month, for an annual sales revenue of only $2 million in 1961.

The Tektronix story was an important omen. HP designers created a notable set of firsts with a series of niche leadership products, but Tek was able to keep HP's innovative edge from eroding Tek profits or sales. It was HP's first experience with a well-funded, entrenched competitor that was willing to go head-to-head. The scope business was vastly different from historic HP experience in complexion, technology, usage, and customer expectation. The crucible of competitive pressure shaped the HP people within it. Hewlett said later, "It was probably better for everyone that we didn't [hire Vollum for HP], because he started that great company and then we proceeded to compete with them, so that everyone won by that."[54] Oliver was not as sanguine: "We didn't come into the oscilloscope field with any significant contribution. We made a pretty good scope, but it had some troubles. Tek had a big effort riding on oscilloscopes, and only part of our effort was on oscilloscopes. We could never leapfrog them. We weren't really making a contribution."[55] Barney didn't mention that his own design was unreliable. Dave simply said, "We did a lousy job."[56]

In hindsight, the HP leadership team missed the point; they focused on the products rather than on root cause. HP pursued microwave test opportunities, ignoring pulse circuit applications, whereas Tektronix pursued switching-circuit analysis. The irony was profound. Terman's

Harvard lab did much of the work with pulse circuits, and Harvard had built the Mark I computer during the war as well. But after the war, MIT seized the initiative to build experimental digital computers, foregoing the communications opportunity. Indeed, one could assert that MIT tackled the more interesting opportunity, whereas West Coast companies (led by Terman and Stanford) were seduced by easy government money in the microwave arena.

Certainly MIT was not worried about playing second fiddle to an upstart West Coast university. All roads led east for a long time. Fred Terman had trained under Vannevar Bush at MIT on radio circuits in the 1920s; Hewlett completed his master's degree there in the mid-1930s. Karl Compton, president of MIT, led the Engineering Accreditation Committee in 1935 that blackballed Terman's program at Stanford because it had too many liberal arts courses. Compton had already set up the Science Advisory committee for President Franklin Roosevelt, and nominated his engineering dean, Vannevar Bush, to head the successor group, OSRD. Bush commandeered the nation's universities for applied war designs, which led him to bring his first graduate student, Terman, back to lead the Harvard Radio Research Labs in early 1942.

Bush, not Terman, wrote the seminal essay for the electronics age in 1945, describing the Memex (*mem*ory *ex*tender) in a powerful *Atlantic Monthly* article in which he foresaw the future of the digital information age, with a computer, digital networks, and massive digital storage at its core. Vannevar Bush's vision hit the popular conscience when his *Atlantic Monthly* article was reprinted in *Life* magazine.[57] It influenced researchers for years, including futurists Douglas Engelbart and Ted Nelson.[58] Heroes of the fledgling computer age—Jay Forrester, Robert Everett, and An Wang at MIT—gave tutelage to Ken Olsen and Gordon Bell, who conceived the Digital Equipment Corporation (DEC) while working on Project Whirlwind at MIT, the first computer that operated in real time, with video display output. Thus MIT led the digital electronics revolution, supporting both IBM and a fledgling DEC, just as Stanford led with frequency domain components for the communications revolution.[59]

In retrospect, it proved difficult to predict the evolution of the new beast electronics, whether analog or digital, communications or computing. Missed forecasts littered the landscape, with comments amplified by the trade press for years. The imperious IBM leader Thomas J. Watson Sr. was often quoted as saying, "I think there is a world market for about five computers."[60] Ken Olsen, founder of Digital Equipment Corporation, the largest minicomputer company, would later prognosticate, "There is no reason that anyone would want a computer in their home."[61] The most respected test equipment manufacturer, General Radio, missed the move to microwave test equipment, even though its designers created most of the product concepts. The new leader of the overall electronics test equipment market, HP, missed the significant move both to time domain equipments and computers, as did its mentor Fred Terman and his university.

Missing a prediction often isn't as important as the later reaction to trends and events. GR never recovered. HP thrived in its focus areas, but never prevailed with oscilloscopes. IBM, DEC, and Tektronix all parlayed their initial lead into a classical first-mover domination for several decades. At HP, a spirited debate got under way. The markets in which the company had invested—both microwave and audio, plus the counter markets—were topping out, or at least so it seemed, with the sales rates of 1953 and 1954, leading to strong discussion about considering other opportunities.

Packard and Hewlett, though feeling rejuvenated by their outside activities, were frankly disappointed by the performance of the company under their protégés. Except for the extraordinary 1945–1946 postwar resizing, 1954 was the only year until the dot-com meltdown that HP revenues and profits were lower than the previous year, a bit of a debacle. Although neither Hewlett nor Packard knew what Tektronix's numbers looked like, Norm Neely's exhortations had concerned them. Figures 2.1 and 2.2 illustrate the numbers as they became known when the two companies later went public. Revenue momentum and profit for HP were downhill, revenue shrinking slightly in 1954 and profit down nearly 20 percent. Tektronix, with new product introductions in late 1953, had a strikingly different tale for 1954. It finished the year with 58 percent of HP's total revenue, and soaring profits—up 106 percent—which were a stunning 131 percent of HP's total profits.

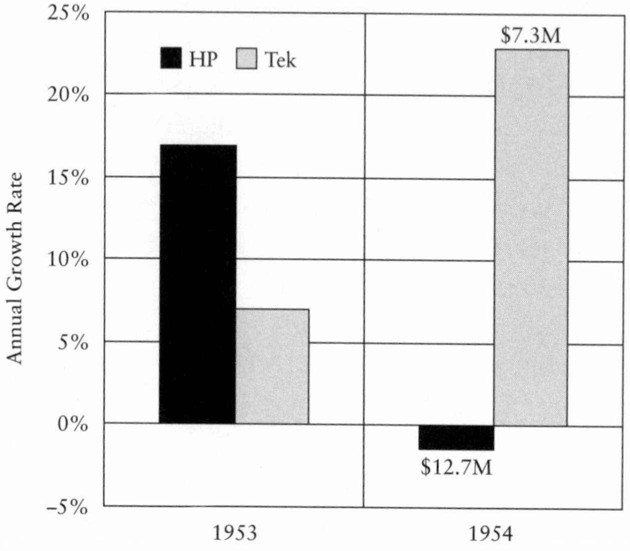

FIGURE 2.1 HP and Tektronix revenue growth, 1953–1954

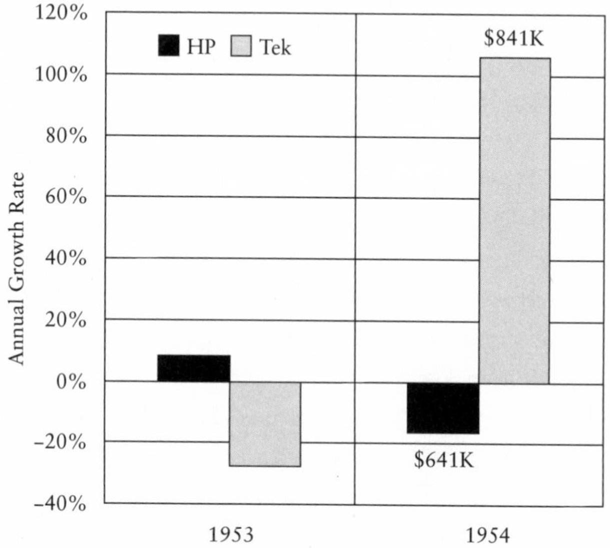

FIGURE 2.2. HP and Tektronix profit growth, 1953–1954

By early 1955, Frank Cavier, Noel Eldred, Barney Oliver, and Ed Porter, the top four executives, had a growing sense of concern. The sales momentum had dimmed more rapidly than anyone dared imagine. Between Norm Neely's warnings and the modest response HP was preparing to the new Tektronix offering, the empowered management team found itself weighed down by their expanded responsibilities. Dave and Bill, though involved, were still spending a good deal of time on their outside activities.[62] And then, an unsolicited buyout offer appeared.

The story might have ended there. Innumerable entrepreneurs have started companies, grown them to some size, and then sold out their position in order to retire young and play golf, sail the Caribbean, or pursue other interests. Many more have started companies and gotten them part way along, only to discover that their enthusiasm outweighed their talents and skills for managing complexity. Very few partnerships develop and flourish over time. Hewlett and Packard managed to surmount all three issues—learning to savor both cattle ranching and public service at relatively young ages; then changing and broadening their focus at their company, developing into superb, self-taught managers; and, finally, strengthening their partnership.

A set of candid discussions in early 1955 led to a meeting of the minds, and with renewed intent, Packard and Hewlett reasserted their leadership without fanfare in 1955, to the relief of the management team. Hewlett concluded his IRE presidency; he and Flora went to Europe to explore his belief that the time was becoming propitious for international involvement. Packard resigned his long-term Palo Alto School Board seat, citing "rising business demands."[63] Perhaps the most remarkable part of the story is the unobtrusive manner in which they demonstrated their leadership. As Packard often noted, they did it "by applying steady, gentle pressure from the rear."[64] The enthusiasm that both Hewlett and Packard brought for redoubling their efforts was predicated on building a much larger and more flexible organization. And they did it together even more visibly and effectively than during the early formative years of the company. By comparison with other strong entrepreneurs, they did it in a very unusual manner. They had rediscovered that they liked time away for their personal interests. They spent many hours discussing and thinking about how they could build an increasingly large company that could be managed to their expectations without them having to spend all of their time and energy running it. Packard noted, with appreciation, "By running the ranches together—as well as the company—Bill and I developed a unique understanding of each other. That harmony has served us well every single day in running HP."[65]

Barney Oliver recalled this shift, telling Dave Kirby in 1991,

> Some rough times in the . . . '50s—Dave took to having staff meetings in his office on a weekly basis. This was something new, a more formal approach to management than we were used to. In that formal setting, his natural and ever-present concern for the business showed up loud and clear. We used to go in there smiling and come out rather sober. I remember joking with Porter and Cavier about how we should put a bucket of red paint outside the door and daub ourselves with it as we came out to indicate how we'd been bloodied.[66]

Ed van Bronkhorst alluded to this period as well, noting,

> Somebody had discussed with them whether they'd like to sell the whole company. And they made a decision that, no, they were going to stick with it, grow it. Part of this was their sense of responsibility to the people they'd hired.[67]

The product focus could have been the first order of business—at most high-tech companies facing an abyss, a redoubled product program would be the natural starting point. It was a candidate for their attention. Both Hewlett and Oliver had a passion for moving the company into scientific measurement, strongly supported by Al Bagley. Bruce Wholey had conceived the notion of combining a power meter and a leveled sweeper, with an automated sweep indexer, to create a spectrum analyzer. Hewlett preferred medical instrumentation, which traced to his father's vocation. Oliver, a physical scientist, was interested in astronomy, physics, and chemistry quite as much as the engineering disciplines. While Oliver acknowledged that oscilloscopes had great value, none of the three was motivated to pursue them. But Hewlett and Packard had larger concerns on their minds.

The two felt very strongly about what they had to do next: they had to develop leadership below themselves, or they'd be forever caught in the conundrum of seeming indispensable. Hewlett especially felt that 1957 was HP's watershed.[68] This was the critical test in his view for how or even whether the company, and he and Dave, could clear the hurdle that trapped so many. *Watershed:* the word connotes much in the arid West. A watershed event is a critical point that marks a fundamental division or a change of course, a turning point.

In his autobiography, Dave singled out several differentiating events in 1957:

- Taking the company public
- Deciding to establish a manufacturing presence in Europe
- Creating product divisions for the company
- Holding the company's first off-site meeting for senior managers
- Introducing a formal set of corporate objectives
- Enormous hiring expansion, with 74 percent new hires (versus a typical 13 percent)
- Occupancy of a new headquarters in the Stanford Industrial Park

Each of these was a significant event. Taken together, they represented monumental dedication to a bolder future, one that could scale significantly while encouraging personal initiative and participation, without the founders being as directly involved as they had been up until now. Insight and ingenuity would be demonstrated as the company evolved over the next decade. In world history similar attempts have almost always been doomed to failure as the enterprise grows larger than something the individuals can manage. As the bolder future of HP unfolded, the initiative, ingenuity, and innovation expected would be the critical characteristic of the HP Way. How the pair perceived the need to restructure their company, and then confidently created an inspired response, is perhaps the most stunning story of Hewlett-Packard's early history.

CHAPTER 3

Scaling the HP Way

When you signed up to HP, certainly in those early days, you signed up to the objectives and to those values. And there's a phrase in Dave's Sonoma talk where he says that people who can't sign up to the profit objective have no role in the management of the company now or in the future. I mean that's calling a spade a bloody shovel. Things were really quite crisp.

JOHN DOYLE (HP VICE PRESIDENT, HUMAN RESOURCES)[1]

JUNE 12, 1957, SONOMA, CALIFORNIA: Attendees recalled the events years later. Frank Cavier said Packard "tried to include everyone in it and have them feel it was the kind of thing they wanted and appreciated and understood and sort of their idea in a way." Al Bagley said, "This guy came down the hill with a stone slab with these things engraved on it." Ed van Bronkhorst, more sardonic, said, "I think [the objectives] were handed down."[2] Cort Van Rensselaer was most impressed:

> [The year] 1957 represented a really major change in the company because Hewlett and Packard came to the conclusion that they really had something that was going to go places. In order to make that happen, they felt they had to change the way they were running the company. They selected about thirty people and said this was the management staff, and then we all went off to that retreat. . . . The main purpose of that meeting was for Packard to tell these thirty managers whom they had chosen what the company's objectives were. Packard wrote the objectives, which have not changed all that much in the ensuing years.[3]

Both Hewlett and Packard felt that the HP Way needed to be codified and documented in writing, especially if the company growth plans were to materialize with the anticipated geographic dispersion. Packard discussed the main points with each of the senior management staff ahead of time, and then produced a written *coda* for the first-ever general managers meeting—known as the Sonoma meeting—in June 1957.

Packard's presentation was refreshing, bold, and even inspired. The corporate objectives were pragmatic, logical, and fair. They stated the priorities of the organization: (1) Profit, (2) Customers, (3) Fields of Interest, (4) Growth, (5) Our People, (6) Management, and (7) Citizenship. The preamble, as powerful as the objectives themselves, described the type of organization Bill and Dave were creating and how the objectives reinforced it. An organization has certain "fundamental requirements: first, the most capable people available . . . second, enthusiasm should exist at all levels . . . third . . . all levels should work in unison toward common objectives."[4] Changing hardly at all for the next fifty years, the objectives have served as an abiding signal of a unique combination of business focus, enlightened corporate self-interest, and citizenship, along with enormous belief in human dignity and capability. John Doyle, who taught them widely for years in the Corporate Training Center, said,

> Dave turned into a great theoretical businessman. He did a lot of reading and quite a lot of speaking. Some of his articles are really important. Once you describe clearly both the goals of the organization and the values that you will use to approach them, then you've done an awful lot.[5]

Expectations of high performance, commitment, and dedication ran through the speech; Dave affirmed that "half-hearted interest or half-hearted effort" doesn't cut it.[6] The objectives were a Bill of Rights, promising people the freedom to work toward goals in ways they determined best. Managers know less than the workers about what's needed: HP intended to let the worker closest to the problem decide.

The second management conference, at Sonoma in 1958, featured two remarkable presentations, one by Packard about people management, and one by Hewlett about international opportunity. Following Packard's corporate objectives talk of the previous year, he felt it appropriate to address the management side. Packard's "Simple Rules,"[7] recorded by the new human resources director, Ray Wilbur, have been called "elegant" and "timeless" by many (see Appendix B). Perhaps most notable about these two meetings, though, is that prior to this point, HP had an entirely oral history—from these meetings onward, the mantra was written, documented, told, and retold. For two men who wrote little over long lifetimes, this was an acme performance.

The Watershed Events

Each "Watershed" event represented substantial change. Decisions to decentralize, to disperse company units geographically, and to compete globally are difficult to implement and arduous to manage today. Fifty years ago, it was audacious in the extreme. In addition, diversifying into new fields of endeavor has been an elusive chimera for many managers and management teams. Deciding to "go public" has its own set of constraints and difficulties, not to mention emotional involvement for founders.

Taken together, the Watershed events remarkably redefined the corporation, putting in place a scaffold for growth that would allow HP to capitalize on opportunity in multiple markets, countries, and technologies. But, in marked contrast to most companies embarking on such change, they combined these new initiatives with something even bolder—Hewlett and Packard consciously chose to do it by delegation rather than direction. This unorthodox decision would permit scaling the HP Way across the globe, even while allowing the two founders more freedom and time for ranching. In many respects, it fundamentally redefined the HP Way, for it really represented much more delegation, more trust, and more independence of action than folk had ever experienced under Packard's

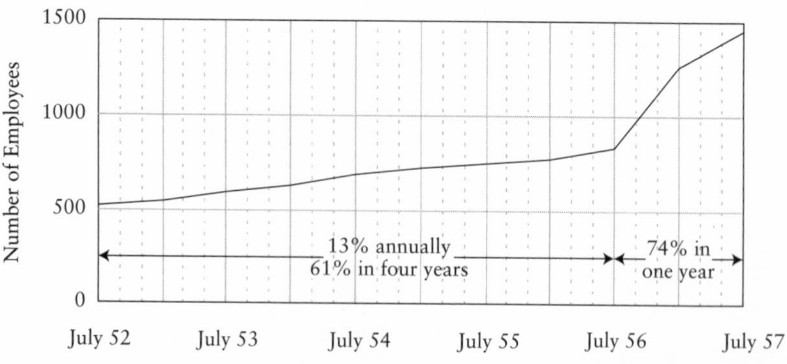

FIGURE 3.1. Hewlett-Packard employees, 1953–1957

baleful eye, whether watching over paper clips and screw sizes or wielding a blood-red paintbrush.

In 1957, the company virtually doubled in employment to nearly fifteen hundred staff. From the start of fiscal 1953 through late 1956, the company grew from 537 to 785 people, a 13 percent annual growth rate. In one year, from July 1956, company employment leapt by 74 percent (Figure 3.1)—no wonder the HP Way had to be written down.[8]

Management Crises

An influential *Harvard Business Review* article in 1972 helped fuel a considered view in HP executive circles that $50 to $100 million in revenue was the magic number—growing to that point was relatively easy with founder management; past that size, companies struggled to redefine how they would be guided. Further, the article stimulated perception that revenues of $500 million to $1 billion would become the next crisis point—this at a time that HP revenues reached $475 million.[9] The thematic points of the article are illustrated in Figure 3.2, redrawn in HP terms (log-linear plot).[10]

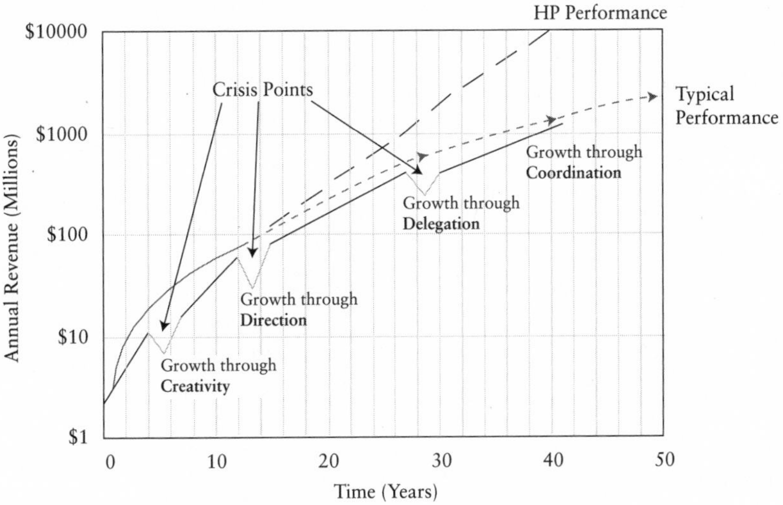

FIGURE 3.2. Management crisis points and revised approaches as function of size

The graph illustrates Packard and Hewlett's remarkable leadership decision. It is apt to describe the era from 1939 through 1952 as a period of "growth through creativity." And the dismal results of 1954 could be seen as a "crisis point," especially when measured against the growth curve of Tektronix. But then an anomaly occurred. Rather than a period of hands-on direction from Hewlett and Packard, the still youthful pair stepped back and tried to develop methods for delegating and decentralizing activities rather than stepping up to the challenge of running them directly—this was the less visible, but extremely vital part of their imaginative solution to the issues of the first Watershed.

Employee Ownership

Hewlett and Packard began experimenting with shared ownership structures when they established the Palo Alto Engineering Company (PAECO) in 1951. This was a novel arrangement whereby they, along with several essential employees, organized a separate company primarily intended to be a captive supplier to HP for many hard-to-obtain components, such as transformers, chokes, and wire harnesses. A bolder proposal—Dynac, Inc.—was announced early in fiscal year 1956. A spin-out corporation in effect, Dynac allowed a number of HP employees a higher equity stake in their success while giving HP a chance to invest in areas adjacent to its main activities. Dynac's logo was the HP logo inverted. Later, when it was found that the Dynac name was trademarked, it was renamed Dymec, keeping the same logo.

The Dynac experiment offered some significant lessons about funding, plus motivating creativity and diversifying into new arenas. More important, it signaled that the founders were ready to experiment with the company itself to deal with the issues raised by the management team.[11] A bigger signal came in mid-1957. They decided to take HP public so employees could build a sense of ownership and equity in the company's growth and success that went beyond the existing incentive with their leadership profit-sharing program. How they did it tells much about the duo.

The pair put 10 percent of their holdings—300,000 shares—up for public sale, but in the process, they gave 55,373 shares away to their employees, prorated as a function of job contribution and length of service. Five vice presidents each received 1,667 shares, and senior technical contributors received 834 shares. Some 31,000 shares were awarded to fifty key employees. At $16.00 per share, Hewlett and Packard gave $885,968 to current employees.[12] They also established a ten-share, ten-year service grant. Although the 1957 *Annual Report* noted that everyone with six months of service was given at least ten shares, John Doyle, vice president of Human Resources, said, "I joined the company right after Labor Day of '57, and I think they went public in late October. Even I was given a gift of 10 shares. Everybody got a minimum gift of 10 shares and the gift was proportional to the number of years you'd been in the company, but zero still got you something."[13] Hewlett-Packard stock was first offered November 16, 1957, on the Pacific Stock Exchange for $16.00 a share. A $1,000 investment in HP stock that day was worth $364,500 on March 26, 1996, the day Packard died.[14]

Management by Wandering Around

At an honorary luncheon for business professor Paul Holden in 1966, Packard recalled standing up with Paul before an assembly in 1942, promoting the novel idea that companies had community citizenship responsibility along with employee responsibility. This day, however, Dave expanded on his views, calling it "The Fourth Dimension of Management," which is "the personal drive and leadership ability—the difference between the great manager and the mediocre manager. . . . Somehow he brings out the best in his people and his organization, and he brings out performance beyond the call of duty. He can do it, whatever the assignment."[15]

For the readers of *Electronic Design* in 1978, Packard spelled out his thesis more clearly:

> You have to get close enough to the people involved so you can get a pretty good sense of who's standing out. You can't go out and ask a man's subordinates what they think of him. They won't tell you. So you need to develop finely tuned antennae. You need the ability to go out in the shop and wander around and sense how things are going. You can measure the performance of a group by financial reports, production reports and all sorts of things. They're all useful. But you get a much better evaluation by being there in person and sensing the situation. A good executive can go into a shop or office and, just by looking around, get a feel of things. It's important to do that. It's not so much a tangible thing as a sense.[16]

The crux, Packard acknowledged, came when someone wasn't doing the job:

So what can we do when we promote a man up to the level where he really cannot do the job? We certainly don't want to throw him out. How do we respond to our own mistake in moving the man to a position he can't handle? It's important to find ways for the man to continue to contribute to the company. The worst thing in the world is to have a company where people move ahead and then get thrown out. That would absolutely destroy morale. You must have a sense of understanding about people. . . . We never want to push a man out—or down. So we try to find something else that's roughly parallel. We may have to tell him that he really isn't doing his job right, and we'll try to find something else for him in the company. We may even have to demote him, but we don't want to demean him.[17]

Acquisitions posed a special situation for HP's approach, to which Dave spoke:

We've had difficulty bringing people in from the outside. There are two reasons. One is that we have an awful lot of good people, so it hasn't been necessary. The other is that we've built what you might call a provincial attitude. All our people are home-grown, so to speak. So somebody from the outside who has not been through this experience finds it hard to get acceptance and to adjust to the way we do things. This might be a weakness. I don't think it is. But it does sometimes seem that you have to be part of the family to move up in the organization.[18]

Divisions

Because of fear that we might lose the personal touch of the small operating units, which we believed was so important, it was decided to divisionalize the company. [This was not] from any then-existing innovative concepts. We were somewhat worried that separating the units, particularly any future geographical dispersion, might adversely affect the valuable exchange of ideas among the engineering teams. Fortunately, this did not turn out to be the case.

BILL HEWLETT[19]

Partitioning anything inevitably creates its own dilemma. The seamless whole has integrity, whereas subdivisions lead to rivalry, infighting, uneven growth, inappropriate boundaries, gaps, and overlaps. Why then do people parse organizations? Because the seamless whole eventually becomes too big, too unwieldy, and too inefficient. Hewlett and Packard at first tried only to parse subordinate activities. Separate organizations—Dynac and PAECO—were initial attempts that bespoke the duo's efforts to decentralize activities with unorthodox organizational structure. But as the company grew, the main product arenas had to be divided. Hewlett's explanation, years later, was elegantly simple: "Most people can keep track of about five hundred names on a first-name basis. Past that, you have to use last names. We wanted to keep the informality and feeling of camaraderie that went with first names, so any time that a group got towards a thousand people, we divided it."[20] HP, approaching three thousand people in Palo Alto, faced a partitioning question.

Both Hewlett and Packard asserted that the company needed to find a model that would support keeping work teams small and focused enough to be nimble and adroit, while hopefully taking advantage of the growing size, strength, and importance of the overall corporation. An issue arose: Along what lines do you cleave? The engineering team favored separating by technology—digital technology differing from analog, microwave differing from low-frequency. Packard, though, was adamant that it should be done along natural customer lines. He proclaimed, "We're not going to organize by the technology. It's by the customers we are trying to please, that's the way we're going to organize it."[21] To begin with, Oliver's central laboratories were split into four instrument laboratories, described as product divisions in the 1957 prospectus—the Audio-Video Division, the Microwave and Signal Generator Division, the Frequency and Time Division, and the Oscilloscope Division. In short order, each team added its own marketing and general manager.[22]

Not everyone approved this move. CFO Ed van Bronkhorst later lamented,

> A registration statement is an incredibly deep description of a company and its operations, including financial statements that go back for a period of years—at least three now and more likely five—a description of the product line and the history of the company. In this case we were required to break the company

down into product divisions, which turned out to be a mistake. From there on, every security analyst in the business wanted that breakdown and it really turned out to be one product line—test equipment and measurement.[23]

Van Bronkhorst's thinking was a view taken in hindsight. All the competitors were in product niches narrower than Hewlett-Packard's. Tektronix competed for years only in oscilloscopes; Narda only in counters; Fluke only in audio; Alfred just in microwave sweepers; Polarad in spectrum analyzers. One could describe Ford Motor's business as all the same—automotive—but analysts have always sought how different segments—pick-up trucks, SUVs, passenger cars—compare to equivalent products from other automotive companies.

At the time, quite separate technology defined the divisions—microwave devices and plumbing were not used in any of the other product lines; quartz crystals and Nixie tubes in counters were of little use elsewhere; circuits with highly tuned signal-to-noise ratio levels were vital primarily for voltmeters; and oscilloscopes had the only need for expensive electrostatic cathode ray tubes. The good news was that not only was the technology separate, so were the customer requirements. Yes, customers might buy more than one instrument, but it was rare for any one engineer to need all of them. A laboratory might, but not individual engineers. Most would need audio-video products, and many required a scope; only specialists needed counters or spectrum analyzers. But when they needed them, they needed the best that they could afford. Even so, for a time, it was not clear just how successful the divisional model might prove to be, nor was it clear how to define success criteria. Interaction with other divisions wasn't viewed as a high priority—in fact, divisions typically were made where the synergy did not seem apparent or even desirable. Overlaps were allowed, even encouraged, whereas gaps were of concern.[24] Bill Terry described it as feudal barony management, which it often was. The view that Hewlett and Packard shared consistently took form: "keep your head down and your feet moving, and take care of *your own* business," even though they'd admonish at nearly every division review that they wanted people to think of HP as "one company."

An International Initiative

Hewlett followed Packard to the podium at the 1958 Sonoma meeting, laying out a plan to expand the company into Europe. Attendees later remembered it as his first major speech to the company. It would prove prescient. When Hewlett urged establishing a European presence, the company had 1,467 employees, all in Palo Alto. Of $28 million in total revenue, just over $2 million was from sales outside of America through agents.

America was isolated economically after World War II. The innovative Lend-Lease program during the war had helped the Allies immensely with war materiel—afterward, Truman and Eisenhower supported George Marshall's innovative Marshall Plan to help rebuild a devastated Europe and Japan. It was a novel idea to aid an enemy after destroying it during a difficult, protracted, devastating war.[25] The Marshall Plan helped to rejuvenate Europe, and by 1957, heads of state from most of Europe were ready to consider an old dream—a United States of Europe. The bellwether event was the 1957 signing of the Treaty of Rome, which led shortly to the European Common Market (and by 1990 to the European Union, with the euro as a common monetary unit).

After World War II, Hewlett spent several months in Japan as a member of Karl Compton's prestigious and clandestine scientific research team. Compton, president of MIT and brother of Nobel Physicist Arthur Holly Compton (who co-chaired the Manhattan Project), provided inspiration for Hewlett to conclude in the early 1950s that in order for HP to do well in a reemerging Europe and Japan, the company would have to have a presence there.[26] Such insight eluded most American corporations for years afterward. When Bill and Flora went to Europe in early 1955 to scope out the opportunity, Bill concluded that it was premature. The Treaty of Rome signed in March 1957 and a Business International seminar in late 1957 that Bill attended, however, gave him "a deep conviction that this was going to be a reality, and it was pretty important for us to develop a presence in Europe."[27]

At the Sonoma meeting, Hewlett outlined the idea of establishing both a European sales headquarters and a manufacturing facility; he personally went to Europe twice, first with a youthful marketing engineer, Dick

Alberding (the only person in HP who spoke German), to assess the situation and hire HP's first *in situ* European, Fred Schröder. His next trip was with his personal attorney Nate Finch, and two HP manufacturing engineers, Bill Doolittle and Ray Deméré, to initiate site selections and start operations.[28] "After a lot of peregrinations" (Hewlett's words), they determined that Geneva seemed to be a good place to locate a central sales headquarters, partially because the Swiss banking laws and incorporation rules were sophisticated regarding trading issues, such as import rule, duties, and customs, but also because it was centrally located—bear in mind that this predated the first commercial jet aircraft. Doolittle set up the Geneva sales headquarters and brought a young sales engineer, Carl Cottrell, from America to manage it for the first four years. Cottrell handed it off first to American Dick Reynolds and then to Dick Alberding before a European, Franco Mariotti, became the European Sales vice president.[29]

Investigating the area around Frankfurt versus Stuttgart, Hewlett was advised to avoid the latter because "ach, those Schwabs [Schwabians] want to work all the time." Bill said that sounded like the kind of people HP wanted, so he directed Ray Deméré to find a place in that vicinity. Deméré and Schröder rented a facility in a town named Böblingen, next to Sindelfingen, ten miles southwest of Stuttgart. Bill, tongue in cheek, later said he thought that Deméré had "rocks in his head" for picking such a small town.[30] Böblingen embraced HP, offering incentives to build there. Today the locale, with HP, Daimler-Benz headquarters, and IBM's European research headquarters, is a major technology center within Germany.

HP, GmbH, opened its doors in September 1959, with Ray Deméré as the plant manager; its first products shipped two months later.[31] Hewlett was adamant that Americans would be temporary employees of the operating units—the goal was to have indigenous management rather than transplanted Americans, another major departure from practices at most international companies of the era. Deméré returned to America within two years to head the transplanted audio-video line in Colorado; local management ran HP Böblingen thereafter. A long line of capable managers developed on the Böblingen site, nurtured by Fred Schröder, including Eberhardt Knoblauch, Klaus Dieter Laidig, and Heiner Blaesser. Pierre

Ollivier, along with Karl Schwartz from America, founded the Grenoble, France, site in 1971, where eventual vice presidents Wim Roelandts and Cyril Yansouni made major contributions.

The Outer Seven countries that didn't join the original Common Market—Great Britain, Norway, Sweden, Switzerland, Austria, Denmark, and Portugal—came together in a group known as the European Free Trade Association (EFTA). In 1961, John Cage was drafted from Barney's laboratory to go to Bedford, England, to develop a second manufacturing site to serve EFTA; Microwave manufacturing engineer John Doyle returned briefly to his home nation to help establish this facility. When the plant grew, HP encountered U.K. planning. The company was forced to relocate, preferably to one of the designated New Towns in northern England. When Dave and Lucile visited the desired locale, Packard said the New Town reminded him of dreary Russian places. He quickly responded, "I didn't want any part of it." Hewlett took Flora to see the same area, and her immediate response was, "In no way you should have any of our people live in this place."[32] The company chose to relocate altogether, to South Queensferry, Scotland.

Thus HP was in Europe. Hewlett was eager also for involvement in Japan; the first opportunity came via Yokogawa Electric Works (YEW) in 1963. The partnership began (analogous to Europe) with product kits being final-assembled, sold, and supported from Japan rather than from America. By 1974, HP had become one of America's top ten exporting companies, even though it was only 225th in total revenues.[33] With just $2.2 million in sales outside America in 1957, by 1980, HP would sell more products outside America than within—$1.57 billion in orders—giving a compounded international growth rate of 33 percent for twenty-three years, growth of 730 times, whereas domestic sales grew only one-ninth as much in that period. Hewlett's hunch proved prescient indeed.

Decentralizing from Palo Alto

Packard, intent on contribution, was also focused on community. He instituted a strong bond initiative for Palo Alto schools while on the local school board; it ensured quality education for the town for decades. In 1953, Noel Porter was elected to the Palo Alto City Council, where he served for the next ten years. A popular activist, he was mayor for an unprecedented five terms. Porter, with Alf Brandin, Stanford's Business Affairs VP, and Jerome Keithley, Palo Alto's first city manager, built an alliance that created the Stanford Industrial Park and the Stanford Shopping Center, each innovative for using dedicated Stanford lands to develop uniquely valuable properties for both business and retail interests.[34] On the positive side of the ledger, the city tax revenues were strengthened; on the negative side, the Stanford Shopping Center pulled clientele from University Avenue merchants, creating a two-decade retail tailspin, while traffic and development growth irreversibly changed the character of Palo Alto. A sleepy little college town became a high-tech powerhouse.

Just as Packard had long stated his belief in community involvement by corporations, he worried about the impact of a large and growing company on the small community of Palo Alto. As the company grew and prospered, Hewlett-Packard began to outgrow its hometown. The first real signal of difficulty for HP was the Oregon Expressway proposal. "A band of outraged residents formed the Committee for Good Government" in opposition to the new City Hall proposal, the new library, and most of all, the condemnation of thirty-one homes for an expressway to the Stanford Industrial Park for new tenants Varian and HP.[35]

Matters came to a head in mid-1959, not long after HP occupied its new facilities at 1501 Page Mill Road in the Stanford Industrial Park. A new editor, Al Bodi, took over the *Palo Alto Times;* he proved much less cooperative than his predecessor, Elinor Cogswell. Many years later, Dave opined,

> At one time there were three of us [Hewlett on the Hospital Board, Packard on the School Board, and Noel Porter on City Council] involved in some of the major city projects. That was when I think the city got a little concerned that we were taking a larger part than we should, so we backed down a little bit.[36]

Bodi was bellicose when interviewed, speaking "spiritedly about how it hadn't been just Dave Packard but also his partner, his production manager, his wife, his attorney, his secretary, and maybe more who were involved in running the town."[37] Packard met with Bodi to no avail, saying later, "That was the end of our cozy relationship [with the *Times*]"; Bodi's retort was that he'd "publish whatever I want."[38]

Packard's response appeared in the 1959 *Annual Report* statement. The 1958 *Annual Report* is sketchy about plans to reshape the company structure, alluding simply to the European sales headquarters and a forthcoming manufacturing site, plus a short note about a new affiliation with the Moseley Company. The next year, a much different declaration appeared:

From 1960 on, the administrative headquarters, the central research and development department and two important manufacturing units will be centered on the Stanford Industrial Park site. Other, smaller units will continue to be operated in the Palo Alto area but the decision has been made to decentralize many operations to provide a better base for future growth.[39]

Hewlett-Packard was taking the growth elsewhere! Both men were concerned about the kind of community in which HP should think about locating; about how to attract superior scientific and engineering talent to a site from national and even international locales; and about the requisite infrastructure such as airports, postgraduate university education, and skilled workforce access. In addition, Packard wanted to take jobs back to his home state, Colorado, and he liked Bill's idea of small, decentralized teams. Bill's vote? Nearby ski resorts![40]

How this decentralized growth would be accomplished was left unstated. Since HP was already organized into project teams, how about moving those units into other geographies? Organizing along customer segment lines allowed a new team near-total control of its destiny. It could still use project teams, with their assemblage of several talents and the responsibility for the product from conception through customer satisfaction. The division team could do the market research that determined the feature-set, and the project-tracking data were still close to the project. In short, the product line separation had already created miniature companies, each a small, self-contained, and reasonably controlled entity. Each new team was told to find its own site outside Palo Alto.

The Audio-Video Division was first to exercise this opportunity, discovering northeastern Colorado in part because engineers Don Hammond and Stan Selby came to HP from Colorado. John Doyle and Selby stopped by on their way home from the 1959 IRE show in New York City; the city fathers in Loveland, Colorado, hosted a welcoming committee that Stan had organized. The decision was quickly reached to begin a manufacturing site there, relatively easy for the low-technology audio-video line.

It seems no one on the executive committee anticipated what happened next. Many customers wanted a variant of the catalog products. Special handling teams had handled customization for all products in the Bay Area, but with manufacturing now moved, it soon proved more efficient to have a few design engineers on site in Loveland for customized "specials." And so it went. The next discovery was the value of having a product manager on-site, and a quality assurance person. Within a year, most of the functions of a full-fledged company had been installed, and the division was on its way to virtual autonomy. Hewlett, passionate about the value of small work units, fondly pointed out that if you eat only with your colleagues daily, you fail to gain a new perspective. He asserted that if lab developers eat with manufacturing and marketing people at nearby tables in a small on-site cafeteria, they cannot help but gain appreciation for those other functions, as well as issues that are happening in the field with products. Shared meals served as a self-correcting communication feedback loop. Hewlett's famous dictum—"marketing is too important to leave up to marketing folk"—was well served by this thesis.[41] Hewlett assumed that any designer would be vitally interested in how his or her product was faring in the marketplace, and would respond to missing product features, useful variants of functionality, or particular issues of quality.

The notion of the triad grew out of this evolutionary learning. The idea was simple enough—each remote operation would have a general manager and a triad staff, the three key folk on whom to rely: the R&D manager (although little R was done in the divisions), the manufacturing manager (because the company produced relatively esoteric manufactured products), and a sales manager, whose job it was to excite the corporate sales staffs to sell the division's offerings. This group of four ran, in effect, their own businesses from a profit-and-loss-statement standpoint, and the triad members were grounded in general management skills rather than functional management specialization. At the same time, they got to where they were as domain specialists, so they were a check if a general manager failed to balance the various issues.

The Oscilloscope Division, younger than Audio-Video, was the second to move from the Bay Area. It selected Colorado Springs, Colorado for its operations, commencing in 1963 with a pilot group and culminating in September 1964 when HP's largest building to date, 137,500 square feet, was opened. Norm Schrock, who with Barney had designed the ill-fated HP 150A oscilloscope, was the new engineering director; Cort Van Rensselaer was the first general manager, Hal Edmondson transferred from Microwave to become the manufacturing manager, and Bill Terry came over from Noel Eldred's organization to become marketing manager.[42]

The Microwave and Signal Generator Division, which remained in Palo Alto, was focused on high-frequency signal generators for the new microwave repeater backbone for national signal broadcast, and for military communications. This division, also producing waveguide sweepers and leveled power meters, embarked on a major new product concept—an integrated combination of a sweeper and a power meter called a spectrum analyzer. The first engineering manager was Bruce Wholey, who brought the Navy sweeper technology to the company right after World War II. When Wholey became general manager, he appointed John Young as his marketing manager, and veteran engineer Howard Poulter took Wholey's role as engineering director.[43]

The Frequency and Time (F&T) Division built particularly useful products for synchronizing clocks for communications networks, as well as tools for extending the new analytical techniques from World War II—radar and sonar. This group, known later as the Santa Clara Division, was managed by Al Bagley. The Frequency and Time Division eventually created more than ten product lines for the company, managed as true profit-and-loss centers. Bagley's staff included Dan Lansdon as engineering manager, Jack Petrak as manufacturing manager, and Ed Smith as sales manager. The division, for several years the most successful in sales revenue and profits, boasted 750 employees and the top two products for HP in 1964—the venerable vacuum-tube counter, the 524D, and the new transistorized version, known as the 5245A.[44]

With about five hundred people per division, it was relatively easy to know most people informally and to gain appreciation for their individual roles and the holistic nature of the divisional task. Some corporate functions were necessary, but they were purposely kept quite lean. Each division was taxed modestly to sustain a small Palo Alto corporate staff; each was allowed to grow mostly via self-generated cash return. Growth begat growth; poor performance was self-correcting. The corporate overhead supported Barney's small cadre of Palo Alto–based researchers looking at new technologies, as well as a centralized standards group and corporate administration.

Impact of Moving a Division

Two divisions moved operations a thousand miles, and two stayed put. As might be expected, the two that stayed enjoyed a more continuous growth curve for the next five years. Much tacit knowledge fails to transfer long distance, and much new learning has to happen simply to get back to baseline. On the other hand, a fresh start can open eyes to new opportunity. Hewlett-Packard leaders spent considerable time trying to understand the teething problems of the two Colorado divisions.

The numbers were compelling. The two divisions that moved to Colorado had slightly smaller revenues than the two that stayed in Palo Alto; six years later, they were significantly smaller. The Palo Alto groups surged at 18 percent per year, nearly their original pace; the two Colorado divisions eked out only a 5 percent compounded rate.[45] Certainly the early years of the Loveland Division were a steep learning curve. In addition to the discontinuities caused by moving so far and having to train a new local workforce, division engineers were preoccupied with issues of digital electronics, busily converting analog instruments into digital versions. A positive discovery was that there were niche markets for the venerable voltmeter line. Relatively low-priced 3½-digit voltmeters (DVMs) became the bread-and-butter line, but four-digit, five-digit, and even 5½-digit machines had useful markets as well, where a truly accurate, repeatable measurement mattered.

HP was not the first company to produce a digital voltmeter—far from it—but by 1965 it had achieved a leadership place in the industry. Given the head start that Non Linear Systems, Electro Industries, Cubic, and Cohu had established before Ted Anderson and Noel Pace built the HP 405AR in 1958, and the entry of subsequent market competitors such as

Dana Instruments, Keithley, and John Fluke Manufacturing, it is a tribute to the attention to detail and quality of the products, the sales and marketing arm of the company, and the superb customer support that HP emerged within the decade as the DVM preponderant choice, with more than 50 percent of the marketplace, just as it had become the vacuum tube voltmeter (VTVM) vendor of choice over Ballantine Laboratories years earlier.[46] Loveland's oscillator line—dubbed Sources—continued to thrive during this period. The two sections, complementing each other nicely, grew at roughly the same rate for a number of years.

The excitement, though, was new applications for digitized voltmeters. They made readings far faster than any human could read and record the data, which put a premium on a data collection storage mechanism. In addition, the sheer volume of data was potentially staggering. Data could be collected for multiple parallel points at once, or logged serially for long data-streams. Automating this data collection and figuring out an effective analysis strategy became a paramount interest for the division.

Meanwhile, the Oscilloscope Division situation differed in two fundamental respects. First, Tektronix virtually owned the market. In contrast to the nascent manufacturers of DVMs, Tektronix had become sizable, its revenues nearly matching the entire Hewlett-Packard Company. And it was managed very similarly, with tremendous engineering capability and a strong employee-centered philosophy. Cort Van Rensselaer set out to transfer the entire Oscilloscope Division, lock, stock, and barrel, whereas Loveland gradually moved departments while keeping the core design team intact in Palo Alto for several years. The negative result was that three of the five key scope engineering managers and a number of scope designers transferred to other parts of HP or left the company rather than move to Colorado.[47]

Just as the seeds of destruction are sometimes found in the height of success, so too does adversity build opportunity. So although the two Colorado divisions hardly grew between 1960 and 1966 while digesting the move and the rapidly shifting marketplace, they were becoming poised to appreciate and take advantage of new situations. For the next six years, their combined growth rate was a healthy compounded 16 percent, versus the 5 percent doldrums of the learning period. The Palo Alto divisions did the reverse: from a quite respectable 18 percent to a mere 6 percent compounded average growth rate (CAGR) during the second six-year period. The Frequency and Time Division, moving fifteen miles from Palo Alto to Santa Clara starting in 1966, found resources and momentum affected by introducing several sophisticated product families—atomic clocks and precision thermometers—that turned out to have surprisingly modest markets.[48]

The Microwave Division posted a spectacular set of gains from late 1964 through 1966 with the new spectrum analyzers, more than doubling to $49 million after three years of stagnation. Alas, the new products were not quite invented, and the subsequent production and quality travail cost the division some significant opportunity for the next three years. Even so, Microwave would double again by 1972, fueled with new sales from such pioneering products as vector voltmeters and network analyzers as well as the more visible spectrum analyzers.

Growth, wherever it occurred, required talented people to solve problems. And they had to learn on the job. Doug Chance, a Stanford MBA student from Princeton, was lured by Doyle to join HP in June 1966, in part because of a recent purchase of a $200,000 Milwaukee-matic, a very sophisticated, computer-controlled, milling machine.

> He convinced me to join as a new engineer and to go through the traditional new engineer training program, which was six months long and you worked through every possible position in the company. You worked in manufacturing specs, you worked in quality control. You programmed the Milwaukee-matic. You worked on the assembly line. You worked on the test line. You worked in the sheet metal shop, and I worked with many of the manufacturing people.
>
> It wasn't Dave and Bill that gave me the first insights into the HP Way. It was crusty guys like Sam Teresi, who was the line manager for the 608 signal generator line. Each new person got his story about how quality was really important, the customer was most important, and we can't let anything out of here that doesn't meet spec.[49]

Chance shared an insightful glimpse of how HP worked at that point:

> After I finished the [training] program, John [Doyle] had me join the production engineering group. I didn't realize that production engineering was sort of a

second-class job in HP. He said, "Oh no, this is where it all happens." Production engineers were on call all the time to go solve the problems that kept cropping up because things weren't necessarily designed to be able to be manufactured well. If some sheet metal part suddenly drifted out of spec, my name would be paged and I'd go to the sheet metal shop. They would explain to me and I'd get the same story, "We can't ship stuff that doesn't meet spec and I know we can re-work this, but I'm not going to re-work it unless you sign off on it and you commit to get the tooling fixed."

The new products gave Microwave a sales resurgence:

[But] the products didn't work. They were great products but the vector-voltmeter had a probe on it that was a little circuit card and it wouldn't stand up to all the pressures. We had to have a recall to fix all these problems. That's when I got to know Dave and Bill; Hewlett in particular was pretty upset—all these great inventions, but they didn't work.[50]

Hewlett created a task force, asking Chance to head it up: "Manufacturing, customer engineering, quality, marketing, R&D, everybody—come up with a process that makes sure it doesn't happen again." The group created a formal cookbook, documenting the lore of new product engineering—criteria for prototypes, pilot run, release process, even obsolescence.[51]

Products, Programs, and Strategies

Notwithstanding more explicit corporate objectives, managing the decentralized company required seasoned managers who implicitly knew the HP Way and could be moved to new locales, interpreting guidelines for charters and product boundaries. Bill and Dave adopted several strategies that proved remarkably effective.

The receptivity of the local community was highly significant to the success for outlying divisions. Most were quite small communities when HP decided to locate there. Palo Alto in 1938 was a small town of sixteen thousand. When HP began in Colorado Springs and Boise, they had populations of less than eighty thousand; Santa Rosa, fifty thousand; and Lake Stevens and Loveland much less than ten thousand. In such environments, a company with a thousand employees has a noteworthy impact on the local economy, and the community's organizations and institutions. In general, HP proved to be a model corporate citizen. Apart from some isolated skirmishes, the corporation's reputation in community after community was excellent. HP employees became ambassadors to most communities, enthusiastically involved in civic affairs: objective number 7 played well.[52]

A division review became the critical approach for keeping a pulse on things; this was an annual trek by Hewlett and Packard and a few of their key staff to each division and site to review new products under development, review operations, and reacquaint themselves with the leadership *in situ.* This was a fundamental part of Management by Wandering Around. Many project managers had their first exposure to Bill and Dave while standing with a prototype, praying that the demonstration would go smoothly.

The division review, the cardinal event of the year for every HP divi-

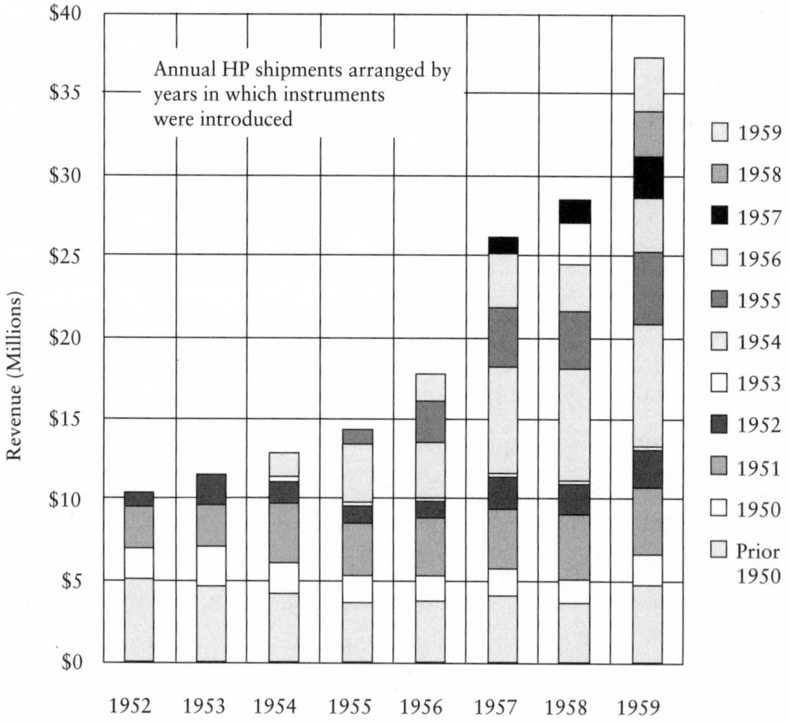

FIGURE 3.3. Corporate vintage chart, 1952–1959.
SOURCE: Cort Van Rensselaer, papers, donated December 6, 2005

sion, featured four categories: (1) a project review, for the principal division projects; (2) division metrics on quality, profitability, and growth (usually in that order); (3) people (hiring, development, and retention); and (4) local issues. Product vintage mattered—consistent investment in R&D was crucial to maintain a dynamic vintage profile of new product introductions. The vintage chart arose, a chart of sales by year of introduction (Figures 3.3, 3.4). The charts quickly revealed the health of new product introductions for both the overall company and each individual division, not only in initial impact, but in lasting contribution to total sales.[53]

Hewlett and Packard enjoyed explaining that the rationale for Hewlett-Packard was contribution. Every product had to offer the customer a clear, distinguishable contribution compared to other equipment or methods. Thus the new product program had paramount status for HP managers. For project reviews, three standard procedures were encapsulated in a "New Product Design Release Criteria statement"—(1) return factor and a Brunnergram, (2) environmental testing and certification, and (3) manufacturability review. Usually the project team made the presentations along with

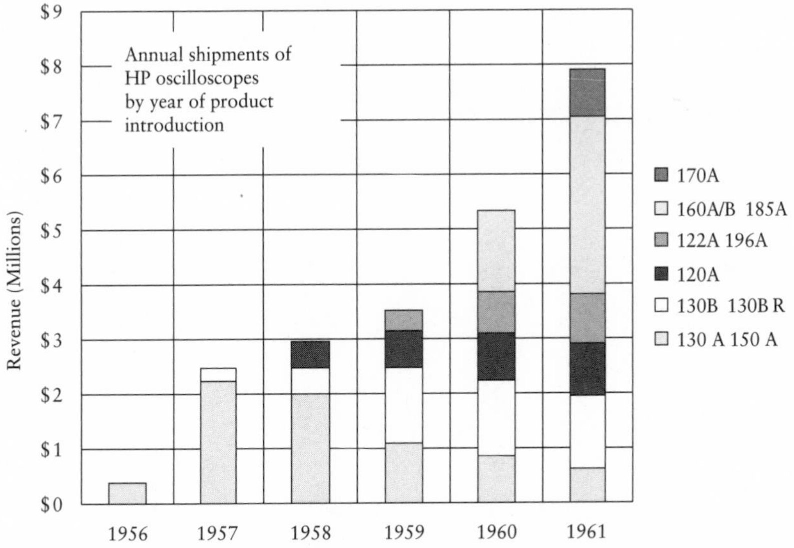

FIGURE 3.4. Oscilloscope vintage chart, 1956–1961.
SOURCE: Cort Van Rensselaer, papers, donated December 6, 2005

a product demonstration, which typically had Hewlett and Oliver, and even Packard, sitting down and rolling up their sleeves to try the device.

Given the strong emphasis on new products, it wasn't surprising that metrics for managing such programs were derived and used. Brunnergrams were named for an early designer, Robert Brunner, who worked on the original HP function generator (HP Model 202A).[54] Teaming with Marco Negrete, a key microwave designer, Brunner arrived at a one-page graphical specification for any project.

The Brunnergram was far more useful for individual project reviews than the overall vintage chart. This unusual graphic worked extremely well for a company with engineering managers who were in tune with the nuances of a project, rather than just the numbers. In the Brunner chart, the horizontal axis is time from the start of the project. Various milestones of the project—breadboard, pilot model, preproduction—are vertical lines. The horizontal lines were the estimated project costs to the milestones. It was vital for a project manager and the team to know what the project value was over time.[55] Anyone could see at a glance that the project shown in Figure 3.5 was on target whereas the project shown in Figure 3.6 was over budget and late. No one enjoyed being interviewed at division review time with a Brunnergram that looked like the second one.

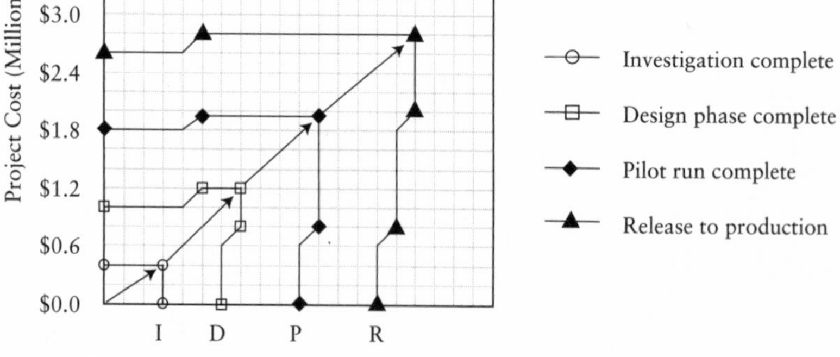

FIGURE 3.5. A satisfying Brunnergram

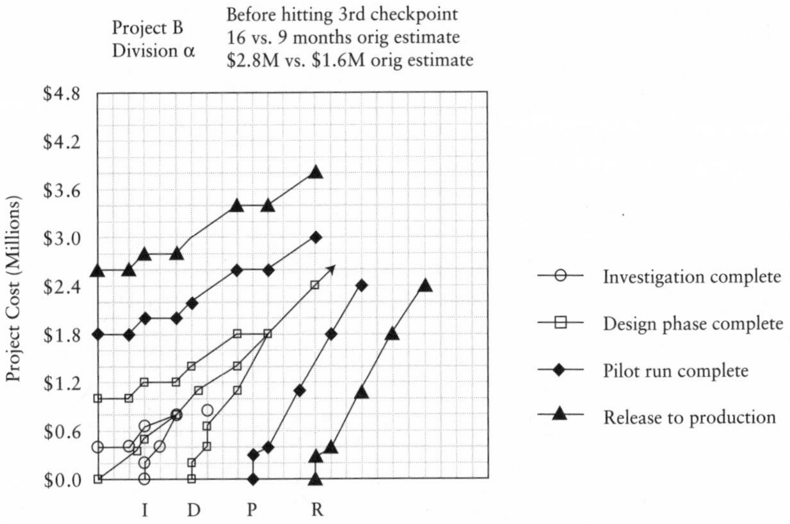

FIGURE 3.6. A disturbing Brunnergram

At the conclusion of a division review, Hewlett or Packard would supply a summary memo, succinct to the point of pithiness. The memos, saved by managers for years, illustrate both the insight and the clarity that the partners brought to the table. Cort Van Rensselaer has a scrawled note from the 1963 Oscilloscope Division review, which said simply, "Next year I think you should concentrate on profits."[56]

Hewlett, asked how he was able to handle the breadth of issues that were revealed in the course of multiple division reviews, modestly said that his major contribution was "to set the meeting date, and then ensure that I held the meeting."[57]

The meeting was a tremendous galvanizing influence, and much additional work—clarifying, strategizing, coordinating kinds of work—got done in thinking about how to handle the review, knowing that questions might well come from many angles. Often forgotten in the day-long technical discussions and demos was the value of the personal contacts that these annual project reviews afforded, especially at remote divisions. The day was usually rounded off with an informal banquet, with the visitors mixing with the participants. This offered a chance for young project engineers to meet the founders in person in an informal setting. Those events were long remembered, a worthy benefit of being put on the hot seat during the day. Much of the camaraderie, loyalty, and affection for the founders and the company traced to these events.

Hewlett and Packard's depth of understanding contributed far more to the success of division reviews than Bill's modest assessment indicates. Walt Selsted said,

> They knew what was going on in every engineering project in the company. They would come by, for example, while we were developing the transports, and later the electronics, and they would come in and ask some questions, which you were puzzled that they even knew anything about. And they showed genuine interest in the engineering project and how it was going, and if you had any problems you hadn't been able to resolve. There were dozens of engineering projects in that company at the time. I was very, very impressed that they knew as much about the projects in the company that they're not working on every day at all.[58]

In 1960, the original four divisions accounted for $52 million of the corporation's $60 million. They had quadrupled in revenue from the trough of 1954, growing at a compounded 26 percent per year for six years. Four new acquisitions accounted for the remaining $8 million in revenue. Six years and a number of acquisitions later, the four original divisions had more than doubled again, accounting for $110 million of the company's total $200 million. After another six years—in 1972—the corporation had grown to $475 million, for which the original four divisions contributed $186 million, up another 69 percent in six years. It is telling that the original product areas were growing at ever slower rates, from 26 percent per year (1954–60) to 13 percent per year (1960–66), and finally to 9 percent per year (1966–72). Without the diversification strategy, HP would have lost considerable momentum; with the additions, HP maintained steady growth.

Scaling the HP Way

Shortly after the end of this period, the employee newsletter, *HP Measure,* summarized the learning from a couple of these divisional moves. The article, constructed from multiple interviews, focused on increased awareness of the contribution opportunity in every job: new ways of handling warranty, new methods for quality assurance, new parts procurement ideas, even new thoughts about defining the role and usage of the HP picnic sites. In effect, managers in these new assignments rediscovered what Dave and Bill had long since learned—that every job matters, which was tremendously reinforcing for the founders' beliefs that contribution can be found in every circumstance.[59] And every group developed camaraderie, a local sense that "we did it" and "we're all in this together." Bill and Dave's goal to keep the personal touch was extremely well served by the divisions sent to the hinterlands.

Maybe, in retrospect, the name badge was the secret. A simple device, a modest name badge—about the size of a stick of chewing gum—was worn by every employee. Your name was prominent, not the company name. You could read a name at a glance from ten feet away. It helped a lot. It facilitated Dave and Bill's desire for informality, the badge serving as either a memory jog or an introduction. The badge was crucial on the day of the division review. Even though the R&D program was the major focus, they'd always include all departments of the division in the review, and invariably there was a plant tour to mingle with folks from the assembly areas—the original Management by Wandering Around. All day, and at the informal dinner, Bill and Dave could address each person by their first name—a powerful positive affirmation, quickly, informally, personally.

CHAPTER 4

Division Renewal and the Corporate Laboratories

The basic operating unit at HP is the product division. It is an integrated, self-sustaining organization with a great deal of autonomy and independence. The divisional concept sprang from the desire to maintain the same kind of atmosphere in a growing company that had existed when the company was much smaller. . . . We still believe that this organizational concept is as valid today as it was when it was first instituted [in 1958].

BILL HEWLETT (1975)[1]

Small companies are alert, nimble—quick to seize opportunity. That is their special advantage. Large corporations lose those qualities while gaining brand, presence, and market share. The first has élan, the second sturdiness and heft. Once a company has attained the latter, the tendency is to protect it at all costs. It seems unnatural to overthrow a winning hand; to transform a successful enterprise; or to renew, refresh, and revise a market position of strength. Somehow, Hewlett-Packard was able periodically to transcend this tendency—renewing and transforming itself with regularity, in division after division, but notably at the corporate level itself. Thus HP's approach and experience with product line renewal and company transformation—among the most dramatic and effective of any corporation in history—is vital to understand.

Organizational choice and cultural evolution go hand in hand. The geographical separation of quasi-autonomous divisions gave rise to an unorthodox organization chart. Figures 4.1 and 4.2 show the organizational difference between HP and Digital Equipment Corporation (DEC) (a more traditional approach)—the HP approach optimizes for customer satisfaction whereas the distributed functional approach encourages technical leadership. Remarkably, this distinction is not widely appreciated nor taught in product management courses or business schools. It is an implicit point in entrepreneurial courses, but such programs seldom deal with scaling to larger organizations. Note that because the decentralized units of Figure 4.1 are essentially autonomous businesses, they can be located quite far apart, even continents away. By contrast, the organizational assumption of Figure 4.2 is that the several units—R&D, marketing, and manufacturing—can get together physically when problems arise. The issue for Fig. 4.2-type companies, though, is that people separated by a few miles aren't much more likely to get together than are people separated by several states.

The quasi-autonomous HP divisions were compelled to be self-sufficient, critically dependent on marketplace success in order to fund their own growth. The fortunate result was that they stayed attuned to shifting trends better than would have a centralized corporation. Nuanced shifts in any division's market position resulted in swift counterattack; the result was continual product line renewal—a subtle shift in product definitions that blurred and then morphed into related but separate product lines (such as

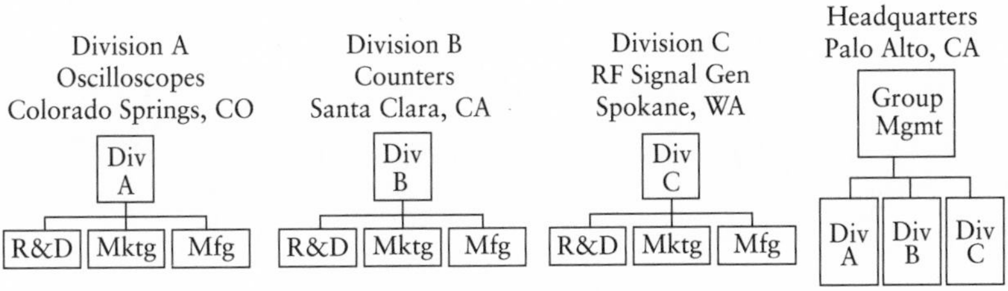

FIGURE 4.1. Hewlett-Packard organization model

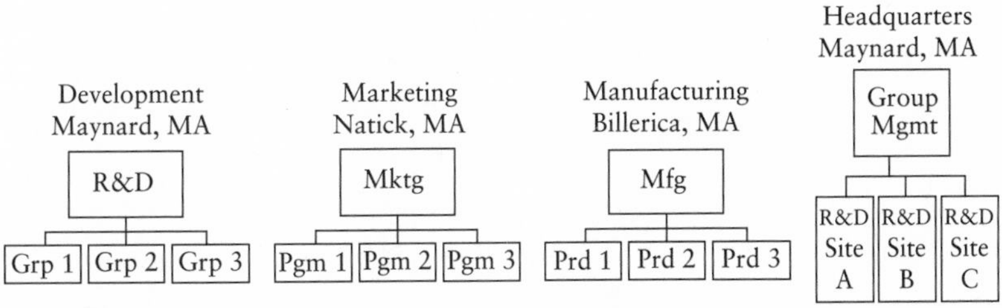

FIGURE 4.2. Digital Equipment Company organization model

voltmeters into data acquisition systems). Some situations were transformations, more like a metamorphosis, such as a voltmeter business spawning a desktop calculator business.

HP's organization reinforced the notion that the business unit is the primary focus—as Hewlett said, all participants in the division are partners, building successful products for customers. Revenue growth becomes a common goal; profits are the metric. All functional jobs exist for their interconnectedness to the business endeavor; none are complete unto themselves. Affirmation and success are measured by overall profitability of the entire unit; patents, which matter most to engineering, are subordinate.

DEC's structure in contrast reinforced the functional department *raison d'être*—that is, research, development, marketing, manufacturing. Performance of each departmental group became the goal, productivity the metric. The geocentric units became the dominant elements, and the synergy to be obtained from the interweaving of all these groups became somewhat elusive. More important than the cultural norms that get established by these organizational structures is the learning that is supported or made more difficult—and the types of corporate knowledge thereby acquired.

Explicit knowledge—knowledge that can be written into process manuals or training courses and taught—is different between the two organizational structures. Figure 4.1-type companies usually have explicit knowledge and metrics for product integrity, failure rates, and customer requirements and satisfaction. Figure 4.2-type companies value explicit functional lore—for example, deep science in a research lab, sophisticated manufacturing, and so on.

Tacit knowledge—knowledge assimilated rather than taught—is used intuitively, but not explicitly described. Corporate standards, morés, culture, and procedures fit into this category for either organizational construct. In recent years, numerous companies have begun to appreciate the issues for and value of making their tacit assumptions more explicit.[2]

Latent knowledge—in effect, knowledge awaiting discovery—will likely be found only by a few questing individuals. In a Figure 4.2-type company customer knowledge or product satisfaction is usually latent for any self-contained research or development lab. A key problem for a Figure 4.1-

type group is that deep science remains latent for a group whose focus is on the marketplace rather than the technology.

Any high-technology corporation must resolve which path is more apt to provide long-term success, as well as which path is more consonant with its historic cultural practices. In HP's case, there was little doubt, and any debate was soon enough dispelled by Packard's view that markets, not technology, was how HP would organize. In the beginning, neither Hewlett nor Packard espoused any particular product vision—they just did "certain obvious things." Twenty-five years later, the process wasn't much different. Hewlett-Packard would, to a far greater extent than practically any other company, allow teams to pursue two competing paths if they appeared to offer opportunity for product contribution. Coordination of strategic focus was modest at best, minimal program rationalization was done, and people risked little retribution for choosing a path that led to a blind alley. Risk-taking in a trusting environment was an aspect of the HP Way that is both crucial to understand and rarely noted.

Most unusual, both Packard and Hewlett were able to allow the managers of these new divisions to run them. Packard was famous for saying, "Hire the best people you can because sooner or later we're going to need them. And don't wait too long to turn something over to them." Many managers echoed Bruce Wholey's observation that Packard had to "let go of things . . . [most] entrepreneurs . . . couldn't let go of. [Packard] really would delegate, he was able to let go."[3]

In its first public decade, HP transformed from a company of $30 million revenue and less than fifteen hundred people, doing all of its business from one small town in America with sales almost entirely in America, to a corporation doing $73 million overseas, nearly $300 million overall, with more than twelve thousand employees, fifteen divisions, and sixty-five field operations in multiple states and nations. HP also significantly broadened its instrumentation product line, embracing medical and analytical chemistry, astronomy, and physics disciplines. But the founders' beliefs, ethos, and creed still resonated strongly, and the diversification had strengthened the character and uniqueness of the total corporation. Profits and growth were as high as ever. The duo had mastered the issues of the Watershed.

The questions to be considered are how did the company choose its strategic direction, and then how did it develop operational skills that were consonant with the unorthodox strategic method adopted? Packard's notion of hiring the best generalists possible and then giving them high levels of responsibility offered much room for contribution and minimized organizational constraints. It gave the company wiggle room. Consistent planning, rote extrapolations of revenue projections, and other hobgoblins of central planning groups never got instituted at HP: the sanguine result allowed multiple adaptations and evolution of the company strategy.

No one legislated the boundaries of division product lines. Division managers often sought an inviolate charter, but Hewlett hated territoriality. He always voted to allow overlaps and cross-divisional competition to flourish, with but one clear rule—if a team had an inferior solution, they were expected to abdicate the field. Bill and Dave insisted for years that the additional motivation of having your own program more than compensated for the costs of duplicated effort, thus providing a highly novel approach for embracing new product ideas as well as productivity approaches. It became more important to make new contributions than to protect turf. Most groups learned to cannibalize their own products rather than let a competitor (including another division) do so.

HP also developed tacit rules of thumb for the overall investment rate. The strong rule for years was that about 10 percent of revenue should be spent on R&D. Hewlett noted that if it was much less than that, competitors began to gain too fast, and if it was much more than that, new products would arrive faster than other departments—marketing, sales, manufacturing, quality—could support them. This 10 percent was further divided into a "6:3:1" ratio, again a tacit assumption rather than explicit. Of the division development resources, 60 percent ought to be working on solid, down-the-middle programs aimed at maintaining and refreshing the current product line that provides some 90 percent of today's revenue. Another 30 percent ought to be working on leveraged development—products that are extension ideas to move the product line into some promising new arenas, usually emerging markets that at the moment might already represent 10 percent of the division's revenues. And a full 10 percent of division R&D resources should be investigative—true breakthrough contributions if they work.

An R&D Manager's View

How did this work in practice? Paul Ely shared his first experience as the Microwave Division R&D manager in 1966:

> When I became an engineering manager, nominally each division got to spend 8.5 percent of prior year revenue on R&D. Corporate labs got 1.5 percent. First observation: You want more money? Grow. It is the only way that you are going to get more money, so all I needed to do to get a bigger budget was to grow. I remember going to John Young [Microwave Division manager] the first time. I said, "John, we've got a lot of things to do, and a lot of good ideas—I need at least another $300K." He said, "You get enough growth so 8.5 percent of your growth is $300K, and you can have it next year, but you can't have it until you do that."[4]

Paul then found that "a hot engineering program that had produced results" might be granted approval to go up to 9 percent or even 9.5 percent R&D. "Very occasionally they would start up a unit with a budget that might get a start-up phase as high as 14 percent, but they wouldn't leave it there very long. It had to earn its way in a couple of years or it was cut back. The divisions at the bottom of the pile got less." The net impact of this was a tremendous sense of control, within limits. "What a great self-regulating freedom-type thing. As an R&D manager or division general manager, I felt I didn't have to deal with these guys [at Corporate]. I had to create success: That is all I had to do. I [did have] to use the sales force, and I had to follow HP policies including policies related to part numbers and so forth."

Paul's thoughts about decisions at the division R&D manager level are instructive:

> We had enough money to have ten to twelve projects going in the lab. I always set aside 15 percent for investigations—"Why don't you look into this or that?" I always had a list of about a hundred possible things to invest in—things that other people wanted, or the sales force told me we needed to do, and a few I had thought up; I'd look at this list and say, "I can do only ten of these." Which ones would I pick? Well, first, I wouldn't pick anything that took a substantial investment and didn't have a 100 percent chance of success. First would be the one that had a wide-open possibility to move us into a new area but wasn't likely to be a big failure if we invested in it. Tenth would typically be something that I had to

do to upgrade a product just to stay competitive or stay ahead in that field. The perspective was that we are going to be number one in every single product line that we have. If somebody outdid us, first we respected them because they were able to do that, and second we figured out how we could have dropped the ball not to come up with these features. That was the perspective. You had to upgrade the product. Why would I invest in something which might have a huge possible return, but certainty of return was low? There was no reason to do that in Microwave. I bet that was true for most HP divisions.[5]

Division Renewal

The Audio-Video Division was transferred to Loveland, Colorado, in 1960. The original two product lines—voltmeters, and sources and analyzers—started with Bill and Dave's first products. At transfer, the entire division had $10 million per year revenues. The compounded average growth rate (CAGR) from 1960 to 1972 was a modest 13 percent. This was a period of product conversion from analog to digital technology. Even though the technology shifted a lot, the measurement contribution did not. But in following years, that technology conversion provided gigantic streams of data from digitized front ends, so data acquisition systems became very efficient, and the growth rate of the entire group rose to 17 percent

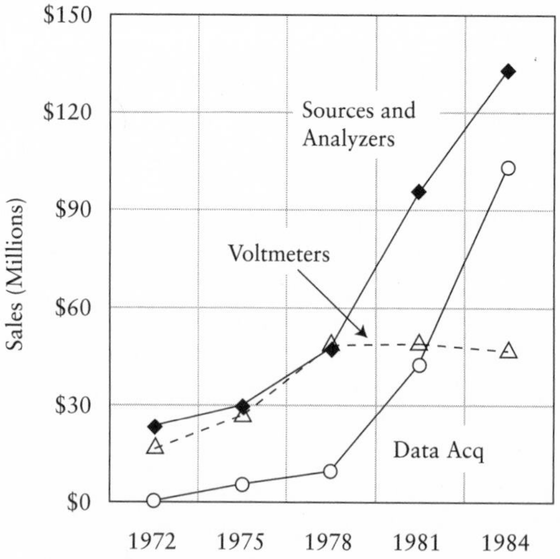

FIGURE 4.3. Loveland product line orders, 1972–1984

CAGR for the next dozen years. But Figure 4.3 shows how it was done—voltmeters slowed a lot more, sources and analyzers were nearly average, and "other" (data acquisition systems) grew dramatically.[6]

This pattern is typical. The corporation managed to continue to grow consistently—it kept the core businesses growing, while taking differential knowledge from those businesses and developing new applications that could grow more quickly. This approach produced a consistent growth rate for a quarter of a century after the first twenty years from when Bill and Dave first got into these businesses. Forty-five years of renewal!

The desktop calculator line at Loveland provided more than growth; it produced transformation excitement. The data acquisition systems were essentially collections of many voltmeters, with a lot of data collection. The computer lines, started because a rugged data logging machine was needed to collect those scientific voltages in varied environments, became novel transformative products for the corporation. And the derivative product line at Loveland—desktop calculators—grew rapidly alongside the voltmeter product line, reaching $300 million by 1984, larger than all of the audio-video lines put together (Figure 4.4). This growth was transformative, taking the Loveland site into very different markets. In addition, it provided a much higher growth rate for the site overall.

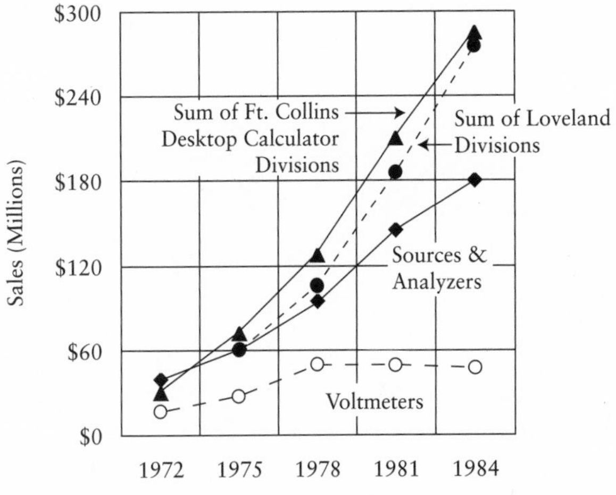

FIGURE 4.4. Loveland core product line plus computing orders, 1972–1984

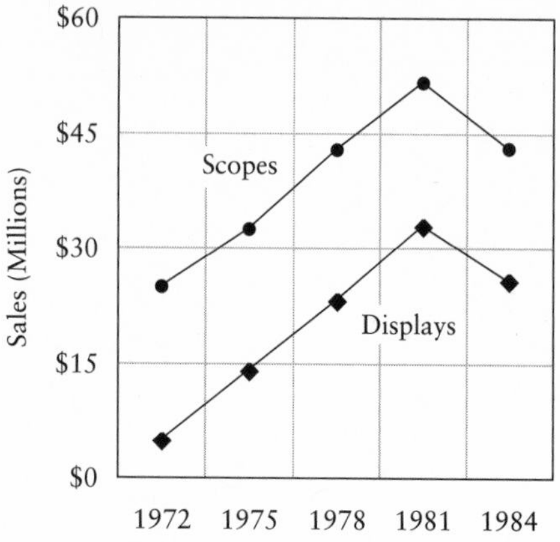

FIGURE 4.5. Colorado Springs core product line orders, 1972–1984

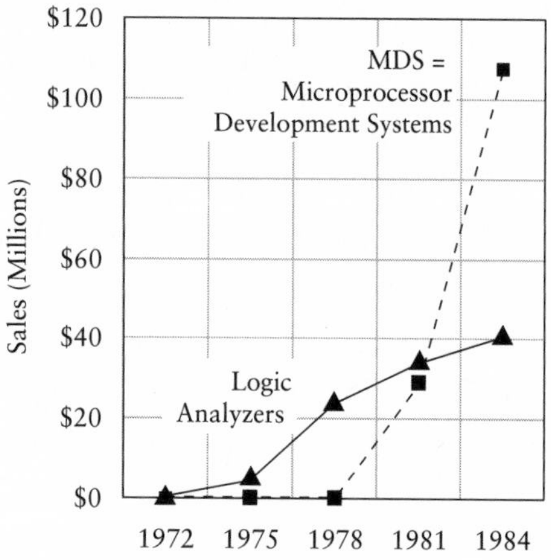

FIGURE 4.6. Colorado Springs logic analyzers and microprocessor development systems orders, 1972–1984

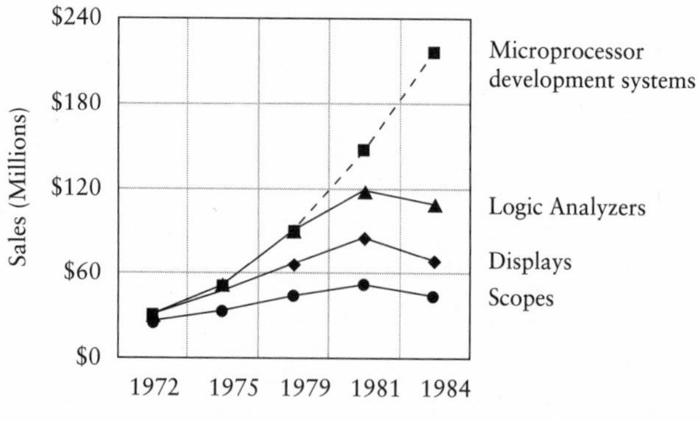

FIGURE 4.7. Colorado Springs total product line orders, 1972–1984

The Oscilloscope Division in Colorado Springs struggled to find a competitive technology edge. HP scopes began in 1955, but after eleven years Tektronix had revenues ten times larger than those of HP scopes. Then HP launched a truly competitive program, the 180A family. Within a year, the Oscilloscope Division doubled its market share. Then designer Al DeVilbiss and project leader Jim Pettit introduced the 250 MHz HP 183A, 150 percent faster than any Tektronix offering.[7] The division couldn't build them fast enough. At last it had a modicum of competitive capability, under new general manager Bill Terry. Tektronix, with unusual ferocity, bracketed HP's new offerings, and the scope wars ensued.[8]

By 1984, the old Oscilloscope Division, now called the Colorado Springs Division, still trailed Tektronix in oscilloscopes, but HP's scope business was scarcely recognizable. The heavy growth was not in scopes, but rather in end runs on Tektronix. In 1966, the division tentatively launched a line of instrumentation displays, a derivative product line based on HP's cathode ray tube (CRT) technology (Figure 4.5). The logic analyzer line began (as a digital scope) in 1973, followed in 1979 by the HP 64000 Development System. Figures 4.6 and 4.7 show how dramatic this introduction was for the division. CAGR for traditional scopes was paltry, especially given the size and growth of the market—Tektronix won hands down. But the other segments exceeded 50 percent total market share against the same competitor and maintained that edge for years. The logic lines were transformative, whereas the display business was renewal.

In Santa Clara, the Frequency and Time Division, heeding Hewlett's desire to move into scientific instrumentation, pioneered many products for physical parameter measurements, including precision frequency sources (for example, atomic clocks), very accurate mechanical measurements (laser interferometry), the first set of logic test tools, and a number of efforts that would lead later to creation of the Electronic Applications Group (for example, mechanical and electrical engineering software design).

As with so many other divisions and groups at HP, the electronic counter parent line grew at a slower rate than its offspring (Figure 4.8). From the divisional standpoint, these were renewal programs; from a wider vantage point, they were transformative because they served the scientific equipment initiative that both Hewlett and Oliver sought.

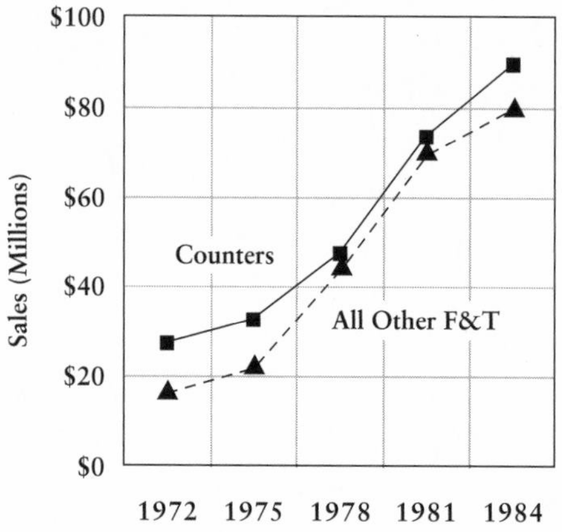

FIGURE 4.8. Santa Clara counters compared with all other Frequency and Time orders, 1972–1984

Division Renewal Versus Corporate Renewal

Three of the four original divisions moved from Palo Alto in the 1960s; the exception for awhile was the Microwave Division, largest of the original four. By 1972, Microwave was easily the largest division within the corporation, as large in revenue as Loveland Division and Santa Clara Division combined. After becoming CEO, Hewlett decided that Microwave too had to cleave.[9] Doug Chance was given the opportunity to split Microwave and take the new division to Santa Rosa, California, about a hundred miles north of Palo Alto. Chance said, "I had the great opportunity in 1973 at the age of thirty-one to be made general manager of two-thirds of the microwave division. . . . It was a great job. It was the largest, most successful division. I was president of the United Way. I was on the board of the YMCA."[10]

In short order, Microwave spun off the Technology Center as well as the new division for the spectrum analyzer line to Santa Rosa. Another division was soon spun off as well, sending Signal Sources to Spokane, Washington. Collectively, these four units were now called the Microwave Group, with three divisions titled by their locale (Stanford Park Division being the original, Santa Rosa Division, and Spokane Division). The Technology Center wasn't really a division, but instead was called an Operation. Learning from both the disruptive Colorado Springs move and the protracted F&T experience, the Microwave team strengthened communication and interdivisional travel to ensure optimum use of scarce resources across multiple sites. Microwave was able to maintain a very consistent growth pattern, exceeding the sum of the three other original divisions in revenue by 1984 (Figure 4.9).

Two consistent characteristics of these renewal activities are noteworthy. First, they were almost always homegrown, even when they had a nurturing kernel from HP Labs. Second, each began as "other," quite small in the beginning compared to the main product line, but relatively soon the baby becoming as large as the parent. Classically, the new product lines spun out additional new divisions as well. For example, the Palo Alto Audio-Video line moved to Loveland, Colorado, and after a few years, it became known as the Loveland Division. As the desktop calculator line blossomed, the Loveland Division split, into a Loveland Instrument Division and a Loveland Calculator Division. Shortly thereafter, the Loveland Calculator Division built a new plant sixteen miles away in Fort Collins, Colorado, which naturally became the Fort Collins Division. Much as did the Microwave Division, the Loveland Instrument Division subsequently cleaved, spinning out the Lake Stevens (Washington) Instrument Division

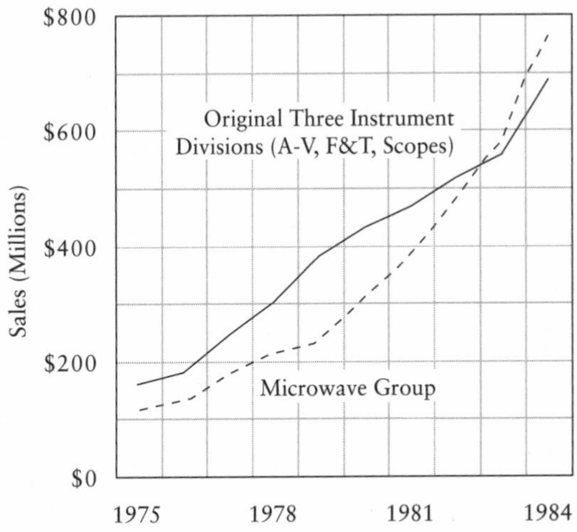

FIGURE 4.9. Three Instrument divisions compared with Microwave Group orders 1975–1984

and the Longmont (Colorado) Board Test Division. These three might have become the Audio-Video Group, except for two things—the focus was no longer just audio-video products, and the three divisions combined weren't large enough or complex enough to require a group level of management investment. Instead, they and the Santa Clara Division product lines and the Colorado Springs product lines (plus a few others from acquisitions) were aggregated and managed within an Electronic Instruments Group.

Continuing the madcap evolutionary pace, the Fort Collins Division continued to grow and subdivide, creating a local Calculator Products Division (a name that too easily could be confused with the handheld calculator products from Corvallis, Oregon), the Colorado Networks Division (also on-site), and the Greeley (Colorado) Memory Division twenty miles southeast. These all started in the Calculator Group (which was all handheld and desktop calculator products), which eventually merged with the Computer Group (a series of divisions with "bigger" computing products—minicomputers, terminals, hard discs (rather than floppy discs), and big impact printers).

Thus, by emphasizing local autonomy in separated divisions, HP built a nearly perpetual renewal machine for more than five decades. At the time of HP's fiftieth anniversary, ninety-one divisions and operations were partitioned across the company, each with its own profit-and-loss statement, nearly all with 15 to 20 percent long-term CAGR and net profits in the 6 to 10 percent range. An astonishingly successful model for a very long time, it relied on a couple of assumptions: (1) it presumed semi-autonomous markets and products, which allowed the company to avoid fractious and expensive interdivisional warfare; and (2) it presumed growth markets rather than static or shrinking ones.

John Young, rather than Dave or Bill, was the one who perceived a need for an intermediate management layer. The creativity and initiative that a local division could generate was wonderful for innovation, but coordinated efforts, especially as products became part of subsystems and more complex aggregations, were greatly aided if the overall market sector were viewed at a higher level of abstraction and integration. These groups became the basis for major expansion in their own right, even as the definitions continued to evolve.

Hewlett was quick to note that divisions seldom diversified into new opportunities, because the focus was on the profit-and-loss statement for the division within a competitive arena, and new investigative work usually fell below the quick-return line. Moreover, as the instrumentation markets grew, competition increased and resources often got funneled directly to answer competitive thrusts. In practical terms, existing divisions would not have entered broader scientific instrumentation fields, such as the medical or analytical fields, let alone an emergent data products arena. Moreover, the company's engineering talent was dispersing from Palo Alto to a variety of remote locations. For larger transformative efforts, the company needed another approach. Hewlett and Oliver looked at other corporate models. Using Bell Labs as a pattern, with a more pragmatic twist, they started a centralized R&D lab at the Palo Alto headquarters in 1962, destined to become a formalized HP Labs by 1966. But first the company had to consolidate its sales force; they had outgrown the representative agent structure.

Integrating the Sales Force

We sell solutions to measurement problems, but it is really an integrated marketing effort to discover, create, arouse, and satisfy customer needs.

NOEL ELDRED[11]

Dave Packard told Howard Vollum's biographer that HP "stuck with manufacturer's representatives far after most companies," probably longer than need be.[12] The symbiotic relationship built over two decades worked well for both sides. Manufacturer representatives differed from today's dealer channels. No inventory was carried; the sale was for a prenegotiated transaction fee. The rep found the prospects, taught them about and got them interested in the product, and then sent an order to HP. When HP had the product ready, it often was shipped to the representative, who took it to the customer, made sure that it functioned properly, and collected the money.

Noel Eldred set the tone for interaction with the representatives. His view was that Hewlett-Packard had a dual obligation—first to the reps to make sure that they were trained and equipped to sell the company's sophisticated products; second, to the customer to make sure that the right high-quality products were purchased. The emphasis was on demonstrating the measurement for the customer. The company participated in two annual tradeshows, the IRE show in New York and WESCON on the West Coast. These shows were major synchronizing events for every lab in the company to have its products done and ready to demonstrate, since these shows were well-attended by leading design engineers and sales rep firms from across the country. HP raced every year to see how its products matched the competition.[13]

The big concern in 1962 was not how to diversify the corporate product stance but how to maintain sales momentum as the selling organization changed. Hewlett urged Packard to build a vertically integrated sales force by acquiring as many of the U.S. sales representative organizations as possible. The company was already experimenting in Canada and with the Geneva sales operation for Europe; this would alter the face of the company forever. Eldred, his hands full with acquisitions, pulled together a remarkable assemblage of talent, promoting John Young, Dean Morton, Bill Terry, Bob Brunner, and Tom Kelley into leadership roles for the new corporate sales function in March 1963.[14] John Young constructed a plan that merged ten of thirteen representative firms into the company, plus two more as buyouts. This was a major step, with plenty of potential to interrupt sales momentum with even the slightest miscues. Affected by the acquisition discussions, HP's growth in 1963 was a modest 7 percent.

Bruce Burlingame had built an East Coast group analogous to Neely Enterprises, but he died well before acquisitions began. The net result was a collegial assembly dubbed the "Nine Old Men," a group of individual office managers who chose to run their respective local territories until a more effective unification was developed. These too had been initiated in classic Packard style—Dave "Tiny" Yewell, a very large man who ran the Boston office, said he'd be willing to set up a company there but lacked funds. Packard wrote him a check on the spot for $10,000 and sealed the deal with a handshake. Yewell Associates was successful in the next few years; the loan was easily repaid.[15] Carl Cottrell, returning from Geneva in 1961, built the Eastern sales region in two years around several small acquisitions in the area.

These purchases began in earnest with Lipscomb Associates in 1962. Earl Lipscomb Associates was headquartered in Dallas, but Earl's reach included Los Alamos and Sandia Labs in New Mexico. In 1963, HP acquired nine sales teams. Norm Neely's Neely Enterprises was the largest of the manufacturer's representatives in terms of sales revenue, offices, and geography. Headquartered in North Hollywood, it spanned the West Coast. Lahana and Company, founded by Pete Lahana in Denver, handled the Rocky Mountain region and the western side of the Great Plains. Frank Waterfall, president of Crossley Associates, was based in Chicago; his team covered the upper Midwest. The founder, Al Crossley, had retired some years earlier. John Bivins headed Bivins and Caldwell, a firm in High Point, North Carolina;[16] Fred Horman ran a nearby organization called Horman Associates in Rockville, Maryland. The RMC Sales Division in New York City; the Robinson Sales Division in West Conshohocken, Pennsylvania; and the Stiles Sales Division in Orlando, Florida, were all smaller, relatively new teams. These firms, along with Tiny Yewell's place—Yewell Associates in Burlington, Massachusetts—were part of the Eastern Seaboard representation.

These sales groups all came together at the annual IRE convention; each of the leaders knew the others well. It wasn't hard, once Neely signed up, for the whole group to join HP.[17] In addition to trade shows and advertising, Norm Neely had conceived the "Neely bus"—a Greyhound bus stripped of seats, re-outfitted with seven different lab stations that exhibited several variants of what the well-equipped design engineer, test technician, or service technician would like to have at his workbench. The bus, driven from company to company, hosted mini-exhibits. Weekly, the bus was driven to a new venue, preannouncing its arrival to customers. The bus driver and a company design engineer staffed the bus each week.[18] It was quite an education for a designer to spend a week on the bus. Trying to be a confident, articulate spokesperson was daunting for most engineers. Bear in mind that universities in America didn't have senior or graduate level classes in measurement science—few even had a conceptual understanding of it. In other words, a bus tour with a senior HP measurement specialist was like a final exam for a course the engineers had never taken.

This instrumentation learning carried over into field engineer training, and even into the vocabulary. The salespeople were not salesmen, they were field engineers; order takers were staff engineers. They were all engineers—Eldred insisted upon hiring only college graduates from engineering schools, a strategic move that paid great dividends as the company grew because of the strong skills base available throughout the company.

Lyle Jevons, one of the first market development specialists, loved HP's first spectrum analyzers; he was dismayed as initial sales proved slower than anticipated. Jevons found that erstwhile customers struggled to appreciate the true value of the new equipment. His conclusion was to show the gear under operational conditions at the customer site, which was, "More often than not, a remote missile range, a radar site, or an air base where conditions were less than ideal for a smooth demonstration."[19]

Jevons pitched his idea to Earl Lipscomb, who headed the Southwest sales region, and Lipscomb provided a loaner Ford van, already nicknamed the Happy Wagon because of its impressive ride characteristics on the rough roads in the desert Southwest. Jevons adapted the Neely bus idea to a specialized van that housed all of the equipment for installing, operating, and maintaining a microwave repeater station; then he put together an itinerary to travel America alone to out-of-the-way places where such stations were being installed (for example, upstate Maine, the Dakotas, Montana, and the Southwest).[20] Jevons earned enormous respect for his missionary-like tours of the country to change the industry morés. After a slow start, the product became HP's first $10-million-per-year product family. Microwave became HP's largest, most profitable division as the first public decade closed.[21]

To augment the sales force, HP established a second repair center in Rockaway, New Jersey, in addition to the Palo Alto facility. These two centers were staffed with 175 technicians and product specialists by the end of 1963, bespeaking a dedication to HP customer satisfaction. HP's sales and support approach was the envy of the industry both before and after assimilating the manufacturer's representatives. Noel Eldred, working with Norm Neely, was the architect of substantial training on both the products and the measurement concepts behind them.

A small monograph titled *How They Sell,* published by the *Wall Street Journal* in 1965, featured HP in the lead chapter.[22] It opened by citing the customer training program delivered to fifteen thousand attendees from some fifteen hundred companies the previous year, immersed for three nine-hour days at HP's Palo Alto headquarters. It went on to note with some astonishment that all of HP's 250 salesmen were college graduates in engineering, while one in five had a master's degree. Even more important, Eldred insisted that the job prerequisite was three to five years of practical engineering experience. People clamored to join the group, but only one of twenty applicants was selected for a largely salaried position.

The HP model was quite orthogonal to most sales environments. Eldred explained,

> We don't sell hardware. We sell solutions to measurement problems. . . . You're calling on smart people, so you have to try to know more about their job than they do. If your technical presentation is skillful enough to make them see a use for your product, generally you've got a sale made. If not, they're turned off completely.[23]

HP Infrastructure for Customer Service

As HP began to acquire the sales reps, the Executive Council became concerned about the efficiency of order processing. "To improve Customer Service was the Number One Objective."[24] With new divisions, new sales affiliates, new subsidiary companies, and new joint ventures complicating the company's organizational integrity, Bud Eldon, HP's first systems and operations analysis manager, was tasked by David Packard to do an evaluation of the problem. The team went further than that—they defined and built a prototype system in four months, augmented it for three more, and deployed it widely across the company in three more. As the November 1963 *HP Measure* article reported,

> With this new system, it is possible regularly to ship instruments the very day a customer gives his order to a sales office. There is no duplication of order editing between sales office and factory, and no possibility of differing interpretations. Since the sales office has all the order information, it can invoice the customer after shipment and collect the payment too.
>
> An interesting result follows: In the customer's eyes the local sales office is Hewlett-Packard—the whole Corporation. The customer goes only one place to get information or place an order or ask for technical help or pay an invoice, without concern about where any item is manufactured or stocked.[25]

Eldon pushed the envelope still further, feeling that

> The overriding challenge (opportunity as I saw it) was to use order processing as a vehicle to tie everything together. Separately, because of my years of experience in production planning, control, and management, I realized that a centralized system should be integrated with production scheduling, inventory control and even purchasing coupled with sales order forecasting.[26]

HP sent direct mailings, a large annual catalog, and a monthly technical publication started by Barney Oliver's group, the *Hewlett-Packard Journal,* to every customer of record. The catalog often exceeded six hundred pages with a print run of three hundred thousand copies. A representative would then call on the most likely prospects, give a demonstration, and even loan a product for a week or two. With such a protracted sales process, it was imperative that the sales force be knowledgeable. It is easy to see why the Tektronix scope success, and its decision to leave the representative organizations, was quickly noticed.

The *HP Journal* was a monthly technical refresher, done as a measurement primer with emphasis on the practical approaches that made the instrument notable. The focus was on the instrument's task rather than the underlying science, as the *Bell Systems Technical Journal* or the *IBM Technical Journal* might seek to do. To publish in the *Journal* became a badge of honor for HP designers, since only innovative products were featured. The catalog, though, was the most impressive customer literature piece. Chock full of measurement concepts and specifications for every product, it was a tour de force publication.

HP Laboratories

It proved difficult for existing divisions to embark on high-risk projects of long duration. They can ill afford to spend much money on basic materials or on technology research that may benefit the whole company, but be of only slight advantage to that particular division.

JOHN DOYLE[27]

With the sales force acquisitions behind them, Hewlett and Packard turned again to the question of renewal. The fledgling laboratory was judged successful, and thus a new organization was created in Palo Alto in 1966, called HP Labs. "The purpose was to carry on basic and applied research studies, to assist the operating divisions in finding solutions to their technical problems, and, if necessary, to develop prototype products in new and promising fields. In this latter role, HP Labs has been immensely successful."[28]

A less visible purpose included providing some consistency for the corporation to avoid replicating common ideas—power supply design, front-panel nomenclature, and cabinets, for example. Barney helped install key research on tools, such as photolithography for IC advances, giving Eberhardt Rechtin a leadership role at HP after his work on global positioning systems in Washington, D.C. Hewlett cut division R&D budgets from 10 percent to 8.5 percent, using the other 1.5 percent to fund this central laboratory. John Doyle, who became head of HP Labs in 1981, said,

> The Labs were formed by bringing together four research and development programs that were already in existence: a CRT lab (cathode ray tube, a television set display), a quartz lab, a semiconductor lab, and an instrument lab. This nucleus was augmented by people from other parts of the company and from outside whose interests lay in a central research function. The hope was that each lab might broaden its own focus, and moreover, that synergy might result from the combination. It took awhile for cross-pollination to occur, but it didn't take long for each lab to extend its contribution into adjacent areas.[29]

Barney Oliver was the logical choice to head the Labs. He'd been at HP thirteen years, following a brilliant career at Bell Laboratories where he held forty-two patents, forty of them sole inventions. His patents were in such disparate areas as television, satellite communications, linear amplifier and pulse circuitry, and oscillographs. He coauthored "The Philosophy of PCM [Pulse Code Modulation]" with Claude Shannon and John Pierce, outlining the basis for satellite communications.[30] At HP, he garnered another eighteen patents, again in wide areas: switching power supply design (a mission-critical, lightweight, high-power computer supply), tactile feedback for keyboards (a crucial contribution for the HP 35), plotter paper movement for HP's emerging printer line, and magnetic coil assembly and geomagnetic suppression correction for MRI.

Oliver's greatest contribution for HP eventually was providing a strong supporting role for the HP 9100A and the HP 35, the two calculator products that shifted HP forever into the data products arena. But that understates his contribution significantly—he was the unifying spirit that helped each lab within the new organization to stretch, as well as interact. Hewlett, a man of deep intellectual range himself, found Barney to be an extraordinary talent, in part because of his wide-ranging interests. He wrote that he had seen Barney as "a scientist, an engineer, an astronomer, an educator, a surveyor, an author, a grammarian, a salesman, and a first-rate repair technician," as well as "a mentor to countless designers and engineers, whom he taught how to convert their theoretical knowledge into simple and elegant designs."[31] On many occasions, Dave and Bill independently averred that Barney did more to contribute to the success of HP than anyone else—a conclusion that fully validated tolerating a perceived prima donna.[32] Not everyone held Barney in such high regard—his acerbic wit and scathing repartee could cut deeply; but under his leadership, the Labs contributed very novel work.

When three of HP's long-term scientific fellows—Zvonko Fazarinc, Tom Hornak, and Len Cutler—compiled *The Selected Papers of Barney Oliver* for HP Labs in 1997, they indexed 279 papers.[33] Barney was prominent at the national level for multiple scientific inquiries—including the integrity of the Space Shuttle re-entry tiles; the Search for Extra-Terrestrial Intelligence (SETI); and the safety of and need for nuclear power—that were vital importance to the national interest. At his funeral service, many HPites were surprised to learn that scientists of the world viewed his HP legacy as a minor portion of his career.[34]

The Instrument Lab, led by Paul Stoft, initiated three notable products—the HP 2116A instrument controller, followed by the HP 9100A desktop calculator, and finally the HP 35 handheld calculator, contributions that dramatically and irrevocably redefined HP's overall mission. None of these were instruments in the sense that the HP divisions understood that term—all would come to appreciate the added value that these computing and calculating engines provided for every HP instrument.

Most HP histories acknowledge the value of HP Labs, citing these fundamental computing products and their impact on HP's evolution. The timing was fortuitous—these products all emerged not long after the formation of HP Labs, giving an imprimatur to Hewlett's idea. The common mythology was that these computer products were the primary HP Labs output. As remarkable as the products were, they were but one aspect of the overall contribution provided by HP Labs. Ironically, the Instrument Lab provided modest contributions thereafter, as other HP Lab sections seized the baton.

The Palo Alto CRT Lab, led by Bill Kruger, was originally established to provide CRTs for HP's oscilloscope division. In classic fashion, the first focus was on technical contribution to the CRT itself.[35] But consistent with a pattern seen often at HP, the important contribution put a refined version into a novel application—the inclusion of a small, bright CRT for text and numeric readout in the first desktop calculator, HP's 9100A—producing the first commercially successful integrated personal computer.[36] At the time, punch cards, ASR-33 teletype terminals, and Z-fold seventeen-inch-wide paper stacks from large, noisy impact printers were the primary interface between computer users and their machines. Several early university pioneers had used CRT displays for computer graphics: Glen Culler, at the University of California Santa Barbara, delivered a few units of the Culler-Fried Graphics Terminal to universities in the early 1960s, and Ivan Sutherland began his ground-breaking MIT Sketchpad work during the same period.[37] When the HP 2116 team assembled, Ed Holland "spent a lot of time looking at different peripherals to attach. For some reason, a lot of people were very negative about using CRTs. The argument was, 'Oh well, the paper tape gives you a printed copy and you could punch out a tape. That's good enough.' . . . Now everybody uses a CRT."[38]

The first computer displays for HP owed their origin to several HP designers from the HP 2116 lab (Kay Magleby, Paul Schmidt, and Bob Grimm) attending Sutherland's graphic demonstration at the IBM Share Design conference in New Orleans in May 1966, plus Chuck House from HP Colorado Springs. The HP 1300A Large-Screen CRT Display debuted months later with a modified TV CRT developed by Milt Russell using concepts from Kruger's lab. In the meantime, Dave Packard and Barney Oliver came through Colorado Springs for a division review. Their reaction to the prototype CRT display box was quite negative. Barney was convinced that Russell's expansion-mesh lens could not be produced reliably with the delicate molding required, while sales manager Bill Terry's market forecast for thirty-two total units was dismal indeed.

Packard's words to the division staff that evening were, "When I come back next year, I don't want to see that project in the lab." The next morning, the project team vowed to have it in production before he returned, even though the production schedule on record was eighteen months away. At the next division review, Packard thundered to the hapless project manager, Chuck House, "I thought I said to *kill* this project," to which the only effective response was to say, "No, sir, you said you didn't want it in the lab—it isn't, it's in production."[39]

Packard, unmollified, demanded to know how well it was selling. The answer was surprisingly positive—not only did Dymec marketeers quickly embrace the display,[40] other American computer labs adopted it. Doug Engelbart experimented with it in his famous Fall Joint Computer Conference demonstration of networked computers in 1968, a show that dazzled the computer cognoscenti.[41] Alan Kay used it for his 1967 Flex Machine, developed under Ivan Sutherland's direction at the University of Utah—the first working self-contained personal computer, by many accounts.[42] Kay recalled seeing HP's 9100A Desktop Calculator advertised as a "personal computer" in March 1968. When the HP35A handheld version came out in January 1972, he was excited, saying, "We wanted the Dynabook to be like the HP calculator except to be a real, live computer. This was the inspiration for all that we were thinking about."[43]

These electrostatic large-screen CRT displays found a variety of novel applications, presaging the computer-human interface issues that would later gain momentum. Hollywood filmmakers used a version for computer graphics, garnering an Oscar for technical production in 1969; the displays were used to monitor Dr. Denton Cooley's first artificial heart transplant surgery in May 1968, as well as Neil Armstrong's foot landing on the moon on July 20, 1969. The Apollo program featured many other HP products as well, notably HPA devices and Santa Clara signal averagers.[44] Years later, David Packard awarded a Medal of Defiance to House for "extraordinary contempt and defiance beyond the normal call of engineering duty," using it as an example to the company of the value of doing your own research and being committed with passion to the project.[45]

When microprocessors came along in the early 1970s, instruments shifted from low-precision analog meter movements (~0.5 percent repeatability measurements) to much more accurate digital numeric readouts (or scalars); shortly thereafter, many designers discovered the power and beauty of graphical, interpretive displays. Thus measurement data were transformed dramatically in presentation format, and the Colorado Springs CRT Lab became a critical vendor of Kruger's original technology to the corporation for a decade (Figure 4.5).[46] Significantly, Kruger's lab was by now working with the semiconductor lab on light-emitting-diode displays (LEDs) as well as liquid-crystal displays (LCDs); these cross-lab efforts would bear much fruit for HP on handheld scientific calculators.

The Quartz Lab, established early by Don Hammond, was retitled as the Physical Electronics Lab in the new organization. Several important products came from this lab before HP Labs was formalized, including precision thermometers, precision laser interferometer work, and frequency standards. The Frequency and Time Division was the natural division channel for these products, and over time, F&T developed its own cadre of scientists and engineers skilled in these fields. Hammond moved on, extending his team into devices, mechanisms, and technologies for printing, as well as transducers and devices for physiologic and analytical chemistry sensors.[47]

My labs had made contributions in the quartz thermometer and the quartz pressure transducer. Lasers had come out about that time, and Al Bagley (division manager of F&T) had twisted Bill and Dave's arms to say, "Why don't we take an atomic light to count meters of length highly accurately. Thus, within one part in 10^8, we could measure the wingtip to wingtip of a Boeing 707, for example. And that was a big step forward, a new kind of product.[48]

Over eight years, distance measuring tool resolution moved from one part in fifty thousand (resolving two inches in two miles) to one part in two million (one-half inch in two hundred miles).[49]

Reversing the direction of inquiry, the team (including Bill Kruger) developed a two-frequency laser interferometer excited by a Zeeman-splitting laser capable of resolving to a micro-inch (0.5×10^6 accuracy) for precision machining. This tool proved invaluable for aligning precision steppers, fueling the famous Moore's Law advances in semiconductor densities that underlay the PC revolution.[50]

Hammond's team required sophisticated measurement tools. Electronic spectroscopy, secondary-ion mass spectrometers, Rutherford backscattering X-ray diffraction meters, and a variety of electron microscopy techniques enabled deep materials research, allowing more precise semiconductor work as well as valuable studies on surface materials such as resists and inks. This work led to efforts on printing and in thin-film memories, as well as glass fabrication technologies. Thus the team became deeply involved with the fundamentals of data storage, printing, semiconductor definitions, and devices for medical and chemical analysis.

A body of patents resulted between 1972 and 1975 with two outcomes: first, a lucrative long-term relationship with Canon Industries in Japan, which led eventually to innovative LaserJet products; and second, a patent-protected, technology-rich understanding of inks and ink-jet technology yielding leading InkJet products. Hammond noted that "the big step forward in my lab was the printer business. We started in the printer business in 1972. It had nothing to do with LaserJet yet, nor InkJet."[51] This was one of those serendipitous combinations—the group became very knowledgeable about inks in order to solve photo-resist surface contamination issues in three-five compound semiconductors. That enabled them to reconsider the Sanborn and San Diego Division slow-drying inks that smudged for physicians doing EKG plots. Years later, these two sets of work would propel HP strongly into a leadership role in printing technologies and products.

The Semiconductor Lab, in existence early, got impetus from the HP Associates (HPA) acquisition. John Atalla, the first lab manager, launched an exotic material science investigation program that provided a base technology for gallium arsenide, gallium arsenide phosphide, and indium arsenide devices. These elements, part of the three-five compounds in the chemical periodic table, were much harder to work with than the better-known four-four compounds of silicon or germanium doped with antimony or phosphorus.[52] Advantages of the three-five group included faster inherent electron mobility (of enormous value in very high-frequency devices) plus the ability to convert electrical signals into light emissions.

Few semiconductor companies were active in these niche areas, so HP Labs was pioneering many concepts without much help from industry colleagues. On the one hand, this was a major disadvantage, but it was a perfectly rational strategy for the purposes of HP devices—to give the instrumentation groups leading-edge technology that they couldn't buy on the market. Eventually, it became the cornerstone technology for HP's Microwave Group, as the team moved to Santa Rosa, California, with part of the newly divided Microwave Division. These devices enabled HP sweepers and network analyzers to push into the 20GHz-40GHz frequency spectrum, ultimately giving HP more than 90 percent of the military communications market, because few competitors could match either the investment or the lore learned over three decades in the business.

Corporate Research Labs

Analysts and corporate managers have been sharply critical of central research labs in recent years—the oft-stated opinion is that such groups have not been adequately productive. There has been a shift toward more applied research to augment existing programs rather than basic or unfettered research.[53] Some technical leaders lament such a shift. For example, dean emeritus Jim Gibbons of Stanford observed in 2006 that each of the major electronics research labs thirty years ago—Bell Labs, IBM Research, HP Labs, RCA Sarnoff Labs, and XeroxPARC—has shrunk by more than half, and many other efforts have disappeared. Alan Kay decries this trend as well, opining that a more favorable climate and expenditure for research into better software methods likely would have produced dramatic breakthroughs.[54] National research leaders David Tennenhouse and Gordon Bell assert that corporate research labs still exert great influence when enlightened corporate leadership supports such activities.[55] These observers cite the burden now being carried by research labs at Microsoft, Google, and Intel.

Perspective on this question is vital. Don Hammond held strong views about HP Labs:

When John Young took over the instrument group, HP Labs had been in business seven years. Every year John would report at the annual management conference how much of the company's total business had come out of HP Labs through diversification. [For example] the first year that he reported, 50 percent of our business had come out of the labs. Narrowly, through the desktop and handheld calculators and the 2100, primarily Paul Stoft's early contribution. The concept was, "Let's make a computer that will interface well with instruments, so that we can build networks, tying together a number of different instruments that can generate data and can do computation and present the data." And, in 1972, my challenge to my lab was, "We've got to be able to do print. We've got to make it a companion product for computers so that we can put the data out and let the information be useful."[56]

Hammond went on to observe that John Young's last report to the annual management conference reported that 87 percent of HP's current business came from ideas initially investigated at HP Labs. Many a good discussion, if not argument, can arise if these numbers are scrutinized; pride factors within divisions run high. In partnership with Chuck Tyler (an HP Labs section manager), Hammond devised an effective technique for working in concert with the divisions:

The division managers were always sure that their money was wasted at HP Labs. You know, it was competition. We were basically taking their money, their profits, and investing it in our ideas instead of their ideas. But several things happened. One of the things that we learned quickly was, if we don't form an alliance with the divisions, we won't have any customers. I used to preach sermons on this subject in the labs. And I'd say, if you don't form an alliance with the division people, your project is going to fail no matter what its technical contributions are going to be. Hewlett put a rule in place: every year a project manager had to call his division and say, "How much were our sales this year in that product that we transferred to you? And how much was the profit total? And then, tell me how much you think our contribution was? Was it half? Was it a quarter? Was it 80 percent?" And we would claim then that we, HP Labs, were entitled to give ourselves credit for half of the profit of that product line, or maybe 10 percent. Sometimes we would just create an ink and we'd get credit for the ink. Or we would invent chromatography and turn it over, and that would be "our" sales. We'd give ourselves credit for that. But if they didn't know these guys well enough to buy them a beer, they weren't going to get credit for that product.[57]

Years later, after HP had diversified into medical and analytical chemistry instrumentation fields, Don Hammond and the Medical Group vice president Dean Morton evolved a collaborative strategy, wherein the Physical Electronics Lab at HP Labs and the medical group operating divisions would meet annually. Dean would start the day with an overview of where the medical products group was focused—what they were doing, what their business was, what the market competition had been, and what the new frontiers were. Then the group marketing people would give three or four talks about their approach and findings. After a coffee break, the HP Labs folk talked about technical arenas that were changing—for example, magnetic resonance imaging (MRI), X-ray technologies, or ultrasonic imaging. Thus strategy groups began to form, bridging the gap between HP Labs and the divisions—in effect, they were piloting a form of technology transfer. These divisions reported to the group vice president. This practice started with medical products, quickly moved to analytical instrumentation, and then spread to subgroups of electronic instruments. As Hammond noted, "It was awkward. It was hard work." But it worked. In the final analysis, three things are needed: deep science, relatively unfettered; broad thinking that can link across seemingly unrelated disciplines and product lines; and a healthy, robust technology-transfer capability. Somehow, HP Labs and HP top management were able to put that combination together, nurture it, and keep it in place for years—with amazingly productive results for the company.

This was renewal—natural, organic, systemic—the HP Way. Pioneered and perfected across many product lines in multiple business arenas, this innovative method stood the test of time for HP's first three decades and beyond. It worked well for evolutionary change. And, since this was the bulk of HP's business for fifty years, the renewal lessons would stand the corporation in good stead.

The answer for planned transformation, on the other hand, was mixed, and the corporation would spend considerable time and energy trying to cope with and take advantage of intended forays into additional markets. Even more important, how did HP fare when it came up against convulsive, wracking change? Disruptive technologies often leave former leadership companies in the dust, as each longitudinal survey of the Fortune 500 demonstrates. The surprising answer, especially given the slow accommodation to planned transformation, was that HP proved able to adapt to major disruptions, and even thrive on them, bringing a unique measure of contribution to the new paradigm. Without the renewal method having been mastered, though, it is doubtful that these bolder attempts would have worked nearly as well.

And as we shall see, the costs of learning how to handle disruptive forces were not insignificant, especially for the leadership. It is tempting to conclude that HP would not have been able to respond to the discontinuities of the convulsive computer era if it hadn't already struggled and persevered through the more modest planned transformations, thereby learning some truly important lessons about how to handle major change. Both renewal and planned transformations thus would become part of the mythic HP story.

CHAPTER 5

Planned Transformation

It would be nice to claim that we foresaw the profound effect of computers on our business and that we prepared ourselves to take early advantage of the computer age. Unfortunately, the record does not justify such pride. It would be more accurate to say that we were pushed into computers by the revolution that was changing electronics.

DAVE PACKARD[1]

David Packard was HP's visible leader for the first thirty years, and 1957 was a vintage year for his leadership. Signal events that year took much thought, time, and energy: presenting explicit objectives for the management team at the Sonoma Meeting, occupying an impressive new headquarters in the Stanford Industrial Park, and taking the company public. Packard was a commanding presence; his size alone gave him instant recognition, and his gravelly voice and assured tone gave him gravitas for almost any audience, such as erstwhile new stockholders.

Bill Hewlett, with little need for the limelight, worked unnoticed in the laboratory. It was only after Dave left for a Washington, D.C., assignment in the Nixon Administration and Bill became the new CEO that he became visible. Hewlett often was the bolder risk-taker, however. His note in 1938 propelled Packard to leave GE and start HP; and his insistence for building an international presence gave HP impressive leadership in building one of the world's most successful multinational corporations. Packard humored his partner on his internationalization dream, eventually spending considerable energy traveling the globe and courting international leaders. But it was Hewlett who galvanized the Sonoma meeting and initiated business efforts in both Europe and Japan.

Hewlett's greatest contribution may well have been his persistent effort to extend the company's product arenas. His pioneering efforts prompted the development and production of the HP 35 Handheld Calculator. He also hired Barney Oliver in 1952 with the intent of adding product lines beyond communications test, but microwave needs occupied much of Oliver's time for the first decade. Then a fortuitous event helped.

On October 4, 1957, Nikita Khrushchev stunned the world with the Soviet Sputnik I launch. President Dwight D. Eisenhower, facing both a challenge and an opportunity for American leadership, chartered a bold path for fundamental research via the Advanced Research Projects Agency.[2] Further stimulation came when a presidential address was sent from the Echo satellite that had been launched into space on August 12, 1960. These events had an extraordinary impact on the electronics industry.[3] They added fuel to Hewlett's desire to broaden the HP instrumentation spectrum. In *Electronic Measurements and Instrumentation,* John Cage and Barney Oliver explain that

> Electronic measurements are of two kinds: those made of electronic quantities such as voltage, capacitance, or field strength, and those made by electronic means of other quantities such as pressure, temperature, or flow rate. Electronic instrumentation (and HP) came of age in solving the measurement needs of electronics itself, but in its maturity it is proving remarkably adaptable to other fields.[4]

Acquisitions

It would be less than truthful to indicate that the Sanborn to Hewlett-Packard transition was smooth and without problems. Frustrations continued to mount between those schooled in the Sanborn versus the HP Way.

JANET DALE[5]

New shareholders in the public company might not have suspected that an acquisition hunt was about to begin. A brief note in the 1958 *Annual Report* described HP buying 80 percent of the F. L. Moseley Company three days after the end of the fiscal year. The other 20 percent was deferred for five years. The *Annual Report* noted that in the past, HP had not used acquisition as a means of growth, that the Moseley Company had had sales in the $1.5 million range per year, and that its product line was "completely compatible with the Hewlett-Packard line. Mr. F. L. Moseley will continue to operate his company as an independent concern, but HP expects to provide substantial assistance to improve the growth potential of the Moseley Company."[6] The HP Virtual Museum website says,

> In 1951, the F. L. Moseley Co. was formed in a California garage to manufacture the first commercially available x-y recorder, called the Autograf line. For scientists and engineers everywhere, the Moseley x-y recorder meant that a means for automatically recording the relationship between two variables was finally available. Friction to heat, vibration to velocity, current to voltage—whatever the variables, the Autograf made it possible to trace them on chart paper automatically, rather than tracking them by hand. HP's Moseley Division later became HP's San Diego Division, evolving to HP's current imaging and printing systems business.[7]

Acquisitions continued with a rush. The 1959 *Annual Report* showed restated revenues for the previous year, something new to HP history. Instead of $30,474,764 in total revenue in 1958 as shown in the prior year report, sales of $35,856,737 were listed, an increment of $5,381,973. That number was both exquisite in detail and significant, representing as it did the addition of several new companies in 1958.[8] By the end of 1966, twelve companies and several divisional units of other companies had been purchased.[9]

Among the first new acquisitions, Dymec and PAECO were well-known at HP, both started and funded by HP executives. PAECO's transformers, coils, and resistors were sold to regional companies, 30 percent to HP. Dymec, created to modify standard Hewlett-Packard equipment to meet special requirements for individual customers, evolved into a systems integrator, combining multiple HP instruments to perform complex measurements.

Moseley, though, was truly independent, as was Boonton Electronics, bought the same year. Moseley Autograf x-y recorders were the class act of the recording industry, used heavily for data-logging of voltages in the evolving process-control industry. Boonton Q-meters were the standard for parametric testing of RLC circuits. Moseley was four hundred miles away, in Pasadena, California; Boonton Electronics was in Boonton, New Jersey, thirty miles west of New York City.

The first three acquisitions went smoothly. Robert Grimm became general manager for Dymec, run as a division. Jack Beckett became operations manager for PAECO, working for general manager Jack Petrak, a long-time HP employee (since 1945). Francis Moseley continued to run his company. Packard's laconic note in the 1966 *Annual Report* read, "Francis L. Moseley was elected to our board in March 1966. He is an excellent addition to our board, with his broad knowledge of the electronics industry, his scientific inventiveness, and his keen insight and interest in our operations."[10] Moseley, as a member of HP's Mergers and Acquisitions team, was often called on during negotiations for companies that HP acquired, to explain how fairly they had dealt with him.

Moseley had become acquainted with both Hewlett and Packard through Norm Neely; he proposed that they buy a small piece of equity for cash, so that he could have some spending money, as he phrased it. Packard and van Bronkhorst described the pitfalls of a partial buyout, including the taxes that he would incur and potential issues with a minority shareholder who might want to direct him more than he desired. Moseley was not yet ready to give up control, which hampered progress until Packard came up with an overall plan that suited everyone.

Packard and van Bronkhorst arrived at a $2 million valuation; Moseley independently came up with $1.5 million. Most purchasers ask the seller to describe his price before proceeding, and the HP team did just that. Moseley said $1.5 million—and the considered response from most executives would have been "bid $1.25 million in return—you know they'll go lower." Instead, Packard intoned, "Well, we think it's worth $2 million." It would have been wonderful to see Moseley's facial expression for that counteroffer! Then Packard continued, "but only if you come with it," solving the question about Moseley being loath to quit. Packard further proposed that Moseley Recorders should become an affiliate rather than a wholly owned subsidiary. A way to do that was to buy $1.6 million worth in cash, and escrow $400,000 in HP stock for purchase within five years, cancelable at either party's discretion. Five years later, the escrowed stock was worth $2.7 million.[11] Thereafter, when prospective sellers balked at a pricing offer from HP, Francis would describe how his situation had unfolded—it invariably evoked admiration.

The Boonton acquisition proved more complicated than Moseley, because of the distance and owner Bob Loughlin's desire to do something different. Packard recruited Bill Myers, the production engineering manager, to run Boonton. Myers, a Princeton graduate, was pleased at the opportunity to learn the expanded role of a general manager; other Palo Alto managers took note. Loughlin's son, Robert Jr., wanted to continue with the new company, and Packard invited him to come to Palo Alto "to learn how we do things," working for Dick Alberding on the U.S. marketing team. The first intercorporate transfer from an acquisition into HP, Loughlin later moved to Moseley, staying sixteen years at HP.[12]

In 1960, two new ideas surfaced. Semiconductors were becoming a hot topic in the "Valley of Heart's Delight," the advertising slogan used to attract Santa Clara Valley vacationers for the previous decade (fifteen years later, journalist Don Hoeffler would tag it as "Silicon Valley," because of all of the new silicon semiconductor companies in the area; the Valley has been known by this moniker ever since). It was clear that there wasn't an effective path for developing sophisticated technology within HP; obviously PAECO wasn't enough. Packard met Jack Melchor, a local microwave business founder (and later one of Silicon Valley's earliest venture capitalists), who proposed a joint venture with HP to develop light-emitting diodes. It became HP Associates, with HP owning 60 percent of the stock and a buy-out clause (today called an exit strategy) at the end of five years. Long-term HP employees Frank Boff and Horace Overacker both joined HPA.[13]

Hewlett had long been enamored of medical electronics; driven by his personal history, along with a belief that electronic measurement opportunities could be quite large, he sought out the Sanborn Company as a new acquisition. The Sanborn Company developed blood pressure and metabolism measurement tools in the 1920s, building a solid reputation in medical circles. John Minck wrote,

> The medical electrocardiograph business was like a razor-razorblade business. Sanborn's product used a recording paper called Perma-paper, a paper sandwich with a black background, covered by a clean white wax coat. The black showed through only when a heated stylus on the end of the recording pen moved across the surface and melted the wax, revealing a stark black line on white. In doctor's offices, any liquid ink process that caused splattered dots and blotches was not acceptable. The Sanborn paper was exceedingly clean, so the record could be stapled into the patient's file folder.[14]

During due diligence for the Sanborn acquisition, Frank Cavier found that nearly all of the profits of the East Coast company were created by sales of the special recording paper sold for EKG machines (a finding eerily foretelling the peripherals story with inks thirty years later). The difficulty was that the paper was produced by yet a third company under patent rights about to expire. Cavier said, "I pointed this out to Packard before they acquired the company. It just made him mad. He was all set to buy this company and didn't want a lot of negative input."[15] The acquisition was made, with much fanfare about the instrumentation opportunity that it represented. The fact that half of the product line seemed to compete with the F. L. Moseley acquisition from two years earlier was scarcely mentioned, and nothing about specialized paper was said in either HP's in-house newsletter, *Watt's Current,* or the *Annual Report.*[16]

The Sanborn experience proved to be quite thorny. When the seventeen-year patent expired "shortly after HP became the new owner, the subcontract manufacturer, Nashua Paper Products, started selling the paper directly to the doctors. A huge amount of revenue disappeared."[17] Within two years, revenues had fallen nearly by half, layoffs were invoked, and tempers ran high. Hewlett and Packard drafted Canadian Bruce Wholey from HP's most profitable division, Microwave, to go straighten things out; it took him many years to do so. Sanborn had an entrenched company management well-liked by employees, who were very set in their ways. Alfred Lonnberg was president, and James Jenks Jr. was board chairman. Packard put Jenks on HP's board and left Lonnberg in charge, until the financial picture dimmed. Sanborn employees equated the profit focus and the layoffs with a clear denial of the Sanborn Way. Hewlett and Packard agreed that it was distasteful to the HP Way too, but the HP Way always was grounded in profitable performance, and they were not about to abridge that fundamental tenet. More concerning was the resistance to change and the reluctance to accept new techniques, new methods, and a new market viewpoint.

Shareholders saw a net growth of 42 percent from 1960 to 1961; deeper reading revealed that the Sanborn acquisition gave HP 70 percent of the total growth that year.[18] The difficulties of the Sanborn product line, though, reduced the value for the overall HP picture—it took seven years for the medical part of HP to return to the revenues Sanborn enjoyed the year that HP bought it, let alone begin to grow profitably. Hewlett noted years later, "Someone at the Harvard Business School had written a case study, under a pseudonym. I think if we'd read that report, we never would have acquired it. When we got into it, we found out that all of those [unappealing things in the case] were true in spades. We had to put Bruce Wholey in to manage [Sanborn], and it was a very difficult assignment." Packard agreed, saying, "Yes, and we spent a lot of time back there helping Bruce."[19]

Undaunted by this setback, HP aimed at another New Jersey target—Harrison Laboratories in Berkeley Heights. Acquired in 1962, this small power supply manufacturer had mastered the technology to build high-frequency switching power supplies. Founder Bill Harrison had capitalized on switching technology using new planar power transistors, along with an unorthodox management style whereby a new designer had just six weeks to get a design into production, or he was out the door. Hardly the HP Way, but the deadline was an effective motivator, and designs got done quickly. Barney Oliver had done some work with the Harrison team while he was still at Bell Labs; he even held some television linearizing circuit patents assigned to Harrison. Harrison Labs later became the New Jersey Division, managed by another Palo Alto transplant, Johan Blokker.

In 1964, John Cage, returning from Bedford, England, to head corporate development, engineered several small acquisitions: Mechrolab, International Control Machines, and Delcon in 1964; Datamec and F&M Scientific in 1965; and the remaining 40 percent of HP Associates in 1966.[20] After Sanborn, none was particularly large. The set in 1964 added $8.85 million in accretive revenues, the high point for all acquisitions except Sanborn (which was $18 million). F&M, a leader in liquid chromatography, enabled HP again to compete with Beckman Instruments. F&M (renamed the Avondale Division because it was located in Avondale, Pennsylvania) became the linchpin division of the Analytical Group for HP.[21]

Delcon produced field-grade telephone test equipment, and after a rocky assimilation, it was moved to Colorado Springs by new division manager Alan Steiner and R&D manager Robert Allen, both of whom came from the Microwave Division. There, Delcon (renamed Colorado

Data Communications Division) eventually became a leading contributor to the emerging digital data communications test arena, with such products as Network Protocol Analyzers.[22]

Buyout time arrived five years later for the HP Associates group; Packard gave the leadership team from Friday until Monday to come up with their valuation. By Monday, they had spent the weekend preparing a forty-page document, which included "both a high-end estimate that the team thought too greedy and a low-end estimate they were prepared to live with." Upon seeing the document, Packard frowned. He said, "Look, I don't want to have to listen to this entire presentation. How's this? Let me make my offer, and if you don't like it, I'll listen." He then offered them 20 percent more than their high-end estimate, amazing the associates.[23]

By the end of 1966, in pursuit of broadening HP measurements beyond communications, twelve companies had been acquired outright; three joint ventures were developed; two overseas divisions were created; and technology from seven other companies had been purchased (this is all in addition to the sales office acquisitions).[24] The federal government's Antitrust Division became concerned that Hewlett-Packard had a monopolistic position in measurement, prompting HP to abandon its eight-year "acquisition kick," as Hewlett would phrase it.[25] Many said that HP would have done it without government pressure because of mediocre results. Packard said, "I'm always amused about these acquisitions, because every time you enter into a discussion, you think that two and two is going to become five, and when you get the acquisition accomplished, you find that there are a good many problems that you hadn't foreseen."[26] Hewlett was equally candid: "It didn't work out very well. We concluded that we could do better with our own resources."[27]

Assimilation: Harder Than Acquisition

Even though the major acquisitions between 1961 and 1966 were in medical and analytical chemistry fields, the organization of HP Labs when established in 1966—the Quartz Lab, the CRT Lab, the Instrument Lab, and the Semiconductor Lab—was aimed far more at the electronic instrument and measurement computing sectors; little new work in the acquisition arena was organized or staffed in Barney's domain. The operating units for the planned transformation, except for Frequency and Time, struggled—during a period when HP grew consistently at a 20 percent rate, the product divisions for Oscilloscopes, Medical, and Analytic all averaged growth only one-third as strong. Medical was the worst casualty—29 percent of total company revenues when acquired, it represented less than 9 percent a decade later. Why the disconnect? Something clearly failed.

Several theories circulated. Some think that an out-of-sight, out-of-mind mentality prevailed, and the Palo Alto–based HP Labs were more in tune with the technologies and enthusiasms prevalent in the Valley than with remote product groups in new fields. Others wondered just who had sponsored the acquisitions, and who picked up the cudgel to make them successful after the initial acquisition enthusiasm waned. Hewlett had been eager to get into medical equipment; Packard was supportive.[28] It was common knowledge that Hewlett's father was a physician. Bill had spent two years working in electro-medical research after college before starting HP with Dave. Dave Packard brought two deals to the table, both via Varian, where the Varian brothers and Martin Packard (co-inventor of nuclear magnetic resonance, or NMR, with Nobel Prize–winner Felix Bloch, but no relation to Dave) had invited Dave to sit on the board. As Varian concentrated more on NMR, it sought to divest its original microwave components line; Dave bought it for HP in 1950 to augment Art Fong's products in the Microwave Division. Martin Packard, playfully saying that Dave was his cousin, introduced Dave to DuPont's research leadership, Crawford Greenewalt and Ray McCarthy, in the early 1960s.[29] Impressed by the opportunities in this field, Dave endorsed the 1965 acquisition of F&M Scientific, a small, leading-edge analytic chemistry instrument manufacturer in Avondale, Pennsylvania.

The acquisitions proved to be challenging for the company—aside from assigning a few managers transplanted from Palo Alto into these several units, it looked and felt to many like a sink-or-swim environment. This is one of the puzzling chapters in Hewlett-Packard history. The founders wanted to be in the medical and the analytical chemistry test markets, even if they were reluctant about the oscilloscope business. But their management style was decidedly low throttle rather than heavy-handed—they had high expectations, but a curiously languid timetable for getting results.

Thus, even though HP broadened into multiple scientific instrumentation arenas over a seven-year period (1958–1965), the acquisition route proved slow in most situations. This was partially because the cultures were seldom in alignment, partially because the entrée product line never proved much more than indicative of the types of products that the company would choose to pursue after the consolidation was complete, but also partially because the company seldom got behind the initiative with its main resources.

Barney Oliver eventually contributed greatly to the diversification effort, but he did so from his own vantage point. His physics training and long association with some of America's keenest space transmission researchers at Bell Labs shaped his perspective on several topics, including radio astronomy; space communications; and physical parameters, such as temperature and pressure. He teamed with Al Bagley, who was actively pursuing concepts for accurately measuring frequency and time (such as quartz thermometers, atomic clocks, cesium-beam standards) for physicists, chemists, astronomers, and many nations' standards bureaus. A fierce, hawk-nosed competitor with Cherokee Indian heritage, Bagley decided, "We should not only make better standards, but make our own quartz crystals so we would be a leader in that too."

A colleague suggested Don Hammond, "the best crystal expert in the world." Hammond sent Bagley's inquiry a "very nice refusal, saying that a company like HP shouldn't attempt to get into quartz crystals." Bagley then asked Hewlett "to see if he couldn't put a little pressure on [Hammond] and tell [him] what a great company HP was."[30] A Palo Alto interview trip with Barney was inconclusive. Barney asked Hewlett, who was on his way home from the New York IRE show, to stop by Boulder, Colorado, where Hammond worked. Hewlett had a telegram from Barney, which he handed to Don at dinner. The blunt wire said, "Dear Bill. I've talked to Hammond. He's back on the fence. Your turn to shove. Barney."[31] It proved sufficient.

Assembling a small team, Hammond built incredible crystal capability for HP. He first built a more stable time source for the counter line, which cemented HP leadership in a high-profile area, adding great momentum and solid profits alongside microwave test products. This line of inquiry led to a pressure transducer still used for down-hole oil well measurement.[32] Hammond, along with a later Bagley hire, Len Cutler, pioneered development first in quartz oscillating crystals that measured temperatures accurately within 0.0001 degree, and then in cesium-beam standards with time interval accuracy to one second in thirty-thousand years (1 part in 10^{12}, or one part in a trillion). The temperature gauge has been used since 1967—over forty years—for measuring ocean temperatures accurately, which has been invaluable to document the nature, extent, and momentum of global warming; it has also measured background radiation temperatures in the universe from space probes, helping to establish the probable origin of the universe.[33]

Post-Sputnik, a much bigger market emerged because satellite communication requires synchronization capability that can only be ensured by atomic clocks. The HP 5060A cesium-beam standard instantly became *the* standard for international time, and was even used to corroborate Einstein's mathematics of relative time and the shifts with time travel.[34] Atomic clocks are also vital in time-critical applications such as space shuttle operations, airplane collision avoidance systems, and telecommunications. The clocks, with periodic advances over the original HP 5060A, today define the world's standard second, and the stability of the world's time coordination. Without them, global communications would be impractical.

Hewlett-Packard engineers, seeking to demonstrate HP's time synchronization capability to the scientific community, devised a series of experiments to illustrate the measurement. The first was in early June 1964, when a highly accurate HP 5060A cesium-beam atomic clock was flown from San Francisco to Washington, D.C., and then on to Switzerland to compare time at the U.S. Naval Observatory in Washington, D.C., to time at the Swiss Observatory in Neuchâtel. Al Bagley and Len Cutler carried the machine in a dramatic demonstration of the value and issues involved in keeping true time.[35] A second trip, an around-the-world affair with one machine, started February 12, 1965, and took thirty-five days and thirty-five thousand miles, during which standards were calibrated for twenty-one groups in eleven countries. The most ambitious was a dual around-the-world trip, when Dexter Hartke and Ron Hyatt went west to east, while Lee Bodily went east to west. The two teams met in Neuchâtel, establishing remarkable correlation for all of the major world time-keeping organizations, as well as verifying the ability of these new machines to operate in less-than-ideal environments—small enough to travel, operate on a variety of power sources, and take temperature and humidity variation.[36]

These concepts were extended with global positioning navigation systems (GPS) based on satellite registry and space telemetry triangulation. Although Bagley and Oliver each had experimental programs under way, both were divested before producing any products. GPS navigation took many years to gain solid returns, but HP's initial efforts paved the way for many people in the world to use these concepts via navigation systems in automobiles. Today, GPS is a fundamental location identification feature for personal digital assistants (PDAs), cellular phones, and Google Earth.[37]

Over the next decade, from 1966 through 1976, each of these new areas of endeavor would bear fruit. Many fundamental technical advances came from activities in each scientific arena, including noninvasive fetal heart rate monitoring and better automated patient monitoring for medicine;[38] significant substance identification and chemical analysis capability for chemists and biologists;[39] substantially better mechanical engineering machining capability through laser interferometry;[40] and sophisticated surveying tools that could resolve one centimeter in two hundred kilometers.[41] Taken together, such products were evidence that HP was no longer just an electronics instrument company for radio engineers, or even microwave engineers. Now HP was building test tools for the engineers and scientists of the world in nearly every discipline imaginable. It had become the scientific instrumentation company.

Evolution of the Medical Group

It took many years to stabilize the troubled Medical Division. Hewlett and Packard sent Bruce Wholey to infuse the HP Way into Sanborn. Sanborn's analog multi-channel recorders were popular at NASA; many in the division wanted to pursue that rather than the medical business. When Dean Morton came from the marketing group in Palo Alto to replace Wholey as general manager in 1968, he sent the remainder of the recorder line to the San Diego Division and focused completely on the medical business, renaming it the Waltham Division.

Over the next decade, Morton worked aggressively with Barney Oliver and HP Labs to develop a wide set of technologies for specific medical problems. HP Labs researchers worked on noninvasive monitoring and diagnostics; their contributions altered the way that clinical medicine is performed today for perinatal medicine, cardiology, pulmonary function testing, anesthesiology, neurology, emergency care, radiology, pathology, and intensive care monitoring. Just as with the original Palo Alto electronics division evolution, the Waltham Division began to spin out additional divisions as well as acquire new capabilities itself. By 1975, the Medical Group had been fully formed, with two divisions in Massachusetts (Waltham and Andover), one in Germany, another in Oregon, and an operation in Brazil.

Simple problems bedeviled the discipline however. Doctors didn't trust electronics, often for good reason. Protection for patients from implanted electrodes had received only modest attention before HP's involvement in medical instrumentation. HP engineers outlined the issues and proposed important new standards.[42] Patient-monitoring tools for relatively simple phenomena—for surgery room, bedside, and the nurse's station—became key contributions. For example, in 1975 Waltham introduced the HP 7822A Arrhythmia Monitor and the multi-station 78220 system, a significant improvement in diagnostic equipment for heart patients. The project leader, Tom Horth, became the R&D manager for the Medical Group, leading breakthrough projects for surgery rooms and after-surgery care.[43]

When HP bought Sanborn in 1961, gross revenues neared $18 million; eight years later, the Waltham Division shipped $23.6 million of product, for an average growth rate of only 3 percent per year (CAGR). Worse, Medical Group sold primarily in the Northeast United States, where the original reputation had been built. To bolster European sales, the Böblingen Medical Division was established; the group quickly found that medicine had regional and local idiosyncratic methods that needed to be considered in product features as well as sales and marketing.

The Medical Group was fluid, nevertheless. Morton shifted recorders away from Waltham, while medical displays were imported. The large-screen displays developed in Colorado Springs proved especially valuable in very bright surgery environments, as well as in multi-patient monitoring for nurse's stations. The beleaguered Colorado Springs Division, fighting a losing battle with Tektronix for revenue and profit, didn't want to cede the very profitable displays to Waltham; Packard intervened, affirming once again that the company was organized around markets, not technology.[44] In addition, HP Labs contributed a slew of new products—a coagulation analyzer, an electromyograph, and a cardiotocograph (a fetal heart rate monitor) in 1967 and 1968. These products gave impressive results during traumatic situations, but difficulty of calibration and operation precluded widespread use. Sales still languished.

In the 1970s, the medical acquisition finally began to contribute to HP revenues and profits. Over the next twelve years, the group recorded a very satisfactory 23 percent compound growth rate, shipping $250 million by 1981 at a healthy 20 percent pre-tax operating profit. New HP patient monitoring systems and a revised fetal heart rate monitor were introduced in 1976, an especially big year. HP Labs, working in conjunction with a noted medical researcher, defined a clever contribution, the blood oximeter, which used technology developed for the analytical chemistry field (spectrophotometry), plus a host of specific contributions, with 2 percent accuracy "regardless of skin pigmentation, ear thickness, or earprobe motion."[45]

Ironically, although the contribution of HP Labs was helpful to this growth spurt, it mattered primarily at a reputation level rather than a sales level. Revenue from pioneering cardiocotography and pulmonary products was only 10 percent of group revenue in 1981—five years later, it had shrunk to less than 7 percent. In contrast, group R&D manager Tom Horth's relatively mundane patient monitoring tools and cardiography diagnostic products averaged 50 percent of sales throughout these years.

Evolution of the Analytical Group

HP had repulsed Beckman Instruments in 1950, chasing the leading chemical instrumentation company out of the electronics measurement field, but when HP acquired F&M Scientific in Avondale, Pennsylvania, in 1966, the tables were turned. Although HP gained a revolutionary gas chromatograph, it was a small fraction of the instrumentation needed for a major chemistry lab. Beckman easily outflanked HP's small cadre of knowledgeable salespeople; the division struggled to gain momentum for years.

Seeking to broaden the line, HP soon added liquid and solid substance measurement. A German acquisition created the Waldbronn Division for liquid chromatography. A new HP Labs idea—spectrophotometry—appeared to offer equivalent analysis for solids. A new division, named the Scientific Instruments Division (SID), was formed in Palo Alto to combine work done at HP Labs, the Microwave Division, and the Avondale Division. New arrival Emory Rogers (from Varian Associates) assembled Avondale, Waldbronn, and SID into the Analytical Group.

In 1973, HP Labs and the Scientific Instruments Division produced the electron spectrometer for chemical analysis (ESCA), which revolutionized analytical chemistry labs. Chuck Tyler led the HP Labs effort in Don Hammond's Physical Electronics Lab; John Hearn led the SID engineering effort.[46] The ESCA allowed very precise analysis of surface phenomena on solids, taking measurements from days and weeks to minutes and hours, and cutting equipment and operational costs as well as size. Rural towns and public health officials now had sophisticated tests that enabled better biomedical diagnostics and pollution law enforcement.

Jim Serum, joining HP Avondale from Cornell in 1973, led an SID team to embed mass spectrometry in a bench-top unit. Serum said, "People did extraordinary things, inventing the impossible. We built the world's first bench-top mass spectrometer. The design of that was beyond revolutionary; when we introduced that in 1976, there was hardly a prouder moment in my life than to watch people's mouths drop open to see the technology."[47] In 1979, the HP 8450A Spectrophotometer, an ultraviolet/visible spectrum (UV/VIS) program for solids started at HP Labs, was introduced from SID, with veteran Dick Monnier as the lab manager.[48]

Much as with the Medical Group, HP Labs's emerging products helped build a very solid reputation for HP among the elite chemists of the world's laboratories, but the revenues were elsewhere. The ESCA, after six years on the market, produced a modest 12 percent of the group's revenue; spectroscopy sold just 4 percent of the group's revenue over its first decade. The big contributors were extensions of the original gas chromatograph work in Avondale; computerized control, miniaturization with electronic design, and much more reliable operation, were coupled with the combinational gas chromatograph and mass spectrometry (GC/MS) product built in SID in Palo Alto. These products contributed two-thirds of the group revenue for the first two decades at HP.

The most impressive part of the two groups, though, was the visible impact on the health and welfare of people everywhere, more than just science and engineering. HP employees with relatives in a hospital being monitored with HP equipment took great pride in the company's efforts; when sprinter Ben Johnson was caught in a drug scandal at the 1988 Olympics with an HP liquid chromatograph, positive public awareness leaped for HP.[49]

Even though the Analytical Group was just a small portion of total HP activity, the "public service" profile had tremendous emotional value for the group. Jim Serum said,

> We always were treated well. I can't tell you how many times R&D managers from the instrument group would say to me, "We're just building another oscilloscope. We're just building another voltmeter. You're building an instrument that detects environmental pollutants. How fun that must be." So we were small, but we were special. You don't have to be big to be special. We earned our profitability. We were a solid, cohesive group. People really envied the kinds of products and the relevance to society.[50]

Evolution of the Components Group

By 1978, the Components Group consisted of the Microwave Semiconductor Division, the Optoelectronics Division, and the Singapore and Penang, Malaysia, Operations (low-labor cost assembly groups). It did not include the HP Labs semiconductor research lab, or the multiple IC design and fabrication capabilities within the Instrument Group or the Computer Groups, of which there were more than a half-dozen (these captive shops were where the significant N-MOS, C-MOS, and SOS work was done).

Semiconductor research facilities are one of the most capital-intensive activities in the world—famously the venture capitalist Arthur Rock (who bankrolled both Intel and Apple as startups) proclaimed Rock's Law, a corollary to Moore's Law, which said, "The cost of capital equipment to build semiconductors will double every four years."[51] By 1971, costs for semiconductor fabrication for HP's diverse needs were sizable. The decision to create the Components Division (and eventually Group) envisioned selling additional output to outside companies to help pay for the operations, generating considerable debate about the risk of selling HP's crown jewels to competitors. The perspective that won had two bases:

1. Since HP would have easy design access for new requirements, it should be able to maintain a competitive edge in any specific device technology.
2. If HP technology was included in competitive products, HP would share in their success, from both profits and expense recovery.

Dave Weindorf, chief engineer at HPA before HP purchased it, became the new division manager. Affable on the surface, Weindorf was a scrappy competitor who relished the opportunity to build an independent business. When asked what it was like to attempt to build a components business within an instrumentation company, he said,

> You're familiar with the term *black sheep*? We felt that way from time to time. We felt that we were out of the mainstream, and we clearly were. We supplied semiconductors to many HP divisions at sharply reduced prices over what we could supply outside. We were growing our business outside. In fact, that was our main thrust. We wanted to become a strong commercial supplier of semiconductor devices, and we did.
>
> We reported to John Young. We invited him once to a dinner with the top HPA managers, and we complained that we weren't getting our fair share of recognition, being this little "off to the side" kind of activity. And he said, in John's inimitable people-oriented style, "You guys are paranoid." So we went about our business and did very well. We became a much larger supplier to the outside world than we did to HP very shortly. Our outside business grew very rapidly.[52]

The challenge primarily was to commercialize specialty devices and technologies. *Commercialize* was a big word; it included writing up more rigid specifications for an external market, developing a marketing staff and a separate sales force, developing manufacturing procedures and standards, installing a full quality control function, and enhancing complete cost accounting. Because the division competed on much different terms—price and volume—from most of HP, it required modification of the normative metrics used to judge divisional performance.

The Components Division was created by acquiring very high-frequency microwave diodes and transistors from the Microwave Division Technology Center and building a catalog of devices for outside sale. The division quickly added optoelectronic devices, transferred from HP Labs (part of the original HPA).[53] Originally, these were simple light-emitting diodes (LEDs), packaged as a seven-segment numeric readout that could replace a Nixie tube.[54] Strings of seven-segment devices were combined to make the HP 35 display. As volumes built, the division learned how to build more efficient devices to increase battery life, as well as more reliable devices for longer service. Weindorf noted, "We did not invent the seven-segment display. We adopted it [from the Japanese] and improved it and made a hell of a fine business out of it. And the same thing with optical isolators. We accepted that technology and improved it and made some fine devices."[55]

Weindorf had been with several companies previously—Sylvania, Hughes Aircraft, Fairchild, and Raytheon—where the leadership style was micro-managing. Constantly defending or presenting your position hardly gave you a chance to make things happen as you thought best. At HP, he found that

> Dave and Bill encouraged innovation. They allowed people wide latitude in exploring different avenues, different product areas, different approaches. HP Labs under Barney Oliver was also a big impetus. He did some very nice work and he organized a good group. Of course Bill Hewlett was always heavily involved in that side of things as well. So I think it was this environment, this attitude on the part of Dave and Bill: You hire good people, and you make sure that they understand your goals, consistent goals, and then you give them the tools and let them go.

Weindorf told a very nice story about trust from the founders:

> We had to make a presentation to Bill and Dave to get a million bucks for a project. And so we went up to the hill and had a conference with them. Dave

used to take off his glasses when he was thinking. Twirling his glasses, he finally turned to Hewlett and said, "Bill, I think these boys know what they're doing. Should we let them go with a million bucks?" Hewlett said, "Yes," and off we went. That was it.[56]

Not only was the trust well placed from the standpoint of getting a proper return, but the investment was the critical element in letting HP ramp up production quantities of LEDs, fueling the HP 35 success three years later. Soon after, Weindorf realized that the offshore cost savings in Singapore and Malaysia were crucial because the division's products required a lot of hand labor. Singapore was doing off-shore manufacturing for several American companies; HP was already stringing core memories there. When core memories were replaced by silicon memory, the Components Division took up the slack, first growing in Singapore, and then expanding to Penang, Malaysia, to assemble optical electronic devices. Clean-room processes were done in Palo Alto, supplying wafers overseas. The chips were cut over there, then assembled and tested. Dick Chang, the manufacturing manager for this activity, provided strong emphasis on costs and productivity, years before the rest of HP grappled with those issues.

The company did not appreciate (yet) the value of the Components Group learning curve. In time, cost-competitive, high-volume topics would interest every HP manager; the Components Division learned some early lessons that would later have value for all. As Weindorf noted,

> The components group was truly quite different—in the products it made, in the way it made them, and in the very cost-conscious market it had. Components and semi-conductor devices are very cost-competitive. The rest of the company really didn't see the same kind of a marketplace that we did. I felt not ignored, not treated unfairly, but just different. In a different kind of a business. Just different constraints. . . . The rest of the company's managers were not particularly interested. They would listen politely, and I guess they kind of understood, but they really couldn't appreciate all the nuances of being in that tough a marketplace. We clearly were not in the mainstream of the company. Sitting in the executive council meetings, we'd go around the table and each give a report on our results. I could stand up and give my report in about five or six minutes, while the other guys would stand up for a half hour or forty-five minutes going into

their stuff. Most of it was frankly not of interest to me. And my reports were not a lot of interest to them either.[57]

The Components Group eventually would become a major contributor to HP revenues and profits, primarily through the LED business as automotive manufacturers adopted LEDs for tail lights. Not counting the captive IC facilities of HP for proprietary leadership in instrumentation and computing, the HP Components Group consistently was among the top dozen IC vendors in the world. With the captive capability, HP had more IC fabrication processes in full-scale production than any other company on the globe by 1980, a testament to the stringent leadership requirements of their products, with a concomitant huge sunk cost to maintain that edge. Such was the price of leadership in measurement, and the corollary cost of technology leadership as HP moved into the computing arena as well.

International Operations

Hewlett's conviction in 1958 that the European market was going to open, along with his belief that a Japanese entrée would have value, led to enormous early success for HP in these sectors. International expansion was aided by fortunate circumstance—English was not a barrier language for most engineers and scientists, so HP was able to avoid costly local language issues for many years. As the company's reputation for high-quality scientific instrumentation continued to rise, sales grew apace.

Both European manufacturing sites began with kits, assemblies of U.S. products already designed and in production. Over time, each facility naturally desired to have hegemony in some product sector, in order to recruit stronger engineering talent. HP transferred its low-frequency oscilloscope programs and its pulse generator lines to Böblingen by the middle of the decade, and the South Queensferry Division moved strongly into digital communications test equipment.

As the company established international manufacturing facilities, the desire arose to have local R&D teams, just as it had for the original Colorado divisions. The company by the early 1970s had enough experience to be more confident about decentralizing R&D. The more difficult question, though, because the overseas facilities produced a product panoply from multiple divisions, was how to focus those overseas labs. Decentralized sites in America focused on one specific product line; that model was soon adopted by the offshore divisions as well. The U.K. operation selected telecommunications, because of the early European emphasis on leadership digital telephony to CCITT standards. With the heavy manufacturing used for oscilloscopes and medical systems that burdened the Böblingen operation, they vied for R&D in these arenas. They pioneered the fetal heart monitoring business for HP worldwide; they also took the Colorado Springs pulse generator business and turned it into a very satisfactory logic signal sources operation. Some activities, as in the United States, were stillborn—the German labs put much effort into noise monitoring for airport noise abatement and auditory testing; they also attempted products in odor measurement. Neither gained traction.[58]

Hewlett was eager for involvement in Japan as well as Europe, especially given his tour there after World War II, when he had the opportunity to meet and work with a number of accomplished scientists. The work of two men in particular would prove propitious for the company in subsequent years—founders Takeshi Mitarai of Canon and Shozo Yokogawa of Yokogawa Electric Works (YEW). In 1961, Shozo Yokogawa sought a partner who could broaden his company's product line. Yokogawa knew Hewlett from his early visit, and both felt that YEW, a quality producer of electrical appliances and instrumentation, would be an ideal partner for HP upon entering a relatively closed society.

The arrangement, a 51 percent YEW/49 percent HP partnership because the Japanese Ministry at the time forbade foreign companies from owning a majority interest, was called YHP. The partnership began (analogous to Europe) with kit products being assembled, sold, and supported from Japan rather than from America. It gave HP a valuable entrée into that market. Japan began a similar charter focus on deep parametric measurements, in particular, the classic RLC (resistance, inductance (L), capacitance) electrical passive elements. By 1966, YHP had introduced the first of its RLC test sets,[59] tools that eventually proved vital for the emerging semiconductor manufacturing field because they could dynamically monitor precise doping depths of specific injected chemicals. Art Fong—Mr. Microwave—had gone back to Stanford for work in digital techniques and software technology in the late 1960s. Transferring to YHP for two years in 1971, he helped the division capture the digitizing wave. The line started slowly, with $3.7 million revenues in 1972, but it burgeoned to a stunning $65 million by 1984—a very satisfying 27 percent compound average growth rate, the highest for any non-U.S.-based division.

YHP recorded 40 percent of its sales in Japan in 1979, stunningly higher than the typical 5 percent for most of the corporation's product lines. Some felt this concentration to be the result of parochial divisional perspective; YHP argued that it was serving local needs very well. Indeed, many local divisions exhibited regionalized success that differed widely and somewhat inexplicably from the corporate averages. The Scottish South Queensferry Division in the adjacent digital communications markets sold 45 percent of its product in Europe, where its sister division Delcon only sold 7 percent. The data communications test equipment business, derived originally from the Delcon Company telephone test set acquisition in 1964, still had 80 percent of its revenue from U.S. markets fifteen years later. The medical patient monitoring business in the mid-1980s (after twenty-five years) was heavily concentrated in the United States (more than 80 percent), even though Europe had more hospitals and people.[60]

The fundamental issue for the business opportunity, though, was whether it was wiser to emphasize regional or local market opportunities, or to expend effort to broaden and balance sales worldwide. Packard and Hewlett leaned strongly toward the view that the tools of the company were generic, and that engineers and scientists worldwide should find them of value. This belief undergirded much of the internationalization. Some fields of endeavor were much more regionally concentrated: Germany's strong optical and chemical heritage gave the Analytical Group regional success; Swiss companies, renowned for pharmaceutical acumen, did likewise; and the broad expanse of Canadian geography stimulated microwave communications research, development, and deployment.

Even though it might seem that low-priced equipment would be especially well-suited to emerging nations, HP's experience in several product lines was that a nation's elite—particularly in India and China—pooled funds to buy a few top-end instruments to conduct meaningful work. India, for example, bought much less than 1 percent of HP shipments annually, but for the new, highest-priced logic state analyzers, universities and government labs in Bangalore alone purchased 10 percent of the world's output in the late 1970s, vying with America's premier engineering school, MIT, for the most units in operation. As a result, in part, of this initial emphasis by the faculty at the Indian Institute of Science, Bangalore became one of the world's premier information technology cities.[61]

Bill Terry sided with Packard's view that the tools of the company are generic, particularly focusing on the Colorado Springs divisions in the Instrument Group—Logic Systems and Colorado Datacom. From 1979 to 1987, the sales shift was noteworthy. The corporate average for the United States, Europe, Japan, and "Rest of World" (ROW) in 1979 was 56 percent, 30 percent, 5 percent, and 9 percent; by 1987, it was virtually unchanged. But Colorado Datacom, highly skewed toward U.S. revenue in 1979, had its profile shift from 80 percent U.S. to 45 percent, while its European share grew from a mere 7 percent to 39 percent—this while maintaining its American market share. This performance profile demonstrated the value of having product divisions worldwide.[62]

Logic Systems provided a surprise. It had been almost exactly the corporate average in 1979 at 55:30:6:9; by putting satellite divisions into Germany and Japan, because of the high interest in microcontroller designs around the globe, it produced a stunningly balanced 38:27:27:8 ratio. Such a profile illustrated the pervasive influence and endemic distribution of the emerging digital design world. No other product line in HP then or later had such balanced regional results. The aggressive marketing tactics with digital design capability extended the digital revolution across the globe faster than might otherwise have occurred, as designers in many countries got access to design methodologies that enabled them to compete more effectively.

The Computing Transformation

Books and museums are wont to describe firsts—who did the most important early work and how it evolved. Such bragging rights confer significant status. Unless, of course, the company didn't optimize the opportunity, in which case vilification or opprobrium is earned: How did they miss that one? The eye of the beholder is crucial. XeroxPARC, for example, created more firsts in computing per design dollar than any other company by a factor of one hundred. Yet the authors of *Fumbling the Future* excoriated both the developers and parent company for failure to capitalize on the breakthroughs. A later work, *Dealers of Lightning,* cast a less jaundiced eye, arguing that the magnitude of the challenge dwarfed expectations that might otherwise seem rational. The most positive view is that a mere handful of researchers with modest resources reconfigured an entire industry, while two hundred billion R&D dollars were squandered at mainline computer companies on more conventional ideas.[63]

Hewlett-Packard, by contrast, is seldom revered as a computer pioneer, even though it is acknowledged to have transformed into a major computer company. But that raises some questions: How did the transformation occur? Did HP do some amazingly prescient things, enabling it to morph from a respected niche electronics company into something much grander? Or did it hold for a moment an astounding opportunity that was missed through inept leadership?

Many critics have been in the latter camp—in 1986, Apple chief Steve Jobs told a Seybold audience that "HP is brain-dead" with respect to its approach to printers;[64] in 2002, Sun CEO Scott McNealy likened the HP-Compaq merger to "the slow-motion collision of two garbage trucks."[65] Prominent writers for the *Harvard Business Review* took shots as well; the January-February 1991 issue featured articles by Regis McKenna and John Seely Brown, and a process step from HP, the Return Map.[66] At a *Harvard Business Review* authors' evening in San Francisco, McKenna extolled Apple and Sun Microsystems aggressiveness while assailing HP stodginess; Brown outlined major Xerox redesigns for productivity and cost savings. During the Q&A period, the "Return Map" article was linked to the relatively unknown Dick Hackborn, whose printer group used this process while building revenue twice as large and growing twice as fast as Sun and Apple total revenue combined—a printer business already larger than the Xerox copier business while Xerox focused on cost savings. The audience loved it, even as the other authors felt skewered.[67]

The Hewlett-Packard Company by 1965 knew what it was, an electronic instrument company defined by a background of building tools for engineers and scientists, and it knew what it wasn't. The thought of entering a world served by back-office machinery was heretical for a couple of reasons: (1) IBM and AT&T were HP's largest customers, and (2) IBM was already known for ruthlessly competing against the "Seven Dwarfs";[68] each was ten times larger than HP and had a far longer pedigree in electricity and radio.

Late in their careers, both Bill and Dave would describe the Hewlett-Packard entrée into computing as less than farsighted. Bill often said that all that happened was that they were "on the nose cone of the rocket as it lifted off."[69] Packard wryly observed that, although he and Bill missed the true significance of the computing era in the beginning, "at least we didn't louse it up completely."[70] Such modesty, though becoming, omits a significant portion of the story. Yes, Hewlett-Packard took a long time to target computing in the classical senses. But HP created more pioneering and trend-setting computers than generally recognized, products that identified the elements of and the issues around personal computing long before such words were used.[71] HP's foray into computing, a classic application of the next-bench syndrome, changed HP irrevocably. To some degree, it was even planned.[72]

The digital voltmeter (DVM) invention, by Andy Kay's small San Diego company, Non-Linear Systems (NLS), started it all. Feeling that the analog voltmeter dial was not only hard to read but very hard to get consistent measurements with, the NLS answer was to digitize the measurement and provide unambiguous numeric readouts. Its first product, in 1953, was expensive ($2,300) compared to HP analog voltmeters ($195). Soon, though, others entered the business and prices began to fall. In early 1956, Hewlett and Packard set up Dynac, soon to become Dymec, a separate company with twin purposes: to integrate multiple instruments into a system and to produce specials, non-catalog items with custom features for individual customers. Just as Norm Neely once stormed into Packard's office ranting about the Tektronix challenge, now he insisted that tying multiple instruments together was imperative, along with a digitizing voltmeter.

HP engineers Noel Pace and Ted Anderson went to work, developing a rack-mount DVM, the HP 405AR, for $825 in 1958. It was an auto-ranging unit with auto-polarity that measured dc voltages from 1 millivolt to 999 volts. It used three one-inch-high Nixie tubes for readout, a distinctive shift toward the digital world.[73] The idea of getting a scalar—a hard, consistent number—instead of an interpreted reading from the movement of an analog dial meter was very appealing. A few designers bought one for their bench; some production lines had enough volume to justify a purchase.

Two new problems quickly emerged. First, the product could make six readings a second, but no technician could write that fast. Second, "dc" was useful, but many voltages were "ac" or had peculiar waveform characteristics. The toughest case was a data-logging situation, simply recording a voltage every five seconds or so, accumulating over, say, twenty-four hours. Such data-logging situations were often in harsh environments, for which voltmeters had been designed. Dymec resolutely set out to provide some quasi-standardized data-logging products, which by 1963 had become the DY 2010 line.

By late 1961, HP had introduced several digitized instruments—an integrating digital voltmeter (the HP 2401), a digital recorder, and a digital-to-analog converter.[74] By using these products with Kay Magleby's sampling scope, automatic switching time calculation became possible. An article in the March 1962 *HP Journal* described this feat, while omitting the fact that it was all done per IBM's request.[75] Then Dave Cochran and Chuck Near at HP Labs in Palo Alto, using decade-counter boards from the Frequency and Time Division and digital voltmeter notions from the Loveland Division, created the highly successful HP 3440A digital voltmeter, launched in 1963 with Noel Pace aiding the Colorado product transfer.

The fully controllable 3440A quickly became a leading voltmeter product, selling some ten thousand units over the next five years.[76] But HP still missed the significance of computerized instrument control; for example, Frank Burkhard's predictive article in the September 1964 *HP Journal,* "Our Preparations at Hewlett-Packard for the Instrumentation of Tomorrow," made no mention of HP controllers in the offing.[77] Few other companies recognized the opportunity: Digital Equipment had sold a few machines for instrument control; Perkin-Elmer had not yet realized the problem.

Hewlett, Packard, and Oliver had several chances to understand the nascent digital field, with its primary component, the computer. Douglas C.

Engelbart, now revered as inventor of the mouse and the first computer networking visionary, tried hard in the spring of 1957 to convey to Hewlett and Oliver his excitement for this new technology. Accepting a job with the company, he belatedly realized that they had no intention of pursuing this fledgling arena; he never reported to work.[78]

HP had another chance to understand it when, two years later, Barney's protégés delivered their sampling oscilloscope to IBM's research laboratories for examining high-speed switching circuits. Kay Magleby, the lead designer, was immensely intrigued by both the products and possibilities of these novel computing devices. His design colleague Dick Monnier soon led the low-frequency HP 140 scope program with several relevant investigations: a four-channel vertical amplifier to view multiple parallel signals, a unique Boolean trigger capability to examine computer switching signals, and the first persistent storage CRT system.

The Oscilloscope Division was slated to move from Palo Alto to Colorado Springs by mid-1964, far from any university or industrial nexus that might further understanding of the newly emergent computer field. Monnier and Magleby weren't interested in geographic relocation, which proved fortuitous for HP computing. Magleby persuaded Bill Hewlett and Barney Oliver to fund a Stanford PhD program in 1964. He studied computer architecture, register design, and algorithmic structures. Returning to HP in Barney's research center under veteran research director Paul Stoft, Magleby built a demonstration computer usable as an instrument controller, able to replace the HP 2010 data acquisition controller. Packard was unsympathetic to the computer; Hewlett was even less enthused. When it was redefined as an instrument controller, however, Packard let Magleby continue. Packard then caught a plane to meet Kenneth Olsen, the garrulous founder of the Digital Equipment Corporation near Boston.

When Magleby began his PhD work at Stanford in the fall of 1964, Digital Equipment Corporation was finishing its eighth year in business, founded by students from Wes Clark's pioneering computer program at MIT. The company had produced the PDP-1 through PDP-6, successive models of the first commercially available minicomputers, and was ready to debut the PDP-8. Not exactly rewriting computing history yet, DEC had delivered only 118 "computing machines" in its first eight years, aside from some PDP-5 run-time controllers.[79] Shown the PDP-8 prototype however, Packard sought to buy DEC from Ken Olsen. A $25 million price was established, but a day later, chilly rapport between the two men and details for how Olsen would participate kept the deal from consummating.[80]

While Packard was in Boston, he also met with the professorial Dr. An Wang, inventor of core memory at Harvard. Wang had built a small electronic calculator company, Wang Labs, which competed with Burroughs for financial tools in the small-office arena. Packard evaluated its new calculator under development (destined to become the Wang 4000) as a possible acquisition, but "decided at the time it would not be desirable for [HP] to get involved in electronic calculators." Wang had high hopes pinned on the 4000:

> The Wang 4000 Computer System was informally introduced at the annual IEEE conference in New York in March of 1967. . . . [It] was formally introduced at the [Business Equipment Manufacturers Association] show in New York in late October 1967. By December, orders had been booked for seven [units]. . . . Clearly the 4000 had a broad potential market.[81]

Note the intimation—nine months of Wang marketing yielded seven orders. Digital Equipment sold 118 computers in eight years. Burroughs built the least expensive mainframes at the time; they sold 106 Datatron machines from 1954 through 1960.[82] Three leading companies had sales volumes of one to two units per month over a decade. No one except IBM had any unit volume. Even IBM's volumes were small. In 1963, a year before System 360 would redefine the market, IBM shipped roughly thirty mainframe systems per month, twice that of the Seven Dwarfs combined. Big firms—General Electric and RCA—began to concede the computer business, just as Magleby's work was coming to fruition.[83]

There was an important signal, though, for those who were able to read it correctly. The DEC PDP-5 and the IBM 1401, as low-cost specialty machines, sold surprisingly well. The transistorized 1401, profiled as an off-line peripheral controller or a department data processing system, produced five thousand orders in five weeks in early 1959, creating a two-year backlog for a machine a year away from production. Renting the 1401 for a modest $2,500 per month, IBM built two hundred machines per month for years. DEC's PDP-5 industrial controller sold up to ten per month at $27,000, while the $300,000 PDP-6 sold only five units commercially in its lifetime (MIT bought another eighteen for research purposes). The PDP-5 success inspired the PDP-8 design that Olsen showed Packard.

Before Kay Magleby transferred to Dymec in 1965, Dymec's Data Acquisition Engineering Lab, headed by Don Loughry, was creating a computer-controlled data acquisition system using a DEC PDP-8 computer. In receipt of two PDP-8s, they had a purchase order for eight more. The plan was to show this system at the March 1966 IEEE show in New York. However, with Magleby's project expected within the next year, that product introduction was cancelled. Instead, HP purchased the assets of Data Systems, Inc., a very small computer division of Union Carbide, hiring four of the five employees. Roy Clay joined Magleby's staff at Dymec to head software development.

FEBRUARY 9, 1967, CARMEL, CALIFORNIA: The Dymec management retreat at the Highlands Inn had an invitation list that included Kay Magleby, engineering manager; Ed Holland, logic design; Bob Gray, memory systems; Dick Reyna, input-output systems; Roy Clay, software; John Koudela, application engineering; and Tor Larsen, mechanical design. Bill Gross, the Dymec marketing manager had Bill Davidow reporting to him for computer sales. Frank Wheeler headed manufacturing, and under him was Bill Abbott, operations manager. Bob Grimm was division manager. It was a small team, especially for a product, the HP 2116A, that portended a profitable future. Given the eventual impact on the corporation, one might expect these names to be revered, honored, and recalled with ease. Would that it were true.

The HP 2116A computer was illustrated on the cover and described in the March 1967 *HP Journal* issue.[84] Packard insisted on calling it an instrumentation controller, but the front panel label said it was a computer.[85] A computer built for instrumentation control created unusual expectations. It required instruments that were capable of being controlled digitally, that derived digitized answers. Computers of that era were large, complex, and notoriously unreliable, installed in specially designed air-conditioned, humidity-controlled rooms. Instruments were used in a wide variety of environments: near dirty manufacturing floors, on airplanes in low atmospheric conditions, even in frigid climes. Thus HP designed the 2116A to work over a much wider range of environments than any other computer.[86] Built to HP's strict quality standards, these products proved to be rugged, long-lasting, reliable machines.

Packard encouraged HP engineers to put the new controllers to work. Kay Magleby teamed with his old colleague Rod Carlson from the oscilloscope days to construct a novel RF vector voltmeter, essentially a pair of voltmeters under computer control to compare phase angle shift through a circuit under test. Improving the ease of such tests, it spawned the Network Analyzer project, fully controlled by the 2116A, described in Paul Ely's first *HP Journal* article, "Signs of Things to Come."[87] Within nine months, several dozen machines were deployed within other HP divisions, embedded within automated measurement systems under development.[88]

The computer launch, though, was difficult. In planning for the sale of the 2116A, the four U.S. sales regions were less than enthusiastic. Eldred finally specified that each region designate one engineer to be that region's computer specialist. Al Oliverio convinced Norm Neely to hire his friend Gene Mylesko as the computer engineer for the Neely (Western) sales region. The engineers took up residence at Dymec, working on applications and the marketing plan before returning to their regions to work with field engineers on computer sales. Over the first year, only five 2116A machines were sold to the outside world, all by Dick Slocum in the eastern sales region.[89]

No one understood software, especially its importance for interfacing multiple products, or the costs to develop such capability. It took three HP designers (Dave Ricci, Jerry Nelson, and Don Loughry) six years to finish a set of standard protocols, the Hewlett-Packard Interface Bus (HP-IB). Loughry soldiered for years to have the HP-IB adopted as an industry standard. Ultimately successful, it became known as IEEE-488 (General Purpose Instrument Bus—GPIB), which still governs basic instrumentation and computing interactions.[90]

The role of supporting equipment—derisively called peripherals by IBM mainframe designers—was also opaque to HP leadership. Storage mechanisms, printers, plotters, data entry terminals, and CRT displays were all used in the instrument world. HP had product lines in most of these areas, but they had specialized roles with analog interfaces ill-suited to this new digital world. Selling a printer or display box was one thing; selling a complete computing measurement system was another.

Dave Packard, over lunch at the Palo Alto Club, replaced Grimm as GM with Jack Melchor. Grimm, reassigned to Noel Eldred, considered opportunities for computer-controlled systems using products from many HP divisions. Grimm vividly recalled an evening when he was working on a block diagram for a big system for an HP customer, and Packard came by and asked what he was doing there at night. Grimm went over the block diagram of the system with Packard, in considerable detail. He concluded by saying, "The problem is no division wants to take on the responsibility of putting the system together because the percentage of their division's products in the system is too low."[91] This led to a second computing systems division, named Automated Measurements Division (AMD), run by Jerry Carlson. Grimm became the new marketing manager—his exile didn't last very long.

The Management Challenge of the Computing Transformation

> *When I see a department well run, a division well run, or a company well run, I never see it done with good judgment, understanding of human values, mastery of management techniques, or vision alone—there is always a fourth dimension added—it can best be described as the strong-minded leader.*
>
> DAVE PACKARD[92]

Tom Perkins drew the short straw. He had joined Barney Oliver as his administrative aide when Hewlett formed HP Labs, where Kay Magleby had started the HP 2116A with Paul Stoft's team. A year after Dymec had launched the computer, Perkins said,

> It had been in the division for a full year and they had not sold a single computer [except] to other divisions of the company for play toys. Dave Packard had a violent temper, and he was not amused by this at all. He called a meeting and probably fifty people came. It went on for a full afternoon. "What's wrong?" Well, everybody attending, of course, was an engineer. So, it didn't have enough index

registers and the I/O was too slow. And it didn't have enough ports—blah, blah, blah, blah. I didn't really know much about computers except that there's this stuff called software involved and they weren't talking about it. I was certainly no expert. But I sat in on the meeting. Finally, Packard says, "Well, Tom?" I said "Dave, when everything else fails, try selling." A week later, he said, "OK, Tom. We want to transfer you out of the labs down to work for Jack [Melchor] and take over the marketing for that division."[93]

Perkins concluded that the only option was to hire specialists, whose first targets were places using IBM computers. Of Marketing VP Noel Eldred, Perkins said,

[He] was absolutely terrified that I was going to offend IBM and it would impact everything else for these little computers. I know there are a lot of stories about Packard on this, about how reluctant he was. But at this point, Packard wanted full speed ahead. Eldred had only about a year and a half to go before he retired. And he just didn't want to rock the boat.

The product, built to HP standards, was very reliable. You could drop it off a truck. It would still work. Once we showed customers how to use it, and helped them with the software, the sales absolutely took off. It went from a terrible situation to the most rapidly growing part of the company. We were growing 30 percent to 40 percent per quarter. We were hiring people and needed money, engineers, space. And [we were] competing with IBM and rocking the boat. I was well on my way to creating my own sales force.[94]

Melchor had a heart attack during this period, and Perkins became the *de facto* division manager. He promptly launched a time-sharing system that would handle up to sixteen Teletype machines at once—which Perkins described as the first actual time-sharing system. It went head-to-head with IBM, at one-tenth the cost.[95]

Eldred just flipped. He told Packard, and Packard came down. He was really angry because I hadn't gotten permission to take over the division, or to do this launch. We'd sold about ten of them. They cost $150,000. And the profit margin was about 80 percent. I took out the books and showed Packard. He walked in with his shirtsleeves rolled up above his elbows and chewing his cigarette and he looked at those numbers and he sort of put the shirtsleeves back down, cigarette out. And he said, "Looks OK." That was the winning of the war in terms of the computer becoming a freestanding business. That was the turning point, just before he went to the Defense Department.[96]

Carl Cottrell, running the Eastern Sales region, described the group:

They really were different. The lab was full of bearded, sandal types. Quite a shock to somebody who's not used to it. It was quite a different language spoken there. We had people to whom the HP philosophy was just totally strange, but we had very, very sharp people. The challenge was to rein them in. Perkins was running the computer division, Bill Davidow was marketing manager, and Jim Treybig was working for us. Many people left and became stars.[97]

Cottrell, the only HP regional sales manager to see the opportunity, said,

When the original 2116 came along, I had some people in sales working for me that had some computer experience. I began to learn that these things couldn't be sold like instruments. But interestingly enough, we discovered how to do time-sharing with it and even some commercial requests. The hottest computer out there at that time was the DEC PDP-8. Already there were lots of PDP-8s in use doing all kinds of tasks, and our salesmen wanted to compete with it. Pretty soon the guys were telling me, "Hey, if we're going to sell these things, we have to be able to demonstrate that they'll do the job. We've got to have a data center." Nobody had ever heard of a data center. So I started a data center. We had the only data center for HP systems anywhere. Pretty soon, we were selling more computers than anybody. We began to learn a lot about what you really had to do to sell this system. Pretty soon we saw that it was obviously going to sell more as a computer than as an instrumentation device.[98]

Perkins's triad staff now included product sales manager Bill Davidow, manufacturing manager Bill Abbott, software manager Roy Clay, and engineering manager Kay Magleby. "That was the core group, all of whom became very successful—every single one of them." Perkins, mellowing in his old age, observed thirty-eight years later, "I was very hard on Hewlett in the sense that I needed so much. I mean we were growing so fast and in those days, all the divisions were treated the same. Everything was percentage management. We just didn't fit; we needed so much cash. And it was different, but a very profitable business."

Perkins described both Hewlett and Packard as consummate entrepreneurs:

They backed their hunches and didn't listen to contrary advice. They just got it done. And they both had a sense of urgency. Now is the time. Not tomorrow. Now. Do it now. This tremendous pace and drive was one take-away. And then the absolute genuine belief in people—it was so sincere.

Discounts were a huge sore point for both Eldred and Packard. Packard, according to Perkins, had a view that the Sherman Antitrust Act precluded discounts, and his ethics just had no room for compromise. Yet everyone else was discounting heavily:

I said, "You know, we have to do this." Packard stood up and actually pounded the table; he got very angry with me and left the room. Hewlett and a couple of others were there; Hewlett said, "Well, Tom, what are you going to do?" I said, "Bill, he's wrong and I'll be back." It took me a couple of weeks to put together a plan, and I got about two minutes into it and Packard said, "Well, you're right." Once he knew that I'd done the homework, he was OK with it. How could you not love the guy?[99]

Bill Davidow described it this way:

Dave thought that we really didn't have an OEM product, we had an instrumentation product. When we signed a deal giving a 20 percent discount for twenty-five units, I had to go talk to Eldred about it. Eldred believed that the only discounts you could give were discounts based on the size of the order. A big HP discount was 4 percent or 6 percent. I had given a 20 percent discount, and Eldred came unglued. Everybody in the business was giving OEM discounts.

The same week I went to U.S. Leasing to negotiate a sale of fifty time-sharing systems and to Dallas to negotiate for a sale of twenty-five OEM computers. I was thirty years old at the time with no sales experience at all. Nobody wanted to touch these deals; The Dymec marketing manager, the area managers, nobody wanted to touch them. They left it to me and I didn't know what I was doing. Fifty time-sharing systems was $3 million.[100]

A case study for the period, endorsed and taught by GM Tom Perkins with the Stanford Business School, summed up the difficulties extremely well, but Packard, a trustee of the University, had the case squelched.[101] Meanwhile Perkins's division relocated to the acquired Varian's buildings on a Cupertino, California, site twelve miles south of Palo Alto.

After Packard left for the Pentagon, Hewlett got nervous with continual forays into the business world rather than the scientific world. This culminated with a forced recall of machines sold to Holiday Inn; Roy Clay was ordered to void the sale. "[Hewlett] called at 10:00 in the morning; by 2:30 P.M., the project was disbanded." Clay left in disgust a few months later, when Hewlett appointed George Newman as the new general manager precisely "because he wasn't a computer guy."[102] There was a lot more to the story, including widespread belief that "these guys coming in from the computer industry didn't understand the HP Way."

The Instrumentation Computer spawned a series of products—the HP 2115A and the HP 2114A were smaller, cheaper versions of the HP 2116A—but the combined set only sold a few tens of units per month, and each of those sales seemed fraught with customer support issues, which the HP service team had not experienced at all. To make matters worse, HP developers had embarked on a very ambitious task—the Omega project—to build a boldly futuristic computer. Too daunting, it died an anguished death in spring 1971. The minicomputer business was tough.

A year later, Tom Perkins left HP to form a venture capital company, and one of its first investments was with project leader James Treybig and two key designers from the Holiday Inn project who founded Tandem Computer. Many at HP felt that they based their product ideas on the early HP contributions. Seven years in, the planned instrumentation controller business was not developing nearly as nicely as folk had hoped when Magleby outlined his idea to Packard. But then, some of the other plans hadn't developed as well as they might have either. Eighteen months into Hewlett's turn as CEO, a nine-day fortnight instead of employee layoffs, a languishing scientific instrumentation markets driven by acquisition, as well as the struggling 2116 family all gave pause to anyone thinking that HP was in full control of its destiny.

The Transformation Factor

Four years later, at the end of 1976, HP had undergone a remarkable transformation. It now looked and acted like a computer company, at least to West Coast folk. The transformation factor—radical capability in new arenas, whether technologies, product sectors, markets, or even the ecology of a city or nation—can be powerful for a company's growth and evolution. Obviously, the divisional structure of HP provided for successful renewal with maturing product lines. But transformation is more than just renewal. Transformation is becoming something significantly more and quite different than before.

The first transformation at HP occurred during its second decade, described earlier as the move from audio-video products into the much-higher-frequency microwave arena. In 1949, audio-video products generated the bulk of HP revenue, 84 percent; microwave products accounted for 12 percent; "other" was a mere 4 percent. A decade later, microwave was larger than audio-video—a clear transformation from a focus on low-frequency tools for radio and television designers and technicians to a company primarily building enterprise-level tools for the ultra-high-frequency communications backbone of the nation.

By 1959 all communications products (microwave and audio-video combined, called the frequency domain), were 71 percent of HP sales, while products for digital circuitry, time-domain, were 23 percent ("other" was 6 percent). Within the frequency domain tools, microwave was up from 12 percent to 59 percent. Microwave had displaced audio-video as the leading program for the company.

Nine years later—1968—acquisitions had changed the scene. Within the company's original frequency domain arena, microwave was now two-thirds of the total. But the entire frequency domain itself eroded from 71 percent to 42 percent of the company, even as it quadrupled in absolute magnitude. The transformation occurred at three basic levels—time domain equipment gained 50 percent vis-à-vis frequency domain products, holding 24 percent of the corporation's total revenue. The scientific instrumentation acquisitions and activities in new areas (medical, analytical chemistry, recorders, and components) proved even more compelling for the company, and, at 30 percent, were now larger than the time domain program. Taking time domain and scientific instrumentation together, scientific test exceeded communication test (frequency domain) by 54 percent to 42 percent (Figure 5.1).

Scientific computing was only 4 percent of total sales in 1968, as the company prepared to launch the first desktop calculator. Lumping all time and frequency domain test together in 1968 (labeled electrical engineering test), it was 66 percent of HP sales. Eight years later, this category had shrunk by more than half, to a mere 29 percent, as scientific computing became an amazing 32 percent along with scientific instrumentation at 28 percent. Another new category—business computing—showed up as well, at 9 percent of sales.

The diversification efforts begun at the Watershed were paying off—the company had been transformed in two decades. Sixty percent of 1976 sales were centered either on scientific instrumentation with computing assistance or computing systems in their own right. This transformative effect was begun and nurtured with a goal to contribute excellent measurement capability to professionals—it expressly was not to "get into computing."

During this dramatic shift, every division spent 8.5 percent of sales on R&D, and every group grew and expanded within its own market, relatively unimpeded by competition from other divisions or sectors for

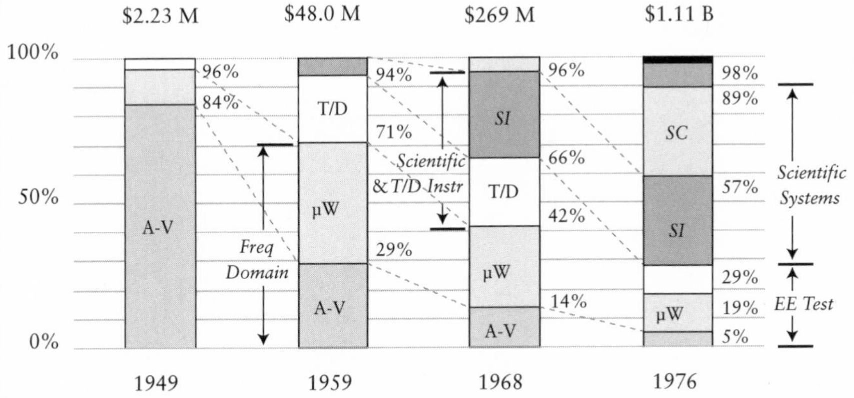

FIGURE 5.1. Three market transformations: Audio-visual to microwave, frequency domain to scientific instrumentation, electrical engineering test to scientific computing

scarce resources. This model empowered small teams called product divisions to invent their way to success in adaptive fashion, following dictates and whims of markets that they had already served. Inevitably, there were groups inventing products that highly resembled each other, and there would occasionally be the charter rationalizing meeting, with lots of discourse and argumentation. But it was remarkably focused outward rather than inward, and it generated multiple creative solutions for the markets the company served. It indeed was planned transformation.

CHAPTER 6

Unexpected Transformation

You know, planning is an exercise in futility. Who could have predicted how the HP 35 would come along and change the company?

BILL HEWLETT[1]

From a small engineering services orientation at the outset, HP had grown enormously—to more than fifteen thousand employees and seventeen divisions around the globe by early 1969. From first revenues for deliveries to the government during the war effort in 1942, Packard led the company through growth of five hundred times in the next twenty-six years—a compounded growth rate of 27 percent for the entire period. Yes, the 30 percent compounded annual growth rate (CAGR) from $500,000 to $15 million for the first thirteen years was a little faster than the 25 percent growth rate from $15 million to $260 million for the next thirteen years, but not by much. The remarkable story was not the magnitude or rate as much as the consistency. "Slow and steady wins the race," said Bill 'n' Dave.

Closing 1966, HP revenue was 10 times higher than a decade before—with profits up 9.7 times, and employees up 12.5 times to 11,309. On the tenth anniversary of going public, a share of stock bought October 15, 1957, for $16.00 was worth $281.60. When the Watershed year began, HP had less than a thousand employees, all working in Palo Alto with no sales force, no divisions, and just a few categories of test equipment for sale. The biggest competitor was Tektronix. The dream was scientific instrumentation—with no thought of computing. With a dozen acquisitions by 1966, HP was a scientific instrumentation force. Both Oliver and Hewlett would be named to the National Academy of Engineering by 1967, a singular honor that was a brilliant omen for HP. With the atomic clock and the microwave test equipment mantle firmly in place, Packard could rest easily—no debt, leadership in every field of endeavor, highest accolades in the land for his designers, and satisfied stockholders.

Where and how did computers enter the scene? Mid-decade, IBM booked $3 billion in computing and another $1 billion in office equipment; the Seven Dwarfs booked another $1 billion in computing, with Sperry-Univac accounting for nearly 40 percent of that total.[2] The PDP-8 had just been introduced by Digital Equipment, spurting the company's revenue to $23 million in 1966. For fiscal year 1967, HP booked $5 million in computing equipment, some 2 percent of its revenue from instrumentation—certainly an inauspicious beginning. Recall that HP turned Doug Engelbart down in 1957 when he'd sought to work on computers. In 1976, the company turned a young Steve Wozniak down when he sought to interest HP in personal computers. An interview with either Hewlett or Packard at the end of the first public decade would not have given an erstwhile investor any reason to think that HP would be a growth vehicle in a high-tech computing market.

A Calculator, Not a Computer

Our intent for the 9100 products was very clear. . . . We were a team of scientists and engineers who wanted to build personal computers for other scientists and engineers. The distinction of being the first mass-produced personal computer is merited by [either the 9100A or] the subsequent 9800 Series, [which] predated the ALTAIR 8800 marketed in late 1974.

BILL HEWLETT, 1985[3]

The turning point for HP in computing came via the fortuitous desktop calculator more than through Magleby's work. In the spring of 1966, Thomas Osborne walked in the 1501 Page Mill Road headquarters front door with a green balsawood model under his arm. Osborne, diffident and not inclined to join a large company, had been shopping his idea around the industry with little success. Meeting with Barney Oliver, he revealed a working machine with floating point notation, which computed accurate mathematic functions rapidly. Using stored program routines called algorithms, the small machine was lightning fast compared to any computer its size.[4] With two mathematicians on his staff—Ron Potter and Len Cutler—Al

Bagley had a project under way exploring similar architectures. Potter had evaluated the work of inventor Malcolm McMillan and two friends for a machine that calculated transcendental functions (for example, trigonometric values). The positive results of that probe sensitized HP to the opportunity now before them. Barney signed Osborne to a consulting contract, and HP Labs combined Osborne's software concepts with ideas already under way for a stylish desktop calculator with a full, algebraic keyboard.[5]

Dick Monnier enlisted as program manager. Working with old friend Bill Kruger, Monnier included an integral CRT display. The HP 9100A desktop calculator launched at the New York IEEE show in March 1968. Barney wrote a lucid history for the September *HP Journal* issue, which also included articles by Monnier, Osborne, and designers Chuck Near and David Cochran. The stunning product was described in Palo Alto at the ACM Personal Computer History Conference in March 1984 as the first mass-produced computer. The *HP Journal* cover showed a fifty-unit production run.[6] Wang's history eloquently captures the impact:

> Just a year after the 4000 was introduced, Hewlett-Packard, a very highly respected manufacturer of high-end electronic test equipment, introduced a calculator that took the world by storm. HP's 9100A offered amazing math capabilities, including comprehensive trigonometric functions, true computer-like stored program capabilities, and a large core-memory that could store data and program steps interchangeably, all crammed into a smartly-styled monolithic desktop unit. To add insult to injury, the 9100A was more accurate, much faster, and also provided extensive I/O interfacing capabilities. . . . Many potential customers looking for a high-end calculator promptly dropped the idea of buying a Wang calculator and got in line to buy one of HP's wonder-machines.[7]

Leadership Renewal

I knew that Bill Hewlett could manage the company just as well as I could and that he had a strong team of management people to support him.

DAVID PACKARD[8]

Packard's long-standing view was that citizenship—both corporate and individual—was an obligation, very much in the Rudyard Kipling *noblesse oblige* sense. Long on record with respect to his view that corporations have an important community role, he also held a fervent belief that individuals have an obligation to society. So when he got a call from Washington, D.C., it was hard to turn down the entreaty.

Congressman Melvin Laird from Wisconsin was tapped by President Nixon in December 1968 to head the Defense Department. Vietnam had become a quagmire for the nation, and the military was beleaguered. The politics of the day were angry, combative, and confrontational. Laird headed the Health, Education, and Welfare group in Washington when Packard served as president of the Stanford Board of Trustees, and Packard had won Laird's respect for a novel approach to funding "bell cow" universities to ensure premier university leadership. Laird invited Packard to become Deputy Secretary of Defense. Packard reasoned, "Lucile thought I needed a change. . . . There were some charities that I wanted to help, and considering all aspects of the situation—including the fact that I thought it was my duty to serve my country—I decided to join Mel Laird as his deputy."[9]

When Bill Hewlett announced at the Cupertino open house (HP had just bought the building from Varian) that Dave Packard was leaving HP to go to Washington, D.C., many didn't believe it. When Bill choked up with emotion, many more were incredulous.[10] Bill—the genial inventor behind the throne—was not only emotionally touched, he was proposing to run the company, something he hadn't attempted in thirty years. Many in the audience that day were concerned. How, they mused, could Packard walk away from something in which he had invested his heart and soul for so many years? After all, fifty-six is a young age for CEOs. Others worried about Hewlett's ability to step in. Would the company suffer? The most common question was, "When will Packard return?"

Packard left for Washington in February 1969, just after the Nixon administration took office. To be appointed, Packard had to turn over his entire estate to a blind trust, forfeit all income for the period (~$7 million in annual dividends), cease all activity with Hewlett-Packard, and agree to disperse all appreciated stock to charity from the trust, should the value rise during his term in office. Packard viewed these strict requirements simply as making sure that no conflict of interest would affect decisions; he had little difficulty deciding that the rules were appropriate.[11]

Hewlett's Inauguration

As Dave departed, before the impact of the HP 9100A was fully comprehended, HP annual computer revenues had just crossed $10 million—a mere 4 percent of the company. The executive team was surprised when the HP 9100A became one of HP's top four products in revenue, averaging two hundred units per month at $4,900 each. Enthusiasm built for this new arena. By the end of that year, computer sales exploded, growing more than 500 percent. Hewlett had a tiger by the tail. The blockbuster product was the desktop calculator, but Tom Perkins had figured out how to sell the minicomputer line as well. Each was a $30 million product line by year's end, and the question for the moment seemed to be, "What now?" Perkins kept pressing, and Hewlett, piqued, brought Carl Cottrell to Palo Alto to manage a new computer systems group, which included two divisions, Tom Perkins running Dymec and Jerry Carlson managing AMD.

Cottrell had managed to get the field forces, both in the United States and abroad, moving in the right direction to sell computers. Data centers became common; people learned how to qualify customers and sell them the right system. Cottrell reminisced,

> In the Eastern region, these guys were coming and asking, "Why is it you guys are successful in selling these things?" I don't know what had happened [in Palo Alto], but suddenly they wanted a new leader for the computer operation, so I got a call. Would I come run the computer operation? I said, "Yes"—it sounded good at the time. These were exciting times, but they were controversial.

Hewlett's staff distrusted the Cupertino MBAs and this new business. The computer managers were bold and brash, and consequently HP's top management went through a period of asking, "Is this really what we want to do?" Cottrell noted,

> Our sales kept growing and other parts of the company had begun to use our computers. That became a major internal market—people all over the company were building computers into their systems and their products. We had battles on inter-company pricing, but the computer was becoming an integral part of HP's life, whether we liked it or not. Quite a few people got dragged screaming and kicking into it.[12]

John Doyle started HP's first off-shore manufacturing in Southeast Asia, which helped Cottrell greatly, as he noted: "We really learned the advantages of going to places like Singapore and Malaysia, where they have highly educated people who needed work and could do high-level work. There certainly wasn't any way you could get anybody in this country to string cores."[13]

Soon, though, things went wrong for Hewlett. First, in early 1970, a year after Packard left, overall HP sales dipped precipitously, as war-swollen government purchases were scaled back across the industry. Computing sales soared for awhile, reaching 20 percent of HP revenue in 1970; but by mid-1971, both DEC and Wang had battled back with a vengeance. Total computer sales were down 12 percent year-over-year.

Aerospace companies laid off thousands. In Seattle, people joked, "Last person out, turn out the lights." In Los Angeles, aerospace engineers began driving taxicabs. Hewlett invoked a novel response: everyone, top to bottom, took every second Friday off, a move that saved 10 percent of salaries, rather than a 10 percent employment layoff. This nine-day fortnight was an unheard-of response to hard times. It lasted nine months, earning wide applause from employees as well as analysts and pundits now noticing the HP Way.[14]

Second, there was trouble with the HP 9100 Desktop Calculator line. Invented at HP Labs, it had been assigned to Loveland for three reasons: (1) they had digital voltmeters to tie to the box for simple data acquisition systems; (2) they had a highly tuned printed circuit board fabrication facility, capable of manufacturing the highly complex sixteen-layer board that provided the core memory with passive inductance rather than magnetic cores; and (3) Hewlett wanted Tom Kelley, a superb marketeer, to launch the 9100. As product sales soared, a new calculator products division was created in Colorado. Spirits were high until Wang mounted a heavy competitive barrage, catching the calculator division off guard. Recriminations flowed as Hewlett sat through an angry division review.

Bob Watson, Kelley's fiery, redheaded R&D director, heatedly said that HP Labs had left the division high and dry, with no follow-on product work, while handing over a product that had to be patchworked in order to put it into production. Watson's words stung Barney Oliver: "held together with chewing gum and baling wire." Barney rebuked him brusquely, saying that the whole idea for the labs was to jump-start new activities, but if the divisions didn't have people capable of taking an idea and doing some decent engineering, then he for one didn't have any patience with them when they failed to make a credible business. For many people in Colorado, this was a first encounter with the irascible side of Barney. The message was: HP Labs does transformative work, but the divisions have to provide sustaining and renewal work.

Noel Eldred, sixty-two, died in December 1970, a third galvanizing event. Noel, five years older than Dave, had been a mentor to Dave and Bill. The urbane Eldred, passionate about Stanford, was president of the Stanford Associates, and had led the largest capital campaign ever run for a university. The computer wars had tired Eldred—resisting newcomers Perkins, his marketing manager Bill Davidow, and the best computer salesman, Bill Krause, was difficult; when old friend Carl Cottrell took over and joined the chorus, Noel took it particularly hard. Eldred's passing was an omen for the old HP. With Dave in Washington, Porter in ill health, and Barney providing little value for business questions, it was a clear changing of the guard.

Added to this mix, the minicomputer team was struggling; they were late to market, and DEC was eating their lunch. Worse, a new aggressive competitor, Data General, had arisen. Its low-priced 16-bit minicomputer was taking market share from both DEC and HP.

MPE—Rx for Business

We're not proud of this product, and we will get it right before we release it again.

DAVE PACKARD[15]

HP's response to this series of difficulties was to go upscale. General manager Tom Perkins had decided almost unilaterally to develop a much more sophisticated 32-bit machine. Dubbed Omega, it had already suffered substantial development delays. Hewlett's exasperation with Perkins finally boiled over. He told Perkins, "Quit fighting me and come on up and help," and then Hewlett brought George Newman in to take Perkins's place.[16] Cottrell, then Computer Group VP, said, "I gave it my best shot, but we made some mistakes and I was over my head, to tell you the truth. And so I was replaced after about two years."[17]

Bill Terry, the ex-marketing manager and division manager for oscilloscopes at the Colorado Springs Division, took Cottrell's place in spring 1971. Terry, fresh from HP's first victories against Tektronix, was a pragmatic, no-nonsense, plain-spoken doer—bright, blunt, unabashed in the face of conflict, and a favorite of the regional sales managers for turning Colorado Springs into a more responsive division. Tektronix had a massive product catalog of similar products, spanning all manner of price points, configurations, and features. To compete with Tektronix, HP had to identify a sweet spot and build a focused competitive program.

That learning would be of little value for Terry's new challenge. There was an array of competitors—not just one—very different from the challenge facing any instrument division. And the combined competitors were huge in comparison. The playbook—the competitive catalog, so to speak—hadn't yet been written. Few people in the world—and no one collectively—knew what a data terminal, a personal computer, a handheld scientific calculator, a Winchester disc drive, or a LaserJet printer was—and no one had tried to build a time-shared, rugged scientific computer with an embedded network database. Off-shoring work from America to developing nations seemed unthinkable.

The biggest difference for Bill Terry, though, was the fact that he was running the Data Products Group, which was a group of rapidly growing divisions with interaction requirements, not just a single orderly division, and the division managers each believed strongly in the HP model of division independence. The idea of groups, first announced by Packard in October 1968 in *HP Measure,* was novel to HP.[18] John Young was the architect of this new group structure; it was described in two stories the next month in *HP Measure.* The first group, to be run by Young, was the Palo Alto Electronic Products Group, composed of the Microwave Division, F&T Division, PAECO, and HPA. The second group, also geographically just in the Bay area, was the Data Products Group, headed by Carl Cottrell and formally announced in May 1969, after Packard had left for Washington, D.C.[19]

In hindsight, each group was abortive because it was only a geographic linkage rather than a business requirements alignment. Calculators in the Loveland Division were specifically excluded from the Data Products Group, for example, which would lead to duplicate efforts for years. The Loveland Audio-Video Instruments and the Colorado Springs Division should have had more synergy with F&T by far than PAECO or HPA, let alone Microwave Division. The idea that divisions within a group would actually do joint activities for mutual benefit was an elusive goal. And every new idea seemed to spawn its own set of beliefs, credo, and mantra, not to mention its own incompatible interfaces and system requirements. Still, it was a start.

No one at HP had either design or management experience with such complexities, and when Bill Terry arrived in Cupertino to head the Data Products Group, he found that the Systems Engineering Division, co-located with the Palo Alto Division, was not part of his group since it "integrated" instruments, not computer systems. The Palo Alto Division, with the Data Products Group, integrated Cupertino Division computers with Mountain View Division disc drives with instruments. Confusing, yes, but to a company still mostly instrumentation, it "made sense."

Events during Terry's tenure—indeed, the difficulties of his reign—led inexorably to a very different group management layer, one that demanded much more synergy and interaction among divisions. It would prove a thorny transition.

When Packard returned from Washington, his first act was to hand the Cupertino Division mantle to Paul Ely, twenty-one months after Terry's arrival in Cupertino. Terry stayed another year in the Data Products Group role before Ely replaced him, and he moved on to manage the newly formed Electronic Instrument Group, which by then did include the Colorado instrument divisions.

History has accorded Ely full credit for creating HP's success in computing, relegating Terry and six previous GMs to also-rans.[20] But the groundwork—the creative spadework, identification of the definitional issues, and incipient developmental and deployment approaches—was virtually complete by the time Ely arrived. In the thirty-three months that Terry ran the group, revenues leapt from $32 million to $160 million, an immodest 500 percent gain.

The challenge was apparent—instrument controllers were becoming very competitive. Competitors had grown from DEC and Data General and three other companies in 1969 to more than fifty in 1971. And three years of flat sales was just about unheard of in HP history. But Terry had to deal with Hewlett's enthusiasm for Perkins's idea of a magnificent 32-bit computer, software-architected by Mike Green. Started in 1969, the Omega machine was boldly ahead of its time. Using a complex, directly addressable, stack architecture, it was meant to be a time-sharing machine for up to sixteen simultaneous users. With re-entrant code capability, it had separation of code and data—a really advanced concept for the day.

Terry discovered soon enough that Omega was sopping up vast engineering resources, resources that were badly needed on the base business products. Bert Forbes, a key architect in the R&D lab, articulated the bigger issue: "The marketing group had decided it had to be leased instead of sold, and if you plotted the cash flow it went about $50 million negative before it turned around." Hewlett and Ralph Lee stopped this program in spring 1971, just after Terry arrived. The design team was stunned—as Forbes related, "It was a really advanced machine and when they killed it, I mean people literally were wearing black armbands for days. Everybody was just unbelieving that such a good thing had been cancelled."[21]

Simultaneously, the 2100 family revision was seriously compromised by a faulty power supply design. Because Omega had used HP's key resources, a consultant rather than an HP engineer was designing the new power supply. Terry brought Dick Hackborn over from the Microwave Division as the new engineering manager; Dick found that the 900-watt power supply intended to go in a space about twice the size of a lunch box in the corner of the computer was an absolute disaster. Terry's emotional account conveys the desperation of the team:

> Poor George [Newman] and I wrung our hands. A representative from Allen Bradley—our biggest customer—came out and we broke the news to him. The guy actually broke down and cried. George and I were thinking, "This is going to cost Allen Bradley their position in the market and it's going to cost me my job."
>
> We went to Barney and said, "Barney, we really need some help. We need a team up here to work on this power supply." I outlined the problem. He said,

"OK." Barney rallied a team of about six or eight people together. He spent a hell of a lot of personal time on it and they designed the power supply. They made it work. It fit in the space. It was marginally reliable because there was so much stuff in it. But by God, it worked. And that got us out of a jam with the 2100.[22]

The good news, once the power supply was small enough to allow the new machine to fit a twelve-inch rack space, was the price, ruggedness, and memory size, plus a terrific new Image database idea, making the machine a real winner in the manufacturing floor and process control marketplace. For the moment, HP's minicomputer business had positive momentum again.

Unbeknownst to Terry, Hewlett had been engaged with Oliver and a small team at HP Labs striving to put the HP 9100A functionality into a personal device. Hewlett called Terry to his office in late summer with enthusiasm; Terry's reaction was "Here we go again." The HP 35 Handheld Calculator launched in January 1972. Sales went crazy—nothing like it had ever happened at HP in terms of volume production, mass-market appeal, sales channel novelty, societal impact, or profitability. But alas, as Terry feared, it distracted him from his main job.

Meanwhile, Omega wouldn't die—vestiges persisted. Bert Forbes had worked with Mike Green on the original 2116, and he and software designer Alan Hewer had designed a pared-down 16-bit machine, appropriately named Alpha (the beginning rather than the end), which soon attracted a number of enthusiastic designers still smarting from Omega's demise. This became the HP 3000, aimed at IBM's low-end machines in the small business arena. The HP 3000 and the HP 35 would pose drastically new challenges for sales and marketing: Each went to new customers via new channels, compared to previous HP computer offerings. It was a wildly divergent time.

On top of this product and channel explosion, a quiet, persistent marketing manager, Ed McCracken, was pestering Terry that customers needed ancillary services and products—peripherals and software. Terry said,

We'd sell somebody a 2100 with a bunch of memory in it for $6,000 to $9,000 and they'd go out and spend $55,000 on terminals. So we finally got a terminal project started. We bought discs from various people, mostly unsuccessfully. We bought tape drives from a number of people; then we hired Walt Selsted and a couple of people from Ampex, and developed our own tape drive. And we started working on our own small discs. And so we started growing our peripheral group.[23]

Bill Abbott, Perkins's manufacturing manager, started the Mountain View Division in early 1969 to build HP's first computer peripherals, with seasoned Dick Monnier fresh from the HP 9100A project, as R&D manager and Ray Smelek, recruited from the Microwave Division, as manufacturing manager. There, Stan McCarthy invented the first tape drive, the HP 7970, which proved to be important because it funded the laser printer development for a decade. Jim Barnes finished HP's first disc drive, the HP 7900A, in time for the new HP 2100 release.

Terry came to see Smelek and Abbott, saying, "Hewlett and I think that it is probably important that we connect our peripherals to our computers. Dave and Bill may not want to be in the computer business, but I do." Terry went on to urge that they relocate outside the Bay Area.[24] Smelek then met with Hewlett, who said, "The only condition is I don't want it in California and I don't want it in Colorado. I have too many eggs in those two baskets that will grow and we don't want any more, so find someplace else." Smelek said,

> We wanted to be no more than two hours away by direct flight from these cities. The first meeting was in February 1972. Four of us visited Boise, Spokane, and Corvallis—Stan Selby, Bruce Wholey, Frank Cavier, and me. In May, we picked Boise, and in September, we started production.[25]

Packard returned to find the company heading into business computing; it is not hard to imagine his angst. For someone who liked to be dominant in a field, it would be sobering to realize that IBM's computer equipment revenues in 1971 exceeded HP's by ninety times, and IBM overall was twenty-two times larger than all of HP. Few at any computer company foresaw the dramatic shifts in competition and technology that the next twenty years would hold. Both challenging and convulsive for HP, they eventually marginalized the company's origins, and forced HP to merge or be absorbed; HP no longer could go it alone. How much of this Packard sensed is hard to know, but he took some uncharacteristic actions, contradicting Hewlett's decisions on occasion and inserting himself back into unfolding events.

The End of the Beginning

HP Co-founder David Packard, Deputy Secretary of Defense for Melvin Laird in the Richard Nixon administration, was back in Palo Alto. In August 1972, five years after the HP 2116A launch and with several marketing missteps along the way, Packard called Roy Clay to his austere office at HP's Page Mill headquarters. Clay had quit HP a year before; he half-expected to be implored to return to the company. Dave began, "Roy, I want you to come back into the company. I want you to get us out of the computer business. You brought us into it. I want you to get us out of it." Flabbergasted, Roy demanded to know why. Packard replied, "We invest in products, not in markets. And if [we] go into the computer business, then we're going to have to invest in markets, and I'm not going to do that." Clay responded that his interest was in computer systems, so he couldn't see a long-term future with HP if he did what Packard asked. Dave stood up, shook hands with Clay, saying, "Young man, you've got the wrong attitude." Packard didn't speak to Clay for five years.[26]

Little did either founder realize that this year—1972—was the end of the beginning. Ignoring a gloomy market research report, the irrepressible Hewlett had launched the pocket scientific calculator—the HP 35—in January 1972, followed by the Alpha, a sharply scaled-back version of Omega, in September 1972. The world accorded spectacular acceptance to the HP 35, with 6 percent of HP's sales and a stunning 41 percent of profits in fiscal 1972. More than fifty thousand machines were delivered, peaking at 2500 percent of forecast.[27]

The Alpha, named the HP 3000 computer system, put HP squarely into the business computing market. After a rocky launch, it became the world's most successful small business systems computer. Following five years of modest growth (11 percent CAGR), HP posted three consecutive growth years (1972–74) with a dramatic 33 percent CAGR, unlike anything since the startup years. Cash was stretched, tempers flared, and hiring burgeoned. The corporation rapidly approached $1 billion in annual revenues, 42 percent of it in computing equipment. In four years, computing grew six-fold, and the corporation nearly tripled. HP was transformed.

From Terry's arrival in February 1971 until November 1972 when Paul Ely came down to Cupertino, a lot had happened. The new HP 2100, with HP Labs's innovative power supply, had more than doubled sales. The HP 35 Handheld Calculator became a cult product, as HP entered consumer retail for the first time. HP confidently leapt into peripherals to compete against a wide array of new competitors. And in September 1972, HP launched its biggest product in history: the HP 3000, intended specifically for department computing. Though scaled down from Omega, it was nevertheless a powerhouse system compared to any previous offering. It even included a unique software package, HP Image, a powerful embedded relational database for the multitasking and multi-terminal machine.[28]

What on earth were they thinking? Terry, not known as an out-of-the-box thinker, had supported what perhaps was the most out-of-the-box thinking ever done at HP in a short period of time. It redefined HP. But just as for Perkins, it earned him little credit. The learning curves were staggering for these multitudinous efforts. To some, it looked out of control; in retrospect, most of HP's first computing attempts struggled.

Even the vaunted HP 35 was hobbled by the company's historic approach to business—"Send us a check, and we'll send you a calculator within six weeks." Terry got involved with Macy's department stores to try to develop a new sales channel; it took a courageous stand in Europe by Dick Alberding to build inventory well in advance of orders, and Terry's bold efforts to call on Macy's, to figure out the new rules.

The HP 3000, though, was the disaster. It hit the market in September 1972, advertised as a 16-terminal time-sharing machine, with a proud new MPE (multi-programming executive) operating system.[29] It didn't work. HP support engineers labored mightily at customer sites to no avail. The system bogged down badly—four users could bring it to its knees. Nancy Anderson, later an HP executive, was selling DEC equipment against it; she called it dog meat. Unlike with its heroics on the HP 2100 power supply, HP Labs lent little help on the larger questions—peripherals, software, and business applications. The first customers—staunch Hewlett-Packard buyers for years—were incredulous; they'd never before had problems with HP products meeting specifications. Packard, returning from his Nixon campaign role, was incensed by the HP 3000 quality issues. By November, he had decided that George Newman wasn't up to the task of running the Cupertino Division (which was responsible for both the HP 2100 family and the HP 3000); Paul Ely would be the next HP 3000 computer executive, working for Bill Terry, who retained the Data Products Group role.[30] Both men were located on the Cupertino Division site; Terry related that "Ely was there about six months and he came to me one day and he said in typical Ely style, 'Bill, this building isn't big enough for the both of us.' I said, 'what do you mean Paul?' He said, 'well as long as you're in this building, I'm really afraid that people from data systems (division) are going to be second guessing me and come over to you and get you to make my decisions.' And I said, 'Well Paul, you know me. I'm not going to make any decisions that you should be making.' He said, 'Yes I know. But it's still a bad appearance and . . .' I said, 'OK. I get the point. I want the data systems division to be successful.' So I moved out and went to Palo Alto headquarters in 3 Upper."[31]

On Terry's watch, in somewhat less than a two-year span, HP's computer business morphed radically. Overall computing revenue tripled, and product complexity expanded by an order of magnitude. Data products (*sans* desktop calculators) were nearing $100 million per year; the new handhelds matched that within eighteen months. The new programs became as large in two years as the entire electronic instrument side of the company had been in 1971. A thirty-two-year legacy was matched in just two. Terry's computing career did not survive the experiment, but he led the maelstrom of one of the boldest transformations in American corporate history.

Ely reminisced about his initial days with relish,

Dave called me into his office, saying "Paul, I want you to go down to Cupertino [HP's new computer division locale]—the company is being embarrassed. We have introduced a product and sold it to people, and the product that we have doesn't meet what we told the customers it would do." And this, he made clear to me, is the ultimate sin at HP. He was personally embarrassed, and it was going to embarrass the company, and he needed that fixed. And he said, "Furthermore, we need to institute a little bit of HP culture down there. We have got too many people from IBM and other places that don't understand what HP is all about, and they got out of control."[32]

Why would Packard, who had been so resolute about staying out of the computer business before his Washington experience—the same man who tried to bring Roy Clay back to get HP to exit the computer business—support staying in this time? An easy answer could be seen on the bottom line. HP, with scant growth for the previous three years, was on an explosive growth track. Never one to ignore business success, Dave was now more interested in getting it right. From Paul's viewpoint, it was just one more interesting task. "There were things in HP that were challenging all the time. There wasn't any difference in the challenges. There were differences in the way the company responded."

What do you do, faced with a situation in which numerous talented managers have failed in the past? Ely listened. "It was my mission to go down and HP'ize it. Dick Hackborn was already there as the R&D manager, and I knew Dick. I had met some of the other key people for casual conversations at management meetings, but I didn't know them very well. So here I am—new kid on the block; I moved my desk overnight." Reflecting thirty years later, Ely was energized:

> People say that I am not a good listener—but my listening ability during the first three to six weeks was uncanny. I would be talking to somebody and they would say a paragraph of things to me and I'd hear five pages worth. After the conversation, I would go back to my office and make an outline of notes of what I had learned from that person. Half of the things in the notes would not even be topics they brought up—things I needed to do, somebody else I needed to talk to. They would say, "When we are working with marketing, something had happened." But in between this, I'd hear other issues coming out. The more people I talked to, the more my list of unstated things that I learned grew. When you are in that mode, it happens this way.[33]

Both Hackborn and Ely discovered that engineering and marketing folk weren't getting along. Marketing was talking to erstwhile customers, making commitments unrelated to the lab projects being built; engineers felt that people in marketing were promoting the wrong product. Also, the cost structures were upside down by traditional HP standards. R&D spent a typical 10 percent of revenues, but marketing was a whopping 14 percent, versus the customary 4 percent. And the Marketing Group was about to move across the street into larger facilities—Paul found this to be out of whack.

Ely quickly decided, "Hey, we need to have our marketing and R&D close together—that is the HP Way. You guys need to talk to one another frequently, you need to get along. You need to respect one another. Until I see that, I am not going to be happy."

Paul felt that the biggest task was to close the loop with the customer base:

> There were roughly fifty customers. I went and personally visited every one of them. Told them the truth, told them what we had and didn't have, when we could deliver what we had, and gave them the opportunity to immediately cancel their order if it didn't fulfill their need, or if they couldn't wait that long. It worked—we lost maybe a third of the orders—the rest said, "We want to see what you have got anyway."[34]

How, and how much, did the founders get involved during the crisis? Hewlett talked with Hackborn to understand the issues in development. Packard quickly developed confidence in Ely's approach and gave him a pretty free rein. Paul said,

> Once I got there [to Cupertino], I reported to Dave once a week on what I was doing to solve the problem with the customers. [Soon] he said, "Paul, I see you are headed in the right direction. Maybe you could give me a summary every couple of months on what is happening and let me know—we just will see you at division review time."[35]

Paul's stentorian voice, ebullient manner, and unflappable self-assurance made him a presence anywhere. He viewed himself as the flag carrier:

> . . . out in front. I create consensus about what I think we need to do in the areas where I need to make the decision and where I don't think I need to make the

decision, I will make sure we have good people who I don't have to worry about, who can make good decisions on their own. That was my style, and you couldn't do that from Corporate.[36]

Four Ely decisions stand out. First was a decision to decouple the various components of the system, so that the classical HP division structure could be operative. This meant disbanding the systems integration function—a notoriously difficult problem for Terry's team. Eventually this would save money, but the concern was that what Packard sought—a better customer experience—would be further compromised. Paul instead thought,

After we finished building a 2100, we would spend a week to a month integrating it to make the software, the peripherals, and everything work together. And then we sent it to the customer and it almost never worked when it got there. Then we would spend another couple of weeks with our field people on site putting it back together and making it work. Maybe four or five months in, I made the decision that we were no longer going to do any factory integration. It is not just that we aren't going to spend the time integrating, it is not doing us any good. It hasn't solved the problem. Our pieces are not as compatible as they need to be. I decided to send [discs] to Boise. The system engineers said, "Oh, you can't do that. We have to interface strongly with the people developing the controller, and we need them to be right here beside us." I said, "No, we need to make discs where there is a known interface that the disc people meet and that your system will meet."[37]

The second decision was to pursue a leadership position for HP computing, ala HP instrumentation. This translated into a strong need for internal innovation—in systems, software, and peripherals, as well as CPUs. Paul voiced this repeatedly: "We need to have products in each of them that are out in front of where the market is and where the products are going." Examples abound—HP was first to use solid state memory (versus magnetic cores) in minis, first to use a microprocessor in pocket calculators, first to shift to the new Canon laser engine for laser printing, first with an embedded relational database.

The third problem was figuring out the sales force needs, and once that was done, figuring out the marketing requirements and the best approach.

In these areas, HP made its most creative and valuable contributions.

We didn't know how to sell them. In 1975, we needed to make a dramatic change. We needed to build a totally different kind of sales force. The story of HP computing—really the story of the transformation of HP—from 1972 to 1983—$100 million to $3 billion—is a story of building the best sales force and the best support organization in the business. We also had good products. But we wouldn't have had any success like we did if we hadn't had the sales force that we did.

We had to experiment. We hired novice salespeople because we couldn't find experienced people who didn't have fixed ideas of how to sell—they were at IBM and they were too highly paid. The instrument sales force said, "Oh no, you can't put new college graduates out selling." Well, we did. Our bigger conflict was a uniform regional sales structure. Our salaries were different, our commissions were different. We gave discounts, and HP never gave discounts. All this created havoc with the corporate part of sales. In a single office managed by the corporate structure, you'd have a district manager for computers and a district manager for instruments; their salespeople got different salaries for the same kind of activity. They called on a different level of people, often on some of the same accounts. These were big issues.

We got the people who were succeeding to write a paper and give a talk at our next sales meeting, once a quarter. There weren't that many salesmen, maybe thirty or forty, so we would have them all in, and they would give a talk and tell how they were doing. Out of this, we developed two distinct sales technologies. One we called "trolling" and one we called "persuading." The way you sold to the hierarchy in large companies was to persuade. The trolling side had geography. The geography might be very similar to the partner account guy's, but the accounts on his list were excluded. Trolling guys would have seminars, and would bring successful HP systems users to present their story.[38]

Ely and the team refined this approach, creating a high-level seminar for managers at HP headquarters, where Ely, Dick Anderson, and Doug Chance talked about HP strategy, approach, and style, while the salesperson would learn who the decision makers were for the account. A critical task was to qualify the customer for its IBM loyalty, often a major stumbling block because IBM service people had long "owned the account." This led to another fateful decision—to "one up" IBM service. "We eventually became rated by J.D. Powers in the latter half of the '70s as the best service organization in the business. We got to 24x7 very quickly; we were the first company to guarantee up-time on our computers. We knew how to build high-quality products from our general HP knowledge."[39]

The fourth and final area of major contribution was to put a systems wrapper on the business. Joe Schoendorf ran business development for Ely in the 1970s; he said,

> Ely was really unhappy with computer marketing. We had HP's classic division structure—too many divisions and everybody was doing his own thing. One of the critical experiments that we ran was to centralize marketing. Ely asked McCracken to run the whole thing. His goal was to take core marketing out of the divisions. I managed the Business Development Group, which meant that we had responsibility for product planning and pricing, core attributes that used to be in the division. This was a very hard cultural change, because the general managers didn't want to let go of anything. They wanted to fight on every point. They didn't want any centralized control. All of them had grown up as old-line HP managers. They wanted to continue to run these fiefdoms; It'd be like having today the Dell printing company, the Dell computing company, the Dell disc company, and the Dell memory company. You wouldn't do that. But that was what HP had, and Paul correctly saw that that wasn't working.[40]

Taken together, these techniques and tactics worked exceedingly well for a long time. For welding group cohesion for marketing, selling, and pricing strategies, the system was uncommonly effective. Paul practiced what he preached. He made decisions and stuck by them. People could trust him to support them if they were following the dictates—second-guessing virtually disappeared from the Computer Group. His stance was that choice between two alternatives is the hard thing—choosing either and then executing that decision well was likely to work out fine. For preserving the essence of the vaunted HP divisional model for motivational innovation, short coupling to the customer, and accountability for schedules and costs, it was a superb choice, unmatched by any of HP's competitors. Rationalizing products and programs proved daunting, however. Although Schoendorf was able to pull the elements for the HP 3000 line together into a systems view, each product family needed the same kind of systems view. Moreover, each family was developing with little synergy to another. That issue, delayed for another decade, eventually would prove nearly fatal.

By the end of 1976, revenue for the four computer product lines was $340 million, matching all historic instrumentation. The venerable HP 2000 family remained the top performer, although sales had been relatively flat for four years; this line peaked over $125 million in 1975, but stumbled badly in 1976, dropping 20 percent as scrappy Data General took a big toll. Desktops from Fort Collins continued to grow nicely—nearly matching the Cupertino scientific computing line. The handheld calculator products peaked in 1974, well over $100 million, but the bloom was off the rose as sales sagged 25 percent in 1976. The slow-starting 3000 line was approaching $50 million, finally. Ely managed the HP 2000 and 3000 lines, each one now with its own division (Data Systems Division [DSD] on the Cupertino site for the HP 2000 line and General Systems Division [GSD] in a new building at the Santa Clara site for the HP 3000). Paul was a natural leader, already generating significant press copy with his brash style. By contrast, the desktop line in Colorado and the pocket calculator line in Oregon were set up as independent divisions, managed in a much quieter low-key manner through the Calculator Group managed by Bob Watson. HP top management seemed to prefer the latter style, staying as much as possible out of IBM range.

Managing the Transformation

IBM decided to fight back against the upstart minicomputer vendors in the spring of 1977. IBM still controlled two-thirds of worldwide computing revenues. *BusinessWeek* profiled a new fighting stance, wherein IBM promised much more aggressive pricing and breadth. HP was mentioned in one sentence: "The giant has also barged into the minicomputer business, threatening to shake up the futures of such companies as Digital Equipment, Hewlett-Packard, and Data General." Founders of both DEC and Data General retorted with saber-rattling; Paul Ely opined that HP was bringing out a line of communications controllers to tie its computers together in a network that connects to IBM equipment. Ely noted that "even IBM doesn't provide that sort of compatibility."[41]

Dave Packard believed that the proper goal in any business activity is either to be or become the dominant player. For the instrumentation sectors in which the company participated—starting with audio-video, then microwave, and finally scientific—HP became *a* leader, and then *the* leader (except with oscilloscopes, and even in that arena, HP was a clear second place). Jack Welch at General Electric famously used the formula of being one of the top two players in any business sector for managing GE's far-flung business empire two decades later.[42]

But the foray into computing equipment challenged Packard's thesis. HP, after a decade, was still a minor player in this business, compared to DEC or any of the five dwarf mainframe vendors left, let alone IBM. But the company's resources were being increasingly aimed at this combative sector. It was a huge upheaval that left many in the instrument groups baffled. They felt abused and unloved. The tail was now wagging the dog. Profits seemed more fragile, more volatile. Uncoordinated programs were frequently at cross-purposes. And the instrument groups (by now considered to include not just the Electronic Instrumentation divisions, but also the Medical and Analytical Groups) clearly had lost their luster in Palo Alto.

Five lines of computing equipment emerged by the end of HP's first decade in computing. Instrumentation controllers split into the Automatic Measurements HP 1000 line and the OEM HP 2000 Controller line from the original HP 2116A. The newer HP 3000 family became a line of department computers, especially suitable for manufacturing data (such as material requirements planning—MRP). Desktop calculators evolved into a very capable line of personal data machines for engineering applications, and the astoundingly popular handheld calculators were quite popular with students and professionals alike. Peripherals were just that—peripheral—developed for each computer family.

Unfortunately, this balkanized approach of niche market success did not add up to an overall strategy of significance. Figure 6.1 shows computing revenues for several companies—Sperry, Honeywell, and DEC—whose products competed with HP. IBM revenues were so much larger that they can't be shown on this scale. While HP computer revenues tripled, growing $1 billion from 1976 through 1980, IBM annual revenues grew by

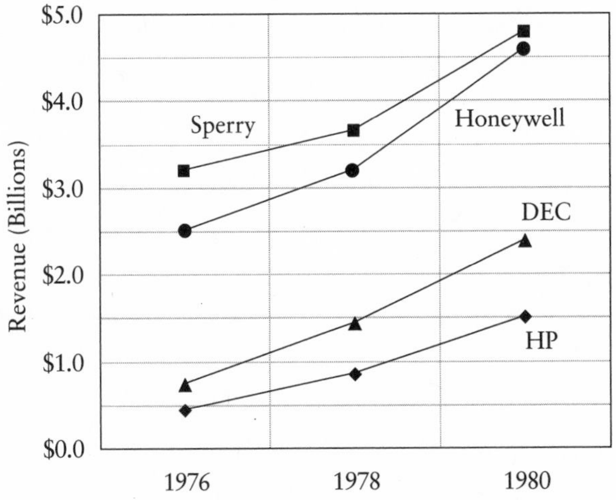

FIGURE 6.1. Enterprise computing company revenues, 1976–1980

$10 billion to $26 billion, and the three other competitors shown had an aggregate growth of $5.4 billion.

Several issues complicated the HP transformation. Except for Paul Ely, HP management waffled when in public—Packard and Hewlett were content to minimize HP's transformation to avoid the risk of irritating HP's biggest instrument customers (for example, IBM). Computing, as a field, was not defined yet in personal terms—it was all about Back Office and the IT departments. For that world, HP produced very little equipment, and even where it did, it seldom enjoyed leadership other than in small, specific feature sets. Thus nearly half of HP's computing revenues were largely ignored by the trade press and analysts.

Within HP, debate raged as to the wisdom of chasing this new arena. First, although HP leadership solidly backed both scientific computing and the new personal machines, competitors were nimble and numerous. Second, the business rules were radically different from those in the instrument business, causing serious side-by-side conflict within HP ranks (about such things as investment rates, pricing models, sales force incentives, and even quality). Third, HP management had always prided itself on technical understanding, but these new technologies were proving arcane and challenging. And fourth, the company struggled for years with how or whether to integrate the calculator activities with minicomputer activities. The resulting long-standing rivalry was often contentious rather than synergistic.

In retrospect, this is a strange story, and a strangely untold story. When the HomeBrew Computer Club (which first met in Palo Alto in 1975) took credit for being the sole predictors of the personal computer age, HP designers were scornful. After all, HP had shipped seventy-seven thousand self-contained "personal machines" far more capable than anything proposed at this assemblage of amateurs. They had specified the design criteria for the Intel 1103 memory chip, and subsequently bought and shipped nearly 40 percent of Intel's memory capacity to their engineering customers for the intervening four years. Steve Wozniak's autobiography comments that, "Before the Apple 1, all computers had hard-to-read front panels and no screens and keyboards. After Apple 1, they all [had screens and keyboards]"—a patently false claim since HP personal computers had featured screens and keyboards for seven years.[43] Wozniak also wrote, "I didn't really think of our [HP handheld] calculators as computers, though of course they were." And HP had already sold nearly a half million of those handheld calculators, from the HP division in which Wozniak was employed.[44]

Bob Frankenberg bridles at such words. He was on the HP team from DSD that built a PC based on a Zilog Z-8 microprocessor in early 1976; Steve Wozniak was on the evaluation team at the Advanced Products Division. APD turned the DSD team down; the team then finished the prototype and sold it to Compression Labs. Months later, Wozniak left HP to start Apple Computer.[45] But perception is everything—and the world did not, and does not, perceive that HP was a leader in computing. Perhaps for HP lovers, this is positive: if HP had been acknowledged as the original leader, the hue and cry about HP fumbling the future might be louder than it was for XeroxPARC.

Questions linger: If it was logical for HP to enter computing because digital voltmeters required something akin to a computer to log data, then might it be logical to ask why the eight leading digital voltmeter companies who beat HP to the DVM market didn't enter computing? This type of question would recur when HP got into peripherals, especially printing.

Why didn't any of the major computer vendors see this opportunity the same way? In retrospect, one must conclude that something odd and unusual occurred at HP several times, enabling it to anticipate new markets and prevail in many instances where other companies missed the signals. In other situations, something enabled it to persevere and endure until winning combinations could be composed, when most companies would cut their losses and quit early. The HP Way includes a healthy component of curiosity, innate skill, and perseverance, but perhaps above all, an ability to "think outside the box" to create transformative solutions.

Personal Computers for Engineers

In the niche that we tried to serve, we had an enormous market share . . . [from] a division whose charter and business goal [was] to sell equipment to be used on engineering and physics and chemistry workbenches.

CHUCK HOUSE[46]

HP needed to become more resilient to seize the opportunities in computing. That story begins with the desktop machines, the HP 9000 family that came from the original HP 9100A. Wang had punctured the HP bubble for the HP 9100A/B by 1971. HP's Loveland Calculator Division engineering manager Bob Watson headed a turn-around product launch—the family of three products numbered 9810, 9820, and 9830, announced in November 1972.[47] There were no microcomputer chip manufacturers yet, so HP synthesized a 16-bit serial microprocessor from MSI chips.[48] The machine used silicon memory—a lot of it. Fairchild Semiconductor defectors spawned a new company, Intel (*int*elligent *el*ectronics), led by Gordon Moore and Robert Noyce, which had just produced a new type of memory chip, called a DRAM, for Dynamic Random Access Memory. Using one-fifth the silicon real estate of static RAM, it offered great cost and size savings, and it saved the young company in the 1969–70 recession. In 1972, Intel would ship one hundred thousand of the new chips, called the 1103 1K-DRAM,[49] accounting for a third of the company's $23 million gross revenue. Selling five hundred thousand chips in 1973 nearly tripled company revenue ($66 million). HP consumed 40 percent of these DRAM chips, mostly for its new 9800 desktop line, as the product line surged from $35 million to $55 million revenue.

Watson determined never to let a competitor beat HP head-on again. Using a new NMOS (semiconductor) facility, the desktop division designed three chips, including a powerful 16-bit microprocessor, labeled the BPC—binary process chip—for a successor product family. Sales burgeoned—a line of products emerged, starting at a $2,900 list price for the 9815—and revenues approached $100 million annually by the end of 1976.[50] More than twenty-five thousand 16-bit proprietary BPC microprocessor chips were shipped to customers in personal computers from HP before Intel introduced its first 16-bit microcomputer 8086 chip in 1978. The 9825 was five years ahead of the IBM PC. The Calculator Division, dwarfing its Loveland voltmeter host division,[51] split off and built a new home sixteen miles up the road in Fort Collins, Colorado.

By the end of 1977, the retitled Calculator Products Division (CPD) had introduced the top-end 9845, advertised as Series 45. Series 45 featured an integrated CRT display, the first large-screen CRT (twelve-inch diagonal) used on a mass-produced computer. Available for $11,500, the Series 45 sold like hotcakes. Revenues for CPD jumped 61 percent in 1978.[52] Within three years, CPD had built and paid cash for three large buildings, launched a successor line based on the 16-bit Motorola 68000 microprocessor, and defined the NMOS III fine-line silicon processing technology for continued chipset leadership.[53] These products, called calculators because of the division legacy, were in fact desktop personal computers for engineers, predating the IBM personal computer for the office by four years.

The 45C debuted in November 1979 with a large color CRT, the first personal computer with embedded full-color display. It gave "engineers and scientists a single compact unit that contains all the elements needed to solve complex design and analytical problems. It has an interactive keyboard, a large memory, a graphic display, two fast processors, a line printer, and dual magnetic tape drives. Standard computer peripherals such as disc drives and plotters can be added if their capabilities are needed."[54] It was the most successful Fort Collins desktop computer ever. Indeed, Fort Collins was for the moment HP's most successful computer division. Figure 6.2 illustrates the revenue growth for the Fort Collins

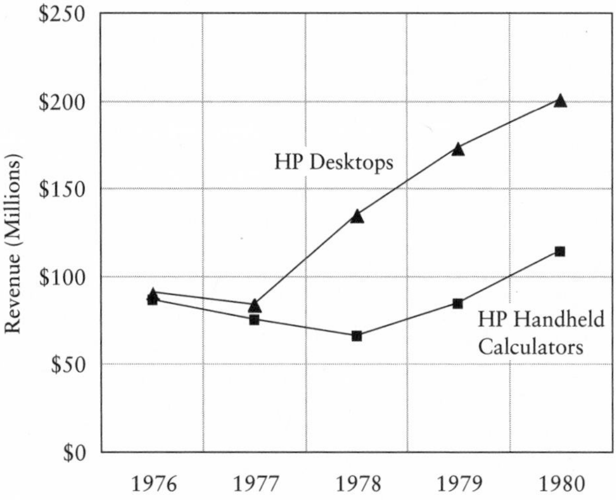

FIGURE 6.2. Orders for the two HP personal computing product lines, 1976–1980

desktop computers alongside the Corvallis Division handheld calculator line. Over time, the Fort Collins team produced six successive waves of world-leading products—the 9100, the 98x0 family (such as 9810, 9820, 9830), the 98x5 family, the 98x6 family (becoming the 200, 300, and 400 series based on successive Motorola MC680X0 processors), the HP "Focus" 9000, and, finally, the RISC-based "Snakes."

You Just Cost Me $395, Sir

The interesting thing to observe about computers and computer technology is that the most significant changes people don't notice. For example, the hand calculator really was a revolution. No one predicted it, no one worried about it. It sneaked up on us and suddenly we all have them, we all use them, and we never thought of it as revolution. It just sneaked up on us.

KEN OLSEN[55]

When Hewlett felt that a shirt-pocket-sized machine with the power of the HP 9100A could be a great product, he urged Paul Stoft in HP Laboratories to consider such a project. Stoft, Kay Magleby's manager when Kay started the HP 2116A, called on Tom Whitney, a young PhD from Iowa State University. Iowa State differed from America's premier universities of that era because it had a computer engineering department. Most others separated computer science from electrical engineering. Tom, trained in both the hardware and the software aspects of computing, was unusually innovative and talented.

Over at Intel, Ted Hoff in 1970 and 1971 had been designing a set of chips for Busicom, a Japanese four-function calculator firm. Just before HP's Model 35 hit the street in January 1972, Hoff had defined the world's first microcomputer on a chip: the resulting 4-bit Intel 4004 was announced in November 1971. Andy Grove was years from his epiphany to change Intel from a memory chip maker into a premier microprocessor company. Designers at HP had already adopted a one-bit serial microprocessor design from AMI (American Microsystems Inc.), which was second-sourced by Mostek at HP's request. Defining four bits as a "nibble," and two four-bit words as a "byte," HP's design team used a word structure of fourteen four-bit nibbles to compose the display register. This novel design permitted high resolution for any computation, with an LED numeric readout digit for each nibble.

Transcendental functions (sine, cosine, tangent, and their inverse) were built in, along with π (the multiplier for the area of a circle if the diameter is known). It was an engineer's dream machine, far more powerful than any four-function calculator. Naming the product was an early challenge. Four pages of suggestions ranged from the fanciful to the sublime, including "Captain Billy's Whiz Bang Machine" and "The Math Marvel." The final prosaic decision was just to go with the model number, which stood for the number of keys on the keyboard.[56] When the HP 35 was put on sale in January 1972 for $395, the most optimistic forecast was for a thousand units per month. The decision to put it into production was made by Bill Terry and Bill Hewlett, who predicted that they could sell ten thousand units over the lifetime of the product, bucking a dismal market assessment by the well-respected local market research firm, Stanford Research Institute (SRI). A feisty Hewlett, showing a prototype to a seatmate on a cross-country flight, heard the stranger exclaim, "You just cost me $395!" That input provided impetus to go to market.[57]

Within weeks, the machines had created a furor. Orders the fifth month peaked at twenty-five thousand units—a $120 million dollar annualized rate at full retail price. For a company with $375 million in annual sales, the HP 35 was a blockbuster. The sales rate exceeded manufacturing capacity at AMI and Mostek so much that orders went unfilled for weeks, even months, in the early days. For the fiscal year ending in October, HP delivered $22 million worth of machines. The second year they sold four times that amount. Bill's hunch had proven correct. At a time when Japan was causing great consternation throughout American industry, HP created pride in U.S. engineering.

To HP calculator enthusiasts, Reverse Polish Notation (RPN) was the most admired feature of the entire product line, even more than the vaunted reliability and the esthetic feel of the keycaps. RPN was a most unlikely concept. It had no marketing cachet, but it became the defining characteristic for HP calculators for years. Based upon a Polish mathematician's insight, RPN represented expressions naturally, without parentheses. Compared to algebraic calculators, RPN notation saves keystrokes (and time) while providing both intermediate answers and the end result.[58]

Alongside the algorithms and miniaturized silicon chips, the HP 35 made distinctive industrial design contributions.[59] Foremost was the sleek packaging, derived from the elegant styling of the HP 9100, fashioned to feel comfortable in your hand. Second was the miniaturized, fifteen-digit, HP LED display, constructed from three five-digit units with a built-in magnifying lens.[60] Third was the solid keystroke feel derived from the oilcan effect, wherein curved metal restrained at the edges can have two stable states—giving a snap click when a key was depressed. Finger spacing on keys and variable coloring for different functions were also critical in this novel, human factors engineering effort.

The calculator's reliability became legendary. One day the design team arrived in Bill's office; reportedly he took the prototype product and threw it against the far wall, to their horror. As he walked over and retrieved it, they were delighted that it was still operational. He smiled, and said, "Good. It has to do that, you know." *HP Measure* trumpeted the results: "Calculator survives being run over," or "HP 35 goes through snowblower."[61] The product was adapted for use by the blind at Opticon, and derivative products were used on space flights as well as the flight of the *Double Eagle* across the Atlantic.[62]

Hewlett was deeply involved with the personal calculator line:

> We had a breakfast meeting with about 200 security analysts in New York . . . shortly after the introduction of the HP 35. On each table we had an HP 35, and it was very interesting to watch the reaction of many of the financial analysts. Although they were familiar with electronics, it was evident that such key designations as "sin," "cos," "log," and "ex" were more a barrier to an understanding of the calculator's function than a help. The one key that was really useful for compound interest calculations ("x^y") was obscure in its use. Right there and then it became evident that what was needed was a pocket-sized calculator designed specifically for the business community . . . that could be readily understood by the user. As we thought more about this problem, it became evident that there was a tremendous gap between the language of the user and of our development engineers.
>
> The answer was to put together a small team consisting of Bill Crowley, from the Corporate Finance Department, who had a long-standing interest in computers, and Francé Rodé, from HP Labs, an expert in programming who was soon to acquire a very good vocabulary of business terms. These two visited a large cross-section of potential business users, and . . . distilled a set of classic problems that they eventually shoe-horned into what is now the HP 80.[63]

By contrast to the HP 35, formulas were built into the HP 80 machine, so single keystroke answers could be obtained by a user once the parameters of the problem were entered. Several significant financial problems were preprogrammed, including time value of money; sum of digits amortization; trend line construction; bond price and yield; accrued interest and discounted note payments; and mean and standard deviation. With the additional functionality, the HP 80 used a color-coded shift key that doubled the number of key functions available—still at the same $395 price.[64]

A month later, HP announced that it was opening urban showrooms for the handheld line. Shortly thereafter, Bill Terry authorized sales through department stores and university bookstores. Forecasts for the HP 80 were as bullish as the earlier HP 35 forecasts were tepid. Why not expect twenty-five thousand units per month? There were five to ten times more bankers, realtors, and insurance agents as there were engineers. Most of them, however, used interest-table handbooks, and the idea of learning and programming multi-step algorithms to calculate interest payments didn't catch on as quickly as HP marketeers hoped. Engineers took easily to RPN, but financial analysts didn't. The resulting training issues bedeviled sales for years. In fact, sales peaked on the HP 80 at roughly two thousand units per month, a mere 8 percent of estimates.

Undaunted, the designers churned out other scientific models. Within the first two years, the HP 45, the HP 55, and the extremely powerful HP 65 joined the original HP 35.[65] The HP 65 (at $795) was fully programmable, with a magnetic card that allowed for program loading, as well as data recording and output. User groups arose, contributing more than thirty thousand programs in nearly a hundred categories. Clubs sprang up on university campuses and in scientific centers such as observatories and national laboratories. Books of programs appeared as well. It was a tipping point for scientific computing.

And then Texas Instruments (TI) changed the rules. TI, one of the premier integrated circuit manufacturers of the era, and proud pioneer of the first handheld electronic four-function calculator in 1967, matched the functionality of HP's machines while dropping the sales price significantly. Hewlett-Packard designers and lawyers discovered relatively soon that TI had indulged in widespread patent infringement, but a task force dispatched to Dallas quickly found that TI's stance was "Tough! We thought you wanted memory chips for your HP 3000 computer line." Faced with such hardball tactics and with little choice—TI was the sole source of memory chips at that point—Hewlett-Packard backed down from a patent fight, electing instead to compete more aggressively on price.[66] Within three years, HP was forced to replace the entire handheld calculator line in response to the significant TI competitive threat.

The new product family—known inside HP as the Nutmeg line—hit the street in early 1975, with three new models—the HP 21A, 22A, and 25A.[67] The HP 21A, a stripped version of the HP 35, had a new price—$125 instead of $395—reflecting TI's competitive pressure. The HP 25A, very similar to the HP35 in functionality, was now $195. When the HP 22A replaced the HP 80, it cut the price point by nearly 60 percent, to $165. In another three years, the E-Series appeared—again cutting prices by more than half. The 31E replaced the 21A at $60, the 37E replaced the 22A at $75. Between 1974 and 1978, unit sales quadrupled, but overall revenue halved. Improvements in the line no longer earned an *HP Journal* spot—it had become a low-momentum, commodity-like product line.

The fourth generation program, though, was well under way. C-MOS technology and liquid crystal displays led to much improved battery life. The HP 41C was the first beneficiary of this shift in enabling technology, producing an outstanding product for serious scientists and engineers, back to a $295 price.[68] Sales revenue nearly doubled in two years with the new line, matching the best year ever at $114 million in orders. The technology move was quickly matched by TI, and the standard recourse—to launch a cheaper series—happened again with the Ten Series, introduced in 1981. Discouraged by the incessant competitive pressure, the shrinking volumes, and elusive profits, HP outsourced distribution, preparatory to abandoning the business. Three years went by, and then, inexplicably, while no one was looking, the HP 12C business calculator became the top-selling full-function business calculator in world history, at more than a half-million units per year. It was the perfect denouement for the unexpected transformation—since no succeeding product came along, textbooks written for junior colleges could now teach the keystrokes that matched the machine in your hand. And this was the lesson—the marketing materials have to match the market requirement, and HP (plus TI) for years out-invented the biggest erstwhile market. It would become a valuable lesson in later years.

For the moment, though, HP had elected to let the high-volume business go. The transformation seemed stillborn to some.

CHAPTER 7

Second Watershed

You never do a person a favor to leave him in a job he cannot do.

DAVE PACKARD[1]

The first Watershed was cathartic, propelling the founders into a new operating mode, breaking the shackles of a parochial company in one town with a dedicated narrow focus. The pressure developed over several years; solution elements came together quickly. The second Watershed was far more protracted. Pressures developed as quickly, but the solution seemed much more elusive. Some recalled the Tektronix debacle that began twenty years earlier; lessons from that experience provided food for thought, including Packard's decisiveness halfway through the period.

MARCH 1965, COLORADO SPRINGS: A Ford Mustang, the new Pony Car that was all the rage in America, pulled up to the curb and parked in the No Parking Fire Zone. A tall man in a rumpled suit climbed out and strode toward the front door. Showing great presence of mind, the front desk receptionist called out on the public address system, "David Packard." The announcement reverberated all over the building. Work stopped. Everyone's lips said it: "What on earth is Packard doing here?" He and Hewlett had just been in town in January for the first program review since the division left Palo Alto, an event culminating with a new building dedication. The dinner that night had been punctuated by Packard's stern admonition to the assembled spouses that their partners would be working long hours for a while, "until we get this business figured out." Hewlett, flush with libation, had gathered uneaten dinner rolls in a plastic bag, handed them to the local general manager, Cort Van Rensselaer, and said, "Here, these might come in handy." It took the edge off a tense moment, but there was no question at the time that Packard was displeased with the lack of progress against HP's chief rival.[2]

Packard's surprise visit culminated with a blitzkrieg move. He removed Van Rensselaer and three staff members, announcing new managers who took over that same day. Employees, shocked by the sudden move, assumed that careers were over for the four.[3] At any other company, they likely would have been finished. But remarkably, Packard, with a different philosophy, had other plans. He put three of them into roles that "better suited their talents," as he phrased it. The wisdom of that move showed up years later, as Cort's career contributed uncommonly well to the corporate well-being. Paul Ely would say,

> People who had done good work and got someplace where they didn't fit well, or weren't able to create the kind of success that the company needed, if the company felt that they had done good things before, and were valuable employees, they would find some way for them to save face to make a temporary lateral move to not embarrass them. . . . Cort's [removal from scopes] was not nice, but he did get the opportunity to do some other really good stuff.[4]

The quintessential test of a policy shows in difficult times. As a general manager, Cort failed the test, and his role was too visible, too public, and too important to have him steal away in the night. There could be no glossing over the fact that he'd been removed, and Packard undoubtedly wanted to use it as an object lesson as well. Yet Packard had something else for Van Rensselaer to do. As Cort observed,

> Ernie Arbuckle [on HP's board] was urging Dave and Bill to have a corporate planning function. Packard came back and personally talked to me about that. We went to dinner, and after dinner we went back to his hotel room and he laid it on me. But the key thing about it was that he had another job in mind. He was saying, "Well, here's another job that you do have the background for." Packard was famous for saying, "If you can't do the job, we'll damn sure find someone who can." The unspoken part was, "and we're going to find a place where you can make a contribution. Because everybody, if they're put in the right place, can make a contribution."
>
> Sometimes the first change doesn't work either. I don't think I had the right imagination for corporate planning. In corporate planning, acquisitions are very important. And from all that I could see, acquisitions were a lot of trouble.

It was the wrong approach. So Hewlett told me that he was relieving me of that duty. It was very abrupt but very positive. There was no discussion about "you've done a good job." It was just "I have decided to do this." He put Austin Marx in charge, and then he got Tom Perkins involved. And Tom was really good at that sort of thing. After I'd been back in Palo Alto about a year, Ed Porter was sent east to salvage F&M Scientific, which had some terrible management problems. Data processing reported to Porter. Packard asked me if I would take over the data processing responsibilities. And I promptly found that was just really fascinating.[5]

Building a Second Career

Van Rensselaer made a huge success of the data processing task, putting HP in the forefront of computer-based order processing and manufacturing systems. He (along with Carl Cottrell, another executive shunted aside from a tough assignment) studied the efforts that Bud Eldon had begun, to illustrate the flow of information required for HP. The resultant Information Architecture diagram gave HP corporate designers a roadmap for order processing, material requirements planning (MRP), and inventory tracking requirements second to none. It was a precursor of the tools that enabled the supply chain management (SCM) industry, thirty years ahead of time. Four systems were defined: two for order processing called Heart and Cochise, a communications hub named Comsys, and an inventory tracking system dubbed Colossus that stitched it all together.[6] The evolution and installation of these systems would give HP managers a secret sauce for more effective business management well in advance of competitors. Van Rensselaer and Cottrell didn't know much about information technology, but with fifty collective years at HP, they knew HP processes inside and out. Cort noted that

I got the feeling, talking to Packard, that he was sort of awed by all this stuff we were doing. There was a lot of fear about the computer business. But by using these products internally, I'd say, "If you asked Paul Ely this question he would say, 'Oh yes, our strategy was to use our products internally.'" He and Dean Morton were good friends, and Paul said if we could use the 3000 in the divisions, we could then prove to our customers that we really had products that could do great things for them. Dean agreed to install a 3000 in the Medical Group; my team had the programming job, for material requirements planning. They converted MRP on the IBM computers over to the HP 3000, installed it, and helped people in the Medical Group get it working. When that was successful, other divisions said, "Oh. We've got to have this."[7]

Cottrell recalled these events with clarity years later:

IT was growing by leaps and bounds in the company, and all of these different divisions were each doing their own thing. John Young became concerned about the increasing use of computers and terminals—terminal usage and costs had just skyrocketed. Asked to put together an IT committee, I had a totally different perspective from the rest of them. I told them right off the bat that I didn't know anything about IT, but I did know how to help get a group together. One of the first things I asked for was a diagram of what we're doing. What happens from the time an order comes into the company, and a product gets shipped out the door? What kind of process does it go through from an IT perspective? We began to document what was really happening in HP. We started describing it to customers—improving business through invoicing, order processing, manufacturing schedules. Cort and I were pioneers in presenting that to customers all over the country. We tried to get across the idea that if you could manage lots of small things, you can run your business better. It is amazing—HP pioneered accounting standards. It was unheard of in those days, but HP accounting people long since had set up accounting standards, so that every division in the company had the same chart of accounts. And in those days we were closing our books in record time. The key was that we had on one piece of paper a roadmap of how it all flowed together.[8]

Give 'em Hell, Dave

Neither Packard nor Hewlett was afraid to change a difficult situation. Both believed strongly in preserving the dignity of the individual if the job wasn't being done well; they differed greatly, though, in their personal interaction style. Hewlett, naturally shy, was seldom upset, although he was unyielding in his technology assessments. Packard could praise profusely, and in the next breath, or so it sometimes seemed, read the group the riot act. Notes and recollections from the 1967 HP general managers' meeting in Monterey, California's languid surroundings reveal that Packard bellowed at his top forty-five managers, "Tonight you have had an overall review of our performance in 1966. Bill [Hewlett] and Van [Bronkhorst] have brought out some of the areas where we have fallen down in our work, as well as where we have done well. I want to spend a few minutes reemphasizing a couple of areas where we have done, in my opinion, a disgracefully poor job."[9] It was vintage Packard—the first two examples he cited were inventory management and accounts receivable, and he went into considerable depth to make the point. It presaged his "Give 'em Hell" speech seven years later, covering the same topics in exquisite detail, with in-depth balance sheet and profit-and-loss study sessions.

Fifteen minutes after denouncing the "disgracefully poor job", Packard intoned,

> We might propose that every division should generate profits at least sufficient to support its own growth. To do this would make it difficult for the company, or even a division, to build strength in a new area. We will talk tomorrow about our strategy for expanding into new markets and new product areas. What I propose is that after we have helped a division to build a good foundation in a new area, then that division or other activity should be able to stand on its own. I don't know that we can define this point precisely, but any division which is in the $10 to $20 million dollar area of sales should be expected to generate profit adequate to finance its own growth, and provide a little extra for seed.[10]

Against this backdrop, it is useful to assess the degree of growth exhibited by the two founders themselves as their roles shifted and the company transformed. Packard's world changed dramatically as he went east to Washington. As Deputy Secretary of Defense, Packard routinely set security meeting agendas with Nixon's Cabinet: Henry Kissinger, Dick Helms, Eliot Richardson, and Lee DuBridge. He worked hard for cost restraints in the armed forces, instituting a "Fly Before Buy" policy to encourage relatively low-priced prototypes—shades of a division review!

Reports out of Washington were not sanguine. The press was vicious, the politics more so. Senator William Proxmire of Wisconsin led the Democratic Party effort to block Packard's nomination, an attack that Packard would never forget.[11] Nor could he ignore the impact on Lucile, who said to Dave, "Each morning when I turned on the radio, they'd be saying something terrible about you, and that spoiled breakfast. Then at noon when I'd listen again, it'd be worse, and that spoiled lunch. Then you'd get home, and tell me what an awful day you'd had, and that spoiled dinner. So when was I supposed to eat?" It was an effective diet—she lost sixteen pounds in twelve weeks. And then she stopped listening to the radio.[12] Asked later about his biggest accomplishment in Washington, Packard wryly quipped, "I gave up smoking."[13]

The times were difficult, to be sure. Vietnam protests had forced President Johnson from the 1968 presidential race; in the campaign Nixon committed to an orderly withdrawal, while Packard and Laird's efforts went into downsizing the military to support increased domestic policies. And then, in 1969, Nixon agreed to secret bombings inside Cambodia followed by an invasion of Cambodia in 1970.[14] The Kent State tragedy happened within weeks, plunging the nation into paroxysms of guilt, anger, and rage. Packard, preparing to give a speech in Palo Alto, was targeted—a Daddy Warbucks as seen by the Stanford student body at Packard's revered institution. The sponsoring group moved the speech to San Francisco—safer for him, they said. He lashed out in the speech, pronouncing Jane Fonda a traitor to the country, betraying his enormous sense of frustration. In December 1971, long before Watergate, David Packard resigned as Deputy Director of Defense and packed up again with Lucile to head for Palo Alto. Ironically, the future was as uncertain in many respects as it had been in August 1938.

Returning, Packard again became chairman of the board, but Hewlett continued to run the company. Some long-term employees were decidedly dismayed by this turn of events, feeling that the company had scarcely done well during Bill's tenure.[15] Much had happened at HP during Dave's absence. His last official picture for the company before leaving, in the 1968 HP *Annual Report,* showed him poking the keys of the new HP 9100A desktop calculator destined to make computing history. The enforced "nine days every fortnight" period during a deep, high-technology recession marred many people's perceptions. When Dave left, computing was just 4 percent of the company's revenue, well into the third year of shipping computers. Under Hewlett's leadership, the historic instrument side sputtered, growing at an anemic 4 percent per year. On the other hand, Medical and Analytical—the acquired scientific lines—had been stalled when Packard left; they nearly doubled under Bill's tenure—from $27 million to $47 million. Though computing revenues flattened just as Dave returned, they had catapulted from $12 million to $64 million during Bill's three years as CEO.

Bill Versus Dave?

Most interesting, and most worrisome to some of those closest to the executive offices, Hewlett had shifted his own perspective. Enamored of the calculating power if not the computing business, he had embraced the nearly preposterous idea of putting the HP 9100A into a shirt pocket, using the new miniaturized integrated circuits. When Hewlett ignored the gloomy market research report from the prestigious Stanford Research Institute and launched the HP 35 a month after Packard returned home, he sent a strong signal to the company about his leadership perspective. Anon, within the year, another landmark product would debut, backed by Hewlett and disliked by Packard—the HP System/3000, a computer that put HP irrevocably into a business arena that both men had studiously avoided for nearly a decade.

The HP 35 and the HP System/3000 caused significant hiccups for HP, both at the outset and over time. But growth rates for HP, stuck at 11 percent per year for three years, became an astounding 33 percent for the next three as a result of Bill's decisions (see Figure 7.1). It was unheard of for a Fortune 500 company to post such gains. The soft-spoken Hewlett disclaimed much credit. By the end of 1974, the company had been transformed. Now reporting revenues of $884 million, with $379 million in computing, the place was scarcely recognizable. And for many, while the revenue gains were spectacular, the resultant changes were not positive.

The most significant complaints were that "the HP Way" was becoming endangered. The long-haired, pony-tailed, sandal-wearing computer developers were led by MBAs who had very different ideas about market dynamics, pricing, and other "learned responses" that HP had accumulated over thirty-three successful years. Fast growth was feared more than slow growth—the feeling was that if computing became "the tail that wagged the dog," a reckoning would come when the competition rose up and swatted the company.

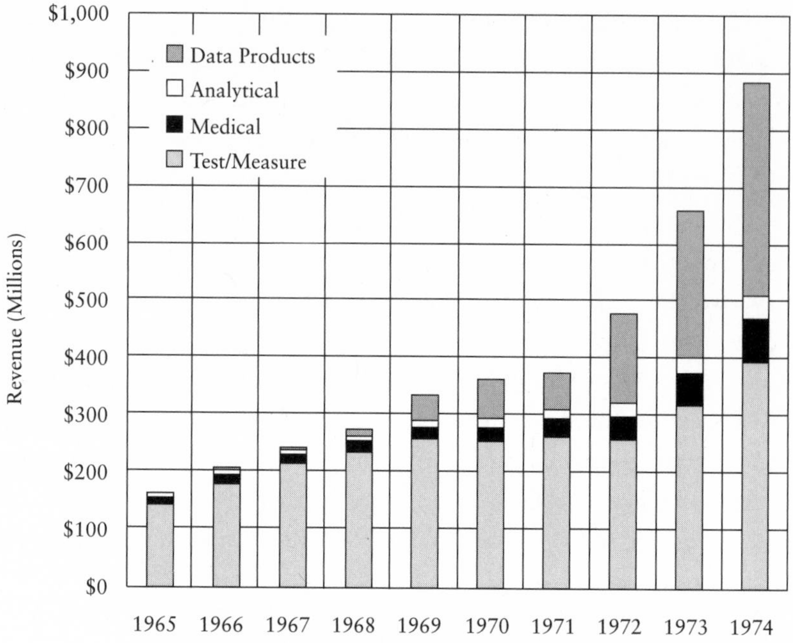

FIGURE 7.1. Market diversification and growth.
SOURCE: 1966–1975, *Hewlett-Packard Annual Report* (1975), 18

The old-line company—some now called it "the staid instrument group"—had grown by a remarkably robust 20 percent per year from 1971 through 1974, faster than the pallid 4 percent of the previous three years. But the computer group, now 37 percent of the total company, had exploded, with a compound growth rate of 57 percent per year for the three years after Dave returned from Washington. Scientific instrumentation—medical and chemical equipment—was solidly on the map as well, growing at 35 percent for the three years. Although Packard had been back for the entire three years, his hand had largely been invisible. In truth, he stepped in five times, twice publicly repudiating Hewlett's leadership, even as he intoned that he didn't mean to criticize Bill because the fault lay elsewhere. His actions sent a curiously mixed message.[16]

Against this backdrop, the partners, if not the partnership, were severely tested. Hewlett had actually taken charge of the company, betting heavily on the data products side after going through the agony of the

1970 recession. Instrumentation suffered worldwide; Tektronix, seriously affected, stagnated for three years. HP, though, surged during this period, seizing the initiative with the new digital capability, producing headlines in new technology arenas.

New thinking, some would say radical thinking, was forced on the company. Tom Perkins, who led the initial sales initiatives for the HP 2116A that established it in the marketplace, was teaching a Stanford Business School case about how a conventional business model could be made to coexist with a revolutionary new concept. He brought some avant-garde consulting concepts—the fabled Boston Consulting Group (BCG) theories about pricing and first-mover advantage—to HP when Hewlett in mid-1970 asked him to "come sit outside my office and help me" rather than continuing to ask for more money to run the division. Perkins reported years later[17] that Bill became a student of such concepts, enough to counter the more conservative Packard's desires when he returned from Washington. Packard was absolutely appalled, both by the BCG philosophies and by the case being taught at Stanford. Few were surprised when he managed to have the case squelched; reading it today, one wonders, "What was the big deal?"[18]

The Shareholder Letters

Bill Hewlett wrote the shareholder's letter for the 1971 *Annual Report,* noting that

> On December 13, David Packard, co-founder and former board chairman of Hewlett-Packard, resigned his position as U.S. Deputy Secretary of Defense. He made immense contributions to our national security and to the attainment of greater efficiency and economy in the defense establishment. . . . Having announced his intention to renew his association with HP, Mr. Packard has been elected to our board . . . and will assume his former role as chairman. Although he will not be devoting his full time to HP activities, that time which he can devote will be of the greatest importance to the company. All of us at HP look forward to having him back with us and . . . I am delighted to renew a relationship that began almost 40 years ago.[19]

The 1972 *Annual Report,* in February 1973, carried a letter "to our Shareowners" from both Dave and Bill, noting that the year was very good, with considerable strengthening compared to the recent recession. The company had restructured corporate operations into groups, and realigned the sales force into eight focused product domains. International activities were highlighted, along with a marked decrease in government-related business over five years—from 40 percent to 25 percent. The founders wrote that

> Demand was particularly strong for our medical instruments and systems, electronic components, and data products, including computers, calculators and their peripheral equipment. Our data products group had orders . . . up 81% from the previous year [and] a major contributor to this . . . was the HP 35, the pocket-sized scientific calculator.[20]

The 1973 *Annual Report* shareowner letter opened by describing "some special problems," including "a shortage of parts and materials ordered from outside suppliers, [causing] frequent changes and adjustments in production schedules, increased work-in-process inventories, and [higher] manufacturing costs."[21] Government orders fell again, to 17 percent; data products sales doubled. After citing the doubling of data products revenue primarily due to the calculator success, the duo wrote that "the systems part of our data products activity was less successful, largely because of problems associated with our minicomputer system, the HP 3000. Placed on the market in 1972, the 3000's initial performance did not meet traditional Hewlett-Packard standards. The product has since been modified."[22] This mea culpa jarred HP veterans.

More concerning was a financial caution that contrasted with Packard's self-funding ideals: "Our substantial outlays for new plant and equipment over the past two years, coupled with rising inventories and accounts receivable, have necessitated increasing use of our short-term borrowing capacity. Such borrowings amounted to $120 million at the end of fiscal 1973. We anticipate that additional borrowings will be required in the coming year, and we plan to place some of these amounts on a long-term basis."[23] In fact, a long-term loan designed by van Bronkhorst and Hewlett and arranged by Dick Alberding with Credit Suisse in Switzerland in February 1974 sent Packard ballistic.[24]

The mythic story is that Packard got back to town almost directly from his work in Washington on a Friday night before the annual general manager's meeting in January, and upon hearing about the debenture idea, said, "Well, wait a minute. You know we don't go into debt. One of our fundamental tenets is to stay out of debt, long-term debt, and so we've got to cancel that." By Monday morning, the decision was made to cancel the bond issue, and Dave personally took up the cudgel to travel the company with a two-hour lecture. He later called the speech his "give 'em hell" talk in his autobiography—one of his legendary actions as the ultimate caretaker.[25]

Several facts get in the way of the myth. First, Packard had been back more than two years. Second, although he raised the topic at the general manager's meeting, he didn't put emphasis on it. The final numbers for year-end close and first quarter weren't yet known. And finally, the general manager's meeting itself seemed to convince him that people had become, well, a bit lackadaisical. Ed van Bronkhorst noted that year-end numbers and more pointedly the first quarter of 1974 numbers gave Packard a rude jolt in early February, while Bill and Ed were working on the debenture idea. Relishing the tale, van Bronkhorst recounted, "My wife had a birthday party for me. People were gathering, and all of a sudden Packard shoved Hewlett and me into my dining room and said, 'Why do we have to have this bond issue?' I said, 'We don't have to if people would just go back to basics and earn money.' He said, 'Well, cancel it and let's go back to making money.'"[26] Hewlett called Alberding the next Monday, saying, "I have a dirty little job for you. I'm sorry. But you have to go to Credit Suisse and tell them we're no longer interested."[27]

There is little dispute about what Packard said in the speech. An unofficial transcript of the original talk, made from an audio recording, was widely distributed (see Appendix C). Packard repeated the speech multiple times at various company sites over the next forty-five days, making it a personal challenge to both get the word out and "look 'em in the eye" to gain affirmation of their support. He boldly took on several topics, including inventory control, new product pricing, and product development schedules. But he reserved his most strident remarks for the areas of fiscal responsibility in terms of accounts receivable, quality control, systems integration, and billing.[28]

Packard made it clear that these were widespread company issues, not just the province or result of growth in the data products sector. He took few questions, and publicly at least, there was no disagreement. Cort Van Rensselaer was one of those very positively impressed: "It was really remarkable how fast that all . . . I mean within six months the problem was solved and at the next management meeting I said to him that I was just so impressed with how you got on top of that and got that fixed so quickly. He said, 'Yeah, but the thing that bothered me was that I had to do it.'"[29]

An epiphany happened all over the company. Middle line-manufacturing managers were invited to the talk, listened for a while, and, yes, internalized the talk. Years later, it still is a vivid recollection for many. There is no dispute that Packard galvanized the company's managers to change behavior. They bought in, and they performed. In retrospect, maybe it didn't matter so much what he said, but rather who was invited to hear him and to feel his sense of frustration and his feeling that we had all let him down somehow. He spent two days in Colorado, one at each division, and as on the day two weeks earlier in Santa Clara, the audience was mesmerized by the energy, the perspective, and the zeal with which Dave Packard addressed the topics—eye to eye, almost nose to nose. "Pappy" (a favorite nickname given him by the old-timers) was back!

Tom Perkins had left HP the year before to start Kleiner-Perkins Venture Partners, using the Boston Consulting Group notions to good advantage. Perkins opined thirty-two years later that for higher-volume, commodity-like products, the learning-curve thesis had proven itself. Bear in mind that when Packard left for the Pentagon, after thirty years of running the Hewlett-Packard Company, the highest-volume company product averaged sales of ten units per day. The handheld calculator that came out in 1972 jumped this number by one hundred times in the fifth month. Learning curves were built on volume, not on handcrafted specials—and the HP that Packard knew best was a specialty manufacturer, not a volume producer.

George Anders, in *Perfect Enough,* argued thirty years later that Packard's talk enabled HP to "hold strong during the coming months as the 1973–75 recession gouged its way through American industry. Other companies went belly-up; HP squeaked through with lean inventories, frugal use of cash, and financial performance that made its shareholders proud." Anders's analysis missed the point—the Rust Belt suffered greatly in this recession, but HP's competitors, IBM, DEC, and Tektronix, made great progress during this period, without any histrionics. And Packard's concerns turned out to be transitory and fixable, unlike the aging infrastructures of the Rust Belt industries that were so vulnerable to newer methods.

Teaching the HP Way

Packard viewed his intercession as vindication—he did still matter to the company; his views of how to run a company conservatively, with proper fundamentals, just needed reaffirmation. Old-timers rejoiced, but not everyone did. Few dared express their views aloud—mostly young MBAs of the day, and the hotshot analysts on Wall Street.[30] Some folk in outlying divisions were miffed. Where had Packard been when Ralph Lee was out rapping people's knuckles to buy more inventory because of the purported critical materiel shortages? Where was Ralph now, to stand up and say, "I asked them to do that"? Analyzing it, John Young and Bill Hewlett concluded that Accounts Receivable was the major culprit, something not taught or measured in any division. As for the BCG idea, no one missed the point two years later when TI used it in calculators to HP's serious disadvantage.[31]

Was Packard's speech anachronistic, out of place from an out-of-step old-timer who just got nervous with someone else at the throttle? The speech certainly demonstrated that Dave still had influence. He could step in and override anyone. Fortunately for Hewlett, these intercessions were infrequent. Dave did get publicly involved once more, two years later when he initiated the Executive Training Program.[32]

Bill Nilsson was the unlikely hero thrust onto center stage. The much younger brother of renowned Nils Nilsson, head of the fabled Artificial Intelligence Lab at SRI, Bill was marketing manager for the Data Products Group in Cupertino when Ely took over from Bill Terry. A thoughtful analytic, Nilsson was miscast for the role that Ely desired. In most companies, he would simply have been one more casualty. But he had seen, up close, the challenging issues; Packard, recognizing that, offered Nilsson a plum—create an HP University that could develop and nurture leadership skills for the coming years. John Doyle, now leading Human Resources, concurred and supported the nascent idea. A broad series of initiatives resulted; courses for the first-time manager, the first-time manager of managers, and, most visibly, for the executive level were instituted, plus initiatives to capture best practice for topics such as manufacturing, quality management, and engineering innovation.

A major training facility, with a leading-edge television studio and eventual satellite-based communication system, was built. Faculty members were recruited from major universities to study and tailor their thinking to HP's special challenges. Bob Waterman and Tom Peters followed Bill Ouchi into HP, concluding that HP was one of those special companies exhibiting rare *excellence* both at their business tasks and in their cultural approach.[33]

The executive course took an intensive two weeks, replete with computer simulations, games, and late-night team projects. The attendees were drawn from all divisions and operations; in many cases, it was the first time that executives met colleagues from different segments or geographies of HP. The degree of insularity that showed up was striking, even more apparent as attendees were drawn from the staffs of the general managers rather than GMs themselves. HP top management was heavily involved, setting the tone, lecturing on their own perspective of the issues for the company, outlining their views of how best to grapple with and resolve the challenges of this new age.

A surprising finding emerged. Accounts receivable, inventory control, and pricing—Packard's classic concerns—didn't make the top ten list. The range of issues compiled at the executive seminar was staggering and insightful. Coordination—or rather, lack of it—topped the list. The growth of the company was so tremendous it was almost threatening; the right hand no longer knew what the left hand was doing. Many leaders in remote locations had little appreciation for, and even less empathy for, the leadership in Palo Alto. A job in Corporate was the bête noire of a career. Thus Dieter Hoehn could tell Marv Patterson that he would be unable to move back into product line operations from Corporate Engineering because he had "corporate stink" all over him after a decade in Palo Alto. Over the same decade, Hoehn himself sat in Palo Alto as a group vice president; those from below heaped the same opprobrium on him.[34] Autonomy had been carried too far. The special strengths of individual initiative, viewed from another angle, were massive hobblers that thwarted coordination.

The lessons from the first Watershed were fundamental to the course. Doyle spent extraordinary time with classes at each level of management, examining the depth of intent in the corporate objectives, with singularly positive impact on a generation of HP leadership. Reinculcating the beliefs and tenets of the HP Way in an explicit way had value that extended well beyond the terse wording in the pamphlet.[35] The class feedback, though, focused more on the second Watershed—what was wrong at HP that the new challenges couldn't be recognized? The Electronic Instrument Group and the emerging Computer Group cultures were clearly in conflict; new growth opportunities were being starved while old-line businesses still commanded the attention of top management; HP had become highly international in sales and support, yet most divisional staffs had scant understanding of issues outside North America. Just who was minding the store?

The Systems Business or the HP Way

In *Bill and Dave,* Michael Malone insightfully analyzed the difference between the two founders. Packard, he wrote, "played a zone strategy, entering new markets very carefully." Hewlett, by contrast, "would always throw deep, hoping for a tech touchdown."[36] The stunning three years between 1972 and 1974, notwithstanding Packard's angry speech, were mute testimony to the success of Hewlett's approach. Hewlett made the bold decision on the HP 35 that took HP irrevocably into the consumer market, as well as the decision to support the Alpha release even as Packard was asking Roy Clay to bail HP out of the computing business. Events inexorably took them into uncharted waters.

The 1972–1974 period was dynamic and tumultuous enough to cause a visible rift between the two founders, but the three succeeding years proved convulsive, revealing a paucity of answers for the next era at HP. From the outside, it seemed to be the best of times. The HP System/3000 recovered from its initial woes, as did desktop calculators. True, "Bill's Folly," which jump-started the company in 1972, the HP 35, and succeeding handheld calculators, had been gutted by Texas Instruments' machinations, damaging both companies. Malone later wrote,

> Texas Instruments, enamored with the controversial Boston Consulting Group learning-curve pricing model, decided to price bomb the market in hopes of

capturing dominant market share. And it did just that. But it was a Pyrrhic victory. TI made itself the industry leader, but so damaged the profit structure of the industry, and so truncated the normal time span from early adopter to commodity product, that by the early 1980's high-end calculators were all but dead as a healthy business.[37]

The TI official history benignly opines that "A worldwide recession in 1974 provoked a price war that staggered the market. . . . The price collapse occurred so quickly that TI's inventories became overvalued, resulting in major write-offs for the company."[38]

Competing views were set forth during this period—each by protagonists with a particular point of view, most of them unalterably opposed to each other. Where was truth in this maelstrom of activity? And more important, what was the future going to hold? The signals were decidedly mixed. The TI battle bloodied the Advanced Products Division, HP's most enthusiastic, forward-looking design team. Moreover, the group moved to Corvallis, Oregon, in mid-1975 in a misguided quest for cost-cutting and autonomy. Malone called this one of the two most significant decisions in HP history—effectively taking HP's best market-savvy team out of Silicon Valley just as the ferment for the personal computer revolution was about to burst on the scene. Packard wondered aloud, "What if IBM gets aggressive? Would it be as catastrophic as the TI onslaught?"[39]

Paul Ely never slowed. His voluble, energetic leadership style added color and excitement, and he exuded confidence. Even though the calculator lines made more money in both revenue and profits than all Cupertino programs from 1972 through 1977, formidable TI and Wang competition notwithstanding, Ely became Mr. Computer for HP more visibly than Art Fong was Mr. Microwave in the previous decades.

Paul had his hands full. The growth rates were spotty; from 1971 to 1974—Hewlett's finest years—the computer lines grew 57 percent per annum versus 20 percent for the venerable instrument lines. From 1974 through 1976, Instrument Group growth slowed to 14 percent CAGR, and Computers, without Peripherals, were even less, plummeting to 13 percent per year CAGR. Peripherals saved the day; new printers, disc drives, and data terminals added orders of $80 million and revenue of $50 million. Net profits were more worrisome; the instrument groups grew a cumulative 21 percent over three years, but Computers, even with Peripherals, were up only 7 percent overall in the same three years. Clearly, more was wrong than just the TI competition.

Hewlett had three new answers being readied, looking for a tech touchdown. One, an impressive calculator-watch, was code-named Cricket and awarded the vaunted HP 01 model number. Second was an incredibly sophisticated surveying tool. Most important, Ely's Cupertino team was finishing Amigo, the most ambitious computer program in HP history, dwarfing the abortive Omega five years earlier. Featuring silicon-on-sapphire (SOS) technology that no other company had yet mastered, it augured to be the flagship personal computer that the industry eagerly awaited. Alas, all three, all highly visible, failed. Hewlett had fingerprints all over the first two, and he had confidently supported Ely with the bold, single-user Amigo computer. Hewlett's confidence wavered, and tragically the love of his life, Flora, succumbed to cancer early in 1977 as well.

There is no evidence that a Pony Car showed up at 1501 Page Mill Road with a lanky rancher to ask Hewlett to step down; one has to wonder, however, if Bill's decision to turn over the reins that spring wasn't governed by dispirited discouragement. Events of that spring and summer in the executive office, out of sight of the rank-and-file, reveal significant discomfort. Young would later say only, "Hewlett is a very nice guy, and a very smart guy. But he's not a very business-oriented guy; he doesn't think a lot about organization. And he came up with a really strange set of proposals. I worked this out and sent them a memo and a diagram on how I thought it ought to be done."[40] In July 1977, Hewlett made Young president; the following May, coincident with a new marriage, to Rosemary Bradford, he stepped down from operations at HP altogether, becoming vice chairman of the board. Rosemary, scion of the Miller Brewing Company and widow of the founder of the company that made the Rainbird sprinkler popular, proved to be a healing ingredient for the genial reticent retiree.[41] Bill simply left—no ceremony, no grand adulations, as Malone wrote, "just a simple announcement, no different from one stating the promotion of an employee to division newsletter editor."[42]

Each of these programs—the watch, the distance measuring instrument, and Amigo—involved extremely sophisticated technology applied in a creative way to tough problems that seemed to represent a great market opportunity. What went wrong? Hubris, perhaps? Inattention to fundamentals? Or too much belief in engineering touchdowns run amok?

Fortunately, the company was not particularly bruised by two of the three failures. For one thing, HP Labs researcher Chris Clare transformed Instrument Group technology skills by teaching colleagues how to use the new microprocessor capability; for the next four years, 1978–1981, the Instrument Group outpaced both its historic average and the stumbling computer engines, growing nearly 24 percent per year versus 19 percent for the Computer Group sans Peripherals. Peripherals, not yet gaining anything from printers, exploded with a 52 percent growth rate, adding $200 million in annual revenue. No one at HP was looking yet at Peripherals separate from CPUs, since they were sold in conjunction with each other. The signals, though, were becoming visible. From a macro level, for board and shareholder standpoints, revenue growth, earnings, and stock price all looked solid. The long-feared CEO transition seemed smooth.

Cricket—monumentally silly in some respects—was damaging to the notion that Bill's market savvy was impeccable; but except for late-night jokes and a lingering malaise at the Corvallis Division, the issue soon ebbed. Barney quipped, "I knew it wasn't going to work when we started talking about it as fine jewelry."[43] The electronic watch business actually became a feeding frenzy in Silicon Valley for a brief period, with more than a hundred entrants. The first casualty was the Swiss watch industry; the second was the multiple players in the Valley. Most concentrated on accurate time, but since even the $5 entries kept better time than any watch in history, that edge soon was superfluous. HP focused, as with the HP 65, on extraordinary functionality for a hefty price—$695. Even the title on the *HP Journal* article seemed breathless: "Wrist Instrument Opens New Dimension in Personal Information. . . . It's a digital electronic wristwatch, a personal calculator, an alarm clock, a stopwatch, a timer, and a 200-year calendar, and its functions can interact to produce previously unavailable results."[44]

The *Journal* article gives pause—for instance, the calendar function description:

The calendar function provides the month, day, and year, but it is often desirable to know the day of the week also. A function has been implemented to provide this information. With any date in the display, pressing the prefix key (Δ) and the colon key (:) converts the date to a decimal display from one through seven, indicating the day of the week (Monday is one, Tuesday is two, and so on). Attempting to perform this function on time or decimal information will cause an error indication. Sometimes it is also useful to know the day of the year. With a date in the display, this function is accessed by pressing the prefix key (Δ) and the slash key (/). . . . In computations involving time, it is often necessary to convert from hours, minutes, and seconds to decimal hours. This is done by the key sequence Δ ÷.[45]

What had gone wrong? How could the division, caught in a dogfight for years with Texas Instruments, learning to stock the shelves at Macy's, produce such a complicated device? The article announced, "The HP 01 is the first of a new generation of wrist instruments." It would also be the last.

As for the $25,000 theodolite replacement for surveyors, Bill Hewlett's heart was in this product, starting with an astute insight in Afghanistan that such a measurement could be a dramatic improvement. It was difficult, but Bill Terry, running the Electronic Instrument Group, decided to stop the program:

Bill Hewlett was a big fan of it. He had one at home so he could survey his lot or his ranch. HP Labs did a lot of development work, and we put [the HP 3810A] in production in Loveland in a separate division. It was a distribution challenge, but we found some people who could sell it. It was a really useful product. I went out one day in the wintertime and spent a day learning how to pull a chain in surveying. Oh, that's a lot of work, versus measuring distance electronically. Originally this thing was pretty big and heavy. The next generation was called BEAR. And it was a bear. As the HP 3850A, it was pretty expensive, but it got a reasonable reception. We were ahead for six or twelve months, and then the competition did things better.

OK, here comes BEAR Two, which was a huge investment, $10 or $15 million—into the jaws of a really competitive market. Bill McCullough, who was in charge of it, said, "Maybe we can start selling boots and pickup trucks and stuff." I had to convince Bill [Hewlett] we were going to exit this. I went to Hewlett and told him the business case. And he looked at me and said, "Bill (Terry), you're breaking my heart. I just love this product. But you're absolutely right."[46]

Terry omitted the story about the angst created by these tools in Washington, D.C. The Defense Department was adamant that allowing cartographers to map the country to one inch within two hundred miles could imperil national security; for a time they sought to degrade HP performance. This roadblock, a small precursor of the rear-guard actions of Hollywood to the onslaught of digital video technology thirty years later, illuminated the fact that once technological progress has been made, it is quite difficult to put the genie back in the bottle.

The third arena, Amigo, was in Paul Ely's domain. Paul, never one to duck the heat, took full blame for the debacle. "SOS [silicon-on-sapphire] was an example of a huge, expensive mistake of mine—nobody else was responsible. I made the decision." It might seem odd that Amigo, bigger than Omega—the erstwhile technology flagship of the computing half of HP—wouldn't have had tough scrutiny from CEO Hewlett, but Ely avers otherwise: "Bill and Dave only made the kind of decisions that were appropriate for each new level. They didn't get involved, they didn't meddle. They got involved to know what was going on, but the decisions they made were the ones that were appropriate at the stage of the company at their level."[47]

One quote from an executive committee meeting stood out: "We're going to invent the Amigo, and it's going to be just as friendly as one of those goddamn Loveland workstations and calculators, whatever we call them."[48] Hewlett had time and again demonstrated his love of the Colorado calculator product lines for their ease of use and key-per-function operation. Tom Perkins much later opined, "Hewlett did not like computers. The perfect computer for Hewlett would have been a thousand keys, just a giant calculator."[49]

Computing was a long way from becoming something understood by "everyman"—computers were still back-office expensive equipment as far as most people knew. But the word was long out in what was becoming known as Silicon Valley that Doug Engelbart, the same man who had turned Barney and Bill down in 1957, "really had something"; Xerox, the big copier company, had built a research laboratory based on Engelbart's theories just up the hill from Hewlett-Packard headquarters. PARC declined to hire the irascible Engelbart, but they did have some first-rate researchers from his team and some leading universities. As early as 1973, the word about a rumored Xerox Alto computer electrified all who knew of it. Hammond's team was tracking PARC's work in printing; the Advanced Products Division (APD) team, building the handheld calculators, was interacting with them on user interfaces; and HP's industrial designers were still in close contact with Carl Clement, who both designed and manufactured the Alto packages.[50]

Ely, trained well in the Microwave Division thesis of winning by superior technology, by 1975 became enamored of the novel silicon-on-sapphire (SOS, pronounced "sauce") semiconductor process. The advantage was much faster electron mobility and hence higher speed. The goal became a 32-bit computer chipset, but SOS did not prove as amenable to scaling as NMOS devices. Thus Cupertino designers unwittingly were handicapped—Fort Collins designers could choose between leading-edge NMOS devices and commercial chips. Ely tied Amigo inextricably to the SOS process, assigning some of HP's best design talent to the task of building a super personal computer. Dave Crockett, a direct descendant of a brother of the frontiersman killed at the Alamo, was program lead. Crockett, an IBM Fellow before leaving to join HP in 1972 at Bill Terry's behest, was a bold, creative manager well-suited to a bellwether product definition. John Couch, who later became the first vice president of software at Apple Computer, was on the software team[51]; Jake Jacobs, an HP 3000 designer, was head of the chip design team; and Larry Lopp, fresh from installing the NMOS II technology at the Fort Collins Division, headed the Cupertino SOS facility. So the team, on the surface—and in hindsight—was as strong as the original HP 2116 team or the Omega team. And HP, with Ely in charge, had the leadership to get it done this time.

Amigo—So Friendly It Never Left Home

Stan Sieler described the program for Answers.com and for Wikipedia:

> The HP 300 "Amigo" was a computer produced by HP in the late 1970s based loosely on the stack-based HP 3000, but with virtual memory for both code and data. Designed as a single-user workstation, it was a commercial failure, massively so, considering the huge engineering effort. . . . The circuit boards were in a floor pedestal, with CRT and fixed keyboard on top. It pioneered such ideas as built-in networking, automatic spelling correction, multiple windows [on a character-based screen], and labels adjacent to vertically stacked user function keys, now used on ATMs and gas pumps. It also featured HP-IB as the I/O bus, an 8" floppy disc, and a fixed 12M Winchester hard drive.[52]

Two issues of the *HP Journal*—June and July 1979—contained fifteen articles penned by twenty-two authors that described the new system.[53] Amigo was a "personal computer designed for the individual worker," with guided "soft keys" for easy user-interaction, "on-board everything" including display, built-in hard and soft disc memory, and a stylish package. Sixteen machines could be networked easily. Priced slightly higher than the Alto at $38,500, with matching specs and a different, much easier interface (by conventional wisdom of the day), it was a major statement by a major competitor in the computer business. Amigo was launched three years before the Xerox STAR, conceived by Don Massaro at Xerox's El Segundo labs embracing elements of both the Alto and the HP 300 definitions. "The competitive landscape of the era was dominated by costly mainframes and minicomputers equipped with time-shared dumb terminals. Personal computers (circa 1981) were simplistic, with limited processing power and the inability to communicate with other systems."[54]

Aside from size, price, portability, software, and success, Amigo was everything a personal computer should be. Spending $40,000 for a personal computer might seem laughable today, but the HP 9845C two years later, a color-display workstation sans networking, sold like hotcakes at $39,500. Ironically, the $33,000 HP 250, sold as a small-business computer, was developed simultaneously by the Fort Collins Calculator Division in one-fifth the time for one-tenth the R&D investment; with European sales via Böblingen's

Calculator Division, it outsold Amigo tenfold. But it wasn't politically correct; moved to Cupertino under general manager Bill Krause, it died of inattention. Two years after debut, an HP 250 *Journal* article appeared two issues before Amigo.[55] Such internecine warfare, unbecoming to a well-managed corporation, increasingly damaged HP Computing. Inexplicably, Hewlett did not get involved. He felt that the loser would abdicate just as in the old days; those days were gone. Something had gone radically wrong.

A Siege Mentality

Cupertino had the feel of an embattled place. Yes, the HP 2000 line had tripled under Terry's brief reign, from $35 million in 1970 to $105 million in 1973, but the next seven years were desultory. Ending 1980 with $141 million in orders, the division had seen seven years at a mere 4 percent growth per year, while fierce competitors DEC and Data General had posted typical 30 percent to 40 percent growth per year. The division had morphed, divided, recombined, and been retitled, now as the Data Systems Division (DSD). The HP 3000 family moved into its own division, General Systems (GSD), two miles away in Santa Clara, California. Figure 7.2 shows this flattening in sales for DSD, as well as relatively slow growth for GSD.

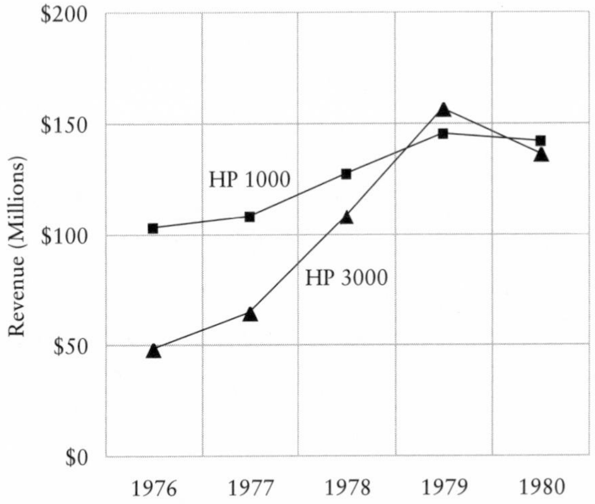

FIGURE 7.2. Orders for HP enterprise computing product lines, 1976–1980

These were strange times in Cupertino, with kind of a Rodney Dangerfield lack of respect for the group that started it all. They listened impatiently to stories about novel machines from a company that professed to change personal computing, as Loveland and then the Fort Collins Division built integrated computers. Cupertino even housed the Advanced Products Division before it moved to Corvallis, for an industry that didn't yet appreciate what a microprocessor was or why it could matter. As HPites, they were proud. The little handheld calculators helped to define a new niche, a precursor to a whole new industry. In the first twenty years of these products, HP sold fifteen million units. But for the Data Systems Division, it often felt like they were toiling in the backwater. The central processing unit (CPU) was but one element of the full system, and HP was organized atomistically. In effect, DSD was building just a box with a microprocessor and some memory chips.

Without input-output data entry, display terminals, and disc storage, the system was hopelessly incomplete. HP had organized each of these elements into separate divisions. Thus, the Data Terminals Division (DTD, nearby in Sunnyvale) and Disc Memory Division (DMD, moved from Mountain View, California, to Boise in 1976) had spectacular growth rates from 1976 to 1980 (doubling every year) while parent DSD wallowed in a no-growth situation. Yet everyone at DSD knew that the DTD and DMD success was governed totally by whether or not the CPU offering was competitive.

At first, this was somewhat moot, since DSD and General Systems Division (GSD) had the bulk of the revenue. In 1976, DSD orders topped $100 million, and GSD orders were half that amount. The combined DTD and DMD order rate was less than 20 percent of the CPU divisions. Four years later, DSD and GSD each neared $150 million—and DTD and DMD matched them. Thus, in four years, the two peripheral divisions quintupled in relation to CPUs. The impact of this transformation played havoc with HP's traditional funding approach. Growing from within, staying within your product line charter, focusing your selling approach on your own product line: all were counterproductive in an integrated systems world. The net result was profoundly demoralizing at DSD.

A Changing Computing Scene

For a company with carefully crafted ratios for managing R&D investments, marketing expenses, and sales commission rates, along with a pacing of product introductions and product longevity, these were awkward predicates. Many at DSD envied the situation at GSD, which controlled the HP 3000. It still had growth momentum, and it had just moved from Cupertino to a back building at Santa Clara, giving it a little more autonomy via a little less visibility. And it had Paul Ely's backing as the next horse to ride. Particularly painful for long-term HP 2000 folk was the fact that they continued to pioneer, leading the industry in one technical feat after another, pointing the way for GSD to take advantage of their work.

The DSD team was strong, and it built on the quality legacy continually. One of the long-time R&D managers, Bob Frankenberg, spoke to the quality instinct:

> We did a lot of pioneering work. We learned about integrated circuit burn-in, high and low thresholds, and all that stuff, and HP became known as the test company in the industry for DRAMs. Everybody wanted their DRAMS qualified by HP because once that happened, everybody else would use them. And nobody else would, if they weren't qualified. This led later on to the issue where all the data that we'd pulled together was shared by Dick Anderson, who said, "Japan is kicking our tail and the domestic manufacturers aren't performing." The analysis was done by the Memory Technology Center in Cupertino.[56]

Frankenberg proudly described elements of DSD's product leadership:

> We made the 21-MX user micro-programmable. We pioneered that, as well as creating writable control store and really taking advantage of memory prices. We were the price leader—we were able to do that because of our testing program. The new DRAMs were much more efficient, and price effective. If you were there first, you could lower your prices and just clobber the other guys. We did that to DEC and Data General on a continuing basis.[57]

Taking a systems view was nearly as hard at GSD as at DSD. And the bigger difficulty was the paucity of leadership in software, a malaise that in many respects persisted for decades. Three executives, Wim Roelandts, Jef Graham, and Nancy Anderson, described this disconnect.

Roelandts joined HP in 1967 in Belgium as a hardware support engineer. He had some training with software, which helped him become a systems engineer as HP 3000s and HP 1000s started to appear in the European customer community. He offered some trenchant thoughts:

I was one of the first people to grow up inside HP with system knowledge and software knowledge. They hired a lot of people from outside to bring knowledge. Most of these people came, stayed a couple of years, and then disappeared because they were frustrated that HP was still a box company. Initially, we brought computer experts in. But they didn't understand the HP culture very well. They are a different breed of people. And HP management didn't understand computers, or systems, or software. So outsiders came in and they didn't understand the HP Way, and the HP Way didn't understand them. After a while everyone got frustrated.

Then we started creating people that were from HP who became more software knowledgeable. But the problem of being a software systems guy in a box company was still a major issue. The box business is really a tactical sell: We have good quality. In software, it's totally different because people are making an investment, and that investment is forever. But the product is invisible. So, you have a bunch of people with long hair, who cannot keep their schedules, and don't produce anything that you can touch, thinking they should make profit, but don't because we give it away.[58]

Graham, then working as a field salesman for IBM in the United Kingdom, visited HP when the HP 3000 really began to have some sales traction:

At IBM, they'd always been about applications. We didn't talk technology. We'd talk about the customer, what they were doing. I came to HP and said, "Can I get a demonstration of the computer?" And they said, "Sure, let's have a look at it." In the demonstration, first, the sales rep got hold of the disc and shook it. Now of course I was horrified. You never shake a disc. My first reaction was, "Why was he still working?" My second reaction was, "Do you have many customers that do that?" It was showing the technical prowess. It's impressive when you do it.

As engineers, you go, "Wow!" But it's irrelevant. The second thing they did was open the cabinet and show me the ports, saying, "Look at these gold fingers on the port." Everything else had copper at the time. Gold fingers, this is how well engineered it was. I thought, "You know I've never looked in an IBM computer." But there's no relevance to that either. So, I said, "Well, let me work with your text editor." The multi-programming executive operating system (MPE) had a most wonderful editor, and it had a relational database called Image. They were the unique things. The sales reps giving the demo didn't know that Image and the text editor were the real strengths. I thought, "I could sell loads of these." My first year selling, I was the top sales rep in the world. I sold $3 million worth of computers in my first year of selling because it was like taking candies from babies. And I didn't shake any discs or open any cabinets.[59]

Anderson joined HP a year before Graham, in mid-1977. She'd developed software for Tymshare and sold computers at DEC against HP. She said,

I sold against the HP 3000 when it was first introduced. It was dog meat. [It] couldn't support four users. It was very easy to beat. And then, there was a new release and I lost every deal to HP. Most of the HP management was following a well-worn path, whereas Ed [McCracken, the GSD general manager] was striking out and finding a new market with new types of customers. It required us to do a lot of things. One was to have a lot of service. HP never had to have a lot of service because we sold to very technical people and we just had conversations between our engineers and our users. Suddenly we also needed a whole lot of application software. So Ed had to solve a lot of problems that seem obvious today. But I can tell you, back in '77, they didn't seem obvious. He was really charting a new course, something that a lot of HP resisted. We came up with the Image 3000 database, a big innovation. We came up with other software such as report writers; there were a lot of building blocks you don't think twice about today. They were big deals then.[60]

McCracken, a shy farmboy who admired fellow Iowan Tom Whitney's engineering skills, brought enormous marketing savvy to HP. When the 3000 division was supposed to move over to the Santa Clara site from the Cupertino site (two miles and one freeway off-ramp away on I-280), no one would move. Ed moved; the division newsletter showed a picture of him sitting all alone in the cavernous facility. Shortly, his team joined him. Ed later would say modestly that it was really helpful to have distance from Cupertino leadership.[61] But he and his marketing manager, Anderson, struggled with manufacturing application issues. She said,

> We'd never really had the situation where an application would drive the sale of the computer system, but we had a big third party named ASK Computer. We were discovering what kind of relationship makes sense because we had a little bit of a love-hate relationship with people like ASK. We had this definite feeling that HP's hardware was all responsible. . . . We couldn't decide how close a relationship to have with ASK, or how our sales reps should treat them. [We had] questions like: Should they actually bring them in to accounts? What kind of discounts should they get? How do we service accounts if they really were ASK accounts and not our accounts? So there were a lot of different issues. ASK was the leading one, but there were a lot of smaller accounts, and then it was a matter of "Gee, is this true generically of all application software or are we just treating ASK uniquely because they are driving so much business for us?"[62]

The Software Issue

Software was an early contributor for HP computer success, even as the company struggled with the topic. Mike Green almost single-handedly wrote the HP 2000 Real-time Executive (RTE) time-sharing operating system before architecting MPE. Operating Systems gave HP CPUs a big advantage. By the time that RTE IV arrived, HP had the most reliable, robust real-time operating system in the industry, which solidified the HP reputation for manufacturing and process control applications. An early version of Image shipped with the HP 2100 before being enhanced by Jon Bale and Fred White for the HP 3000; as both Jef Graham and Nancy Anderson reported, these were crucial distinctions.

Interex, an HP users group, appeared on the scene by 1974, spearheaded by Doug Mecham, who wrote the first HP 3000 System manual. Interex provided a wonderful meeting ground for independent software vendors (ISVs) who spent a lot of time building drivers, hardware tools, and performance enhancers as well as software application tools. Abacus,

Adager, Allegro, American Management Systems, ASK, Gentry, LARC Computing, Quasar, and SD&G were never household names, but these companies built powerful HP software, and in the process created much enthusiasm and loyalty among the HP user community.

Inside HP, however, there was ambivalence, if not antagonism, toward these companies. Doug Mecham wrote a letter to long-time CFO Frank Cavier on February 13, 1976, copying thirty-one HP managers:

> It is clear to me that these statements [in the *Annual Report*] epitomize the HP NIH factor and show a lack of understanding of the user's viewpoint. HP has rarely listened, communicated with, nor sought users' ideas except in very limited situations or under duress. Paul Ely has specifically stated to the HP 3000 Users Group Directors that "We do not need you." . . . During my two-year tenure as president of the HP 3000 Users Group, the rapid change of HP management has made it difficult to develop stable Users Group-HP interface [and] HP middle management seems to have a problem in communicating with users on the user level. It is difficult to express the frustration that is felt when HP does not appear to be very interested. It would appear that HP designers have very little comprehension of the user frustration caused by simple little problems. I sometimes get the feeling that HP is afraid of users and wished to hold them at arms length.[63]

Cavier didn't know much about computers, but he knew this was a hot potato. He gave it to Packard rather than Hewlett. David Packard wrote back on February 25, 1976:

> I have had an opportunity to read your thoughtful letter, [and] I wish to assure you that the suggestions you have made will receive careful consideration, and that some of us in this company are very appreciative of these most important contributions. We hope also that you will continue to speak up when you see ways in which our people can improve the job they are doing.[64]

Why did the ISVs stay with HP then? Jack Damm at Quasar (later sold to Cognos) said, "We got 'shared computer time' when that was expensive. So did ASK." Grace Gentry, founder of Gentry Systems, said with much energy that "HP didn't lie to clients; we dropped the other two vendors." Alfredo Rego at Adager felt that "DEC and DG isolated the lab guys, but when I visited HP, I got to the 'low-level' guys." Martin Gorfinkel at

LARC said "HP called on us. HP was way better to deal with than DEC or DG. Their prices were exorbitant, but the quality of the machines and of our dealings was important to us."[65]

The die was cast. HP itself would continue to struggle with software issues, especially whether or not to build applications for sale. But its user community found solutions that worked, and that was good enough.

Transformation—Indeed

Seven managers in seven years followed by one manager for a dozen years took the computing side of HP from $100 million to $3 billion annual revenues, 50 percent larger than all of HP's historic instrumentation. Ely's leadership and inimitable style made the difference.

Graham, who was HP's most successful European salesman for the HP 3000, noted that

> Paul had at least three opinions about everything; often they weren't based on facts. One would be absolutely spot on and the right thing to do, one would be OK, and one would be awful. And the difficulty was knowing which one it was. But Paul was a strong statement leader who would push and push and push. If you don't have somebody with a vision saying, "This is where we're going. This is what we're doing," it's very hard to go there. Paul could be pretty controversial and difficult, but he was a very strong leader.[66]

Joe Schoendorf worked for Paul in several roles, including Group Marketing. He said,

> Ely got it right, because he had the chutzpah to run over the people who got in his way at Corporate. You had a lot of the old guard sitting up there either in administration or in other businesses, all guys that didn't know a damn thing about the computer business. They were used to being good general managers, but not starting new businesses. That generally takes rule-breakers. Ely was a really quick learner and he was street smart. He would engage constantly. He interacted and he learned and he would challenge you. Paul would look at you in a meeting and say. . . . "You know, that's exactly the wrong way to think about it." He loved to do that in front of a large group of people. And while you'd say, "That's not HP," it made you rise up and challenge him back. He wanted people to think out of

the box. Previous managers wanted everybody to think in the box. They wanted to use the instrument rules in the computer business. Ely came in and said, "I've watched ten years of failure. We need a new set of rules."[67]

As the company struggled with the second Watershed, it seemed CEO Hewlett needed a new set of rules. Decisions from the first Watershed, such as local autonomy and delegation, weren't working in this new systems world.

CHAPTER 8

The Secret Sauce

In today's world it is difficult to conclude that there is any business or industry not influenced by rapidly changing technology—and, if anything, the pace is quickening. But this emphasis on short-term profits is most disastrous—failing to build long-term strength into an organization. This weakness is evidenced by such things as inadequate personnel development, failure to recognize the importance of research and innovation, and the absence of well-developed long-range plans which are understood and accepted by the organization.

DAVE PACKARD (1983)[1]

Efficiency and productivity experts are continually paring excess expense and redundant activity, in a never-ending quest for greater return on investment. And in the short term, they often succeed. Although such efforts are not unknown at HP, there has long been a profound additional component. HP's secret sauce, the differentiator giving it long-term competitive advantage, came from employee creativity, dedication, and drive for excellence. The corollary was that HP employees often defined and built company-wide solutions as well as specific products and technologies that were amazingly effective, giving the company unusual capability. Always managed tightly to a rigid profitability expectation, Hewlett-Packard has been lavish with its long-term investments in people, products, systems, and structure. The movie *Standing in the Shadows of Motown* celebrates all of the backstage support team—the analogy is apt for an HP repaid handsomely by its employees at every level.[2]

David Packard's tenure as chairman of the Hewlett-Packard Company spanned fifty-five years, affording him many opportunities for speeches regarding the unique insights that he and his partner, Bill Hewlett, gleaned over the years. Invariably, the conversation got around to a few well-worn phrases:

- Whatever the requirements of the job, we start with good people. We get them to understand what we want them to do and then we leave them alone.[3]
- You need to develop finely tuned antennae. You need the ability to go out in the shop and wander around and sense how things are going. You need what we call the fourth dimension of management—Management by Walking Around.[4]
- The hardest thing to do is to define the problem and start tackling it.[5]

Hewlett-Packard people have defined problems again and again in terms different from those of their competitors, coming up with solution after solution for the corporation that have proven novel, inspired, and apropos. The secret sauce was seldom articulated, but it was widely understood throughout the company. An aura, a mysterious capability seemed to envelop the company, shielding it to a significant degree from the travails and difficulties experienced by others. It isn't hard to understand, but it requires a different perspective to believe that it works as well as it does. It grows out of the HP Way, and out of the objectives: give someone a job, set high expectations and clear objectives, and get out of the way.

A Single Parts-Numbering System

HP's first twenty years were intimately tied to Stanford, Palo Alto, instrumentation—and the presence of Dave and Bill. The first Watershed diluted each of these bonds—but although the HP Way, with the Corporate Objectives and the Eleven Rules, was a substitute, it ran much deeper than that. HP had long nurtured a culture of consensus; less acknowledged was a common way of doing things, methods that got exported to the decentralized locations and embedded in the acquisitions.

One of the principal differentiators for HP was the overlay of corporate consistency on top of localized initiative. At HP, everyone agreed on one common parts-numbering system for purchased parts; a corporate standard paint color for cabinets; a corporate standard lettering for front panels; a finance chart of accounts; and consistent price sheets from country to country. These elements of consistency didn't just happen. More to the point, they didn't happen at all at most other companies. HP, for all of its purported local autonomy and driving of decisions to the lowest level, enjoyed a strong corporate consistency, which provided an uncommon overall effectiveness.

Hewlett and Packard insisted on elements of uniformity, but standards were enforced by lieutenants—and their contributions were so culturally attuned and so pervasive that it seemed unremarkable at the time. Few "historic moments" acknowledge how this happened or who led the charge. Some examples, though, give life to three precepts. First, anyone could try out new approaches—this was evident in contributions from assembly workers (for example, the invention and application of lazy-susan assembly stations in Palo Alto in the early 1950s). Second, new ideas were broadcast—not only was insularity frowned upon, praise (and, more important, time) was given for sharing ideas with others and helping their adoption. Thus disciples taught the Microwave Division project management methods to other divisions (such as Jerry Boortz and Dar Howard for the Oscilloscope Division). Third, and maybe most important, a few corporate departments codified emergent methods into guidelines that, in effect, put a kind of franchising in place, so that any new site, division, or operation could start full-blown with consistent procedures, processes, and vocabulary. The method was both efficient for individual operations and able to leverage corporate strength.

A few stories illustrate how guidelines worked. When Cort Van Rensselaer in 1948 designed and installed the Kardex that linked marketing forecasts, manufacturing schedules, and inventory purchasing, he had little reason to anticipate the eventual importance of the derived decisions. As fate would have it, he was involved again as two different technology improvements loomed. The decision to standardize a parts-numbering system for the corporation was fundamental. It began when Dymec and PAECO were integrated with HP in the late 1950s and continued with the acquisition of Moseley, Sanborn, and other companies. Although standardization might seem like a simple and rational decision, it was not the conventional wisdom. Even today, General Electric reportedly has some forty-three different parts-numbering systems across the company. In fact, it is much easier, not to mention cheaper in the short run, to let new acquirees keep their own systems intact. The problem is that it becomes nearly impossible to discern, let alone administer, opportunities for consolidated ordering, whether to obtain higher volume discounts, to arrange preferential shipping schedules, or to manage inventory levels. More insidiously, quality issues that surface in one site don't transmit across the company. Every problem has to be discovered and solved anew. In 2008, powerful MRP and CRM systems (manufacturing resource planning[6] and customer relationship management) are deployed to try to manage such complexity, but they can work only if the requisite foundation has been laid.

Corporate Quality

I am on three corporate boards of directors, and I was embarrassed the other day when Fortune magazine said we had the worst quality of the three.

DAVE PACKARD (1983)[7]

From the beginning, superb product quality was paramount at HP. When Barney Oliver gave the development lab responsibility for products from inception through production shipment, he and Ralph Lee established a "Production Readiness" team whose job was to test all new designs rigorously to ensure that they met the corporate standard. Strict environmental testing to explicit design specifications, clear performance feature test requirements, and a rigorous manufacturing specification package were crucial for any new product. Radio frequency interference, drop tests, and wide altitude and temperature excursion limits were all assiduously imposed—and products were tested far beyond the published specifications. Products were built to Class A, B, or C environmental specifications. These conformed to military criteria, and although HP only built commercial equipment, Hewlett decreed that every new design had to be at least Class B. This meant, among other things, that a product must meet full performance specifications over a temperature range of 0° Centigrade to 55° Centigrade (from 32° Fahrenheit to 131° Fahrenheit), up to 95 percent humidity.

Many HP products were even more rugged, handling temperatures from 0° to 150° Fahrenheit. Though it was hard to imagine someone standing in a room with such temperature extremes, it wasn't hard to conjure an image of a customer trying to use a voltmeter outside on the Alaska DEW Line. HP CRTs had to work up to a fifteen-thousand-foot altitude without arcing—something that the Japanese plasma panel television makers knew, but the Koreans did not when widescreen wall displays became popular in the late 1990s. The unhappy result: a high number of shattered glass displays in ski resorts around the world.

Incoming vendor parts were subjected to stringent evaluation and certification. Then and only then was a part number assigned, with appropriate documentation to find equivalent parts from other vendors. This was a costly up-front process, but it was imperative to guarantee the implied trust for users of HP equipment. Hewlett and Packard both were clear that if HP equipment failed, it was not just the cost of repair, nor even the product or brand reputation that was at stake. More damaging was the loss of confidence in the entire measurement process. HP's quality emphasis was highlighted in 1980 in a speech by Dick Anderson, by then a Computer Systems vice president in charge of the HP 1000 and 2000 lines of manufacturing test computers. At a forum in Washington, D.C., his topic was the stunning difference in quality between Japanese and American vendors of integrated circuits. American vendors, notably Intel, were at first enraged, then sheepishly apologetic, and then energized into reaction and repair.[8]

By 1980, Japan had totally dispelled the notion that Japanese goods were cheap and shoddy. Instead, in a remarkably short time, "Made in Japan" came to mean the world standard of quality for products ranging from steel, automobiles, and heavy machinery to cameras, scientific instruments, and electronic gear. For American and European firms that used to control world markets in these fields, the transformation was calamitous. In semiconductors, where virtually all of the basic technology was created in America for transistors, integrated circuits, and microprocessors, Japanese competitors had moved up so far and so fast that U.S. firms went to Washington for help. The Semiconductor Industry Association, a leading U.S. electronics trade group, asked the federal government to help combat unfair Japanese competition. They argued that predatory trade and pricing practices, together with massive Japanese government assistance, were responsible for the rapid growth of the semiconductor industry in Japan.

T. R. Reid, in an American semiconductor industry exposé, wrote an article titled "Meet Dr. Deming, Corporate America's Newest Guru," in which he cited Anderson's speech:

> The Japanese moved ahead in semiconductor sales at least in part because they moved ahead in semiconductor quality. Evidence was set forth in an infamous—or famous, depending on your point of view—meeting of electronics industry executives in Washington, D.C., in March 1980. Among the papers presented was one known today as "The Anderson Bombshell." Richard W. Anderson, an executive at Hewlett-Packard, spoke on his company's experience with Japanese electronic devices. He explained that HP began in 1977 to produce a computer that used Random-Access Memory (RAM) chips which store 16,000 digits of information. Such memory chips—known in computerese as "16K RAMs"—were invented in the USA. But American suppliers could not produce enough acceptable 16K RAM chips to meet HP's needs, so the firm somewhat reluctantly turned to Japanese manufacturers as an additional source of supply. Hewlett-Packard gradually began to realize that there was a significant difference in the Japanese memory chips. They were far more likely than the American product to pass HP's standard factory inspection. And the computers in which they were installed went much longer without a memory failure than did comparable machines using American memory chips. In sum, Anderson said Japanese firms were producing higher-quality chips at about the same price as the American product.[9]

Reid's story referenced Dr. Edward Deming, but it didn't do justice to the emotional situation. First, for a decade HP had been the top purchaser of memory chips from American semiconductor manufacturers—Mostek, Texas Instruments, Motorola, and Intel—along with microprocessor chips for the handheld and desktop calculator lines. Second, the higher-quality Japanese chips were more than 1,000 percent better at initial inspection, and 500 percent better over time—not just a little bit, but a whole lot better![10] Given the raw TI patent infringements and the angry feelings between the two companies in the handheld calculator business, and the head-to-head competition between HP's Fort Collins NMOS II shop and Intel to build more capable microprocessors, Anderson's criticism had all the earmarks of a vendetta rather than an objective, disinterested, third-party report. The difficulty was the data. And the data traced to that fundamental work in corporate quality assurance—work not done with nearly the same rigor at any other U.S. computer manufacturer.[11] But then, virtually every other computer manufacturer was building equipment that, at best, met Class C environmental specifications—meaning that they worked only in a restricted temperature and controlled humidity environment. HP, following Hewlett's dictum, built its controllers and all succeeding computing equipment for Class B, figuring that these machines, just as instrumentation, might well be deployed in manufacturing environments.

Anderson also had the advantage of a long-standing HP Computer Group quality audit function in the Memory Technology Center (MTC) to assess and verify the conclusions that he presented in Washington. Bob Frankenberg started this unique group in Cupertino, and Gordon Goodrich and Tak Watanabe were the principal engineers who did the pioneering work. Once again, quality audit groups, often seen as impediments to fast action from a division perspective, were important to HP strength.

Packard, a staunch supporter of quality efforts, gave Ken Sasaoka, Y-HP's president, the podium at the next annual general managers' meeting. The group heard an even more improbable story. Sasaoka-san described his manufacturing operation outside Tokyo to a hundred managers:

> We have built our Printed Circuit fabrication line from cast-off equipment from other HP divisions, when they wanted to upgrade their manufacturing capability. We didn't have funds to buy new, so we took the old equipment. Here are our quality statistics. We reject forty boards per million, and we plan to improve that by a factor of two next year. The best U.S. division is rejecting five hundred boards per million.

Then Dick Anderson came to the podium, retelling the semiconductor story.[12]

Packard concluded the three-day meeting with his own postscript, building on the recent inaugural *Fortune* "Most Admired" story that ranked HP the third-best quality company in America. The ranking provided pride for everyone in the room until Dave intoned,

I have always felt that HP should represent the highest-quality products possible, and Bill shares my concern. You have all heard him describe how fundamental it is that our products never cause a customer to lose confidence in the measurement itself. Well, I am on three boards of directors, and we have the worst quality of the three. I have spent years telling the people on those boards about my views on quality, and I looked like a fool when this report came out. I want you all to be number one—*do you understand*?

Afterward, one reckless division manager said jocularly, "Dave, I hope Boeing stays number one forever, as much as I fly on planes for HP." The patriarch didn't smile.[13] Most attendees thought that being named number three in quality of the top one thousand companies in America was damn good and should have earned high praise rather than brickbats.

Ken Sasaoka, an urbane, pleasant man on the surface, had shown a tougher side to Packard some years earlier, insisting that HP wasn't trusting their Japanese partner fully because they still used American leadership. Packard had given him the reins, only to have Sasaoka become something of a thorn at HP headquarters, adamant that HP divisions were shipping unreliable and unfocused products to Japan that his customers wouldn't buy, accounting for poor performance by the Japanese subsidiary. Sasaoka got two Colorado managers to travel to Japan, one on behalf of Logic Analyzers, and the other for the Fort Collins computing lines. The disturbing findings propelled Craig Walters into a new Corporate Quality Manager role. Sasaoka's pressure got results.

Quality would become the bête noire of American industry over the next decade. Philip Crosby wrote a book titled *Quality Is Free,* expounding the idea that the costs of bad quality exceed corporate profits in many cases, and that the cost of fixing the problems ahead of time in design will in the long run be invisible on the bottom line. A retired *Fortune* editor, Jeremy Main, devoted five years to a book, *Quality Wars,* that indicted American industry in general, not just semiconductor manufacturers. Motorola by 1990 had gained much fame for its Six Sigma practices, a concept that AlliedSignal and General Electric later adopted widely with hugely successful results. But Main found that at Motorola, one lone individual had stood up in 1979, essentially as a pariah, to argue the case, and it took years for him to prevail.[14] The same was true at North American Rockwell, then the world's largest cell phone manufacturer.

Corporate Groups

Jeremy Main's book described HP practices only briefly. Consistent with the understated nature of everything it did, HP was not yet publicizing its extensive activities. When John Young put Craig Walters into a strengthened corporate oversight role, the two came up with a challenging goal for every product line in the company: improve quality by ten times, or 1,000 percent, in five years—everywhere. Some demurred. The exasperated Logic Systems Division general manager gave Young graphic examples of divisions with awful quality records compared to others—his point was that quality at the least should be improved to some normative number. But Young was wise enough to sense a crucial element about corporate groups—fiats are tough to impose, and seemingly arbitrary numbers would be resisted even more. Instead, the thinking went—let each division decide its own metric, in light of what mattered to its customers, and then simply figure out how to improve that by ten times. The idea, Young said, was that superficial efforts cannot yield a ten-fold improvement, so it enforces rigor and out-of-the-box thinking, while leaving divisions in charge of their own affairs. Craig Walters's group, then, existed to do two things—collect the metrics and display them in a visible way for all to see the results (both for those who were improving, and those who weren't), and collect and share best practices widely.[15]

This model proved extraordinarily useful. Every department and function of the company—corporate parts inventory management, sales force automation, corporate communications, quick turnaround integrated circuits, and next-day order tracking—instituted productivity and quality improvements years in advance of competitors, at relatively insignificant expense compared to the value. How these groups chose their focus, where they got their guidance, and the results that they realized are huge parts of the secret sauce recipe.

Evidence all around the company indicated that Bill 'n' Dave's fundamental belief in people was well placed. Those closest to the problem learned and understood the issues, just as Packard had always insisted. For example, in the early 1960s, when Dave asked Bud Eldon to consider how best to coordinate orders with shipments as HP prepared to buy the sales reps, Eldon concocted a bold plan to try to integrate not only order processing but inventory control and production scheduling—something not done anywhere at the time for a decentralized set of operations.

Eldon, who seldom asked permission but on occasion begged forgiveness, lured Matt Schmutz back to HP from a short venture as a stockbroker to supervise the data center. Eldon hired Les Oliver to build the sales office system, Peter Brink from Microwave to design the production control system, Bob Puette to build the inventory control system, and Dick Hackborn from Paul Stoft's group in Barney's centralized lab to define a unique order forecasting system. Eldon said,

> I hired Hackborn into my group to keep him from leaving HP to get a PhD degree in Operations Research at Stanford (my department paid his tuition, as well as his part-time salary); I asked him to develop an HP comprehensive forecasting system, to tie into my order processing system.[16]

Alas, the system was ahead of its time. These expensive and strange new tools (mainframe computers and quite sophisticated software for the day) caused a negative reaction with many managers and staff in the newly acquired sales offices and the remote operating divisions. One of the first of many such reactions to centralized efforts in Palo Alto, it would hardly be the last. When Noel Eldred waffled, and Noel Porter allowed remote divisions to choose their own degree of compliance, Eldon moved over to Bagley's division to manage the facility move to the Santa Clara site, and the experiment continued at a much more modest rate.

A decade later, the requirement had become impossible to ignore—HP had fragmented to more than twenty manufacturing sites and over a hundred sales centers, while the new product families that HP built required integrated shipments from several divisions for a customer's order to be filled. This time, several Palo Alto managers who had worked on the first system decided to re-tackle the issues of coordinating orders and shipments.

Led by Bay Area Electronic Data Processing (BAEDP)[17] manager Matt Schmutz, Bob Puette and Bill Johnson defined a bold and comprehensive order processing system dubbed Heart to symbolize its central value to HP. Needing European involvement, they got Dick Alberding to volunteer Geneva-based Hans Vogel to help. Vogel, fond of early histories of America, named his portion Cochise, after the famous Comanche Indian warrior.[18] Les Oliver, from the original team, did an international implementation to handle Asia and the rest of the world.

Comsys

Not long after Heart and Cochise were up and running, Rich Nielsen realized that HP headquarters was being inundated by magnetic tape mailings from each of the far-flung sales offices—more than one hundred sales offices in more than forty countries. The tapes were generated by HP minicomputers in the sales office; mailed tapes were reloaded onto headquarters HP minicomputers for downloading. Nielsen concocted an idea for electronic transfer of the data, using a long-distance connection over a phone line between the computers, thereby saving a lot of time and certainly a lot of mailing and tape costs. Asked if the solution was suggested by supervisors, or by Dave or Bill, he replied, "No, of course not. This was our problem, and it was our idea how to solve it." A classic HP contribution.[19]

Nielsen, a Stanford graduate in computer science, thought that a dial-up modem might work—at 1200 baud, it was outrageously slow by today's standards, but it did the trick. At first bedeviled by a series of problems, he persevered and worked out the kinks, eventually building a robust system that allowed both order transmission and e-mail to ride in piggyback fashion. *HP Measure* ran a story in April 1974, "Fast as a Speeding Electron . . . the Penny Post Rides Again." It described the communication system, Comsys, built by the Corporate Marketing Services Group.[20] In 1977, realizing that a corporate support group product offered sufficient value to take to market, the Computer Group launched it as the HP 2026, and *HP Measure* again ran a story, in June.[21] In November 1977, *HP Measure* published a story about the Information System architecture at HP, and in December 1978, another story ran, about the $20 million in savings that HP e-mail provided that year, on a framework of 130 HP 2026 minicomputers from 105 locations worldwide.[22] Finally, in 1986, a definitive *HP Journal* article outlined the HP Word capability of the corporation, documenting the complexity of this enterprise-level system.[23]

Here, Let Me Show You How . . .

An untold story within the HP 35 handheld calculator design team proved as significant for designers as Comsys was for operations. Bill Hewlett's little marvel inspired a host of instrumentation engineers in the early 1970s. The visible result was a total revamping of the company's product lines into equipment with keyboards, CRT displays, and embedded microcomputers that provided phenomenal new capability. Correlation functions, comparative results, and complex calculations became standard in nearly every product line. Competitors were caught mostly unaware, and they certainly lacked the investment wherewithal to compete broadly during this renaissance of electronic and scientific instrumentation.

In many respects, this was Hewlett's finest legacy. Instrumentation sales soared, from $500 million in orders in 1975 to $1.2 billion in 1979, a compounded average growth rate (CAGR) of 25 percent for all of the company's myriad voltmeters, spectrum analyzers, frequency counters, medical bedside monitors, and scopes. Computers—including the famed handheld calculators and peripherals—grew only slightly faster—from $350 million to slightly more than $1 billion in orders, which compounded at 31 percent per year. Instrumentation was now $200 million larger than the Computer segment, versus $150 million four years earlier. More important, HP held hegemony in the instrumentation marketplace as never before, and profits flowed accordingly.[24]

The hidden contribution was ASM design (algorithmic state machine design[25], an esoteric set of words describing a computer programming methodology). ASM design, although not taught as core curriculum in American universities in 1970, had been used to great advantage by Tom Osborne and Dave Cochran on the HP 9100A Desktop Calculator. Hewlett urged Barney Oliver to create a major product initiative to take ASM technology and apply it to HP's core business in scientific instrumentation. Chris Clare penned a small monograph about ASM design used by HP Labs designers:

The lessons I learned about how to design logic were valuable. The lab director and especially Tom Osborne said, "You seem to really understand this. See if you can put together an explanation of how this works and how the design technique works." So, I took it on as a project; it took six months full time. I wrote a textbook on how to design logic using these techniques. I worked with the people who did the *HP Journal,* and they helped put together a book, and then I went around for a year, training all the engineers in HP about logic design. All the things you wished you'd learned in school about logic design, but didn't, or maybe all of this stuff that you thought you learned, but here's a new way to look at it.[26]

HP published Clare's revised manuscript as an in-house document, which later became a McGraw-Hill book.[27]

Then he and Tom Whitney, the unassuming program manager for the HP 35, toured the corporation, talking to packed audiences of design engineers at every stop about these new computing marvels in a chip, and how to embed them into every instrument that the company produced. Clare signed up enthusiastically:

I did a one-week intense course. Engineers said they felt like they were at the end of a fire hose, just getting an incredible amount of information in a short period of time. The premise was that logic design is just a realization of an algorithm that you want to accomplish. You design the algorithm, and then you can implement it in an unlimited number of ways. The book was called *Algorithmic State Machines.* The idea was to design hardware as if it were software. The whole book was on how to represent your algorithm in such a way that you could directly translate it into hardware. It opened a lot of engineers' eyes to the fact that logic design wasn't a bag of tricks, but actually was a systematic design methodology. This was all prior to wide use of microprocessors, that interim stage between just hooking logic gates together in some manner rather than actually being systematic about it. Eventually the book got published by McGraw-Hill. It gave HP a huge lead over all the other instrument companies. It was a jump on what was being taught in schools at that time.[28]

The pair was an improbable duo for causing a design revolution. Whitney was a diffident, shy project leader, whereas Clare was a classic engineer. Each had, at best, modest speaking skills. But their topic excited staid HP designers. They began by focusing on the single-bit microcomputer chip and its unusual 4-bit width, 14-nibble serial word structure, and how the algorithmic design approach and this strange architecture yielded the classy HP 35. Demonstrating some unusually interesting examples, their palpable enthusiasm grew with questions, and they became, for engineers, pretty animated. They'd conclude by leaving copies of the book, a few microprocessors, and a promise to answer any later questions.[29] Learning how to program these new microprocessors gave HP designers some awesome digital design techniques that enabled HP to lead the shift of analog instrumentation to digital instrumentation, with much more accurate answers as well as smaller, lighter, more compact designs.

A Jump Start on the Competition

The Digital Revolution, as some called it, was jump-started for HP by the Santa Clara Division (formerly Frequency and Time) in three important ways. First, its products pioneered digital readouts—for example, the numeric Nixie tubes, as well as decade counter units, which became a basis for HP digital products. Second, it led the company in new technology adoption on two significant fronts. The algorithmic studies that led to the desktop calculator were first done by Al Bagley's team, giving Barney Oliver impetus when Tom Osborne walked in the door. The first silicon processing fabrication work within HP was done at the division, led by redoubtable Ed Hilton. Hilton's work, focused on commercially centric processes and appropriate design tools, was a counterpoint to HPA work in exotic materials and specialty devices. This work would be extended significantly by Merrill Brooksby for VLSI (very large scale integration), resulting in leadership tools equivalent to the best at Bell Labs and IBM, and far ahead of the commercial semiconductor vendors. Third, the next-bench syndrome spawned a fledgling effort in digital test tools led by creative Gary Gordon. This group pioneered a series of simple, incredibly useful probes and clips, and HP's first logic analyzer, the HP 5000A, which detected and displayed serial data bitstreams.[30]

Ironically, the Oscilloscope Division, long the doormat of the Instrument Group (and perennially the lowest in profit level of the entire corporation), would also become a vital contributor to the instrument renaissance. First, the electrostatic cathode ray tube (CRT) would transform numeric displays into alphanumeric and richer, two-dimensional plots. Second, their designers invented multi-channel signal capturing systems to watch the proliferation of signals coming from the new integrated circuits. The resultant set of products, known as logic analyzers, became the design tools of choice for ASM design techniques.[31]

Logic analyzers came in several flavors—timing analyzers, most useful with random logic designs and for designers who thought conventionally in the time domain; parallel state analyzers, which captured and displayed parallel signal logic state flow as Chris Clare's ASM book described; and serial state analyzers, which were most useful for serial data ports, such as the ASCII busses by which most peripherals interfaced with computers. This latter group today is known as network analyzers and network protocol analyzers, and the first two, often combined in one product, are simply called logic analyzers. Logic analyzers would be singled out by a large reader poll for *Electronic Design* in 2001 as one of the fifty top electronic products of the 20th century, alongside television, AM and FM radio, CDs, cellular telephones, and personal computers. Hewlett's oscillator was also cited, along with the HP 35.[32]

ICs, ASM technology, and CRT graphics, coupled with new tools that facilitated ASM designers, transformed the instrument business and allowed HP to gain market share at the expense of its historic competitors in this arena. Nonetheless, the Instrument Group could not, as Hewlett forecast, "burn out the ball bearings in the cash register" as the HP 35 had. Virtually all of a modest market is still modest.[33]

Leitmotif

MAY 17, 2004, NEW YORK CITY: From a *BusinessWeek* cover story on industrial design: Management consulting companies (e.g., McKinsey, Boston Consulting, and Bain) tend to look at the corporate world through a business-school prism. By contrast, IDEO advises clients . . . about the consumer world through the eyes of anthropologists, graphic designers, engineers, and psychologists. Frog Design won fame for its design of the acclaimed portable Apple IIc in 1982, Sun's SPARCstations in 1986, and the NeXT cube in 1987. IDEO, a merger between David Kelley Design, which created Apple Computer's first mouse in 1982, and ID Two, which designed the first laptop computer in the same year . . . has designed hundreds of products and won more design awards over the past decade than any other firm. Once best known for designing user-friendly computers, PDAs, and other high-tech products, by showing global corporations how to change their organizations to focus on the consumer, IDEO is now a rival to the traditional purveyors of corporate advice: the management consulting companies.[34]

AUGUST 23, 1961, SAN FRANCISCO, CALIFORNIA: The 3rd Annual Industrial Design Award Program gave an Award of Excellence to Hewlett-Packard "in recognition of outstanding achievement in industrial design for its novel electronic enclosure system." Carl J. Clement Jr., director of the program, was thrilled. Design awards are one thing—consumer sales success is the goal. And sophisticated industrial design has become *de rigueur* for the computer industry. Unwittingly, HP was a pioneer here as well, starting with the Clement Cabinet, introduced at the March 1961 IRE show, cited by IDA, and then in 1962 for a *Fortune* magazine award. Packard said, "Our products had an elegance and finish which will be hard to duplicate. Carl Clement's new cabinet system was the hit of the show. It was considered by many to be the most impressive contribution to the packaging of electronic instrumentation that has ever been made."[35]

Clement would have an enduring influence, not only at HP but on the computing world. Clement Designlabs, established in 1970, responded to a request for a design of the "Replacement for the Pad and Pencil" issued by Alan Kay's team using Doug Engelbart's prototype as the design metaphor. The XeroxPARC Alto would become the most important single design precursor for personal computing. Clement's winning five-page design specification drafted for Bill English at XeroxPARC on June 29, 1972, bid a mere $4,340 for Phase 1. Clement's company produced all two thousand Altos, one of which graces the Smithsonian Institution's permanent collection today, along with the predecessor mouse for IDEO's design,[36] yet the common mythology is that none of it profited Xerox shareholders.[37]

XeroxPARC anthologies, written by computer scientists, tend to focus on the memory space, the CPU architecture, and the bit-mapped pixel display, taking the unusually attractive package for granted, just as did HP chroniclers with the HP 9100A CRT display.

One passage in *Dealers of Lightning* gives insight to the design:

> There was the marvelous sleekness of its engineering: Alto was like a fine timepiece somehow assembled from pieces of stray hardware lying around the lab. The display monitors were appropriated from POLOS, its specially ordered video display terminals still sitting in boxes. In almost every respect the Alto design was so compact and uncomplicated that, while prototypes were still scarce, engineers desperate to get one were invited to come into the lab and assemble their own.[38]

The Alto introduced two new terms—*GUI* (graphic user interface), pronounced gooey, and *WYSIWYG* (what you see is what you get), pronounced wiz-e-wig. GUI's quickly replaced text-based screen editors, putting a little picture or icon on a screen to represent a document. GUIs transformed not only the appearance of a computer screen but its ease of use and understanding. WYSIWYG referred to the important (and difficult) notion of printing a page that looked identical to the screen.

Analogous to the HP voltmeter saga, the question facing Xerox was simple: "Where does all the paper go?" The tale usually revolves around personalities and the missed opportunity: PARC invented Ethernet and the laser printer, and turned Alan Kay's Dynabook into a personal computer, yet none of it profited Xerox shareholders. Much bad press for innovative research labs in fact stems from the erratic and spotty performance of PARC for its parent.[39] But that criticism misses two points. The first is "Why did they do what they did?" The second is "How did they do what they did?" Only after those two questions are answered is it even relevant to ask what was done later with the contributions.

PARC's secret sauce revolved around a "why" question. Xerox rented copy machines for a nominal sum, selling copies at a nickel per page. Annually, the Xerox forecasts for how much paper would be sold were low. The amount of paper being sold just grew and grew. Where on earth were all the copies going? PARC hired a wide range of talent to figure it out. Thus the credentials of Lucy Suchman, Stuart Card, Eleanor Wynn, David

Thornburg, and Mark Stefik differed greatly from those of John White and Stig Hagstrom, let alone Alan Kay, Butler Lampson, and Adele Goldberg. Most of these names are missing in the standard PARC anthologies, but each mattered for the PARC-driven paradigm shifts.[40] The remarkable fact was that PARC leadership included industrial design, cultural anthropology, sociology, and fine arts backgrounds in the mix. And they figured out where the paper went, from desk to desk, from desk to file drawer, and significantly, from office to office. These findings led to key redefinitions of how to author, store, and distribute documents—ironically, they have not slowed the flow of paper: the paperless office remains elusive. At a 2009 conference, one wag observed that the "paperless office will happen about the same time as the paperless bathroom."[41] These findings well served CEO Peter McColough's fervent hope and desire that Xerox define, design, and build "the architecture of information."[42] Indeed, the Alto—with its GUI, WYSIWYG, sleek design, and compact capability—would transform both computing and office work forever, with an R&D investment less than 2 percent that of the cumulative leading computer companies.[43]

Industrial design, still novel when PARC instilled it, was nascent in 1951 when Carl Clement joined HP. Few schools taught it, and fewer companies acknowledged its value. Frank Lloyd Wright's bold architecture and Henry Dreyfuss's stylish designs for everything from locomotives to telephones inspired a group of budding designers, including Charles and Ray Eames and Eliel Saarinen's son Eero. The Eames duo and young Saarinen won the 1940 Museum of Modern Art competition for a sculpted chair design; Eero won the prestigious design competition for the magnificent St. Louis arch in 1947. When Raymond Loewy designed the elegant 1953 Studebaker Starliner coupe, the discipline thrived. Carl Clement, a radar technician during World War II, was fortunate during this era to be a student at the University of Washington with its pioneering industrial design group. Taken by the power of design, he took a job at HP, but they really didn't know what to do with him, so he "worked as a design draftsman by day, and did the industrial design work at night."[44]

HP had three hundred employees when Clement started designing the wraparound cabinet and bezel that housed some of the equipment in the famous HP product picture—everything made by the company—

that graced the 1959 *Annual Report,* as well as Packard's autobiography. The picture showed 373 products, with very little similarity in packaging. There were wooden boxes, metal transit cases, *zero* cans, and eight different sizes of wrap-around cabinets with distinctive bezels, the result of Clement's first attempt to create a common product identity. In 1957, Packard, enraged by the disastrous HP 150 oscilloscope fiasco, made worse by a nearly impenetrable cabinet design, asked for a new cabinet to facilitate easier service. While he was at it, he asked Clement to give the company's products "a more uniform look." Clement's boss, Barney Oliver, did not support the new design, however. He and Ralph Lee stopped Clement and developed their own answer, a clamshell one-hinge kludge. At a review, Hewlett asked Clement to comment on the design. Clement, saying nothing, rolled in a cart with a Tektronix Model 545 on it, produced a dime from his pocket, and demonstrated how the covers could be taken down in ten seconds, providing access to the entire circuitry. Hewlett voted instantly for Clement's proposal; Packard privately rebuked the officers for stifling creativity.[45]

Clement's penchant for elegant design was reflected in HP industrial design and human factors engineering for decades. Alan Inhelder became group manager when Clement departed; Inhelder led a design team fourteen years later for a revised cabinet to meet stricter environmental constraints.[46] Inhelder, who also designed the sophisticated triple-stack keyboard layout of the first programmable handheld calculator, the HP 65,[47] had a simple goal: "bringing coherence to design elements such as color schemes, human factors, and enclosure form as some 24 HP divisions independently design their own products."[48] Tom Lauhon, responsible for building sites, logos, and signage, had another design group at Corporate as well, led by Jack Magri.

Both Inhelder and Lauhon showed early interest in digitized typography, abetted through their Stanford connections. XeroxPARC designers had invented the document metaphor—with file and folder icons—but the world at large didn't yet know about it. Lauhon met a reclusive European, Jan Molenkamp, at Stanford, who was teaching typography to a youthful David Kelley. Molenkamp had first come to America for a degree at Yale University; after graduation he returned to Europe via the Yale typography lab in Basel, Switzerland, funded by IBM, AT&T, and RCA, all of whom saw promise in digital printing and digital font design. After a short stint there, Molenkamp migrated to Stanford. At HP, Lauhon encouraged Magri to fund Molenkamp for three years in the early 1980s to create a small group to build a type library, which was a host of complete digital character sets for a wide range of typefaces.[49] The work, scarcely appreciated at HP corporate headquarters, was nurtured by Jim Hall, the R&D manager at HP's Boise Division. Begun in response to issues raised by EPOC Laser Printer customers, the solution would prove vital in differentiating the as yet unanticipated low-cost LaserJet family.

JUNE 1, 1990, GREAT FALLS, VIRGINIA: For the second time in two years, HP graphics artist and user interface designer (and leader of HP's Corporate Engineering Industrial Design team) Barry Mathis got a letter from the Industrial Designers Society of America. This one opened, "It is with great pleasure that the jurors bestow the 1990 Gold IDEA to the HP Visual User Environment . . . with over 535 products, VUE 2.0 stood out." The three-dimensional elements of VUE—called Motif—had won the year before, not long after the design swept the OSF Graphical User Interface (GUI) competition against forty-two other entries.[50] *BYTE* magazine also selected Motif as its User Interface Software of the Year in 1990. Once again, HP had solid reason to be proud of the industrial design and human factors heritage begun forty years earlier. When Microsoft later embedded the "New Wave look-and-feel" of the Motif design widgets into Windows—Windows 3.1—it gave them near parity with Apple's MacIntosh GUI, and ignited a patent suit filed by Apple against Microsoft and HP over intellectual property rights for industrial design.[51] To many observers, it was a laughable suit—the common Silicon Valley view was that Apple itself had stolen the Xerox PARC GUI design shamelessly; to sue others for building an open systems software design tool was ludicrous. In a fast-track decision, the judicial system agreed with HP and Microsoft that the suit was groundless, and the suit was tossed out.

SEPTEMBER, 1998, PALO ALTO, CALIFORNIA: When Agilent was being divested from HP, a joint committee for intellectual property met yet again to resolve patent ownership for the two companies. One patent remained at issue: number 4,479,197, issued October 23, 1984, to George Haag, Doug Fogg, Gordon Greenley, Steve Shepard, and Duncan Terry at HP's Colorado Springs Division, which described a "pull-down stack" whereby a small window on a display screen could be "opened" by a cursor to reveal a list of multiple choices (for example, countries and states). This patent, of fundamental importance to all computer screen application design today, had been HP's "most valuable" patent for cross-licensing revenue over the previous decade. Nonetheless, because it had been created for logic analyzers long before personal computers were popularized, the patent was given to Agilent.[52]

Industrial design, psychology, cultural anthropology, the fine arts—and a healthy mix of "not invented here" coupled with user need—HP designers have had an impact on HP products and the computing world in ways scarcely realized or acknowledged. Not a bad legacy for a radar technician and draftsman. Quite an imprimatur—*leitmotif*.

Honors Co-Operative Learning

The Stanford Honors Co-Op program, created by Hewlett and Terman, enabled local engineers from a dozen Silicon Valley companies to pursue advanced degrees at company expense, on company time. Initially these students came to the Stanford campus to be in the classroom with regular on-campus students, which was acceptable when the program was small. But as demand for the program grew, it became necessary to consider alternatives that would not require all co-op students taking a course to attend lectures on campus. This requirement led, in the late 1960s, to the creation of a closed circuit TV network at Stanford that could connect the live, on-campus classroom with access points in special rooms at each participating company. This solution worked well for a time, but it was only available to companies within a fifty-mile radius of the Stanford campus, that being the limit on closed circuit TV broadcasting allowed by the Federal Communications Commission. There then arose a problem of how to solve the continuing educational needs of Honors Co-Op students whose work locations were outside the fifty-mile broadcast limit. Jim Gibbons, later to become dean of the Stanford School of Engineering, conceived of a new approach to distance learning that was compatible with the existing closed circuit TV approach but not limited by the broadcast requirements of the FCC. Gibbons described its evolution as follows:

I was serving on the Nixon Science Advisory Panel in 1972. We were studying, among other things, the impact of television on education. During World War II, several hundred experiments had been funded either by the Ford Foundation or the U.S. Department of Education to study the potential of television as an alternative to classroom education. These experiments covered the full width and breadth of education from Kindergarten through Baccalaureate, and every subject from fine arts to mathematics and science. The overall result of these experiments was that, as far as student learning was concerned, there was no significant difference between a live classroom and its televised equivalent. This result had a predictable effect: Those who supported televised education said, "See, it's no worse than a classroom and it can be less expensive. So we ought to do much more of our education with TV." The position taken by those supporting education in a live classroom was just the opposite: "See, it's no better, and we know the kids better, so let's stay with what we have." So nothing ever happened. I remember getting on the plane after many months of reviewing this data, thinking that, if you use technology correctly, you should get better results, not just equivalent results. So that starts you down the path of wondering what is wrong with a classroom that you could hope to improve with television. And eventually you realize that, truth be told, a conventional classroom is not necessarily a good learning environment. So rather than use television to replicate the classroom experience, we should use it to improve the learning environment in a way that is difficult in a normal classroom situation.[53]

Gibbons experimented with a model in which videotapes of the live classroom lectures would be provided to small groups of remote students who would be assisted by a mentor as they watched the tape. The mentor was not to be the equivalent of a faculty member but rather was to help the students as they watched the faculty member on the video. Gibbons sought mentors from the engineering staff of the companies where the students were employed. The mentor perhaps had experience in the field, or might have had a similar course earlier in his or her career and now wanted to review the material. Gibbons said,

We created a very successful learning environment by allowing any student to ask any question he or she had at any time. When questions arise, the mentor stops the tape, and the group works on the question until they have it resolved to everyone's satisfaction. Most of the time the students can answer the questions themselves. The mentor is supposed to help only if the students cannot figure it out themselves. If the mentor does not know the answer either, he gets in touch with the faculty member who gave the lecture, saying, "Look, we've got this problem and my group can't solve it." But by the time he calls, the question he is asking the faculty member is not usually the same question that led to stopping the video in the first place, because the group has reformulated the question into a better and most often deeper one. So, we created what is now called a collaborative learning environment, and we proved that students learn significantly better in that situation than they do in a live classroom, at least for the sorts of material we were providing.[54]

Gibbons himself taught this way for many years. His ready answer to a mentor, wherever the mentor might be (in the United States or not) was to say he'd call back in a couple of hours with recommendations of other ways to look at the question, other sources to read, and some additional problems to work. "In other words, my remote classes used my knowledge of the field better than my on-campus classes did because of the way they engaged the materials."

Thinking back to the time he thought of this scheme, Gibbons said,

I wrote up this idea for Nixon's science advisor. We called it "Tutored Video Instruction," though "Facilitated Video Instruction" would have been a better term. In any case the idea would most likely still be buried in the archives of the White House, except that [HP CEO] John Young called [EE chairman] John Linvill and said, "We're getting ready to move a division up to Santa Rosa and we are hiring young engineers for that group. We'd like to offer them an opportunity to keep their education up to speed with master degree-level courses from Stanford, but Santa Rosa is outside the radius of the broadcast license." John Linvill's response was immediate. He said, "Well, Jim Gibbons has this new idea he calls Tutored Video Instruction, if you would like to try it." So the first application of TVI was for HP Honors Co-Op Students who were now living and working in Santa Rosa, seventeen of them.

Gibbons found tutors at the HP Santa Rosa site. They had to have taken the course in the last two years from the same faculty member now teaching it, and made an A in the course. "I ran out of those tutors pretty quickly; then I had some MIT grads." Gibbons soon ran out of those as well, and then he hired a guy from Purdue, who couldn't get into the MIT or Stanford graduate program because of his GPA at Purdue, but he had done well in the course at HP as a TVI student.

I thought, "OK, let's see how he can perform as a tutor. And the result was: best tutor ever for that course! Why? Because when someone in the class would ask a question, the tutor remembered having some of the same questions himself, and he'd say, "Oh yes, I understand that question. I had it myself when I took this course." Whereas, these sharp guys from Stanford and MIT would say, "Well what's the problem here?" From that experience we learned an enormous amount about how this system works.

Gibbons went to great lengths to protect the experiment—same homework for all, sent back to Stanford to be graded by the same graders; every exam was proctored on-campus, "because I knew if they did well, my faculty colleagues might say, 'Well, they're up there cheating on the exams.'" After two quarters, they had a lot of data: The HP employees at Santa Rosa outperformed the on-campus kids hands down! It wasn't even close. And the HP TVI students also outperformed the HP students in other locations taking the course by closed circuit TV. Of significance, those same students who were partway through their master's degree had been lost in the crowd when studying with live television.

The HP Santa Rosa team then proposed another test of the system to Gibbons, saying,

If you really want to do an unusual experiment, we've got a couple of people here who don't have an undergraduate degree from anywhere. They left high school, joined the Navy, learned electronics on shipboard, came back and did a couple of things here and there at some community colleges. But over time they have become fabulous bench engineers. If we could put some academic underpinnings underneath them, we'd be doing something really great.

Gibbons went for the bait, noting that at Stanford you don't need a bachelor's degree to sign up for a master's degree. To his and HP's delight, it worked. He said,

The only college degree these students have in this world, as far as I know, is a master's degree in electrical engineering from Stanford University. Their performance was half A's and half B's, which is exactly the Stanford on-campus average. Every single HP TVI student performed at or above the campus average, while those studying from the closed circuit system were somewhat below the campus grade point average. Barney Oliver got excited, saying, "Jim, this is fabulous. We can locate a plant anywhere we want and not be outside the radius of the Stanford education system."[55]

Jim Barnes, R&D manager for a nascent division at Boise, signed up. Barnes would use the program extensively to recruit new graduate engineers to the remote Rocky Mountain town, saying, "By the way, we have a Stanford master's degree that we're offering if you can qualify." This was magical in the late 1970s—you could earn a Bay Area salary, live in a relatively low-cost, semi-rural environment, and gain a prestigious graduate degree from Stanford if you qualified to enroll. The word spread quickly—Guadalajara, Tokyo, Grenoble—everywhere Hewlett Packard had an R&D lab. Gibbons said,

I've got a wonderful chart showing where Stanford master degrees are being earned by people around the globe. Now think about this system. You put together the students. These lectures are Stanford lectures. They're in English. But you're in Tokyo, Japan; the language is Japanese, right? The mentor is on the HP staff. He's an engineer, and he is Japanese. He knows the course broadly, and that's all he needs, because he's going to call the faculty member if he's got a problem. But in Japan, when the students stop the tape for these discussions, they're in whatever language you want. So they're in Japanese. Or if the course is being offered in Grenoble, the discussions are in French. So a lot is happening here. The material is being delivered in English. You're learning from lectures in the English language, which is improving your grasp of English. And you're stopping it all the time to ask questions, all in your native language. Barney's first reaction was "We can put a plant anywhere we want it." And the second was, "Why are we doing anything with live television? Why don't we do the local stuff this way?"[56]

The key was that the TVI students did significantly better than their on-campus counterparts. Some students were still studying from live television. It was a great experiment, because there were classroom students, HP live TV students, and HP remote videotape students. The experiment ran for eight years. Astonishingly, every single quarter for eight years, the Tutored Video Instruction students outperformed the on-campus students as well as the live TV students.

[The difference in performance] was significant. Over this longitudinal experiment, the average score of all TVI students for their master's degree was six A's for every four B's. The average on campus is six B's for every four A's. That's a huge swing. The academic credentials of these on-campus students were significantly better than the academic credentials of the TVI guys, because they're selected that way. This was the introduction of collaborative learning. Gibbons and his colleagues created an intellectual community out of these students, with their mentor, allowing them to learn at their pace, repeat what they did not understand, and so on. Now the system has propagated around the globe for engineering education broadly. It may never have happened without HP making this move. Now you've got engineers everywhere who have the same basic education. This is Hewlett's point. He said, "All of our engineers have to learn to communicate with each other across their language barriers. But they've got the same quality of education that we all understand. So, they can talk to each other technically."[57]

The actual impact went deeper than that. HP engineering leadership noted that American engineers who traveled to the Bristol, England, lab; the Hachioji, Japan, lab; or the Barcelona, Spain, lab found colleagues that used the same vocabulary, studied from the same books, and had the same professors—the resultant shared skill set greatly facilitated joint engineering efforts. The outcome was especially impressive to young engineers being recruited by the company. In remote places such as Guadalajara, Bangalore, Penang, Karlsruhe, Grenoble, and Bristol, not to mention U.S. locales in Oregon or New Hampshire, the program gave young engineers a window to one of the finest research universities of the world without leaving home. The self-effacing Gibbons said, "We never really did publicize our learning experiments broadly. We wrote one paper about it for *Science*. And, you know, people are surprised usually."[58] An HP audit of the program in 1982 revealed that it was one of only a few truly differentiating contributions for keeping HP designers current. That was not surprising, because the program had been tailored expressly for HP needs in far-flung places where advanced university work was sparse—this was an early extremely powerful e-learning experience. The bigger impact, over time, was that HP engineers could combine on virtual teams—linked by teleconference and Comsys—with efficient shared skills.

Lingua Franca

All of these stories—one common parts-numbering system; Dick Anderson and semiconductor quality; Heart, Cochise, and Comsys backbone; the Corporate Executive Training program; industrial design and the Clement Cabinet; Motif and a 3-D look-and-feel; Clare and Algorithmic State Machines—have common themes. Each resulted from leadership close to the problem; each was unique for its day by comparison with other companies in HP's sphere; and each provided a unifying vocabulary for the increasingly far-flung corporation.

The logical next extension of the Heart system, once Comsys was in place, was to redistribute the answers to the supplying divisions. By 1974, a division manager in, say, Colorado Springs would have a report, every single business day, of sales of the division products the prior day, sorted by office around the globe, with the quoted price, the customer name, and the expected shipment date. Not unlike the FedEx idea two decades later, orders from the world were collected overnight in Palo Alto, aggregated and then disaggregated and sent in logical packets to the myriad worldwide operation centers that designed, produced, and shipped the products. Talk about a revolution in knowledge! Every division manager now had a direct link to the salesperson who had just collected an order. The enterprising division managers had their marketing manager on the phone with the successful salespeople to discover the elements of the sale. Waiting for an annual meeting to learn the situation in the field became instantly obsolete; trying to query through the three or four layers of distributed field sales management to find out truth when a problem arose was no longer necessary.

The linchpin was the Bilzer Report, named for Maria Bilzer, the clerk who prepared the monthly summary report for more than twenty years, a consolidated paper document data repository. It contained the order dollars for every product line, sorted by sales region or country, by sales force, comparing actual orders to the forecast for the current month and for the year to date. This treasure trove showed up at every general manager's desk three days after month-end, starting in 1974 when the Heart system was first complete.[59] General managers would use the report with their staffs to analyze strengths and weaknesses in various regions of the world; the more competitive of them would map their respective sales versus other divisions of HP in the incessant divisional rivalries that naturally arose.

The Nilsson training program was corollary reinforcement—now executives from around the globe knew each other, or at least knew someone local who knew the right person. It was social networking thirty years ahead of its time, and the linked person had already taken the same courses in HP lore, history, style, and process. Bonds grew quickly, and learning time was truncated.[60] Efficiency and effectiveness dramatically improved. Then Hank Taylor, running the Palo Alto communications network, became enamored of satellite television and the possibilities of video-conferencing. HP already had a history with the innovative Stanford University Honors Co-Operative program of distance learning that augured well for the new, expensive technology. Taylor experimented for five years before he proposed a video-linked network and won acceptance for it from John Young and the executive committee. Roxanne Hiltz (*The Network Nation*) had already proclaimed HP's e-mail network to be the second-largest corporate communications network on the globe (1981); with these voice and video connections, it had arguably the most comprehensive network in the world, amazing for a company ranked sixtieth in revenues in American industry.[61]

A number of important efforts grew out of this networking effort. First, at the instigation of John Young, Corporate Engineering hosted a seventeen-site, twelve-hundred-person virtual meeting in April 1984, which included many members of the executive committee (Young, Morton, Doyle) as well as Bill Hewlett himself. Over the course of a four-hour meeting, more than two hundred dial-up questions and editorial comments flowed in, responding to the twenty presentations. A crucial finding: a topic could generate caustic commentary among a wide set of potential users, who had great fun with the topic until the division whose talents were being maligned would join in. Suddenly, the meeting took on a more professional tone, much as Internet chat rooms get policed today by the membership. As the group in the meeting grappled with one thorny topic, it became clear that no one had an answer. Over the next few days, a steady stream of suggestions and observations came in to Corporate Engineering, which reframed the problem dimensions, prompting a stronger effort for solution. As one member put it, "Until the meeting, I just assumed that this was being taken care of, and that my input was not of much value. It was a great synchronizing event to show us (a) that no solution exists; (b) how much it matters to the company; and (c) that my input might be able to help."[62]

The video linkage was not an insignificant project. It deployed on a K_{μ}-band satellite channel, with seven uplinks and three hundred downlinks. Any HP engineer in the world was within a two-hour plane ride of an uplink, so modest travel and time effort could in fact link two teams in a virtual face-to-face conversation, and any number of viewers could be invited into the conference as well (and they could participate via audio link). To be sure, even as today, some participants had to meet in the middle of the night; time zones still challenge synchronous "virtual meetings". The system cost $40 million to construct—wags called it "one aquarium"[63] in value. It gave HP a mechanism, albeit imperfect, to enhance conversations a decade before the world had the Internet on which to build easy e-mail links. Of course, Comsys gave HP its own HP InterNet already, with high usage by 1975; once Bert Raphael, Tony Fanning, and Mark Laubach finished building their computer teleconferencing and e-mail bridges on TCP/IP, tying together the UNIX community with the business community in 1985, HP's teams were linked solidly.[64]

Movers and Shakers . . . from the Design Lab

At Hewlett-Packard, the strong legacy was that projects got defined at the designer level, and strategies frequently evolved bottom-up. Bill Hewlett's curiosity, Don Hammond's work in quartz crystals, and Len Cutler's cesium beam and rubidium standards gave the world atomic clocks and precision parametric instruments for astronomers, oceanographers, and cartographers. Each of these folk, recognized with major scientific awards, has been exalted in HP history. But the myth says that it mostly stopped there—that once HP got into the computing business, it became a different place, driven by high-volume, consumer-like products, and the engineering acumen and recognition ebbed.

This change, seen as a destruction of the HP Way, especially disturbed old-timers. Bruce Wholey, enchanted with HP in 1946 when he came to Palo Alto to transfer a Navy lab microwave sweeper, enjoyed a thirty-nine-year productive career, providing leadership for microwave spectrum analyzers and also the Medical Group. Wholey, like many, was troubled by changes wrought by the computing business to the HP Way:

> I've come to believe that there isn't anybody who knows what the hell the HP Way is any more. They've all been there so little time that they don't know what it is, and there are no words that can tell you. The thing that really bugs me is a bunch of personnel people who tell you that this is the HP Way, and they've been there less than a year—they've got all these quotes—it's a bunch of bullshit.[65]

Wholey reacted to downsizing and restructuring that included key officers and contributors when Hewlett handed the CEO job to John Young in 1978: "They don't have the sensitivity to people they used to have. People have become numbers. That's a pretty sorrowful situation, and it goes all the way through the place. Overall, it's, 'Well, he's got to go. Let's get rid of him.'"[66]

Some metrics, such as membership in the National Academy of Engineering (down from sixteen to two in the past two decades) certainly support this chary view. Research VP Joel Birnbaum said it differently: "There used to be these two demi-gods. Now all we have are us twenty pygmies."[67]

On the other hand, newcomers were still able to define their own careers and to make a major impact on HP for years. To that end, it is worth considering the career impact of three scientist-engineer designers who joined HP well after the handheld calculator had redefined the company. Jim Serum, Neerja Raman, and George Craford were typical engineers who joined HP forty years after Bill and Dave started their partnership. In their accomplishments, they were anything but typical. Their stories are relevant today to both HP and Agilent. Jim Serum reported,

> When Hewlett and Packard got into the analytical chemistry field, they went looking for people who knew the business intimately from an application scientific

point of view. I wasn't interested in leaving the university, but when they finally got me down to Avondale and talked to me about setting up a laboratory, I loved the people and the camaraderie, and I decided to try it for a year. Almost exactly a year later, I was invited to come back to Cornell as an associate professor, and I turned it down very quickly. I was just immensely content at HP. It was an interesting self-analysis—with the opportunity to go to a first-class institution again, I turned it down. What was it about HP that was so compelling that I could turn down my career aspiration?

It was two things—the teamwork that was involved in problem solving, whether it be a customer problem, a research problem, or a business problem, was terribly exciting to me. When there was a problem, people worked on it as a team and solved it as a team. I didn't realize how important that was to me as a scientist and a professional. The other thing was that I have always been, even as a general manager, a scientist first and a businessman second, believing that if you understood the customer, matching the technology products to customer needs, your business would do well, and so I was never a number cruncher. I always worked very hard to understand the relationship between the products and the customer needs, and in the context of that, HP was doing world-class research and development in analytical tools that rivaled any research university in the country. Not only could I enjoy the people I was working with, I could be doing it with enough money to do what I needed to get done, working with world-class tools.[68]

Serum, named co-chair of HP's R&D council by Joel Birnbaum, led the company into biotechnology in the mid-1990s—today a major business for Agilent Technologies. Serum, very active in science education and technology development throughout his career, chaired the National Institute for Standards and Technology (NIST) review board 1997–2001. Today he serves as chairman of the NIST Visiting Committee for Advanced Technology, and he is a National Academy of Science National Associate.[69]

Neerja Raman, an analytical chemist, joined the Scientific Instruments Division (SID) in 1985 after stints in academia and at startups. Her perspective is instructive:

When I joined, I was the first Indian and one of two technical women. Everybody had an open mind; you were always judged by your work. SID was small, but I felt it had the stability of a larger company with HP behind it. At the same time, it was small enough that I felt that whatever I had to say would be heard by people who were going to be making the decisions. I was very technical, but so was everybody I dealt with. Even in marketing, you had to explain the analysis.[70]

The week after I joined, SID went on one of the abbreviated programs—work five days and get paid four. Even though I was new, and it impacted me directly, I thought that was a good thing. I could have been one of the first persons let go if it had been somewhere else. To me, that made a huge impact, HP really stood by its values. We're here and we'll grow the company. I didn't hear any complaints.[71]

Raman would stay at Hewlett-Packard until 2005, when she joined the Stanford faculty to pursue educational science programs for her native India. Significantly, in 1990, she transferred from SID to HP Labs, contributing heavily in imaging, graphics, and eventually the video communication tools known as HP Halo. Her impact was felt over twenty years—in Analytical, Peripherals, and Computing.

Slight and soft-spoken, the archetypical research scientist George Craford began his professional career as a research physicist at Monsanto Chemical Company. He advanced to the level of technical director of the Electronics Division before joining the Hewlett-Packard Company in 1979. He later became the chief technology officer at Philips Lumileds Lighting Company, spun off from Agilent in 2005. Craford's research has mainly focused on the development of visible light-emitting diodes (LEDs) using a variety of compound semiconductor materials. He first became known for the development of nitrogen-doped gallium arsenide phosphide (GaAsP) technology in the early 1970s, which became and remains one of the dominant commercial LED technologies. At Hewlett-Packard, Craford's group pioneered the development of aluminum indium gallium phosphide (AlInGaP) LEDs, as well as aluminum gallium arsenide (AlGaAs) and indium gallium nitride (InGaN) products. Each of these esoteric combinations yields a different, valuable light-emitting quality.

Craford, an IEEE Fellow and member of the National Academy of Engineering, received the IEEE Morris N. Liebmann Award, the Holonyak Award of the Optical Society of America, the Welker Award of the International Symposium on Compound Semiconductors, the Material Research

Society Medal, an IEEE Third Millennium Medal, the Electronics Division Award of the Electrochemical Society, and the Distinguished Alumni Award from the University of Illinois College of Engineering. In 2002, Craford received the National Medal of Technology from President Bush. His accomplishments, honors, and prestige are in Barney Oliver's league.

The Secret Sauce and the HP Way

HP was fortunate to have far-sighted, commonsense leadership. Remarkably, common sense in such situations is uncommon. And that is perhaps the chief characteristic of Hewlett and Packard and the company—their instincts for commonsense decision making, especially in longer-range strategic issues, set a pervasive tone for the company. Without it, people would not have risked, stretched, or taken on bold longer-term assignments. Fundamentally, the secret sauce boiled down to how best to empower what Packard called "enterprise." The example he often used was the low efficiency of collective farming in Russia and other controlled economies relative to the productivity of individual farmers, particularly in America. He concluded, "A company structured to maximize individual freedom, and the opportunity for reward identified with personal performance, will develop a high degree of enterprise among its people." He argued passionately that "the opportunity for the individual, for every individual, must be established and jealously guarded, the opportunity for the individual to benefit personally in proportion to his or her good work."[72]

Lucile Packard, Flora Hewlett, Bill Hewlett, and David Packard (from left) handing out Christmas profit-sharing checks—1947.

Courtesy of Agilent Technologies.

Dedication of the "HP Garage" as the "Birthplace of Silicon Valley"—1989.

Courtesy of Agilent Technologies.

Leadership for the first thirty years. The Executive Committee—1958: Barney Oliver, Frank Cavier, Noel Eldred, and Noel (Ed) Porter (from left).
Courtesy of Agilent Technologies.

373 products in the HP product line—1959.
Courtesy of Agilent Technologies.

Communications Test Equipment

The Audio-Video test products of the 1940s: 202D audio oscillator, 350 B attenuator, 400A AC voltmeter, 450A companion amplifier, 200C audio oscillator, 320A distortion meter (wood box) (from left).

Courtesy Marc Mislanghe; The HP Memory Project.

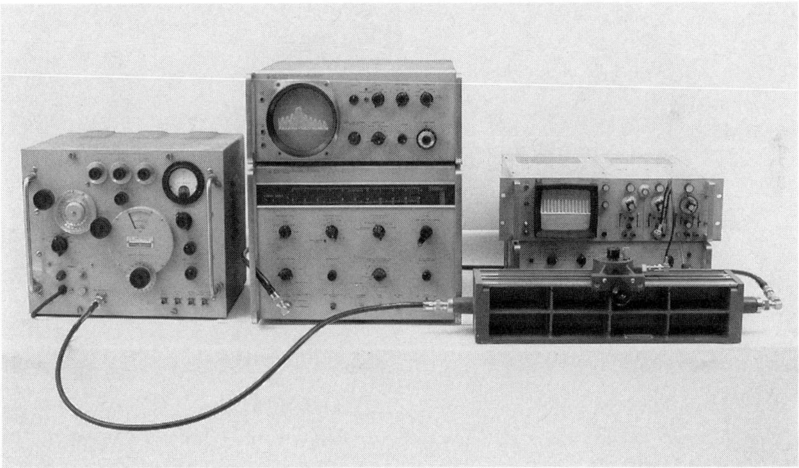

Microwave test equipment circa early 1960s: 616B signal generator, 8551A spectrum analyzer, 805C slotted line, 1200B oscilloscope (from left).

Courtesy Marc Mislanghe; The HP Memory Project.

Scientific Instrumentation

Nurse's twenty-four-bed station from the Medical Group—1972. Courtesy of Agilent Technologies.

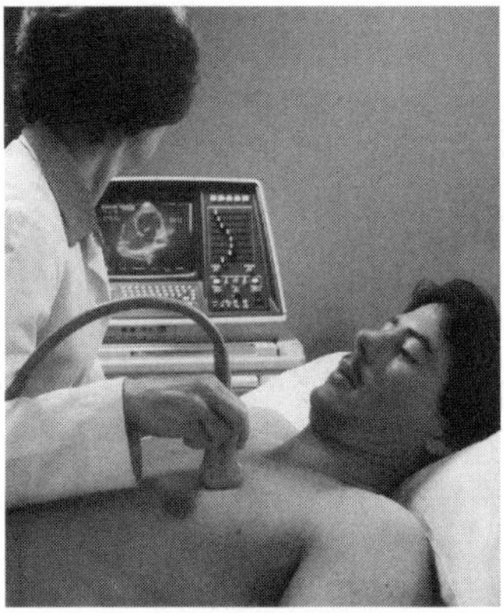

Ultra-sound imaging system—1982 HP Labs and the Medical Group. Courtesy of Agilent Technologies.

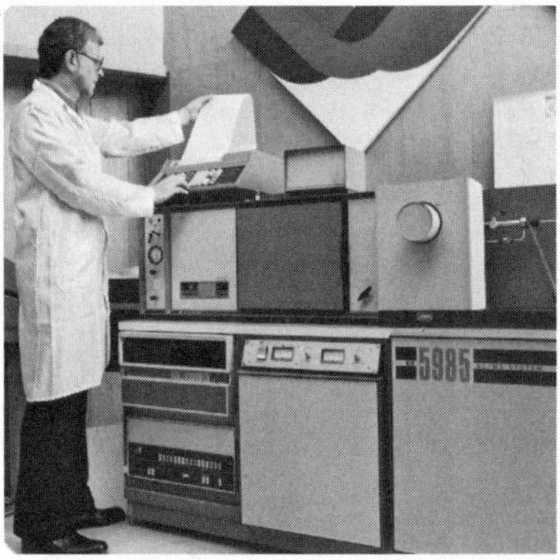

HP 5985 bench-top GC/MS—1982 Analytical Chemistry Group. Courtesy of Agilent Technologies.

Scientific Computation

The HP 2116 computer—1966: An instrumentation controller from HP Labs and Dymec Division.

Courtesy of Agilent Technologies.

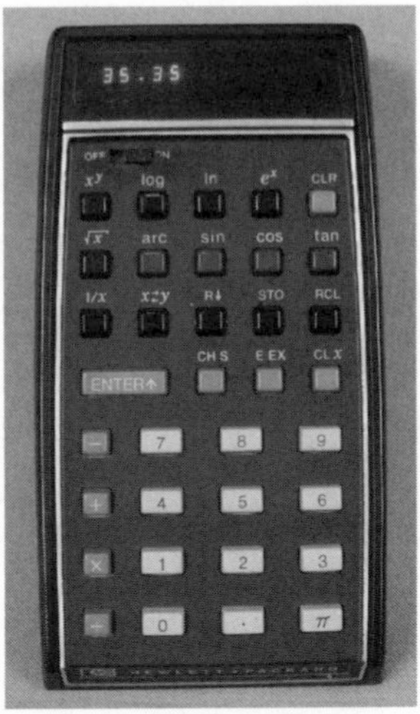

The HP 35 scientific calculator—1972: A handheld personal computer from HP Labs and Advanced Products Division (APD).

Courtesy of HP Computer Museum in Australia.

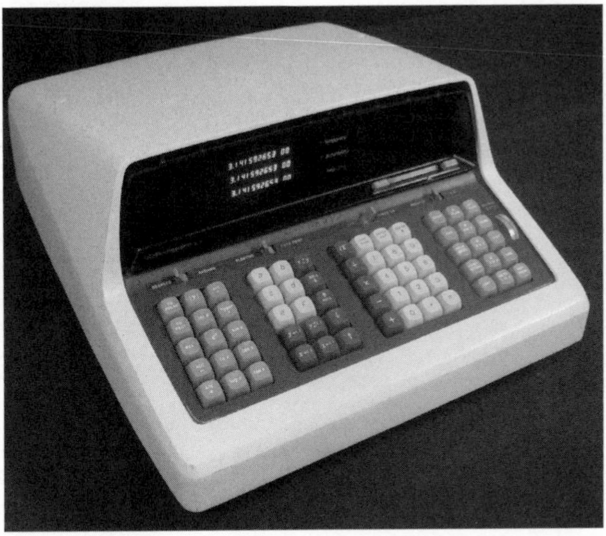

A new electronic calculator with computer-like capabilities—1968: HP 9100A from HP Labs and the Loveland Division.

Courtesy of HP Computer Museum in Australia.

Business Computation

HP 2640A intelligent terminal—1975.
Courtesy of HP Computer Museum in Australia.

HP 3000 business computer system—1972–1975.
Courtesy of HP Computer Museum in Australia.

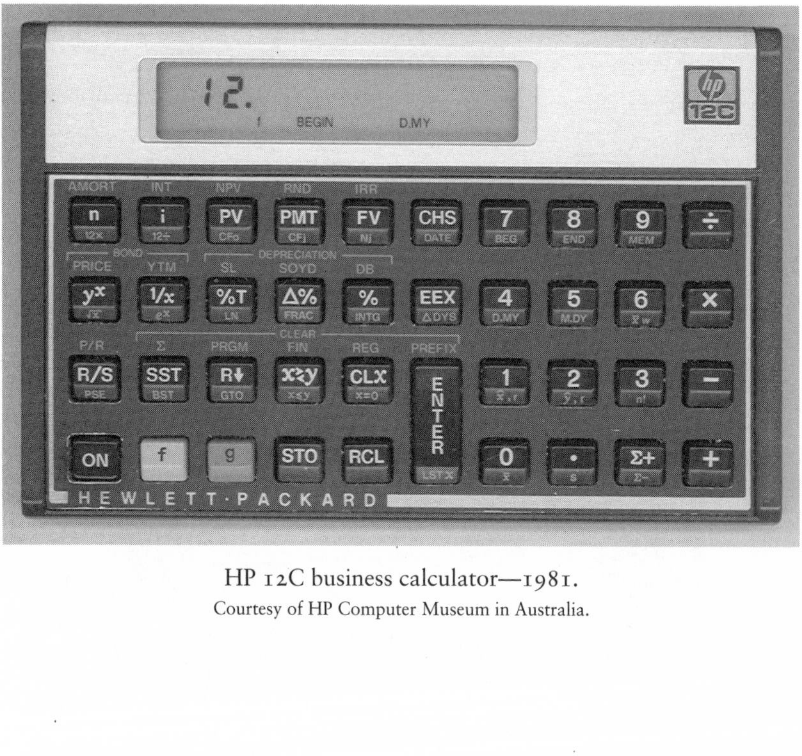

HP 12C business calculator—1981.
Courtesy of HP Computer Museum in Australia.

Key Products of the 1980s and 1990s

HP 9836A—1981, engineering workstation, $11,950.
Courtesy of HP Computer Museum in Australia.

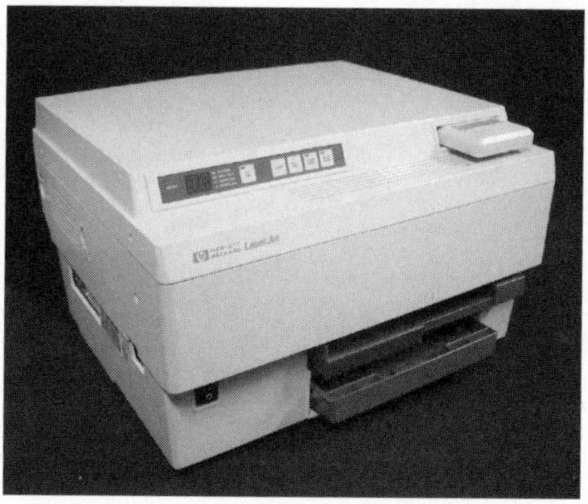

HP LaserJet—1984, $3,495.
Courtesy of HP Computer Museum in Australia.

Precision Architecture: HP-PA 8400—1986, the first Spectrum machine, $113,500.
Courtesy of the Computermuseum, Stuttgart, Germany.

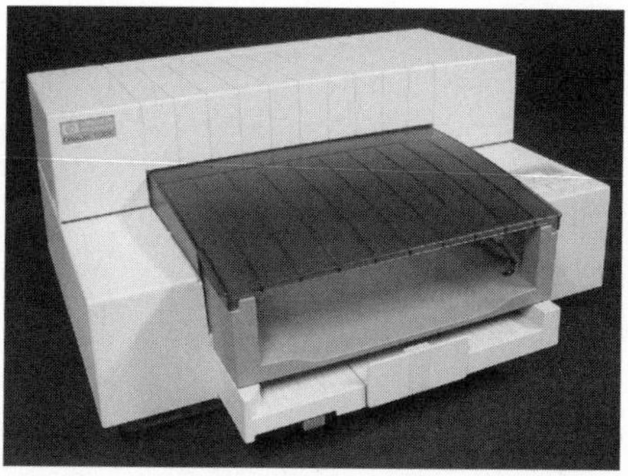

Finally . . . an InkJet That Works: DeskJet 500C—1992, black and white and color on plain paper, $995.
Courtesy of HP Computer Museum in Australia.

HP CEO Leadership

John Young,
1978–1992.
Courtesy of Agilent Technologies.

Lew Platt,
1992–1999.
Courtesy of Agilent Technologies Corporation.

Carly Fiorina,
1999–2005.
Courtesy of Carly Fiorina.

Mark Hurd,
2005–.
Courtesy of Hewlett-Packard Company.

Agilent CEO Leadership

Ned Barnholt,
1999–2005.
Courtesy of Agilent Technologies.

Bill Sullivan,
2005–.
Courtesy of Agilent Technologies.

HP Strategic Leadership

Paul Ely,
Computer Group.
Courtesy of Paul Ely.

Dick Hackborn,
Peripherals Group.
Courtesy of Agilent Technologies.

HP R&D Leadership

Barney Oliver,
National Academies—1959 Engineering, 1967 Science.
Courtesy of Agilent Technologies.

Joel Birnbaum,
National Academy of Engineering—1989.
Courtesy of Joel Birnbaum.

CHAPTER 9

Disruptive Forces

We thought the PC would amount to [sales of] a few hundred thousand units. None of us thought it had the power to restructure the entire computing industry and economy. [PC] microprocessors then were basically a sideline for us. They were not our core business. Very rarely do you foresee these kinds of things.

ANDY GROVE[1]

The Computer History Museum Silicon Engine Timeline,[2] an impressive list of daunting accomplishments, gives a clear picture of the inescapable fact that much time, multiple perspectives, and many people necessarily contribute to the creation of something as complex as our computer-based information age. Picking out one significant fact in this rich panoply is ludicrous, and yet people try to do just that. "Here, this is the turning point," they exclaim. For semiconductors, the product for which Silicon Valley was named, the key event cited is the Nobel Prize–winning work of Jack Kilby at Texas Instruments in 1958 for an integrated circuit. Because he died too young, Robert Noyce of Intel was not included in the prize, but his fundamental contribution of manufacturing processes to realize Kilby's idea was the engineering impetus for an explosion of device creativity in memory circuits and computing elements.

Paradigm-shifting changes would occur in these solid-state physics techniques. Some are well-known, but many other high-technology applications are not acknowledged, even if they are almost equally fundamental. On a gray afternoon in February 1963, one seemingly obscure event was reported in Malcolm McWhorter's first-year graduate electronic circuits class at Stanford University. McWhorter, a sonorous junior faculty member, allowed the class to be interrupted by two Honors Co-Op students from Sylvania Electronics, who outlined their findings of that morning. The students had successfully fabricated a gated flip-flop from six transistors, with no resistance elements, using the transistor-transistor logic (TTL) ideas of Fairchild Researchers R. H. Beeson and H. W. Ruegg, who had published in the already prestigious International Solid-State Circuits Conference (ISSCC) the year before. James Buie at neighboring Signetics already had filed for a patent application, but none of these researchers were yet aware of that fact. McWhorter led the class in analyzing the circuit—and voilà, it worked, both theoretically and in practice.[3] The resulting device became the storage cell for a "1" or a "0"—the most elemental forms of digital numbers. The world now had a practical memory cell and from it a new form of circuit design would emerge—digital, rather than analog.

Through the use of these concepts, solid-state memory became possible. It was eventually fast and cheap enough to compete with core memory, memory defined by switched electromagnetic fields using very small iron donuts or magnetic cores strung laboriously into threaded arrays after inventions of An Wang at Harvard and Jay Forrester at MIT.[4] Intel Corporation would spin out of Fairchild expressly to build "large memory ICs," by which was meant arrays comprising these gated or bi-stable flip-flops: "Silicon gate technology combined with a three-transistor per bit design allowed Intel to produce the i1103 1K DRAM in half the die area of competing products in 1970. At an unprecedented low price of one cent per bit, Intel aggressively pursued replacing magnetic core technology for computer main memory."[5] A dense, fast, inexpensive storage cell was crucial for digital electronics to emerge.

An equivalent dense and inexpensive controller was also needed. Fortuitously, Ted Hoff at Intel was able to cram all of the computational logic of a four-bit computer onto one chip. He and colleague Federico Faggin built the Intel 4004, done under contract for Japanese business calculator firm Busicom. Fortunately for Intel, Busicom declined to proceed, selling the rights back to Intel. The mantle passed from Fairchild device innovation to Intel manufacturing skill.

Ten-year veteran Jim Pettit was one of the first at HP to comprehend the dual opportunity of these critical innovations. Hired by Dick Anderson from HP Colorado Springs in January 1972, Pettit was briefed in his first Bay Area week by the brash team at Intel about their new 4004 microcomputer. Usually unflappable, Pettit, developer of HP's first four-channel oscilloscope and leader of the highly successful HP 183 oscilloscope for IBM performance measurements, was dazzled. Returning to his old haunts at Colorado Springs, he enthusiastically told Dick Cochran, Bruce Farly, Bill Farnbach, and Chuck House what he'd seen and what he thought it portended. Farnbach, with long experience designing HP sampling scopes, understood and shifted HP logic analyzers to synchronous sampling. This seemingly simple act enabled the Logic team to become the number one digital systems measurement leader, besting old nemesis Tektronix with a design tools shift destined to rewrite electronics and computing history.

Intel chips would lead that revolution. Gordon Moore had stated "Moore's Law" in 1965, working from Caltech professor Carver Mead's calculations. The Law predicted an astounding logarithmic factor of improvement—the number of devices per chip doubling very eighteen months—from Moore's standpoint, this seemed possible for three decades.[6] Moore and partner Robert Noyce impressed the industry with this bold prediction: no one imagined that it would really work that way, or if so, that it would work for as many years as it did.

The 4004 that excited Pettit was a primitive IC with only twenty-three hundred transistors. As Intel designers outlined the possibilities—that the next device would double the power, and the one after that would quadruple it—he grasped the potential impact on the computing world. He was one of very few at the time. Most designers used integrated circuits only as enhanced circuit design elements, still using analog design techniques.

Pettit had managed the fledgling Logic Analyzer team in Colorado Springs before heading west; when he left, the group was designing multi-channel scope-like tools with logical trigger circuits to enable a designer to see complex difficulties with asynchronous logic designs—for example, race conditions, switching transients, and jitter. Farnbach's inspired answer ignored switching issues, focusing only on the resultant signal after it had restabilized. This tactic gave a significant distinction between logic timing analyzers and logic state analyzers, a paradigm shift difficult for most experienced designers to accommodate, but one that students of Chris Clare's algorithmic design course could readily appreciate.[7]

Clare reported that Stanford professors didn't get it either. His course gave students

> a year or two lead on a way of thinking about things. . . . It was extremely well received by the students who felt they finally got it. They figured out how to design logic, compared to what was being taught in schools at that time. I did teach a class at Stanford . . . but my methods were too far astray from the classical terminology and way of doing things. The administrators of the EE department said, "It's a little bit too unconventional."[8]

Intel itself didn't know what it had. Dick Anderson's 1980 bombshell announcement that Japanese IC quality surpassed U.S. vendors angered Intel managers. But that was nothing compared to Intel angst when the Japanese turned memory chips into a commodity and ruined Intel's financial health. As Richard Tedlow described in a 1991 *Fortune* article:

> The company's top executives simply could not believe the growing evidence that they were being out-competed in a market they had created. Intel was the memory company, period. Its chips were in the best minicomputers. . . . Intel kept denying the cliff ahead until its profits went over the edge, plummeting from $198 million in 1984 to less than $2 million in 1985. "Welcome to the new Intel," Grove said in a speech not long afterward, to rally the troops behind the decision to exit memories. "Intel, the memory company, is dead," he explained, but there was another product on which it could stake its future: the microprocessor. Invented at Intel in 1971, it had spent the 1970s timing traffic lights and helping bacon packers slice their bacon into even strips. Not all that exciting . . . but once IBM chose Intel's microprocessor to be the chip at the heart of its PCs, demand began to explode. Even so, the shift from memory chips was brutally hard: In 1986, Intel fired 8,000 people and lost more than $180 million on $1.3 billion in sales, the only loss the company has ever posted.[9]

Eight years after Jim Pettit's insight, Don Estridge at a skunk works IBM operation in Boca Raton, Florida, selected the relatively prosaic Intel 8088 microcomputer chip (twenty-nine thousand devices) for the first IBM PC. Learning of this project from IBM CEO Frank Cary, IBM Research vice president Joel Birnbaum had been enraged that it was being done without his knowledge. A *BYTE* magazine history notes that

> Don Estridge and his team considered using the IBM 801 processor and its operating system developed at the IBM research laboratory in Yorktown Heights, NY. The 801 [from Birnbaum's lab] was at least an order of magnitude more powerful than the Intel 8088, and the operating system many years more advanced than the DOS operating system from Microsoft that was finally selected. [But] ruling out an in-house solution made the team's job much easier and may have avoided a delay in the schedule.[10]

. . .

AUGUST 12, 1981, NEW YORK CITY IBM Corporation today announced its smallest, lowest-priced computer system—the IBM Personal Computer. Designed for business, school and home, the easy-to-use system sells for as little as $1,565. It offers many advanced features and, with optional software, may use hundreds of popular application programs. . . . "This is the computer for just about everyone who has ever wanted a personal system at the office, on the university campus or at home," said C. B. (Buck) Rogers, Jr., IBM vice president, General Business Group. "Its performance, reliability and ease of use make it the most advanced, affordable personal computer in the marketplace." IBM has designed its Personal Computer for the first-time or advanced user, whether a business person in need of accounting help or a student preparing a term paper. An enhanced version of the popular Microsoft BASIC programming language and easily understood operation manuals are included with every system. They make it possible to begin using the computer within hours and to develop personalized programs quite easily.[11]

A Microsoft PC

Somewhat surprising for a man who had spent his career selling big iron, IBM VP Buck Rogers sounded enthusiastic about this new PC. But over at Intel, Andy Grove was not impressed. Six months later, in January 1982, Grove stood with founders Gordon Moore and Robert Noyce at Intel's annual management meeting, listing the top fifty products for Intel's microprocessor sales. The IBM PC didn't make the list. A year later, *Time* magazine named the PC "Man of the Year," yet it took two more years before failing memory chip profits forced Grove to realign Intel behind the microcomputer, and another two years to get revenue and profits back to normal. In other words, it took sixteen years for the company that created the key chip for the PC revolution to understand its importance. The growth in chip capability in those sixteen years—from the 4004 to the 80386—was staggering. The devices on one chip had grown a hundred-fold, from 2,300 to 275,000; clock speed had increased from 106 KHz to 16 MHz, one hundred fifty times. Moore's Law has held for more than thirty years, yielding a CPU chip with an amazing 1.72 billion devices by 2006.

Larry Ellison also "got it," describing it to an IDC conference in Napa, California, in April 1987, fifteen minutes before the scheduled OS/2 1.0 introduction by an IBM Personal Systems Division VP. Ellison's brilliant analysis: "The world thinks of it as an IBM PC, but in the year 2000, the world will realize that it is a Microsoft PC, for which IBM supplied the first compatible hardware." Computer companies—IBM, DEC, the remaining Dwarfs, Wang, HP, and Data General—were still dismissive. If Clayton Christiansen had thought to include it, the situation could have been one of the best case studies for his insightful book *The Innovator's Dilemma,* about how sometimes the simplest innovations become industry giant killers.[12]

The significance of the PC was largely ignored at HP as well. Bob Frankenberg labored to make the New Wave program for the PC the preferred user interface for HP business systems in 1988–1989, but HP overall did not embrace the PC as a fundamentally strategic element until 1995; even then debate was acrimonious. That year, Dick Hackborn observed for an HP Archives interview that two schools of thought emerged at HP. The conventional wisdom supported the tightly integrated enterprise computing model, while the other embraced open, piece-parts, tinker-toy, low-end computing, or more accurately, consumer electronics. At HP, only the Handheld Calculator group and the low-end printer divisions of HP's Peripherals Group really grasped the fundamental importance of applying a consumer electronics mentality to enterprise-level system components. More remarkably, these portions of HP were virtually alone among the world's computer companies to do so.

PCs were perhaps the most visible products of the disruptive forces seen in technology circles, but there was also evidence that the merging of the communications and computing paradigms was forever altering strategies, tactics, and structures on a global scale. Competitive pressures mounted and speed of response shortened; everyone at all levels of HP had to think about their jobs and about how to contribute ideas for improvement.

No Computer Scientists?

Disruptive thinking often starts in research universities. Two miles away from HP headquarters, the verdict was unexpected, but crystal clear. John Doyle listened in amazement. The Stanford Computer Integrated Systems (CIS) committee was adamant—no one at HP was deemed qualified to serve on a computer science architectural task force for Stanford University in early 1980. Doyle, a Stanford engineering graduate and by now vice president of Human Resources for HP, was quite proud of the computing contributions of the company, and he naturally assumed that the university appreciated the value and worth of the company's programs as well. Baffled, he inquired more deeply. After all, Stanford and Hewlett-Packard were practically synonymous terms in the Valley in 1980—Hewlett and Packard were the biggest benefactors of the university, the company was easily the largest on campus land, and Stanford alums were prominent throughout HP. Packard had been on the Stanford Board of Trustees for years, replaced just recently by HP's new CEO, John Young. Trustees, though, aren't on the leading edge of fundamental research. The Stanford group patiently told Doyle that HP had indeed been a stellar products company, especially in measurement instrumentation, but was absent completely in discussions concerning computer systems, Reverse Polish Notation notwithstanding. The Amigo failure wasn't even mentioned.[13]

The topic had to do with high-end computer performance, as it might be implemented in silicon chip designs. The world would later know the field as reduced instruction set computing (RISC) architecture. Stanford would become known as one of two leading protagonists of RISC chipsets. John Hennessy, selected as president of Stanford in 2002, would develop a version that competed with the cross-bay rival University of California at Berkeley and the chipset designed by Dave Patterson. Hennessy's chip would be manufactured by MIPS Inc., later bought by Silicon Graphics, and Patterson's chip would fuel the designs at Sun Microsystems.[14] All of these developments lay well in the future, however, as did the IBM PC. No one in this group considered the toy Intel or Motorola microprocessors; Doyle himself helped convince parochial Intel leaders to join CIS. For now, the buzz was all about John Cocke and his colleagues at IBM, known to be working on RISC ideas patterned after the architecture of the fabled Illiac IV at the University of Illinois two decades earlier.

Doyle met that day with John Young, and the two agreed that Stanford had a point. Young in particular was troubled by the quixotic manner of his old colleague, Paul Ely, and the dysfunctional strategy of his group. Every program grew in response to customer demand, the degree of commonality was next to none, and customers were getting tired of the inconsistency. Growth, although still strong, had slowed.

The company complexity continued: in the September-October 1980 *HP Measure,* the new "Company Organization Chart" was unveiled. It showed an Instrument Group under Executive Vice President Bill Terry, a Computer Group under Executive Vice President Paul Ely, and a potpourri grouping of the Analytical Group (three divisions led by Lew Platt), the Medical Group (four divisions headed by Dick Alberding), the Components Group (three divisions headed by Dave Weindorf), and Personal Computing Products (one division and two operations) all managed by Executive Vice President Dean Morton.

The Instrument Group had two subgroups—the Microwave and Communication Instruments Group with seven divisions reporting to General Manager Hal Edmondson, and eight Instrument Divisions, each titled by a geographical name, reporting to Bill Terry directly.

The Computer Group now consisted of four segments—the Technical Computer Group with five divisions, headed by Doug Chance; the Business Computer Group with four divisions, headed by Ed McCracken; the Computer Peripherals Group with four divisions, led by Dick Hackborn; and the Terminals Group with three divisions, headed by Bob Watson. In fact, the Instrument Group, astonishing as it might seem, was growing as fast as the Technical and Business Computer Groups combined. Worse for the Technical and Business Computer Groups, a myriad of midrange adversaries had arisen, nearly all with faster momentum than HP.

Young and Doyle decided to launch a search for a person who could change the direction of the Computer Group, which in itself was a challenge to imagine. They pondered where best to focus—on group management, systems development, or computer research. Given the strength of HP semiconductors, they decided to focus at the architecture level, much as Stanford was doing. That decision led them directly to Joel Birnbaum, the head of IBM's Computer Systems Research Lab in Poughkeepsie, New York. Birnbaum, Cocke's supervisor, was himself a keen researcher, and his team had stunned the computing world with surreptitious discussion about RISC performance the year before at the International Solid-State Circuits Conference.[15]

Birnbaum, forty-three at the time, was on the fast track at IBM. Working directly for Ralph Gomory, EVP of IBM Research, he was widely viewed as the heir apparent. Ambitious, articulate, and urbane, he had just remarried, to Eileen Shelle, a diva on the U.S. and European opera stage. With her, he was seen in New York, London, Milan, and Vienna.

When Frank Bacci (a corporate recruiter hired by HP) called, Birnbaum was not interested in the recruiter's story. He listened politely, but was dismissive of HP as a potential computer contestant. They didn't make the radar at IBM. Looking them up, he found that they were fourteenth in terms of revenue for U.S.-based computer vendors, something like twenty-fifth in the world. HP hardly seemed the place for the technical leader of the largest computer company on earth to go to advance his career.

The search team turned elsewhere. Over six months, they found five other promising candidates. None had nearly Birnbaum's stature in terms of appreciating the new architectural opportunity, even though most had racked up more years of managerial success. Doyle and Young urged the recruiter to try again for Birnbaum. Bacci placed one more call, and to his surprise, Joel agreed to come out to interview for a day with HP.

Anon, Birnbaum arrived, and met with Doyle and Young directly. He appreciated their earnest manner. Young and Doyle were of like mind that HP had very able designers and solid technology, but the current Computer Group leadership had been singularly unable to craft an overall program that integrated their several efforts. As Joel described RISC technology, they seemed uniformly enthusiastic that it could be the solution to their dilemma. After lunch, Joel was ushered in to see Barney Oliver, whose job, it seemed, was the one for which they were interviewing him. Joel was forewarned about this pugnacious old warrior. Telling two colleagues at IBM that he was going to interview at HP, John Cocke said, "He's going to give you the Barney Oliver interview." Joel said, "What the hell is that?" to which Cocke replied, "Get ready to take another PhD exam." Joel's rejoinder was "Bullshit. He's not going to give me any PhD exam." He walked in to meet a scowling Oliver, arms folded, with "a million gadgets all over the place. 'Sit down,' [Oliver] commanded in a Jehovah-like booming voice; then we go through about all the pleasantries that he could handle, which was maybe eleven seconds."[16]

Oliver proceeded to fire a set of questions at Joel. First, he brought out a large printed circuit board (the famous sixteen-layer inductive memory board for the HP-9100A calculator), and asked, "What do you think of that?" Joel missed the point of that artifact, to which Barney said, "You obviously don't know anything about hardware." He followed that salvo with a question about some semiconductor chips—silicon-on-sapphire (SOS) semiconductor chips—to which Joel responded, "'We've done lots of experiments with that, and I think you're betting on the wrong horse.' He really got pissed." Handing Joel a large integrated circuit, Oliver fired back, "What do you see there?" Joel said, "I kind of looked at it, and I don't know much about circuit design and logic design. I never designed a chip. I never designed a board. And I said, 'I'm sorry, I really don't know.'" Barney's rejoinder was curt: "Well, do I need to count the pins for you on the bus? It's a 32-bit computer. The first." He was showing Joel the N-MOS III Chipset for the HP-9000 family, designed and produced by the recently renamed Desktop Computer Division in Fort Collins—this was HP's hardware CPU *du jour,* following the very dismal results of the SOS chips.

Joel by now had his dander up, and he replied,

"Gosh, I understand that. So how wide is your bus structure to feed it?" And he looked at me blankly. I then said, "What operating system are you going to run on it?" He said, "Well, we've got five operating systems." And I said, "Five?" He said, "Yes, we've got Rocky Mountain BASIC. We've got this, we've got that. We've got MPE." I said, "What the hell are those things? You know, the software is going to determine this, and I'm very impressed that you have the technology to do [this chip], but just because you've got a fast chip, doesn't mean that the computer is going to be fast." Barney had zero patience for it.

Puzzled by this behavior, Birnbaum decided to play along for awhile. Barney hauled out a beautifully machined brass mechanism on a lovely wooden base, which looked to Joel like a working model of a steam engine. Again, Barney asked, "What's that?" Joel said, "I figured I'd make light of this, here comes my PhD exam. But he was just . . . really annoying me. I said, 'It is some kind of an engine.' And he said 'What kind of an engine do you think it is?' I said, 'Barney, I don't do engines,' thinking he would laugh. He didn't laugh."

And then Barney tried his famous "go to the blackboard" routine. Barney had mastered the art of the stand-up oral exam at both Stanford and Caltech in the 1930s, and honed his skills with Claude Shannon, John Pierce, and John von Neumann at Bell Labs. Dr. David Tuttle still used this intimidation technique on Stanford graduate students in the 1960s, with Barney's enthusiastic support.[17] Barney said "It's an external combustion engine. I'm kind of interested in seeing the way you think. So why don't you go up to that blackboard and derive the duty cycle for that engine, and figure out its entropy." Joel said he "vaguely remembered twenty years before taking a thermodynamics design course where you did this kind of crap, and I suppose there was a time in my life where I might have been able to do it, but I certainly couldn't do it then. And I probably couldn't do it under that kind of scrutiny anyway."

Joel, incensed, replied in even tones:

Well, you know, Barney, it's been a long time since I took thermodynamics, and it's a reasonable question, but I think I'm not going to make a lot of progress on it. But I'll tell you something—while I'm doing that, why don't you go over to the other blackboard and design a second-level cache, because I've been working on that, and that's a very interesting idea in which you have two levels of interactive memory, which you'll need for your 32-bit computer because it's going to die of starvation with that silly little bus structure you have.

Barney's frown deepened and his face reddened, and Joel thought "he was going to leap up and take a swing at me, and then he sat back in his chair, and broke into a great guffaw of laughter—he just kept laughing." The bluff called, the two had a very productive forty-five-minute discussion about computing.

Birnbaum returned for one more visit. Eileen had just received an invitation to sing in San Francisco. She had never been to the Bay Area, and Joel offered to go out with her to spend three or four days in the City by the Bay, one of his favorite places. When the call came, he quickly concluded that an interview would pay for the trip, and after all, there'd be no harm done.[18]

This time, Joel reviewed the efforts in HP Labs, which he regarded as naïve and academic, quite in alignment with Stanford's assessment. But their enthusiasm and spirit appealed. Packard was out of town, so Birnbaum did not meet the patriarch on this trip. In meeting Bill Hewlett, Birnbaum's first reaction was

> What a great man. And then I said to myself, if I were to come here, it'd be the same thing as at IBM. I got to IBM after the two Watsons were gone. I got the caretaker guys, John Opel and Frank Cary. . . . Here [Bill and Dave] are retired and they got John Young, who looked like every IBM business manager I'd ever seen. Talking about ROI and ROA—I hardly knew what they were. [But] I said to myself, it's sort of crazy, it's this little tiny company. But it could really grow.[19]

Joel and Eileen toured San Francisco, including tourist stops in Napa Valley and Monterey. Eileen loved the visit. Joel was at least intrigued. He drew up a comparative list of what he liked and didn't like about his IBM job, surprising himself at how many negatives made the list. Foremost was the fact that the company was ignoring his group's work. RISC architecture was extremely powerful, so much so that it augured to reconfigure the very structure of CPU design, and in doing so, to cannibalize the current revenue basis of the IBM juggernaut.

The IBM executive committee saw no value in such a move, especially while the company's competitors were so ineffective. To an engineering purist, such business reluctance is usually anathema. To Birnbaum, once RISC was a known method, it was just a matter of time until someone produced equipment using it, and it had better be IBM rather than a competitor. But the work was now several years old: Joel detected no desire to capitalize on his team's contributions. For researchers, this neglect is the kiss of death—how can you get excited about coming to work on the next great thing if your superb work on the last great thing was ignored?

Try It for Two Weeks

Hewlett-Packard gave Joel an offer—doubling his salary, increasing his stock options, giving him a sizable starting bonus and a remunerative relocation package, and promising him a new computer research lab. The proposal commanded Joel's attention, and over the course of several telephone meetings, they hammered out an agreement that Joel accepted. Under its terms, John Doyle would replace the retiring Oliver as head of HP's Research Laboratories, which would allow Joel to focus on the computer systems research effort for which he was uniquely qualified. To the outside world, this move would be viewed with incomprehension, but to HP leadership, it was not only sensible, but imperative in order that Joel's efforts not be diffused.

Joel wasn't convinced, especially because Doyle was currently VP of Personnel, hardly the qualification Joel was used to for leading a major research laboratory. He had little understanding yet of the way in which Packard, and in fact the company, picked its senior leadership, and how they managed—generalists all, with the willingness and skill to learn on the job and contribute uniquely to any assignment. HP's formula had worked well. Joel's reaction, though, was to say, "I'm not cashing in a set of IBM executives who tell me nice work but no thanks, for some personnel vice president who is going to tell me whatever, who is not even qualified to tell me. At least the IBM guys were qualified." Doyle assuaged his fears, however, and they struck a deal.[20]

One hurdle remained: resigning from IBM. Major corporations are very possessive of their best talent, and IBM had long identified Joel as top talent. So when he told his boss that he was resigning to join HP, Gomory was extremely upset. First, he cajoled, saying that he'd retire and move to a national job in Washington, D.C., to free up the job heading all of IBM research—a three-thousand-person activity—Birnbaum was his choice for that job virtually immediately. Second, Gomory raised Joel's salary by 150 percent, going 25 percent above the HP offer on the table. The latter move, though, backfired. Birnbaum coolly replied, "You've been underpaying me all these years." Unsuccessful, Gomory did get Joel to agree to meet IBM's president Frank Cary. Cary came to his home on a Sunday morning, and they talked for three hours.

Birnbaum poured out his frustration with IBM regarding his RISC designs; Cary told him of the Boca Raton personal computer project. Joel, incredulous that such a program was under way without his knowledge, was angered by the fact that he was not included in the strategic decision. But he was soon stunned to hear Cary promise him that he could have an equivalent division for RISC products, and he'd be given a free hand to try to assail IBM's big machines head-on. Joel, intrigued, listened to Cary describe how that could happen. By the end of the three hours, they'd defined a new division, located it fifteen miles from Poughkeepsie in buildings just being completed for another purpose. It would be staffed with two hundred hand-selected employees from Joel's lab of six hundred, plus two hundred more to be drawn from product divisions at Joel's behest. Joel was in heaven. But now he had to call HP and renege.[21]

He called Doyle. John, totally sympathetic, said, "You'd be foolish to take our offer if they're going to offer that." Doyle then said, "Do me a favor. Are you at home today? I'd like to have Dave Packard give you a call." Joel, nonplussed, agreed to take the call. Birnbaum said, "Dave Packard called. I'd never met him, but I certainly knew of him; he was doing his aw shucks, Jehovah-voice too. Not the same as Barney's, but the same antics."

Packard was not seeking a quick fix—in fact, he viewed computers as a twenty-five-year quest, one that he said would fit Joel's career just about perfectly. Packard said that he wanted to have HP become the top computer company in the world, something Joel hadn't heard from the others. Packard asked Birnbaum to outline Cary's proposal, to which he said, "Frank is a good friend of mine, and a really fine man. If he tells you that's what he wants to happen, you can absolutely bet, one hundred percent, he's going to follow through and he's going to try to make that happen. You've got a marvelous offer there and it speaks very well if they think enough of you to do something like that." Joel expected the conversation to end there. But it didn't. Packard lingered, and then said,

> Joel, I've got a much smaller company and I started this company. Frank Cary didn't start IBM. If I tried to do something like that in HP that was totally different from HP, the company would reject it. You just can't change a company culture. So I don't think you're going to be able to do that. I don't think it's going to work. But you shouldn't take my word for it. I could be wrong. So here's what I propose. John Young and I are going to Washington in two weeks, taking the company plane. Instead of going back to Washington, we'll land in White Plains. Why don't you tell IBM you haven't made your mind up but you think you're going to stay, and try to make it happen. Try for two weeks to assemble the people; we'll go out to dinner. If you think it is working, obviously you'll stay. If not, our offer is good. You tell me.[22]

Packard called again ten days later to say that the trip was delayed by a week. Joel, meanwhile, was encountering enormous push-back. The Boca Raton experiment worked because it was clandestine and almost thirteen hundred miles away, not fifteen. No one could fight an unseen, unknown foe. Joel's new program was visible, worthy of full frontal attack. He later said, "I spent the worst three weeks of my life. It was just a total disaster." Dave never took the trip, but John Young did. Birnbaum said, "When we met, I said, 'I'm yours!'"

Packard did not spend time describing to Birnbaum just how hard it would be at HP to buck the culture, and Joel didn't ask. Certainly at the Labs, he had freedom to create his own culture, his own program. It developed fairly well, on a reasonable time scale, especially with a few lieutenants from his old IBM lab. But the Cupertino group was having none of it. RISC was theoretical, and HP always had prided itself on doing rather than researching. And the RISC program was—well, risky.

First of all, RISC was a long way out. Second, it purported to be all things to all people, something any rational person knows to take with a grain of salt. Third, every business line had a general manager whose job depended on selling something today. Every product line had to keep its offerings fresh. Worse, something grand would instantly make obsolete products just sold.

Birnbaum reported to work in Palo Alto in January 1981, coincident with the annual general managers' meeting down in Monterey, California, at Pebble Beach. Not Invented Here (NIH) was a virulent disease at HP by this time, in many ways a classic derivative of the individualistic creative spirit that Oliver and Hewlett cherished. Transplants at high levels—Dave Crockett from IBM, Eberhardt Rechtin from the Department of Defense, and Jim Bell from Digital Equipment Corporation—had all been emasculated. What chance would Joel be afforded? Yet Birnbaum marveled instantly at the open, creative, spontaneous, accepting culture. Certainly Birnbaum's early encounter with Barney was hardly auspicious. What Joel didn't yet appreciate was the degree to which Barney himself was viewed as both an anachronism and a detriment to HP computing. Bob Frankenberg said it in an agitated passionate mode:

> We were really pissed at Barney. Barney was a guest speaker for the sales force in Cupertino in '78, DEC had just introduced the VAX. He came down and said, "Here in Cupertino, the geriatric ward of the computer industry."[23]

Frankenberg, running the next-generation development project in Cupertino R&D at the time, later became a Computer Group vice president for HP before becoming CEO of Novell. His emotion was high twenty-five years later, telling his reaction:

> Geriatric group? We work our ass off to keep this thing alive and HP Labs is supposed to be doing the front work for us, and you haven't done [anything] in computers. That was our response. People in Cupertino saw the need to make the change to a 32-bit machine, but they were so wrapped up in making the 3000 work that the right work didn't get done ahead of time. HP Labs didn't do anything in that space—because there wasn't anybody at HP Labs that knew anything about computer architecture. Then we started these efforts [in Cupertino], and HP Labs competed and management wasn't making choices. So there was a continuous hassle.[24]

The first night, Birnbaum encountered Al Bagley in the Pebble Beach bar. Bagley's opening salvo still smarted twenty-five years later: "I'll come see you in your office in a month, if you're still here." The acerbic Bagley went on to say that there were twenty-five thousand antibodies in HP getting ready to reject him. In many respects, it was one of the gentler introductions. Paul Ely came out swinging, but Joel found the sparring to be engaging and productive.[25] Joel stayed well past the month—he stayed eighteen years directly, and six more as a senior consultant. Lots of work was left to do, but the second Watershed had been approached and mapped. Dave Packard again put a characteristic stamp on HP. This time Bill Hewlett was in full accord.

A Clash of Cultures

Bill Terry felt the change as soon as anyone, maybe sooner; he described it as a very human sort of thing. The Instrument Group operated by one set of ethos, Computer Group by another. But the differences were circumstantial and environmental—not malevolent, as some believed. As Terry told it:

> Instruments was a group of people who had worked together for quite a while in most cases. Turnover was relatively low. I used to tell stories in a difficult circumstance and say, "OK, about next year, remember in 1968, when the world was going through this situation and remember what happened to us? We're going to have to do the same thing again." And they'd say, "Yes, you're probably right, boss." I'd give that same speech in Cupertino, and after I got through, somebody would say, "Who's that guy?" They were a whole bunch of strangers and they didn't know the lore; they didn't understand the analogies. So you'd have to go at it a different way.[26]

The Instrument Group and Computer Group, although they differed greatly, were first cousins by comparison with cultures at other computer companies. When HP entered the computer business, the high-technology sector of Corporate America—including AT&T and IBM—operated with a systematic product development process derived from the military electronic systems constructed at the MIT Radiation Laboratory and several government agencies during World War II. These programmatic methods had layers of managers, large staffs, and several hand-offs from concept team to design team to development team. Specific techniques, known as PERT charts (program evaluation review technique) or CPM (critical path method) diagrams, became commonplace approaches to design and decision making. Although Bill Hewlett and Barney Oliver had abandoned this methodology in the late 1950s in favor of a much more nimble and efficient project management structure, the projects for which they had done so were minuscule by comparison. Scaling up—the bugaboo of organizational structures—was much more difficult for larger computer systems than anyone in the "old HP" imagined.[27]

For the instrument business, virtually every new engineer came fresh from a college campus, without preconceived ideas about how to operate within a company. And the company, growing slowly and patiently over four decades, had time to teach by example. But HP made its entrée into computing with experienced people from other companies, designers who brought methods from their previous assignments. Thus the disconnect between the HP culture and the new computer folk that Dave Packard found so distressing wasn't just due to the external manifestations of long hair, sandals, and work hours—it was a wholly different approach to scheduling, managing, and organizing development work. It was complicated, for a complex problem; Packard liked simple approaches for simple problems. While Bill Terry allowed early Computer operations to run this way, Paul Ely had forced the Computer Group back to the highly divisionalized, project-centric "HP model."

Bill Hewlett and Dave Packard shared Ely's enthusiasm for this local autonomy model, but as John Young became CEO in 1979, contrary evidence had become compelling. Paul Ely's team was struggling. As John Young put it:

> We were probably about the fourteenth largest computer company. We had 16-bit computers when everybody else had already gone to 32, DEC leading the parade. We had the 3000, the 1000, and the 9800 family, different operating systems and associated networking within each. And Barney [Oliver] never believed in systems at all. There was zero effort in anything at the systems level. There wasn't a single person in the corporate laboratory who knew anything about operating systems or networking. This was really a tough, tough time. You're faced with either disappointing an awful lot of historic customers, deciding you really can't make it in the computer business, or you're going to have some tough times to really get from here to there.[28]

Coordination among divisions was implicit in HP's model, evolved for the Instrument Group via occasional coordinated efforts between divisions that shared technology, such as high-frequency sampling heads for the Oscilloscope Division and Microwave's spectrum analyzers. The vital metrics, though, were divisional revenue and profit, not cooperative activity. HP, especially the Computer Group during the 1970s, was so consumed with explosive growth and new challenge that it failed to construct communication mechanisms required if it were to expect its managers to cross-pollinate or collaborate on multi-team programs. Divisional managers had not been taught that their interconnection role was as vital as their local role. The reward system and historic culture were skewed completely toward divisional rather than group success. This would became a bigger crisis for HP than Packard's historic concern about asset management.

The problem, in hindsight, might easily be seen. HP acculturated its professional workforce for forty years into a well-oiled, nearly monolithic culture, even though the corporation was widely dispersed around the globe. The Stanford Honors Co-Op master's degree program, a big part of the secret sauce, was one of many elements that ensured a consistent vocabulary, skill set, and value system. An HP study, done for the Accreditation Board for Engineering Technologies (ABET) annual conference in 1980, found that 71 percent of HP's 123 R&D directors held a science or engineering degree from one of three premier U.S. universities: the University of California at Berkeley, MIT, and Caltech. An astounding 43 percent of HP's top 700 corporate managers held a degree from neighboring Stanford University. For many years, HP was able to attract the best and brightest students from America's finest universities for its relatively modest recruiting needs. Analysts attributed this and the very high retention rates to the great working conditions and fringe benefits, but more important, the work itself was highly motivating, extremely sophisticated, and narrow in focus (which meant that few alternative job offers were available). Turnover for the professional staff was practically nonexistent, less than 2 percent per year.[29]

Growth was a consistent 20 percent per year CAGR for those same forty years, seldom deviating from this average. Personnel growth could be moderate, with maximum acculturation time. The hiring needs were simply the growth rate less any productivity increase plus the attrition replacement. For HP, with typical annual 10 percent productivity increases, new employee needs averaged 11 percent of the workforce per year, which was one new employee for every nine on the payroll. This rate gave plenty of time and adequate resources to teach the HP Way.

And the HP Way that was taught had a couple of interesting fillips. Mavericks were not just tolerated, but encouraged in many places. Some managers were exceptionally able to create incredibly innovative employees, and some policies bore unusually high-impact fruit. The first attempts at the Honors Co-Op program had disastrous results, as five of the first six graduates left HP as soon as they completed their advanced degree, paid for by HP. Packard, incensed, stopped the practice momentarily, but relented when Kay Magleby didn't want to go to Colorado Springs, and was going to leave HP to get a PhD at Stanford. Paul Stoft went to bat for Magleby—the sanguine result was the HP 2116A. Similarly, when Dick Hackborn was going to leave Stoft's group to go to Stanford for a PhD, Bud Eldon went to bat and got his work funded. Hackborn's contributions would repay HP for its consideration many times over.

At first, seasoned HPites filled many of the new Computer Group management jobs, especially those who had learned computing issues already. Carl Cottrell, learning about data centers, became the first Computer Group VP; Bill Terry, learning about computer testing from his Colorado Springs assignment, became the second. Matt Schmutz became the HP 3000 group general manager from his learning at BAEDP; Dick Hackborn became an engineering manager for Bill Terry and Paul Ely before becoming Disc Memory general manager. Bob Puette moved from BAEDP to build computer-based instrumentation, then led the Personal Computer Group starting in 1986, before leaving to become president of Apple USA in July 1990.

As the Computer Group side of the company found itself thrust into a much more competitive, faster-paced arena, all bets were off. Experienced leadership had to be brought in, as did employees in general. Attrition rose to 9 percent in the Bay Area—low by the standards of many other companies, but huge in HP history—and growth rates surged to an average 40 percent CAGR. Now 40 percent new employees were required annually, two new employees for every five on staff. Training time and access to lore was shortened radically, never mind the faster competitive pace and changing-nature job. Just finding people became a huge task, and the notion of hiring the best and brightest became attenuated. For the period from 1978 to 1980, HP hired one out of every nine California college graduates in computer science, recruiting heavily at vocational colleges such as San Jose State, Humboldt State, Chico State, and California Polytechnic at San Luis Obispo to fill the needs. Not surprisingly, the cultural norms of HP clashed with the experiences of the hired managers from other companies, who argued passionately that the reason they were needed was that HP's way had proven inadequate to the challenge. More than from the mergers and acquisitions challenge, and more than from the decentralizing thrust, the HP Way was at risk.

The HP Way in Practice

Even with tumultuous growth, traditional HP values surfaced again and again in numerous small and large examples—examples that could be noted, described, and instilled into the lore of the company. When asked about "management by wandering around" (MBWA), Byron Anderson, GM of the Spokane Division in the 1990s, began by reflecting on the HP Way during a tough period at the Santa Rosa Microwave Devices group:

> Reagan's Star Wars defense business was booming. It was a crazy time [for our division]. A lot of individual effort went into making the new IC technology, which changed the performance bar by significant orders of magnitude. We went up through 40-gigahertz, and a lot of really very important things happened. It was one of the reasons we were able to do the things we did in the computer business, because we were just "printing money." We had a significant market share. People needed what we had. We ran the EPI machines with special lots to find those fifteen or twenty transistors that would make the output stage of a driver section on a source that would get you 10-milliwatts at 10-gigahertz because it was worth $20,000 more. It was an unlimited opportunity for special performance, and the organization rose to the occasion. . . . It's sort of a higher calling. No one told us to do that. It was just kind of in our genes.[30]

One insightful story—although it created some momentary problems—concerned off-shoring and outsourcing in the mid-1980s. Sken Chao in

Taipei managed printed circuit board purchases for the Data Terminals Division. His suppliers, mom-and-pop shops around Taiwan, told him that HP's specifications were ridiculous, because they demanded 30 mils[31] of gold plating on the connector strips compared to 15 mils on boards for IBM, DEC, Wang, and Wyse printed circuit boards.

Chao was quoted 40 percent savings if he'd authorize thinner plating levels. He checked with the Roseville Division, who had product responsibility for the specific boards in question. They said, "Sure." A few months later, when an HP corporate engineering employee was in Taipei, Chao proudly related this story while sharing news that Taiwan had just displaced West Germany as the number two producer of printed circuit boards in the world behind the United States. As it turned out, the visitor, though shocked to find that Taiwan had come so far in the marketplace, was equally surprised that the design spec had been so easily modified. The employee knew of tests at HP Labs with a printed circuit board being repeatedly inserted into a connector while testing electrical continuity. The test result, over thousands of insertions, was a need for 30 mils plating.

The result, published in 1966 in an HP Labs whitepaper, became a guideline in the 1967 *Corporate Design Standard Handbook*. The terminal was designed in 1983 by people not yet in school when the insertion tests were done. The instrument groups, for whom the standard had been derived, accepted the finding and the guideline. But the computer group was caught in a fiercely competitive environment in which 40 percent savings on an expensive element such as a motherboard mattered a lot. So, at first blush, Chao was a hero, and the division in effect knighted his efforts. He was rightfully proud.

The rub came a few months later, when failure rates of data terminals soared out of sight. The failures traced to intermittent connector contacts. Customers using HP terminals in manufacturing, where the HP 1000 family had earned a strong quality reputation vis-à-vis DEC, were incensed. The altered plating levels and the connector continuity were correlated; corrosion in a manufacturing environment rather than plug insertion frequency was the issue. The result was the same. Plating levels of 30 mils provided a safety margin for years while a 15 mil plating level was breached within a matter of months.

Chao, somewhat mollified, accepted the higher cost burden at first, but then went to work on the group successfully to ask for an office-grade design separate from a manufacturing-grade unit. This example illustrates various employee contributions (1) at the buyer level (Chao, with PC board suppliers); (2) at the research level (HP Labs in 1966); (3) at the quality-monitoring level, to find and correlate the failures early in the cycle; and (4) in seeing a possible product distinction to serve two markets, one very cost sensitive, the other a harsh environments market. The illustration also reveals some of the special strengths that HP built and illuminates some tough issues of coordination and multifaceted goals that bedevil a larger company.

Discussion Forums

President Eisenhower initiated the Interstate Highway system in 1955—inspired in part by his difficulties in moving an Army troop convoy across America in 1919, and his perception of the effectiveness of the German Autobahn in 1944. The impact on America's transportation and commerce, not to mention the ancillary recreation and travel industry, has been incalculable. Jet fleets did the same for global commerce starting in the 1960s. Analogously, the world has embraced Internet communications—first with Web 1.0 browsers and information search, and then with Web 2.0 interactivity using social networking software (ubiquitous e-mail, chat, conferencing, blogs, and Wikis) in the first decade of the 21st century. It is hard to imagine how difficult it was to connect separate groups of people prior to the World Wide Web, first conceived by Tim Berners-Lee in 1990 and made generally accessible by Marc Andreasson's 1993 Mosaic Web browser.

For HP, an interactive communications backbone was fundamental to the company's ability to perform, because HP was more geographically dispersed and subdivided in operational units and sales, service, and support offices than virtually any other company on the globe. Company leadership and employees had no way to appreciate just how different HP had become in this regard from other corporations of the day; like the proverbial fly in the vinegar bottle, they had no context for comparison. But there were signals. Whether in IT, where faster data transfer of sales data was needed, or in design, where a common Lingua Franca lent value, or in Nilsson's executive seminar laments about consistent communication, the need for a regularized, easy-to-use communication system had become paramount. It was this need that led Hank Taylor's group to add to the video, voice, and e-mail infrastructures inaugurated by Comsys in the early 1980s. Enhanced communications gave HP some critical competitive advantages as the company experimented with building collegial groups across distance.

The Western Behavioral Sciences Institute (WBSI) created the first distance learning computer-conferencing system to support an alternative MBA in strategic studies in 1982. Attendees included Bill Johnson (B. J.) from Digital Equipment and Chuck House from HP, along with Dennis Hayes, founder of Hayes Modem, and Stewart Brand, who had profiled XeroxPARC for *Rolling Stone* magazine. House and Johnson agreed to install computer-conferencing software as an experiment and to share the sociological lessons that resulted.[32] An Industrial Research Institute membership starting in 1984 allowed House to form a virtual team with R&D leaders Roland Schmitt and Fred Geary of General Electric, Lew Lehr and Les Krogh of 3M, Ian Ross at Bell Labs, and Dan Stanzione at Bellcore. This became a loosely federated core experimental group wrestling with the import of and lessons from innovation in this "digital world."[33]

It was experimental, not conceptual. As such, it was exploratory, adventuresome, and pioneering. Amid conflicting advice, the Corporate Engineering team—Bert Raphael, Tony Fanning, and Mark Laubach—brought five different e-mail systems together with an overlay interface, allowing all of the company's people to communicate. They evaluated two leading university computer-conferencing systems, Confer and EIES, installing Confer to give discussion forum capability to HP employees.[34] The results, surprisingly positive in terms of participation, were subject to varied analysis by top managers, evincing a lack of understanding about what this new participative world would bring. Many employees were excited—HP again was experimenting boldly, building cross-divisional discussion.

Confer enabled many groups to share and archive information that was otherwise hard to coalesce. Disenfranchised groups were the most enthusiastic—for example, Quality Assurance people, Productivity managers,

Human Resource specialists, and legal groups—because they had minimal travel budgets and only a few colleagues in any given locale. Confer gave them a tool to create a widely distributed HP "community of practice."

Terrill Hurst, in charge of mechanical engineering systems at Corporate Engineering, saw a way to coalesce the company's mechanical engineers (MEs). He built a virtual community on Confer, seeking to coordinate computer-aided design tools across the company. MEs often felt like second-class citizens in the hierarchy of HP design engineers, especially compared to the far more numerous electronic engineers (EEs). With this communication tool, however, the ME community found its voice, becoming more assertive about their needs and their value.

The Mechanical Design Division (MDD), a small division at Böblingen, Germany, formed to develop ME CAD tools, was developing a two-dimensional graphical drafting package (ME 10) and a three-dimensional solids modeling package (ME 30). Hurst was able to get MDD to support a beta-release distribution of ME 10 for the HP MEs; almost immediately the Confer conference heated up with critique and advice. Soon, the HP ME community caused a firestorm, pronouncing the product unfit for release to customers because of critical flaws. The division was caught off-guard by this unexpected help, both in terms of the volume of input and the strident nature of the commentary. Dick Moore, group manager and vice president for all engineering systems, stormed into a management council meeting to demand that Confer be removed from the company, and engineers within the company be disbarred from pre-release software. A strong-willed leader in the Paul Ely mold, Moore was widely seen as an engineer's enthusiast. But he ignored these engineering inputs and barged ahead with the ME 10 launch. The product cratered in the marketplace, just as HP users predicted.

The skirmish was a symbolic prelude to a fundamental shift going on at HP. A mechanical engineer from Princeton and Berkeley, Moore had led many HP products and groups, including the HP 970A Digital Multimeter at Loveland, the original "marks on paper" plotters at the San Diego Division, and the HP85A personal computer at Corvallis, before becoming vice president of the IC/EE/ME Computer Aided Design Group created to market internally developed tools for sophisticated designs.[35] Moore, no less than Bagley or Ely or a dozen other key managers before him, felt he was in charge of his fiefdom—that was the implied promise and privilege of the decentralized HP Way for a local management team. But just as the Myers filter had been inserted and resisted before release twenty-five years earlier, Confer provided a new communications capability that enabled user testing in addition to environmental testing. The eventual happier ending was that HP MEs helped MDD with feature improvements. The revised product enjoyed solid commercial success. HP designers began to appreciate the value of additional perspective from their colleagues.

The geologic rift—a tectonic plate collision of sorts—at HP resulted from John Young's decision to develop an activist role for Corporate contribution. His conclusion as the new CEO was that Hewlett's laissez-faire approach to divisional management issues missed opportunities for synergy. Young had already persuaded Hewlett and Packard to insert a group structure to help guide and coordinate multidivisional product strategies. Now, abetted by John Doyle, a Microwave Division lieutenant for Young in the mid-1960s, Young began to construct or strengthen Corporate teams at headquarters to create and regularize process strategies. Corporate functions such as Communications, Data Processing, and Quality Control already existed, along with nascent teams for Business Development, Manufacturing, and Engineering issues. The change was to bring senior managers from around the company in to build strategic strength into these functions, in effect trying to create more of the "secret sauce" components for the company. Key employees were recruited from divisions throughout HP.

Young turned to some of his most trusted advisors to implement these changes. As personnel vice president in the 1970s, John Doyle had initiated innovative training practices. As the new R&D vice president in 1982, he commissioned a newly formed group to "do research and development on the process of research and development," consistent with Young's goal.[36]

The group, known as Corporate Engineering, instituted many productivity processes that are now widely used in American industry, such as software code coverage methodology, Return Maps, and efforts to shorten dramatically the fuzzy front end of innovation. They also contributed standardized designs such as OSF Motif screens and LaserJet fonts for personal computer and printing lines. In conjunction with Corporate Manufacturing, pioneering work was done on smooth integration of computer-aided design tools, CAD-based parts, and inventory control. Linked with Hank Taylor's Corporate Communications team, this group helped design the HP Corporate Internet, the e-mail connectivity, and video-links, and experimented with the Confer system.

The collision with divisional autonomy was inevitable, with long-ranging implications for the corporation. The ME 10 fracas was but the tip of the iceberg. John Doyle and Bill Terry each defended the program against the vehement charges of interference posed by Dick Moore, on the basis that more information by early-bird users had to be of value. The admonition to Hurst and others in the Confer experiment was to put safeguards in so that division sensitivities wouldn't be hurt too seriously.

Charlie Elman, at Corporate Engineering, with an assignment to focus on engineering productivity, argued that productivity is affected quite as much, if not more, by motivation and morale as by tools and processes. Using Confer as an archiving chat room to collect and post commentary from employees around the globe on topical issues, he launched the HPC:MOTMOR Conference, "a public conference on Motivation and Morale within HP, including the related issue of productivity."[37] The "conference" was stunning for its wide-ranging perspective and its candor. It also created controversy; HQ leadership coached Elman to soften the inflammatory commentary. Twenty years later, it is fascinating to see the stresses and strains on the HP Way, and accommodations being made to adjust to this new reality.

Within a year, 127 separate threaded discussion topics were spawned, with nearly five thousand contributions from eight hundred engineers in sixty-five divisions. Participants had to use their own name and location, so contributions undoubtedly were less chary than in some of the extant anonymous bulletin boards and chat rooms. Elman spent a lot of time with erstwhile commentators, assuring them that candor and openness were not only appreciated but desired. The record, archived for posterity, was an opportunity for post-analysis and interpretation, revealing much divergent opinion, even acid commentary in places.

Some topics drew heavy involvement while other threads thrived only briefly. Insightful analyses were found in threads such as "Ways of giving employees recognition," "Why don't HP engineers pursue patents?" "Are engineers being stuck in positions which do not utilize their skills or interests?" and "Community involvement among HP employees." The most energized thread, with 142 entries in less than five months, was "Has the HP Way changed?" The consensus was, "Yes." Some of the answers sound surprisingly modern:

1. "The groups that experienced the most growth (i.e., Computer Group) show the least application of the HP Way vs. the groups that had a tradition and grew slowly enough to absorb and 'convert' newcomers."
2. "Interfacing between these different teams feels like moving in the midst of separate competing companies sharing only a logo; although day-to-day work would benefit from more coordination and information sharing, they see each other as 'us' vs. 'them.'"
3. "To me and lots of newer people, it's as vague as saying 'Christianity' or 'Buddhism' or 'business' or 'religion.' Frankly, I think that to each person talking it really means nothing more than 'what I like(d) about HP.' I was introduced to it by someone who told me it was ineffable and can only be absorbed rather than described."[38]

The HP Way was still ineffable, treasured, and seemingly at risk. Newcomers still find HP and the HP Way to be incredibly positive, affirming, and hopeful—old-timers often view the current changes as putting it in a casket.

Computer Group Tension with the HP Way

When the Stanford Computer Science CIS committee dramatized HP's paucity of computer architecture leadership to John Doyle and John Young, the resulting HP search effort for new leaders revealed that building a systems company was a clear mismatch for Paul Ely's considerable leadership strengths. Nonetheless, Young promoted Ely to executive vice president in late 1980, consolidating the design teams at Cupertino and Fort Collins as well as their sales forces. Ely said, "John was concerned that we still had two computer families and he felt strongly that the people at Loveland had the right approach to this new computer; he was pushing hard a project under Fred Wenninger."[39] Young tried to cajole his long-time colleague into focusing on the bigger picture, but Paul was not easily persuaded. Young imposed a new obligation on Ely—moving his office. Paul recalled,

> When I moved to corporate headquarters I lost control of the computer business. In 1980, I was made executive vice president, and John insisted I move from Cupertino. In a typical day, I would have at most a third of my time to pay attention to computer activities. For example, I sat in on every single division review for every division in the company, whether it was in the United States, Europe, or Asia. The travel was enormous. There was no way I was running the computer business the last few years, which frustrated me immensely. It was a business that needed the Dave Packard type of decisions, and they weren't being made.[40]

Although many commentators have written about Ely's personality—"the loudest, the brashest, and the toughest of the new generation of HP superstars"—few tackled the obvious rivalry and profound difference of approach between Young and Ely. When Ely joined the company, he audaciously told the founders at a small dinner party that he intended to have their job within a decade.[41] Ely worked for Young at the Microwave Division, and after five years in the Computer Group, he again reported to him when John became president. With huge ambition, gigantic skills, and a stunning track record by most standards, Ely had considerable reason to desire more control and freedom, if not the ultimate prize. Indeed, it was a mystery to some why he hadn't come up higher on the list for consideration as CEO when Hewlett retired, but Dave and Bill picked the urbane Young over the "fiery, difficult, and unpredictable" Ely.[42]

Paul Ely wasn't expecting much from Joel Birnbaum and his new research lab in early 1981, nor were the extant divisions looking for HP Labs help; they had their own projects under way. They weren't looking for reorganizational help either. Project failures such as Amigo notwithstanding, the prevalent view was that HP divisions had an inviolate charter based on historical product line definitions. Sales success was the prime metric. Joel Birnbaum, newly arrived from IBM, faced a daunting task.

John Doyle, replacing aging Barney Oliver as head of HP Labs and vice president of R&D, encouraged Joel to build a first-rate research team in Palo Alto. Bill Worley, who had already resigned from IBM Yorktown, joined Birnbaum as the new RISC architect. CPU performance analyst Tony Lukes, an HP alumnus, came home from IBM Santa Teresa Labs. Joel attracted noted artificial intelligence researcher Ira Goldstein from XeroxPARC, along with Bert Raphael from SRI.

Birnbaum thought, erroneously, that he had been hired to oversee the computer fortunes for the company. After his first Cupertino review in early 1981, he said, "I must have been crazy to think I could do this, because it was much more entrenched than I thought." He inherited a lab of sixty engineers, whom he found illiterate with respect to classic computer understanding. He lamented, "They were working engineers. Most of them didn't go to major conferences. If they went, they came away with what some professor in Illinois, Princeton, Harvard, or MIT—who had never built a real computer and certainly had never had to sell or service one—was writing papers about."[43] Adopting Lord Kelvin's perspective, Birnbaum urged developers to build a prototype RISC machine and measure performance precisely, with special logic state analyzers co-developed with the Logic Systems Division in Colorado Springs.[44]

The experimenters were "really smart guys. We measured everything; we didn't take anything for granted. We found out a lot of work on any computer is just too complicated to be intuitive." Many months later, they knew which instructions were the right ones, how big to make the cache structure, and the degree of branching that various programs incited. After profiling numerous business and scientific programs, they had characterized workloads enough to freeze the instruction set. Then they tackled multiprocessing environments. Birnbaum said,

> We had to characterize the machine, to optimize how fast and how wide the buses have to be. The key fact that emerged was a real surprise. Something like every fourth instruction is a branch. Computers really don't have big long strings of code that go linearly; in fact, they go all over the place, for one job. If you now have multiprocessing computers, which of course is what we have, you have four, ten, twelve, even twenty instruction streams, each of which is branching all over

the place. So if you want to solve one critical problem, you have to do what is called branch prediction. You can't just have the machine wait to see which way the branch goes—you've got to take a best guess at where the branch is likely to go, and start executing down that branch and then be able to back up in the once out of ten times that it didn't go that way. So you need to build architectures that gather statistics of the job that refine it in real time.

All of this was unheard of at HP. They had no concept of how to do this—and yet they were really smart, really confident, very creative super engineers. I had an ethics problem. Cupertino was working on a much smaller variant of IBM's Future Systems work, where ten thousand engineer-years were squandered on a system architecture that didn't and couldn't work. I was its chief opponent there. But because of my exit terms from IBM, I could not tell HP this won't work.[45] I went to Bill Hewlett about all this; he gave me some of the best advice I had ever gotten.

[I said] "I see all sorts of things that I really shouldn't be talking about, and yet I know that HP is going to waste a couple of years and a lot of dollars and we're going to come up empty." I didn't know him well; he said, "How do you know?" I said, "Because IBM already did it." And he replied, "So maybe we will do it better. Maybe we will do it different. Maybe one of our young guys will have an idea they didn't have. What makes you so sure that because they couldn't do it, we can't do it? Pay attention to your ethics, but don't be so damn certain that you know the answer because you are going to get a lot of surprises here. This is a company with great engineers, and great engineers who run into problems behave differently." Boy, was that true![46]

The official story, told in business analyses about HP's computing catharsis, is that John Young understood the dilemma the company faced with four mainline CPU systems, sought out someone who could rationalize them, and gave him the reins. After some effort, the new program was ready to supersede the 1000, 2000, 3000, and 9000 families with a scalable architecture that was both faster than any of the predecessor equipments and fully backward-compatible. A brilliant management strategy! Birnbaum said, "Ah, would that it were true!"

What really happened was that Doyle and Young gave Birnbaum time to prove his thesis, letting him build a focused lab to conduct architectural research in scalable systems. But they gave him neither connection to Ely's teams nor any promises of merged technologies. His lab created experimental systems to tackle questions unanswered at IBM or anywhere else and made the critical performance measurements; they were able to demonstrate outstanding results to the Cupertino teams for each extant product line (such as five-times to eight-times higher performance). Birnbaum was ecstatic about the findings. HP Labs tested and proved that a COBOL-compiled RISC machine was plausible, even though IBM was certain that it was not feasible, because of sophisticated issues such as variable-length and runtime-modified instructions. HP Labs also built a real-time machine, thought untenable with RISC. This was all done with young designers who didn't know these things couldn't be done, as Hewlett shrewdly observed. Joel was especially proud of the optimizing compiler team, noting, "I later came to think that the optimizing compiler group here was better than the very famous group that I had at IBM. They never got as famous. . . . But boy, they were good."

The Cupertino leadership came to a major program review and listened, but they didn't buy in. The executive committee interviewed widely, then Ely and Young told Birnbaum, "What you guys have done is quite a tour de force, but this [group] is the horse that brought us here, and the [Cupertino leadership] tell us we can do it, and we are going to go with it. Vision is the machine of the future." Birnbaum was crushed. He considered leaving HP, feeling that it was the same story he'd heard at IBM—great company, put together a crack research team, solve major problems for the company, and the company votes to put it on the back burner. Fortunately, Eileen urged him to wait and see what might happen.

A week later, I had my monthly meeting with John Young. He did a really wonderful thing which I have never seen written up in any other business case. Probably he didn't tell them, and I refused to be interviewed. He said to me, "I know you must be really disappointed. It is a fine piece of work and we are going to reward all your people for it." I am thinking, "John, I didn't come here for a stock option." But he said, "We talked about it a lot after you left the room, and we don't really know whether they are right or you are right, so we want you to go full-steam ahead. You keep working on that as if you are on the toughest, tightest possible schedule for that to become the main line."

And then he said another wonderful thing: "By the way, you are not alone. That is not a united front down there. When you talk to the engineers, there are a lot of questions in a lot of people's minds as to whether they are really going to pull this off. Because every time they turn over a stone, there is another stone underneath it. They are getting in deeper and deeper. So I would like to ask you to do two things—build a team to the size that you think it needs to be in order to be ready to transfer into a product division as soon as you can—in other words, act as if we had said 'yes' to your deal as opposed to 'no.' I will make sure you have the resources in HP Labs. And the second thing is, I want you and a few of your key people like Bill Worley to come to all of those reviews and I want your candid appraisal."[47]

Birnbaum and Worley relished this golden opportunity. Joel's view of the Cupertino team was that

They were not totally convinced that they were going to succeed, but we were 100 percent certain [that they wouldn't]. We had done all the measurements and we knew their architecture about as well as they did, and it couldn't work. And they couldn't recoup fast enough. We went to the first meeting, asked a lot of hard questions, and embarrassed a couple of people. We were told afterward by Paul Ely and John never to do that again. Which pissed me off at the time because I thought that was why we were there.[48]

HP Labs Leadership

Young counseled Birnbaum not to embarrass anyone in public—"That is not consistent with what Dave, Bill, and Barney did." While HP old-timers couldn't recall Barney Oliver showing a gentle, kind demeanor during reviews, it was a wise admonition. Told to moderate his sidekick's hard-driving New York approach, Birnbaum took the message to Worley, who conceived the idea of providing index cards with questions for the executive committee "to take to those reviews, figures of merit as to how the project progress was going." The team put together "six or seven key tracking parameters, each of which has a long story behind it." Birnbaum shared the story for each parameter with Young, whom he called "an engineer and a smart guy."

Thus the Executive Committee could ask the questions, and Joel consulted in the background. Vision just kept slipping and slipping. Nevertheless, Cupertino kept going ahead, while Birnbaum's team was "getting to be kind of an open secret in the valley." Birnbaum and crew, though, were focused on a big problem of their own—could they really put the capability of each of HP's three product lines together into one common architecture? Birnbaum recalled,

HP had for a decade been selling these machines, and they had to have a path to move people onto the new architecture. I had lived through taking people off the IBM 360 and 370, and it was a nightmare of hand-holding, hand-compiling, rewriting code, validation, and testing. A lot of those people were never happy. We had what was called emulation mode, in which they could run like the previous family of machines. For example, a very complicated payroll program could run on a 370 emulating a 360, emulating an 1130, emulating something that came before it. Five machine families since the code was first written. It'd be slow as hell, correct but slow. The alternative was to rewrite a million lines of code. IBM could get away with that, but HP couldn't. We needed to have a way to transition people from the current machines. HP had very high customer satisfaction on all three of those machines. It had to be something they would like really better. How do you do that? That was an unsolved problem in the computer industry—this was HP's dilemma. Thus we needed to be able to build a common architecture that stayed simple but took on three really different characterizations, plus we really wanted to do online transaction processing [OLTP].[49]

HP Labs, venerated in HP history, is given credit for initiating or catalyzing most of the company's current product directions. When John Young turned over his CEO role to Lew Platt in 1992, he estimated that 87 percent of the corporation's product revenues stemmed directly from work begun at the Labs—an estimate that both Don Hammond and John Doyle proudly cited numerous times. But research labs differ radically from product development labs. Goals, perspectives, and values are attuned to new ideas, not new products. Birnbaum, in the same job at both IBM and HP, was uniquely able to draw sharp parallels:

I felt very strongly that the only difference between the two companies, [was that] the IBM guys were better, deeper, and more thoughtful in science, especially in the science of computing, and in the science of information and mathematics. The HP guys were a hundred times better engineers than the IBM researchers. The real difference was the coupling between the labs and the company, the way in which the labs were viewed by the company, and the way in which people would collaborate to make an innovative idea come true. But especially in the way . . . the executives didn't think a lot about taking money from instruments and using it to fund the computer business. I found the IBM research culture immensely more "out there and off beat" than HP, which was kind of white shirt and tie, good engineers sitting at benches doing their jobs. There were a few guys a little off the beaten track, but there were a thousand stories about weird stuff at Yorktown. And with this towering patriarchic, tyrannical figure of Barney Oliver over the whole thing, sort of terrorizing everybody, HP Labs didn't do anything risky.[50]

Rosanne Wyleczuk, documenting and teaching tech transfer concepts to a new team at HP Labs in 1999, commissioned multiple interviews: divisional viewpoint, HP Labs members, Hewlett, selected outside third parties. Divisions often were chary about the Labs, saying that they provided nothing specifically valuable, and the Corporate taxation kept the division from doing fundamental research. Pioneering groups (for example, Logic Analyzers or Network Analyzers) tended to have this view. Even these groups felt that HP Labs provided significant constructive criticism for division prototypes. One R&D manager said, "They were always 30 percent-plus of my beta sites, and 25 percent-plus of my first fifty unit sales—their inputs were invaluable as early indicators."[51]

Notably, the Labs pioneered devices; spectrophotometry, medical transducers, HP's first computer, desktop and handheld calculators, and the Spectrum architecture.[52] Contributions ranged from really stimulating conversation to immense insight into new arenas and combinations of ideas. The work on inks, paper manipulation, and laser printing established a huge base for later HP profitability. On balance, though, some things were easier than others. Systems views are harder to create than product views, software contributions are harder than hardware, and products are easier than processes. Perhaps most profound, the distinction between pragmatic engineering and innovative science is a major demarcation between HP Labs personnel and divisional development staffs. Hewlett himself valued research, saying that "only one out of six Labs projects should become economically successful—higher transfer rates indicate either too meek a goal or a division strategic failure."[53]

A Lonely Vigil

At one level, Young's task was straightforward. Vote for the new HP Labs creation and have Cupertino finish the engineering. Hewlett, though, had observed that "It is rare to hand off new product ideas and have them accepted. It is much better to start a new division." But in this case, the old division was half the company. No ground rules or homilies existed.

John Young had a very full plate, and it was a lonely vigil. Hewlett had withdrawn from the company almost completely; Packard was involved only occasionally, mostly nostalgic for days when simpler solutions were enough. The board was not helpful—only a couple of members were conversant with complex business issues. Fred Terman, nearing the end, had trouble focusing on systems issues; Luis Alvarez, eager for instrumented scientific pursuits twenty years earlier, was currently interested in paleontology and a theory about dinosaur demise. Not only was the computer future cloudy, with fractured leadership and Birnbaum's dilemma, but tectonic shifts were under way—at HP, in technology, and in the wider industry. International competition was, of a sudden, enormous. The Japanese seemed to have a chokehold on the Rust Belt, and now were focusing on consumer electronics and computing. Within HP, increasingly the Instrument Group seemed, well, peripheral. Computer peripherals, not CPUs, by 1982 were the ascendant products. But if CPUs didn't sell, and HP peripherals were inextricably tied to them, the company would be in trouble.

If John wavered on Packard's charge to become number one in computing, no one noticed it. The die was cast. Disruptive forces, externally and internally, would forever recharacterize the Hewlett-Packard Company. Semiconductors, PCs, and RISC machines, along with monumental peripheral contributions, were about to create a convulsive wave destined to redefine method, success, and the HP Way.

CHAPTER 10

Marks on Paper

HP introduced its first laser printer, the HP 2680 laser printing system. We were developing what we thought was really a breakthrough product. It was phenomenal in terms of what we could print. We had a poll in marketing on how many we'd sell the first month. The forecast was seventy-five. Actual sales were zero. We also sold zero in January and February. Finally in March, Dan Schwartz sold our first trade unit to AAMC in Washington, D.C. This was the struggling beginning of the laser printer revolution within HP.

JIM HALL[1]

DECEMBER 7, 1980, BOISE, IDAHO: The introduction of the HP 2680A was a defining moment for HP, eventually to have much more influence on the world than even the HP 35 Handheld Calculator. Demonstrating fully digitized printing, formatted dynamically by a computer, it augured to revolutionize printing. The code name said it all: EPOC, standing for electrostatic printing on command.[2] HP was not first. Both IBM and Xerox had machines on the market, priced between $350,000 and $500,000 each.[3] HP's new product, designed to interface only with the HP 3000, sold for a mere $121,000.[4] Few buyers, though, lined up at first, even before they learned that the machine required an HP 3000 print server at $165,000 to feed it with the right data. Similarly, few erstwhile buyers found out that the Xerox and IBM configurations exceeded $1,000,000 to work.

EPOC was epochal. Its power was awesome compared to anything previously available for anywhere near the price. Text and graphics were crisp, beautiful, and malleable. A wide variety of font selections lent a sophisticated air to the printed page, unimaginable with the Z-fold computer printouts from line printers. The EPOC printer, with a Canon engine under the hood, took the team more than five years to invent after signing the Canon contract. As with desktop calculators, the development team quickly started reengineering the product—the goal: reducing the price by ten times.

To Canon's dismay, the next solution used a Ricoh engine. The price dropped to $10,000, the size shrank by 80 percent, and the development took only two-and-a-half years—but the product proved unreliable. Jim Hall, HP's redoubtable development manager, ruefully acknowledged years later that it too failed.[5]

The EPOC project team, Hall recalled,

> was mostly made up of kids right out of college. This was their first project. It was a real family affair; we went to the Boise Little Theatre as a group every month. It generated personal friendships that endure today. People still look back at that project as something very difficult, but a real fun project. People put in tremendously long hours and effort into pulling this thing off. We had twenty-five to thirty engineers working on this, which was a huge project for Boise Division.[6]

Jim Hall was the persevering one. He worked for Jim Barnes, who worked for Ray Smelek, who worked for Dick Hackborn, who worked for Paul Ely, who worked for John Young, who worked for Bill Hewlett, who worked for Dave Packard. Hall, with two clear laser printer product failures, surprisingly was allowed to keep inventing in this same arena. He was left, though, with only five engineers; he had little choice but to borrow from previous work and from partners. Somewhat surprisingly to Hall's small group, the Canon team came back to Boise in early 1983, this time with a dry toner solution that was both simple and elegant. Pride and relationship, always paramount for the Japanese in business dealings, had been seriously damaged with Canon when HP decided to go to Ricoh. Hall put uncommon effort into placating and working again with Canon. It yielded a product called the HP 2686A, later renamed the HP LaserJet.

Smelek managed the Boise Division. Hackborn also lived in Boise. Smelek stood alone, however, at the January 1984 Silverado general manager's meeting: "I said we're going to introduce this product in about three months and we know we can sell fifty thousand, and they laughed me out of the room. We'd never sold fifty thousand of anything." The Corporate Engineering director the next day named the LaserJet one of the top ten new products of the company. He said, "I probably had twenty people afterwards say, 'You idiot—that LaserJet isn't ours and it's horseshit stuff and it's for a market we can't serve. Why would you select something like that?' And I looked at the list some years later and thought, 'That's the only one that made any sense.'"[7]

LaserJet sales soared, establishing HP firmly in the driver's seat for printing peripherals in the computing industry within eighteen months. Needing to sell thousands per month, HP sold nearly a quarter million units that first year. Between LaserJets and the InkJets introduced four years later, HP sold three hundred million printer units over the next twenty years.[8] In 2008, the pace approached two million units per week—an amazing one hundred million units per year.

Business writers have an atavistic need to find and exalt heroes, and Hackborn was conveniently available in 1992 when the world was finally ready to notice. Michael Malone added color to the LaserJet fable in *Bill and Dave,* describing how Canon came calling in 1984 and "ran into a growing and dangerous attitude—spawned in part by the HP Way—that anything not invented at the company couldn't be very good, [but] HP was so desperate to get out from under its dependence upon Diablo, that the Canon delegation met with a positive reception. They left with a deal to provide the CX [laser engine] to Hewlett-Packard." The essay described how HP Labs vetted the work before assigning it to a division for completion, fortunately Boise, "which was serendipitous because it was led by the most interesting new executive in the entire corporation: Richard Hackborn." Unfortunately, much of this story derived from "web historians" who got virtually every factoid wrong.[9]

Canon had originally approached HP with respect to the EPOC work because the dyslectic Bill Hewlett had befriended Canon's founder, Takeshi Mitarai, when he toured Japan in late 1945 and wanted to learn Japanese kanji. Mitarai, recalling Hewlett's story about an intervention getting him admitted to Stanford University, called Hewlett in 1964 to ask for similar assistance at Stanford for his own son, Hajime.

Canon, founded in 1933, had produced the world's first focal plane shutter camera, and with it, Japan's first 35mm camera. Like HP, Canon is a proud engineering leadership company, which by 1980 was renowned for its cameras and lenses. Canon also capably led in the computing arena, producing not only many laser engine patents, but both the world's first electronic handheld calculator (licensing Texas Instruments patents) and the first laptop computer, in partnership with IBM.[10] As John Young retired from HP, the 1992 Fortune International 500 list had HP eighty-first at $14.5 billion and Canon eighty-third at $14.2 billion revenue U.S.[11] When Hajime Mitarai died suddenly in 1995, the *New York Times* obituary noted that under his leadership, "Canon last year earned more American patents than any company except IBM. In 1992, it ranked first in number of American patents obtained and has consistently been in the top five."[12] Fortunately, the Canon team acknowledged in 1983 that HP Boise had excellent design instincts, and that HP's marketing view held promise. In addition, they agreed that their original, cheaper alternative was inferior to the dry toner process, and that the Boise engineers had made the unpopular Ricoh decision on the basis of engineering requirements rather than intentional affront to Canon.

JANUARY 3, 1983: *Time Magazine*'s "Man of the Year" was the IBM PC.[13] The first LaserJet was conceived as a cheaper print engine for the HP 3000 family, but the world morphed during development, moving dramatically toward PCs. Hall noted,

> The PC revolution was really taking place, and we kept saying, "Boy, it sure would be nice if we could sell this on a PC." Somehow we thought that if you're going to attach a peripheral, it ought to cost at most one-fourth of a PC. And back in those days a reasonable PC sold for about $3,000. Could you really sell a peripheral that was comparable in price to the PC you're going to hook it to?
>
> HP was preparing to introduce the HP 150 TouchScreen personal computer—HP's foray into the dealer channel, and into the personal computer business. The 150 team had the same misgivings we did: "This thing is too expensive. Maybe you could come with us on some dealer visits. We've got a two-hour schedule, we'll give you ten minutes at the end." The typical scenario was that HP would start out with reasonably high-level managers in the dealer chain, and within thirty minutes, they'd meandered out. By the end there were no high-level people left for the LaserJet presentation. We'd start, and the people there from the dealer said, "Wait, wait. Stop, stop." They would run out of the room, getting some of

their managers back. They were so excited about the LaserJet that it really turned us on. Maybe the LaserJet actually could do something in the dealer channel. We were really encouraged.

Product development, start to finish, took just a year. Pricing the product was the key. Of course, we had negotiated with Canon and tried to get the cost as low as we could. But it looked like it was going to sell for $4,000 if we used a typical HP pricing model. We really wanted to sell it for $3,500. But that $3,500 price was only going to work if we had volumes in the thousands per month. Hackborn wasn't involved, but [Paul] Ely took a gamble on us and let us price the product at $3,500, which could have been really bad if it hadn't been a success. And, we didn't have a great track record.[14]

MAY 22, 1984, LOS ANGELES: HP unveiled the LaserJet at Spring COMDEX.[15] Hall described the scene:

We had our booth set up, and attendees had not been allowed to come in yet. There were several companies that introduced a printer based on the Canon engine at the same time we did at that COMDEX show. But most of them, as soon as they saw our booth and saw the price we were going to sell the LaserJet at, just went home. They closed their booth and left. They didn't even stay for the show because they were so blown away.[16]

Two Sides to Printing

The product took off, but HP itself yawned. The sales force sold some, but because the printer wasn't interfaced to the HP 3000, that channel didn't develop. Dealer channel sales mounted, and the company noticed, but sniffed that it was really an OEM (original equipment manufacturer) product, with little HP contribution. It took five years for *HP Measure* to run a story about it.[17] Hall, incensed, said,

HP's CEO actually went to HP Labs and told them, "Don't work on anything that has anything to do with laser printing, because we're not going to be in the laser printing business very long. It's going to go away." I never could understand why we couldn't get enough traction with the labs. Even in the later days of LaserJet, you could see that people did not ever want to let us invest very much in the business because they knew that the business was going to go away.[18]

Hewlett, an early proponent of laser printing as well as Canon engines, had long ago retired and left the group to fend for itself; Ely was there for the pricing argument, but left within the year. Dick Hackborn and his superb group engineering manager, Bob Watson, bet almost entirely on color inkjet printing, seeing the LaserJet as a short-term expedient entrée before a classical HP program with a sustainable R&D patent portfolio could take its place.[19]

Carly Fiorina noted years later, "We had to eliminate the internal competition that existed between these [LaserJet and InkJet printer groups]. Carolyn [Ticknor] and Antonio [Perez] could no longer agree. Their mutual distrust and dislike were apparently well known to the broader organization."[20] In fact, as with many historic HP rivalries, the printer fight had been brewing for a very long time. Hewlett's dictum about the loser withdrawing from the playing field had never been tested by two very successful programs head-butting for years. The scars ran deep.

Described by associates as friendly, straightforward, and expansive, Carolyn Ticknor was a long-term HP loyalist, starting in BAEDP in 1977, gravitating first to Networks and then to HP's printing side. By the time that Fiorina arrived in 1999, Ticknor had full responsibility for the $20 billion global Imaging and Printing product line business, HP's largest and most profitable. Ticknor's perspective was that she led the integration of LaserJet, InkJet, and the Imaging product lines to leverage and capitalize on HP's leading market share position while creating two new growth market initiatives in digital imaging and commercial printing.

Ticknor had embraced Bill Bondurant's color study (described later in this chapter), spearheading product development and successful worldwide launch of the first color LaserJet and multifunction LaserJets (print, copy, scan, fax). She supported the "distribute, then print" vision that has become the basis for today's digital printing, which grew LaserJet revenue from $3 billion to $9 billion and increased its global market share from 40 to 60 percent.[21] Ticknor, well liked and respected in the Peripherals group, retired in March 2001 just as the dot-com frenzy peaked. As events unfolded over the next year, Fiorina might have rued her leaving.

Expansive and easygoing were not terms often used about twenty-five-year HP veteran Tony Perez, but he was universally admired as a results-oriented scrappy competitor—a perfect protégé of his own mentor, Richard Belluzzo, who was Dick Hackborn's right-hand man for years. Perez came up through the InkJet wars, fighting for dealer space, razor-thin margins, and media attention. In the five years Perez headed the InkJet group, the installed base grew from seventeen million to one hundred million printers.

His departure, simultaneous with that of Ticknor, took him to a private company first, and then to struggling Eastman Kodak in 2003. Two years later, he was elevated to CEO and chairman of the board for that venerable company, to which he recruited key HP executives including Philip Farasi, William Lloyd, and Jim Langley, among others. Like Ticknor, he had many fans in the Peripherals group; when he left HP, it was not viewed with equanimity.[22]

A Long Slow Road to Leadership

HP peripherals—printing specifically—trace back to a much earlier time; the long, slow learning is fundamental to how printing eventually became a $30 billion revenue line with solid profits for the corporation. Printing began with acquisition of both Moseley and Sanborn, recounted earlier, including the ill-fated specialized paper that Sanborn licensed from a third-party. By the time Dave Packard left for Washington, D.C., the Sanborn and San Diego divisions accounted for 10 percent of HP revenue; each team had just launched one new product of consequence. The Medical Group built an eight-channel recorder (HP 7848) featuring a pressure-modulated inking system and contact-less pen-tip position feedback, while the Moseley Division (relocated to Rancho Bernardo, California, and renamed the San Diego Division) produced a low-voltage electric writing system without ink (HP 7100A). Three *Journal* articles—July 1967, October 1968, and December 1968—extolled the engineering contributions of these products.[23] Don Hammond's team at HP Labs was beginning significant work on printing methods, inks, and mechanisms. They were doing sophisticated modeling of ink-squirting methods that were calculated on a leased Cray Computer; Bill Hewlett and Barney Oliver were keen to include hardcopy output for their prize desktop calculator. The first significant peripherals for the computer lines were also printers—the HP 9120A Printer and the 9125A Calculator Plotter.[24] HP's later dominance in printing traces to the basic research on inks begun in order to understand and solve issues around photo-resists, crucial for semiconductor manufacture. It was made all the more essential by HP's resolute focus on the easily contaminated Three-Five class of semiconductors in order to meet unique microwave frequency, light-emitting diode (LED), and SOS requirements.

When central processing units (CPUs) were the primary focus of computing in the late 1950s, the mainframe CPU group at IBM had dubbed all other equipment ancillary, peripheral, or incidental. The name peripherals stuck, even though the structure changed with minicomputers. Although most mainframe and minicomputer suppliers included peripherals in their lineups, none ever escaped the view that they were incidental to selling more CPU systems. This undervaluation in retrospect is more astonishing than the fact that no other voltmeter company had the prescience to enter the ruggedized computer data-logging market. As Ed McCracken noted, peripherals could be more than 80 percent of the system revenue; with this thought in mind, he had commissioned a line of data terminals in late 1973. Jim Doub headed the HP 2640 Data Terminal Project that launched in March 1975, followed by the HP 2644 in December. Peripheral revenues soon dwarfed the CPU business. The signal could well have been read more clearly.[25]

Tape Drives for Instrumentation

The computer peripherals story at HP started with tape drives rather than printers. Ironically, the two would long be economically linked. It began with Walt Selsted, chief engineer at Ampex in Redwood City for years. After Ampex founder Alex M. Poniatoff retired in 1955, the company did well for awhile, and then in 1960 had a disastrous year, leading to the third CEO in six years.[26] After a major disagreement with the new CEO, Bill Roberts, about the potential Japanese threat to video recording, Selsted left in 1961. HP had been using Ampex tape transports to build instrumentation recorder decks for several years, but Roberts, piqued at HP's competition, had discontinued the line. In 1962, Selsted talked with Barney Oliver as well as Hewlett and Packard, and he joined HP in order to reengineer an instrumentation tape transport and recorder. Significant progress was made over the next two years.[27] Selsted said,

HP needed this transporter for the instrumentation business to record what was going on with all sorts of things that they wanted to record. It wasn't just music or voices. The machine handled ten-, twelve-, or fourteen-inch reels, with a half-inch to one-inch wide tape, depending on how much capacity you wanted in the machine. They were in a rack about seven feet high. I have no idea how many they made, but I know that there were quite a few out in the military installations that I visited later on.[28]

Selsted's machines were analog, though, unsuited to the unfolding digital world. Uninterested in making the shift, Selsted left HP. John Cage, returning from his U.K. assignment, bought a small digital tape drive company called Datamec, started by people who had left Imtech in the mid-1960s. At Barney's suggestion, Cage hired Dick Monnier from HP Labs to run R&D; he hired Ray Smelek as manufacturing manager. John Doyle brought Smelek from the Microwave Division to Bedford, England, in 1964; Smelek had managed the move from Bedford to set up the South Queensferry (Scotland) Division in 1966. Monnier had managed the highly successful HP 9100A project at HP Labs; he brought Stan McCarthy from the Waltham Division as a project manager.[29]

The division had two vacuum column tape drives under development. McCarthy invented the first tape drive, the HP 7970A, which funded almost all of the laser printer development for years. Tape drives, though not exciting, yielded surprisingly good revenues and substantial profits because the field was not as hotly competitive.[30] At Hewlett's instigation, Smelek took tape drives to Boise six years later, leaving disc drive development in Mountain View. An inveterate nomad, Smelek moved a decade later to Greeley, Colorado, setting up a new division to build floppy disc drives and scanners. Smelek subsequently moved to Bristol, England, to develop digital-audio tape (DAT). Smelek commented, "The DAT ultimately became my real cash cow. We made tons of money on that product."[31]

Asked, "Why Boise?" Smelek had a ready answer: "The truth of the matter is Doyle picked Bristol because it was home, and Stan Selby picked Loveland because it was home. I picked Boise because my kids liked it.

They were in high school, and you can get a driver's license at fifteen. The Bogus Basin ski resort is right in town. We joined the golf club for $900. That was the real reason." How did he select the printing charter?

HP had no idea what to do with printers, and so we picked the 7970 and moved it and some old punch card readers that nobody wanted. I had to have some products with some cash flow, and we've got to be in manufacturing. While all this planning was going on, (Paul) Ely switched out of Microwave and came down to the computer business. I was on my way out the door, and he said, "Ray, I don't know what the hell you're going to do in Idaho, but I'm up to my ass in alligators so you just go do what you've got to do." He had just recalled the 3000. Well, a week before that a guy from a company called Tally came to see me about a printer head for a dot-matrix printer. About to go bankrupt, he said, "I need to save this company." I ended up giving the guy a contract to buy two hundred printers in return for manufacturing rights.[32]

The first line printers shipped in May 1974. Smelek's Boise Division reached $20 million revenue in 1975, split almost evenly between digital tape drives and line printers. The San Diego Division, building strip-chart recorders and graphics plotters, was one-third larger but with no growth for four years. By contrast, desktop calculator printers were growing; and some handheld calculators needed printing capability. The HP 9100A had a companion printer unit, the HP 9120A, which enjoyed modest success. The next unit, the novel HP 9866A Thermal Line Printer for the HP 9830A Desktop Calculator, was described by designers Dick Barney and Jim Drehle in the May 1973 *HP Journal*; its successor, the HP 9871A, a new daisy-wheel character impact printer designed at Loveland for the HP 9825A three years later, was an immediate success.[33] The November 1976 *HP Journal* described the first of a series of small, light-weight thermal line printers for the handheld calculator line. These devices (the HP 91A/97A) came from the Corvallis Division, with veteran mechanical designer Bernard Musch leading the design.[34]

By 1976, peripherals, including printers, were starting to be noticed at HP. The new Data Terminals line booked $17 million in 1976, $5 million more than Disc Drives. Jim Barnes, the disc project manager for HP's first disc, the 7901A, had moved to Boise as Smelek's R&D manager in

1973. The Mountain View Division had just debuted the HP 7920A in late 1976, a 50 MB drive that gave HP a much stronger footing.[35] The Boise Division grew 10 percent with tape drives slightly larger than printers. Dick Hackborn, with Paul Ely's blessing, transferred the rest of the Mountain View product line to launch a second division in Boise in November 1976, using the infrastructure that Smelek had already developed.[36] Monnier, the Mountain View R&D manager, transferred to SID Analytical Instruments.

The newly named Disc Memory Division (DMD) and Data Terminals became the two fastest growing product lines at HP, with orders nearing $200 million and $180 million respectively in 1981—five years' growth at an average of 90 percent per year. In addition, Moseley's strip-chart recorders and XY plotters became important items for HP, selling $100 million revenue per year by 1980. Adding in printers, recorders, and tape drives, Peripherals grew from about $60 million in 1976 to nearly $700 million in five years—a 63 percent CAGR. From an insignificant 5 percent of HP in 1976, Peripherals overall burgeoned to 19 percent of HP sales in 1981, helping to fuel overall corporate growth from $1.1 billion to $3.6 billion at a quite remarkable 26 percent CAGR. Yes, the novel handheld calculators had transformed HP, but even that five-year period showed slower growth at 24 percent—and handhelds after five years were but 8 percent of the company.

The Boise Division, though, was hardly sharing in the success of Peripherals. Their growth rate, 33 percent CAGR, was outstanding by comparison with the Instrument Group, historic HP standards, or even CPU divisions, but they slipped from 40 percent of all HP peripherals to 14 percent in this five-year interval. Disc drives were more in the mainstream than tape drives; and graphic recorders seemed more in vogue than line printers. Data Terminals were building a life all of their own. As for printers, Ray Smelek noted that it wasn't for lack of trying:

> In early '75 Bill Hewlett called me and said, "I just met the guys from Canon, and they have a laser printer that you guys should take a look at." Jim Barnes was my R&D manager. We went to see this thing and it was a great big box—I mean, it was huge, with a liquid toner base that used jet fuel to carry the toner

which went on the paper, then you dry it and it catches on fire. And Jim said, "Oh, man, this is going to be a challenge." We teamed with HP Labs to learn more about it, and they said, "Well, it is pretty tough," and we had to find someone to run this project. Barnes and I went all around and talked [to HP managers] Bob Watson and Rit Keiter, the guy that ran Santa Rosa . . . and nobody wanted to do it. We ended up in the microwave lab and we found Jim Hall, and Jim said, "I love a challenge. We'll take a look at it." And he came back with this write-up of all these challenges and I thought he was going to say "No," but he said, "Let's go get it."

The task took a Herculean five years, longer than any project in HP history except for the original Spectrum Analyzer. Smelek said,

Hewlett and Packard both loved it, and so did Paul Ely. They would come to review and shake their heads. "When are you going to finish it?" They saw the opportunity to print with no constraints. It didn't have the noise of the impact printer. It could do forms. It revolutionized the way to print. HP Labs helped a lot. Don Hammond was a lot of help on the technology. They developed all the optics for that machine, and they developed a seamless print drum. So it was Canon, HP Boise, and HP Labs. It was Canon's baby from the very beginning, and they provided a lot of the technology. [We did it with about] a two-page contract, and I learned years later that it has never been changed. It's the way Hewlett and Packard used to do business.[37]

It is hard to re-create a feeling for those times now that printers are ubiquitous, but typically, big impact printers, devices with an individually molded character at the end of a long rod for each character, resided in a noisy print room. The rods were stroked, and the character struck a ribbon that deposited ink on the paper—typewriters were built this way for nearly a century. IBM improved the typewriter design in the late 1960s with the Selectric, which used a lightweight aluminum ball that could be rotated and swiveled electronically to find the right character. Diablo invented the daisy wheel printer a decade later; it used a rotating disc with the characters along the perimeter. Each of these was an electromechanical wonder, and each gave high definition to the character, because curved-line edges could be easily molded. But the digital world sought something faster, less noisy, and more reliable. Nonetheless, two successive failures by Hall's laser printing team certainly dampened enthusiasm at HP.

Dot-Matrix Line Printers

Duncan Terry, an early "digital scope" designer at Colorado Springs, transferred to Boise in 1975, working on dot-matrix line printers while Hall's team toiled on the laser machine. By 1980, the Boise Division had tripled its business in line printers, from $10 million to $30 million, but tape drives had quintupled in the same period. Jim Barnes's main team had by now incorporated SOS technology—at Paul Ely's insistence—into a new family of dot-matrix line printers, much faster than the mechanical hammer devices known as impact printers, which were slow and made a lot of noise. The resultant family—the HP 2631A and 2631G printers, and printing terminals HP 2635A and 2639A—were proudly described in the November 1978 *HP Journal.* Duncan Terry led the low-cost version, the HP 2608A,[38] directly confronting Ely about not using the SOS chipset at a division review:

> Paul Ely sat across the table from me once in Boise, saying that if I didn't use his silicon-on-sapphire microprocessor in my printer, he would bill the SOS entire development cost to our division. He was mad. I didn't do it, and he didn't bill it, but he openly threatened to bill me and our division the entire $100 million development cost.

Asked how he was able to defy Ely, Terry matter-of-factly replied,

> I'm not sure he ever really knew whether I had one in the product or not. We'd see Paul Ely just like we used to with Barney, at division review time. They came in at division review time with their agenda, and they reviewed your projects. The time he did that with me, I laid out for him why we were choosing a simple microprocessor. We were trying to drive cost out of the box. He questioned that, and then he came over to meet with me later at my desk. He said he wanted me to use SOS, and I told him I couldn't because it was too expensive. He informed me, loudly, that I didn't understand the economy of scale in HP, and that I was thinking too parochially and that he wanted me to use SOS. I said I could not create a product that we could price to sell if I did it, and that I wouldn't do it. That's when he got

mad at me, and told me "You'll either do it, or I'll bill the whole damn division." When the next division review came around, those products were already out and selling. . . . He only saw us once a year and so you could get away with it—actually inside HP, you can get away with a fair amount since it doesn't stay highlighted all the time. If it comes up only once in awhile, you can kind of get away with it, because by the time it comes up again, things are already accomplished.[39]

Mavericks existed all over HP, making many good decisions. They still do.

The Boise Site—Discs in the Ascendancy

The disc drive business, compared to the printer business, seemed to explode. Dick Hackborn, known early for his brilliant strategic capability and revered by his Cupertino R&D team for a cajoling, easygoing style even under duress, was viewed by top management with some distrust—especially when he aspired to run a division. The HP division manager mold was quite clear about propriety and style. Bill Terry said, "There are these thirty-five checklist items, for which you have to have an 'A' or 'B' in each one." Hackborn had a number of 'A+' grades, but also some 'D's'. With Ely's strong endorsement, though, Hackborn finally persuaded Young that he should be given a chance. By mutual agreement, it was a long way from headquarters, on a minor-league program. Disc drives—the big washing-machine-sized products with little strategic content in them—were chosen, and Ray Smelek (who had managed the disc drive business previously) had already built infrastructure in Boise, reducing startup costs and travails. The new division started in November 1976.

HP 3000 sales were finally burgeoning, and each new installation seemed to have an insatiable need for additional fast-access bulk memory. DMD booked $20 million in orders in 1977, slightly exceeding its next-door neighbor's tape drive revenues. By 1980, the disparity in storage methods was huge. DMD's orders had catapulted by seven times, now 300 percent of Boise's tape business. In 1978, DMD introduced a licensed Winchester disc drive for the ill-fated Amigo, built to nonstandard size and specification.[40] Fortunately, the division had made its mark in revenue growth already, and riding the Winchester technology gave DMD even more cachet—at the end of 1984, orders soared well past $300 million, the largest single product line in HP. The products that led this remarkable surge were documented in *HP Journal* articles, and DMD leadership gained considerable recognition across HP. Hackborn's baby had exceeded the HP 3000 in revenues, as well as the Microwave Sweeper and Network Analyzer revenues whence he came.

Oddly, for all the revenue growth, DMD generated little enthusiasm or interest in Palo Alto or Cupertino. This was backroom stuff[41]—rooms full of disc drives might be big revenue, but no one touched it, felt it, or even sensed it. Storage was still a peripheral thought. When computer people thought about storage and product line contribution, small storage—tape cassettes, eight-inch disc drives, even five-inch drives—was more in vogue, especially with the new Intelligent Data Terminal line next door in Cupertino. And other new divisions—Greeley, Colorado, for example—were springing up to serve that need. The excitement was still with CPUs, as the Cupertino management saw it. Only Data Terminals could challenge that view.

Inkjet Technology—Another Protracted Birth

As DMD and DTD flourished, the Boise Division struggled. Some dot-matrix printers launched in 1980 gave the division a little life—sales of printers managed to grow again at a 20 percent per year rate for the next four years, even as the laser engine efforts failed twice. This success was fortunate because the mainstay—tape drives—stalled, growing at a meager 10 percent CAGR. The excitement in printing was now directed toward inkjet technology, but it wasn't at Boise. In 1969, Loveland had established the technical feasibility of a disposable ink cartridge with the HP 9125A plotter for the original HP 9100 calculator line.[42] Even earlier, Robert Sanderson's HP 7848A Recorder had established the superiority of ink versus treated paper for the medical field. Don Hammond's group at HP Labs had profiled inks in the early 1970s. For fiscal 1980, Ely formed a new Peripherals group under Dick Hackborn, coordinating the two Idaho divisions—DMD with Disc Drives (which Hackborn handed off to Doug Spreng) and Smelek's Boise Division, with Tape Drives and Printers—along with a new Greeley Printer Division under Tom Kelley and the Vancouver (Washington) Printer Division under Jim Doub. Vancouver and Greeley focused on smaller equipment—peripherals more suited for desktops than for enterprise computing. This shift augured to open a new line of thinking for HP.

By 1980, Corvallis badly wanted to improve its printing capability for the handheld line. They recruited Duncan Terry as project leader, with Frank Cloutier as the principal print head designer for a new InkJet printer. Terry related,

> A lot of people inside HP wanted to kill it, but Dick Hackborn supported InkJet even though it was an embryonic technology. At that time, they were kind of like the early laser printers. They were huge things, with lots of tubes, and they had ink that would run all over everything. They were generally viewed as a royal pain in the neck, but we were particularly intrigued for the desktop, especially for calculators, because this stuff could be small and light as well as fast. The idea came together in Corvallis for the disposable printer heads. We patented the idea of a disposable inkjet head that Frank Cloutier put together for us. He created the disposable head and I had a project team for the printer. We all knew it should be a full page 8.5-inch by 11-inch printer, but in Corvallis we were constrained to do only portable products, so the printer had to fit in a briefcase and work off batteries or else we wouldn't be allowed to do it. And Vancouver didn't want to touch InkJet at all. They had no interest in it at the time. So we went ahead and created a printer that literally fit in a briefcase. We had to put in a set of batteries although we knew it would virtually never be run off batteries, but we did put together a nine-dot head printer, so it was an embryonic beginning. The print quality was nothing like text quality, but it was enough to demonstrate the viability of the disposable head.[43]

The San Diego Division (SDD) emphasized scientific computer graphics rather than text for many years. Dick Moore, running SDD, had redefined their perspective, adopting a vision of "marks on paper" after his arrival in 1973. Moore had earned his stripes at the Loveland Division, pioneering a leadership handheld multimeter in 1972.[44] Considering overlapping projects in printing and plotting at several divisions to be dysfunctional, Moore persuaded the Fort Collins Calculator Products Division(née the Loveland Calculator Division) to let SDD build a dual-purpose line. The resultant flagship products, introduced in 1976, were the HP 9872A and the HP 7221A, sister products for four-color plotting that served both desktop calculator and instrumentation worlds.[45] These two products, along with a follow-on graphics and text machine—the HP 7245A—propelled SDD from an atrocious growth rate of 3 percent per year (1972–1976) to an outstanding 39 percent per year (1976–1980).

The 7245A was the first SDD product to feature quality text imaging. It used a half-shifted character row with a 7 × 9 dot-matrix character—resultant characters were very high-quality 14 × 9 dots, nearly as good as impact printer images.[46] Many enhancements followed—the HP 7225A in November 1978, and a continuous-feed mechanism for S-versions in November 1979.[47] The crucial product, though, proved to be the HP 7225A. This product featured a novel paper movement schema invented by HP Labs's Larry LaBarre, whereby grit wheels (with sandpaper-like texture) rapidly rotated, and the paper whipped speedily back and forth, because the paper had less mass and weight than the print mechanism. LaBarre thought of that because he once had been a logger in the Pacific Northwest, impressed that huge logs in the water could be spun and manipulated by men wearing spikes.[48] The culmination of SDD's work would be the PaintJet, introduced in August 1987 with high resolution.[49]

Becoming the Personal Computer Group general manager in November 1979, reporting to Executive Vice President Dean Morton, who managed the Medical, Analytical, and Components Groups, Dick Moore focused first on the desktop computing opportunity rather than the printing side when the HP 85 was introduced in January 1980—but he did get the briefcase-sized printer for the top-end HP 41C to use the dual 5 × 7 dot matrix array of the 7225A to improve character definition.[50] The HP 85 printer, by contrast, went back to a thermal print head to save weight and cost on HP's first avowed personal computer. It didn't prove popular.[51] Meanwhile, Duncan Terry and Frank Cloutier persevered. Terry observed that

> Dick [Hackborn] became an even more active supporter of the technology, and he continued to fund it to the point where eventually Jim Doub at Vancouver Division couldn't fight it anymore, and decided he'd rather own it. They took the technology up to Vancouver and turned it into a real printer [the first ThinkJet, released in 1984 after the LaserJet], which is what they should have done in the

beginning. But again, it was a case of a technology that was actively opposed by the division that should have it because it wouldn't do quite what their own technology would, and they didn't have the resources to put on it to develop it. So we did it another way, at another place, and then they took it over and dominated the industry [after another four-year drought].[52]

Hackborn, starting in November 1980, encouraged experimentation and allowed a lot of ambiguity. The Vancouver Division, for example, touted only the development of a character thermal printer, a graphics thermal printer, and a wire-matrix printer in a feature article about their division in the January-February 1982 *HP Measure.*[53] Bill Bondurant, hired by John Young from the General Mills consumer products research group in 1981 as a marketing focus group expert, noticed in 1984 that the computer divisions were insistent that "We don't sell printers by themselves, we sell printers as an add-on to a system, and what we're trying to do is sell systems." Bondurant, noting that Hackborn had a different point of view, said, "I realized that this dissension set up an opportunity."[54] Bondurant continued,

We did a major study for Hackborn to try to understand the dimensions of commonality and strategy for these different categories of plotters. And we came to some insights on that. We segmented those between the systems business and the standalone business. The standalone business just had enormous potential. We didn't get a huge reading on laser printing in that first study, but it was enough to encourage them to shift more resources into that area.

The real breakthrough . . . came later [1986], which is interesting from an organizational point of view. A subsequent study indicated a huge potential for color. The plotters had color, but none of the printers did. LaserJets were going gangbusters, but those were all black and white. Nobody else in the business had successfully sold a color printer. Notably, IBM had failed selling a color printer. This study indicated that if you could build a color printer product that had the print quality and price point of the LaserJet, and maybe a few other things, you could essentially restructure a whole market. In other words, the whole purchasing paradigm would change.

It was a worldwide, massive study, and we got results. I did a preview to the marketing management team in Boise. I was expecting to hear, "This is very interesting or here is how we could use that." Instead, they said, "You can't show that to anybody. I mean, look at what's happening, our laser business is doing capacity, you just would disrupt that. We can't afford to be disrupted."[55]

Bondurant was incredulous. He said, "You don't understand. This is the future. LaserJets will continue to be a growth opportunity for whatever period of time, but there is another opportunity. Yes, it might be a bit disruptive but if you see it first, you do something about it." The team reply was disconcerting, but intent. "You can't show those results." Bondurant went away. A couple of months later, after a visit to Boise, Hackborn saw Bondurant and said, "I thought you guys were going to have this study. Whatever happened?" Bondurant replied, "Well, you know, I showed the results to the team, and they said that it wasn't really useful. It wasn't helpful."[56]

Vancouver Division had already tried—and failed—with the first ThinkJet in 1984. Introduced as a low-end color printer, it lacked several things. An unusually candid *HP Measure* article in 1992 noted, "ThinkJet was a 96-dot-per-inch (dpi)—i.e., draft-quality—printer. It required a special clay-coated paper. The ink needed a certain amount of time to dry, so you couldn't just grab the copy out of the printer. And it wasn't waterproof, so whole pages vanished when the coffee spilled, and labels ran in the rain."[57]

Nonplussed, Hackborn pressed to see Bondurant's results. His response was, "That's huge, that's wonderful. That's exactly what I was hoping for. We have all this technology." Bondurant said, "I was persona non grata for a long time with that team—for a year or more. Ultimately they acknowledged that it was right. It had identified the color opportunity, which was a really huge thing. HP, to its credit, figured out a way to capitalize on that."[58]

Vancouver Division introduced the DeskJet at 300 dots per inch in 1988, followed by the DeskJet Plus (1989), the DeskJet 500 (1991), and the full-color DeskJet 500C for $995 (1992). The DeskJet 500C was the big hit. By the end of 1992, HP had sold nearly five million DeskJet printers, almost matching the LaserJet cumulative sales. Bondurant described the strategy:

> We simulated in our study the possibility of a color product just like the LaserJet. The color laser wasn't ready, so they shifted the goal over to the InkJet group in Vancouver Division. We built a simulation model on three pieces of info. One was all the characteristics of a product that potentially could differentiate it in

the marketplace—hundreds of features, actually—and how valuable each of these characteristics are to an end user. And then how that particular end user perceived the existing alternatives. From that, you could model what his or her purchase patterns or decision-making process might be like. Then you do that not just for one but for a thousand people who represent a population. Our study revived Vancouver, which was producing dot-matrix. . . . They were about to be phased out. They were searching for a new base of interest. Hackborn was clearly, in my interactions, the visionary. His operational team looked to him for that. The mistake I made was in expecting the operational team to respond, when I really should have gone to Hackborn, or somebody else that he designated to be in that role, maybe an R&D strategic person. While I got into a little bit of trouble, eventually they got over it, and they used not only that study but a bunch of other stuff that we'd done as thoroughly as anybody in the company.[59]

Inkjet Technology as a Breakthrough Technology

Most of the tale just told is of which divisions vied for inkjet product development, and how Bondurant and his team struggled with market definitions. But fundamentally there is no story to be written unless the invention team is unusually adept. Most anthologies fail to get beyond recitations of who was CEO, what the board intended, and who the maverick program manager was in order to appreciate the true value of the innovation culture.

Fortunately for the inkjet story, as well as for students of innovation, Harvard business professor Lee Fleming teaches "Commercializing Science and High Technology,"—and he brought a decade of engineering experience to bear, having worked in HP's printer divisions from 1985 to 1995. He posed an important question to open a 2002 article that described the HP inkjet invention story in depth: "Which firms are more likely to invent technological breakthroughs?" He notes that HP

> increased its odds of success by generating many high-variance inventive trials; it mixed and juxtaposed diverse technologies, professions, and experience, managed by objective and collocated. The firm exploited this variance with effective selection processes, strong socialization norms, deep experience with the components of invention, rapid prototyping and testing, and scientific knowledge and method.[60]

Just as with laser technology, Canon beat HP to the first patents; and just as with laser printing, the two companies soon decided to partner rather than compete. Fleming noted the long effort that HP expended in printing prior to inkjet, interviewing many developers across HP, including the principals for most of the twenty-three *HP Journal* articles covering eleven printing technologies brought to market. Fleming sagely observed that "these represented only the commercialized technologies that the HPJ staff chose to highlight."[61]

Fleming did yeoman work to extract the essence of the early inkjet innovations as seen through the eyes of John Vaught and Dave Donald, two researchers at HP Labs. Both members of the early HP 2680A EPOC team in Boise, they were befriended by Larry LaBarre when they transferred to HP Labs in 1977, and they were granted substantial resources and advice from Howard Taub, one of HP Labs's senior managers. And, in the end, they created the important elements of how best to form and squirt a droplet of colored ink that helped the divisions to create the "marketing miracle" that became the legendary HP printing engine. Which of course is only part of the story, but without this ingredient, the rest of the story could not happen.[62]

Low-Cost, High-Volume "Commodities"

Hackborn supported a lot of technology innovation, but more important, he was also following closely the evolution of the dealer channel for IBM and Apple PCs. Bill Bondurant was assigned to Alberding's new marketing committee for printers in 1985. He noted that

> The focus was still on computers, but it was shifting heavily to include peripherals. It became clear that you had to think through the whole process, and part of what's critical is the delivery of that system. And the whole value chain option was one that Hackborn drove. We did a study for him and his group to figure out how to organize the presentation of printers in the dealer channel. It turned out to be helpful—there tended to be price value points for a bundle that made sense. . . . They went for the very organized presentation of products and marketing material that nobody else managed to have. One of the key factors to their success early on was they took an unorganized industry, the printer industry, with a million different kinds of printers. Either the dealer had to figure out how to

present them or the end user did. HP organized presentations so decisions were easier to make and you could fit the product to the user.

They were geographically apart from most of the company. They were also psychologically apart from much of the company. They saw themselves as setting the pace for what HP was becoming, and they wanted to become a leader in the application of these kinds of capabilities. It served an internal competitive side. We were trying to demonstrate early on to the people that we worked with what the role of marketing can be in a process, so that you started out with a deep understanding of what the world would let you do, and that influenced your entire plan in not only developing products but also delivering products.

I went back months later, and they had seriously taken this stuff and gone way beyond. They had their business plan in electronic form, and they used to take it to these meetings where they had to make group decisions. They would refer to the business part of their marketing plan throughout that decision-making process—is it on strategy or off strategy? Do we have to change it?

One of the things as an outsider that I thought was really terrific about HP in general was that they looked at marketing like an engineer would. The emphasis was on systematic problem solving, rather than just on the creative aspects of marketing. When people talk about marketing, they have a sense of the advertising and creative aspects, but they don't think about the process, working for first principles and moving a business in a direction to make it more appealing to the world. That is one of the things that made HP a successful marketer. That fit well with the culture and style of the company.[63]

Evolution of a Marketeer

Dick Watts started at HP in 1968, working for the South Queensferry lab on a digital signal analyzer (DSA). Upon completion, his management said,

"Why don't you put one under your arm and go over to the States and see if we can sell this thing. Train the sales force and be the U.S. resident marketing applications engineer." It was a product that had some fairly weird applications in low-frequency signal analysis, doing things with acoustics, vibration analysis, physics, and astrophysics—things that were pretty unusual for the mainstream test and measurement business. It was a lot of fun, because salespeople would call up and no one would have a clue what this product does, but I'd think it might fit here. They'd take me into a NASA facility or a physics or geology department—say, someone doing earthquake studies. Because the sales force was basically afraid of the product, I was always welcome to do the demo. At twenty-three years old, this was a blast, and a great way to see the country. I decided very soon that I wasn't going back if I could possibly help it.[64]

Watts, a U.K. citizen, joined a small group in Palo Alto titled Import Marketing, the marketing team for all of the overseas divisions that sold products in the United States. This gave him a very different perspective on the divisional-corporate relationships as well as the United States and overseas roles. After eight years, he joined the Santa Clara Division, for the Fourier Analyzer product line (similar to the DSA products he brought to the United States). Marrying a local woman, he got a valued green card and became marketing manager for the division, selling atomic clocks and other arcane instrumentation.

In 1984, the Engineering Design Systems Group was formed, with the intent to develop and sell application software for HP Engineering Workstations (the HP 9000 line). Watts was recruited to go to Fort Collins (which his wife henceforth referred to as foreign service) as the Design Systems Group marketing manager. Following three years in this job, he returned to Palo Alto to work for up-and-comer Lew Platt, who had just become the Technical Computing Systems (both engineering and manufacturing systems) Group vice president. This group made the 9000 family of workstations, the engineering solutions product lines (electronic, mechanical, and software development), and the 1000 family and related production test and automatic test manufacturing systems. Watts said that after five years of group and sector marketing experience,

I was pretty anxious from a personal career point of view to get back into a line job because these group marketing jobs had been pretty much staff roles, where I felt very much like a consultant. I had been [seeking] more direct line responsibility, and [in 1989] one of the major McKinsey-led reorganizations resulted in putting the sales forces back under the product businesses, having been centralized for many years during the 1980s. The field was split into four groups: the test and measurement business (including Medical and Analytic and Components) under Bill Terry, which later became Agilent; the second, called Commercial Systems, reported to Doug Chance, which was all the business systems divisions; third was Lew Platt's Technical Systems; and, the fourth was Computer Products, which was the low-end, fast-growing small printer and PC business under Dick Hackborn. Hackborn wanted someone to run his sales force, which was heavily dealer-reseller channel focused, very different from HP's normal mode of operation; he asked me to run that.[65]

Watts would do two critical tasks for Hackborn. First, he built the Computer Products sales force—a heavily dealer- and reseller-oriented operation—for four years, from 1989 to 1993. The printer business grew from $2 billion to $15 billion in those four years. The channel was constantly morphing—from "mom and pop" stores to superstores and major chains. Watts worked closely with Hackborn on a wide variety of strategic issues, both for the products and the sales and marketing side. Then, when Bob Frankenberg departed HP to become CEO at Novell, Hackborn selected Watts to head the PC business, doing

the classic group job—marketing, manufacturing and engineering, and R&D; all the businesses broken into about six divisions, covering everything from calculators to desktop PCs, servers, notebooks, and some associated networking businesses. That was a lot of fun. Because Packard had left, we were going through some interesting changes at the very top of the company. It was clear that HP had found the formula for low-cost, high-volume distribution businesses.[66]

Vancouver Division had become a believer. In the sense that Jim Pettit, Chris Clare, or eventually Andy Grove would use the term, they now "got it." Jim Browning, Vancouver's manufacturing engineering manager, said in 1992 for *HP Measure,* "Originally, we thought we were in the computer business. We didn't know we were in the consumer electronics business. I think we're all pretty sure now."[67] HP would never be the same.

The Story Behind the Story

Peripherals have remained peripheral for both financial reporting and history books. The world writes about Moore's Law for semiconductors. The lower Bay Area is called Silicon Valley, named for the chips rather than the peripherals defined and built in the same valley. Intel's fortunes are followed assiduously; few people can name a leading peripheral vendor. When Apple changes microprocessor vendors, it is big news. But for impact on the world—indeed for the dramatic Information Age revolution that the world has experienced, peripherals—in particular, disc memory and print engines—are the central story. Moore's Law famously drove the semiconductor industry, but the value and pervasiveness of a laptop PC, or of cell phones and PDAs, would be inconceivable if those components had experienced only equivalent gains to semiconductors in density, cost, size, and weight.

Consider, for example, the scaling improvements of the microcomputer that have fueled today's laptop computers. The microcomputer chip driving the latest laptops in 2007 has ten thousand times as many devices as it did when the IBM PC was introduced. It costs twice as much per chip (OEM cost); the chip itself is ten times larger and five times the weight. Using HP's finest product at the time—the HP 7910 Winchester disc, which was a momentous breakthrough compared to previous equipment in size, weight, and cost at the time—as the equivalent starting point, disc memory capacity has increased twenty-thousand times, cost has dropped by thirty times, and the weight and size have dropped by two hundred times. A typical three-pound laptop at $1,200 would instead weigh two hundred pounds and cost $10,000. The laptop industry would have developed more slowly! Similarly, LaserJet engines have reduced in cost by a factor of three hundred, decreased size and weight by a factor of fifty, improved print resolution by a factor of ten, and added color, while still printing as many copies per minute. InkJet printer improvements are even more dramatic, with color resolution improved fifty-fold, a capability that has seriously altered wet-chemistry photography (as can be seen in Kodak, Fuji Film, and Agfa products).[68]

It would require far more than one chapter to cover the impact of peripherals on HP, the industries involved, and the user community. For example, HP participated heavily in disc storage design and manufacture for nearly two decades, building some breakthrough products on occasion, including the world-leading Nighthawk 1.8-inch disc drive in 1989, but in a cathartic move in 1993 (after an abortive attempt to buy a major competitor), abandoned it. Ironically, Jon Rubenstein, one of the original developers of HP's 9836A leading edge personal workstation in 1981, would seize upon Toshiba's "breakthrough" 1.8-inch disc drive in 1999 to envision and build the stunningly successful Apple iPod.[69]

Clayton Christiansen focused on disc drives, analyzing the brutal competition for his insightful book, *The Innovator's Dilemma.* Predatory pricing tactics, relatively low barriers to entry, and invisibility of brand uniqueness for OEM components made profits illusory—just as Intel found in memory chips, but managed to surmount in microcomputer chips. On the other hand, HP built a unique and extremely lucrative digital-audio tape (DAT) business for archival storage and backup protection; Ray Smelek and John Stedman moved from Boise to Bristol to build one of HP's most successful divisions in the mid-1980s.[70]

Almost always, two or three companies with rough parity divide large markets. Think, for example, about manufacturers of automobiles (for example, GM, Toyota, Daimler-Benz); computers (HP, Dell, IBM); airplanes (Boeing, Airbus); or heavy equipment (Case, John Deere, Caterpillar), let alone razor blades or cereals, soaps or candy bars. Somehow HP, in its best moments, wound up with market shares three times to ten times the size of the second place vendor. What is truly wondrous is that HP has done this now for twenty years in printing and imaging, besting some of the most formidable worldwide technology competitors (Xerox, Canon, Epson, IBM, Dell, and Kodak) to get there. Mere marks on paper indeed!

CHAPTER 11

We Need to Be Number One

If you're going to be in this business, we need to be serious about it. We need to be the Number One computer vendor. It will take us twenty-five years. We'd better get started.

DAVE PACKARD (1980)[1]

Ivan Sutherland left MIT in 1968, recruited to the small University of Utah computer lab by new chairman Dave Evans, leading to the forging of a highly respected computer graphics group. Alan Kay's revolutionary Flex Machine and Dynabook—the latter becoming the first personal computer, by many standards—emerged from the lab, as did object-oriented programming. Jim Clark, who later founded Silicon Graphics and Netscape, designed his first graphics rendering software algorithms for Evans and Sutherland (E&S), a company started by his teachers. E&S built stunning computer graphics machines dedicated to flight simulators for training jet pilots and Hollywood special effects.[2] Other noteworthy students of this pioneering program included John Warnock, Adobe Systems founder, and Ed Catmull, co-founder of Pixar.

Except for E&S, these companies were still far in the future. Beehive Medical Electronics was the first University of Utah spin-out company to have an impact on the computer world. It emerged from the University's renowned Medical Informatics group, led by Homer Warner. Combining ideas with those from Evans's lab, Warner and fellow physician Don McQuarrie built CRT graphics displays to replace teletypes.[3] They couldn't build them fast enough for an industry that was ready to change how people interfaced to computers. Harris, Cromemco, and Altair used them, as did Ed McCracken for the HP 2615A.[4] Beehive, however, struggled to meet HP's burgeoning volume and reliability requirements.

Jim Doub, hired by McCracken from Bagley's Frequency and Time Division, where he had been building nuclear magnetic analyzers, developed a superb intelligent terminals program, described in the June 1975 *HP Journal.* For HP, reliability was as important as screen editing, and their new line of display terminals exhibited high-quality performance in customer environments.[5] HP data terminals, known for reliability and unusually nice interaction modes, quickly became big business. Beginning with first-year orders of $17 million, orders doubled every successive year under general manager Jim Arthur and R&D manager Doub. Within five years, they exceeded HP 3000 CPU revenues. Peripherals were becoming central.

The HP 2640A, the flagship product, was priced at $2,640; in November 1975, the HP 2644A was announced at $5,000, adding important storage capability. Interactive terminals operated very differently from classic terminals because they had an internal microcomputer. They could function in their own right as a local computer, while also tethered to the CPU over a network connection.[6] Terminals were gaining smarts and CPU independence.[7] The 1977 catalog debuted three international machines—the 2640C, N, and S—that provided Cyrillic (Russian), Norwegian and Danish, and Swedish and Finnish alphabets, respectively. By November 1977, with the HP 2648A, there were ten models in the family.

Using internally developed SOS and CMOS technologies, the 2648A was the most powerful terminal yet. Buyers flocked to it. With two on-board microprocessors for both alphanumeric and graphical capability on the CRT screen, the machine was a full precursor for a personal computer with word processing and spreadsheet packages.[8] The final machine in the series, the popular HP 2647A graphics terminal, priced at $8,300, offered terrific graphics tools.

> Sophisticated graphs and charts can be generated while requiring little or no programming experience. A menu is provided to lead the user through a question and answer session about the data. By completing the form and a few keystrokes, the user can display his data by using bar charts, pie charts, semi-log and log-log charts or regular linear charts. Automatic data labels, legends, and titles are also

provided. This feature makes chart generation friendly and easy to use with or without a computer.[9]

By mid-1979, the emphasis was shifting to cost and footprint. The HP 2621A debuted at a price of $1,450, almost 50 percent lower than the price of any previous HP data terminal. With a larger screen, smaller desktop footprint, and fully detached keyboard, it proved very popular for HP 3000 office users. The next year, a novel machine arrived—the 2626A—in which display memory and the screen could be divided into four independent workspaces. Significantly, the terminal featured eight thousand hours mean time between failure (MTBF) as a design criterion.[10]

The Data Terminals Division (DTD), without quite realizing it, was knocking on the door of a new class of stand-alone equipment—personal computers. The divisional perspective, although still tethered to the CPU, increasingly featured local processing power. The next spring (1981), the Corvallis Handheld Calculator Division, led by GM Dick Moore, proudly introduced the desktop HP 85 as "HP's first personal computer"; founder Bill Hewlett demurred, claiming in a 1985 article that the HP 9100A twelve years earlier was "HP's first personal computer," a fact that HP's Virtual Museum doesn't acknowledge.[11] The reason may well be that Hewlett focused on the machine functionality, whereas most PC definitions specifically mean microcomputer-based machines with independent operating systems, such as CP/M (control program for microcomputers, sold by Gary Kildall at Digital Research) or DOS (disc operating system, primarily known as MS-DOS, from Microsoft).

DTD marketeer Fred Gibbons had an idea in late summer 1980:

I proposed turning [the terminal's microprocessor] into a personal computer running CP/M, because you can get lots of software to work on that. We started getting this thing going, but then some big boots started coming down. Who had control of this project? Was it Jim Arthur in the data terminals division? Was it the computer division? What's this all about? And suddenly I found myself in the middle of a political mess. I was pretty naive about that stuff. And I couldn't find a champion for this little project.

Suddenly I heard about this thing called venture capital. So I thought, "I can fight to build a product from HP—this CP/M-based computer—or I can go to Steve Jobs." I live here in Palo Alto. I don't have any responsibility, no parents. So I left HP. Leaving HP is not an easy thing to do—you had to go see Ed McCracken, Paul Ely, and Al Oliverio. They made you walk the hot coals before you left. And I walked the coals because they had done well by me. Nonetheless I left and started Software Publishing.[12]

Gibbons persuaded DTD project leader Janelle Bedke and HP Image manager John Page to join him and build graphics software for the Apple II. Gibbons was not the first computer visionary to leave HP. A small parade of HP's best software developers had already begun to leave the Cupertino site under Ely's regime. The key section manager for languages and operating systems for HP Cupertino, Bill Foster, left to start his own company, Stratus Computer, after the HP 3000 Series I debuted in 1976. Key software developers John Couch and Jim Gross left DSD and the abortive Amigo project for Apple in 1978 at Tom Whitney's behest, after he had left HP to become Apple's first R&D vice president in 1977. Ken Fox, DSD's R&D manager, left in 1979 to join ASK Computer, "frustrated by HP's lack of willingness to grab onto the software side of things."[13]

The bigger problem in Fox's view, shared by many interviewees, was that

[Top managers at HP] didn't know anything about software . . . [nor] much about the computer business. Ely wasn't a computer jock either, but Ely was a smart guy and a quick study. I was in charge of the WideWord machine, and I went up to talk with John Young. He asked me why there were three or four such projects, saying, "We've got the Amigo." I said, "That's not a 32-bit computer, it's a 16-bit computer." And he said, "Well, Dave Crockett says it's a 32-bit, and you tell me it's a 16. Who do I believe?" I thought "Oops; if you can't figure that one out."[14]

In November 1980, Jim Arthur was named to head Ely's Computer Marketing Group; Doub moved up as well, becoming the Vancouver Printer Division general manager. But Srini Sukumar, Prem Kapoor, and Lance Mills were all strong, bold managers in DTD's R&D laboratory. Why didn't they and DTD make more of a run at the personal computer business? One answer is that DTD folk couldn't shake tethered thinking. Consider advertising for the HP 2382A, a smaller, cheaper version of the HP 2621A introduced in mid-1982:

> The HP 2382A Office Display Terminal is a block/forms mode display terminal for office use. The 2382A consumes less than a cubic foot of space, which makes it ideal for the office desktop, yet provides many of the high performance features available in larger HP terminals. Non-computer professionals and infrequent computer users, such as managers, will find the 2382A's small size, simple styling and easy-use features the correct solution to their data processing needs.[15]

A year later, the company would fashion two variants of a personal computer, using the 2382A package. The first, the HP 120, although a CP/M-based machine from DTD, was primarily recognized for its devotion to being a block/forms mode terminal. Block mode transfer was a design artifice to get around inefficient disc memory transfers for disc-based machines; while efficient for data transfer, command-line editors were usually tied to block-mode transfer operations rather than single keystroke editors. The HP 120 Personal Office Computer Product Data Sheet was quite explicit:

> By pressing the "Remote Mode," a user changes the Series 100 computer from a standalone computer system to an interactive computer terminal. Either of two RS232C communications channels can connect the system to a remote computer. . . . The Block/Format software utility allows Series 100 computers to operate as block mode terminals with applications using V/3000 software for data entry.[16]

The description was telling: when you want to do real work, shift back to block mode and upload your data to the CPU! The division was doing too well at its main task to think about the problem from the user perspective. As 1984 ended, HP had sold a half million terminals in a decade, with twice the revenues of handheld calculators.[17] DTD built new terminals to better serve the group to which they were already selling. By definition, they were selling data entry peripherals for time-shared CPUs to workers beholden to IT directors. As late as 1992, IT and MIS directors were still bitterly complaining in professional forums that people were using PCs independently on their own data at their desks rather than the protected, sanctioned, privileged data in the corporate databases. The irony was that most early PC users were more inclined to use them for memos and letters than for data massage.

As division sales thrived, graphing solutions such as the HP 2647 and 2648 were minimized; multiple-screen windows such as on the 2626 were set aside altogether. Some analysts opined that HP missed the personal computer revolution because it moved the Calculator Division to Corvallis, thus missing the ferment of Silicon Valley as the PC fever erupted. In fact, DTD was in a position to see it much more clearly, but their incentive to chase it was too low. With success fully in hand for their main business, they couldn't step outside of their comfort zone to recognize the new opportunity.

Mavericks seldom get a chance to lead unless help is urgently needed. Churchill's brand of leadership for England, recall, was only sought in crisis, never in peacetime. Such paradoxes are seldom taught in entrepreneurial programs or business schools, but it is abundantly clear from HP's history that the most creative contributions occurred in units that were starving rather than in groups flush with cash. Leadership at DTD was winning, not losing. They were heroes, extolled for being far-sighted, bold, and decisive, and for growing revenue remarkably well—HP promoted them into bigger roles, unaware that they had missed the biggest opportunity of all. Meanwhile, mavericks within DTD got short shrift. No one needed paradigm-challenging ideas, not when the current paradigm was working so well.

Ignored mavericks can simply leave, taking the idea to a new company where the idea may be deemed valuable rather than as a disruption to the status quo. HP was not alone in missing big signals, and DTD certainly was not alone among HP divisions in missing the personal computer revolution. Without question, however, DTD designers came closer to understanding this than anywhere else in the company—much closer than either the Corvallis team or the Fort Collins team—because they were dealing with business users, not engineers. It is noteworthy that when HP finally did recognize the PC opportunity three years later, the insights came primarily from the successor DTD leadership.

Standards, Standardization, and the HP Way

When John Young became CEO in 1978, he focused on the lack of standardization across HP. Standardization, necessary to eliminate the cost of duplicated effort, was crucial for the company to realize consistent solutions. Young stimulated much broader capability in the corporate and group roles, but Ely had returned traditional divisional autonomy to HP computing, enhancing local initiative and innovation, and the two goals were mutually exclusive. The concern at headquarters focused on the fact that HP couldn't afford three different computer systems, each with their own unique operating system, peripheral interface, and application program languages and code sets.

The problem went much deeper. Divisions vied with each other for the best answer rather than supporting each other with compatible systems. Steve Joseph at Corporate Engineering found that the print heads and print driver protocols from the leading seven printers of the company from four divisions were all incompatible with each other. In 1986, Joseph hosted a corporate-wide meeting at which Boeing's corporate IT vice president, John Warner, who was the world's largest purchaser of HP printers at the time, spoke. Warner ended his speech (with Dick Hackborn seated in the front row) by saying, "I am going home to stop purchases of Hewlett-Packard printers until this issue of incompatibility is resolved."[18]

Graphical User Interfaces (GUIs) and WYSIWYG (what you see is what you get) were the new buzz-phrases introduced by the Xerox Alto, and popularized by the Apple Lisa and Macintosh. Within three years, a dizzying twenty-two independent designs of "standard interfaces" were in production from HP divisions, with up to seven different symbols for any given function.[19] HP design standards were unequipped to deal with this explosion of creativity.

Customers, confused by such disarray, suffered even worse when software was involved. HP proudly rolled out the Manufacturing Productivity Network (MPN) for Doug Chance's new Computer Products Group (the old Technical Computing Group) in 1983. On the floor of the Dallas Convention Center, two SMU students naively took their computer program homework assignment from booth to booth, where eager HP salesmen helped them. The program had to be rewritten six times in order to execute a simple twelve-line mortgage amortization program on different computers. A subsequent Corporate Engineering study found that seventeen incompatible BASIC dialects were being shipped to HP customers; efforts to rationalize this madness began immediately. The backlash in Cupertino was strong enough, though, that John Doyle felt obliged to defend it, proclaiming, "This isn't all bad—Burroughs couldn't invent seventeen dialects."[20]

Meanwhile at the High End

HP's biggest machine—the HP 3000 Series 64—was announced at the end of 1981. If HP lacked a 32-bit machine, available from all other competitors, why not label a 16-bit machine with a Series 64 name? The *HP Journal* story opening was decidedly upbeat:

> Large enough to handle the entire data processing needs of a good-sized company, this newest member of HP's business family has 2½ times the processing power of the HP 3000 Series 44, previously HP's largest. . . . For example, Series 64 can have 144 terminals attached to it, while the Series 44 can accept only 64. Series 64's greatly improved performance [is due to] faster operation and parallel operation. Faster operation comes from the use of emitter coupled logic (ECL), the fastest commercially available integrated circuit logic families, and from some advanced memory units. Parallel operation is made possible by a pair of arithmetic logic units, or ALUs, that share the calculating and decision making that are the basic functions of a computer. . . . The Series 64 can execute well over a million instructions per second (MIPS). . . . Since it is an HP 3000, the Series 64 can run programs written for other HP 3000s . . . [and] it qualifies for HP's money-back guarantee that it will be operational at least 99% of the time.[21]

Although the computer business was now more than half of the company, aside from Ely, no operational manager at headquarters understood it. It wasn't clear, though, that Ely had the right recipe either. Putting critical mass together to build an effective 32-bit computer architecture and supporting system had proven unachievable. Bob Frankenberg, a stalwart developer in Cupertino responsible for many HP 2000 line (21MX, 21LC, 21e) extensions, said,

[Young] hired Birnbaum, and Birnbaum brought in Bill Worley. We've got three competing designs now—the HP Labs-Birnbaum Spectrum effort, WideWord, and Vision. Amigo was another system development, aimed at highly interactive single user environments. Amigo actually started out as what one would call today a personal computer that grew into a $40,000 single-user monster. Young did wake everybody up to this mess. He insisted that we figure out whether it was going to be Vision or WideWord or RISC.

There were several task forces evaluating each one of these. The conclusion was to go with Spectrum. We were [way] behind; we had to have something revolutionary, and we needed to devote a full team. In fact, some of us thought "over-devote." We had to have strong efforts to keep the 1000 and the 3000 alive, and we needed to free up a significant number of people for Spectrum.[22]

In Search of Excellence

Feeling that HP was being end-played in its biggest overall opportunity, in 1983, Young commissioned the McKinsey Consulting Group to look at HP to assess market dynamics, and to help conceive the right structure for moving ahead. Bob Waterman was the lead consultant on the project. The most visible outcome was the book *In Search of Excellence,* by Waterman and his associate Tom Peters, with a chapter analysis about HP. Dick Alberding, just back from Geneva, headed the internal group:

I got to know Bob Waterman and Tom Peters and that whole bunch really well. We were confusing our customers by how we were selling computers, instrumentation, and instrumentation systems. We had two or three alternatives presented to us. One was to spin out test and measurement. Another was to spin out computers. Give it a new name. Maybe you could acquire something in the process. The third alternative was to reconfigure marketing and selling to accommodate a direct and an indirect sales force for test and measurement, along with a direct and indirect sales force for computer capability system. We selected that third alternative because the mind-set and the willingness of Packard and Hewlett specifically to spin out either one or the other, just wasn't there.[23]

The third option was, at one level, quite simple. HP had never emphasized marketing and sales as a discipline in the same manner as manufacturing and R&D. HP's first marketing vice president, Noel Eldred, had set the tone. Salespeople were engineers too, on salary with modest commissions. Advertising wasn't nonexistent, but it was polite, urbane, understated—just like the company. What was needed, argued the consultants, was a strong leader—someone who would stir the pot and change things. Funding would be dramatically increased. The company needed to take off the gloves and join the fray. Alberding argued for Ely:

> Paul was significantly burning bridges with John Young. My recommendation to John was that Paul should run the sales and marketing side. We needed a leader who was going to knock some heads. It would have been easy for Paul, and it would have taken the Paul-John conflict and put it off to the side. It didn't work. John said, "Well, I've got a new job for you. You're going to do the one you want Paul to do." The politics at that point was pretty confusing. Spectrum wasn't happening and the computer stuff was in trouble. And Dave [Packard] was losing patience.[24]

Young's decisions, in addition to enhancing marketing and sales, took Ely out of his computing role, divided the Computer Group among three other executives reporting to John Doyle, and placed Paul in charge of three smaller groups—Medical, Analytical, and Components. This courageous and bold set of moves generated both admiration and criticism. No matter how it was cast, it was guaranteed to drive Ely out of HP—a move clearly supported, if not embraced, by the founders. Analysts were puzzled—who now had the charismatic aura?

Young's strategic moves were documented in the July 1, 1984 Organization Chart, published for the company in the worldwide news magazine for employees, *HP Measure*.[25] Avid chart watchers were amazed to see Bill Terry back in charge of half of HP's computer business—the HP 9000 families for engineering, and the HP 1000 and 2000 families for manufacturing. His lieutenants for these assignments—Bill Parzybok for engineering, and Lew Platt for manufacturing—were both rookies to computing, coming from solid HP instrumentation backgrounds.

John Doyle had the HP 3000 family and the incipient personal computer business, in addition to networks and peripherals (without data terminals). Doyle, who started in Microwave in 1957 as a manufacturing engineer, had never run a profit-and-loss business for HP. Rising through manufacturing ranks, establishing facilities for HP in South Queensferry, Scotland, and Penang, Malaysia, Doyle briefly left HP, then returned in staff jobs—corporate development director, VP of Corporate Personnel, and finally replacing Barney Oliver at HP Labs in 1981.

Doyle's staff were all Microwave-trained as well—Doyle had hired Doug Chance as a manufacturing engineer, while Hackborn came over from Eldon's Corporate IT group to run an R&D section for Paul Ely; and Cyril Yansouni immigrated from Egypt via Belgium to Stanford, becoming a Microwave development engineer working for Paul Ely. While each man had a significant challenge, Yansouni won the PC role that drew the most attention from outsiders.

1984—*The Golden Age of Electronics*

The IBM PC had been gaining both acclaim and adherents at every turn in the twelve months since *Time* magazine named it Man of the Year (January 1983). HP's entry, the Corvallis HP 85, had turned out to be a terrific dud. Incredibly slow, it was hopelessly incompatible with business conventions. Proud HP was being humbled by upstarts in a business that the company rightfully felt that it had pioneered and led for years. Recognition of that fact was totally absent in the trade press, but those in the Silverado auditorium knew it only too well.

Ely had organized a Personal Computer Group in mid-1983, led by Cyril Yansouni, who combined elements of DTD and DSD along with low-end peripherals. Yansouni had the chutzpah to lead. Years earlier, he had applied for the division manager job for the Grenoble Terminals Division while still an R&D manager in the Santa Rosa Microwave Division, and when CEO Hewlett turned him down because he wasn't French, he angrily told the founder that Hewlett himself wasn't following the HP Way. Hewlett, incensed, threw him out of his office, but later realized his mistake, and Egyptian-born Yansouni got the French task. Now, Yansouni had a true hotseat job.

The HP 150, defined as a successor PC to the HP 120, was a crash project under project leader Srini Sukumar's guidance. Via HP Touch, a novel touchscreen with softkeys, in classic HP fashion it sought to define a unique capability for the PC user. The singular contribution of the HP 150 turned out to be its decision to focus on the dealer channel, breaking the traditional tie to the CPU that hobbled the DTD management team. Introduced in September 1983, it carried high hopes. McCracken, Yansouni, and Young were exuberant, even exultant, at the meeting. HP had finally gotten it right. Or so it seemed.

An Epoch of Incredulity

SEPTEMBER 1983, PALO ALTO, CALIFORNIA: "HP Announces the 150 Personal Computer." Featuring a novel touchscreen, a built-in printer, and a new 3.5-inch diskette, a pioneering personal computer was introduced at $2,795 to the dealer channel to challenge the $1,565 IBM PC and nearly two hundred other competitors on the market. McKinsey's brash consulting marketing team set a goal of 22 percent of the $7 billion PC market for HP's new PC chieftain Cyril Yansouni.

JANUARY 22, 1984, SUPER BOWL XVIII AD: "And, you'll see why 1984 won't be like *1984*." Broadcast but once, during the Super Bowl, "Beyond 1984" is one of the most famous television commercials ever run. Directed by Ridley Scott (who made the science-fiction classics *Alien* and *Blade Runner*), the spot features a female athlete smashing a large-screen image of an Orwellian Big Brother, a crude allusion to IBM. The Macintosh, announced two days later at a price of $2,495, used the same 3.5-inch diskettes as the HP 150 but substituted a graphic iconic mouse interaction versus a traditional command line text interface.[26]

JANUARY 23, 1984, NAPA, CALIFORNIA: On the big television screen, the gorgeous Monarch butterfly stretched its wings, flew lazily around the computer, and lit, ever so gently, on the keyboard. At the tony Silverado Country Club, Computer Group marketing vice president Ed McCracken revealed for the HP annual general manager's meeting his intended launch of a $25 million TV advertising campaign, a first in HP product history. People admired the ad, but the squirming in the room was evident. McCracken turned over the podium to fellow vice president Cyril Yansouni, who boldly portrayed HP Touch as the differentiator that would enable HP—from a standing start (a mere 1 percent of the personal computer business at the time)—to take 22 percent market share within a year. McKinsey consultants had generated this forecast with considerable confidence, following many strategic sessions and focus groups. To close the meeting, John Young scoffed at George Orwell's famous diatribe, *1984*, which proclaimed that computers would spell the end of human creativity. John announced solemnly to the crowd that this was "the golden age of electronics." Some demurred, unsure about this brave new future. Doug Chance said it best: "I thought we might be in trouble when I realized that the twenty-three-year-old account manager for McKinsey had been my paperboy only a few years earlier."[27]

HP Touch, Touché

Most of the attendees at the Silverado meeting had watched the Super Bowl the day before. At least half of the group had seen the solo Apple ad that appeared during the third quarter, describing an imminent Macintosh computer. Voices buzzed all around the room as the audience gathered. Few of the one hundred fifty attendees previously knew of the Macintosh computer; only one or two had seen one.[28] Most, though, were certain that it was either insignificant or distracting. Their arrogance was amazing.

A year later, the Macintosh had sold two hundred thousand machines while the HP 150 was selling forty thousand machines, more than half of them for HP CPU terminal support. Uncharacteristic quality problems forced multiple HP 150 re-work recalls. The fly-back transformer in the power supply caught fire in multiple machines; the telephone modem connection froze multiple-button office phone sets; the clever and virtually useless touch screen—the rationale behind the light touch of a butterfly—cost 40 percent of the machine. McKinsey's forecast was dashed quickly when customers found that the 150 couldn't use application software packages in dealer stores because HP didn't have an industry-standard disc format.

Musical Chairs

MAY 1984, MOUNTAIN VIEW, CALIFORNIA: "HP Executive Joins Silicon Graphics Inc. as CEO." Ed McCracken, passed over in the summer 1983 shuffle of HP's Computer Group, left the company where he built the HP 3000 into the industry's most successful departmental business computer. Most recently, McCracken had commissioned the HP TV ad for the HP 150 touchscreen computer, which was upstaged immediately by Apple's incredibly successful "Beyond 1984" commercial run once during the Super Bowl.

JULY 1984, PALO ALTO, CALIFORNIA: "HP Board Approves Reorganization Plan." John Young unveiled a bold reorganization, which moved Paul Ely from leadership of the Computer Group (which he had led for eleven years) to managing three Corporate functions and the three smallest groups (Medical, Analytical, and Components). John Doyle, with three lieutenants—Doug Chance, Cyril Yansouni, and Dick Hackborn—was named to lead the revamped Computer Group.[29]

DECEMBER 1984, PALO ALTO, CALIFORNIA: "Official at Hewlett Joins Convergent." Six months after HP reshuffled the Computing organization for the second time in a year, Paul Ely left the company where he had led its Computer Group for eleven years."[30] Ely, whose devotion, passion, and immense energy had been singularly focused on computing for a decade, looked askance at this turn of events. While a quick learner, he had little taste for running the ancillary groups of HP; more important, for a man who viewed leadership as a singular task of grabbing the sword and riding forth to do battle, it felt like HP was abdicating the field. Many analysts had no trouble agreeing with him.

SEPTEMBER 26, 1985, HP MEASURE: "HP Introduces the Vectra Personal Computer." The *Measure* article, sent to all HP employees, was unusually candid:

Before 1983, Hewlett-Packard had tiptoed around the personal computer market with offerings aimed primarily at users already familiar with the company and its equipment. With the release of the HP 150 in the fall of 1983, however, the company felt it had the product it needed for the general public. The general public wasn't so sure. Those who wanted to take their brand-new HP 150s and go off in a corner somewhere and use them to process words or do the books could be forgiven some confusion. After all, here was Hewlett-Packard promising to set them free with a jewel-like new computer featuring a user-friendly touchscreen, the footprint of a toe-dancer, and a butterfly. But they quickly learned that their

MS DOS machines couldn't run all that marvelous MS DOS software that was becoming available to those who'd purchased IBM PCs. Even less available to HP 150 users were the accessory cards that let them add such functions as RAM-disc and print spooler. And when the hardware and software finally did appear, they were accompanied by steep prices. Bill Bondurant, HP's marketing research director, said, "There was a strategic mismatch. We invented a product that fit with our installed base, whether we acknowledged that or not. We presented it as a mainstream PC; it really wasn't.[31]

FEBRUARY 1986, PALO ALTO, CALIFORNIA: "Cyril Yansouni Rejoins Old Boss at Convergent." The head of HP's Personal Computer Group, Cyril Yansouni, left to become the COO at Convergent Technologies. Yansouni, nineteen years at HP, had recently led the introduction of the Vectra PC after disappointing product acceptance for the HP 150.[32]

Postmortem

The HP 150 design, development, introduction, and product failure was analyzed and documented by Professor Charles Holloway at the Stanford Business School a decade later. It was a much more specific and stronger indictment of HP processes and leadership than any previous analysis. He described it as a tremendous example of bold but botched change at the venerable company.[33]

> The real challenges . . . were as much managerial as technical. . . . HP had virtually no mechanisms in place . . . to do cross-divisional development. Furthermore, the HP 150 represented HP's first entry into the consumer marketplace, its first use of dealers as a distribution channel, its first attempt at building to inventory in a centralized warehousing structure, its first strong need to work closely with corporate procurement to ensure quality from suppliers, and its first introduction of design for manufacturability on a product that would be assembled worldwide. In retrospect, this represented an overwhelming set of largely new managerial complications.
>
> Given the complexities . . . strong leadership and commitment were clearly required. Unfortunately, although there was strong commitment [from] the project team itself, leadership from senior management was inconsistent or came in bursts. . . . The lack of clear leadership, or of a consistent champion, in upper management

[meant that] the project manager was unable to maintain control . . . as his decisions were often over-ridden by his superiors. The corporate players were not close enough to the project to know all its intricacies, but nevertheless intervened.[34]

Perfect Enough?

Holloway's analysis was skillfully presented. The product development itself indicated wider problems for HP. Coordination issues across HP presaged the enormous problems that the Spectrum team would face. The most challenging note was that episodic, relatively uninformed top management involvement emasculated the project team; this issue would plague HP over the next two decades—it was a near-total inversion of the Ely leadership issues.

An internal postmortem found that at product launch the members of the design team averaged only fifteen months since college graduation—corporate leadership as well as pundits from the Instrument Group found it ludicrous that such an important program was staffed with novices. The untrammeled growth rates in the Computer Group, however, coupled with high attrition of seasoned veterans, left little choice for the division. Srini Sukumar had a pithy comment: "No senior designer knew what a PC was, anyway."[35]

It was tempting to believe that the embarrassing quality gaffes traced to this naiveté. It was worse than that. DTD for years had exhibited cavalier disregard for corporate quality and environmental standards with impunity because DTD top management refused to correct them. A year earlier, also during a Super Bowl weekend, HP's Corporate Engineering director found that HP's 2647 Graphics Terminal emitted enough radio frequency interference (RFI) to jam television set reception for two blocks around the neighborhood. Apple and Atari home computers followed HP design specs, causing no interference, whereas HP terminals, including those developed as personal computers, failed the test.[36]

Two decades later, George Anders would quote Carly Fiorina's comment in a similar situation: "It's perfect enough."[37] Indeed, for the typical DTD customer, the quality of HP terminals was unparalleled. Terminals were peripheral devices with little fail-safe impact for either vendors or users; HP had entered the business precisely because Computer Terminal Corporation (supplying the HP 2600A) and Beehive Medical Electronics (the HP 2615A vendor) built inherently unreliable products. By the time that Sken Chao experimented with connector gold-plating thickness in Taiwan a few years later, DTD and HP had earned huge respect from customers for high-quality terminals. Users weren't aware that they didn't meet tight Class B corporate specifications. A remarkable Stanford University study in the early 1970s concluded that quality, more than any other one factor, best determined long-term company profitability.[38] The concept, embedded in Bill Nilsson's Executive Training program, stimulated John Young to declare a "ten times improvement in quality in five years" goal, managed by HP's soft-spoken Corporate Quality director, Craig Walters.

Walters's findings were remarkable—MTBF varied by more than twenty to one across product lines. Anecdotes abounded—five dead terminals in a room of thirty machines, three crashed discs in an array of twenty, software upgrades that crashed the system and erased old applications. Yet Young thought that demanding an absolute quality level would yield three potential problems: (1) great divisions would have little incentive to pursue continued improvement; (2) poorer divisions would feel undue pressure from Corporate to perform miracles; and (3) more likely than not, the divisions with the best quality programs would be wasting money on quality goals well in excess of the needs of their customers.

The implications for the corporation were both subtle and profound. Quality, always the linchpin for the Instrument Group because a professional user cannot abide uncertainty with tools being used for validation, took on a different meaning when clerical office productivity was the intended usage. For most HP instrumentation, designs were evolutionary with relatively slow replacement cycles for equipment selling in modest quantities. In contrast, the Computer Group quality metrics had to be balanced against time-to-market, cost, and fast ramps to maximum shipments. Design issues in new circuitry—for example, the modem conflict—are tough to predict; fast-track programs that include new functionality are particularly prone to disaster.

Design teams, like strategists and marketeers, struggle to understand new paradigms. A new paradigm means that something is radically altered—the product concept, the usage model, the customer base, or the environment.

A lot of old assumptions will be proven incorrect or disabling. For example, as noted, when DTD's terminals became personal computers able to be used at home, RFI interfered with neighborhood television reception and therefore environmental specs mattered. When the Logic Systems Division adopted a shared-disc model for the HP 64000 Microprocessor Development System, up to six expensive peer-networked CPUs shared one disc so that multiple professional software developers could write code for one overall program. Six highly reliable boxes now relied on one low-quality system element—a clear use-case paradigm shift.

Despite Professor Holloway's assertion, HP had mechanisms in place for cross-divisional cooperation, including cross-charging of R&D expense and shared manufacturing and support costs. The HP 64000 project five years earlier, for example, used components and design capability from fourteen autonomous divisions to construct HP's most sophisticated computer-based system at the time. Much learning from that tour de force buttressed the 1982 Corporate Engineering productivity report.[39]

The underlying assumption in the cross-divisional mechanisms, though, was that all divisions were peers, with shared values and metrics. A corollary was that enough time and energy was available within the cooperating division for it to contribute some effort for the requesting division. But the competitive pace of the marketplace limited both the ability and the willingness of a Computer Group division to work with another division while their base business seemed totally at risk. Thus when the new Personal Office Computer Division sought a less-expensive modified keyboard from the Fort Collins Desktop Computer Division, the response was tepid. Fort Collins engineers didn't care whether the keyboard cost $20 or $100, because they used one keyboard for each $40,000 system. When the Sunnyvale volume estimates were ten times as many as Fort Collins currently made, it only sharpened the dichotomy. Fort Collins management felt like the division was being demoted to keyboard component vendor.

It also worked the other way around. When Femcor, an acquired small McMinnville, Oregon, division of the Medical Group, pioneered surface-mount technology (SMT) for Medical monitoring, a Corporate Engineering newsletter, *HP Network,* extolled its success. For the next year, the small division hosted more visitors per week from the rest of HP than they had developers working on the technology. They pleaded, "Call off the dogs."[40]

So while things needed only to be perfect enough for the situation at hand, when a dynamic paradigm shift was under way, and things weren't perfect enough for a changed expectation, pundits within HP had a field day. It was often easy to presume that the difficulties traced to underlying disregard for lessons long-ago learned at HP, rather than to tectonic shifts. Just as HP underestimated the oscilloscope meaning for electronic design, it struggled to appreciate the implications of the new personal computer for users; CPU-centric systems; and quality, cost, functionality, and compatibility issues.

Staying Alive Awaiting Spectrum

While the personal computer developments generated the most press coverage, HP's bigger challenge remained the enterprise-level computing systems for which Joel Birnbaum and his RISC architecture ideas had been recruited. Bob Frankenberg, DSD's R&D chief, chaired HP's Engineering Productivity Task Force in 1981, focusing on software issues. He'd graduated from project leader to R&D manager in Cupertino, handling the Vision team and maturing greatly during the Vision-WideWord-Spectrum infighting. Coming to appreciate Birnbaum's perspective and contribution, he knew someone had to handle the bridging requirements. The loyal Frankenberg stepped up:

> Ed McCracken asked me to take over the HP 3000 lab from Dave Cochran. My first day, the job was to cancel Amigo. Bill Richion was to buy us out of the places that we promised things we couldn't do, and I delivered the message. Paul Ely had just been an avid supporter of this whole thing. It didn't endear me to Paul to call it off. There were some wonderful innovations in it. It had a mouse, it had icons, it had a guided syntax softkey tree. Xerox Star rightly gets a lot of credit for being the pioneer in that space. But [Amigo] embodied a lot of those kinds of capabilities. A lot of those guys went to Spectrum; some of them left.[41]

The task facing Frankenberg, once Spectrum was staffed, was to keep the 3000 alive. The lab "cranked a lot of product out the door, including getting the 3000, Series 68 fixed [four years in development before Frankenberg arrived] and doing the 70, which was a higher-performance version of it. We even did a single chip version of it, called Mighty Mouse [HP 3000, Series 37]." This machine became an amazingly popular small business machine, filling a gap that the HP 250 had identified. The 250, invented at HP Fort Collins, then sent to HP Böblingen, had been reassigned to Cupertino by Ely and merged with the HP 300 team. Frankenberg said, "It was a very nice little machine. We had a lot of devoted OEM's; ultimately with Mighty Mouse, we got them a 3000 that they could move over to. We made Basic work nicely on it, and that was the transition path for them." Once this was done, the HP 250 was killed.[42]

In 1984, John Doyle pulled together some IBM managers alongside some of the Cupertino stalwarts, and they, along with Joel Birnbaum and his HP Labs team, set out to finish development of the RISC ideas. The Spectrum family would become known to the world as Hewlett-Packard Precision Architecture (HP-PA), so named because of the extensive measurements done during research.[43] Thus Spectrum, the scalable RISC architecture, was adopted as the panacea, integrating all three lines and adding functionality—provided it worked. Nancy Anderson, marketing manager for General Systems Division, became a keen admirer:

I'm sure you've heard about the sparse matrix. We had three computer systems, and each one had a matrix of needed things—a range of disc drives, all the different peripherals, all the different software. . . . The matrix of things that was needed for each one of these was sparse, because every compiler had to be redone for each one of these systems and every disc drive needed a separate driver. . . . During the budgeting process, they decided at a pretty high level that we were just going to stop development on all the future 3000s, 1000s, interims, and all that stuff and move to Spectrum. That was a really gutsy move. I thought that was very bold on Young's and the board's part.

And yet the way they did it was remarkable. It was a "go slow to go fast" process where they rolled it out slowly to each level of management, and made each level of management feel that we were really helping decide whether or not to do this. They would go through the whole decision process at each level of management [so] when you were finished you would feel like it was the right thing to do. As painful as it is, this is the right thing to do. I remember Birnbaum saying that at IBM they would have brought everyone into an auditorium and announced the change and it would have been over in a day. Even though it took a lot of time, I thought it was my decision at the end.[44]

Anderson was sobered when she first heard of this "go slow plan." She spoke later to the feelings that she and her colleagues had upon hearing the news:

Our first reaction was, there's no way we could keep our customers at bay for two or even three years without a performance enhancement. We'll be out of business before Spectrum. If you cut off our engineering, we'll be out of business. That's what I personally really thought at the time. But then they gave us the time to say our concerns. And people started saying, "Well, what do we do to make sure we can hold onto the engineers that just spent three years of their lives developing something that was going to be released in six months? What do we do about that? What do we do about the customers who think they're getting a performance enhancement in six months and who say they can barely live six months without more performance?" By the time they finished my level, I was on the team, and I was ready to sell my team.

But it was so hard. . . . [For example] I came out of the first meeting, and I had to go talk to one of our largest customers—General Electric—and they were saying, "We're dying. We are out of performance. Tell us." And I had to tell them about the plan that had existed before the meeting I had just had.

Nobody on my team knew. I couldn't say anything. That whole week we were going through this, I had to keep telling customers that these products were coming out. [But] this horrible, tumultuous, emotional time allowed us to get everybody on board and then figure out our plan and then be able to go to the General Electrics of the world and explain to them that it was really going to be better for them in three years, because we were going to have more of the system that they needed. And just plead with everybody to stick with us that three years, and tell them what we were going to do to try to get through that period. I remember Joel saying it was the exact opposite of the way IBM did it. IBM would have done it fast and then would have had a lot of trouble with the implementation because so many people would be in "malicious obedience" mode.[45]

Asked specifically, "Did it come through like they said it would?" Anderson replied,

It did come through. Everything happened. A lot of people started saying—and in the press, there were lots of articles saying—you know this RISC architecture that Joel and his team had come up with, "It's great in theory and it's great for certain kinds of applications but not commercial applications." A lot of HP's technical people in the field would say, "I don't believe this will work because . . . ". For three and half years there were naysayers, a lot of press that was negative. And it played to what HP was best at—people came up with ideas for short-term upgrades.

As Hewlett said, "Great engineers who run into problems behave differently." GSD engineers gulped, dug in, and started proposing ideas. Nancy Anderson marveled,

When you're in a box like that you ask, "What are we going to do? We'll lose our major customers if we don't have a performance upgrade." Our designers [made] some board upgrades that we had not thought were even possible, and then one person came up with the idea of some software caching, and that again was very controversial. A lot of people said, "It will not work. It won't do anything. In fact it will probably slow the system down." One engineer came up with this; he worked with four people—[and] one year before Spectrum came out we made about $30 million in profit on that software solution. We did all these little projects because we had very little staff to work with, and they really pulled things out. In my mind, that's what HP's great at.[46]

The Spectrum Management Challenge

The IBM-versus-HP culture shock reverberated as the Cupertino team mushroomed. John Doyle hired George Bodway from the Microwave Technology Center to head core IC and platform development. Wim Roelandts hired Dan Warmenhoven and Alain Couder from IBM for networking; software guru Jay Richards rejoined Birnbaum as well from IBM. Designer Sam Prather had been at Amdahl, and network researcher Steve Markman arrived from Bell Labs. The practitioners who were brought in knew only top-down design. Eerily, they went back to the early days of the Computer

Group. Old-timers recoiled—the new Young, Birnbaum, and Doyle model looked like a replay of the approach that Perkins, Davidow, Magleby, and Clay had imposed in the early days of computing at HP.

Doyle, who had led Corporate Human Resources for four years, and HP Labs for the next four, had a strong background in infrastructure strengths and values. His appetite for conflict and chaos was low, but conflict and chaos reigned in the Cupertino computer divisions. Doyle's approach was to impose more business rigor on the senior computing team—exemplified by the Ten Step Planning Process—and at the same time backing managers who had come from IBM with complex system-management tools and the vaunted IBM Phase Review process.[47] Doyle expended much personal energy, defining and teaching this more regularized planning process reminiscent of his previous approaches, including roles at Corporate Training, Corporate Engineering, and HP Labs integrated circuit (IC) leadership. Doyle was a rational manager, a craftsman in the *Gamesman* sense.[48] He was one of the "Microwave Mafia"—Young's old division—which believed market domination was the primary goal of business.[49] The Ten Step Planning Process, along with the CBEC (Computer Business Executive Committee), proved ponderous, especially for successful division leaders. Some even found it glacial. Cyril Yansouni, vice president for the Personal Computer Group, said,

> They thought they were going to fix the problem that we're having in the company and the computer industry by having us do a lot of reports. Every month we had to write a book. I said, "I'm losing; I can't stand it anymore. This is so unproductive." It was the worst time of HP, in terms of bureaucracy. I remember telling my wife, "I spent today, the entire day, in the boardroom in Building 20. There are no windows. Nobody ever talked about customers, about competition, about anything that mattered to our success; it was all about internal issues. Report to some committee, some personnel policies on this, on that, on the other. There was nothing constructive." From a personal computer angle, everything was driven by customers, every day the competition is beating on you.[50]

The corporate solutions—in training, engineering tools, and manufacturing process—were defined and built by senior managers who had grown up within HP. The good news was that these experienced managers could see both cost duplications and structural difficulties that dispersed divisions had with communications, standards activities, and shared resources. The bad news was that, although they built some novel and capable systems for the corporation that were embraced and valued by many divisions, these solutions were too often ill-defined for the time-urgent, complex management problems of the besieged Computer Group—disappointing and even angering desperate Cupertino managers. The newly arrived IBMers tackled the second kind of problem the best way they knew how—with oversight committees and classic bureaucratic control, to a considerable degree re-creating the morass into which Ely had stepped years earlier. Cultural war was the inevitable result.

John Young assigned Dean Morton to mediate and asked him to chair the CBEC. Soft-spoken and mild-mannered, Morton took a simplistic view of the problem:

> It became more difficult in the computer business to coordinate activities. The competitive juices were derailing what needed to be done, and they got in the way of efficient deployment of resources. The CBEC was just an executive council, put together to bring the heads of the major divisions together to talk about things, to be sure that there was communication and cross-fertilization. The marketing programs particularly were coordinated. HP always valued independence, being able to run a division and call your own shots, but pragmatically that behavior had to be modified when you got into the computer business. It was a matter of resource allocation and setting priorities and getting people to agree to [them]. We tried to manage it as a whole that really needed to be pulled together for maximum effectiveness, but without stepping on everybody's toes and trying to do a command-and-control kind of management structure. I think it did some good. I don't think there is any question about that. But those battles continued.[51]

Bill Bondurant was the Marketing assignee, and he noted that

> Morton was a skeptical person, not dictating vision necessarily, but setting general direction and then watching the format and making adjustments and changes if things weren't going exactly right. If they were going well in an area, he gave that more recognition. It was great leadership in the sense that all the

systems weren't necessarily in place to pull off this stuff. He had to make some decisions that were anti-cultural, that required some leadership. It was a very tough time. The minicomputer business could have gone down the tubes. HP would have been a much different company today if that decision had gone the wrong way.[52]

Other observers were not so sanguine. Mike Malone wrote that when Young selected suave Dean Morton as COO rather than the prickly Ely, it was "Young's single biggest mistake . . . a trajectory that would ultimately lead to a corporate crisis and the end of Young's career."[53]

The net result was considerable dissatisfaction. The much higher interaction and compromise requirement of the IBM methods raised frustration levels for long-term HPites within Bodway's new Information Technology Group. Sam Prather and Jay Richards, key managers in the new Cupertino-based Information Software Operation, became the Philistines in the temple—they in turn were equally quick to criticize the well-intentioned but primitive corporate systems designed to help. Palo Alto management and customers alike chafed over late deliveries and broken promises. The Medical and Analytical Chemistry divisions were critically dependent on Computer Group products, and slipping schedules led to raw emotions there as well. How had Hewlett-Packard gotten to this place—internecine warfare, ineffective product development, and stalled business effectiveness?

The predicament traced back in many respects to the failure of Amigo. Reading the Amigo spec sheet in 1979, Alan Kay at XeroxPARC was concerned that it seriously clouded PARC's future. Asking for a demo at HP Cupertino, he was relieved to find that although many at HP were aware of the Alto and the Dorado work, and although the Amigo outshone the nascent Star on paper, HP's icons, their use of softkeys, and the level of understanding of both networking and application software was primitive by comparison with the office metaphor then being developed at PARC. No one at HP was worried, however. No one believed that Xerox could ever sell what they were inventing. Both groups were correct. John Couch left HP to join Tom Whitney at Apple after Amigo foundered, where he led the ill-fated Lisa project. Still too high-priced and plagued with very slow software execution times, the project failed to ignite the personal computer boom. But a year later, Apple got it right with the Macintosh.[54]

Hardware improvements kept HP Computing alive as CPU divisions awaited Spectrum. Frankenberg feared the future more, thinking about how all the software might move:

> We had a really big problem with Spectrum. All of the application software we had was very dependent on the 3000 architecture, such as HP Office and HP Word, done in the U.K. at the Pinewood Division. We had millions of lines of code, and one of the intractable problems in moving people to Spectrum was how to move all that stuff over. It was spaghetti code. [I tried] to figure out how to get all this software ready to go onto Spectrum in an easy fashion. We created a program called PC Central. We used what later became called Client-Server computing, to put all of the functions that could be logically done on a PC on a PC, and all of the server functions, as we later came to call them, on the 3000. We rewrote those things so that the huge mass of code in HP Word and HP Access, etc., were separated that way and rewritten before they had to be moved to Spectrum. We moved the entire base over, and then pushed PCs as the way that you do office functions, instead of terminals. It all worked. Actually I think we anticipated the true PC revolution. We were one of the pioneers in the Client-Server definitions. We took it one step further and said, "Really, the best word processors are the ones that are running on PCs." We integrated those, so that people could gracefully come out of HP Word, HP Graphics, and proprietary spreadsheets. We got ourselves out of this hole of all these proprietary office application tools, while other folks including IBM had a big problem with that.[55]

Frankenberg argued that his group's effort never got a lot of credit outside. It was one of those internal transformations that no one knows about because from the external user's view, it didn't change a lot. He said, "In fact, that was the idea. But architecturally it was radically different. We got a lot of attention when we became the leader in office software as PC functionality moved up and HP integrated other people's stuff. Others followed, but we by far were the leader in doing that. It is ironic that it happened partly because we had to make the change due to Spectrum."[56]

Spectrum Arrives

FEBRUARY 25, 1986, PALO ALTO, CALIFORNIA: After two years of speculation and concern, HP officials unveiled the new Spectrum computing architecture, in a fanfare-rich worldwide television show (a press conference, really) for HP leaders and key clients. Called Hewlett-Packard Precision Architecture (HP-PA), the novel technology was described by CEO John Young, chief architect Joel Birnbaum, and other key members of the team.

> The HP 3000 is a general-purpose multiprogramming machine, designed for the interactive, transaction processing environment of business and industry. The HP 3000 family of computers includes several models. The newest high performance members of the 900 Series HP 3000 family are based on HP Precision Architecture (HP-PA), a highly flexible computer design that can meet current user requirements and requirements arising during future growth. HP-PA is based on Reduced Instruction Set Computer (RISC) concepts with added extensions for a complete system. This increases computer performance by reducing and simplifying the computer instruction set. HP-PA eliminates system overhead associated with conventional computer microcode by directly implementing computer instructions in hardware. The uniformity of HP-PA instructions enhances pipelining, providing higher performance by overlapping execution of multiple instructions. Many technologies can implement HP-PA; highly integrated VLSI designs can be achieved by eliminating the chip space required for microcode.[57]

Bill Worley, the chief HP-PA architect, had written about Spectrum features in an August 1985 *HP Journal* article, and he explained some of the key features again for the press conference. As described in the HP 3000 Introduction manual, "the high performance resulted from the memory hierarchy design and the use of optimizing compilers. Processor waiting time for memory accesses is minimized due to the fact that all instructions execute in a single cycle—the first modern computer machine to do so. Fast, wide bus structures ensure that the machine is never I/O bound. Moreover, the machine has separate instruction and data caches, allowing a much higher bandwidth between memory and CPU. Optimizing compilers generate efficient object code, allocate registers, and schedule instruction sequences to maintain efficient pipeline operation."[58]

The point of the press conference was to position future gains for the customer base, to assure them that the new capability was both imminent and powerful. Imminent meant end of year, and indeed some machines shipped by November 1986. A panoply of speakers did a creditable job—Young, Doyle, Birnbaum, and Worley among them. Packard was asked to comment at the end, giving a benediction. Had he not taken one of his contrarian stances, the whole show would have been upbeat. Important customers were quick to catch Dave's solemn tone, though, as he mused that the program was in its infancy and had a long way to go to be complete. One more time, Packard's integrity and blunt honesty and modesty reaffirmed the fact that this was still his HP, still not into flash, marketing hype, or empty promises.

Selling a Better Mousetrap

Young, commenting much later, talked at length about two issues—how hard it was to find ways to keep the customer base enthusiastic during the long dry spell, and then, to his surprise, how hard it was to sell HP-PA once it was available for sale. Dealing with the surprise, a variant of the unshakable HP belief that building a better mousetrap will inevitably catch mice, was an important evolution for HP:

> There were a lot of elements to holding on—getting out and seeing customers and getting them thinking about these ideas; trying to use quality ideas to improve our effectiveness for volume manufacturing; talking about time-to-market. All those things, I think, helped us stay in business long enough to learn how to do this, and finally win in the marketplace. HP emerged in the '90s as a really effective computer systems company. Getting to where we ended up was a tribute to a hell of a lot of people working really hard over a whole decade. It was hard work, believe me, just getting customers. I spent an awful lot of my time being the chief salesman, cold-calling these people, people we'd never talked to before. CitiBank, AT&T: these got to be really big customers for us. Boy, I was out making calls everywhere. But it was a very, very tough time. I remember having a big launch of the Spectrum products, and they were pretty good, but they were a lot

of homemade integrated circuits, a lot of complex stuff. It gave us fits to get the operating system to work as well as it needed to. It was a lot of tuning to get it to be really competitive.

We got some help that you didn't expect to get from DEC being unable to make these transitions to a larger company. IBM didn't push this end of the line, because they didn't want to cannibalize it, so we had some room to maneuver. And so, by the end of the '80s, we had a very strong position in the business. We were the number one RISC computer company, including workstations, and we were the number one UNIX vendor the year I retired in 1992. It was a very hard decade. I look at the competitors and the nameplates that started out in those eras . . . and we started at fourteenth and we wound up at third or something. Having to work on improving your ability to compete became kind of a theme. And I was quite visible, testifying on this sort of thing.[59]

Two unlikely heroes emerged in this period—men known for other pursuits in the old HP—Carl Cottrell and Cort Van Rensselaer. Together, they had designed the Corporate Information System in a later assignment. Carl said, "We built a slide show that explained how the HP systems architecture (e.g., Heart, Comsys) worked; Young used to call me over to his office and say, 'Will you run through your little pitch with this guy?' It would be the president of some company."[60] Satisfying for both men, they became extremely effective salesmen in top-level discussions with Fortune 100 leaders in the 1980s, when John Young was struggling to implant the HP-PA machines. Their stories of "how we did it" turned the tide. John Young lauded their contributions, noting that

I was trying to figure out how to run a whole company, particularly applying this quality defect idea in all processes of the company. We rolled that idea up and started having seminars here in Cupertino, to which we'd invite a lot of high-powered people to come. We had a lot of great data. That was one of the most powerful selling tools ever . . . because we had zero credibility in big corporate IT places. These were IBM-owned—every company, outside of the lab or the factory floor. If you're going to break into where the real money is in the enterprise, you've got to go up against IBM. You couldn't go sell a Spectrum, you couldn't sell a product. You're selling an answer to a business problem—so you have to tailor the presentation to the corporate communications and inventory guys and corporate manufacturing. Cort Van Rensselaer, Carl Cottrell, Hank Taylor, and Sally Dudley had credibility. On a daily basis HP could get sales from around the world—product by product, office by office, the next morning. The notion that you could get that in 1975 was crazy for any other company. We had the order processing system, the order transmission system, and the e-mail that layered on that. It was the leading-edge worldwide system. It was remarkable. We absolutely had great control of our business.[61]

Workstation Aberration

While HP Cupertino was busily trying to finish Spectrum, Fort Collins had been upstaged—thrashed, actually—in the engineering workstation business. Apollo Computer in Boston, built by William Poduska and some folks from DEC and Data General, had grown spectacularly. Sun Microsystems, *Sun* an acronym for Stanford University Network, was started by four unlikely partners: Andreas Bechtolsheim, a Stanford PhD student from Germany, who created a workstation from off-the-shelf components for his own use in his graduate work; Scott McNealy from Stanford, scion of William McNealy, who co-managed American Motors with George Romney; William Joy, a Berkeley student who had a large role in rewriting the UNIX Operating System licensed to UC Berkeley by AT&T Bell Laboratories into the Open-Source Berkeley UNIX (BSD); and Vinod Khosla, a venture capitalist from India working in the Sand Hill Road community. Sun, starting two years later than Apollo, had surged to the forefront and was vying with DEC by 1987.

The Fort Collins Systems Division was absorbed with the deeply integrated Focus III microprocessor chipsets strongly advocated by Fred Wenninger. When that colossal experiment failed in the marketplace (inexplicably, from the point of view of the Fort Collins marketeers), the division found itself behind the two upstart rivals who had selected Motorola's new 16/32-bit microcomputer, the 68000, for their machines. Motorola, chasing Intel's 8086 microprocessor, put seventy thousand devices on their chip (versus twenty-nine thousand for Intel), with a key 16 megabyte linear address space. Almost immediately, it became the dominant workstation standard, as well as the basis for the best graphics and GUIs in personal computers (including Atari ST, Amiga, and Macintosh).

HP Fort Collins had used the Motorola chipset in the low-featured HP 9826, introduced in 1981. Playing catch-up, it put the HP 9836 Engineering Workstation on the market in 1982, using the same Motorola microprocessor. Alas, the division made three fundamental errors with this machine, which cost it the leadership position against its rivals. First, it failed to bet on networking, still believing in the individual desktop metaphor. Apollo built a very robust local networking capability, which became their chief competitive advantage with a full suite of network administration tools that complemented a very effective engineering lab infrastructure. Called Domain, it supported team collaboration on hardware or software engineering projects.[62]

Second, HP's machine was optimized for hardware engineers rather than software developers. It had a low-resolution monochromatic or color CRT (512 × 390 pixels) instead of the exquisite gray-scale high-resolution CRT (1024 × 768) on the significantly cheaper Sun offering. This decision coincided with a tremendous surge in software application developers, both on campuses and in industry, for which Sun enjoyed near-monopolistic hegemony. DEC had won the college campuses years earlier with huge donations of DEC VAXes for computer science departments; Sun now was able to displace many of those seats under a bold University Associates program instigated by Sun VP Bernie LaCroute, who had come to Sun from DEC. Even at HP, software developers began bootlegging Sun and Macintosh machines for work.

The networking issue was fixable simply by using standards. Apollo had a proprietary version of IBM Token Ring that worked exceedingly well for local area networking (within a building complex). Sun adopted the increasingly popular TCP/IP, which became the winning hand for the Internet backbone a decade later. HP doggedly stayed with its proprietary instrument perspective, wed to homebrew HP/IB and the nearly useless RS 232 serial interface.

Fixing the CRT design would have been amazingly simple, as numerous critics pointed out, but the beleaguered and obstinate division leadership resolutely ignored Bay Area input, not to mention the HP software engineering community. The net result of these two decisions doomed the third, even if HP had understood how to deal with software applications.[63]

The third decision, of course, was to compete, via the Engineering Applications and the Manufacturing Applications groups, with the emerging third-party software vendors. These vendors included ASK Computer, Mentor Graphics, Cadence Systems, and Valid Logic, plus new database companies such as Oracle, Ingres, Informix, and Sybase. HP Corporate had a very hard time deciding whether or not to compete with these upstarts—the obvious issue was why Mentor Graphics would port to an HP workstation instead of or in addition to an Apollo workstation when HP's Engineering Design Systems Group was trying to be its major competitor. Apollo and Sun avoided channel conflict, and their growth rates and much better tuned featuresets offered much more excitement than the combined sales for HP.

First Bill Terry and then Lew Platt ran these groups, with lieutenants Bill Parzybok as the Design Systems Group VP and Brian Moore running the Manufacturing Systems Group.[64] Managers for divisions in these groups, as well as the Office Products Software Group, found that (1) the computer sales forces gave their software away to win the hardware business; and (2) competing workstation vendors didn't want to host their products. Worse, HP top management couldn't figure out how to reward these divisions with shared revenues and profits because HP revenue-sharing models were built on archaic manufacturing cost transfer rates rather than development investment (such as R&D, marketing, and support). Dick Hackborn resolved nearly identical problems in the Peripherals Group, but it took lots of Palo Alto time and battles. The VPs charged with these responsibilities abdicated, dooming HP's entries in these arenas, even though in several cases, the actual products were world-class at the time. HP has not yet recovered in software. Over the 1988–1993 period, two-thirds of the vice presidents, division managers, and R&D managers for these software divisions left HP to join independent software vendors (ISVs), often as CEOs, almost always as officers (including Dick Moore, Dan Warmenhoven, Alain Couder, Dennis McGinn, Bill Parzybok, Chuck House, Bob Kadarauch, Dave Dayton, Sandy Chumbley, Jef Graham, Nancy Anderson, Jay Richards, Sam Prather, and Bob Frankenberg).

Personal Computers Go Mainstream

Investors dissecting the 1988 *Annual Report* would have been sick if they knew Packard's 1981 dictum: "We need to be Number One in computing." Birnbaum came into a company that, although number fourteen in computing measured by overall revenue, was a leading factor in minicomputers (number two), engineering workstations (number two), data terminals and personal computers (number two), and calculators (number one). Birnbaum's scalable architecture thesis, intended to bridge from super-minicomputers to personal machines, had been applied only to a few minicomputer machines after eight years of development. Annual sales for all of the minicomputer CPU lines of the company (for example, the 1000 and 3000 series) was nearly flat, in the low $500 millions since the Vision decision four years earlier. Grudging respect, though not granted, was due the Cupertino team for holding the fort. The issue was that DEC had grown enormously, from an overall $5.584 billion to $11.475 billion in the same interval.

The bigger miss for HP, a huge miss, was in personal computers and workstations. Sunnyvale and Corvallis dropped the ball in PCs and terminals, allowing Compaq, a new clone company based in Houston, to whip them hollow, while a nascent Dell caught them from a standing start. HP parlayed nearly $400 million in 1984 into roughly $650 million by 1988, while Compaq exploded from $329 million to $2.07 billion. For the next two years, HP Personal Computing grew only $25 million; Compaq grew forty times more, adding $1.03 billion. Dell sold $69 million in 1986; four years later, they nearly caught HP at $546 million. These numbers weren't in the Chuck Holloway analysis, nor in the self-satisfied Vectra *HP Measure* article.[65] The defense for HP managers in this arena was that the other companies were growing by shaving margins, essentially building a nonprofitable business. Packard, who fumed that "the only thing worse than a little shitty business is a big shitty business," must have raged when he read Compaq's 1988 first-quarter press release, with 108 percent growth rate in revenue, 133 percent in profits, and 10.6 percent net profit percentage.[66] The fact that Compaq was still only 20 percent of HP's overall size did not mollify the chairman.

APRIL 22, 1988, NEW YORK CITY "Texas Instruments Net Down, Compaq's Up." Texas Instruments Inc., a major computer chip [maker], today reported a slightly lower net income for the first quarter, while the profits of Compaq Computer Corporation, a rapidly growing computer maker, nearly doubled. The companies said demand surged for their major products. . . . Compaq's net income more than doubled, to $46.8 million, or $1.21 a share, from $20.1 million, or 56 cents a share, in the period last year. Sales rose to $439.5 million from $211 million.[67]

The Acquisition Trail

Engineering workstations were the biggest disaster, since HP once had had a huge lead. Fort Collins, well-funded in R&D, spent enormously on Wenninger's N-MOS III silicon IC family for the HP 9000 that debuted in 1982. It failed nearly as completely as Amigo, for many of the same reasons, but especially due to conflict with independent software vendors (ISVs). The overall product line managed to grow from $275 million in 1984 by about $200 million four years later. Meanwhile, Apollo grew from $81 million in 1984 to $392 million by 1987; Sun exploded, from $38 million in 1984 to $1.05 billion by the end of 1988.

HP bought Apollo Computer in mid-1988, briefly leapfrogging Sun Microsystems to become again the highest unit-volume workstation vendor. Joel Birnbaum, opposed for weeks, acquiesced when it became clear that HP would abandon the space if the deal fell through.[68] Dean offered,

It was a big mistake. Lew and John and I were all proponents of it. We were losing market share rather steadily; Apollo had some interesting products and some major customers, including Mentor Graphics. I don't know whether it was just a bad idea or we didn't execute it well. One thing is very clear, it's very hard to integrate different technological approaches and to get full leverage across the whole product line. Different microprocessors and operating systems give huge compatibility issues. They were three thousand miles away, and . . . the Fort Collins team, whom they were supposed to integrate with, weren't what you would call the strongest of team players. They made it very difficult, unnecessarily so. Given all that, I made a mistake in being such a strong proponent for it. . . . But once the die is cast, there you are. We were stuck with it. It wasn't fatal. The cost was $700 million, which was a lot of money in those days. It didn't show up anywhere in the numbers and we worked our way through it. And we got some good people. But on balance, I think it was a mistake.[69]

. . .

MAY 1989, PALO ALTO, CALIFORNIA "HP Won't Abandon Apollo Users." "We're very committed to the Apollo line, both existing machines and those in development," said Dick Watts, computer products sector marketing director for Palo Alto, CA-based Hewlett-Packard.[70]

Two years later, HP/Apollo sold a combined $725 million, retreating in fact, whereas Sun Microsystems grew to an astounding $2.45 billion in 1990. Even niche player Silicon Graphics (led by ex-HPite Ed McCracken) grew from $22 million in 1986 to $520 million by 1990. Worse, key HPites fled to the competition. A fine graphics designer from Fort Collins, Warren Pratt, went to Silicon Graphics, as did Howard Smith, the GSD R&D manager. Mike Ramsey and Tom Jermoluk from HP Cupertino joined them. Mark Tolliver, a long-term HP UNIX marketeer, joined Sun later, becoming its VP of marketing in the mid-1990s. Most of the significant Apollo software designers were driven out, as Bill Kay and other HP top managers made it clear that the Fort Collins "individual workstation" concept rather than the networked cluster was the winner. Atria Software in particular, with Paul Levine's leadership and David LeBlang's brilliant software designs, bought the Apollo EE Domain software for configuration management. They built a leading middleware company over the next seven years, before merging with Reed Hastings's Pure Software to form Pure Atria.[71] If it had not been for small printers growing from $11 million to $2.2 billion, an incredible five hundred times increase in six years, HP shareholders might have been incensed.

And then, HP made two positive moves. First, Sun combined with AT&T to try to co-opt UNIX. John Doyle, in a move as bold as his support of the CIS initiative at Stanford to open the decade, organized the Open Software Foundation (OSF), blunting the thrust of the new leader. John Young called OSF "one of the most significant events ever to occur within the computer industry. Membership in the OSF leaves plenty of room for competitive differentiation."[72]

Second, Denny Georg from Fort Collins led a multidivisional team, using a new set of HP-PA chips, that yielded a new HP Apollo 9000 Series 700 workstation family informally called "Snakes," coiled to strike in the marketplace. Georg's challenge was "to coordinate, motivate and focus the work of 30-plus functional organizations." It was a gritty performance, resulting in a fabulous breakthrough befitting the original Fort Collins leadership legacy. One writer enthused in *Personal Workstation Magazine* that the machines are "the last word in raw performance for a while . . . no one is even coming close."[73] Andrew Pollack in the *New York Times* reported that it was "a sign of renewed vigor and confidence throughout the proud and tradition-rich organization that has been suffering from missed opportunities and unsatisfying financial performance."[74] The highly respected SPECmark measurement yielded extremely competitive RISC numbers.

Spectrum, after ten years, demonstrated leading-edge performance for the entire industry. HP still had a chance.[75]

CHAPTER 12

Looking Forward

There is no point in looking backward. All of our challenges lie in front of us. I think we should concentrate on looking forward. It doesn't matter to Bill and me personally what happens in the next twenty-five years, but it matters greatly to us what happens to you in the next twenty-five.

DAVE PACKARD (1990)[1]

The fiftieth-anniversary year, 1989, should have been appropriate for a celebration of just how far Hewlett-Packard had come. But enthusiasm was strangely muted. By the late 1980s, many employees were increasingly aware that things weren't working as well as they once had. The board and the executive committee saw a shrinking growth rate and reduced profit margins. Divisions experienced bogged-down schedules; everyone was hostage to the Computer Business Council release plan. Many divisions simply had no idea which ingredients to value—if profits were impossible to obtain because the corporation wouldn't let you sell your software, how could you be held accountable for a profit-and-loss statement? Exit interviewees spoke the unspeakable: HP had lost its élan, the *joie de vivre* was gone.

Some remembered the euphoria a few years earlier. Rejecting Orwell's dark vision of Big Brother taking over, CEO John Young had named 1984 the Golden Age for HP and for electronics. Easily the most profitable year in HP modern corporate history at 11 percent net profit, it followed a string of ten great years. In 1984, the first RISC computer was nearing completion, the 32-bit computer-on-a-chip from HP Fort Collins had just been released, and HP had recently shipped its ten thousandth HP 3000.[2] Then something went awry. The HP 9000 failed to attract third-party software, the Spectrum/MPE release didn't work, and Sun Microsystems and Apollo Computer challenged and bested HP engineering workstations.

Against this backdrop, the company approached a fiftieth anniversary with trepidation. Thankfully, in late 1988, RISC machine quality improved and sales jumped. Already involved in lukewarm planning for summer picnics in 1989, general managers viewed the January meeting guardedly. No one, it seemed, expected an upbeat meeting. But the news—one million LaserJets shipped, plus a working HP-PA system—with an uplifting start in orders, gave energy to the annual meeting. After two-and-a-half days of unexpected elation, Dave Packard walked to the podium to close the meeting with one of his annual "thank you" benedictions.

An eyewitness account of Packard's remarks revealed disquieting concern (see Appendix C; "A Founder's Benediction"): Dave's dour soliloquy dampened the ardor. Packard seemed grumpy at an odd moment—yes, DEC had caught and surpassed HP in total revenues, and HP net profits were down 15 percent from the previous eleven-year average. Worse, revenue growth had stumbled, from an average 23 percent per year to a dissatisfying 10 percent—lower than any single year since Hewlett's nine-day fortnight in the 1970–71 recession. But 1988 was back on track. It appeared that HP was righting itself after a protracted siege when the HP 3000 was under pressure and the long-awaited HP-PA program stalled. Revenue growth at 21.5 percent was bested only in 1984 for the whole 1980s decade; profits were back above 8 percent. Packard did softly say he felt that he could speak for both himself and Bill Hewlett, recuperating from a heart attack, in saying that things appeared to be back in good shape, and how pleased they were with the recent signs of progress.

But Dave exploded when he talked about HP Labs and their flawed fiber-optics research program. Intoning that it takes twenty-five years to come out on top, using the LED business as his example, Packard tackled the company's big bet—Spectrum. Packard's projection jolted his hearers: "We can now begin—*begin*—to participate seriously in the computer business. And if we do our jobs diligently, we can indeed be a, if not *the,* world leader in computing equipment in just another fifteen years or so." Who in the room truly believed that?

No betting person that day would have subscribed to Dave's assertion that IBM, invincible in 1988, would be surpassed by HP within the next fifteen years. Birnbaum perhaps would have once dared to think it, but he was now eight years into the quest at HP, chastened by the extraordinary difficulties. Young, almost certainly not—an abortive experiment with "rows and columns" management had made him more dubious than ever about the struggle between divisional autonomy, initiative, enthusiasm, and the need for system integrity that seemed so culturally bound in this aging company.[3]

A simple perusal of the revenues and profits of IBM and DEC versus HP computing for the previous four years (Figures 12.1 and 12.2)—never

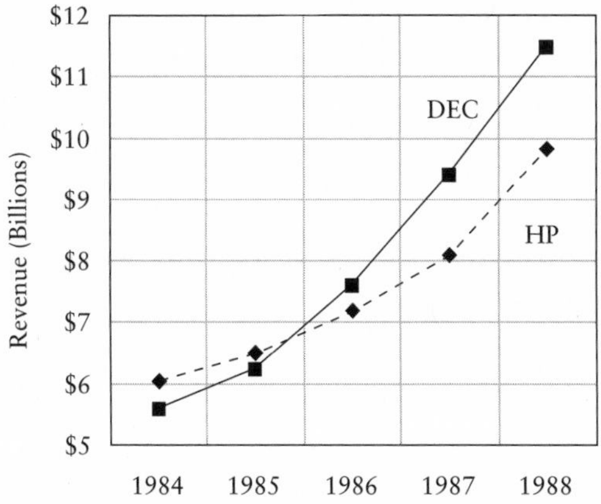

FIGURE 12.1. HP and DEC revenue growth, 1984–1988

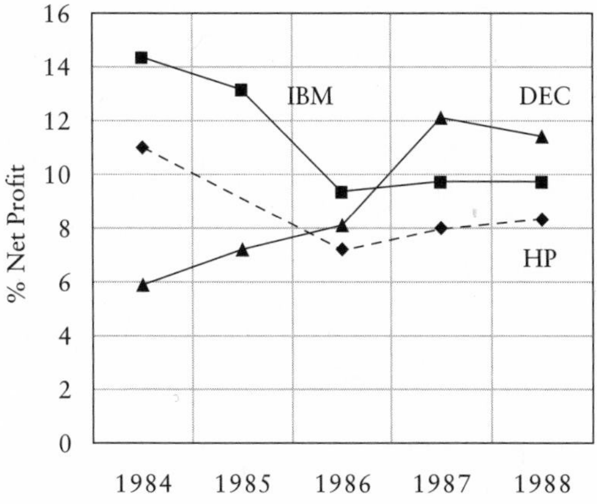

FIGURE 12.2. IBM, HP, and DEC profit, 1984–1988

mind issues of the IBM PC or a Macintosh versus the HP Touchscreen—would have quelled enthusiasm. Catch IBM? DEC was the worry; they had just caught and surpassed HP overall, and HP computing was only half of the company.[4] And IBM had added nearly as much revenue in the previous five years as the combined HP and DEC computing totals.

As the spring unfolded, groups and teams around the globe fashioned picnics and parties to celebrate the milestone. Dave and Bill, truly beloved elder statesmen in their legacy company, attended many events. Employees greeted them everywhere with extraordinary enthusiasm, but too often the founders heard frustration: "We can't get decisions made; the company is no longer quick to market; HP isn't responsive to customers; the HP Way is disappearing."

Answering the Fire Bell One More Time

An apocryphal story asserts that a long-term, low-level employee sent David Packard a note that broke the camel's back. The note indeed was sent, but numerous cathartic moments exist in various people's memories over a four-month protracted period while both Dave and Bill mulled the wisdom of stepping back into harness. Goaded into returning to save the ship, the duo swung into action. Packard launched his campaign in his home state of Colorado, giving a provocative speech in Fort Collins in August 1990 (see Appendix C, "Management by Wandering Around") that promised to "sweep the company clean of bureaucracy."[5] Hewlett simultaneously visited the Boise, Idaho, divisions, with deep inquiries of key employees. The actions were undeniable—implying strongly that CEO John Young's tenure was at an end. Wistful accounts reveal that the duo labored mightily, and through hard work and inspiration, rallied the company from the abyss and saved it from mind-numbing bureaucracy at a time of crisis even more compelling than the cash crunch of 1974. How many times in the history of the Hewlett-Packard Company had these warriors changed the focus or sharpened the perspective? It is a gripping story, with melodramatic moments.

Just as with the 1974 "Give 'em Hell" speech, the facts are complicated, and the results debatable. First, the bureaucratic committees had been largely disbanded eighteen months earlier. More telling, from the time of the Fort Collins speech, it took Packard another two full years to change the CEO. When Packard finally did ask the board for permission, a frustrated Hewlett tossed a pencil into the middle of the table, saying, "Packard, I was there years before you on this one."[6]

Packard's Colorado speech galvanized Palo Alto. John Young and the executive committee angrily sought a videotape of what he said, without success. But the story spread like wildfire. Three days later in Cupertino, Young gave an hour-long speech to HP's Software Productivity Forum. Hundreds of developers heard Young give a classically solid analytical presentation about opportunities in the software field, and what he expected HP to do with them.

The first question challenged one of Young's tenets, not unlike the questions that Packard had gotten earlier in the week. The brusque answer began, "Where you are wrong is . . ." There were no more questions.[7] John's irritation had boiled over. Publicly humiliated, Young weighed his options, packed up his office, and resigned. Packard, with a history in his early career of being way too hard on people, grumbled and met with his CEO for rapprochement; Young went back to work at Packard's behest.

During the next few weeks, stories of seeing the stooped septuagenarian shuffling into his office at 1501 Page Mill Road circulated. Packard ardently courted Dick Hackborn, who rebuffed him. Young's description: "Dave said, 'Well, I'm going to help you.' I said, 'That's fine.' But, he had no idea what to do. This was very sophisticated stuff that he hadn't been involved in. So I assigned Dean [Morton]and Pete Peterson [Human Resources vice president], between the two of them, to answer any questions . . . and just keep him occupied, while we got things back on track."[8] Young then installed Platt and Hackborn as co-COOs, while continuing the bureaucratic sweep that he had started the year before. Twenty years later, Young was sanguine:

> There was a lot of frustration on my part, too. I could have been more forceful in making these things happen, but I was trying to get Hackborn to take on PCs, which he desperately didn't want to do. Finally I bludgeoned him into doing it, because it was the key to cleaning things up. That transformation from having one Chief Operating Officer to having two was key. It cleaned things up. Then I could really work with both Lew and Dick, and things really started running. By

the time I left in '92, it was in pretty good shape; in the next few years when Lew came in, I thought it went very well.[9]

Joel Birnbaum, HP's senior vice president of research throughout this period, had a birds-eye view:

They were involved in a fatherly way. They did indeed make some visits to the divisions. *BusinessWeek* had a wonderful time with the controversy.[10] My own view of that stormy time was that John Young had laid almost all the seeds for fixing the problems. There was some friction between them, and it eventually led to him leaving and Lew Platt coming in. But I never really thought they had done all that much, frankly.

John thought we had too many layers of management. It had gotten popular in the company to have councils, so they had a million different councils. John was hard at work, streamlining the plans for fewer products, eliminating products, getting manufacturing done elsewhere where it made sense to do it elsewhere. Not just to make it at lower cost. He understood the problem well and he was taking aggressive action.[11]

The Competitive Challenge for HP

A key problem for Young was the fragmented nature of HP's key competitors. The reorganization at the end of 1990 was revealing. Bill Terry was now the executive vice president for the Measurement Systems Sector, which comprised four groups: Medical (run by VP Ben Holmes), Analytical (led by VP Dieter Hoehn), Components (managed by VP Bill Craven), and a newly combined Test and Measurement Group under Ned Barnholt that brought the former Microwave and Communications Group back together with the Electronic Instruments Group. For this Measurement Systems Sector, disparate companies in various segments mattered, none of them competing in more than a small niche.

Dick Hackborn headed another new sector, the Computer Products Sector, which combined his old Peripherals Group with the Personal Computer Group, since both primarily sold their products through the computer dealer channels. Within the Peripherals Group, printer competitors were separate from disc drive or tape drive manufacturers. Both were distinct in general from the PC vendors.

The computing world too was pretty fragmented—Apple built only personal computers; Sun focused only on workstations; Stratus and Tandem built only high-availability large-database systems. HP's Computer Systems Sector, led by Lew Platt, was a generalist company, along with IBM and DEC, in a world of specialty niche players.

Generalists have a hard time matching the unique capabilities of niche players—for example, personal computer folk saw little need for unique silicon technology, but a huge need for dealer channel pricing strategies and heavy merchandising; the Microwave instrument divisions and the Computer Systems Sector divisions had nearly inverse views, competing heavily with major technology investments. Twenty years later, the HP slogan—HP Invent—is a misnomer for the Personal Computer Group: even design is outsourced to Asian companies; R&D is a miniscule 0.7 percent of revenue, less than one-tenth the old HP average.

Young's bigger problem was Packard, who became increasingly frustrated in 1990 and 1991 as the computing industry suffered a major recession. The four hotshots of Silicon Valley relational database companies—Oracle, Ingres, Informix, and Sybase—nearly bankrupted, collectively losing $200 million dollars in a business not much larger than that two years earlier. Larry Ellison of Oracle barely survived a board attempt to remove him; all of the other companies deposed their CEOs. It was a vivid precursor to the dot-com meltdown a decade later. And Packard, an absolutist, held up the numbers for his CEO; by the end of 1992, HP's growth rate had dropped dramatically, from a typical 22 percent per year to three years in a row that averaged 11 percent CAGR, as low as Hewlett's first three years at the helm. Profits attenuated radically, from 8 percent net to 3.5 percent over the four-year period (Figures 12.3 and 12.4).

Figures 12.3 and 12.4 are revealing for HP's numbers, but measured against IBM and DEC—the two leading companies targeted by the ambitious Spectrum program—HP performance from 1990 through 1992 was actually terrific. HP exceeded DEC and IBM average profitability by an astounding 16.5 percent in 1992; revenues grew 13 percent as IBM and DEC were flat. Young could have been praised highly for outperforming his major competitors dramatically. Instead, Packard was incensed. More a student of HP history than of contemporary competitors, he

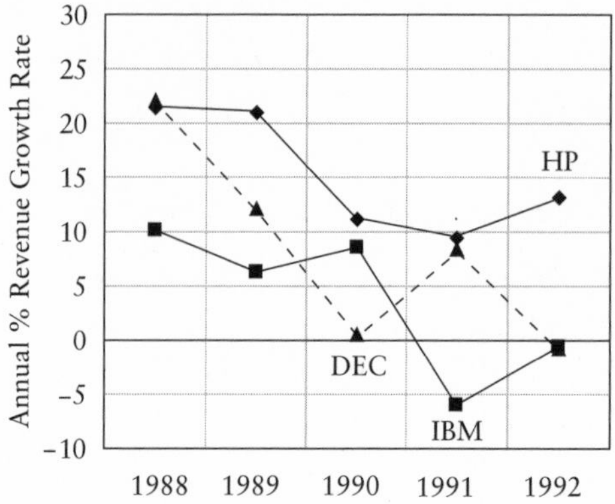

FIGURE 12.3. IBM, HP, and DEC revenue growth, 1988–1992

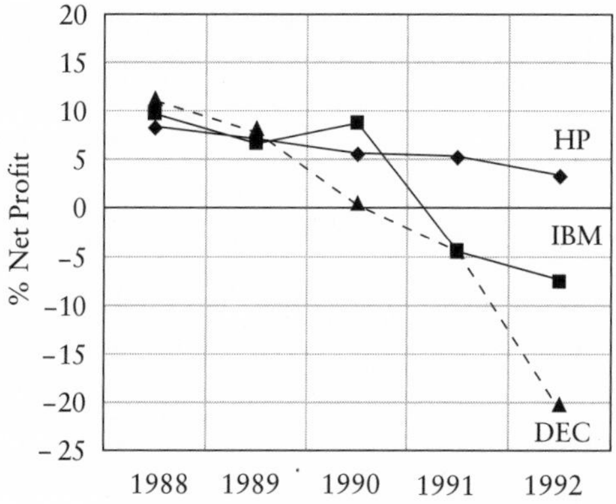

FIGURE 12.4. IBM, HP, and DEC profit, 1988–1992

had the view that five of Young's previous seven years ranked among the lowest in both profitability and growth rate in HP history. Packard went on the warpath.

Recognizing a Restructuring

An encomium for Packard at his death has become the conventional wisdom re HP history: "In the late 1980s as if reflecting the growing age of its founders, Hewlett-Packard began to slowly rot from the inside. . . . Sclerotic, flat-footed giants like Wang, Data General (DG), and DEC—were sunk or left crippled in the water."[12] None of these companies was an apt comparison with HP, however; a different view is mandatory to understand this period. The computing industry was being savagely restructured. Spectrum—a scalable architecture from low to high performance—was one approach. Edge computing—workstations for professionals, and personal computers for office workers—was a new challenger. Networked clusters of many edge machines, coupled together in a client-server arrangement, and peer networks eventually, was yet a third version. And these all became somewhat mixed up, blending and merging and redefining almost annually in performance races, as silicon processing power soared.

Some companies were sclerotic—DG had 50 percent of the workstation business and $1.2 billion in sales in 1985; sales flattened and profits disappeared at that point when Apollo, Sun, and Silicon Graphics redefined the business. By 1990, the others had grown from $1.3 billion to $4 billion in this space—even HP, with a $400 million acquisition, grew from $500 million to $1.3 billion while Data General stagnated.

Some companies were bureaucratic—Wang and DEC both had become hobbled by top management policy and stifling committees, not unlike the problem that Young tackled at HP. Wang had grown enormously on dedicated word-processing machines for office work—they simply couldn't fathom the notion that the low-cost IBM PC would displace their capable machines. The IBM PC, Apple, Compaq, and Dell were head-on threats to Wang. Wang revenues stalled in 1986, and the company had $1.1 billion net losses in the next four years.[13] Wang's sales, 49 percent of the independents' total in 1985, eroded to 21 percent by 1990. Founder An Wang died brokenhearted in 1990; his company declared bankruptcy in mid-1992. HP data terminals and PC sales in this space were a mere 7 percent of Wang, Dell, Compaq, and Apple in 1985, and 6 percent in 1990. HP didn't factor into the business. This wasn't sclerosis or bureaucracy. HP leadership couldn't decide how to deal with this disruptive PC world; in terms of price, features, and marketing, it was alien to most HP experience.

For a company that emphasized engineering excellence, next-bench syndrome market research, and growth from within a divisional structure, the paradigm shift of the PC revolution was nearly antithetical. A business environment in which feature differentiation was a handicap rather than an advantage, and speed of development, price competition, and market understanding were paramount, was just not HP culture. Not unlike Intel leadership, the HP executive committee misunderstood the extent of this shift.

Help came from an unexpected source. DEC leadership, particularly Ken Olsen's autocratic style, proved unequal to the structural shifts of the industry. DEC struggled as badly as HP with the meaning of and best strategy for the personal computer. Both companies launched myriad offerings, none differentiated effectively, with each robbing the company of critical marketing mass. Meanwhile, Prime Computer, Tandem Computer, and Stratus were taking market share from DEC's upper end, and the open-systems approach that Sun Microsystems espoused was punishing at the low end. When HP's Spectrum Architecture finally proved enterprise-ready in 1989, DEC's revenues, escalating at 25 percent per year in the 1980s, suddenly and irrevocably flattened, and the company, unable to halt the expense flow, quickly found itself in serious financial difficulty. Its answer—the 64-bit DEC Alpha, a predecessor to the HP/Intel Itanium—was a costly abortive effort that consumed the company's resources. HP-PA was the death blow for DEC. Birnbaum's arrow found a victim, even if it wasn't the primary target when he left IBM to join HP in 1980.

HP-PA Comes of Age

If viewed from the vantage point that Birnbaum was hired to solve a particular problem, HP-PA had proven worthy. The scalable line integrated the multiple conflicting lines of equipment, ending the bizarre complexity of the earlier era, and, in addition, it provided a logical upgrade path for enterprise-level customers. The Spectrum architecture demonstrated stunning performance leadership against all comers with the Snakes program, as did new applications such as online transaction processing and real-time control.

Young did encounter enormous difficulty selling the HP-PA concept to the Fortune 100 enterprise IT managers, who perennially found that buying IBM was safe while other purchases were often costly detours. But, in sharp contrast to understaffed efforts in the PC side, significant investments were made in a performance-tuning center and a migration center, plus customer seminars extolling HP's productivity processes. Birnbaum commented with enthusiasm and animation on some of this work:

Half of our work, which never got any publicity and HP could have made an incredible name for itself, was migrating customers from the old systems. Yes, Spectrum improved the cost performance ratio, and yes, it made HP an effective computer company in a variety of fields, but the real [contribution] is that we achieved the absolutely best transition from one machine to another. If you build an emulator of a previous machine, you have to emulate not only the instruction set, but all the special cases and the special states that the machine can get into. Eventually the emulator becomes more complicated than the target machine. That is the way PCs go from one generation to the next. They use as much as a quarter of the chip real estate to put hardware emulators in place. That's the way Intel PCs operated. They had the benefit of just one operating system from Microsoft, at least until recently. We needed to support that same kind of migration for a broad set of issues. We looked at a lot of different ways of doing that. I knew we could deliver the cost performance because we had already done that in the lab. I knew we could scale across the applications; I was a little worried about real-time, but clever guys figured out a way to do that. But how in the hell were we going to get the customers off their current machines without consuming the entire HP support structure and taking so long in the process that IBM and everybody else would just come in and scoop up all the customers?[14]

The Spectrum Achilles Heel

IBM was already spreading FUD—fear, uncertainty, and doubt—in the HP customer base. Spectrum was two years behind schedule because of the years that were lost with the Vision decision. Birnbaum was, of a sudden, terrified:

We knew what to do but we didn't know how to do it any better than IBM or anyone that had ever done it. And it just seemed like it was going to ruin the whole thing. So, on one side, I was getting positive surprises that Spectrum was faster than we thought, it was better than we thought, it was easier to scale than we thought, its cost was lower. Everything about it was great, but it was like starting from scratch and HP couldn't afford to start from scratch; we knew customers would run away. So that was the really hard problem. And I started really losing sleep about it. I just didn't know how we were going to get out of that. I started hiring consultants asking for help, and I was really getting very depressed. Nobody in the company knew anything about it outside our lab. They weren't sophisticated enough to ask the question. It was like seeing a light from the railroad train coming down the track at me and it is getting bigger, bigger, and bigger. What a mess. And I said "Oh boy, I really screwed up.[15]

Serendipity, good fortune, or the fabled HP Magic Stardust showed up just in time. A long-time HP lawyer-engineer, Ron Griffin, went to Birnbaum's office to plead for Birnbaum to interview a neighbor's boy from San Diego. Griffin had never met Birnbaum, but he told him, "this kid is so smart, he loves computers so much. He went to UCSD and he was one of the top students there. He graduated two years early and he would just love to work for HP, and I think he has a master's degree and he really, really likes the idea of working in research. Do you think you could use this guy?"

Joel demurred, saying, "Ron, frankly we are so behind the industry that we are either hiring guys with PhDs because they have three or four years of research experience, which we need, or we are hiring guys that have the equivalent who are working in other companies because we can't afford to do on-the-job training. I am sure he is really a bright kid . . ."

Thank goodness Griffin was persistent. He told Joel that it would break the kid's heart if he couldn't even come up to talk to him. Joel acquiesced: "I was interviewing a hundred guys a month anyway. I spent almost every lunch, most dinners, and every breakfast for twenty years recruiting or selling. I said, 'Ok, have the guy come up.'"[16]

The kid [Dan Magenheimer] walked into Birnbaum's office a couple of weeks later, whereupon two key software designers, Bill Worley and Michael Mahon, said, "This kid is really special, hire this kid. He is really bright, and he just loves computing so much. You will see he is going to turn out to be really good. We can send him over to Stanford later for a PhD."[17] It carried the day.

Joel got rhapsodic about Magenheimer:

He really loved languages and compilers. We put him in the optimizing compiler group and he immediately started making contributions. He was very different in his manner, very respectful and quiet, but one day he walked into my office and said, "You know, Bill [Worley] has these lunches, talking about our big problems: how we are going to have to transfer this into an installed base? Everybody keeps talking about how hard that problem is. I would like to work on that, and I really have an idea that I think might work." And I said, "Oh really. Great, what is the idea, Dan?" He said, "Object code translation."

I said to myself, "The oldest idea in the world, tried by a hundred thousand people." I had a whole group working on that in IBM at one point. But I had learned my lesson (from Hewlett) about not telling people that it's been done and failed. And I was not supposed to talk about IBM. So I thought I will ask him three key questions. I figured, "I kind of hate to do this to him, but he can't go charging down this trail."

Joel said that Magenheimer, who looked only about twelve years old to Joel, leaned back and said, "I've read a lot of papers about those problems; in fact, I read a lot of papers that your group at IBM published, but you know, the world has really changed. We know so much about optimizing compilers now, and we know a lot about program analysis. I've been doing some of this at home at night, and I figure with a pretty good translator, we could get it down to maybe five times longer." And I said, "Yeah, that is about consistent with what my group at IBM found." And he said, "When we apply our optimizer to it, it drops to twice. And our machine is four times as fast, so that means we will go twice as fast as our original code. I think that any customer will be happy with that performance, don't you?"

And he gave me three examples of things that we didn't know how to do five years before. The whole field had progressed; now there were whole conferences on optimizing compilers. He said, "That is how you get performance." I thought, "Wow, this kid is really thinking." Whereupon he said, "I have written some little routines to demonstrate how instead of just translating the instruction, we will translate a whole subroutine. So we can handle this." Then to the third question, he said, "Yeah, I've thought a lot about that; we can do an evaluation suite that works like this." I said, "Dan, you just became a manager!"[18]

Migration Centers

Using the optimizing compiler technology, Birnbaum and his team helped set up a network of migration centers. Coca-Cola provided a typical example, coming in with a full application suite. HP told them that in less than one week, HP could migrate all of their applications. Birnbaum said,

That was a claim so outrageous, it became a part of the sales handbook for IBM and DEC that HP was such a naive bunch of guys. "One week! It has never been done in less than six months." In many cases, after HP got good at it, we did it in a day. We moved people in a day. That not only saved us, it let us build a sales steamroller. There were indeed some special cases where it took three or four months, but everybody was expecting it to take much longer. Bruce Campbell, a very energetic and charismatic manager, ran the migration center. Once we saw how successful it was, and once the business just started coming in like crazy, I kept saying to the HP communications people, this is the best thing that we have done. This is an absolute breakthrough: you take your application, stick it into the machine which grinds away for minutes and it comes out with everything ported. The rest of the day it is tested using some other very novel technology. You get a performance profile right away. HP never published it. They never ran an ad. The salesmen, of course, were all over it. It was one of the great stories of the whole experience. It totally saved my job. Without that there was nothing.[19]

Birnbaum and Young didn't share the Migration Center story widely, nor did Denny Georg share the Snakes development story widely. Thanks to the breakthroughs of each, HP-PA blossomed, giving HP computing breathing room. Years later, Georg would talk more freely about some of the unique challenges of the Snakes program. He said,

Dean Morton called me and wanted me to become program manager; they were on their second program manager at that time, and there was a lot of activity but not much result. And I was as close to burnout as I had ever been, from my previous job working with Hitachi to license the HP-PA chipsets. It was a really significant learning experience for me, having to negotiate in a different culture. People practiced in negotiating with Japanese companies had written some really good books. I read them, and I started attempting different negotiation styles—and it really worked. With Japanese negotiating, sitting and having a lot of silence is part of the negotiation process. Americans typically don't have the patience to do that. Once I learned how to do it, it was amazing. We did complete the negotiation with Hitachi successfully.

I was in Hawaii, closing this negotiation. It was John Young and I, plus two people from corporate development, and a couple of attorneys. Literally, John and I were doing the work. I got a call from Bill Kay, the workstation business unit manager, who said, "We really want you to do this. We really need somebody who's willing to come in and take over this program and make it work." When I got back to Colorado, I said, "Ok, I think I can do this." I needed to have a goal that would motivate me.

At the time, we had an excellent Motorola 68000 workstation program. HP had bought Apollo Computer, which had been successful in workstations with a proprietary operating system, architecture, and their own 68000 program. This project, called Snakes, was to create a RISC workstation. Sun was starting to eat our lunch with the SPARC chips from MIPS, which executed industry-standard UNIX software with third-party applications (Mentor Graphics or Cadence) that ran on multiple vendor platforms. Specialization in software, standard platforms for that software, and then competing based on your ability to deliver those standard platforms, was starting to become a trend in the industry.

I'll never forget, I spent a half a day in my office at home on a Saturday, and I wrote about five slides, which were the objectives for the program, the first order of strategy, and then what some of our tactics were going to be. And I met with a few people who became critical to the program. I probably met with about thirty people—various section managers and lab managers across HP, in Oregon, in California, and people in Boston who had been part of Apollo. I asked each of them, "How do you want to contribute? Here's our challenge. Our challenge is to build an industry performance leading workstation at a competitive price point and make a real statement about Hewlett-Packard being in this business." I met with them kind of one-on-one and tried to engage them with my proposal and get their support, their buy-in. I made an enormous amount of notes, and it's probably still part of some lab notebook that's in HP. But I kept track and 90 percent to 95 percent of the people said, "Look. That sounds great. We want to be part of this program. We want to make HP successful."[20]

Organizing for Success

Georg went to work, organizing teams of people to meet weekly. There were teams for networking software; teams for storage systems; and people responsible for system quality, including very key people out of Apollo.

They met weekly, for the most part in San Jose in a conference room at the HP hangar. From literally blank sheets of paper in May of 1990, HP introduced the workstations in March of 1991. Georg said,

> It was intense. I don't think I've ever worked harder, and I don't think a team that I've been associated with has ever worked harder. But we basically went through a lot of putting the issues on the table, prioritizing the issues, working the issues, deciding, and then moving on. It was about that time that I think somebody applied the moniker "Czar"; I was making sure that the program kept moving.
>
> You know, we made a lot of decisions based on a mix of the team's intelligence and intuition. When you're going to move fast, you can't always wait for all the data. You have to be getting data, making decisions, and moving forward. This included a new microprocessor, new IO system, and a whole new industrial design. This was one where we took a break from HP tradition. We hired an outside design firm, who came up with a very attractive industrial design.
>
> I would call it a pseudo-division. It was not a division. It was a program. But it was very important to move R&D teams close together for rapid decision making with some financial authority and decision-making power. I didn't want to have to take going to an outside design firm up to a division manager. And they were incredibly supportive.
>
> There was a time in the middle of this program where things got a little tight and I have to admit I was running on fumes. I can remember at a review where we basically demonstrated some part of this first workstation. We made three, but some part of the first one was working spectacularly, and the performance was beyond what anybody had thought possible and it was way, way beyond a competitive point.[21]

Georg noted that while the teams were all excited, the top management response to their excitement was "well, we need to have more control." Georg said, "Wait a minute. We got here by some amount of controlled chaos. We didn't get here by a lot of management control. And we're not going to be able to finish on schedule."

Bear in mind that there were still competing HP workstation entities who were trying to satisfy customers and run their business, while in parallel, Georg was trying to get this program to deliver these industry-competitive workstations based on RISC out the door.

Part of the design was a new internal microprocessor, but there was also a co-processor to do floating point, designed by TI (Texas Instruments). Within a ten-month period, Georg and his team had negotiated getting the co-processor designed, built, and interfaced to the HP microprocessor. Georg said,

> We were pushing the envelope hard. Part of that push was getting this new co-processor done, and the thing that moved the schedule from February to March was we just couldn't get the yield up on both our microprocessor and TI's floating point co-processor to the point where we could ship in volume. We made a decision fairly late in January that we were going to delay the introduction from February to March. I'll never forget. It was so disappointing to the team. But we used that time to refine our capacity so that when we could introduce, it was going to roll in volume. The team could have taken a great defeat in that, but they didn't. They just put their heads down and we introduced the products in March.[22]

Georg was part of the team that introduced Snakes to the sales force at a huge meeting in Las Vegas, where he observed that, "One of the things that HP as a company has is an opportunity to be the company that replaces a competitive product with an even more competitive product. You want to be the one to replace your product, not your competitor."

Both Birnbaum and Georg bespoke the belief that there was a new kind of teamwork at HP, working across divisions and entities. It was time for HP to build a competitive workstation, and everyone—engineers, project managers, and section managers—was excited.

After Snakes was done, in April of 1991, HP made a decision to combine all the workstation businesses, naming Georg R&D manager for that business unit. He described the new role:

> It was an opportunity to get the people who were at Apollo, working on their own workstations, to aggressively become part of the HP Company that had acquired them. For quite a while I'd leave Fort Collins, drive to Denver on Sunday night, and fly to the East Coast. I'd spend Monday and Tuesday in Chelmsford [Massachusetts], working with the team there. Tuesday night I'd fly to California and work with the California teams on Wednesday and Thursday. Thursday night I'd fly back to Colorado to work with my team on Friday and be home for the weekend.

It was a really interesting time because we were building new models, trying to move our customer bases to their future. We were recruiting new software partners. We were taking key software partners that Apollo had, like Mentor Graphics, and moving them onto a consolidated single UNIX called HP/UX for our workstation business. Wim Roelandts was at that time responsible for all of HP's computer businesses. I had R&D, and Mark Tolliver had marketing and sales. When we first went to Chelmsford, we were (what's the best way I can say this?) "Those HP Guys." But we got the team signed up and engaged. And I was really proud of that team because they came back and they did another variation of a PA-RISC workstation, which was their first contribution to the PA-RISC area, past the original Snakes program. And they did a great job of it.[23]

At the end of the Snakes program, Dave Packard sent a letter to Denny Georg, Mark Tolliver, and Fred Schwettman (who ran the IC processes for HP-PA) saying that, while a lot of credit has been given to the Apollo team, he personally wanted to let the three know that he, Dave, recognized that the credit for pulling this together went to a lot of employees who were a part of HP. For Georg, this was especially meaningful because "There were a lot of people that were trying to prove that HP wouldn't have done as well without Apollo in the workstation program. And yet, Packard was the first to say, 'Wait a minute. There were a lot of people from HP that helped make this program successful too.'"[24]

Packard, connected enough to appreciate the magnitude of the Snakes achievement, still did not seem assuaged with the overall progress rate of the company. Combining the success of the Snakes program and Spectrum with HP's installed base, plus the ability to capture IBM and DEC converts via the migration center should have created great enthusiasm. Why wouldn't the story have gotten a more sympathetic hearing? There are several plausible explanations. Old-timers at the fiftieth-anniversary picnics were vocal, and letter writers and commentators were complaining from their points of view, deep in the trenches, that the place was being mismanaged. Ambiguity or differing points of view can be tolerated most of the time, but two instances caused particular angst—vying for scarce resources was a perennial battle, and inordinate dependence of one group's success upon another group's deliverables caused undue friction. The resources needed for the Spectrum rollout were monumental, and Young was faced time and again with decisions to fund it at the expense of other groups and programs. The medical business in particular had heated up and HP computers were central to that strategy, so late delivery of scalable 32-bit equipments was keenly felt in that arena. So, too, the PC business, where Compaq especially had given HP's relatively tepid efforts a hard time.

When things aren't going well, assigning blame and naming scapegoats become easy traps. Packard historically had exhorted employees to focus externally rather than fight internally. But even he was prone to take sides during this period—voting, for example, against the personal computer business for profitability reasons, and against separate software divisions because of the complex dealer channel issues that they created. More important, while Packard was listening to the common person as he had espoused for years, most of them were disconnected from the sophisticated systems issues with which HP now needed to succeed. For those few who could remember it, this was strongly reminiscent of the original battles over Bud Eldon's Palo Alto team trying to get the new sales organizations to use a corporate order processing system in 1963.

A Challenging CEO Environment

Perception is often stronger than fact when it comes to evaluating management performance. And political decisions are different than factual analyses. Packard had made the decision to switch CEOs in 1990, but his choice, Dick Hackborn, had refused the offer to take over the company. Through all of 1991, the mainline computer companies were in distress, and business pundits and the trade press were harsh.

MAY 31, 1991, ATLANTA: "IBM's Akers Should Resign." IBM Chairman John Akers . . . has taken to criticizing employees en masse for complacency. He should take his own advice, and quit. . . . It's true that the world has changed on IBM . . . with changes which have roiled the computer industry the last 9 years. But IBM has been behind the curve consistently—on laptops, on Unix, on lower-priced PCs, on workstations. . . . The acquisition of Rolm was a colossal flop. The only moves which IBM has made in the last 10 years which worked—creating the

PC and the R6000—were forced on it, and done by small groups working outside normal channels. . . . To survive as a giant company, IBM must change. But John Akers won't be able to handle that transition. If John Akers won't quit, IBM's board should . . . fire him.[25]

JUNE 1991, PALO ALTO, CALIFORNIA: Eric Nee, in the avant garde magazine *Upside,* published a crisp, analytical, fifteen-page assessment of the role that Packard was playing to rejuvenate HP. Building on Richard Pascale's bold claims in an HP case study, Nee proclaimed it imperative that "HP must find replacements for John Young and Dean Morton who can bring back some of the aggressiveness and vision that have been missing for much of the last decade," a reference to the departed Paul Ely.[26]

When dismal second-quarter results were given to the board in May 1992, the patriarch was apoplectic. Emboldened by such editorials, and visibly enraged, Packard unilaterally took charge of the transition plan, leaving Young on the sidelines. Two years after the Colorado speech, Packard led a palace coup at the board, emphasizing that Young had instituted the mandatory sixty-year retirement age to get rid of Hewlett and Packard's staff in 1979. Using the phrase "He who makes the rules must live by them," Packard got board approval to remove Young at age sixty and again offer the CEO slot to Hackborn. To Packard's astonishment, Hackborn again declined. Packard labored and cajoled to no avail; Hewlett blithely observed that, "For a job like this, you shouldn't have to talk someone into it."[27] Packard finally settled on Lew Platt as the logical next step, although he still wanted Hackborn involved. He seemed not to understand the animosity between the two, and Dave Packard—famous for "wandering around"—curiously seemed oblivious to the schism that existed between Hackborn and much of the company.

Bill Terry related the denouement as he experienced it:

Margaret [Paull, Packard's personal secretary] called and said, "I want you to come to Mr. Packard's office at 9:00 tomorrow morning." It was Hackborn, Platt, Packard, and me. I'm wondering, "Why am I here?" It was Dave's sensitivity—keep everybody on board. So Dave said to Dick, "Dick, I know you don't really want to do this. But is that your final answer?" And Dick said, "Yes, Dave. That's my final answer." I forget exactly Packard's words to Lew: "You're the next best candidate to do this. Will you do it?" And Lew said, "Yes." And he turned to me and said, "Bill, what do you think about all of this?" And I said, "Well, I think Lew could do a fine job. I'm sorry in a way that Dick made that decision, but I think Lew will do a fine job." And so he said, "All right. That's fine. Let's get on with the job." The meeting took maybe a little over four minutes. And the three of us walked out together, Lew, Dick, and me. We didn't say much to each other, except Dick said, "Well, I'm going to go back to Boise and enjoy myself," and Lew kind of gulped.[28]

Ironically and coincidentally, the same day that Young's retirement was announced, the Digital Equipment board of directors fired their enigmatic and bellicose founder, Ken Olsen. Digital had flattened in sales during the 1989–1991 recession and lost a whopping $617 million in 1991 (Figure 12.4), pocket change alongside IBM's $2.8 billion loss, but stunning compared to historic patterns. DEC's losses in 1992 would match IBM's $2.8 billion loss in 1991; IBM would lose another $13.1 billion in 1992 and 1993, and its board accepted CEO and chairman John Akers's resignation effective March 31, 1993.

JULY 17, 1992, WASHINGTON, D.C.: "DEC and H-P Both Lose Heads." On Thursday the founder of pioneering computer company Digital Equipment, 66-year-old Kenneth H. Olsen, announced that he would step down as president and chief executive of his company effective October 1, 1992. Palo Alto, California-based Hewlett-Packard announced that after a 14-year stint at the head of that company, John A. Young is retiring.

Digital is expected to announce dismal quarterly earnings next week. . . . Mr. Olsen's imminent retirement was not expected by industry observers. A DEC manufacturing vice president, Robert B. Palmer, was named to succeed Olsen as both president and chief executive, pending approval of the board of directors. Lewis Platt, presently executive VP at HP, will replace Hewlett-Packard's retiring head John Young effective November 1, 1992.[29]

The Digital story took all the business headlines; HP was merely changing the guard. Again, dirty laundry wasn't washed in print; the smoothly managed, understated corporation had pulled it off once more. DEC's and IBM's economic woes were well understood on Wall Street by this time. HP seemed somewhat immune, more distant, so circumstance helped keep the facade in place. Eric Nee's resourceful journalism had dug out the essential story a year earlier, and Mike Malone celebrated Packard's intervention as *the* saving factor for HP.[30]

John Young and the Silicon Valley Forty

The aftermath provided more drama for HP followers. Packard was a rock-ribbed Republican, who had run Nixon's 1972 reelection campaign in California. Presidential campaign politics in 1992 were destined to play a role in John Young's final days at the company, adding overtone to the denouement ceremonies and appreciation for Young's years of work.

Dave Barram, HP's Computer Products Group controller, joined Silicon Graphics (SGI) in 1983, a year before Ed McCracken was recruited to SGI as CEO. Later moving to Apple Computer, he was Apple's vice president of corporate affairs and had gotten to know Bill and Hillary Clinton along the way. Enamored of Clinton's possibilities if he decided to run for presidential office, Barram recalled,

> Six of us were at this breakfast meeting just before Clinton announced in October 1991. I said, "I think you would resonate with the leaders of Silicon Valley companies. Would you like me to help?" And of course, what's he going to say? I went home and thought, "I've got to do something here." I had been talking to John Sculley a little bit. John was a Republican. John Young and virtually everybody that I finally got to sign up were Republican. But they were the kind of Republicans that I could have been: sensible, moderate, business-oriented. The first thing I did was that I organized a Saturday morning 9:30 meeting with Bill Clinton, governor of Arkansas, December 7, 1991, at the Cupertino Inn, at the corner of De Anza Boulevard and Interstate 280. It's just a little motel. I said to Bill [Clinton] the night before, "None of this late crap," that he was notorious for. I said, "These guys don't come [to] hear politicians, and they don't come out on Saturday mornings. You're not going to be late." So he shows up at 9:25 (when I told his close friends this, they were amazed). I introduce him and he talks for twenty minutes, half an hour, and then he answers questions for another hour and a half. Now, this is forty CEOs. McCracken was there,

John Young, John Sculley, Chuck Boesenberg. . . . At the end of the meeting, I happen to look over, and John Young is taking notes. I thought, you know, he's taking notes because he sees something in this guy and he wants to be sure he gets it right.[31]

Barram followed up with a few letters to keep attendees interested, but saw their despair when the Jennifer Flowers story and Clinton's draft evasion issues surfaced in January and February. He saw Young in March at a luncheon, and Young asked, "How's your boy doing?" Barram nonchalantly replied, "He's doing great. He's going to win this presidency." John just smiled. In May, Clinton called Barram and said, "I would like you to do a technology policy for me." Barram immediately called Young and Sculley. He recalled,

We had a dinner at Sculley's house with John Young and a couple of other people. And Young said, "There's a group in Washington—the Competitiveness Council"—through which John had worked really hard to teach George Bush the elder about technology and never got anywhere. Young said, "Let's use what they have there." So we built a technology policy over the summer, and I faxed it back and forth to John. This was before we did e-mails. He'd comment on it, and we ended up building a nice technology policy. Clinton was going to come out here September 13 [1992], and I wanted to get all these guys together to endorse him.[32]

Barram had to work hard on John Young, saying,

John, I think that this guy is important to the country because he will push technology in ways that haven't been done before. You saw George Bush not do it. And your voice—if you endorse him—will be really important; it may be one of the most important. It's something you can do that will be more powerful than almost anything else you can do in national affairs.

Young did endorse Clinton during the visit, which impressed Barram:

He knew that he would get a lot of crap if he endorsed Clinton. He was going to retire soon anyway. If he had another five years to go, I'm not sure he would have done it. But that's not fair to him, because he was courageous to do it when he did it. But I never will know the level of pressure that he had or maybe felt or imagined he was going to feel. And so he had to have nerve. Remember, Packard was a very staunch Republican.[33]

Young reasoned that Clinton was going to be far better for technology than Bush. He had lost hope that Reagan and Bush would ever get it. Young told Barram that he had "argued the best arguments I can ever make. I have set up the Competitiveness Council. I brought a roundtable, and they don't get it." And Clinton did deliver—Barram was proud that they built an advanced technology program: "There were $10 billion spent in corporate R&D and $10 billion in government labs. We got $200 million to get this stuff commercialized."[34]

SEPTEMBER 17, 1992, SAN JOSE, CALIFORNIA: "Executives for Clinton have Blundered," said the indignant letter to the editor, from David Packard. "I am very disappointed that John Young, John Sculley, and many of my other good friends in the Silicon Valley industry have been caught in the updraft of Bill Clinton's hot air balloon."[35] John Young stands by his decision still:

I was very unimpressed with Bush's domestic policies, as were a lot of people. And from my personal orientation point of view about competitiveness, the Democratic Leadership Council's program for which Clinton was head of the board—I thought their positions on a lot of things for domestic policy were absolutely right on. Barram was a friend of Bill Clinton, and I went to some meetings and ended up meeting with Clinton. He persuaded me that he was working on the things that I thought were going to be important in domestic policy. It didn't end up that way. But [setting aside what happened in Washington] . . . Dave [Packard] was such a Republican through and through, he just couldn't handle that. And probably if I wasn't very close to retirement, I probably wouldn't have openly supported [Clinton].[36]

OCTOBER 29, 1992, NEW YORK CITY: Calvin Sims, writing in the *New York Times* the weekend before the presidential election:

In some instances, top senior executives who have come out for Governor Clinton find themselves at odds with executives within their companies who support Mr. Bush. For example, John A. Young, president and chief executive of Hewlett-Packard, who has voted Republican his entire adult life, has said he endorsed Mr.

Clinton because he believes the Governor "understands business and technology and the need for a motivated, highly skilled work force."

But David Packard, the company's chairman, favors Mr. Bush, saying in a statement: "Clinton talks about the future, but his ideas come from the past—and his tax proposals will kill America's technology companies."

Mr. Young is chairman of the Council on Competitiveness, an independent research group which has made recommendations to the Bush Administration over the years without much result. Mr. Packard, in a recent interview, offered a possible explanation of why Mr. Young would support [Clinton]: "If Mr. Clinton is elected, Mr. Young would have a chance at becoming head of the Commerce Department."[37]

Clinton was indeed elected president of the United States in a close contest, days after John Young retired from HP. When Young did romance the notion of joining the administration, Packard threatened to revoke his retirement package. Knowledgeable observers were stunned. Barram said, "I don't know why Packard would do that to his CEO, unless he was drifting in and out of complete lucidity. John had already been through hell getting out of HP."[38]

Jef Graham, an incredibly loyal HP executive, is still incensed. He said,

I went to Young's retirement party, and it really upset me. Remember, these were the days when a number of Silicon Valley CEOs had supported Bill Clinton. Packard was extremely Republican, and he wrote that letter to the *Mercury.* I don't think he forgave John Young for that. When John retired, at the retirement party, people were coming over to John while Packard was holding court in another part of the room. It was insulting to Young. I think he did it entirely intentionally. And not to have kept John on the board, and provided some continuity as chairman, but to collapse all those positions—crazy. He forced everyone out—Alberding retired, Bill Terry retired, John Doyle. . . . Very influential people, they all retired. He should have put some of them on the board, particularly Young. Some of the guys could have kept a watchful eye on things, but the weight all collapsed to Lew. It put too much pressure on Lew. Packard stayed a bit long in charge, and the board let Packard make some decisions that he shouldn't have made.[39]

Dick Alberding, on Young's staff at the time, was nonplussed:

> It was sad. It was really unfortunate. No question that Lucile was a cushioning force, who was now gone. As was Hewlett. But you can only cushion half of the blows, as they say. You can't stop them totally. And I always used to smile when somebody would speak with glowing terms about the warmth and the kindness of Packard. Now, he could be that. But wow, could he be vindictive.[40]

On November 1, 1992, Lew Platt replaced Young as CEO, five months after the board backed Packard's plan. The HP transition again was handled with aplomb, understated and circumspect—until Packard grew incensed with increasing public criticism of paternalistic boards around the country and the populist turn of the election. Without consulting anyone, in a fit of rage, Packard took the issue public. He sent a letter to the *San Jose Mercury-News*, explaining why HP changed CEOs, just to make sure that everyone knew he and his board were still active. Why Packard felt a need to do this, given his long history of avoiding the limelight, is hard to say. Some opine that he felt personally wounded by the harsh stock market treatment that HP stock had endured; others offered that he felt personally attacked and had risen to the bait. Many thought him just becoming more querulous as his faculties diminished. Some felt that his anger came from his rightist political views and his feeling of betrayal by his CEO. *Forbes* was thrilled to feature a quarrelsome interview with both founders.[41] Young's cryptic answer, with a smile, as to why Packard took this route: "Lucile had died.[42]

Because Packard had been trying for some considerable time to change things, only to be frustrated again and again by Hackborn's reticence, the accusation that he was asleep at the switch, merely accepting his CEO's graceful retirement, belied the dangerous precedent his actions set—encouraging zealous, possibly malignant, board oversight.

Young, the architect of HP's organizational structure during growth of one-hundred times—from $160 million to $16 billion, elaborated:

> There is a mythology that Dave and Bill knew how to do it and I didn't know how to do it. But we didn't learn how to run the systems until very, very late in life. We spent an awful lot of the '80s trying to learn how to run a systems busi-

ness. When I [became] CEO, we were probably the fourteenth largest computer company—way the hell down the line. We had 16-bit computers when everybody else had already gone to 32.

We had three different operating systems. Barney never believed in systems. He didn't like them at all. And there was zero effort in anything at the systems level. We had great products from HP Labs, but there wasn't a single person in the corporate laboratory who ever knew anything about an operating system or networking, or any of those things. This was really a tough, tough time. You're faced with either disappointing an awful lot of long-time customers, deciding you really can't make it in the computer business, or you're going to have some tough times to get from here to there. Part of it was the technology. No less of [a problem] was going from these divisions to learning how to be a systems company. That was probably even harder than doing the RISC processors. It was anti-cultural.

And [we had to do it] with a lot of people that I don't think were all that good at what they did, just because of the history of it, a lot of half-homegrown people who really didn't know about computers.[43]

New management was appointed; old leadership left the company. Packard swept the board clean, dismissing Young and enticed his two executive vice presidents, Dean Morton and Bill Terry, to retire. He asked Dick Hackborn, Platt's rival, to join the board. Naysayers had a field day as a fresh team took the field. The company's approach to business, however, didn't change dramatically, although its economic fortunes did revive for a while.[44]

The organizational shift from Young to Platt would be the last engineered by Packard. Packard, CEO for thirty years, was chairman spanning an amazing fifty-five years. The combined record of Young and Platt—twenty-one years in the CEO office—continued the legacy well past the founders' own energy and perspective; were it not for the John Wooden factor (who can match the mythical hero?), both men might be remembered as exceptional leaders through challenging times.[45]

Less charitable observers opined that the founders themselves would have been found wanting in these much more sophisticated times. After all, the company Platt turned over to Carly Fiorina was one-hundred-fifty times larger than the company that Packard turned over to Hewlett. The founders, now finished, each placed family members on the board and retired—Packard to write a taciturn memoir, Hewlett preferring to leave his place in history to others.

The Mythic HP Way

How did the upheaval come about? How could a revered founder become so upset with his company's leadership, especially when by almost every metric available, the company was performing better than its major competitors? What tipped the balance? The answer may lie within the hallowed cultural element of HP—the fabled HP Way—and the degree of reverence with which the aging patriarch viewed the legacy.

The HP Way had by 1990 become fully mythic. In 1975, Hewlett assigned Doug Chance the task of making the elements of the HP Way more explicit; thirty years later, Chance opened an interview with the startling words, "I thought that you might be interested in the day we invented the HP Way, June 15, 1975." When the interviewers expressed surprise, he went on to say, "We didn't really invent it; let me clarify what I mean there."[46] For the annual GM meeting at the Silverado Country Club in Napa, California, in January 1975, Hewlett asked Chance to run a two-hour workshop on the basic question, "As the company's growing and becoming much more complicated, how do we keep the HP Way?"

Chance took out the August-September 1973 *HP Measure* issue, entirely devoted to the HP Way:

> It interviews Dave and Bill and all the good old boys, and it interviewed John Young and Bill Terry, then it talks about tomorrow, and then the last page is the letter from [Hewlett]. They're all kind of rambling . . . platitudes and homilies and . . . great stories. But there was never anything written about the HP Way that was succinct; there wasn't any slide that described the HP Way.[47]

Chance took similar words in the several articles, underlined them, and built a ten-point slide transparency (pre-PowerPoint!). The words are familiar to HPites today: (1) belief in freedom; (2) respect and dignity, individual self-esteem; (3) recognition, sense of achievement, participation; (4) security, career development; (5) insurance, personal worry protection; (6) shared responsibility, helping each other; (7) MBO, decentralized operations; (8) informality, first name, family-oriented, open communications; (9) a chance to learn from mistakes; and (10) training and education, counseling.[48] Chance said,

> I made that into a slide and sent a letter and a copy of *Measure* to the participants who would be at the meeting, and at the beginning of the meeting, I said, "Here's the slide I made and how I got the slide. Why don't we take the first thirty minutes to discuss the slide? Do you want to add anything?"[49]

After a few modifications, the group turned to the topic of HP getting bigger and more complex. "How do we maintain the HP way?" Hewlett said, "We're getting bigger; 58 percent of the people have been here less than eighteen months." Any group of people who have worked together have traditions—and the group concluded that at HP all of this falls under the general heading of the HP Way. The group concluded that although the HP Way isn't tangible, it is unique, based on sound principles, and not directly transferable. Most important, it's dynamic.

A month after Fiorina's removal, Chance said, "There's every reason to believe that a dynamic HP Way will work in the future."[50]

> So what is it? It's the policies and actions that flow from the belief that men and women want to do a good job, a creative job. And if they're provided the proper environment, they will do so. Closely coupled is the HP tradition of treating each individual with consideration and respect, and recognizing personal achievement. This sounds almost trite, but we believe it. And then Hewlett said, "Let me give you some examples of concern for people. It wasn't necessarily written down that we'll never hire or fire. It doesn't say profit sharing has to be, or medical insurance. But we believe in management by objectives, as well as sharing the burden. Help each other. It's a spirit. It's the team. Informality; we're on a first-name basis."[51]

At the end of the retreat, Packard said, "That slide that Doug had there was useful." He told Ray Wilbur, "We've always talked about this HP Way thing, and it's not really clear what it is. I think we need to reappraise it and write it down, and I'd like to see you put it into some of the training materials and see if we can institutionalize this as we go forward." The computer group began to use it; later, corporate training and development and the management training program used it. A corporate brochure was eventually developed. "That's how the HP Way came about." The workshop results, broadcast widely, were published in the July 1975 *HP Measure.*[52] Chance said,

> Here's the important part—when people start whining, I always say, "Well, you know I invented the HP Way." It always shocks them. They go, "Yeah, right." And I say, "No I've got the slide to prove it." Maybe the current management teams and the current board of directors would find that it would be useful if they got the slide out. And then do like we'd done—use a development process to go through and evaluate and discuss.

Doug quoted Hewlett's own words: "It's dynamic. It should change with the time. You can't be in a huge computer business, and have it exactly the way it was for the test measurement business."[53]

The HP Way included a strong open-door element. No manager could reside behind a closed door and ignore concerns of his or her people. Everyone knew that anyone anywhere could walk in with a problem to Bill or Dave, or any other level of management, without recrimination, and expect them to take some action. This privilege could not be abused—ultimately the accuser would face the accused, and the issue would have to be resolved. But it worked well for years, and it was deeply ingrained into HP employees at every level.

During the Golden Age, much change was occurring at HP. IBM people took over leadership of the Computer Group, replete with a different, more adversarial culture; the Peripherals Group (at least the LaserJet side) disdained the tried-and-true vertical integration that HP had carried to extremes in its component technologies and integrated circuit facilities. Systems integration issues across multiple divisions, groups, and sectors hobbled independent action, resulting in stifling reviews and committee overview. CPM diagrams and PERT planning along with five-foot-by-twelve-foot printouts of spreadsheets written in ten-point fonts now were management tools. Old-timers were horrified; newcomers were merely mystified. Many long-term employees started sending notes to Bill 'n' Dave—"Hey, come back, something terrible is happening to your company."[54]

Packard's speech in Fort Collins signaled the beginning of the end for Young—but ironically, for Hewlett and Packard as well. A decade after

Birnbaum joined Hewlett-Packard, it was no longer a quirky bit player in the computing world. Packard's Colorado speech was not known to the business press, but the resultant actions raised visibility. The company could no longer operate in the background, insulated and unexamined by external commentators. The next two CEOs—Lew Platt and Carly Fiorina—would govern on a much more public stage; the modus operandi of the company would become a large part of the story, enhanced by the increasing numbers of HP alumni who spread the lore, the intrigue, and their adaptations of the HP Way widely throughout the electronics industry.[55]

Robert Grimm, who started in 1951 and retired in 1989, observed that the computer world changed things dramatically for HP: "We all think the world of Bill and Dave, but I don't think they had the right answer to it either. It was a very, very tough time."[56]

CHAPTER 13

Strategic Turmoil

Lew Platt set a new tone for HP leadership at the top. Taking up the cause of the HP Way, he became the most ardent and articulate CEO supporter in HP history, even more than the founders themselves. He worked tirelessly to define, model, and extend the values and ethics of that credo, focusing on women and on disabled, disadvantaged, and minority groups as areas of concern. Platt's personal history energized his beliefs, much as Hewlett's history infused medical instrumentation goals.[1]

And the fates were kind—for a while. Most CEOs know that company performance for their first two years is largely predetermined by momentum and the products and services already in place when they arrive. Motivation can be improved, and some rules and procedures modified, but the basic product flow, both of products in production and those in near-term release, determines a company's competitive stance and fundamental cost structure.

Platt's first three years were a honeymoon (Figures 13.1 and 13.2), as HP-PA computing and HP printer revenue surged against IBM and DEC.

Traditional computing was convulsive for the leading vendors between 1992 and 1995. When Platt became CEO, HP had just finished the 1992 fiscal year with $16.4 billion revenue, one-quarter of IBM's $64.5 billion. IBM was again profitable—Lou Gerstner's strong emphasis on consulting services helped IBM recoup almost half of the $16 billion lost between 1991 and 1993. DEC, nearly as big as HP in 1992 at $13.9 billion revenue, had stopped growing at all; more important, they were still hemorrhaging cash, losing more than $5 billion in four years. In the next three years, HP nearly doubled its revenue, to $31.5 billion; profits quadrupled from $549 million to $2.43 billion. On a logarithmic revenue plot, a few people could now imagine that HP might fulfill Packard's goal of catching IBM.

Lew Platt joined HP's Waltham Division in 1966, hired by Dean Morton and Bruce Wholey to manage the facility. He would joke later that he was hired as the custodian, a peculiar job for a new graduate fresh from Wharton Business School with a mechanical engineering Bachelor's degree from Cornell. He did consider resigning after a year, when no advancement path loomed, but a heart-to-heart talk with Dean Morton led to a fast-paced variety of management posts and the general manager position at the Waltham Division by 1974. He moved to Avondale (PA) briefly, and then to Palo Alto as general manager of HP's Analytical Group from 1980 to 1984.

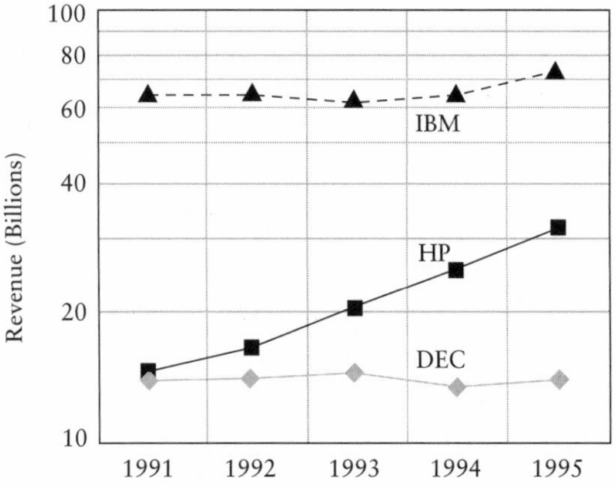

FIGURE 13.1. IBM, HP, and DEC revenue (semi-log plot), 1991–1995

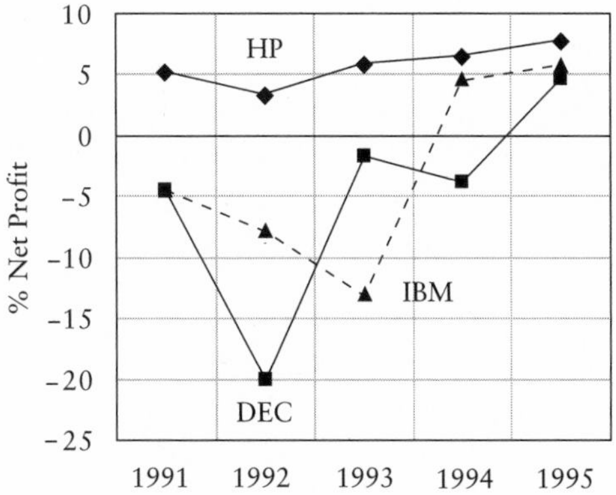

FIGURE 13.2. IBM, HP, and DEC profit, 1991–1995

When John Young revamped the Computer Group in 1984, Platt was elected Manufacturing Products Group vice president. He became executive vice president in 1987 when Young moved him to oversee the Computer Products Sector. In the 1989 restructuring, Lew became head of the Computer Systems Organization. Platt was elected president and CEO of the company and a member of the board of directors in November 1992. The board elected Platt as its chair when David Packard retired from that post in September 1993.

Once becoming CEO of HP, Platt became a director of Pacific Telesis and Boeing and a member of both the Business Council and the Business Roundtable in Washington, D.C., following in the footsteps of Hewlett, Packard, and Young. The bigger opportunity, on an international stage, came in 1995 when President Clinton appointed Platt to the Advisory Committee on Trade Policy Negotiations, in which he served as chairman of its World Trade Organization Task Force. WTO, launched in 1995 after five decades of U.S. Senate political wrangling, set goals to increase international trade by promoting lower trade barriers and providing a forum for trade issue negotiation. At first, global stature rose for both HP and Platt, but the WTO soon became a target for protest groups coalescing around job outsourcing issues and the influx of cheap foreign goods.

As Figure 13.1 indicates, HP made strides in mid-range computing as IBM staggered with the uncertainty of CEO turnover and a fragmented strategy. Dick Lampman, who later headed HP Labs, reported that by 1995, the server side of HP was convinced that they "had IBM on the ropes."[2] Computing VP Wim Roelandts concurred, adding a strong observation:

> By the early '90s, DEC hit the wall, and IBM was in trouble. IBM changed management, and they were going to split up that company. Through these tough times, the key reason for our success in networking was the adoption of open standards. IBM had SNA. DEC had DECNet. DEC also supported SNA, because everyone connected their mainframes to IBM. We were number three, so we had to support our own Advance Net, which was our own home-brewed networking, and DECNet and SNA. Concluding that there is no way that we can survive here, I made the decision to move to ARPA and OSI networking.

We were the first company in the world to move to open systems networking. That created tremendous momentum. The others now became the proprietary guys and HP became the open systems company. It worked very well in networking. Then we did the same in systems by supporting UNIX. Not only for workstations and technical applications, but also for commercial. That was a tremendous success. HP was the only company that really supported UNIX as a platform at the time. DEC was against it because they had their own operating system. IBM was against it. Sun supported it only for workstations, not for commercial applications. By 1993, we were the number one UNIX supplier in commercial systems. From '92 to '95, we grew market share. We grew almost as fast as the Printer Group, and we were the second most profitable after Instruments. It was a $6 billion-plus business. Then we began a strategic relationship with Intel to do the WideWord architecture, which became known as Itanium. HP would have become the number one computer supplier without any doubt.[3]

This optimistic view masked some difficulties. While HP-PA had proven its worth, HP was again late in the next-generation architecture race. MIPS, founded by John Hennessey from Stanford, had been shipping a 64-bit chipset to Silicon Graphics since 1991, and Sun Microsystems, via SPARC Technologies, had a 64-bit chipset based loosely on David Patterson's Berkeley designs in production by 1993. DEC's Alpha was heavily funded from the outset of Robert Palmer's tenure in 1992 when he replaced founder Ken Olsen. Birnbaum, returning to run HP Labs in late 1991, supported Bill Worley, the original HP-PA architect, who teamed with Bob Rau to design a true 64-bit architecture to serve as the successor for HP-PA. Worley was strongly supported by Josh Fisher, the VLIW (Very Long Instruction Word) definer who had joined HP Labs; thus, a second HP WideWord project was begun.

The extensions and ramifications of this chipset proved both dramatic and sobering—the most significant of which was the realization that HP could not easily afford to manufacture the chipset unless they could sell it broadly—the same thesis that had been used in part to justify the Spectrum HP-PA, which proved false when the Wintel platform (Intel chips and Microsoft Windows operating systems) became the dominant low-end platform. Worley and Birnbaum had been down this path before, and they now sought to find a way around it.

After considerable debate, Platt's team approved a delegation going to Intel to propose a partnership—a major long-term partnership whereby HP would design the architecture and instruction set, and Intel would merge it with the fabulously successful Pentium family, while providing major manufacturing resources. Worley led the delegation, and a joint partnership was announced in June 1994.[4] At least for the moment, it appeared that HP's server lines had a strong future.

Ignorance Is Bliss

John Young's tenure ended with a perceived crisis of bureaucratic regimentation, which Young himself had largely eradicated before handing over the reins. A classic CEO, Young combined urbanity and a patrician demeanor. Viewed as a rational and thoughtful architect, he was often considered decisive, but almost never charismatic, warm, or empathetic. He did, however, drive a corporate consistency, often when few people perceived the need—his hiring of Bill Bondurant was a classic example of his farsighted vision. When Bondurant hired Davis Masten to conduct a survey of HP top managers in 1987 to ask them what contributed to the HP brand, Masten interviewed 410 executives throughout the company before anyone gave him the expected answer: that the consistent look and feel of the products—package color, style, shape, knobs, and CRT screen graphics—was paramount.[5]

Lew Platt, by contrast to Young, embraced the underdog, appealing to the rank-and-file, describing and extending the HP Way tirelessly, making it more visible, more explicit, and more wide-reaching. Platt's actions and words rekindled lots of enthusiasm, unleashing tremendous local initiative. Remotivated people set about fixing the bureaucratic overlay that Young had crafted. Modified processes, new approaches, and creativity flourished again throughout the company; Corporate functions retreated to sharply constrained activities. Divisional enthusiasm rose, and the groups felt more empowered to do their own thing as well. The change was refreshing, in the view of most employees. From another vantage point, it very nearly killed the company.

Unfortunately, system infrastructure is seldom well understood by users—it exists, and is used, or it doesn't and isn't missed—unless some comparative norms are used. So it would be with HP in a perennial contest between corporate consistency and local initiative and contribution. "Corporate contribution" was derided more often than not, even when it was the most effective and rational approach.[6]

Overnight, incompatible processes and systems sprang up. The core elements of the HP secret sauce—the common "look and feel" that contributed so much to the brand, the unifying common parts numbering system, the consistent MRP and inventory control systems, the corporate-approved design tools, and even the carefully constructed common communication system, were all swept away in a wave of creative zeal that amounted to a purge, resulting in an equally strong backlash under Carly Fiorina to reinstall consistent corporate systems.

The result of the unleashed creativity was not surprising. When Eugenie Price, the talented and experienced HP Labs librarian, served on the ACM Digital Libraries project, she knew of the NSF-funded Digital Libraries research activity led by Stanford professor Hector Molina-Garcia under IEEE sponsorship. But when ACM tried to sell her a corporate membership in the resultant portal service in 1996, she was unable to do more than buy one copy for HP Labs. ACM was told to call on some twenty-five additional divisional libraries to cover other HP professionals. At best, only 60 percent of HP professionals would then have the high-value service. More important, instead of $25,000 for a corporate license for all of HP's professionals, it would have cost at least $156,000 to buy twenty-six copies, one for each existing division library. The party line was that maybe some divisions wouldn't need one, and they should be allowed to expend their discretionary dollars for their true needs.

This example might seem trivial, and some people could argue that professional paper archives had little value for their design staffs, but no division staff could argue that they didn't need manufacturing information systems. Here too, the carnage was rampant. Debra Dunn observed, "When Carly arrived, we still had eighty-three very autonomous business units, even after the [Agilent Technologies] divestiture. It didn't make sense from a cost structure perspective. We had eighty instances of SAP, for example."[7]

Rather than a few-hundred-thousand dollars, this was an additional several-hundred-million-dollar expense, one which prevented consistent purchasing. No one seemed to recall that Colossus had done the job far smoother and cheaper. As e-mail systems got more robust, even the corporate communication system—admittedly an expensive backbone, but one of HP's flagship differentiators—was dismantled. When Fiorina arrived at HP, she was astonished to find she couldn't talk to everyone simultaneously. She did say that someone told her HP had had the capacity in the past.[8]

Platt believed deeply in the Packard philosophy of small autonomous units performing more nimbly and effectively when "corporate" stayed out of the way. Dismantling the corporate infrastructure was a manifestation of that philosophy, one heartily endorsed by the aging chairman. Unfortunately, in endorsing individual contribution, exalting local initiative, and reinstilling Packard's love of small, simple organizational units, Platt lost control of the company. The lessons, by no means obvious, are profound. It was very late in HP's evolution to experiment so profoundly with a federation of divisions rather than a corporation.

MC^2—A Study in Leadership

The biggest challenge for Platt arose around product strategy. Joel Birnbaum, a proud scientist, shared Barney Oliver's attitude about management: respect had to be earned rather than simply accorded as a function of rank. His initial encounters with Lew Platt, when Platt was assigned by John Young to run the Computing Group in 1988, were not pleasant:

> Suddenly, as CEO, Lew was now my boss again. I said, "What are you going to do in the next ten years?" He replied, "I haven't had much time to think about it. What do you think I should do?" I proposed that we adopt a theme for the company—MC Squared (MC^2). It became the watchword of the company strategy for five years. It stood for measurement, computing, and communication.[9]

Birnbaum proposed that Platt organize HP to produce unique products at the intersection of sensors and measurement, combined with communication and computing. These were businesses that HP could enter without having to establish partnerships; it could move rapidly and natively in a way that others would not be able to match. The potential for higher profits was enormous, but speed of execution was the main advantage. Platt loved it. Birnbaum said,

> We announced it—and many new businesses started to emerge. Digital photography was one, sensors in cameras, automotive systems for Ford where they plug their cars in for deep diagnostic work, and a lot of the stuff for the phone companies. We became number one in selling computers to phone companies in that era. There were a lot of successes. The key was MC^2. This was an astonishing and unprecedented time in history because each of the three was undergoing a revolution—not an evolution—at the same time.

In computing, chips were on a relentless march, new technologies were on the horizon for storage, and personal computing was proliferating. In communications, the fiber-optic revolution meant that bandwidth was becoming free and universal; the glacially slow telecommunications companies were finally converging to serve the Internet-connected world. And in measurement, more quietly, micro-sensors, especially embedded and biological sensors, which could be organized into sensor networks, were now widely available, and measurement and test products were already becoming systems and solutions rather than isolated things.

The company that Young handed over was sound in retrospect. John noted that circumstances helped—DEC struggled to make the transition, IBM waffled at the low end:

> IBM really didn't push this end of the line, because they didn't want to cannibalize it. So we had some room to maneuver. By the end of the '80s, HP really had a very strong position. We were the number one RISC computer company. The year I retired, we were the largest UNIX vendor. But I look at the competitors and the nameplates that started out in those eras . . . it was a very hard decade. We started with such a disparity in size. Getting to where we ended was a tribute to a hell of a lot of people working really hard over a whole decade—it was hard work, believe me.[10]

A Monumental Disconnect

Although Lew brought strong concern for the HP Way to the CEO office, he lacked the strategic focus that both Young and Hackborn exhibited and prized. He profited for the first three years from the increased success of the Spectrum HP-PA family against IBM and from continued growth in the printing and imaging business. Birnbaum and Lampman kept driving for the MC^2 idea; And then, surprisingly, the MC^2 strategy collapsed. Joel lamented,

Lew killed it. He had to lead, and he was unwilling. I was so naïve that all I ever thought about was the technology. You'd think that I would have learned by this time! Lew was a wonderful, high-integrity man, but he didn't have the confidence or the leadership that a guy like Jack Welch or John Young would to say, "Do it." He acted like it was mine, and not his: "We are going to kill it. We aren't going to talk about it any more. If anyone wants to do it, they can do it." He said, "I am just here to cut the cake and hold the coats. HP always has been that way. It is a collaboration of democratic enterprises—our strength has come from our liking of each other, and our loyalty to each other, and if anyone wants to do it, I will never stand in the way but I am not going to force an organizational structure which does it." It was disastrous.[11]

Birnbaum was incredulous. "HP was at the forefront of all that stuff. Unfortunately, what I didn't think about was that you can't do that without creating an organizational structure that supports the integration of the technologies." Joel slowly and painfully realized this was a monumental disconnect:

Lew said that has to evolve by the individual people wanting to work together and doing it. "We are not going to create a corporate entity called MC^2." The most significant case, which eventually led to its failure, was the Medical Instruments Division. Once the largest in the world, they wanted to go into remote distributed medical measurements using computers and the Internet to do remote physicals, battlefield medicine. . . . But it needed major support from the Computer Group. I started making speeches—"If you want to do MC^2, you have to create an integrated company or you have to free the separate components to choose partners that are also competitors." If the HP computing business won't work with our Medical Group, then they should be free to work with DEC and IBM. The executive committee listened to that, and said, "That is OK." But the culture of loyalty, friendship, and trust was so deep that, with very, very few exceptions, nobody ever did it. They just couldn't imagine helping DEC to sell workstations against their own workstation divisions to doctors, hospitals, and medical organizations.

Divisions make your bottom line work, but the city-states that promote it cannot become a united nation. The system world is increasingly connected, so you won't be able to make the investments to compete with them unless you become integrated. Only three companies in the world were in the forefront of each of those businesses—IBM, AT&T, and us. IBM had no measurement capability. DEC had no measurement. AT&T really had no computing. The leader of the new paradigm of computing—distributed computing based on RISC computers, on high-speed networks, with critical open software—was HP. That was how we had become a great computing company.[12]

With Lew's abdication of leadership, Hewlett-Packard devolved into a holding company, as Platt demanded little synergy between groups. Such an arrangement was a logical derivative of the highly autonomous structure favored by Hewlett and Packard, setting the stage for a Hydra-like leadership structure that in many ways persists. Hackborn had ruled the Peripherals activity with strong adjudication; but when he retired, that group quickly took on the same character—exhibited in the internecine battles between the InkJet and the LaserJet groups.[13]

The Wintel Battle

Packard appointed Hackborn to HP's board in 1992 when Platt became CEO. Lew harbored deep concern about Dick, commenting that "He knows a lot about running a business. He doesn't know much about running a company." The relationship between Platt and Hackborn, never smooth, became confrontational over the computing futures issue. Hackborn was reading the industry data differently from others. HP had been remarkably unsuccessful in personal computing, after two significant forays—the HP Touchscreen and the HP Vectra. Packard nearly persuaded the board to ask that HP cease and desist in early 1991. When Packard sought out Hackborn about becoming CEO to replace Young, Dick deflected his request by asking to have a try at the PC business. Hackborn recruited Bob Frankenberg to take on the challenge.

Frankenberg, who had just restructured the $500 million Network group and generated huge profits for a change, signed on. HP PCs in the dealer channel were down to a mere $80 million annual run rate, less than handheld calculators, logic analyzers, or a dozen other instrument divisions. Even counting the shipments tied to HP 3000 system sales, they ranked twenty-fourth in the world, behind most Taiwanese clones. Frankenberg recruited a solid team, including Jacques Clay, Duane Zitzner, and Khaw Cheng Joo, who quickly assessed the difficulties and put them into four main categories. First were the twin facts that HP product introductions were usually last to market with any new microprocessor chip and were overpriced compared to the main players by nearly 30 percent. Second, HP was primarily using two high-cost manufacturing centers, one in Sunnyvale, California, and the other in Singapore. Third, the company was still trying to add differentiating features, thinking in classical HP fashion that these were desirable and could command higher prices. Fourth, and maybe most important, the company had never spent much time with the dealer channel asking, "What do you really need?"

The group made some immediate changes. First, they reduced design cycle time to three months from a leisurely eighteen months, making significant cost-cutting steps in the process. The most important factor, though, in Frankenberg's assessment, was a decision to provide some major changes for dealers, including a first for HP of "flooring demo units" to help cash-strapped dealers with inventory carrying costs. HP's traditional management triad—an engineering, marketing, and manufacturing leader on a project—was modified, adding a distribution manager and a sales promotion manager to the team from the get-go. This was big, fast business—requiring fifteen thousand units in dealer hands by introduction, three months after the project definition. Four years later, as Frankenberg departed HP to become CEO at Novell, HP had risen to the number seven supplier rank, growing the dealer channel business nearly ten-fold in four years. More important, they had taken a loss leader, and turned it into a profitable line above the corporate average. Webb McKinney took over; HP moved to number five the following year. Hackborn felt vindicated when he retired from HP in November 1993, but he continued to chafe as Platt still favored "big iron."

A year later, Hackborn and his protégé, Rick Belluzzo, tried to persuade the board that although HP was gaining in servers and larger systems, along with Sun Microsystems—while IBM and DEC were stumbling—the story was really in the gains that Intel, Microsoft, and Compaq were posting. Hackborn had reason to know—his Printer Group sold in the same dealer channel, and through that connection, he had gotten to know the Microsoft team. In fact, Steve Ballmer and Bill Gates tried hard to lure him when he retired from HP; when that failed, they put him on Microsoft's board of directors.[14]

In 1990, Microsoft released Windows 3.0, the first attractive graphical user interface (GUI) that they shipped. It was warmly received; ten million licenses were sold within six months. No software package had ever had sales approaching that magnitude. Apple sued both HP and Microsoft for infringing their Macintosh screen metaphor. HP was included because the New Wave GUI using the award-winning, three-dimensional, iconic Motif "look-and-feel," done for the UNIX OSF group, emulated the Macintosh screen. It was a curious mixture of emotions at HP, especially when Microsoft appropriated the 3D look and feel in Windows 3.1 the next year.[15] In a rare, fast-track ruling for the industry, a superior court judge threw out the basic suit by the end of 1992; the Wintel platform (a combination of Intel chipsets and Microsoft operating system software) burgeoned while the Macintosh advantage dissipated.

The chief purveyor of the Wintel platform was Houston-based Compaq, building IBM-compatible PCs. Compaq, after enduring the ousting of founder Rod Canion and a workforce reduction of 12 percent in 1991, exploded in revenue from 1991 to 1995 by a factor of five, becoming half the size of HP at $16.3 billion with 5 percent net profits. In 1994, Compaq surpassed IBM itself in PC shipments while IBM was trying vainly to make their own operating system, OS-2, succeed over Windows. Dell Computer, begun in Michael Dell's college dorm room in Austin, Texas, as a mail-order Wintel supplier in 1984, posted an impressive $5.3 billion in sales at 5 percent net profits in 1995. The component vendors—Intel and Microsoft—also had substantial growth over three years—$5.8 billion to $16.2 billion for Intel, and $2.7 billion to $5.9 billion for Microsoft.

Hackborn and Belluzzo argued that Wintel was the future of computing, and urged Platt and HP to join it wholeheartedly. Hackborn demanded a full-on assault, using the dealer channel strength already built by the printer divisions. It was a persuasive argument. Birnbaum's bet—a scalable, top-to-bottom architecture—had proven illusory at the bottom end, because of the extraordinary success of the Wintel platform and the inability of HP to establish high volumes for HP-PA chipsets. Roelandts and Birnbaum agreed that PCs mattered, but countered that traditional HP values—innovation and the chance at higher profit margins—would suffer. They further argued that a PC-centric view was superficial, noting that many back-end business tasks were far too computer-intensive and customer-support intensive to be served by a small-box strategy alone. A central part of their thesis rested on IBM's profitability recovery, a story not yet well known.[16]

Belluzzo argued for a blended approach. There was an old saying at HP: "When HP comes to a fork in the road, it takes both paths," letting the market decide rather than make a clear choice. He offered the following:

> The strategy was that UNIX and Windows systems would coexist and that the vast majority of customers would create a heterogeneous environment. HP should deliver both, while recognizing that over time the Windows (and now Linux) world would take on a larger role. But since we were losing money in the UNIX business (outspending Sun and driving lower revenue), we had to manage our UNIX investment better, gain more leverage between UNIX and PC servers, and build an integration offering that would allow for the heterogeneous model to work (to be built around Openview). The integration piece would allow for more value and better margins.
>
> In fact, history now shows that this was totally right. HP is the server leader as a result of the Compaq merger, and it is dominated by PC servers, not proprietary UNIX. Sun is dying. The new HP team gets this and has driven solid results.[17]

The HP Board Gets Involved

HP's board members were not sophisticated—they understood well the destructive contention between Platt and Hackborn, but they saw the argument almost solely as a UNIX versus Windows debate. Among the members, only Hackborn and Jay Keyworth were strong technologists. Most were Packard appointees selected for political or friendship reasons, or they were family members seated to ensure the legacy. Hackborn persuaded the board, and Platt acquiesced. The shootout was quick. Platt merged the Computer Systems Group into the Computer Products operation, moving Roelandts under Belluzzo on August 28, 1995. To many, it seemed an odd choice given that Belluzzo appeared to be Hackborn's spear carrier in the board campaign to get Lew to abandon this program. Belluzzo felt cornered by the tough challenge of dealing swiftly with the bloated UNIX cost structures and Hackborn's strident stance. Roelandts resigned, becoming CEO at Xilinx by January 1996, saying, "Lew decided that UNIX was going to be dead and that the future was going to be Microsoft and PCs. That was pretty disappointing for me, to be honest with you. I decided it was time for me to move on."[18]

Peter Burrows wrote, "Belluzzo insists that he never intended to trample HP's UNIX business, but that business quickly lost momentum—just as the Internet boom was about to send demand for such systems through the roof."[19] Belluzzo in 2006 was unrepentant:

> The company is caught in a commoditized hardware business, and they need to take it to the next level. They don't know how to do that. They don't have the courage. Dell changed the economics of the business. The company has increasingly commoditized its standardized offering; there's just not much money to make in that business. It's just that simple. That business model is not conducive today to the HP values of innovation and making a contribution.[20]

An op-ed *BusinessWeek* piece in 2005 mused about Hackborn's role behind the scenes:

> While Hackborn's visionary contribution in printers is undeniable, many wonder if he led HP in the wrong direction in the computer business—away from systems based on proprietary HP technology and toward more commoditized gear, such as Windows PCs, a market dominated by super-efficient Dell. Some critics say Hackborn's influence has pushed HP away from its roots as an innovator and relegated it to being a distributor of less profitable products.[21]

Platt would later say that he regretted the Wintel decision more than any in his career. He was not satisfied with the result for the systems side, even while acknowledging that changes were necessary. When Roelandts departed abruptly following the Wintel decision, Platt asked Dick Watts to run CSO, the Computer Systems Organization with the Spectrum family, the Itanium partnership, and the UNIX operating systems, HP's most complicated business by nearly an order of magnitude.

Watts had earned much respect while running PCO for Belluzzo when Bob Frankenberg left to become CEO of Novell. He built a strong dealer channel, a task well-suited to his amiable cajoling style; but he had never run a systems business before nor dealt with attendant interlocking political issues. It overwhelmed him:

That was a very big challenge because it was a highly vertically integrated, very large organization, not really in tune with the much lower-cost leaner and meaner nature of the PC business where companies like Dell and others were teaching people how to do it. We had a lot of internally focused issues—cutting and trimming, and realigning organizations. You had a division producing, for example, the RISC architecture chipsets. But they actually did not have revenue in the normal sense because it didn't really sell anything. Instead of having a real internal corporate transfer, or attempting to build the customer focus, it was all, sort of, "Well, we'll take the revenue at the end of the pipe when the customer buys, to be divided up between the various players." Unfortunately, we would spend more time arguing about that than we did getting the order in the first place. It was pretty frustrating.[22]

Watts was surprised to find vestiges of the Engineering Design Systems Group still around:

I was amazed that the mechanical design division—MDD, the software division doing 2D and 3D mechanical drawing systems—was still there. HP should not have been in that business if we really wanted to be a mainstream platform supplier because it competed directly with the people we needed to develop the applications on our platform. So we spun that off, outside the company.

Watts was even more surprised by—and ill-equipped to deal with—a lot of internal issues (cutting and trimming, realigning organizations, and refocusing groups):

I was only there for about a year—I tried to put a set of business metrics around parts of the organization that really had lost touch with the customer. For example, there was the consulting services business. We gave it its own P&L. There was Open View, which was the system and network management business. It too was measured more as a cost center, so we made that a stand-alone business.[23]

Platt, losing patience as implications of the Wintel decision unfolded, reassigned Watts to revamp the sales force along the lines of Young's disastrous approach in the late 1980s. Watts said,

Lew asked me to run the sales force again when he wanted to put it all back together under one customer-focused organization. Customers had been complaining that the PC sales force, the Systems sales force, and the Printer sales force were all coming and giving them different stories, so we had another try at putting it all back together. That was not what I really wanted to do; there were lots of internal meetings and haggling with divisions over how much they were going to pay for selling costs and how we were going to tie this back to the P&L. It was pretty frustrating. I left in the middle of '98, and went to a startup.[24]

Bondurant agreed that Packard had an influence on the company with his intervention in 1991. But the impact, as it played out under Lew, was not what was intended:

By the late '80s, no real decision making was happening; Packard came in and cleaned up some of that. It is a different company today from what it was in those days, culturally and otherwise. It is much more hierarchal, a top-down company. It shifted under Lew. The Wintel decision was a complete debacle. Where's the business leverage that comes from putting box companies together with the same distribution and the same sales strategy? There's no leverage there. What surprised me most? Hackborn's response—he was always the brilliant strategist. I never saw him lose contact before.[25]

Between the time that Watts moved to Hackborn's group and the Wintel decision, only six years had passed, but it was as convulsive for top management continuity as any period in HP history. Doug Chance departed to become CEO at Octel Communications; networking specialist Dan Warmenhoven (one of the IBM transplants) left for a CEO role at Network Equipment Corporation. When Roelandts took Chance's spot, many in the second tier left. Two-thirds of Birnbaum's Computer Engineering Council left HP within an eighteen-month period, including Frank Carrubba, Jay Richards, Alain Couder, Chuck House, and Bob Frankenberg; all took executive roles in other high-tech firms.

Though it seemed remarkable at the time, similar leadership turnover had characterized each shift in HP's computing perspective. The minicomputer leadership team—Bill Davidow, Mike Green, Jim Kasson, Dennis MacAvoy, and Jim Treybig—left when Packard brought in Paul Ely in 1973. In the early "personal computing" era, another group of extremely capable leaders—Janelle Bedke, John Couch, Dave Crockett, Bill Foster, Ken Fox, Fred Gibbons, Jim Gross, Bill Krause, John Page, and Tom Whitney—left. When Young shifted Ely out of computing, it wasn't long before Ely departed, followed shortly by VPs Ed McCracken and Cyril Yansouni and some highly visible performers such as Joe Schoendorf.

Each time, though, the company spawned new leadership from within, and the next HP computing chapter invariably was even more positive. The net result in Silicon Valley was dissemination of the HP Way throughout computer companies of the Valley; while this had occurred to a limited degree on the instrumentation side over the decades, the evolution was much slower and the consequent leadership disruption less pronounced. The Wintel decision would leave deeper scars.

A Strained Partnership

Wim Roelandts watched the dissolution of the UNIX initiative with dismay, but even more concerning for him was the progress rate of the HP-Intel partnership.

> Precision Architecture RISC was a very good architecture—a very, very good architecture. It was masterfully done. It really gave us tremendous advantage in the market. But it doesn't translate to commercial success without someone driving it. Intel was looking for a systems partner. We had the systems knowledge, which is operating systems and compiler knowledge—things in which Intel hadn't much experience. We could supply that. We had a very strong compiler team. We had a very good operating systems team. We had a very, very strong CPU development team in Colorado for high-end computing, for performance chips. That combination together with Intel's low-end volume capacity and its manufacturing skills, should have dominated the industry. But once the systems part disappeared, there was nobody to talk to Intel anymore, and then Itanium slipped and slipped. When it came out three years late, it wasn't competitive.[26]

Birnbaum had committed himself—first to Spectrum and HP-PA, then to MC^2. From his perspective, the second was easier than the first—by quite a bit. The latest turn of events did nothing to reduce his anxiety, especially after Roelandts left:

[Lew Platt] began dismantling the company into separate parts, where everybody had to have their own balance sheet. He even went so far as to name each of the sector heads CEOs. When Carly arrived, we had five CEOs plus Lew. There was a CEO of printing, a CEO of computing, a CEO of services, a CEO of instruments, and so on. Carly said to me after a week, "The 'C' stands for 'chief.' There is one chief. . . . There are not going to be any more CEOs. There are going to be five executive vice presidents, whatever you want to call them. How can you guys have ever spun-off Agilent? How did you do that?" I opposed the [Agilent Technologies] spin-off so much that I was asked to leave the executive committee the last six months that I was here. And they spun it off a week after I retired. That was probably a coincidence, but that was how it worked out. I thought that was throwing away HP's trump card.

The tragedy is not only that HP could have surpassed IBM—that would have been easy. But more so, HP could have been a major force in three or four massively growing businesses that had to do with information utilities and the so-called persuasive computing revolution if we had not lost our courage. If we had stuck to the MC^2 notion we would have been number one in biomathematics, number one in security. We would also have had major new businesses in anything that had to do with distributed sensing: for example, health network or *in vitro* monitoring. The fact that we allowed them first to remain splintered by not forcing integration and then to actually spin-off the thing which was our uniqueness, for no reason, was lunacy. The board, even more than Lew, was guilty. They had all drunk the Wall Street Kool-aid—just an act of spinning it off will make the stock rise and will make the people think you are really moving forward. Ned [Barnholt], who ran instruments, was initially wildly opposed to it. Somehow they convinced him that it was a good thing.[27]

Losing Traction

Sometimes events turn on the smallest of signals. Chaos Theory attracted many converts in the 1990s—the famous example used was that a butterfly flapping its wings in Asia inexorably, though unexplainably, affects weather climates in California.[28] Lew Platt might have felt that his Wintel decision set in motion a paradigm shift in computing, as the computing world began to move away from stand-alone equipment, whether mainframes or servers or even desktops, and turned to a networked world. The new paradigm was based not on a proprietary DecNet or SUNet, but on the Internet. Sun, with a net-centric strategy and superbly tuned Web servers during this period, thrived, whereas HP found itself increasingly marginalized, especially as HP UNIX server leadership faltered. From 1996 through 1999, the Hewlett-Packard juggernaut careened downhill.

For HP critics, the HP Way became the whipping boy as the company struggled, almost as though the products were fine, and people just became complacent and somewhat inept. But the product shortcomings and the strategic decisions were tangible. Spectrum floundered after Roelandts left; the joint HP-Intel IA-64 Itanium chipset took years to launch; and Dell's sales model proved far more efficient for commodity PCs, virtually destroying profitability chances for HP's Wintel offering. New businesses no longer seemed to gain traction in HP to serve as the renewal fuel. Yes, the HP Way was "in the way," but such a superficial catch-phrase does not help analyze the true complexity and difficulty that HP faced.

Stunningly, the marketplace was finding that HP machines were performance-bound, surprising in view of the HP-PA architecture's power. Worse, Itanium chips expected from the Intel partnership had not materialized, and the field reports were truly dismal.[29] The PC business, though growing smartly in revenue under Webb McKinney's leadership, encountered tough profitability issues, as Dell and Compaq proved fierce competitors with lean cost structures. Even the Instrument businesses stalled. Wherever Platt turned, even in the imaging and printing profit margins, he heard discouraging news. But as CEO, you still have to present a positive image and a confident air.

The Sheffield Address at Yale

FEBRUARY 20, 1997, NEW HAVEN, CONNECTICUT: For Immediate Release: Lewis E. Platt, chairman of the board, president and chief executive officer of Hewlett-Packard Co., will present the next Sheffield Fellowship address at Yale University on Friday, February 28, at 4:30 P.M. in Sudler Auditorium of William Harkness Hall, 100 Wall St. His talk, titled "Managing Innovation: An Oxymoron?", is open to the public.[30]

The Sheffield Fellowship was established in 1996 to honor the Sheffield Scientific School at Yale. Founded in 1852 to train engineers, the school produced some of the greatest inventors and industrial leaders of the 19th and 20th centuries before it was absorbed into the growing Yale Faculty of Arts and Sciences in the mid-1940s.[31]

Platt began in his inimitable conversational tone:

I was talking to one of our R&D managers the other day about the importance of the young engineers we recruit, and she summed things up this way: "People right out of school are important members of a project team, because they don't know that something is impossible to do." And that's the beauty of the close interaction between the academic and business worlds. Universities are the birthplaces of many creative new ideas. Industry is the proving ground where the value of those ideas gets determined by people's willingness to pay for them. Separately, academia and business are incomplete. Together, they form a complete cycle.

Bill Hewlett tells an interesting story about that dynamic tension between the creativity that leads to innovation . . . and the hard-headed practicality required to bring a product to market and earn the profit that makes possible the next round of creativity. In a 1986 speech on creativity to MIT's commencement class, Bill recalled the time he quoted Thomas Edison to an HP engineering manager. You've probably heard Edison's famous quip . . . "There ain't no rules around here. We're trying to accomplish something." When Bill said that, the HP manager replied, "Don't say that. Creativity is what screws up my engineering schedule." Bill's next comments were eloquent, so let me quote him verbatim: "These two comments say a great deal about the creative process. It works well when it is not too structured. But, in the long run, it must be tamed, harnessed, and hitched to the wagon of mankind's needs."

That discussion sets up the question I'd like to explore with you today—namely, how HP manages to both stimulate creativity and harness that creativity to produce real products, on time, and on budget. Thus, the question my speech title poses: "Is the term 'managing innovation' an oxymoron?"[32]

The Lightbulb Business?

Lew described historic HP inventions at length (see Appendix D) and added a pseudo-forecast: "Looking forward, we've just perfected blue LEDs. And that means we can combine the colors to produce white light. Remember the advantages—energy efficiency and, essentially, no need for replacement. Will HP go into the lightbulb business? Stay tuned."[33] For the astute HP observer, Platt was tantalizing in the Sheffield address. The light-bulb business? What was he talking about? And where would it lead? This sounded far afield from the HP of personal computers, LaserJet printers, and enterprise servers. Speakers often reveal their own biases and perspectives unwittingly in public addresses—in the Sheffield address, Platt put remarkable emphasis on the ancillary side of the $40 billion company he headed. He never mentioned Spectrum or HP-PA, Birnbaum's capstone, and he omitted the LaserJet side of the printing business, much more vital for the enterprise side than the consumer side of the company. Nor did PCs, the troublesome low end of computing, get mentioned. Platt spent more than half his HP career on the East Coast, in the Medical and Analytical groups, and fully half of his Palo Alto time was concentrated on those groups or the abandoned Manufacturing Systems Group. At one level he was giving voice to the areas he best understood, and presumably, the societal value of those product sectors outweighs in many respects their business revenue potential. At another level, though, it revealed discomfort with the current HP stance in Enterprise Computing, by now in near-total disarray with Roelandts gone, Birnbaum distressed, and Hackborn in control.

The numbers are interesting, put alongside the speech. The 1996 *Annual Report,* published ten days before the talk, cited Computer System sales of $31.5 billion, $3.9 billion Instrument Group sales, and sales of Medical, Analytical, and Components taken together at less than $3.0 billion. The bulk of his talk focused on 7 percent of the company's product profile. Stay tuned indeed!

Birnbaum was a willing and eager but eventually frustrated accomplice. He noted that

> In the labs, we had a lot of bio-instrumentation, human gene tools, the next generation of medicine, pharmaceutical equipments, etc.—whole businesses could

be built on that. Biological assays working with Affymetrix and interesting inkjet printers that could make gene chips by spraying the four genetic bases, instead of four ink colors. Fluidic micro-processors, and things like a chemistry lab built on a chip. There were many others as well, but they all required somebody to say, "Hey, this is a new business. And it is going to take three to five years before it is really profitable." But they were unwilling to do that. That has to come from a few leaders who have belief in it—it can't come from a caretaker mentality that says, "I've got to preserve the quarterly results for the analysts so our stock price won't fall."[34]

Was the Sheffield speech a Freudian precursor of Platt's waning confidence in his primary business strategy? Was he wishing for his own version of Hewlett's touchdown play? Unfortunately, the white light LED strategy to which he alluded was disquieting as well—multiple companies had gained cross-licensing access:

LEDs used to be constrained to low-value uses such as system indicator lights, because of poor light output and limited colour palette (mostly red and yellow). Technology breakthroughs boosted their brightness dramatically in the 1990s, however, and the development of blue and green LEDs based on gallium nitride expanded the available colour spectrum. Japan's Nichia [Corporation] produced the first white LEDs in 1996, by coating blue LEDs with phosphors that give off yellow light, which combines with the devices' blue rays to create white light. After years of litigation and eventual cross-licensing, numerous companies now produce white-light LEDs, using variations of that technology or combining multiple red, green and blue LEDs. . . . Optical components analyst Jagdish Rebello estimates [in 2004] that "It will take five to 10 years to reach the goal of LEDs that equal the performance and cost of conventional lighting."[35]

The Dot-Com World Meets HP

The performance problem of HP computer servers was most surprising. Amid the confusion, two HP researchers—each with strong instrumentation backgrounds—tried to dissect fact from fantasy. Nina Bhatti started her career at Tektronix in 1985, designing software packages for the DAS 9200, Tek's answer to HP Logic Analyzers. Moving to HP a decade later, she teamed with Jim Salehi to investigate issues of latency and slow response time.

Monitoring websites, we discovered that a lot of the latency performance issues were delays from the web server, not the network. When you wait for a page to load, you're waiting for the total round-trip—the network's request, then the server reply, and then the return trip. And everybody said, "It's the network, the network is terrible." What we found is that most of the time when people encounter big delays, it's the server.[36]

The duo, in HP Labs, might have been expected to study the problem, but Nina said, "As a purely academic researcher, I might do that. But HP sold servers. As a researcher who's industrially focused, if I can give HP a distinguishing feature for their platform versus Sun's, I've contributed more than with pure research." The pair decided to design software that would enable higher performance. They wanted to guarantee that HP servers wouldn't fail, or become overloaded by temporary peak loads, while delivering really low latency and advertised capacity.

We basically created a set of technologies able to recognize how much traffic was coming in, reorder the traffic to handle priority requests based on a number of criteria, and really make sure that we were monitoring the server itself, so that if we're getting overloaded, we could take action. We could guarantee throughput even when we were being bombarded by either spam attacks or a lot of low-importance tasks.

It detected overload requests, redirecting loads elsewhere to stabilize the server response. It was soon developed as a product, under the name Live-Lock, for Web Quality of Service (QoS).

We spent about a year and a half, really revolutionary in thinking about server questions. That's an example of looking for an opportunity and figuring out how to create a solution that could give us something new in the positions that mattered in our market. We transferred this to a division. Basically, it was a really cool thing that became a product that gave HP something to take to the market. When you're late for the party, you'd better bring something good. Sun was already in the network server business. So HP had to bring something to users. And this was a promising feature that we could give them.[37]

After the Web QoS work, Bhatti and Allan Kuchinsky teamed at HP Labs to begin an e-commerce study, one of the first of its kind. The question that sparked the investigation was "How fast does the response have to be?" It initiated some fundamental research. How fast the response needs to be determines to a substantial degree how much computing power you need and what architectural topology is most appropriate. Bhatti, pleased with the outcome, noted that

What we wanted to figure out was how much response time is needed for people to continue to shop at your site. We did a controlled study with a system that would control the loading of their Web pages. And we put them through these loops where the latency would be varied periodically. They had a little icon on their screen that they could click when they thought it went too slow. We were able to graph when people said it's too slow with the latency that we'd give them. It tells you how much response time minimization is needed before they'll stop shopping. We published and patented a very new result—the longer you're in a session, the more picky you are about performance. You become more intolerant. And, the longer you are in session, the more likely you are to be a revenue-generating person, because you're not just looking at one or two items and browsing. You're really doing something.

We were able to recognize long sessions and expedite those requests before others. If you just came to my store, I'm going to ignore you a little bit. If I've got someone who has a big shopping basket, I'm going to take care of that person. We tried to do with a Web server what a shopkeeper would do.

A by-product of this work was the discovery that people who fill a shopping basket, but who cannot check out for some reason, get really annoyed. They probably won't shop again at your site, concluding that security might be infringed or that the company is somehow unreliable. Worse than a lost sale, this is a lost customer.

We also found people have mental models of how long they think each operation should take. When visiting a Web page about a product, they expect that to be fast. If you're calculating sales tax and shipping charges, they're pretty tolerant. So it allows you to have more programmatic control over latency to reflect the user's expectations. In the Web QoS product, we shipped software that went underneath the Web server—a little additional software package that you install.

> Unfortunately, HP thought, "This will just move more iron." They didn't think about it as a product on its own, whereas Netscape would have thought about it as a software enhancement. They'd funnel it as part of the Web platform, as a distinguishing feature.[38]

Too frequently during the 1990s, HP was unable to take advantage of HP Lab research into Web-enabled solutions. Don Hammond's sage cultivation advice for his HP Labs teams twenty years before—to make sure that there was a closely coupled receiving division or group who supported the research—no longer seemed sufficient to transfer significant work into market value. Asked how technology transfers from HP Labs worked, Bhatti replied,

> A lot depends on your relationship with the division, if you can find one. If you find one, sometimes they just don't have the ability to invest in it. That's a systemic problem—you don't necessarily have a product group that has the ability to even take it in. It's really bizarre. HP will go buy a company—that is easier for them than it is to take that technology from HP Labs and actually create a product around it. We spent all this time and . . . quit investing in it. About this time I actually left and went to Nokia.[39]

A Crisis of Confidence

Although the Wintel battle caused the executive team angst, and response to the dot-com sea-change yielded inconclusive debate, another topic generated consternation. George Bodway, the former head of HP's Microwave Components Division and the Spectrum chipsets, managed Platt's business planning office. He hired ex-Booz Allen Hamilton consultant Jim Mackey, who put together an impressive collection of historic product line data for some of HP's greatest success stories before turning his attention to the Fortune 50. The disturbing findings showed that no one escaped the "curse"—the flattening of sales between $50 billion and $100 billion. First published in the 1998 Corporate Strategy Board study, "Stall Points, Barriers to Growth for the Large Corporate Enterprise," Mackey's report said,

> This remarkable research in partnership with Hewlett-Packard examined the point when growth "stalls" to near GNP rates and found "(almost) all large

companies stall, most with very little warning . . . only a handful have been able to maintain anything resembling an unbroken growth run since entry to the ranks of the Fortune 50." [It is] extremely rare to maintain double-digit top-line growth above $20 billion in revenue, a ceiling that has crept upward across time. . . . Most compelling is . . . [that] stalling companies lose over half their market value; very few [have been] able to recover.[40]

Clayton Christensen's widely acclaimed book *The Innovator's Dilemma* (1997) had just been published. It captured the mood in the executive offices at 3000 Hanover Street in Palo Alto. As Polly Labarre wrote in *Fast Company,* Christensen had argued that

Successful companies tend to swim upstream, pursuing higher-end, higher-margin customers with better technology and better products. They boost profitability and shareholder returns, and they reflect good management. But they can also open a vacuum that disruptive upstarts may rush into with completely different offerings: worse, but cheaper and more convenient products. Dominant companies often ignore these disruptive innovations because they don't interest their mainstream customers. But in so doing, they miss the next great wave of industry growth. "By doing what they must do to keep their margins strong and their stock price healthy, every company paves the way for its own disruption."[41]

Labarre cited Christensen's proud intervention at Intel at Andy Grove's behest, forcing the company to look hard at the low end, and then protect it with a new creation that undercut its own Pentium, the Celeron. Alas, CEO Hector Ruiz at Advanced Micro Devices (AMD) didn't read Christensen's book, attacking the Pentium with the Athlon at the top end rather than the low end. In effect, AMD took a page from an earlier playbook, DEC's strategy against IBM with the VAX/780, keeping the instruction set compatible while adding a virtual memory extension. It proved disastrous for Intel—and for Christensen's thesis—not only stunting the Itanium 64-bit adoption on which HP's top-end machines were reliant but gutting Intel's thought-leadership and huge profit margins on its bread-and-butter Pentium line from 2003 through 2006. As for the Celeron, it bombed. Many CEOs were frankly tickled—rather than business management by theory, the school of hard knocks seemed more valuable.[42]

To the HP board, the Wintel vote to move HP into the low end was congruent with Christensen's thesis. The printing side, too, seemed aligned with the Christensen thesis. HP printers relentlessly drove prices down and down, maintaining and even increasing their market dominance—and their proprietary ink supplies became an increasing part of HP's profit margins. In actuality, this strategy was probably more like the Boston Consulting Group approach that TI had used against HP calculators. The Instrumentation side of HP, though, still a third of the employees and 20 percent of sales, had not been able to escape the trap. Medical and analytical systems in particular were caught exactly in the bind outlined in *The Innovator's Dilemma*; one could argue that components were being rapidly commoditized as well. Platt revived the idea to divest Instruments, as an anachronistic appendage from a historic past. Birnbaum's vision of MC^2 now fell on deaf ears, and Ned Barnholt switched his view—instead of opposing divestiture, he began to see that it was his best opportunity.[43]

Platt had long been managing the business as a consortium—but his entire staff was clear about the issues that rose to the fore. As Belluzzo described it,

> There were three things that we had to deal with. First, we had to recognize that a lot of the business was becoming commoditized—the PC business was the issue of contention. And we had to become more compatible. This was at odds with both Bob Wayman and Ned Barnholt. They said, "Just because you guys can't figure out how to innovate in the PC business, don't drive us through all these cost changes." So there was no desire to simplify the company, to reduce the cost structure. There were a number of things, which now the company has done, but when I proposed them back in 1997 and 1998, it was just a total war. People said, "No way, you guys just want to be like Dell." Well, we really didn't want to be like Dell. We just wanted to survive to fight another day.[44]

Belluzzo elaborated on the second point, saying that both HP Labs and the business units had not delivered: "The track record was atrocious for innovation. It should be a company with just two or three areas we were going to bet on, and go make it happen. Instead it was this . . . potpourri." It wasn't for lack of good ideas, he stressed, but rather lack of strategic focus. "The labs would come over with new innovations, and one by one these things would die." Belluzzo's answer was to become more strategic, pick the bets and put a focused team in place to achieve results. "Lew couldn't handle that. The Internet question, in particular, was really fascinating. We struggled with 'What does that mean? We're in systems, are they vital for the Internet? But what does that mean?' Even Joel was really kind of lost on that."[45]

The worst charge was that "All we have is a tired computer systems business." Noting that this dilemma presaged the Compaq merger idea by four years, Belluzzo took umbrage in particular with David Woodley Packard's propensity to "play that quote back in a disgusting way for years afterwards." To Belluzzo, the point wasn't that the commoditized hardware business was where the company should focus, but rather that "a new software layer is going to be the new point of contribution value. We haven't been a software company, but we have to become a software company, or else we're going to be a Dell in the computer systems business. And we need to figure out those ingredients."[46] But Lew and his senior staff—Ned Barnholt, Doug Carnahan, Bob Wayman, and Rick Belluzzo—were tacticians. Only the disempowered Birnbaum brought technical insight or vision. With no fireball like Ely, no master strategist like Hackborn, no touchdown quarterback like Hewlett, the company needed the decisiveness of Packard or the persistence of Young. Belluzzo adopted a unilateral acquisition strategy to try to break the logjam.

M&A—Acquiring a New Strategy

On April 27, 1997, Hewlett-Packard announced that it was buying VeriFone for $1.18 billion ($1.29 billion by the time the transaction closed) in a stock swap. "HP said the e-commerce pioneer will operate as an independent subsidiary. The new unit will use technology developed by both companies in an effort to accelerate development and deployment of online commerce and smart card applications for consumers and businesses."[47]

Belluzzo imagined that HP could become known for enabling and guaranteeing secure payments. With six million point-of-sale (POS) terminals, VeriFone should have been an ideal early experiment, with intersections between several HP technologies and product segments. He argued that

"VeriFone was intended to be the foundation for building a leadership position in secure payments—from the edge (payment terminals) to the core (backend systems). This end-to-end solution would have given HP the ability to deliver solutions to retail, financial services, and web based 'new retail.' This was a tremendous opportunity."[48] Belluzzo, hopeful, "charged into the deal, and yet there was this passive-resistant culture where nobody would stop you but they said, 'I'll get even with you.' And that turned out to be a train wreck. Wayman and Barnholt and Carnahan—Lew's whole staff—were opposed."[49]

VeriFone, more than twice as expensive as Platt's ill-fated Apollo acquisition in 1988, yielded even worse results. John Sheets, a long-time manager at VeriFone, came to HP excited about the chance to put real muscle into the company. Within a year, he was profoundly disillusioned, saying, "No one wanted us—we were amazed."[50] Belluzzo tagged Glenn Osaka, head of Enterprise Systems, to manage the team; Osaka left HP shortly thereafter. Belluzzo abandoned ship nine months later; Sheets and his colleagues found neither another sponsor nor a synergistic home within HP over three years. In the early HP days—acquisitions in Medical and Analytical, for example—it was perhaps a positive thing to be left alone to develop the business at a moderate rate. But the VeriFone case led to emasculation, with no synergy and little enthusiasm. Magazine pundits were acidic in their analysis:

> Software and acquisitions have never been HP's strong suit. In the past, software has existed at HP as a means to sell more hardware, not as a strategic infrastructure play. As for acquisitions, HP hasn't done a good job of integrating companies once they are acquired. Witness its $1.3 billion purchase in 1997 of electronic-payment company VeriFone. HP executives have acknowledged that they kept the company at arm's length and failed to capitalize on its assets. HP sold VeriFone in May [2001] for an undisclosed amount of cash.[51]

Belluzzo's precipitous action sealed Platt's fate and his own:

> It was a strategic debate, and we just couldn't get anywhere. And the politics between Dick and Lew . . . I was right in the middle of things. If I tried to get Dick to help me . . . then Lew would be more distrusting. And Bob Wayman was Lew's

trusted assistant. I finally realized one day, I'm going to fail at this. Should I sit here and ride this thing to the end and fail? Pretty brusque at the time, I thought I'll just go somewhere else.[52]

Thwarted completely, Belluzzo soon resigned. The dilemma for Belluzzo—seeking the safe zone in the no man's land between Dick Hackborn and Lew Platt—was shared by many. Dick Watts worked for both men; his views about Platt, echoed by many others, are insightful:

Platt spent immense time consciously talking about core competencies and core values—measuring them, surveying their use, and getting people to put them on objectives. He had a broader sense of what the business was all about in terms of customers and employees and the philosophical side of it, and the benefits they gained from either doing business with us or being employed by us, than anyone else I've worked with. [He was] very approachable, very personable. You never found anybody who found Lew abrasive or hard to deal with. Very high integrity, but he wasn't intuitively technical. He struggled most for not having a sense of the right strategic drivers in the computer business. That wasn't his comfort zone. He could help people rationalize and work their way through decisions surrounding an issue, but it just wasn't intuitive for him.[53]

Packard said, "All of our challenges lie in front of us. I think we should concentrate on looking forward." But looking forward with Lew in the driver's seat was very different than with resolute Young, risk-taking Hewlett, or decisive Packard in command. Values, legacy, and history are crucial, but most companies ask, "What have you done for me lately?". That question would be asked with increasing frequency at the end of the decade.

CHAPTER 14

Amicable Separation

If the Agilent split had been done fifteen years earlier, there would have been way less issues in the company. But at any rate, when it was done it was a good decision.

PAUL ELY[1]

In January 1998, Rick Belluzzo, known as "Rocket Rick," left HP to become CEO of Silicon Graphics, replacing ex-HPite Ed McCracken.[2] The board was stunned, no less than Platt—Belluzzo was widely viewed as the heir apparent. HP officials stolidly explained that his departure was not a surprise, since he had often voiced a goal of becoming a CEO. Journalists George Anders and Peter Burrows each explained in detail that it was in fact a major surprise for Lew Platt, as well as a critical tipping point for Dick Hackborn.[3] Hackborn chafed, as did Belluzzo and Birnbaum, about missed opportunity, about tectonic shifts in the computing landscape, indeed about a leadership crisis. Anders and Burrows—both hard-bitten Valley journalists—conducted many interviews, and a spate of articles during this period revealed some of the tension at the top of the company. Yes, Platt had elevated the work-life issues for employees, and yes, HP routinely was rated highly by magazines such as *Working Mother.* But his team was getting ragged—bench strength was thin as defections continued, and no one had much *joie de vivre.* Platt's first-string team, as the company entered fiscal 1998, was Barnholt, Belluzzo, and Carnahan. By coincidence, Belluzzo's abrupt resignation came the same day as Doug Carnahan's planned retirement.

The next board meeting was contentious on multiple fronts. Particularly to Hackborn and Jay Keyworth, HP seemed to be missing the Internet boom. It was painfully obvious that no one on Lew's team was ready to be considered for CEO, throwing any pretense of succession planning into disarray. The kinder, gentler management style had done nothing either to help strategic initiatives or to rationalize operations or process issues.

Meanwhile, there was competitive turmoil. While the executive committee had gotten involved with the Wintel threat, there had been considerable evolution at the upper end of high-performance computing. Silicon Graphics had opted in 1988 to use the MIPS RISC processor designed by Stanford computer scientist John Hennessy for their blindingly fast 3-D workstations; SGI bought MIPS in 1992 to answer HP and DEC homebrew RISC chips, introducing the world's first 64-bit chip, the R4000, in 1994. They bolstered their top end by buying supercomputer manufacturer Cray Research in 1996 for $740 million. Simultaneously, CEO Robert Palmer was trying to salvage DEC with the Alpha chip, which debuted in 1995. Alongside these initiatives, HP's response with Intel for WideWord was a belated effort.

HP-PA leadership was by now hollow—and the founder's son, David Woodley Packard, who had been installed on the HP board at the same time as Walter Hewlett in 1987 to provide some family legacy for the board, was openly critical of both the Wintel focus and the declining fortunes of high-end computing for HP. Rick Belluzzo described it as having to endure Packard's jibes "in a disgusting way for years afterwards."[4] True, HP had dabbled in the high-performance end, buying Convex (a superminicomputer manufacturer in Texas) in 1995 for $150 million, a wholly inadequate thrust against SGI. Meanwhile, Compaq, which had been the PC leader, was becoming much more aggressive, buying Tandem Computers and its fault-tolerant capability and reputation in 1997 and then swallowing DEC in 1998 for $9.6 billion, the largest acquisition in computer industry history to that point. The irony was profound; the largest Wintel company on the globe was buying companies to compete in the space that HP had just relinquished in order to focus its Wintel efforts.

JUNE 15, 1998, HOUSTON, TEXAS In a defining moment for the computing industry, Compaq Computer Corporation unveiled its strategy for combining the strengths of Compaq with those of its recent acquisitions, Digital Equipment Corporation and Tandem Computers, to lay the "cornerstone for the new world of computing."

Eckhard Pfeiffer, Compaq president and CEO, speaking at a press conference June 12 after the completion of the acquisition of Digital, underscored two major points:

Our commitment to our customers is to provide more choice, more power and more freedom than ever before, and the Company is committed to extend industry standards into the enterprise. Compaq is the undisputed leader in industry-standard computing through its market share of Windows NT, SCO, UNIX, and NetWare. The Company plans to extend its leadership position in Windows NT through the continued deployment of application solutions, dedicated enterprise sales teams and its field service and support organization. Compaq employs more NT-certified engineers than its next three largest competitors combined. Compaq Computer Corporation, the world's largest computer manufacturer, is a Fortune Global 200 company and the largest global supplier of personal computers.[5]

"Largest computer manufacturer"? What was that all about? By a cute definitional trick, counting unit sales of computers and excluding revenues from equipment rental and consulting service aspects, Compaq did pass IBM and HP. The claim forced the HP board into yet another round of assessment; the results were not satisfying. Two other analysts at the start of the year had proclaimed the death of UNIX workstations: "In 1996 only 716,000 PC workstations shipped versus 712,000 UNIX workstations. For 1998, In-Stat forecasts 1,858,000 PC workstations compared to 734,000 UNIX workstations. In 1996, IDC says UNIX workstations were $11.5 billion in revenue. In 1998 that number will drop to $10.9 billion. Shipments of PCs will rise from $3.6 billion in 1996 to $6.8 billion in 1998."[6]

But all was not smooth in Houston either. Three days after Pfeiffer's strategic press conference, Compaq filed its earnings report. Analysts assailed the "new leader" (for example, Lawrence Fisher, *New York Times*):

The challenges going forward are to maintain sales momentum amid tough competition and to successfully integrate Digital into Compaq. Compaq, based in Houston, said last month that it was closing six plants overseas and eliminating 5,000 jobs, including 1,000 at its Houston headquarters. The company is planning to cut 17,000 jobs as it absorbs Digital and another recent acquisition, Tandem Computers. The cuts will leave Compaq with a work force of 67,000. For the quarter,

Compaq lost $3.63 billion, compared with earnings of $257 million, or 17 cents a share, fully diluted, in the quarter a year earlier. Consolidated revenue rose 7 percent, to $11.52 billion, from $10.79 billion in the second quarter of 1997.[7]

Computergram, in the United Kingdom, filed a sardonic editorial:

The combined charges will push Compaq into heavy losses for the year to December 1998, as it axes an estimated 17,000 employees from a combined workforce of 82,000. The DEC deal was hailed as the biggest merger in computing history. . . . Now the associated provisions that Compaq is pushing through in the second quarter of 1998 will probably hold the record for the biggest ever charges made following such a deal. In comments made to Reuters in Munich, Germany, CEO Eckhard Pfeiffer unwittingly explained the reasoning behind such a gargantuan charge. "Given the magnitude of the restructuring charge we are taking, it will make the year negative, but you have to look at the difference between net and operating results," he said. Pfeiffer is asking for the suspension of disbelief. The $3 billion write-down of DEC's assets and the $1.7 billion cost of laying-off staff will negate Compaq's entire net earnings since 1993. . . . But, says Pfeiffer, we should only look at the figures before the charge. In a sector littered with these charges, which are all, to a greater or lesser extent, intended to distract analysts and investors from including such costs in their earnings models, this stands out as an all time low.[8]

Against this mixed backdrop, the HP board agonized. Hackborn, like Packard eight years earlier, began interviewing employees around the company. Board members fretted about the lack of PC and Internet momentum. Platt authorized Richard Hagberg to conduct an exhaustive psychological study with the executive team, akin to a failed experiment by John Doyle twenty years earlier. Reported to the board January 16, 1999, the results were damning. Hagberg intoned that the HP Way had become an entitlement, blunting the historic competitive spirit into a nasty case of passive-aggressiveness, wherein people agreed but then followed their own persuasions. A key example: Belluzzo's eviscerated VeriFone acquisition.[9]

Board displeasure grew. The psychological assessment didn't instill confidence, nor did Jim Mackey's somber analysis, that large companies almost always level in their sales. Press coverage that year was ominous—Compaq bought a defunct DEC, while Silicon Graphics dismissed McCracken and stole Belluzzo from HP, followed by a truly disastrous SGI fourth quarter, reported July 24, 1998.[10] By HP's January 1999 board meeting, the numbers were compelling. Although HP had been a growth leader vis-à-vis IBM, DEC, and even Sun until 1997, among these enterprise computing companies, HP no longer stood out in growth rate (Figure 14.1). The Wintel world was dramatically worse, showing two years of desultory growth for HP, while Compaq and Dell scored tremendously (Figure 14.2).

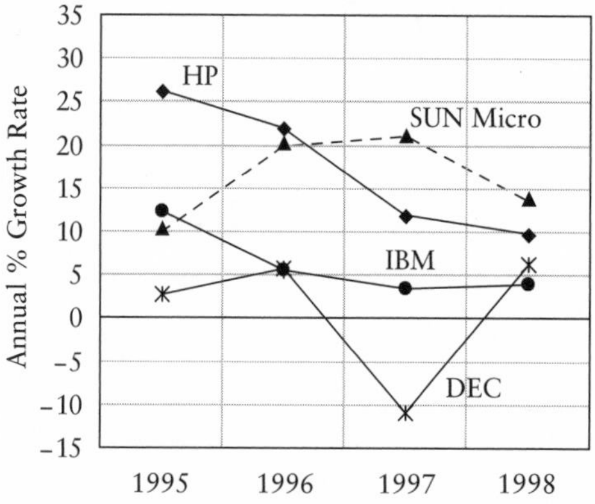

FIGURE 14.1. Growth rate per year enterprise computing vendors, 1995–1998

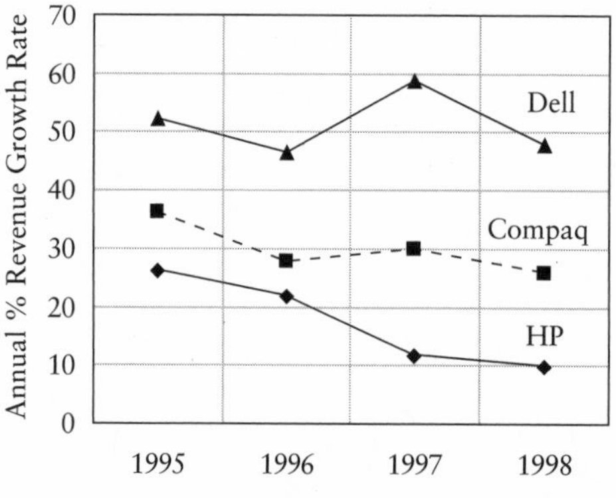

FIGURE 14.2. Growth rate per year PC (Wintel) computer vendors, 1995–1998

HP's net profit numbers, though not catastrophic, were now 15 percent below the consistent average; both growth and profit numbers were even worse when Instruments were included—enough reason for Platt to resurrect the idea of divesting the very different, slow-growth Instrument businesses. This time Barnholt was ready:

The reason HP split is that we had too many business models being managed under one roof. Duane Zitzner, who ran the PC business, would come to Platt's staff and say, "I'm trying to compete with Dell, and they don't pay their engineers what we pay, they don't provide retirement plans for their engineers, and they don't have a central research lab. I want to change all that so I can go compete with Dell." And I'm sitting there saying, "Hey wait a minute, time out. I want the best engineers. I want to pay them at the high end of the curve. I want the best benefits possible and central research is growth." Those two models are in constant tension.[11]

Agilent Technologies Goes It Alone

NOVEMBER 18, 1999, PALO ALTO, CALIFORNIA: Agilent Technologies closed its first day of trading at $44.75 a share, an increase of 49 percent from its opening price. CEO Ned Barnholt outlined the four key HP attributes of greatness and what he hoped to achieve at Agilent Technologies, when the Instrumentation side of HP was cleaved away:

Number one is a decentralized management philosophy and structure. The decisions to enter businesses, or what products to develop, very often weren't the decisions of Dave and Bill. Dave and Bill didn't sit there and say, "Invent a printer." It was people in the organizations that came up with the idea for printers. It was multiple people, in multiple divisions. We had a decentralized structure where people were encouraged to come up with those kinds of ideas, and pursue new business opportunities. The distributed philosophy encouraged entrepreneurship and independence of thinking about growing and building a successful business—that was a lot of the impetus for growth.

Second was the culture of innovation. From the day I joined, it was pounded into me about making a contribution. And not a contribution for contribution's sake, but a contribution that really meant something to the world. We really believed we had the opportunity to change the world through our measurement technology. We were providing new insights that let people come up with new advancements in technology. In computation we were providing capability, speed, and functionality people didn't have. In printers, we were providing printing technology at affordable prices. That culture was pervasive. It was part of the HP way. It was part of the fabric of the company; if you were in R&D, you knew that you didn't do "me too" products. You were constantly challenged to come up with contributions. I'll never forget my first division review as an engineer. I was showing some circuit design I had done to Dave and Bill and the first words out of their mouths were, "Help me understand the contribution."

The third thing was a commitment to advanced research. It was insightful for Dave and Bill to recognize that as they started to develop a decentralized divisional structure, they needed to keep a percentage of the research and development budget at HP Labs looking for breakthrough ideas. Over time, the divisions became more incremental in their thinking. So the lab's job was always to keep looking over the horizon at new technologies, new business opportunities. It wasn't one person responsible for new business planning.

The fourth is extremely important—hiring and retaining the best people. When HP went on college campuses, we generally got to pick from the top of the class. And HP did a lot of advanced things to retain people: medical benefits, good salaries, picnic sites, and retirement plans. But more important for top people was providing an environment where people just really liked to come to work every day. It was energizing. That environment allowed us for many decades to attract and retain top talent.

When we separated from HP, people asked, "What's going to be new?" I said, "We're going to bring the best of the HP Way." To me, the best of the HP Way was two things: it was this culture of innovation and making a contribution. And it was the deep valuing of people. Respecting, trusting, rewarding, recognizing, and creating that environment where you can attract and retain top talent. That was the magic of HP.[12]

HP divested Agilent Technologies in a two-step process—first was a spin-out of a separate company, partially owned by HP, which was fully separated six months later.[13] The initial spin-out, an $8 billion dollar revenue startup, was accorded extraordinary value by the stock market. The stock price soared to $161 per share, giving a market valuation of $85 billion, an amazing ten times the revenue for a company whose product lines had not experienced a 20 percent annual growth rate for two decades. But this was a strange time—Cisco became the highest valuation company on the New York Stock Exchange, with revenues one-eighth of General Electric's.[14] America's most popular stock, owned by 4.6 million shareholders, was Lucent Technologies, spun out of AT&T by three people, including a master marketeer named Carleton Fiorina.

JANUARY 5, 2000, NEW YORK CITY: Lucent Technologies announced an earnings shortfall, which caused a 28 percent price correction, erasing $65 billion of value in the $38 billion revenue company.[15] Just four days after the much-feared Y2K millennial date elapsed safely, this stunning correction raised concern that the high-tech sector—with extraordinary stock inflations over the past year—might face rough times.[16]

The dot-com meltdown came suddenly. In mid-March 2000, the NASDAQ index plunged 33 percent. In retrospect, it was silly to expect Web-based businesses to replace all the bricks-and-mortar companies who were too stodgy to realize what was about to hit them.[17] Amazon.com led the way with book vending, and AOL even bought Time Warner—a company with ten times its revenue—on the strength of its inflated stock valuation. But Pets.com, Webvan, and a thousand other notions disappeared in short order. Tulipomania was a favorite euphemism of the day, and most folk nodded knowingly and shrugged or winked, usually not mentioning how much of their own money had been invested in such illusory ideas.[18]

Then, in September 2000, a second tsunami hit the blue chips. Cisco and Intel each provided updated earnings forecasts with cautionary notes. And the market for technology stocks, fueled by big requirements for the dot. com company infrastructures and the worrisome Y2K forecasts, suddenly sneezed, caught cold, and then pneumonia. Agilent Technologies announced a $3.4 billion revenue quarter on November 20, up 36 percent, observing that this was the best quarter in history, and projecting growth in 2001 at 20 percent. Three quarters later, they reported a $1.3 billion net order quarter. The most serious blow came in Agilent Technologies' optical test business, a $1 billion dollar revenue line that collapsed by 90 percent in three quarters, reported in August 2001, weeks before the economic damage caused by the tragic 9/11 terrorism event, which later took much of the blame.[19]

The markets didn't know how to respond, especially with the compounded impact of the 9/11 event. Blue chip technology companies, the most widely held stocks in American portfolios, were savaged. In six months, Lucent, the core of the old AT&T, plunged 97 percent; other technology stocks followed. Sun Microsystems, HP's chief midrange computer competitor, collapsed 96 percent; Agilent Technologies stock fell by 92 percent; and Hewlett-Packard dropped 91 percent. Three leading lights of the new order—Cisco at 87 percent, Oracle and Intel at 82 percent—suffered only slightly less. Motorola, becoming a world leader in cellular telephony, was clobbered by an 86 percent reduction. IBM at 59 percent drop, General Electric at 62 percent, and Microsoft at 63 percent held up better; but collectively, investors in these three companies lost $1 trillion in value. Corning Glass—a $4 billion company in business fifty years when it produced the first glass for Edison's lightbulb—had its stock fall calamitously from $106.63 to $1.33, suffered the worst indignity as its emergent fiber-optic cable business cratered.

Agilent Technologies had freedom, but the giant HP corporate safety net no longer existed, and cash mattered in a different way. When they had been part of HP, the gripe was that HP wouldn't provide investment money beyond the normal "grow from within" dictum. Once freed, there wasn't enough cash to invest in meaningful ways without violating the Packard "no borrowing" edict. And some groups—Medical, Analytical, and Components—seemed stalled in growth.

Out from Under the Shadow

[Nearly] 80 percent of Agilent's orders and revenue this quarter came from our communications and electronics businesses, where orders grew 62 percent, and revenue increased 44 percent. These growth rates have accelerated despite this quarter's tougher compare. Our biggest challenge is to ramp capacity to meet this unprecedented demand.

NED BARNHOLT (2000)[20]

AUGUST 21, 2000, NEW YORK CITY Agilent Technologies Inc. reported this week that its orders increased 44 percent and its net revenue was up 28 percent in the fiscal third quarter ended July 31. Net earnings, which include the costs of branding and operating independently, grew 15 percent and earnings per share were 33 cents, the Palo Alto, California–based manufacturer of test and measurement equipment said.

"This quarter Agilent achieved record orders and revenue," said Ned Barnholt, president and CEO of Agilent, adding that the company is continuing to work with its customers to build next-generation wireless, optical and data networks. Total orders for the quarter were $3.2 billion, up 44 percent over the same period last year; revenues were $2.7 billion. "Given our excellent position in the communications and electronics markets and our strong backlog levels, we continue to feel comfortable with fourth quarter earnings per share of 39 cents, before restructuring," said Barnholt. "For fiscal 2001, we are raising our guidance from 15 percent to at least 20 percent growth in net revenue."[21]

Those who computed the numbers, though, found that the other part of Agilent Technologies—Medical, Analytical, and Components—suffered seriously in the third quarter: Orders were down sizably, and revenues declined dramatically.

Agilent Technologies Tries M&A

NOVEMBER 27, 2000, SACRAMENTO, CALIFORNIA Agilent Technologies announced its biggest purchase since divesting from Hewlett-Packard, buying Objective Systems Integrators (OSI) for $665 million. OSI, based in Folsom, California, makes software for communications networks.

OSI has recently reported a recovery in its earnings after a period of troubled financial reports. The purchase is projected to increase Agilent's revenue by only 1% next year. But Agilent gets about $618 million in goodwill, other intangibles and in-process research and development. The acquisition of OSI is expected to enhance Agilent's product lines with key technologies and industry-leading expertise, and will augment its worldwide customer base and industry presence.[22]

Asked about the key technologies that OSI brought to Agilent Technologies, the head of Agilent Laboratories (the Agilent successor to the storied HP Labs), executive vice president and CTO Thomas Saponas said, "I found out about the acquisition the morning of the public announcement. That's how much I was in the loop on it."[23] What was going on?

Heir to the legacy of Barney Oliver and Joel Birnbaum, Saponas was HP's first White House Fellow,[24] a man with a solid creative history, a quick mind, and a hair-trigger temper. Agitated, he related that

I immediately went to my computer after Ned told me. It was a public company. They're in the telecom business. Three years running, revenue $67 million all three years—unprofitable all three years. Through the biggest boom in telecom, they were stagnant; this is '97, '98, and '99. We paid $700 million for $67 million in revenue. The next year it was about $14 million in revenue. It really angered me that we would make that big an acquisition and they didn't want my input on it. . . . It would seem to me that at a minimum the group GM who did it would have to be accountable. Dave would not have fired the guy in charge—but [he] would have put him in charge of doing good somewhere else, something he could do.[25]

. . .

APRIL 11, 2007, BANGALORE, INDIA Sobha Renaissance Information Technology (SRIT) today announced a definitive agreement to acquire Objective Systems Integrators, Inc. (OSI)—a global supplier of Telecom Operations Support Systems (OSS)—from Agilent Technologies, a Fortune 500 American corporation. The key factor influencing the decision is the strategic fit with its Telecom BSS business.[26] The OSI sales price was not disclosed.

Agilent Technologies Tries Divestiture

The Medical Group—flat at $1.5 billion in revenue for five years—was the first large casualty. Three giant corporations—Siemens in Germany, Philips in the Netherlands, and GE in America—upped the ante, using mergers and acquisitions to build medical divisions three to four times as big as HP's Medical Group. Dean Morton, on Agilent Technologies' board, and once HP's Medical Group GM and vice president, lamented the decision:

It's one of the consequences of HP's philosophy of "stand on your own pedestal." If you grow by making money, and you invest according to what you can afford, which seems to be prudent for the operation, it works unless others play by different rules. GE acquired Medtronix, who was a big competitor in the ICU field. They acquired some ultrasound people. They put together a very strong imaging base. And they invented the CT scanner. Siemens did the same sort of thing, as did Philips. Then the market changed a bit, and the decisions that used to be made by the surgeons or by the anesthesiologists in hospitals are now being made by the board or by capital committees. The ultrasound business, very important for HP's Medical Group, was just one piece of a broad imaging product line that other people were beginning to put together. So it was increasingly a competitive problem. We always dreamed about technology transfers between analytical products and medical instrumentation. It never amounted to much. And you just can't force these things.[27]

Ned Barnholt elaborated on Morton's comments in 2007: "We were trapped by our legacy of 'no borrowing.' The other competitors didn't play by those rules, and we just got end-played." It is hard to discern a leadership stance of the type that Packard, Hewlett, or Ely—or, for that matter, Fiorina—would have taken. It is hard to build a leadership company with such a caution, and equally hard to sustain one. Agilent Technologies abdicated the arena.[28]

Ken Ferry, vice president and GM of HP and then Agilent Technologies Healthcare Solutions Group, was responsible for sales, service, and marketing for the fragmented patient monitoring, cardiac ultrasound, defibrillation, diagnostic EKG, and information technology solutions. Ferry brought his strong concern to Barnholt that the medical instrumentation industry was consolidating, and HP/Agilent Technologies was becoming squeezed. Five major segments existed—Computer Aided Tomography (CAT), X-Ray, Magnetic Resonance Imaging (MRI), Patient Monitoring (PM), and Ultrasound (US). HP was very strong in PM and US, moderately involved in X-ray, but absent in CAT and MRI. If the top three firms were strong in all five categories, what chance did Agilent Technologies have for the long term? With the reduced reserves, moreover, could a low-investment strategy resolve the missing elements? Barnholt's conclusion was, "No"—HP's forty-year history in the medical field had been marginalized.

In retrospect, big may not be better—Ferry, Stacey Stevens, and Jeff Barnes were the leadership staff at Agilent Technologies who joined the Philips team after the sale. Four years later, the three bolted Philips to join iCAD Medical, a $20-million company that is an industry-leading provider of Computer-Aided Detection (CAD) solutions that identify pathologies, helping to pinpoint cancer earlier.[29] Michelle Barkley, an eighteen-year veteran of heart transplants with famed pioneering doctors Michael DeBakey and Denton Cooley, observed this trend: "It used to be that Hewlett-Packard Medical Group provided the best displays for our work; by the mid-1990s, though, SpaceLabs and especially Marquette Medical Systems were getting very competitive. Then GE bought Marquette in late 1998, setting the stage for marginalizing HP Medical."[30] Barkley decried HP's decline, and the subsequent industry consolidation, while praising new smaller innovative medical companies, such as Abiomed, a Texas pioneer in artificial heart technology, headed by two former GE Medical executives, which doubled in revenues to $50 million annually in three years. Bill Terry agreed in late 2006. He wondered aloud what Dave or Bill might have thought about all of this—why couldn't HP/Agilent Technologies keep the innovation and renewal in this arena?[31]

Barnholt offered an alternative view in 2007. He noted that the sale was arranged before the dot-com meltdown, but consummated well into the morass of red ink that flowed directly thereafter. The sale saved Agilent Technologies from a fatal cash flow crunch as events unfolded.[32]

Renewal with Resizing

AUGUST 21, 2001, PALO ALTO, CALIFORNIA Agilent Technologies Inc has reported a smaller-than-expected loss in the company's fiscal third quarter, but it also announced plans to cut 4,000 jobs, or 9 percent of its workforce, to restore profitability as soon as possible. "This is by far the worst industry downturn I've seen in my 34 years with the company," said Ned Barnholt, president and CEO of Agilent. "Extraordinary business conditions, unfortunately, require unusual actions." Agilent said it expects a slight increase in total orders during the current fiscal quarter, but another drop in revenues—to the $1.3–$1.5 billion range—will lead to an expected loss of $0.50–$0.70 per share, excluding restructuring charges. The Palo Alto–based supplier of test systems, semiconductors, and instruments reported a 33 percent sequential drop in total revenues to $1.8 billion in the fiscal third quarter, ended July 31, compared to $2.7 billion in the prior quarter. Compared to a year ago, Agilent's revenues were 25 percent lower than $2.4 billion in fiscal Q3 of 2000. Including one-time items, the company's net loss reached $219 million, or $0.48 per diluted share, compared to a net income of $155 million, or $0.34 per diluted share, last year. "Based on our outlook earlier in the year, we implemented a variety of aggressive cost-control measures—including a temporary 10 percent pay cut—to try to avoid layoffs," Barnholt said. "The measures to date have had a positive impact, but the business environment in our key industries continued to deteriorate this quarter. And the outlook going forward is for a slow and gradual recovery."[33]

The news was treated sympathetically in many places. Under the headline "Tough Time, Tough Choices," Trish Saywell wrote for the *Asian Times* on September 13, 2001, "The axe has finally fallen at Agilent—[will] they retain their recent rating" as the #2 employer in The Best Employers in Asia survey?" Her conclusion: Sure! "There's no doubt that Agilent has worked hard to treat its staff well," she wrote as the opening for a strong interview with Agilent Technologies' Ee Bian Tan, president of Agilent Singapore and Malaysia. A series of humane steps was chronicled, including job placement help and a competitive severance package. "Even the best companies have to make difficult decisions, especially in a climate as tough as this one."[34]

Just as had HP employees in 1971, Agilent Technologies employees recycled equipment parts and cut back on travel, long-distance calls, and work supplies. Nonetheless, the company had grown by five thousand workers, to forty-seven thousand employees, in its first year, plus another five thousand temporary employees. Selling the Medical Group moved five thousand people; laying off the "temps" got rid of another five thousand. The next step was a 10 percent wage cut, emulating the famous nine-day fortnight strategy. The August 2001 layoff of four thousand was the toughest move to date. More than eight thousand people were laid off in 2002. The February 2003 announcement signaled the final four thousand people to go.[35]

The press reports and the later assessment were amazingly positive:

> The response of employees to the layoffs was remarkable. The general impression of the employees was that Barnholt had done all he could to save their jobs, and those who were laid off stuck with their jobs, working hard, until the end of their last day with Agilent. The Hewlett-Packard Way had paid off in employees who were not angry with the company and thus would be willing to be rehired by Agilent should the company manage to end its steep decline.[36]

Agilent Technologies' management shared an internal survey:

Nearly 90 percent of employees thought that those who had been laid off had been treated well; this resulted in a high level of motivation among the employees who remained. Barnholt made an extraordinary effort to explain it, saying later, "How you communicate bad news is an important challenge, because how you treat people who leave has a great impact on the attitude of those people who stay." By 2004 Agilent Technologies had only 28,000 employees, but the company seemed to be stabilizing."[37]

Nonetheless, enormous structural havoc had been wrought. The semiconductor operations were still struggling—Agilent Technologies' market share had dropped precipitously during the interval, and the business was still as cyclic as ever. The Medical Group had been a mainstay of the company for forty years; the Communication Group had been the stalwart leader since HP's inception. All of these groups were in disarray. Senior management had retired, discouraged by the sudden turn of events; critical engineers had left as well. The future didn't seem nearly as exciting somehow in mid-2004 as it had in early 1999.

Opting for a Safe Haven

JANUARY 19, 2005, PALO ALTO, CALIFORNIA: The Agilent Technologies board announced that Ned Barnholt, sixty-one, would retire on March 1, handing the reins to Bill Sullivan, who had become Agilent Technologies' COO after leading the Components Group. The team had hunkered down, sold off the legacy medical systems, engaged in three disabling layoffs, and endured much criticism during the intervening three years, as sales eroded and profits were wildly erratic. The team and the board had lost patience; the charge for Sullivan was to stabilize earnings and the employee base—growth would no longer be the Agilent Technologies watchword. Sullivan didn't waste any time. Over the next six months, he divested four groups from Agilent Technologies, some nearly sacrosanct.

JUNE 24, 2005, SAN JOSE AND PALO ALTO, CALIFORNIA Symmetricom Inc. (NASDAQ: SYMM), a worldwide leader in precise time and frequency products and services, and Agilent Technologies Inc. (NYSE: A) today announced that they have entered into a definitive agreement pursuant to which Symmetricom would purchase Agilent's Frequency and Time Standards product line (for) approximately $8.0 million in cash.

Agilent's Frequency and Time Standards product line includes the 5071A Primary Frequency Standard, one of the highest-performing commercial cesium standards available for timekeeping. The cesium clock, accurate to one second in 162,000 years, is used in government laboratories worldwide. Customers include national time authorities and measurement institutes, such as the U.S. Naval Observatory and the world's time authority, Bureau Int'l Poids et Mesures (BIPM), in France (BIPM provides the internationally recognized definition of a second of time). The U.S. government also uses Agilent's precision timing instruments for satellite communication ground stations and precision navigation.[38]

Tom Steipp, one of Hackborn's managers, joined HP to market Disc Storage in 1979. He rose to general manager through a succession of positions in storage, then networks, and finally Federal Government Systems—a classic HP career story. Scientific-Atlanta attracted him from HP to lead the industry's first cable modem solutions in 1996, where he saw the fundamental importance of the atomic clock technology to the worldwide communications backbone. When the CEO role at Symmetricom became available in 1998, Steipp seized the opportunity, even though the group competed directly with HP. Two years later, gloating with the chance to buy the Agilent product line, Steipp said, "The acquisition of Agilent's cesium products strengthens our technology leadership in high-precision timing. Having the high-performance products and expertise will allow us to leverage our R&D investments in cesium for the benefit of both Agilent and Symmetricom customers. We are committed to further advancing cesium atomic oscillator technology to serve our customers' requirements for precise time and frequency."[39]

Bob Burns, vice president and general manager for Agilent Technologies' Nanotechnology Measurement Division, was supportive, even as he rued the shift:

For more than 40 years, scientists and technicians around the world have trusted Agilent's atomic cesium clocks—they are the most precise cesium-based timing tools commercially available. As Agilent focuses on new market areas, we are pleased to transition this important world-leading and historic product line to Symmetricom, where our customers will find continuity with a company that understands their needs and can provide them with strong worldwide support.[40]

Having engineered an equity partnership with Philips in 1999 for white light LEDs, Sullivan moved quickly to consummate a total divestiture. Some despaired—Roland Haitz, his former CTO, agonized that Agilent Technologies was selling out a huge future revenue stream.[41] Ned Barnholt, in a private conversation, said, "I'd never have supported that move," but reversed himself two weeks later, saying, "I did tell Bill [Sullivan] that if he could get $2 billion for it, he should do it—he got $2.7 billion!"[42]

AUGUST 15, 2005, PALO ALTO, CALIFORNIA: Following much speculation, Agilent Technologies confirmed that it would sell off its semiconductor business unit:

Private equity firms Kohlberg Kravis Roberts and Silver Lake Partners take control of Agilent's semiconductor product group in a $2.66 billion cash deal. While Philips has bought out the company's stake in Lumileds, the remainder of the Agilent chip business has been snapped up by two private equity firms. Apart from LEDs and fiber-optic components, Agilent also manufactured GaAs-based E-mode PHEMTs at its six-inch wafer facility in Fort Collins, Colorado. Market analyst Stephen Entwhistle said, "Agilent has struggled against incumbent GaAs power amplifier (PA) suppliers in the cell-phone handset sector. In its most recent quarter . . . the semiconductor group saw a 2 percent drop in revenue year-on-year to $458 million. But orders were up strongly, to $499 million, an 8 percent sequential growth."[43]

. . .

AUGUST 15, 2005, PALO ALTO, CALIFORNIA Co-incident with announcing the sale of the Components Group to a private firm, Agilent Technologies announced that Philips will acquire Agilent's 47 percent share of the Lumileds high-power LED joint venture for $950 million. From August 2004, the joint venture reported sales for 12 months of $324 million (up 28 percent) with an operating profit of $83 million. Philips paid six times the LED revenue for Agilent Technologies' half, for an industry already seeing "major over-capacity," a remarkably healthy price by the historic record of the semiconductor industry.

AUGUST 15, 2005, PALO ALTO, CALIFORNIA: In the third of three major announcements, Bill Sullivan described the pending spin-out of Verigy Corporation, based on Agilent Technologies' Automated Test Division under Jack Trautman. This division, reporting $900 million in revenues for 2004 (down 2 percent year over year), was set up as an independent corporation. On March 9, 2006, Agilent Technologies filed papers with the SEC for an IPO, which took place on June 13, 2006, at a $15 opening price. With 58.5 million shares, the company was valued at $877 million, just about 1:1 for its revenue; it closed the first day at $14.33. Reuters reported February 23, 2007, that Verigy shares rose 27 percent to $23.96 in morning trade on the Nasdaq, having gained almost 45 percent since its IPO in June 2006, thanks to a strong earnings and revenue report.[44]

Page 3 of Agilent Technologies' 1999 *Annual Report* proudly carried one sentence: "Agilent is a *diversified technology company* whose products and solutions revolutionize how people live and work." Page 4 has two sentences, commenting that "Agilent has more than 20,000 products, 42,000 employees, and customers in 120 countries. We *innovate* like a start-up and deliver as a global company."[45] By contrast, CEO Bill Sullivan on Page 1 of Agilent Technologies' 2006 *Annual Report* described the new focus: "a pure-play measurements company" with two business groups, "electronic measurement, which includes general purpose test and communications test; and bio-analytical measurement, which includes chemical analysis and life science." The announced 2007 goal was "to attain higher sustainable profitable growth."[46]

Agilent Technologies today is a mere shell of its former self—$4.97 billion 2006 revenues versus $10.9 billion in 2000.[47] Employees—full-time and temporary—have declined from a peak 52,000 to 18,700—21,500 departed in one of the three successive debilitating layoffs, and the rest went with groups sold to other companies. Agilent Technologies still continued to garner positive press. The company proudly noted in the 2002 *Annual Report* that Agilent Technologies ranked high as one of America's Best Places to Work—thirty-first, up from forty-sixth the year before—and other countries ranked Agilent Technologies even higher.[48] The 2003 *Annual Report* was "pleased to note" that *Fortune* still ranked the company in 2002, while China and Taiwan each rated Agilent Technologies the "Best Employer in Asia"; both *Careers Magazine* and *Disabled Magazine* gave plaudits as well.[49] *Business Ethics Magazine* publishes an annual "100 Best Corporate Citizens" list; Agilent Technologies was ninth in 2004, a proud listing worthy of Hewlett and Packard's insistence on absolute integrity.[50]

When Sullivan became CEO, Agilent Technologies promoted Patrick Byrne to Sullivan's old job—senior vice president in charge of the Electronic Products and Solutions Group, 70 percent-plus of Agilent Technologies' revenue. Byrne, twenty-two years with the company, had breadth, an incisive mind, strong ethics, and a balanced perspective on business requirements coupled with R&D investments. Byrne reemphasized a classic HP / Agilent Technologies attribute, innovation for new markets: "Emerging technology trends include: (1) Pervasive mobility; (2) The integration of mobile technology with enterprise applications; (3) Recapitalization of defense electronics to meet homeland and mobile security needs; and (4) The conversion of radio frequency signals to digital signals."[51]

In the understated manner of old, however, Byrne resigned without explanation from Agilent Technologies on March 31, 2007, and Sullivan added his responsibilities to his own. No national or Bay Area paper carried the story; the *North Bay Business Journal* (Santa Rosa coverage) merely said "Agilent Plans Unaffected by Byrne Exit."[52]

FEBRUARY 7, 2007, SANTA CLARA, CALIFORNIA: Agilent Technologies' Life Sciences and Chemical Analysis business (LSCA) won the prestigious 2006 Company of the Year Award from the influential *Instrument Business Outlook* newsletter. LSCA was headed by veteran Chris van Ingen, who joined HP in 1977 as a mass-spectrometer sales engineer in the Netherlands. Named the Netherlands country manager for LSCA in 1981, he moved to Avondale (PA) in 1984; in March 1999, when Agilent Technologies was formed, van Ingen became vice president of sales, support, and marketing for LSCA. Appointed VP-GM of LSCA in 2001, he said, "It's gratifying to be recognized within the industry as a global leader, so we're honored to be named for this award. The achievements outlined by IBO are the result of hard work on the part of Agilent Life Sciences and Chemical Analysis employees around the world, and they deserve all the credit."[53] The IBO award praises Agilent Technologies' bio-analytical measurement business for transforming itself into a powerhouse in the years since Agilent was founded in 1999. Citing the introduction of the 1200 Liquid Chromatograph Rapid Resolution System, and also a new series of high-end mass spectrometers "that instantly changed the competitive landscape of the LC/MS market," the article said that Agilent Technologies' bio-analytical measurement business, after years of being considered a bit conservative and slow moving, is today "aggressive—even audacious—and surprisingly spry."[54] Van Ingen too retired at the end of fiscal 2007, giving Sullivan a whole new team.

Though less than half the size it was six years before in both revenues and employees, Agilent Technologies had more cash at the end of 2007 ($2.3 billion versus $1.0 billion), the same amount of working capital, and 70 percent of the equity value of the 2001 ending numbers. Operating profit was the highest percentage in Agilent Technologies history, higher than the boom year in 2000. In retrospect, Agilent Technologies fundamentally reshaped itself in this first decade. Although both the Medical Group and Analytical Group were stagnant, the two groups differed in the size and number of major competitors. T&M, ATM, and Semiconductors all proved volatile, T&M tied especially to Communications, which has been stabilizing. Semiconductors always have had a boom-bust type of activity. Now only two segments remain, both in the Instrument Group. Retired computer executive Paul Ely, still inordinately proud of the old HP, is laudatory: "They've done well."[55]

CHAPTER 15

Indigestion

In my experience, more companies die of indigestion from trying to seize too much opportunity than die from starvation for lack of it.

DAVE PACKARD (1986)[1]

Two events eleven years apart, Lew Platt's Wintel decision and Mark Hurd's pretexting revelation, serve as bookends for the most tumultuous period in company history for the HP Way.[2] Firing two CEOs, hiring two outsiders to run the company, enduring two enormous merger proposals—one erupting into a fratricidal ownership fight between the families and the board—and finally a public debacle over board leaks propelled the HP board of directors into the limelight. The spectacle was disturbing.

Some found blame quite easy to assign. Paul Ely, the most confrontational and assertive leader in HP history, pulled no punches: "Bill and Dave felt that the HP Way and the HP spirit were so deeply ingrained in the company that their presence wasn't needed, that it would continue to exist. They were wrong. It didn't take Carly very long to get rid of it."[3] Ely faulted the board in three regards—first, for removing Platt ("Lew Platt did an excellent job as CEO and I think the criticism that he got in the press when he was forced out was totally undeserved. . . . If they had left Lew alone, things would have been fine."); second, for hiring Fiorina ("Hackborn could have known that he was mixing oil and water to put her in the company."); and third, for taking so long to remove her ("I can't think of a good thing that happened during all those years.").[4]

Others faulted individuals. Joel Birnbaum, distressed by Platt's disavowal of MC^2 and the subsequent divestiture of Agilent Technologies, supported the shift to a new CEO, and he found Fiorina's style a breath of fresh air for research. Rick Belluzzo, who resigned in disgust from Platt's staff, indicted the events surrounding pretexting:

I am so furious at this whole situation, with this scandal. . . . I'm shocked at all the HP people that I talk to who still don't take this thing seriously. They still say that the media is out of control and it's no big deal. And I'm shocked. . . . The worst of it is that the company lost a lot of its ethical edge for awhile. For several years, it seemed that HP would say, "You've been awarded the business," but you know they're awarding somebody else too. And they were really telling you: "You make the investment," and three months later they would say, "We decided we don't want you anymore."[5]

Ethical violations are the most egregious transgressions imaginable to the HP Way—Belluzzo's indignation went far beyond the pretexting lunacy, however, to a basic observation of a change in the ethical character of HP employee attitudes as exhibited in supplier and customer interactions. This change, perceived widely amongst suppliers, seemed to trace back to a post-Compaq merger era, an unwelcome consequence perhaps of the more aggressive methods embedded in the style of the Houston company. A corollary of the *Bill and Dave* version of the HP Way is that it has to be protected in every interaction by every employee of the company. Who protects and guards these behaviors? And, if they are abridged, what corrective mechanisms are activated? Belluzzo himself noted that these excesses have been curbed, that by mid-2008 the company seems once again to exhibit a much more balanced, more stable ethic.[6]

It is vital to distinguish between change and ethics. Packard noted on numerous occasions that change is usually opposed most by those who led the last change. The opposition by old-timers when HP Cupertino tried to take the company into the computer age was fierce, and couldn't be breached until Paul Ely's brash leadership won the day. Time would establish that those being rebuffed were competent, capable, enthusiastic change agents, well able to lead in other companies once freed from the HP old-timer conservatism. Likewise, the winning minicomputer leadership hobbled those who sought to lead a personal computer revolution a decade later. It would blunt the PC impact on the company for a critical decade. This resistance to change cropped up, in another place, for the idea of networked workstations. Mark Twain wrote that the only two constants were death and taxes—Packard opined that "Those are minor individual events. The true constants are change and conflict, and the latter almost always arises between those seeking change and those resisting it." He went on to observe that the goal within a company ought to be to fight the competition, not colleagues.[7]

The whole company resisted Hewlett's enthusiasm for the HP 35 handheld calculator until it became wildly successful. The early peripherals work was not popular with either the Instrument folk or the CPU design teams, and the notion that terminals could become autonomous, even driving a personal computer revolution, was heresy. The printer revolution, especially the LaserJet families, was widely viewed across HP as aberrant; John Young and the executive team sought repeatedly to rein in Hackborn's activists. Hackborn often went back to Packard and Hewlett to verify that he was working within the spirit of the HP Way; he and his staff continued to assert that the company didn't know how to stop the Peripherals Group from succeeding, even as the hurdles that they had to overcome were substantial. This learning crucible helped to create a siege mentality in the Peripherals Group.

Selecting . . . an Outsider

JANUARY 18, 1999, PALO ALTO, CALIFORNIA: The terse HP announcement revealed that the board, tired of the deteriorating financials, concluded that no insider could change things sufficiently. Platt, stung by the rebuff, acquiesced.[8] Jeff Christian, an aggressive headhunter, took Lew Platt's phone call in March 1999. Platt, introduced to Christian by venture capitalist (and ex-HP Computer Group marketeer) Joe Schoendorf, had used Christian on several prior assignments before Platt found himself at the mercy of the HP board, seeking his own replacement six years ahead of schedule.

Christian was an odd selection, an outsider both to the Valley and to significant CEO searches. His retention was greeted by the Silicon Valley network with disbelief; he reveled in the chance to bell the cat. Christian, a hard-charging workaholic, put enormous energy into the search, turning up names one might readily anticipate, but also a real surprise—Carleton S. Fiorina, known as "Carly," recently lionized by *Fortune* magazine as "The Most Powerful Woman in America," outranking even Oprah Winfrey and Martha Stewart.[9] This was celebrity country, not Wall Street or Silicon Valley. "Just who is she anyway?" was the first reaction. But when Carly surfaced, she was endorsed by Lew's team. Ned Barnholt, on Platt's team, described her:

> I knew Carly long before she joined HP. She was the assigned executive to HP from Lucent. I was the assigned executive from HP to Lucent. So she and I arranged a lot of meetings with Lew and Rick McCann [Lucent CEO] and others. When we announced the [Agilent Technologies] split, she was the first one I called. Hiring Carly was a clear signal by the HP board that they really wanted to emphasize the consumer aspect of the company. Carly is probably one of the best marketeers I've ever met.[10]

Fiorina was the antithesis of Platt—bold and instinctive, even clear and commanding in initial interviews. She did not appear indecisive, agonized, or hobbled by doubt. Some worried—she was, after all, an outsider in every sense of the word. She was not an internal candidate who knew HP, she was decidedly not an engineer, she was not a westerner, she was not male, and she was not introverted. She was—gasp—a marketeer, an impeccably garbed marketeer at that. The contrast to ex-HP CEOs, or to the peer group of Silicon Valley CEOs for that matter, was stark. Other reputed candidates—Ed Zander from Sun Microsystems, Paul Otellini at Intel, Ray Lane from Oracle, Rick Belluzzo at Silicon Graphics, plus Ann Livermore, Carolyn Ticknor, and others within HP—were full-fledged Silicon Valley club members even if they didn't meet every single criterion. The committee was delighted. The issue, they felt, was that HP had been led by introverted nonmarketing engineers for too long. It was high time to join Corporate America as a premier Fortune 20 company with topflight leadership.

Carly Meets the HP Way

The interview process was illuminating. Only four members of the board were involved. Making a move that might give pause, the board deposed its chief and then allowed him to head the search committee. This board had been selected for its toadyish support of the HP Way and insider leadership for years. Schisms were already developing, however, that would soon surface and fracture the board. Fiorina would write in *Tough Choices* that she doesn't recall the family being involved; Walter Hewlett, son of founder Bill, didn't even attend the first meeting she had with the full board. It seems unusual in retrospect that the families, with four of the fifteen board seats, handed over control to an outsider without much more than a cursory look and tacit approval. It also helps to explain the overt mistake that Fiorina made vis-à-vis the Compaq bid.

Fiorina attentively agreed with the HP board during her initial interviews that Hewlett-Packard needed major surgery. Examining the annual 10-K and quarterly 10-Q detailed financial filings (public documents required by the Securities and Exchange Commission) from 1996 through 1999 revealed a troubling situation dating from Lew's fateful Wintel decision and loss of crucial leadership in the server side of the business. Roelandts, Birnbaum, and Lampman were proven right: UNIX servers with high profit margins thrived in the new Web-based server-farm world, and the commoditized, hotly competitive PC business produced dismal margins at best. HP blew an out-and-out UNIX lead badly in three short years, going from number one in the industry under Wim Roelandts to a weak number three in UNIX servers and a minuscule eighth in network servers. Sun grabbed nearly all of the business for the Year 2000 buildup as well as the massive server farms constructed for the dot-commers, growing at an amazing pace for a large company (30 percent CAGR). IBM, given a chance to rally, restored luster to their larger servers, placing a round of even more capable multiply connected or clustered machines (called "n-way," where n is an integer usually from 4 to 64). HP had left the barn door wide open; the horses were gone. Only DEC did worse, capsizing completely.

The PC business was still struggling, despite Hackborn's enthusiasm. The company was gaining in market share, but HP had yet to figure out how to make money in PCs. The printer position in the dealer channel helped situate PCs, but this was not of much value against the emergent mail-order e-commerce model that Dell was exploiting.[11] Webb McKinney had gamely taken over this business, and although he found a niche in home computers and with companies standardizing on Web servers, the cost envelope was bloated, to date producing disappointing earnings. Hackborn and Belluzzo had not anticipated that this business would become commoditized so quickly, or that the razor-thin margins would preclude any significant value even for the winner.[12]

Printing—the darling of Hackborn's renaissance for HP—was still in full control. Or was it? The revenue line growth was now a meager 4 percent per year, rather than the 20 percent rates that marked the first half of Platt's tenure. And profits, even with a truly dominant position, had eroded badly, from 15 percent operating profit to 8 percent in the same three short years. Worse, the LaserJet and InkJet lines were in full competition with each other, not only avoiding common designs for some semblance of synergy but fighting each other for shelf space and ad coverage.

When Fiorina joined HP, services were mostly a relic of Bill Terry's decision—against huge criticism from the sales teams, customers, the press, and the rest of the executive committee—to task Roger Costa with making a profit on repair. Thank goodness for that bold move! It gave HP a profitable, if small, business in services. But it was hardly the consulting arm that IBM was constructing.

Against this backdrop, Fiorina went to work, arguing that each arena made sense strategically and each could be galvanized. She even went on record that the Agilent Technologies divestiture was unnecessary—that Birnbaum had been right. The split was too late to undo, and she wisely elected to play the hand that she had been dealt. But in retrospect, some wondered, "What if?"

Repairing a tired, strategically bereft company can take one only so far. And it can proceed only at a certain pace, especially if the players are the same team that was fielded for the previous three years of combat. Debra Dunn (no relation to board member Pattie), served as Lew's chief interlocutor with the HP board. Dunn, with HP for more than sixteen years at this time, had seen the company grow, stall, wrestle with the question of systems versus products, and struggle to find meaningful leadership in the vein of the old HP. Describing herself as a corporate rebel for years, she now was an insider, too nuanced to accept the stark black-and-white stereotypes being portrayed:

> Everybody had these ludicrous ideas about Bill [Hewlett] and Dave [Packard] and the HP culture. That kind, gentle, loving behavior was not the way the company

was run. But that, of course, was what Carly was encountering. The reaction to any minor thing she wanted to change was "This is not the HP Way. This is going to destroy the HP Way." It was absurd.[13]

The HP Way, Version 2001.1

In her first two years, Fiorina got more ink for HP from the business press than John Young and Lew Platt together had accomplished over two decades. Bojana Fazarinc, a twenty-six-year veteran at HP responsible for brand advertising for Lew Platt, says that she learned more from Fiorina in weeks than she had in years. She even got her favorite slogan, "HP Invent," endorsed.[14] The coverage got HP noticed—some thought that ink in the press for this staid, sclerotic company was needed more than ink in printer cartridges.

Four areas stood out in Fiorina's first year—(1) repositioning the product strategy; (2) a new thrust and energy for marketing and press coverage; (3) assessment and correction of the atomized corporate infrastructure; and (4) rebalancing the leadership team. On this latter point, Fiorina did not bring in cronies from her previous companies, as so many outsiders have done with mixed results in the Valley. She did, however, empower some newer talent within the company, notably some of the senior women managers, including Debra Dunn. One of very few women to become a successful HP division manager, Dunn became general manager of HP's Executive Committee for Platt in 1998. She led the Agilent Technologies spin-off process, as well as HP's new business creation function. Fiorina appointed her vice president of Strategy and Corporate Operations in 1999, responsible for corporate strategy, development, communications, and brand management, along with corporate philanthropy and government affairs. Dunn, plus VPs Carolyn Ticknor, Ann Livermore, Allison Johnson, and Susan Bowick, gave Fiorina a strong staff with a sizeable number of women—a novelty not only for HP but for the high-tech computing world. Fiorina achieved visibility, yes, but not necessarily admiration. She realized that this placed a different standard of expectation—an unrealistic expectation—on the team, and it became oppressive.[15] Dunn, more clear-eyed, perhaps, noted that much was structural, not amenable to simple declaratives. Observing that the biggest issue was the radical autonomy of eighty-three divisions, she also said,

> The other issue was the sales side. Carly was out talking to customers all the time. They consistently expressed frustration: "We have a parade of people at HP coming to meet with us. They don't even know each other half the time. It's taking an incredible amount of our time. We call to have a meeting and twenty people show up." Customers were really unimpressed with the way we were managing the customer-facing activities. Thus, driven from operational inefficiency and a desire to radically improve the customer experience, we went way the other direction—reducing the number of P&Ls, and targeting some processes that needed to be global corporate functions, against huge resistance the whole way.[16]

Onstage, Fiorina was a presence, unlike any previous HP CEO, and quite a contrast to the jeans-wearing, techno-nerd CEOs in the Valley. Carly had a strong command of facts, numbers, and strategy. She sounded great. And then, something went awry. Unctuously flattering for the first year, press stories soured, coincident with Fiorina's failed PricewaterhouseCoopers acquisition attempt and a disastrous quarter, which she optimistically and mistakenly proclaimed a speed bump. The dot-com meltdown was well under way, and the press critics surfaced, focusing on style—Fiorina's hair, clothing, and perks—as much as substance. She fumed.

> NOVEMBER 27, 2000 Carly Fiorina has brought some glamour and excitement to old-line computer-maker Hewlett-Packard. But last week the chief executive suffered her first humbling setback—and it was a big one. With the transformation of the company at stake, HP badly missed Wall Street's earnings expectations for its fourth quarter.
>
> At the same time, HP lost the opportunity to buy the consulting arm of PricewaterhouseCoopers, a move that would have quickly given it the firepower of 31,000 consultants to take on e-business giant IBM. For Fiorina, acquiring PwC was an important step in an ambitious design to reinvent Hewlett-Packard for the Internet age. . . . But Wall Street was never sold on the benefits—or the lofty $18 billion price tag. HP's stock has fallen 36 percent in the two months since the company acknowledged it was in talks with PricewaterhouseCoopers.[17]

Though no journalist stepped forward to say so, the stock in fact had fallen less than equivalent competitors. Agilent Technologies saw its stock price drop 27 percent on one day, July 20th, when the company announced a probable third-quarter earnings shortfall due to Medical Group and Analytical Group order rates. In September, Intel's stock price fell twice as far as HP's—down 44 percent versus 22 percent (see Appendix E). No articles exclaimed that Agilent Technologies' and Intel's strategies were hopelessly flawed, or that their equally new CEOs had been humbled. Nonetheless, for Carly, the honeymoon was over.

Three years later, George Anders wrote, "When stock trading opened the next day (September 11, 2000), HP shares fell 3 percent, amid investor jitters that the acquisition would hurt the company's short-term earnings," while Peter Burrows wrote, "It might have been a great idea, but analysts hated it."[18] The data do not support the chary critiques. HP was simply caught in the large-company dot-com meltdown with hundreds of other high-tech companies. Perhaps more surprising, no analyst would assert that Fiorina's idea to buy PwC's consulting segment was prescient, rather than misguided. Lou Gerstner had already refashioned IBM more along the services vector, but the stunning success that it would prove to have for IBM overall was yet in the future.

Dot-Com Disaster

The dot-com meltdown was a crushing blow to Silicon Valley—neither Fiorina nor any of her Silicon Valley associates could comprehend the magnitude of the disaster. The common criticism—and the prevailing belief among many HPites years later—was that Fiorina didn't appreciate the gravity of the situation. Her tactics were seen as bullying her staff for better numbers. George Anders captured the essence of Fiorina's dilemma:

> Fiorina was vulnerable for three reasons that had nothing to do with her immediate job performance. As the shortest-tenured CEO of the bunch [versus Chambers at Cisco and McNealy at Sun], she couldn't remind people of all the good things that had happened earlier in her watch. As the lone woman in command at such a giant corporation, she couldn't blend into the background in Silicon Valley. And as a charismatic leader who came to Hewlett-Packard with an im-

plicit promise of better days to come, she became a tempting target of scorn when things got worse.[19]

Ironically, while IBM's hardware sales were cratering (falling 65 percent), service revenues would grow by 50 percent and profitability nearly quadruple from 2000 through 2007. From that perspective, an $18 billion stock swap for PwC might have been wise rather than too expensive. Analysts, focused on short-term results, couldn't envision the opportunity. Two years later, when IBM was able to buy the PwC unit for a mere $3.5 billion, critics scornfully recalled Fiorina's high offer. Only one analyst, Jonathan Eunice of Illuminata, noted that "everyone is less valued right now. Everybody was buying with highly inflated 'Monopoly' money two years ago." No one went back to do the calculations—if they had done so, the equivalent HP stock at that point was a similar $3.8 billion.[20] But by then Fiorina was dealing with a more serious problem.

DECEMBER 6, 2000, NEW YORK CITY: "Fiorina remains confident that her company will meet Wall Street forecasts of between 15 percent and 17 percent revenue growth for fiscal year 2001—numbers the company released three weeks ago in an effort to guide analysts in the face of its rapidly deteriorating stock price."[21] Just two weeks earlier, Barnholt at Agilent Technologies had proclaimed, "For fiscal 2001, we are raising our guidance from 15 percent to at least 20 percent growth in net revenue."[22] Peter Burrows, in *Backfire,* chided Fiorina, citing SoundView analyst Mark Specker's derision about her judgment, but did note that "Over the coming months, many CEOs repeatedly revised their financial targets as the economy went into a recession." Specker reversed himself later when Fiorina beat all of the Valley's CEOs to a realistic appraisal of the dire situation.[23]

FEBRUARY 7, 2001, NEW YORK CITY: Veteran Silicon Valley journalist John Markoff filed a surprising *New York Times* report from the Cisco earnings meeting:

> Silicon Valley bellwether Cisco Systems [with] 44 consecutive quarters of revenue growth, shocked financial analysts . . . by saying today that it expected revenue to decline next quarter by as much as 5%. . . . But Cisco executives, who have repeatedly told Wall Street that the company plans to grow by 30% to 50% a

year, took pains to point to slowing purchases by American telecommunications service providers and manufacturing companies as the reason for Cisco's pessimistic forecast. "While we were pleased with certain areas of our business," said [Cisco CEO] John Chambers, "this quarter was even more challenging than we anticipated in light of the abrupt economic slowdown in the United States." During a conference call with financial analysts this afternoon, Mr. Chambers said that although the next several quarters would be challenging, he expected the downturn to be a short one. Cisco said that it expected its growth would be flat or would decline 5 percent in its third quarter and that growth would be flat in the fourth quarter. But it still expected total revenue growth for the year to reach 40 percent.[24]

. . .

MARCH 22, 2001, HANOVER, GERMANY Departing from the hype of her fellow technology leaders, Carleton Fiorina on Wednesday offered a starkly pessimistic appraisal of a technology industry still grappling with a staggering collapse. Ms. Fiorina, one of the most powerful women in American business, sounded a note of sharp pessimism not only about prospects for her company but for the global economy. Few other leading companies at CeBit matched her candor and pessimism—most executives still seemed full of hope.[25]

. . .

MAY 10, 2001, GREENBRIAR, WEST VIRGINIA At the annual CEO Business Council, Scott McNealy, chairman and CEO of Sun Microsystems, called the computer maker's forecast of 15 percent revenue growth in 2002 "a rough estimate rather than a specific target since spending in the technology market remains in flux and too difficult to accurately predict. Guidance is probably too strong a term any more—wild-ass guess."[26] Sun's fiscal year had been satisfactory, but its last quarterly earnings report was off 43 percent.[27]

. . .

JUNE, 2001, BOSTON, MASSACHUSETTS: *Fast Company* founding editors Alan Webber and Richard Taylor tried to make sense of the situation, in an editorial: "Our Forecast: Pragmatic Optimism."

This just in! According to Cisco Systems CEO John Chambers, his company has just been hit by a "100-year flood." No wonder he feels like he's been cast in the role of Noah, doing his best to keep the company afloat after the deluge. But this wasn't just a flood: It was a massive, sudden, unpredicted downpour that hit Cisco by surprise. In a five-day, December period, the company's orders dropped . . . from 65 percent growth to flat or negative growth. Chambers's forecast: pragmatism mixed with smart risk taking.

According to Intel CEO Craig Barrett, the bad weather that has struck the Internet won't dampen Intel's enthusiasm. In fact, Barrett says, Intel is putting its chips on the Net. The company's goal is to convert itself into a 100 percent e-business and to use the power of the Net to cut error rates and increase speed. Barrett's forecast: steely-eyed optimism with increased speed.[28]

HP Public Relations—Internally

As the economic climate worsened, the mood shifted. Outsiders had criticized HP CEOs routinely, from Packard's early pronouncements about civic involvement to Platt's tepid dot-com response, but internally, HPites had always supported, even revered, their CEO. But a new tone surfaced, wherein early supporters of Fiorina shifted their view.

According to many, Fiorina violated the egalitarian spirit of the company. She eschewed, for example, Lew Platt's penchant for flying coach rather than business class on company business, and then spent lavishly on new corporate jets to whisk her hither and yon. Carly's mannerisms did not sit well with the rank-and-file. Never mind that HP had a thirty-year history with a corporate jet fleet, housed in the HP hangar at the San Jose airport; that Packard and Young had driven more upscale cars than their staffs for years; and that the company leadership for years had flown business class, especially for long-haul trips essential to manage the far-flung global enterprise.[29] The mythology ignored this reality, just as it suppressed knowledge of prior layoffs. And the new communication tools—e-mail and chat rooms—were ablaze with sarcastic and caustic stories.

Old-timers especially became critical of the outsider, complaining that Management by Walking Around had seemingly disappeared. At a particularly well-reported luncheon hosted by Rosemary Hewlett at the founder's home in mid-2000, Fiorina had inadvertently angered the crippled founder and some of the invited "old guard." Some attendees thought her naïve and forward. "Obsequious and condescending," said others. According to some attendees, Bill Hewlett demanded to be removed from her presence, in an awkward denouement to her comments directly to him. Others weren't as certain of the cause of his discomfort. Fiorina described the luncheon as an "ordeal by fire"; the oldtimers described it as compelling evidence that a discerning Hewlett found her lacking.[30]

Debra Dunn, with long experience near the executive office, had rare insight:

> First of all, unlike [Bill] Terry, [John] Doyle, and [Paul] Ely, all of whom I have great respect for, I probably have a more balanced view of Carly [Fiorina] because I worked with her really closely. I appreciate some incredible strengths that Carly has, and also some limitations. Carly came to HP genuinely wanting to prove that you could be successful in the computer business and maintain the core values of the company. She genuinely embraced that as a mission.[31]

A local journalist, Joselyn Dong, penned a piece after the Compaq battle titled "The Rise and Fall of the HP Way." Dong cited Al Bagley, who said, "She isn't around like she ought to be. I don't think she is comfortable walking around . . . and hearing what people really think. She's got a lot to learn."[32] Bagley, who hadn't worked for HP for the previous fifteen years, failed to mention that the common HP joke in the 1960s was "What's the difference between God and Packard? God is occasionally around." In some private circles, the old pejorative epithets about "Young's imperial presidency," or the derision about the posh Hanover Street headquarters—the Taj Mahal or Galactic Headquarters—were recalled.[33]

Fiorina seemed consistently to jab the "old guard," most notoriously when she revoked their "retired employee" status. Some fifty-seven hundred people learned in early 2001 that they were no longer ex-employees of the Hewlett-Packard Company, and hence no longer either welcome at retiree events or qualified for employee discounts on HP equipment. Instead, they now were considered Agilent Technologies ex-employees. Thus instead of buying a computer or a printer at reduced prices, an ex-Agilent Technologies employee could buy only Agilent Technologies instruments at a discount. The group had an estimated twenty-three thousand offspring and relatives still working for the two companies, most of them shareholders in Hewlett-Packard, so this was a particularly maladroit political move as events unfolded. Though the decision was quickly reversed, the emotional damage had been done.

Consolidation?

Fiorina quickly decided that the dot-com disaster provided a masterstroke opportunity. No one questioned that she was bold and that she could get "outside the box" to put exciting goals in place. In the face of a rapidly declining financial situation, she rekindled a mega-acquisition notion. A big merger or acquisition was not the obvious play from almost anyone's perspective. Fiorina was convinced that the heady growth days were over and that racking change was about to overtake the entire group of companies. The time was at hand for a major industry consolidation move. The scenario demanded action: consolidate or wither. But HP's history—from Sanborn to Apollo, let alone the recent VeriFone fiasco—was hardly affirming.

Hiring McKinsey—*de rigueur* since the John Young days—led to the logical conclusion that HP shouldn't be broken up any more than IBM should have been when Gerstner arrived. It followed, in the wake of the PwC situation, that a focus on the computing business was the only place to make a significant move. HP had the imaging world already—no major move could be made.[34] And the synergy between the two arenas, as Joel Birnbaum insisted for years, could still be made, but only if HP were competitive and sizable in computing. And though HP had gained dramatically in market share, it still failed to be a serious entrant in personal computing.

Compaq was the only force in PCs besides Dell; its acquisition could help the Services side that Ann Livermore was struggling to improve. Compaq had been wounded more than HP by the downdraft of the initial dot-com meltdown (revenues down 15 percent versus 7 percent; earnings evaporated even before the 9/11 event). Compaq, with three-quarters of HP's revenue in 2000, imploded in the dot-com meltdown. They grew increasingly concerned, even desperate, and Fiorina sensed it. Dell was trouncing them in their core business. The compound growth rate (CAGR) for Compaq revenue from 1997 through 2000 was a very tidy 20 percent, versus HP's sluggish 10 percent. In their core business, however, it was only 2 percent, versus Dell's outstanding 37 percent. The acquisitions were not being integrated, and the DEC base business was faltering in the dot-com meltdown.

Acquisitions architect Eckhard Pfeiffer had been fired by the board in April 1999 because of the earnings shortfall and Dell's success. His replacement, CIO Michael Capellas, was an outsider in the high-tech world, without Fiorina's charisma or command of detail. As late as January 29, 2001, Capellas was "standing by his forecast of growing earnings by 20 percent to 25 percent," even as he reported a $672 million loss in fourth quarter 2000.[35] Fiorina, in *Tough Choices,* wrote:,

> Realism was what we needed most. Our board had to understand how tough this would really be. It was clear the market didn't understand what was actually happening in the technology space. In the summer of 2001 [no] Wall Street analysts were talking about structural change in the industry. . . . Accomplishing this merger would require incredible skill, energy, commitment, and will. The integration would be hard, selling the deal would be hard; dealing with people's emotions, as they fully comprehended what it all meant, would be hard.[36]

Fiorina had little idea of just how hard it would prove to be. Events in the next few weeks damaged Fiorina's credibility badly. Even if she called the depth of the technology train wreck sooner than her peer CEOs, it left the question of what to do. Wall Street always has a ready response: layoffs. It had become a truism by this point that the best way to raise a stock price was to announce lowered earnings, along with a plan to lay off 10 percent of the workforce. Moreover, CEOs had become high-profile authors. Their books sported titles that were the antithesis of the HP Way—*Only the Paranoid Survive, No Excuses Management, Straight from the Gut,* and *Execution* don't sound paternalistic, and they weren't.[37] Investors seemed to relish such hard-nosed management, even as employee trust and loyalty was abridged.

Meanwhile, over at Agilent Technologies, the disarray was even deeper than at HP. Barnholt first resorted to the time-tried nine-day fortnight pioneered by Hewlett in the 1970–71 recession.

APRIL 18, 2001, BUSINESSWEEK: It's better to have all employees bleed a little than a few bleed to death. That's the view at Agilent Technologies, the large test-and-measurement equipment maker, that on April 5 [2001] announced a companywide salary reduction of 10% for its 48,000 employees. Unusual in a time of unimaginative daily downsizings, that move is getting applause from management experts—for purely practical reasons. "Many times, companies will lay all these people off, then the economy gets better and they have to do rehiring," says Kelly Mollica, associate professor of management at the Babcock Graduate School of Management at Wake Forest University in Winston-Salem, N.C. By holding onto workers now, Agilent is positioning itself to strike aggressively when the economy rebounds. The cuts took effect for the company's 200 senior managers April 1 and will kick in for the rest of the workforce May 1. Expected to save $70 million per quarter, they will last until July 31, the end of Agilent's third quarter, and could be continued beyond that date. (CFO Robert) Walker won't rule out layoffs if demand doesn't bounce back.[38]

Six weeks later, on June 7, 2001, Fiorina announced an analogous program for HP. The press saw it as a non-event, no longer novel since Agilent Technologies beat them to it by seven weeks. And then came the bombshell: Fiorina bowed to the inevitable and laid off six thousand workers.

JULY 27, 2001, LONDON On Thursday morning, after HP announced it would lay off 6,000 workers, the angry spouse of an HP employee sent a fiery email to CNETNews.com. She was bitter because her husband—who generously agreed to a 10 percent pay cut to help HP save money—is now in danger of getting a pink slip. "I realize every tech company is facing tough times, but I really felt this cut was unfairly done. I feel it was an underhanded threat to get them to take the cuts in pay even though they said it was 'voluntary.' Who is going to say 'no' when layoffs are looming?"

The plan was not supposed to generate such rancour. When HP chief executive Carly Fiorina unveiled a cost-reduction strategy based on voluntary cutbacks, they asked all workers—from administrative assistants to senior executives—to sign up. . . . Surprisingly, about 80,000 people—86% of HP's work force—chose one of the first three options, HP spokeswoman Suzette Stephens said. [The plan asked that employees take one of three options: a 10 percent pay cut through the end of October, or eight days of vacation, or a 5 percent cut and four days of vacation. The program was optional: employees could chose anonymously to keep their full pay and vacation benefits without any repercussions.] That will save HP about $130 million between now and the end of the fiscal fourth quarter in late October. Senior executives were "overwhelmed" by the response, Stephens said. She chalked up the high participation rate to the computer giant's corporate culture, known as the HP Way . . . invented about 60 years ago, when Stanford University buddies Bill Hewlett and Dave Packard . . . worked out of their garage, which has since been dubbed the "penultimate nerd site" and the birthplace of California's Silicon Valley.

Few other companies could pull off a similar voluntary cost-cutting campaign, said Art Resnikoff, a corporate consultant and psychologist. "It's contrary to the survival of the fittest theory but it's not contrary to HP's corporate culture. If Intel did this, the results would be very different because they're much more internally competitive and political. If you look at the principles that go back to the garage, there really is a sense of collaboration: [There is] this attitude that 'if we keep each other happy, we'll in the long run be profitable because we won't have turnover and we will have consistency.'"

Despite its success, executives announced this week that the voluntary cutback program alone could not save as much as HP needed. Executives emphasised that the cutbacks were a short-term cost reduction strategy, but over the long term HP needed to reduce its work force. Although the voluntary program saved $130 million through October, 6,000 layoffs will save HP $500 million annually. The layoffs will also help the overstaffed company to get its work force on par with leaner computer companies, such as Dell Computer. Psychology experts question how much longer HP can keep asking workers to tighten their belts.[39]

"Chainsaw Carly" became Fiorina's new nickname.[40]

Three weeks later at Agilent Technologies, on August 21, 2001, Barnholt laid off 9 percent of the team (versus 6 percent at HP), in the midst of the same nine-day fortnight strategy. Instead of vilification, he won an Innovation Award from the Great Places to Work Institute:

During the 2001–2002 tech slowdown, Agilent Technologies showed how to weather a recession while maintaining high levels of credibility and trust. After earnings plummeted, management instituted a 10% salary reduction . . . and candidly explained the company's situation to employees. . . . These gestures showed management's commitment to avoiding layoffs. . . .

By August, it was clear that layoffs were necessary. CEO Ned Barnholt broke the news to employees in a worldwide employee announcement that was candid and direct . . . before speaking with investors or the business press. After the announcement, the news was posted on the company's online newsletter; business managers hosted coffee talk [events] to give employees an opportunity to hear full and clear explanations of the layoffs and get questions answered face-to-face; frequently asked questions were posted online and candidly answered by management. Employees knew the reasons for the layoffs and felt grateful for candid communication.[41]

No one wrote about the irony. One a hero, the other a villain? For the same actions, in the same catastrophic situation. What was going on?

The sociologies of HP and Agilent Technologies differed. Agilent Technologies' troops had been through a number of wars together—instrumentation for HP had been under siege for two decades; now that Agilent was financially adrift from "the mother ship," it had to solve the ills of the economic downturn alone. Also, Agilent Technologies was a small player against very large competitors in the medical and semiconductor businesses. Draconian moves could be defined and understood as necessary predicates for forestalling a truly dismal future. And Barnholt's credibility was unquestioned—he had been around forever and knew the lore and the HP Way deeply. HP vice president Webb McKinney, on Fiorina's staff, said it well later: "Agilent handled their layoffs in a much more personal and HP-like way. There were stories of Ned talking with people being laid off, and helping them take boxes to their cars."[42]

Fiorina had no reservoir of trust. Moreover, many HPites saw no good reason to support layoffs, as they perceived that their product sector was still doing quite well. Their disgruntlement resembled the Instrument Group's ire years earlier when John Young used their profits to fuel Computer Group expansion. Not surprisingly, the Peripherals divisions in Boise and Corvallis were the most virulent opponents of the "Carly Way." Once targeted by the rest of HP for violating the HP Way with their unusual business approach, they were now the bastions of preservation for those ways.

Not Your Father's HP

John Toppel, HP's alliance manager for the go-to-market relationship with Deloitte Consulting, had a wry observation about Carly's dilemma in mid-2001:

> In May, she told us that we needed to get rid of seventeen hundred people from Marketing, and in true HP fashion, people set out to do just that. Within a month, we had gotten rid of seventeen hundred Marketing folk—they had all been recategorized and retitled into support roles, production, and other corners of the company. No one had left the company. She lost it when she learned this—her next move was retaliatory.[43]

The concerns about Carly's East Coast style—the limos, the company jets, even the dress code—proved mild by comparison with issues of executive compensation and job security. Exorbitant incentives, bonuses, and rich stock packages were the new entitlements in the dot-com era. John Young noted in a *Vanity Fair* article that Fiorina's $70 million hiring package exceeded his lifetime earnings,[44] but it seemed curiously quaint alongside *BusinessWeek*'s special 2002 report on executive pay:

> Oracle Corp. chief executive [Larry Ellison] earned a special place in the history of executive compensation last year with the $706 million he pocketed from exercising long-held stock options. It . . . constitutes the single biggest one-year haul of all time.[45]

Both the board and Fiorina, challenged on the pay issue, responded that all her hiring package did was provide parity with her unvested options at Lucent. There simply was no way to hire someone without "truing-up" her equivalent earning structure; an equivalent package would have been needed for any of the external candidates the board considered.

Layoffs, though, were the more volatile issue. Fiorina announced the plan to lay off six thousand workers on Wednesday, July 26, 2001. Two weeks later, jaws dropped when some people were told on Tuesday that Friday would be their last day; others were told on Friday that their employment was over, and they were unceremoniously escorted out of the building without a chance to pack their things or say goodbye to colleagues.[46]

> Executive programs director Mr. [Joe] Podolsky calls it a "wrenching situation" because of the way it was handled. "In the past, department heads weighed in on where cuts could be made and employees got a three-month grace period to find another job. The August layoff was none of that," Mr. Podolsky says. "The decisions were top-down, direct managers were told who to lay off, and people were given no opportunity to look for jobs. They were told on a Tuesday and were out on a Friday." In a January 23 [2002] town hall meeting, Ms. Fiorina said the management "did not do a good job of implementing" the August layoffs, but said she did not apologize. She had little option in 2001—a year when tech layoffs were prevalent—HP [had] a new reality from past halcyon days.[47]

Double-Down with Compaq

Announced on September 4, 2001, the HP-Compaq merger news was explosive. Outrage didn't take long—the stock dropped 19 percent on announcement day.[48] HP old-timers gravely commented to zealous journalists that HP had never succeeded at the M&A business. Never mind that HP had by now bought the technology, the people, or the assets of more than one hundred companies—bringing the all-important fuel that powered initiatives along the way. When some alumni were pressed on this point, they conceded that, yes, maybe that was true, but *big* mergers didn't work well, and this was big, almost two equals in fact, and *that* would make it much harder.

On September 11, 2001—a mere week later—the terrible shock of the terrorist attack on the World Trade Center and the Pentagon shook the Western world. High-technology companies were jolted, and Carly's bet was now in jeopardy. Pundits arose en masse—as Peter Burrows later wrote,

> Everyone seemed to regard [the merger] as a disaster. . . . Investors from coast to coast began spitting HP out of their portfolios as if it were a moldy piece of fruit. . . . In late September, HP stock skidded to $12.50 a share, partially because of investor jitters about the deal and partially because of a wider sense of despair sweeping through the United States. Terrorists had demolished the World Trade Center a week after Fiorina and Capellas announced the merger agreement.

Anthrax scares broke out soon afterward, darkening the national mood. At a time when even the most routine activities, such as opening the mail, seemed scary, hardly anyone was inclined to endorse a giant and risky combination.[49]

Hyperbole, it seemed, but again the data didn't show it. Agilent Technologies, Sun, and Intel stock all fell much further during the next thirty days than HP stock. Appendix E shows that by the end of September, each of the three stocks fell 50 percent further than HP's. And none of them was proposing a "giant and risky combination" like HP-Compaq.

Debra Dunn, reflecting on the events leading up to the merger, stated,

Carly is a person who really likes to win, not uncommon among CEOs. But she was not embraced by the employees. It was pretty dramatic the extent to which many people, particularly in places like Boise and Corvallis, didn't want to change. They resented having an outsider brought in to run the company, so while she really was trying to go down this path—"We've got to make changes from a business perspective because we're not competing successfully. We've got to move more quickly. We've got to do a better job of satisfying customers"—she was getting so much pushback from so many corners of the company that I think she then decided, "This culture has to change. This culture has calcified, and it really has to change." I think she felt that changing evolutionarily . . . wasn't going to cut it. A merger was the vehicle for radically disrupting the culture and shifting people's attention from just whining about the good old days to much more significant concerns.[50]

Boise and Corvallis—bastions of the Computer Peripherals activity—were holdouts? These divisions were Hackborn territory. He had virtually handpicked Carly; there was enormous self-interest at stake for him and the company for which he had built such a legacy. Did she block him out, did he decide to cast her to the wolves, or was it a missed opportunity that neither perceived to be critical? Or had he himself been too long gone from his old redoubt to rally support for her? Some suggest it was simpler than that—computers were "old-school" by now, and to go acquire three retread companies to add to a failing strategy inside made no sense.

Tandem was the smallest unit of the proposed acquisition. Tandem had a culture not unlike HP, built on excellence in a product niche, with consistent HP Way–like belief in people and quality products, but their product sector had been assailed by a number of lower-price competitors, and they were struggling with the increasingly marginalized value of their unique and powerful Non-Stop database. The historic leadership at Tandem, originally from HP—founder James Treybig, Mike Green, Dennis MacAvoy, and Jim Kasson—had retired. Tom Perkins, with much HP experience, had been chairman of Tandem from its inception. He joined the Compaq board after the acquisition and helped with the proxy battle for Carly.

Digital was another matter. DEC, the proud leader of the minicomputer revolution, had been caught in a decision paroxysm, paralyzed by conflicting arguments for higher-performance silicon-led enterprise solutions versus the ubiquitous low-end PCs running on standard Wintel machines. When the DEC board evicted their embattled founder and CEO Ken Olsen on the same day that HP issued a statement about Young's retirement, it was not done with much grace, and the scars of that confrontational battle still persisted.

In sharp contrast to HP's board forcing Platt's decision for Wintel, DEC's board voted for Robert Palmer, who embarked on an expensive 64-bit silicon solution, called DEC Alpha. Within three years, DEC was hemorrhaging cash, and Compaq prevailed as the buyer in a brief bidding war. The question was, "What have we got?" And the answer seemed primarily to be an installed base of disgruntled enterprise IT managements, locked into the proprietary DEC systems with little prospect for upgrades and modern feature-sets.

The biggest asset was DEC's extensive service and support structure. DEC for many years had earned a sizable fraction of its total revenue from its services side. This began oddly—both DEC's PDP-11 line and the VAX 780 line had enormous product functionality leadership, coupled with relatively modest quality. They garnered a huge installed base, which required consistent support effort. DEC shrewdly turned a major product liability into a significant source of continuing revenue. In 1970, DEC service revenue was 6 percent of product revenue; a decade later it was 36 percent. In 1987, it was 50 percent, and by 1993, it had peaked at an astounding 89 percent. HP by contrast had always focused on high-quality equipment that needed much less maintenance, so its sales were much more dependent on product upgrades and new design wins. DEC's advantage was that of "first mover"—get the installed base, and multiple good things happen. It is hard to dislodge the installed base, especially one built on a proprietary platform, so product upgrades and service created an annuity for years and years. When IT groups figured out that easy migration to HP's Spectrum family, with its performance-centric, scalable open-platform attributes, was feasible, and Sun workstations were also open-platform structured for engineering groups, the question for DEC was, "What now?" The company culture, built around historic product-functionality leadership restricted Palmer's choices.

Of the three, Compaq was the most unlike HP. On a napkin at lunch, Rod Canion had conceived of a clone company building cheap knockoffs of the IBM PC in 1982. Catching a wave of buying enthusiasm, his company became an overnight sensation, helped immeasurably by the fact that the Microsoft software operating system made clones a practical solution even more than had been true for Amdahl versus IBM CPUs. Spending far less on R&D than any of his competitors, Canion craftily built a copycat company that was nimble in product turnaround, with thin margins and a strong attention to the dealer channel. It proved immensely effective for nearly a decade, until Michael Dell pioneered a direct sales model that undercut Compaq. Canion was replaced in a palace coup by Ben Rosen, his funding partner, whereupon management turnover plagued the company, coincident with the DEC, HP, and IBM malaise in the early 1990s. Rosen's successor, Eckhard Pfeiffer, was forced out in 1998 after embarking on acquisitions to broaden Compaq customer appeal. CEO Michael Capellas had been drafted from the CFO ranks in a bid to restore some fiscal responsibility to a fragmented company.[51]

Backfire

Perceptions are often stronger than facts, and political decisions are different from factual analyses. This time, scion Walter Hewlett would provoke the political drama. The industry was in turmoil, as Fiorina said. But the data were debatable.

For those who held the old paradigm of an enterprise computing center—the IBM, DEC, and HP-PA Spectrum view—Compaq now looked like a formidable player. They had bought DEC and Tandem in fire sales and had grown topline revenue at 20 percent per year for several years during a period that IBM only grew 4 percent per year and HP 10 percent per year. Moreover, the brash Houston company proclaimed when they bought DEC that they were now the world's largest computer company, a claim based on ignoring IBM services and HP peripherals revenue. Even so, by the end of 2000, Compaq's total revenue was 87 percent of HP's and 48 percent of IBM's.

For Wintel observers though, it was clear that Dell trounced Compaq between 1998 and 2000, adding to their PC business by $19.5 billion in revenue from a $12 billion base, while Compaq could only muster a $1.7 billion increase on a $24 billion base. Dell's 37 percent compound growth rate swamped Compaq's meager 2 percent; Dell was now 27 percent larger than Compaq's PC lines. It was a shocking comeuppance for the one-time PC leader; no computer company had ever squandered such a lead so quickly.

All companies lost momentum in the 2000–2001 downturn year. When Fiorina conceived the merger idea, quarterly reports were showing the trends although final results were not yet known. Overall, the average shift was down 25 percent. IBM was best, shrinking only 7 percent; Sun was down 14 percent, HP was down 18 percent. These were the best three. Compaq was down 34 percent, and Dell dropped a whopping 39 percent.

Increasing anger of employees was the most concerning. The merger announcement followed only five weeks after the July layoffs. The fallout from that was reaching a crescendo on company communication systems. The Chainsaw Carly moniker sounded even more accurate as HP's Human Resources director, Susan Bowick, made the decision to "tell workers of plans to cut 15,000 jobs, or 10 percent of the combined workforce" when the merger concluded. With the recent layoff still fresh on people's minds, the ills of Compaq in the marketplace and the cultural differences between the two companies well-known, Bowick's announcement stoked the fire against Fiorina. When the 9/11 terrorist attack cratered business more than the dot-com meltdown, and in November, the beloved founder's son, Walter Hewlett, announced his intention to fight the deal, the wolves came out. Internal HP attitude surveys shifted suddenly, from 89 percent favoring the merger to only 55 percent. Bowick insisted that it was essential to be up front with workers. "One of the things you want to do is build trust, even if it's bad news," Bowick said. It proved to be a serious tactical error, at least for the short term.[52]

It is one thing to read the data. It is quite another to have to reconcile long-held opinions and values with the stark reality of drastically changed conditions. Walter Hewlett, some would say, succumbed to nostalgia and mythology, challenging the HP board's actions. Others viewed him as the board's only sane member, turning him into a martyr.[53]

A family feud unfolded, unprecedented and tragic for the company and its employees, alumni, and friends. Enmity and bitter recriminations flowed, mortally wounding long-term friendships. Walter Hewlett lobbed the first grenade, giving Fiorina a mere half-hour notice with no chance of negotiation before publicly announcing his opposition to the merger. The HP board, stunned by this unexpected move, responded with a below-the-belt *Wall Street Journal* rebuttal about Walter's ineptitude for business. After all the bear-baiting that Sun CEO Scott McNealy had unsuccessfully tried with Fiorina, it was shocking that she allowed a *Wall Street Journal* ad that besmirched the Hewlett scion. In defense, she said with some vehemence that he had sideswiped the deal, her leadership, and the company's momentum. The facts support her contention.[54]

Even the board was impressed by Fiorina's extraordinary resolve. Evidence abounds that Hewlett's move, especially when coupled with the Packard Foundation's agonizing decision to support it, demoralized the board, leading to a full reappraisal for abandoning the deal.[55] Led by Hackborn, the board determined that the deal still made sense, that HP required it in order to persevere with any chance of true industry leadership, and they concluded that the case could be won with shareholders. It is notable that Peter Burrows, in a chary book about Fiorina, took time to write, "She was likeable, and remarkably informed and eloquent when giving her pitch. At times, her ability to read investors was downright mystical." He cited Mike Winkler, a Compaq executive who hadn't known her: "She's a woman of steel. She simply will not let herself or her operation fail. She's not mercurial or emotional in any way. It's that Maggie Thatcher constitution."[56]

The Food Fight

No one anticipated the depth of emotion that many HP employees and the sizable HP alumni community would muster. The ensuing brouhaha engulfed Fiorina, the management team, and the board in a public relations disaster. Members of the board—led by Phil Condit and Sam Ginn—publicly impugned Hewlett, excoriating his business sense and his motives. Condit, who had known Platt well (Boeing and HP had enjoyed interlocking board memberships for years), would shortly face and lose to his own detractors at Boeing, brought to dock by numerous unethical and illegal behaviors of that company under his leadership, but not before his actions saddened reverent HPites everywhere and cheapened the HP board still further.[57] Ironically, Lew Platt was later pressed into service at Boeing as chairman, where he succeeded admirably in restoring investor and employee confidence.[58]

Uncharacteristically, Fiorina made several tactical miscues. First, she failed to make entreaties to the Hewlett and Packard families. When the Compaq merger arose, she declined to meet with either family to describe the merits of the case. Granted, Walter Hewlett was still on the board, but a courtesy call might have saved much later embarrassment—the heirs did, after all, still control a lot of stock (18 percent of the total) via either family or foundation holdings. One might think there was adequate time for amends—after all, sixty-three days elapsed before Walter called Fiorina just thirty minutes before announcing his crusade to the world.

Nor did Fiorina court any of the retired HP executives in town. Two ex-CEOs and multiple former vice presidents lived within fifteen minutes of her office. They all had close ties to the founder families, all of them knew Compaq and its mélange of company acquisitions, and each could have been a potential ally in a difficult transition. But Carly had not sought to build bridges; it soon became too late. Not surprisingly, ex-executives arose, at first individually and then en masse, to rage against her folly. Lew Platt agreed to serve as CEO if Walter's desires prevailed with shareholders. John Young granted a lengthy interview to *Vanity Fair,* which ran alongside stories from Dominick Dunne and other celebrities, wherein Young sniped at Fiorina's AT&T accomplishments.[59]

In retribution for these treasons, during a remodeling phase, the ceremonial offices of ex-officers John Young, Dean Morton, Lew Platt, and Bill Terry were remanded. Terry said, "We all used to have offices here on Page Mill Road. We were down in that building for about six or eight years. And then Carly threw us out. It didn't cost the company anything. The total space was just about as big as this living room." When they protested that Packard had granted them office space for life, the alleged retort was "Packard's dead."[60]

As the battle wore on, it became increasingly obvious that no matter who won, the company had lost its luster. Furious employees and ex-employees filled the Cupertino auditorium on March 19, 2002; invective filled the air. Muddied, sullied, and still combative, Fiorina emerged in an eleventh-hour scramble for votes with a narrow victory. Who hated the deal most? Old-timers! HP employee-voters were actually more supportive than Agilent Technologies employees who held HP stock, among whom eight out of nine voted "no."

MARCH 19, 2002, CUPERTINO, CALIFORNIA: "Hewlett-Packard claimed victory Tuesday in its hotly contested battle to merge with Compaq Computer, while opponents maintained that any such declaration is premature."[61] Even the victory was tainted— a dramatic shift of forty-nine million Deutsche Bank votes on the day of voting cast suspicion on the process, especially when an insider in Corporate headquarters released a surreptitious voice-mail message from Fiorina to CFO Robert Wayman, which urged currying votes with some major shareholders amid threats of retaliation via withheld business. Walter Hewlett sued for a court ruling to void the vote.

William Shiebler had become the new president of Deutsche Bank Americas three days before the HP vote. A close friend of Massachusetts Governor Mitt Romney, and co-organizer with Romney of the 2002 Winter Olympics for Salt Lake City, Utah, Shiebler had an impeccable ethical career over many years of involvement with Wall Street. Stunned by the "home office" about-face, he confided privately that this was a highly irregular action.[62] A protracted legal battle ensued, and acting with dispatch, the courts upheld the transaction. A year and a half later, three Deutsche Bank officials were found guilty of misdemeanors and barred from the industry henceforth. No one at HP was sentenced, or even taken to trial.[63]

Fiorina won. She had a narrow margin but a win nonetheless. How did it turn out? Opinions vary. Ned Barnholt, openly skeptical at first, "thought it was a bad strategy and combining these two companies is just . . . the toughest thing anyone had ever thought about doing. Poorly executed, it will just run the company in the ground." He later noted that, "to HP's credit, it's probably been the best-executed big merger ever. You could easily use that superlative—in the high-tech industry, there's never been one pulled off so well."[64]

Tom Perkins in 2006 offered,

> The Compaq merger was brilliant. I don't know where HP would be without Compaq right now. They'd just be printers, period. And with Compaq they're pretty much market share leaders in servers, and very close to Dell in size in PCs. The service operation is very strong. That merger really made sense. Carly took an awful lot of gas on that. But she was right.[65]

HP leaders from previous eras were more reserved, and generally unforgiving. Five years later, Dick Alberding said, "I'm obviously not a Carly fan, although I have been mesmerized by her speaking ability numerous times." Paul Ely remained recalcitrant; Bill Terry offered, "The Compaq deal brought some strange people to the board," while agreeing that it had worked better than he might have thought. John Doyle was vitriolic: "The HP Way died with the Compaq merger. . . . It was an absolutely grotesquely bad decision." Dean Morton viewed the HP Way at Agilent Technologies as intact, but quite fragile and nearly extinct at HP.[66]

John Young, like Barnholt, familiar with the unique pressure that a CEO must endure, was more circumspect. He observed that corporations of this magnitude are difficult to manage, let alone control, and the evidence was positive in revenue and profitability trends under both Fiorina and Hurd.[67]

Craig Samuel, at Compaq when the merger was announced, spent five years as HP's service sector chief knowledge officer; later he was Unisys vice president of innovation:

> When the merger was announced, people were saying, "Was this the right thing?" I could understand the logic. I could also understand a lot of the criticism. Was it

the right thing to do? It's difficult. It wasn't just market share. It wasn't the sum of two parts together. A plus B equals something less than the combination of the parts because we lost some share. But it clearly added some capabilities that didn't exist in both companies. There were synergistic areas. Compaq was very strong in business PCs. HP was very strong in consumer PCs, and with Imaging and Printing Group. So there was on paper, a very understandable logic about the tapestry and how it would fill in the gap. Of course the secret sauce is the execution.

If you look at it three or four years later, it's going remarkably well. And it was the largest technology merger in history at that point. It's arguably very successful today. Certainly Mark [Hurd] has really brought in very shrewd operational experience and perspective. And he's simplified, he's rationalized the complexity, and he's increased the agility. This was started by Carly. It wasn't all Hurd. Carly had started on these initiatives, in fact made great progress. But she still had market pressure about whether IPG should be spun off like an Agilent-type entity. Even six months ago there would be . . . "Unlock the value, right?" But now the stock is at 36.5 . . . and suddenly that squealing has stopped.[68]

True Believers

Eric Hoffer was a San Francisco longshoreman in mid-century America who wrote insightful prose at night after laboring daily on the docks. In a remarkably pithy book titled *The True Believer*, he wrote in 1951: "A mass movement's appeal is . . . to those who crave to be rid of an unwanted self. The true believer cannot be convinced, only converted." Groups thus impose, wittingly or otherwise, "a fact-proof screen between the faithful and the realities of the world." A group's "faith should not be judged by its profundity, sublimity, or truth but by how thoroughly it insulates the individual from himself and the world as it is."[69]

HPites in many respects are True Believers. CEO Mark Hurd sensed this in June 2007, when he sold the historic Little Basin recreation site in the Santa Cruz mountains and weeks later revoked Gold Badge privileges to wander HP hallways unescorted. These two actions provided much grist for the HP Alumni and Retiree Club chat rooms, plus highly critical columns in the *San Jose Mercury News*.[70]

Why are such issues so emotionally charged? Little Basin usage had dwindled to near zero, and an employee survey taken months earlier indicated profound lack of interest in the site as compared to tickets to local amusement venues. Moreover, the site wasn't sold—it was transferred to the Peninsula Open Space Trust, to be available in perpetuity for HPites and California citizens. In Dave and Bill's era, such a farsighted action would have drawn enthusiastic raves. Likewise for the Gold Badge decision. One of the real privileges granted by Dave and Bill, a Gold Badge—a gold-plated version of the classic name badge—granted a trusted ex-employee a lifetime privilege to wander throughout HP buildings. In an era of cost pressure, terrorism, and domestic violence escalation, is it so hard to register at the front desk? Packard likely would have just adopted a new policy, and if anyone questioned it, would summarily have stated, "That's the way it is here."[71] Perhaps Camelot was so perfect, for so long, that any change is seen as an assault on a whole way of life, a simpler and purer life, which is being forever abridged. Barnholt reflected on this:

> It would be nice to see the "good old days," but I don't think the "good old days" were ever that good. One of the advantages of being with a company for forty years is [that] I can remember when I had been with the company ten years, people started talking about "the good old days." And then again at fifteen years, and at twenty years. The good old days are always better. And they're always trying to go back to the good old days. The HP Way that's going to make HP successful in the next thirty years is going to be different from what we knew . . . [but] if you define the good old days in terms of deep respect around people . . . [HP] can still achieve that. But it's going to be different.[72]

Within HP, the furor calmed quickly, as immense tasks unfolded:

> "I have lots of friends who are retired from HP—almost all of them [were] against [the merger]," says Mr. [Joe] Podolsky, who support[ed] the merger. "They are referring to their memory of what The HP Way was. The company was really different then. Whatever The HP Way was then and whatever it is now are different. Change is inevitable."[73]

Merging Two Cultures

The server initiative gained momentum from the merger. Compaq shipped the DEC-developed Alpha Server systems with the industry's first 64-bit, 1GHz processor in 2001; IDC ranked them number one in High

Performance Technical Computing. In 2002, the new HP displaced IBM as number one on the TOP500 list of the world's most powerful computer systems. HP also announced breakthroughs in molecular electronics from HP Labs efforts begun under Birnbaum; HP and UCLA netted four key patents. For the next two years, HP again ranked as the number one supercomputing provider on the TOP500 supercomputer list.[74] The company had a chance to reestablish the leadership it had in 1995 under Wim Roelandts.

The hard work of integration was still ahead. Fiorina named Webb McKinney to head the cultural merging effort. McKinney had led HP's PC efforts in recent years, so he had more knowledge of Compaq than most HP managers, and his roots went back to the Instrument Group at the Santa Clara Division. Systems integration occupied much time for the two companies coming together, as did the selection of leadership in office after office, and reconciliation of competing product lines. But the most important elements were psychological. Healing time for HP employees from the bruising proxy battle was the most critical issue. For the moment, Fiorina's board was solidly behind her, exultant in their surprising victory.

CHAPTER 16

Who Decides Who Decides?[1]

SEPTEMBER, 1983, BEIJING, CHINA: By the time the story circulated in Palo Alto, it was averred that when David Packard proudly took the HP board to China, ready to show off his latest coup—opening this vast land to private enterprise—a giant snafu occurred. Arriving a couple of hours after the board members and the executive team had checked into the hotel with their spouses, Packard encountered angry board members and CEO John Young in the lobby, along with the hapless country manager, who had assigned the rooms with baths to those with HP titles, whereas board member rooms had baths down the hall. Everyone had unpacked before the imbalance was discovered. Several board members and their wives were quite upset—after all, chairmen or CEOs and their spouses from such corporations as Chevron, Boeing, Ford Motor, Avon, and Boise Cascade are accustomed to the best accommodations. Young, confronted with the situation, had attempted unsuccessfully to shift folk without unduly upsetting the executives and their spouses. Tempers were flaring in the lobby when Packard walked in. Towering over everyone in the room, he listened patiently for maybe thirty seconds, then turned to the assembled group, calmly said, "That's the way it is here," and walked away. No one challenged him. Of such heroics are legends made.[2]

Who decides the big questions? Who decides who decides them? And who decides how the decision turned out? The performance of a company and its leadership can be and is continually assessed by many disparate observers. Rather than "What have you done for me lately?" a board must ask, "What will you do for me next?" At least thrice the HP board has decided that a new CEO could lead the next HP challenge better than the CEO incumbent; all three replaced CEOs had wanted to continue, confident in their own ability to manage the complexity.[3] To make CEO replacement decisions, and then to select the replacements, is an awesome responsibility. The question is worth asking today: Is the present management taking the company where it should and could go? And if not, who could do it better?

To pose such a question, and to presume to be able to answer it, requires some degree of certitude about what constitutes "right." The difficulty for HP's board today is the inescapable fact that HP historically has succeeded against the odds, against the prevalent thinking, and against the considered wisdom. And therein lies the dilemma. Can a board, especially this board, escape its own perceptions and the hardened views of analysts and pundits enough to chart its own course, or will it fall prey to becoming ordinary, hobbled by mediocrity, and thus consign the company and its leadership to the same fate? Were the board somehow to develop enough character and clarity of purpose to chart its own course, how confident can it be in the outcomes? Indeed, charting the course of the company is an awesome responsibility, shared to a very high degree by the CEO and executive staff. And history, along with a myriad of HP employees and alumni, will judge those decisions, make no mistake about that.

A Critical Trade Press

In Search of Excellence (1982), coupled with an innovative *Fortune* "Most Admired" list, thrust the modest Palo Alto–based company into the limelight. Once there, it couldn't deflect the spotlight. Seers filled pages of *BusinessWeek, Fortune,* and *Forbes* over the next twenty-five years, usually foretelling woe and impending doom for the too-nice company for any number of reasons: sclerosis, paternalistic or idealistic management, stodgy engineering, bureaucracy, mal-adaptiveness, employees who believed in entitlement rather than creativity, innovation for its own sake, and, worst of all, inept management.

This last charge, inept management, has been a favorite. Every HP CEO, including Packard and Hewlett, has been repeatedly subjected to it. Journalism requires a story, just as the Nobel Peace Prize requires a war. Unless a company has troubles, the story is not interesting; without a war to be ended, no Peace Prize candidate can emerge. But for a company that has morphed so often, done so well, and been led so consistently by so many different CEOs on its way to stardom in high-technology revenue leadership, something is being missed in the assessments. Maybe, in fact, there is something to the HP Way—it must be stronger and more resilient even than anyone suspects. There might be something in the ethos that, as Paul Ely said, "brings out the best in folk, and makes them better people for the experience."[4]

Journalists, in chasing the sensational story, often miss the most important shifts. Bill Hewlett's second Watershed travails didn't garner lines in any biography; and Paul Ely, whose efforts carried the two of them a very long way, was both celebrated and vilified for his fiery approach and stentorian voice, but the tectonic shift that led to the denouement of his story at HP was largely unrecorded. Platt and Fiorina each defined major new elements of the HP Way—extending its reach to women, to people of other nations, to merger partners, and to part-time workers—but these don't make the list either. Who decides who decides proper success criteria?

The PC Challenge

Fiorina must have paused, thinking about the PC challenge. Platt had told her in their first meeting that "No one would set challenging goals at HP. . . . He felt powerless to drive the company . . . because of its highly decentralized nature and structure. The culture was both a great strength and a source of weakness, and certainly an impediment to change . . . [and] that the upcoming [Agilent Technologies] split would be traumatic."[5] The question everyone could have asked was, "What will HP do with this PC opportunity?" But instead the question was, "Why did Carly want to chase this garbage business?"

First, the two companies had to be integrated, a process predicted to be virtually impossible. Every big merger or acquisition in the high-tech sector had struggled. Fiorina knew the AT&T-NCR failure firsthand; Michael Capellas knew the Compaq-DEC issues intimately; the Unisys result, merging Burroughs and Sperry-Univac, was hardly a model.

In early conversations with Fiorina and Capellas, Susan Bowick, HP's senior VP of Human Resources, stressed cultural issues as the biggest disablers. CNetNews reported,

> Bowick likens mergers to an iceberg. The tip is made up of the sorts of financial goals and organisational structures that always get top billing. But the things

below the surface, such as how workers communicate and what words they use, are just as important. To help organise those that are staying, the company is putting its entire work force through a training dubbed "Fast Start," designed to explain the company's new organisational structure as well as allow workers to confront concerns about their new co-workers. . . . The day the merger was completed in May, all workers had HP badges as well as access to a unified HP.com email system. Bowick said: "We're eating our own dog food."[6]

. . .

OCTOBER 15, 2003, HOUSTON Bob Napier, the executive who led the merging of the computer systems of Hewlett-Packard and Compaq Computer, died on Monday after a battle with cancer. He was 56. Napier garnered praise for having many of HP's computer systems integrated on May 7, 2002, the day "the new HP" was launched. On that day, employees arrived at work to find they had a single email system, combined corporate and internal Web sites, and a unified help desk. "Bob was a great leader and a great friend and colleague to all of us," Fiorina wrote in an email to HP employees. "Bob was one of those rare individuals who could both challenge and support, who was both tough and compassionate. He made us perform, he made us think, he made us laugh."[7] Fiorina noted that "229,000 e-mail boxes, 232,632 accounts, 220,000 desktops, 1,093 network sites, and more than 7000 applications" were integrated in one day.[8]

Bob Napier's contribution wasn't just a lone-wolf act. It was a conscious decision made by HP's merged leadership. The company pioneered cultural due diligence as well as operational due diligence with the merger. Headed by Webb McKinney, who had led HP's growth spurt in PCs from 1996 through 1999, and Jeff Clarke, Compaq's CFO who joined from a long career at DEC, the integration team fashioned a merger that became the envy of corporate strategists worldwide.[9] Mergers take a while to settle in, and this one was no exception. The merger, however, also had to deal with an IT industry that continued to ail. Some called it indigestion, but it more correctly was profound restructuring. Just as HP competitors General Radio in 1955, Data General and Tektronix in 1985, and DEC and IBM and Wang in 1989 saw revenues flatten irrecoverably, the 2001 malaise stopped Intel, Sun Microsystems, IBM, and Agilent Technologies for years thereafter; even growth at Cisco, Dell, and Microsoft was severely stunted.

In contrast to this dismal picture, the new HP (NYSE ticker symbol HPQ instead of HWP) showed serious competitive spirit, whether in overall revenue growth, in GAAP profits, or most clearly in the hotly competitive personal computing space. At a 2007 Kellogg Conference on corporate governance, Fiorina cited four leading indicators to track: customer satisfaction, rate of innovations, diversity, and ethics. She focused briefly on Dell:

> Customer satisfaction metrics tell you whether customers will continue to buy in the future or whether they will begin to seek alternatives. If customer satisfaction is deteriorating, a revenue or margin decline is inevitable. It may not happen next quarter, it may not happen next year, but it will happen. Had investors really been paying attention to Dell Computer's customer satisfaction metrics, they could have seen it coming. Beginning in about 2003, HP's customer satisfaction metrics were improving every single quarter. It was public data. And Dell's were deteriorating every quarter. It was only a matter of time.[10]

Dell, the leader in PCs for nearly a decade, began losing share to HP starting in spring 2004. Over the next eight quarters, Fiorina's conviction that the customer satisfaction index was a precursor came true, as the Austin company's performance eroded. The financial numbers became suspect as well by mid-2005, a problem that showed when Dell failed to file year-end audited results. In early 2006, HP's personal computer business emerged as the leader in revenues and units. The wheels really came off at Dell in 2007; Hackborn's championing of Wintel, the perseverance of Carly and her board in the merger fight, and Hurd's steady operational hand prevailed.

OCTOBER 17, 2007, SAN FRANCISCO, CALIFORNIA "Hewlett-Packard widened its market share lead over Dell in worldwide personal computer shipments in the third quarter, while Dell returned to growth after several quarters of declines," researcher IDC reported Wednesday. "HP shipped 19.6% of all personal computers in the period, a 33% leap from the year-earlier period; the gap between HP and Dell widened to 4.4 percentage points from 3.2 points in the second quarter."[11]

End of an Era

Sales vice president Peter Blackmore provided the straw that broke the camel's back, although neither he nor Fiorina probably realized it at the time. When the Compaq merger took place, Michael Capellas's departure seemed a foregone conclusion. But Blackmore's position was solid, and he ran the sales teams well until a third quarter 2004 sales shortfall, the second in two years. Carly, steely-eyed, replaced Blackmore and his whole team forthwith. The issue, rather than her action, galvanized the board against her over an agonizing six-month period. Alone, Pattie Dunn delivered the news to Fiorina on February 7, 2005: Fiorina was through. It was three full years from the merger fight before the board terminated Fiorina. The pundits hailed back to the Compaq merger and the family feud, calling her demise inevitable. But it was more complicated; the outcome really turned on the question of what a board does and should do with respect to guiding and shaping a company strategy, and then monitoring and ensuring the results.

Three years is a long time in the Valley and in the high-tech world. It was, for example, only three years from the acme years of both John Young and Lew Platt that the HP board ended their careers. John Akers retired in disgrace from IBM three years after its high point in revenues under his leadership. DEC's best two revenue and profitability years ever were in 1987 and 1988; Ken Olsen was fired three-and-a-half years later after winning international accolades for the 1987–1988 comeback. Ed McCracken at Silicon Graphics delivered 52 percent growth and 10 percent net profits—bests on both scores—as SGI attained $2 billion in 1994; three years later, he was fired. Rod Canion had many great Compaq years—1989 saw 40 percent growth to $2.8 billion, two years before he was cast away when Compaq lost its way. Successor Eckhard Pfeiffer in 1997 delivered 30 percent growth in revenue (to $31 billion) and the highest profit on record (7.7 percent); fifteen months later chairman Ben Rosen removed him. No CEO escapes the question, "what have you done for me lately?"

The tendency was to blame the firing on Fiorina's polarizing style; she was not winning many popularity contests inside HP at the time. Craig

Samuel, a Compaq executive who stayed at HP for five years, reflected eighteen months after Fiorina was replaced:

People viewed Carly as a rock star. She was impressive. She was very capable, but she was out ahead and the rest of the company became further and further detached from her. Somehow, it wasn't the right values. She'd say, "Charge. We're going to take that hill," and you look behind you, and no one's there. She outran her team. I heard this a lot. And perception is reality. One of the complaints was that Carly was very much focused on building Carly's image. And that caused a lot of animosity and bad feelings because they didn't feel she was doing the right thing for HP. The Compaq folks felt less concerned about it. But the HP premerger personnel had many heartache moments about this. This alienated her greatly from the troops.[12]

Franz Nawratil pointed out that Carly was forced to react to an enormous amount of external garbage "which was spread by analysts and by other people about HP being in deep trouble and the HP Way doesn't work any more, etc." Nawratil, a silver-haired, kindly HP veteran born in Czechoslovakia, began as HP's first manager in Berlin, selling voltmeters in 1964. Franz spent many years leading various computer initiatives, as DSD general manager and later Computer Group marketing manager; he finished his career in 2000 as VP for European Operations. Passionately, he said,

I am still close in touch with at least the European part of the headquarters here and some country organizations; I believe today, and I see it myself, that the HP Way is coming back. The inherent strength in the HP Way was that it survived the Carly years. It came out stronger today than anybody would have been able to make it without being so much questioned.

It needed the challenge . . . to really sharpen the focus. We have been overconfident, self-confident that we had the formula and we knew exactly what was right and what was wrong. And that is not true. We knew in general terms where the compass needle was pointing, but we weren't quite sure where the cliffs were and where the currents were. So the challenge to the HP Way proposed by Carly was a needed one to bring out the best of what it is.[13]

Rick Belluzzo, once Platt's heir-apparent, and twice interviewed as a likely CEO successor, said:

There is all this fanfare about Carly, but nothing has really changed. People say the HP Way is how you treat your people, but the strength of the HP Way was the ability for people to argue and fight and have courage in the sense that they were doing the right thing for the company and however it turned out, it was mostly going to be OK. It changed—it became more punitive—and then people started leaving the company over those battles, whereas in the earlier days people tended to survive them if you had the courage to try to help change the company.[14]

Belluzzo may have hit the nail on the head. Tom Perkins, concluding that the company needed additional strategic guidance, was willing to re-join the board and lead a new strategic business committee with Keyworth and Hackborn. Apparently engendering huge jealousy in some circles on the board, it was the precursor event for the concerns that led to the pre-texting decisions. The firing of Fiorina and the pretexting debacle are linked events, as some would tell the story. It leads to this question: How will the board guide the executive team and HP's future? They started by hiring Mark Hurd as Fiorina's successor, an almost direct antithesis in style.

The Queen Is Dead, Long Live the King

No one really knew Mark Hurd when the board appointed him CEO of HP. Called the "Un-Carly" in the trade press, Hurd had a low-key, understated approach. Craig Samuel's quick take:

Mark was very direct. Very pragmatic and very straight. He came across as very genuine and cordial. He is a very effective, straight-talking CEO, somebody who can really get the operation going. And he's had the ability to execute that. The employees like Mark. Mark is well-liked because he has said what he'd do; done what he said; and got the stock price up, higher than any of us thought possible in this short time frame. He has been very direct about his plan and the responsibilities every employee in the company has. He's connected very well with the employees.

What of the HP Way? A lot of the HP Way was damaged, and some would even say destroyed, during the Carly era. She basically took issue with the HP

Way. But did the HP Way need revamping? Yes, it did. But the way it was handled was part of the reason for so much resentment. Mark has come in, and I don't hear too much about the HP Way, but you know he's certainly not trying to destroy it. . . . It's implicitly accepted. The HP Way and the open-door policy are two critical hallmarks of the company—the open-door policy is still cherished.[15]

Nawratil, with a European perspective and a pre-Carly perspective, observed,

From 1991 on, we suddenly became an American company running a globalized business, while before we were very much a global company [such as] the whole idea about setting up international divisions, giving those divisions their own R&D programs, or allowing them to have one to support them. The growth of divisions in Europe and the Far East created a worldwide catalogue of products and solutions. During that time, we also had a very international management team in Palo Alto and an even more international board.

We somehow lost the interchange of ideas, problem solving, and talent sharing when we started verticalizing businesses. When the businesses were running their own show, the European sales manager of [each] business was invited to the U.S., but not the country general managers. The country GMs suddenly were left out of the communication. Communication broke down and very often. [Jim] Arthur and others told them this is the way things are going to be done worldwide, period. And the moment you have country managers meeting customers and not being able to talk about HP business, they lose credibility very rapidly. Lew [Platt] avoided the issue. With Hackborn, it was impossible. When Carly came in . . . they didn't invite the country manager to [meet with] a customer. She made the presentation. She made the promises. But nobody knew what the hell was going on. We couldn't do any follow-up.

You can run a products company on individual performance, but not a systems company, which has so many facets that need to be in sync to solve a customer problem. If you want to sell a printer to a consumer, you can do it with individual performance. If you want to sell a heavy-duty enterprise system, you'd better have everybody playing together. Otherwise your customer is going to go crazy. Mark Hurd is bringing back the idea of teamwork. He's winning with the idea of the solution business.[16]

Pretexting and the HP Way

Hurd's "winning" ways quickly became overshadowed, however, when the CEO, the board, and by association, the company, were implicated in the pretexting controversy.

SEPTEMBER 6, 2006, PALO ALTO, CALIFORNIA In a filing with the SEC, HP acknowledged that it investigated its own board of directors to discover who leaked information that led to a News.com story about HP's future strategic plans. HP also said that the outside firms used to obtain the identity of the source of the leak might have used a technique called pretexting to obtain phone records of calls made by HP directors from their home phones and cell phones. Pretexting is one form of a new phenomenon called "social engineering," a fancy term for a person gaining unauthorized access to private information by pretending to be a person with such authority. This in HP's case involved intentional ID fraud by hired sleuths for the purpose of gaining unauthorized access to telephone records and bank statements of reporters, directors, and employees.[17]

Public outcry was immediate and visceral. Rick Belluzzo, interviewed weeks after the scandal broke, was enraged by the situation. He was even more shocked, though, by the reaction of HPites who viewed it as a media witch hunt rather than a serious breach of ethics. Fred Vogelstein, in *Wired Magazine,* caught the shifting mood a few weeks later:

> Until recently, the world hadn't heard a peep from former Hewlett-Packard CEO Carly Fiorina, and for good reason: Few wanted to hear from her. When she was fired 18 months ago, her five-year tenure was widely characterized as a disaster. She had put the company through hell—a megamerger, huge layoffs, countless reorgs. Yet it all seemed for naught. HP's share price and business still seemed moribund. Now she's written *Tough Choices: A Memoir*, a blunt, 300-page book telling her side of the sordid tale.[18]

The preponderant view of the press, as well as that of HP old-timers, and especially the Peripherals Group at HP, is profoundly negative about Fiorina. Inside HP, "off the record," our interviews revealed surprisingly significant support for her approach and achievements, if not her style, from employees at every level, including several senior vice presidents.

These polarized emotions likely will remain unaltered, but other interpretations surface.

Susan Harman, an IPO investment banker who took Cypress Semiconductor public, is one of many professional women who think much of the furor surrounding Fiorina was gender bias. She cites a well-documented case at Harvard Business School in which male students displayed profound deep-seated biases. In the T/Maker software case, test groups of women students made little differentiation in the leadership of "Heidi" or "Howard" Roizen, whereas for their male counterparts, the more aggressive they thought "Heidi" was, the less they liked her, while "Howard" (for the exact same facts) was seen as more genuine and less power-hungry and self-promoting.[19]

JULY 23, 2008, SAN JOSE, CALIFORNIA: Chris O'Brien, the hard-hitting business journalist at the *San Jose Mercury-News,* had the temerity to write a column titled "Was Sexism 'A Factor' in Firing of VMWare CEO?"[20] O'Brien challenged the Valley leadership for the disparate handling of near-simultaneous firings of CEOs Hector Ruiz at AMD and Diane Greene at VMWare. Greene was summarily dismissed sans any significant benefits from the very successful startup she led; Ruiz was elevated to chairman with a huge severance package and ongoing sinecure even though AMD was enduring near-fatal economic performance. O'Brien, citing a number of historic cases, engendered a polarized series of blog responses. One of the calmer inputs came from Marguerite Wilbur, who wrote, "Thank you for bringing to light another example of sexism in Silicon Valley. Sexism is prevalent in the valley, particularly in the technology industry. The industry's acceptance of it stifles creative and exciting female minds every day."[21]

Though there are questions lingering about whether sexism played a role in Fiorina's demise, there is little argument about the impact she had on HP. Without her bold leadership, the Compaq merger likely would not have happened. Without the cultural emphasis, the merger likely would have foundered. Without that successful merger, HP could easily have slipped into an also-ran position, dissolving into atomistic parts just as Agilent Technologies disintegrated. Yes, her style was confrontational, and the HP Way—especially the noncontroversial, nonconfrontational, conservative side of the HP Way—was boldly challenged. But as HP loyalist Franz Nawratil observed, that challenge put teeth into the slogan again. Finally, under Hurd, the company image is again understated—just like always.

Press Time for Silicon Valley

When Fiorina was being excoriated for excessive pay, it was not yet known that greed was being coupled to systematic graft at nearly two hundred Silicon Valley companies, with widespread stock option backdating to ensure huge gains. Several Pulitzer Prize–winning *Wall Street Journal* stories in 2005 and 2006 reported the stunning extent of these practices occurring in 1997–2002. One analyst reported that 23 percent of some 38,500 option grants had been manipulated, with estimated total net worth "improvements" approaching $100 billion.[22] Subsequently, HP's chief corporate counsel, prominent lawyer Larry Sonsini of the firm Wilson Sonsini Goodrich & Rosati, came under fire for his firm's seeming complicity in the practice.

MARCH 29, 2007, SAN FRANCISCO, CALIFORNIA: "Options Morass Deepens at Wilson Sonsini," wrote Justin Scheck for *The Recorder,* the San Francisco Bar Association newspaper:

> Wilson Sonsini Goodrich & Rosati has spent the past year trying to back away from the metastasizing stock option backdating mess, but an internal e-mail now in regulators' hands is making it difficult. In a 2004 message, Wilson Sonsini lawyer Roger Stern asks his partner to dig up a document from the time when a client was "using the time machine to pick low strike prices."
>
> Across a swath of companies at which Sonsini had a leadership role, options were misdated on his watch by executives or lawyers close to him, by company officials consulting with Sonsini's firm, and—in the high-profile Pixar case—by Sonsini himself. Prominent among those companies are Brocade, Juniper Networks, Apple, and Pixar, as well as KLA. Complicating matters is the fact that, according to SEC records, Sonsini and his firm may have profited immensely from stock awards by companies that admit to rampant options improprieties.[23]

Fiorina vehemently noted in mid-2007 that Hewlett-Packard had assiduously avoided any such illicit activity, even as it became the Silicon Valley norm; moreover, in sharp contrast to many others, notably including archrival Dell Computer, no earnings misfilings have ever emerged from the company where Packard set the ethical standard. Pretexting, although hard to defend, did not seem nearly as reprehensible as these offences.[24]

Silicon Valley changed irrevocably when the venture capital community burgeoned in the late 1970s. Big annual bonuses, new job payola, and stock options—especially stock options—became the new currency. These perks were especially dramatic for those in the Valley with credentials and a risk-taking mentality. The whole system seemed antithetical to the HP Way. When Ken Fox, DSD R&D manager, joined ASK,[25] some of these problems were revealed:

> ASK at that time was fifteen people, and profitable. [CEO] Sandy Kurtzig said, "I'm looking for a VP of R&D, and I talked to people at HP and your name keeps coming up." I took the job. Several people at HP tried to talk me out of it. Dick Anderson sent me off to talk to Doug Chance, who told me that basically ASK was competing with HP's manufacturing software and they weren't going to last long. And then he said, "Well, are they giving you any stock?" And I said, "Yes, I got a reasonable stock option." And he said, "Well, HP's starting to do that too."
>
> Now I was an R&D manager, and we were just starting to get [very small] stock options in HP at that time, whereas out in the industry, lots of other people were already getting healthy stock options. Doug's view of my stock options at ASK was, "Well, you know the market value of that isn't worth a damn." I had done an analysis of what I thought the stock was going to be worth and wrote it out for him. He had started this part of the pitch by saying, "Our goal is to have people like you with stock options within x years, be worth a million dollars." And I said, "Well, I'll be worth a lot more than that at ASK a lot quicker than that." He said, "I can see you're just in it for the money!" I said, "I didn't even bring the money up. You did." That conversation tipped me toward leaving.[26]

Sally Dudley, an HP quality leader for years, managed corporate compensation in her last role before retirement. Along with COO Dean Morton, she fought the trend toward big executive bonuses. She said,

> I really learned over those years that we would be seriously in trouble if we ever put bonuses in place. Eventually I lost that battle, and in 1997 they started doing bonuses. Within the first month of the announcement, a business manager in

Singapore was quoted saying, "This is great—before, I had to manage a lot of different aspects of my business. Now I can optimize for three or four measures." This all basically says, "You should be concentrating on the money." That was a crucial psychological error on HP's part.[27]

The structure of bonuses changed during Platt's last years, making them more in line with the big executive bonus structures of the Valley; Fiorina added fuel to the fire by changing the sales compensation structure when the Compaq merger was completed, because of the substantial difference in how the two companies operated. But it remained for Hurd's team to do the final insult to the egalitarian HP Way of rewards—changing the stock option program so that only high-level managers qualify for awards that used to be granted for contributions at every level of the company. These topics are seldom in the press, but they make a profound difference in the attitude, loyalty, and "family" feeling within a company.

Press Time for the HP Way

MARCH 30, 2005, CHICAGO, ILLINOIS: "HP's Hurd Lets Us Pretend Compaq Never Happened." HP's board hired Mark Hurd as the company's new CEO for three main reasons—he's duller than Carly Fiorina, he's supposed to have more operational expertise than Fiorina, and he's not at all associated with the Compaq acquisition. . . . Hiring reason number three stands out after Hurd today held his first press conference. The subject of the Compaq buy only came up once or twice during the event—a rarity in HP Land. The failures, the successes, the analyst scorn, the employee loathing all belong to Hurd but aren't of him. He didn't create the mess. He has to clean it up. "I can think of few companies that have such a strong foundation of talent, leading edge [research and development] and enviable market position," Hurd said, during the press conference. He's right too. It's not like Fiorina turned HP into a total disaster from a financial point of view. HP had its up and downs during her tenure but quite a few major tech players still have their pre-bubble CEOs in place and have not performed as well as HP in recent years. It's that Compaq albatross hanging around Fiorina's neck that pushed her onto the exclusive unemployment line reserved for fabulously wealthy business superstars. She just couldn't escape the Compaq baggage. . . . Hurd will be loved for taking a bit of pressure off HP.

"The one thing that has probably always stood out to me is the passion of HP's employees. When I look at HP, I see a company that is fundamentally sound."[28]

. . .

AUGUST 3, 2005 LOS ALTOS, CALIFORNIA: "Impact of HP Layoffs on Area's Workers Unclear." Hewlett-Packard's stock is up on Wall Street, but employee morale is low at the company's headquarters on Page Mill Road. Some employees at the technology giant's business park in Palo Alto received pink slips the same week that Mark Hurd, the company's new CEO and president, announced he would be cutting 10 percent of the HP workforce . . . nearly half of the reductions will occur in back-office support functions. Those include IT, human resources, finance and marketing, with the remainder inside the business units, [said] an HP spokesperson.

HP has advised its employees not to speak to the media without the company's permission. One nine-year employee who spoke on the condition of anonymity told the Town Crier that since the Compaq merger orchestrated by former CEO Carly Fiorina, things at the company have taken a turn for the worse. "From a business perspective there's no easy way to fix this," the employee said. "I think Hurd is trying to do the right thing, but the jury is still out. I think people will feel motivated if they survive the cut and the cut is fast." The increased workload from waves of layoffs under Fiorina and watching executives walk away with millions while employees waited for formulaic raises, not only sunk workers' good feelings about the company but caused dissatisfaction to swell, the employee said. "A lot of employees feel like they're being managed based on fear. The family feeling isn't there anymore."[29]

MARCH 12, 2007, NEW YORK CITY: The *Forbes* cover proclaimed, "Tech's New King—HP," and author Quentin Hardy duly noted that HP had just surpassed IBM as the largest high-tech company, by revenues, on the planet. Hurd's operational skills drew admiration along with a folksy, no-nonsense, low-profile style—"arriving without bold proclamations or sweeping plans." Echoing Packard's sentiments, Hurd said, "Without execution, vision is just another word for hallucination."[30]

A grousing IBM sales vice president fumed that "HP is fundamentally a printer and PC company—they are not really an enterprise player. We're not arrogant about this, but we have immense capability."[31] The numbers though, had to be disturbing in Armonk, New York. IBM's enterprise hardware revenues were only 10 percent larger than HP's in 2006. Moreover HP's servers and enterprise peripherals had virtually constant revenue since the merger with Compaq four years earlier, while IBM's had shrunk by 29 percent. The *Forbes* article, noting that IBM had 53 percent of its revenues from services whereas HP's percentage was but 17 percent, failed to mention that HP services were growing half again as fast as IBM's. Software, one-fifth of IBM, only grew 6 percent per year over six years, but CTO Shane Robison and CEO Mark Hurd busily bought software companies, including Mercury Interactive and Snapfish. And HP's April 25, 2007, Neoview announcement must have caused angst in Armonk.[32]

MARCH 19, 2007, NEW YORK CITY: The *Fortune* "Most Admired" survey appeared; no computer company was in the top ten. HP was a distant fifth among computer companies, behind IBM, Apple, Xerox, and Canon. IBM led the overall list the first four years it was published (1983–1986), but made the top ten only once more over the next twenty years. Dell made the top ten a total of seven times—with a first place finish in 2005. With the recent financial difficulties and ouster of the CEO, however, Dell fell all the way to eighth place in computing companies alone, well below HP, which finished a dismal 225th on the overall list—its worst finish in twenty-five years (Agilent Technologies remains unlisted). As HP's recent business success becomes more appreciated, and as residual ill will ebbs, it might not be a stretch to assume the *Fortune* list will show a resurgence of admiration for HP.[33]

The HP Way Reinterpreted

A (large) number of ex-HP employees assert that HP has lost its way. Alumni Association Bulletin Boards and Chat Rooms give them voice.

MAY 7, 2007, PALO ALTO, CALIFORNIA: HP ALUMNI ASSOCIATION POST, FERNANDO GOMEZ PANCORBO: As a field engineer in Mission Critical Services, I spent many nights working with customers (some of them really angry) to fix problems. It was a time where HP was trying to expand the services side. The Management By Objectives aspect of the company was marvelous, I could call anybody when I had a problem (no matter the time of day). As I got more senior, I received many calls of entry-level engineers who were stuck, with a customer shouting at them, and I was happy to help. When I moved to Cupertino, I kept the same passion, although it is true that in Cupertino, there were a bunch of, to put it politely, fossilized people who needed some action. Before the merger, I always had the feeling that if I delivered, I was going to be fine since the ultimate goal was to produce results. The merger changed all that dramatically; the mood of the office became full of fear.

People you could trust before became paralyzed . . . about the layoffs. The process [seemed] totally random. People got fired for being too good; people left because they couldn't take it anymore; young bright people got laid off just to be hired by pre-IPO Google. After the first couple of rounds, you couldn't trust anything, not even your performance and dedication. I heard similar stories from other groups in Cupertino and my colleagues in France and Madrid.[34]

. . .

SEPTEMBER 19, 2007 WAUKEGAN, WISCONSIN: HP ALUMNI ASSOCIATION POST, CINDY HOSSZU: The HP I worked for and believed in is really gone, and it's been gone for quite a few years. When the early retirement was announced, I was so happy to get the opportunity to move on and to do something more gratifying. Most of the managers I respected and loved working for are gone too. The new management teams at HP are very different and, quite frankly, I don't want to work with them. What HP wants now is people that will do as they are told—people that will do whatever it takes to make their numbers. Most of us wouldn't do that. I am proud of the values that HP instilled in me. . . . I truly believe that those principles were good ones and I don't think they need modifying. Unfortunately, we can't go back and infuse those in power at HP to believe in them. However, I do believe that in time history will prove that what Bill & Dave lived and taught us is a better way.[35]

And yet, interviews at HP in 2007 found that many HP people were as proud of their company as ever. An MIS controller in Roseville worked four days a week from home as her baby neared a year. After ten years at HP, she was still enthusiastic. A researcher in HP Labs, angry about some specifics, lashed out in a private setting but realized quickly that others might mistake his frustration with a supervisor for a deeper angst about the company, whereupon he went to great lengths to explain the positives.

A Corvallis Division design psychologist raved about the science behind the Halo room design and the willingness of his management to endorse his avant-garde ideas. A salesperson from France bubbled with excitement about new products.

We interviewed many "generational" families in our research. Some of the younger generation went to work for the company only to resign and go elsewhere, explaining to a surprised older generation that "It isn't the same company you joined." But others went to work for the company and love it today even though the older generation argued that "It isn't the same company as when I was there." Sometimes in the process, it was quite disconcerting, even enraging, for the older generation to learn how positive their younger counterparts felt about today's HP Way, while they themselves were certain that it has been unalterably desecrated.

More surprising, though, was to find that every generation felt similarly—that the HP Way they'd come to know, love, and trust was changing. Doug Chance led the general managers' group at Silverado for Hewlett in 1975 because of concern that things were getting worse. John Doyle commissioned an Open Line survey in 1979, which collected 7,966 responses in America—HP was in the top 2 percent of employee attitudes. Management was endorsed at 67 percent compared to a national norm of 46 percent, yet employees rated job security at 55 percent positive, 4 percent below the national average. An *HP Measure* article explained the discontinuity in soothing terms: "Concerns didn't involve worry about losing one's job, but rather related to rapid changes in organization and technology as well as relocation of divisions."[36] Back then, "out-sourcing" meant sending the division to Colorado or rural Washington, or sometimes overseas. If your specialty was computer graphics displays, in a decade your job moved from Palo Alto to Colorado Springs to Waltham, Massachusetts, to San Diego to Sunnyvale, California, to Fort Collins, Colorado. When the product line moved, you either moved with it, or found a new line of work. Duncan Terry moved four times to four western states because of his passion for low-cost printing. The worst, perhaps, was the small business computing group who built the HP 250. The product home base moved to and from Germany, Fort Collins, and Cupertino a total of five times before it was made obsolete by the Mighty Mouse program in Roseville, California.

When Lew Platt became CEO, Packard's challenge to him was to restore the HP Way. Both founders felt that the bureaucracy and centralization of the company imposed in order to succeed at the enterprise computing business had damaged the core of HP's value system. Platt embarked on a serious quest, which he reported early in the president's column of *HP Measure:* "There is a very troublesome trend in HP now, and that is the increasing number of people who think that the HP Way is either dead or irrelevant. . . . I think a lot of our people are having trouble distinguishing between core HP values and practices. . . . We must re-emphasize, renew and reaffirm the HP Way today. . . . We ought to be praising our people as well as challenging and criticizing them."[37]

The HP Way relies on success—it is hard to maintain enthusiasm and a positive attitude in the face of downsizing, outsourcing, and wholesale loss of jobs. Fewer than 15 percent of today's Hewlett-Packard employees (pre-EDS merge) were with the company when Packard died in 1996. Seventy percent have joined via or since the 2002 Compaq merger, never mind the proposed EDS acquisition. At Agilent Technologies, less than half the remaining team predates divestiture in 1999. It may be natural to assume the culture weakened dramatically in each case, with dilution and distance from the founders—setting aside tremendous differences in a company four hundred times as large as the one Packard ran before he left for his Washington service. Nonetheless, employees at all levels of each company, including newcomers, have sought Packard's modest book. Citations, reviews, and purchases have risen markedly after Hurd's arrival. New HP employees—hard-bitten DEC and Compaq veterans—seem to identify with, embrace, and even emulate the HP Way.

HP Values Reinterpreted

In many ways, the difficulty that Fiorina encountered at HP traced to a cultural approach at odds with the HP Way. Paul Ely summed it up this way: "What I knew was the environment where she came from. It was the antithesis of the HP Way—backbiting, internal politics, no integrity. The comments that my friends on other boards made about Carly was that she was the best practitioner of those things, and you could tell by her public image when she got here. Cosmetic detail wherever she went."[38]

Lew Platt came back fighting mad from his first trip to Asia with Fiorina, because she was cavalierly promising major concessions to heads of state with respect to trading rights and new plant locations. Advised to be more cautious, she retorted, "They'll not remember what I've promised." Platt and Alan Bickell, HP's senior intercontinental VP, knew HP's reputation, and they felt it dying. Platt went back to the board at the first meeting after she took over, saying "We've made a big mistake."[39] They listened, but voted for Fiorina.

Simplistic overviews are not particularly helpful for dealing with myriad details that bedevil any organization, small or large. There is a tendency to think that boardroom drama, merger and acquisition strategies, and bold leadership are the pivotal elements of a company's evolution. Those may be instrumental, but they are usually insufficient to explain either a successful situation or a failed one. Operational soundness, daily, is far more important in the main; without it, no strategy can succeed for very long, no board decision can be implemented, and no leader can expect followers. The secret of the Hewlett-Packard Company and its Agilent Technologies alter ego largely traces to the operational instincts put in place as part of the HP Way—drive decisions to the lowest level, execute crisply, strive for excellence, and serve the customer.

Decisions cannot be driven to the lowest level unless the people at the lowest level are trusted. If the people at that level are capable, but not trusted, it is difficult to expect them to strive for excellence. They wind up trying to curry favor to be allowed to do what they know must be done, rather than spending time on doing the best possible job. If skill and talent and judgment are missing anywhere in the management chain, the system fails for that branch. Most important, it is reciprocal: If the company doesn't trust and support its people, it cannot expect their loyalty and trust either.

Trust becomes paramount in the world outlined in Thomas Friedman's popular book, *The World Is Flat*. He explains that global enterprise, with virtual teams meeting electronically rather than physically, is becoming a normative organizational approach. People on three continents, with widely varying lifestyles, beliefs, and cultural values, work together on common objectives without ever meeting face to face. There can be no supervisory oversight in the traditional sense. Several large corporations—Intel, IBM, Microsoft, Cisco, Sun Microsystems, and HP—independently reported stunning findings to several forums during 2006.[40] All have large professional staffs, and all have large outside contractor staffs in addition. The teams on which these folk work are increasingly dispersed across the globe. The traditional model of two teams, each with a central locale, trying to work together is vanishing. These teams instead are loosely coupled, often comprising six to ten people located in as many sites. Studies have revealed that 75 percent of professionals at these companies work on one or more such teams weekly, two-thirds of them on three or more teams. Most amazing, one out of five employees has not yet met a manager face to face. Social and psychological questions arise, and issues of productivity and effectiveness move front and center. In a flat world, an HP Way becomes vital—not just useful or hygienic, but vital. Reciprocal loyalty and trust are required.

And in part, HP is helping to engineer that flat world. When Fiorina arrived, she was dismayed that no worldwide communication system existed—not realizing that Hank Taylor's world-class capability had been dismantled during Platt's regime. Birnbaum and Dick Lampman showed her some innovative HP Labs work in Fred Kitson's lab by researcher Susie Wee; Neerja Raman's lab had related technology. Energized by Steven Spielberg's Dreamworks vision, Fiorina boldly supported developing a product from their "lifelike, lifesize teleimmersion" project derived from Bran Ferran and Danny Hillis's work at Disney Imagineering and Applied Minds, Inc. The analogic result was HP Halo, an imaginative solution for telepresence, which debuted in mid-2005 from the Corvallis Division. Described in Tom Friedman's award-winning book, it works in real time, with indiscernible latency.[41] Halo was introduced at a pricey $550,000 per room; HP has reduced the price by 45 percent in two years. With breakthrough digital technologies, "what if" HP produces price reductions analogous to those of calculators and Laser printers?[42]

HP Citizenship Faces Challenges

HP has compiled an attractive record for its concern with both the environment and the well being of people, whether vendors, workers, or customers. HP led a Pacific Industry and Business Association effort in 1995 to spur suppliers worldwide to reveal and document environmental practices in a consistent manner; more recently, the company adopted a policy called "Supply Chain Social and Environmental Responsibility" requiring supplier codes of conduct. And HP and Dell Computer have stood alone in their industry to establish a "manufacturer's responsibility" approach to recycling rather than the "advanced recovery fee system" that gives manufacturers incentive to dump product in underdeveloped regions.[43] Bruce Piasecki, a noted environmental journalist, goes further still, stating that "HP's entire product line is beginning to reflect social concerns such as reducing energy use, affordability, and the maintenance of privacy, [while] IBM and Dell still see these challenges as involving trade-offs."[44]

But HP's care for ecological concerns predated even these advance efforts. In February 1967, *HP Measure* headlined "Pollution," in a story describing the newly acquired F&M gas chromatograph to aid in the war on environmental pollution.[45] A similar *HP Measure* story in November 1967 announced the HP 8051A Loudness Analyzer, to "fight Noise Pollution."[46] Such stories, three years before the first Earth Day, speak to HP's seventh objective, citizenship. HP equipment early established important normative baselines for scientists studying all manner of issues, from atmospheric and oceanic temperature gradations that early on helped to validate concerns about global warming, to composition of organic compounds and trace elements in materials and foods and their evolution, consumption, and accumulation in the food chain. Graphical correlations between alfalfa dehydrators, smoking drivers in air-conditioned closed-cab tractors, and emphysema death rates for Great Plains farmers, or the connection of colon cancer incidence with the diet of people regularly ingesting both gulf shrimp and Wisconsin-fattened beef regularly were possible in 1971 using graphical analytical tools that HP calculators facilitated.[47]

In January 1975, an article titled "Golden Treasure of the Trash Barrel" described an innovative recycling program for HP, aimed at recovering precious metals from plating shop wastewater.[48] A cost-saving effort by Norm Schrock in Colorado Springs quickly expanded corporation-wide to include environmental pollution reduction. The savings were not insignificant—more than $100 thousand per month was recovered the first year. The fact that HP was becoming a better environmental citizen was an even more compelling story. John Young joined Denis Hayes's board for Earth Day 1990, helping to bring a stronger message to the global HP community.[49]

The Analytical Group, now a cornerstone of Agilent Technologies, contributed much to world scientists working in such arenas. When SID pioneered the Spectrophotometer, it gave public health officials a mobile device capable of monitoring sporadic emissions from companies practicing episodic rather than regular discharges of pollutants. The Waldbronn acquisition of liquid chromatography technology enabled the tools that became standard for sports testing, but it also provided easy diagnosis of food substances and trace elements. An example was the inadvertent discovery of a trace carcinogen in orange juice concentrate made by a worldwide manufacturer. The development team had pioneered a much more sensitive (10x) tool, which gave a spectral plot of the contaminant in concentrate from one of three vendors. Consultation with HP Palo Alto folk led to the decision to share results with all three manufacturers, without identifying the culprit, tactfully saying that "a new testing technique has revealed disturbing results (enclosed) on some of our samples, but we don't know whose samples are which. Could you please send us new sample material; you are also invited to our labs for analysis and understanding." Nearly immediately, "clean" samples arrived from all three vendors.[50]

Citizenship contributions have taken a wide variety of forms. Legions of employees have volunteered innumerable hours for civic groups, charitable causes and organizations, and public service. Some have had a strong scientific component, such as the study commissioned by Hewlett with his chief pilots to equip airports with side-ranging Doppler radar that documented the first recorded microbursts—the very dangerous downdrafts responsible for the crash of Delta Airlines Flight 191 at Dallas-Fort Worth in 1985 that killed Don Estridge, leader of the IBM PC team.[51]

Dave Cochran, Len Cutler, and Barney Oliver turned their attention to the Bay Area Rapid Transit (BART) collision issues a year after completing the HP 35 handheld design.[52] The January 1974 *HP Measure* described the BART effort plus the deployment of HP equipment to understand macro-weather. Barney Oliver also served on the Space Shuttle program, detailing the safety issues of the reentry tiles, and raising the hackles of senior NASA officials. Packard's quiet decision to nuclear-harden the Santa Rosa gallium-arsenide facility, which produced 90 percent of the very high-performance chips for military communications, was unheralded and virtually unknown at the time. Local officials were amazed at the company's extraordinary use of concrete and the depth of the excavation; Doug Chance and the management team, unaware of the design issues, knew of the cost overruns.

Two other forms of citizenship stood out—contribution to the scientific community, and contribution to the educational community. HP-Agilent scientists and engineers provided leadership for professional societies around the globe, notably supplying five IEEE presidents and one ACM president from their ranks, along with sixteen National Academy members circa 1990.[53] Such activities helped HP appreciate the fragility and value of the IT world beginning to unfold. The Bay Area EDP group constructed a dual IT backup system in Loveland, Colorado, to preclude loss in the event of a catastrophic earthquake or other event in the Bay Area. Completed by 1976, this system was fully redundant for order processing and operational transactions. Analysis of company preparedness in 2002, after the 9/11 terrorist attacks, revealed that a very small fraction of U.S. firms were so equipped twenty-five years later. Via the HP scholarship program and the equipment donations program, HP led in educational contributions. The Public Management Institute in 1990 singled out HP as "the most generous corporation" in the world, for its donations in 1988 of $55 million, 92 percent of it to universities and schools. The contributions were sizable at 4.4 percent of pre-tax earnings; the next year, *HP Measure* reported that donations rose to $74.5 million.[54]

Some commentators chide HP, saying that it once pioneered leading-edge benefits, but no more.[55] The criticism seems curiously short-sighted. Under Platt's leadership, much attention was given to recruiting and promoting both minorities and women, and substantial efforts went into developing a stronger telecommuting employee workforce—some metrics indicate that HP is the most virtual large corporation around.

Fiorina believed in this vision as well. Debra Dunn teamed with social economist Keith Yamashita to publish a ground-breaking *Harvard Business Review* article about a "living lab" in Kuppam, India, where HP is helping people overcome barriers to social and economic progress while learning how to compete better in the region and around the world.[56] Titled "Microcapitalism and the Megacorporation," the article spoke of highly courageous leadership for HP. The article energized campuses globally fueling widespread debate about e-inclusion in time for Friedman's highly popular globalization thesis.[57] When Fiorina proposed products, services, and concern for working conditions targeted to reach the underprivileged four billion people who have not experienced personal electronics, HP escalated the stakes, combining classic HP citizenship values in a manner befitting the HP heritage.[58]

OCTOBER 12, 2003, GENEVA, SWITZERLAND: ITU TELECOM 2003, CARLY FIORINA KEYNOTE. There are two types of games that motivate businesses, countries, and people. There are "zero-sum" games, and there are "non zero-sum" games. Zero-sum games are contests in which one person's gain is another person's loss. Translated to economics, this is the belief that for one country to win, another must lose. But in non-zero sum games, one person's gain is not necessarily another person's loss. For one country to move ahead, another does not have to fall behind. . . . Looking back on human history, the moments when our world has made the greatest social and economic progress, are those moments when new technologies came along that permit or encourage new, richer forms of non zero-sum interaction. In other words, looking back on all the great advancements through the ages, there are moments in history—from the invention of the wheel, to the Silk Road, right up through the automobile, the airplane, and the Internet—where technology makes it possible for everybody to advance together, if everybody is willing to do their part. We are at one of those moments in history. The vast potential of this industry to bring social and economic progress now has moved beyond the hype, and is within our reach. The real challenge for this industry is not a question of technology—it is really a question of leadership. A decade from now, we are either going to be able to tell a glorious story of empowerment and opportunity, or we are going to look back on missed opportunities and talk about what might have been.[59]

Services . . . from HP Labs

Joel Birnbaum, talking in 2006 about future scenarios for HP, became expansive:

> Instead of selling [commoditized] printers, the business was in the ink, and the way you sold more ink was initially through photography—one image is worth twenty text pages. More important, printers would be embedded in ways that have nothing to do with what printers do today. As a trivial example, we could very easily build a small printer in every TV set with a slot in front that was connected on a network so when you are watching the ball game you push a button and print the player programs, or watching the shopping channel you get the coupons to go to the store. HP could sell a printer to almost every television set in the world, and charge a monthly service, which we could split with DIRECTV. There must have been ten of those kinds of things where . . . the technology doesn't exist. For example, people use magnets on the refrigerator as a home message center. Why not refrigerators with writable touch screens, networked to grocery stores, your office, and your car? Another example: the world's worst gas chromatograph, to sell for $20 to $30. You take it to the supermarket like a pen, and it lights a couple of lights and tells you which melons are ripe, which salmon is freshest, etc. With different tips, it is a shopping pen for a wide variety of tasks.[60]

. . .

SEPTEMBER 12, 2007: "HP Technology to Help Deliver Medications." The technology behind that inkjet printer on your desk may soon deliver drugs painlessly into your body, potentially replacing the need for traditional hypodermic needles. The system is based on the same technology developed by HP to make InkJet printers heat up ink and precisely squirt it onto paper. Under the agreement, HP will license the technology to Crospon Ltd., a small Irish medical device maker. Over the next several years, Crospon will seek government approvals and secure agreements with pharmaceutical companies, with plans to start selling a patchlike drug delivery system in about four years.[61]

Micro-needles, from inkjet printers!

Procter and Gamble (P&G), a conservative old-line company, is renowned as a marketing firm and an ardent experimenter with high-tech "toys"—partaking of 3-D simulation virtual worlds with fanciful synthetic shopping experiences, the company has invested in immersive cave environments, Virtual Worlds, massive multiplayer gaming, and other esoteric technocratic arcana for market research purposes.[62] These two P&G characteristics came together in a most surprising way when the company proposed to switch its IT outsourcing to HP in 2003.

HP won the $3 billion, 10-year IT operations outsourcing deal in short order, having only entered negotiations early this year. HP was not even a dark horse last summer. . . . The plan calls for HP Services to take on 1,850 employees from 50 countries in P&G's Global Business Services unit. Covered under the outsourcing agreement are management of P&G's IT infrastructure, data center operations, desktop and end-user support, network management, and some applications development and management for P&G operations in 160 countries.[63]

MAY 6, 2003, SAN JOSE, CALIFORNIA: A prosaic HP announcement emerged:

On the heels of finalizing its largest services contract with Procter & Gamble (P&G), HP today announced it signed more than 200 managed services contracts in the past 12 months. As part of the agreement, P&G will benefit from some of HP's industry-leading technology solutions, including the adaptive infrastructure capabilities provided by the HP Utility Data Center (UDC) and Adaptive Network Architecture. With UDC, P&G will be able to rapidly deploy and manage servers in its IT environment, providing greater flexibility to quickly respond to changes in its business and IT environments. The HP Adaptive Network Architecture services provide a policy-based architecture to allow P&G to easily and rapidly add and reconfigure networks from its corporate backbone. "HP Services will give P&G the flexibility to respond rapidly to changing business needs such as rapid changes to business processes, speedy entry into new markets and strengthened ability to execute acquisitions quickly," said Ann Livermore, executive vice president, HP Services.[64]

Left out of the announcement—but critical to the deal—was a creative offer by Fiorina and Shane Robison to offer HP's famed research laboratories to P&G researchers for project consulting on issues of mutual interest. The few researchers at HP Labs who even knew of this proposal were puzzled, but no one objected. The contract consummated, that portion was forgotten for a time. HP Services had been building momentum since the Compaq merger, with major wins at Ericsson and Bank of Ireland, plus Telecom Italia, Cathay Pacific, and a host of other leading international companies. Most were IT management services, but some, such as the Shanghai General Motors (SGM) contract, were more consultative (for example, to optimize the company's supply chain management system, with Deloitte Consulting deploying the solution). By 2006, services were becoming a major component of the HP strategy.

Enter the creative minds of HP Labs. Nina Bhatti, an HP Labs researcher, became disgruntled and left HP when the QoS software technology was starved as a result of the company's weak infrastructure for turning software contributions into products. She found, however, that HP's environment offered more freedom of independent action than she had appreciated while she was within it. Within two years, she returned, soon attending a desultory review with the P&G folk, with uninspired ideas about short message service (SMS) messages on a phone to stimulate buying behaviors. She left the meeting imagining difficult buying situations she had encountered. Cosmetics came to mind. How might one use new imaging technology to help the cosmetics industry treat its clients more satisfactorily?

The idea was slow to catch on. HP has been a bastion for white male engineers and managers for seventy years, and HP Labs, although more equitably balanced for ethnic background, was still primarily a man's world. More important, the magic elixirs needed—the technologies to be brought to bear—were complex, multifaceted, and never focused on the type of problem that Bhatti proposed to solve. In short, the problem statement and the eventual success were in the best tradition of HP—find the person closest to the problem and give them resources to solve it.

Bhatti thought to shake up the cosmetics industry, especially the foundation colors, tints, and creams sold through either drugstores or high-end department stores (such as Neiman-Marcus, Bloomingdale's, and Marks and Spencer). Drugstores provide no help for the purchaser, but department stores act as an incestuous cabal known for pricey products, haughty sales attitudes, and low customer satisfaction. Earlier attempts to broaden the appeal—mail-order and home products—suffered from a lack of sophistication in actual selection and usage. Colors matter. Selected carefully, they can be quite enhancing. But like house-paint selected from a color chip, the applied cosmetic color seldom looked as hoped.

Bhatti's solution combined four types of technology, much of it HPL-patented, into a brilliant collage. Women, with nothing more complicated than a mirror and a cell phone camera, now can get a customized color chart for their own faces, sophisticated enough to be specific for cheek, forehead, and chin, with one-touch ordering from P&G online services at a fraction of the cost and none of the snobbery and high-pressure tactics of the current buying experience. Known as Color Match, the technology was introduced to the world in May 2007, with anticipation about its potential to expand the market.[65]

What technologies did Bhatti employ, and more important, how did she come to see that her idea had merit? Maybe most significantly, what does it say about the spirit of inventiveness and the ability to turn ideas into products at HP today?

First, the technologies were wide-ranging, never brought together before. They combine mobile phone communications, color calibration of images from any camera from ubiquitous color bars in magazines, location of a face in an image, and statistical classifiers that can compare a color-corrected image to exemplars.[66] The system behaves as a cosmetics expert. The color chart is used to normalize for illuminant and camera color sensitivity. Product enhancements—identification and security studies at HP Labs (for example, facial recognition); digital camera improvements; deep studies of the composition of creams and their properties under varying light conditions like the ink research from years earlier; and, significantly, because this innovation might become standard for many vendors, not just P&G, the databases of creams, supply chain management, and customer fulfillment offer rich opportunity for personalized marketing and delivery systems.

It is a testament to Bhatti's dedication and perseverance that HP Labs supported the project. During an interview while the project was still flying below the radar, she began with the travails and barriers, then abruptly shifted course to a self-deprecating stance. She was able to see that her project was such a novelty, such a breakthrough in thinking, and a wild combination of techniques that in retrospect it seemed implausible even to her.[67]

Enterprise Software

Shane Robison, HP's chief technologist, has said HP doesn't need to explore transformative technologies any longer at venerable HP Labs: "HP has plenty to do, simply executing against its current strategies." But he resolutely describes a vision for enterprise software contributions, including social networking, auction forecasting, and other knowledge intensive information services.[68] Services? Yes, but not as they were previously envisaged in the IBM consulting context. These services are a unique HP blend of technology, people, and autonomic agent backbone. In short, it is a classic evolution of HP, and possibly a transformation even while not really seeking one (just like the last five). Will enterprise software prove as transformative as the scientific instrumentation that emerged when electronics was applied to medicine? Or as convulsive as the computing that emerged from the voltmeter renewal? On the surface, it seemed unusual that HP acquired the software testing company Mercury Interactive. Agilent Technologies is the test instrumentation company. But for a vision that embraces providing robust, secure management services for IT, Mercury Interactive fits—beautifully.

MAY 2, 2007, HP PRESS RELEASE, PALO ALTO, CALIFORNIA: "HP Names Dean of University of Illinois at Chicago . . . as Director of HP Labs." "Prith [Banerjee's] energy, vision and combination of high achievement in scientific, academic and entrepreneurial settings make him an outstanding choice to lead HP Labs," said [Shane] Robison. "Technology is at the core of HP, and Prith's mandate is to ensure that HP Labs continues to be one of the world's leading research organizations."[69]

Replacing Dick Lampman as research senior vice president and director of HP Labs, Banerjee has a great challenge—to uphold the inventive legacy of Kay Magleby, Don Hammond, or Dave Cochran, with the stature of Joel Birnbaum or Barney Oliver—but this time with the onus of a large corporation with little taste for launching small nascent businesses. HP Invent describes the desired innovation processes: unfettered on occasion, unexpected often, world-changing more frequently than one might anticipate; except for one caveat—adoption of HP Labs ideas within HP product divisions.

Licensing inventions, even for sizable royalty expectations, is very different from developing businesses around those breakthrough ideas. The microprobe, Color Match, and HP Halo all have threads related to HP's business models, but they are threads, not necessarily ties that bind. In earlier times, it took creative division managers, or creation of a new division unfettered by a historic market, to capitalize on the energy, insight, and bold innovation from HP Labs. Why will business development differ this time? And what can be said for the role of serendipity?[70]

DECEMBER 12, 2006, NEW YORK CITY "HP is focused on organic growth and doesn't expect to do huge acquisitions, with a few rare exceptions like its $4.5 billion purchase of Mercury Interactive," said Mark Hurd at HP's 4th Quarter 2006 press conference. The purchase continues a stream of smaller acquisitions, some of them quite innovative and exciting in their own right. Like the "old HP," the company tries to identify an arena of interest, locate the crucial technologies and players, and build synergy around them.[71]

Massive Multiplayer Games

SEPTEMBER 28, 2006, PALO ALTO, CALIFORNIA HP today announced it has signed a definitive agreement to acquire VoodooPC, a leader in the design and manufacture of high-performance and personalized gaming computer systems. HP will form a separate business unit within its Personal Systems Group focused on the gaming industry. VoodooPC co-owner Rahul Sood will become chief technologist for the unit and co-owner Ravi Sood will become the unit's director of strategy. Both executives will report to Phil McKinney, who will become general manager of the gaming business unit while maintaining his current role as chief technology officer of HP's Personal Systems Group.[72]

. . .

JANUARY 5, 2007, LAS VEGAS, NEVADA Anil Desai flew directly from Taipei for the show. The largest trade show on the globe—the Consumer Electronics Show, known this year as CES 07—was about to feature his new products, HP's most serious entrants in the consumer electronics field—digital television and home entertainment systems. Asked about the HP Way, he smiled broadly and said, "It's like it used to be. We're back to being an engineering company." Desai, an electronics design engineer hired in 1978 for HP's Data

Terminal's Division, worked for Bob Chin. Chin, then just moving to Data Terminals from the ill-fated HP-01 project, has now been at HP thirty-three years. Desai spoke for both, saying that HP has undergone wrenching change; he gave Fiorina credit for giving the company a much-needed swift kick into higher gear, along with a tonic dose of marketing skill. Desai exulted that the company's roots in solid products are being reaffirmed; he and Chin are unconcerned that "times are different"—in fact, they embrace the changes as evidence again that HP "has what it takes."[73]

At CES 07, the Voodoo booth drew heavy crowds. Voodoo has taken home the Editors' Choice award the last three times in a row for the Ziff-Davis competition called "The Ultimate Gaming Machine Showdown."[74] Rahul Sood and Ozzie Diaz, chief technologist for Mobility and Wireless in Shane Robison's Office of Strategy and Technology, proudly pointed to some unannounced curvilinear screens in the booth that were hosting a Voodoo road-racing contest for show attendees, proclaiming this a natural alliance of HP Labs technology, Voodoo gaming, and the new HP Gaming Division. These screens, invented for collaborative experience, showed the games well. Philip McKinney, PSG CTO, and Paul Campbell, founder and vice president of the Gaming Division, sounded a clarion call reminiscent of the "old HP"—"we're serious, and this will be a major initiative." Asked about HP leadership, they each wore a broad smile; one ventured, "Let's just say, it's great—our executives have been fully supportive of our innovative approach to entering the gaming market through invention, acquisition and incubation of a small team with loads of passion."[75]

Irwin Sobel, a contributor to the HP Labs curved screen display at CES 07, joined HP in 1982 to work on robotics. With HP Labs ever since, he has worked on a wide variety of challenging assignments. He is particularly proud of Adaptive Lighting. HP's advertising says it thus: "What you see is what you get" (a parody of the old WYSIWYG notion for PC screens converting to the printed page)—HP's Adaptive Lighting Technology automatically makes your pictures look like what you see with your own eyes. It automatically balances the dark and bright areas in a photo while maintaining the overall contrast. Adaptive Lighting Technology adjusts the lighting differently for every shot, and even works well in difficult lighting environments. The result is that you can now see details normally lost in the shadows.[76]

Sobel, a mathematician by training, has done algorithmic design work for thirty years in a variety of application areas. Taking advantage of a chance to work alongside John McCann, the gifted research director working at Polaroid Corporation for founder Edwin Land, Sobel realized that McCann knew how to brighten dull images on Polaroid prints so that higher contrast was available for items in shadows. Sobel, with McCann's support, figured out how to express McCann's knowledge mathematically, and over a five-year period was able to help an HP colleague, Bob Sobol, incorporate the algorithmic work into HP's printing and imaging software. The irony: in the meantime, Sobel's supervisor lost patience with a lack of discernible output and sent him packing. As it turned out, another HP Labs manager, Fred Kitson, at the time was willing to give Sobel a respite and safe haven—the rest, as they say, is history.[77] Mavericks still survive at HP.

A Massive Services Gambit

In May, 2008, HP announced its intention to acquire EDS for $13.9 billion, in a deal that would double HP's services business and revive EDS's position as a leader in global technology services. The acquisition had the potential to catapult HP's annual revenue for services from less than $20 billion to nearly $40 billion and to position HP as the second largest services provider in the world. HP stated that it would establish a new business group, to be branded EDS and located at EDS' Plano, Texas, headquarters, and that EDS would continue to be led by chairman, president, and CEO Ronald Rittenmeyer, who would report directly to Mark Hurd.

EDS, the feisty outgrowth of maverick E. Ross Perot in 1962 when IBM snubbed his strident view that software applications and software IT services were the future, had long enjoyed consulting success under the able leadership of Mort Meyerson. Perot brought zeal and passion to the company, while Meyerson lent a polished, dignified demeanor that was crucial for the Fortune 50 customers. In 1984, General Motors bought EDS for $2.4 billion, only to have Perot become a dissident board member upset with the ponderous pace of the stodgy Detroit company. He launched a new, competing company, named Perot Systems; GM spun EDS out. EDS thrived for the next fifteen years; Perot Systems never got momentum.

Ann Livermore, a leading inside contender for HP's CEO job when the board dismissed Platt, was appointed Services executive vice president in 2001 by Carly Fiorina. By 2003, her division had grown from eighth to third place among American consulting companies in service revenue. When HP beat service leaders IBM and EDS for multi-billion-dollar contracts with Procter & Gamble and Ericsson, and won the overall customer satisfaction survey conducted by *Information Week*'s research survey of seven hundred IT professionals, jubilation ran high within HP that Fiorina's backing of the PricewaterhouseCoopers deal was actually wisely conceived, even though the deal wasn't consummated.

Hurd, in announcing the EDS purchase, praised Livermore's team; the facts, however, were that HP's services sector had stalled after 2005, growing only modestly in 2006 and 2007 to $16.6 billion. For 2007, EDS had revenues of $20 billion; Perot Systems did just one-tenth of that. EDS however, experienced profitability issues from 2005 onward, as revenue gains stalled. Their profitability sagged from 12 percent net to 6 percent, while IBM maintained 14 percent net on their services business. HP Services achieved 11 percent net, helping HP's overall 8 percent net profit even as the hotly competitive PC business, growing faster, had low 5.6 percent margins.

Significantly, the EDS management team won the rights to manage Livermore's team, rather than the other way around. But that didn't last long. On December 6, 2008, Rittenmeyer announced his retirement as of the end of the calendar year, and Hurd folded the independent EDS unit under Livermore.[78]

The trick will be to integrate the two groups. The bigger issue is the dramatic shift in the balance of HP employees, from a design and manufacturing company to a services provider. On the surface of it, assuming constant revenue from the merged operations, services is on track to become the leading sector of HP business for the first time—a classic transformation! Appendix A illustrates the company's transformations; a most remarkable aspect of the Hewlett-Packard business evolution. Usually a redefinition of terms accompanied the transformations; for example, discovering that tools for radio and television designers were not unlike tools for AT&T long-distance telephony if it was called "the frequency domain." Similarly, computer peripherals became "printing and imaging," becoming larger than the computing engines that spawned them. The Compaq merger allowed the redefinition of computing into personal terms more clearly than HP had for three decades; the EDS acquisition will recharacterize much of HP going forward.

Within one decade for this seven-decade company, the tumult for employees has been profound. Consider, of 125,000 employees who had known HP history and lore, 52,000 were divested with Agilent Technologies. Three years later, 65,000 Compaq employees joined with 90,000 HP employees, and 20,000 of the combined set were excised. Now, 140,000 newcomers will join 170,000 melded workers, to grapple with "the HP Way," the "Compaq Way," the "DEC Way," and the "EDS Way." Megamergers can work, but the cultural adaptations are nontrivial experiments. What is to become of the HP Way in this brave new world?

One of the hallmarks for HP is that it learns from its experience. Hurd has embraced the same cultural integration methodology for the EDS merger that Fiorina's team used with Compaq. The costs are huge in terms of devoted time, time away from families, and "primary jobs" that have been set aside, but integration teams have spent enormous face-to-face time in group after group, to establish and build the trust and camaraderie vital to the integration of HP and EDS groups so crucial to success of the combined services venture.

Foretelling the Future

ACM, the leading computer science professional society on the globe, proudly hosted the "Next Fifty Years" futures conference in January 1997 with HP as a lead sponsor. No one, not even the first five acclaimed speakers—James Burke, Gordon Bell, Joel Birnbaum, Carver Mead, and Vint Cerf—predicted the imminent explosion of the World Wide Web. Cerf outlined the thesis, saying that within twenty-five years, the three basic communication networks—for data, voice, and video—would converge. But, he later observed, it took twenty-one years for his baby, TCP/IP, to be given "product of the year" status, quipping that it was "old enough to vote." ACM's president, touring the world the next year to extol the conference results, repeatedly had to defend why this group missed the Web explosion.[79]

If futurists notoriously miss the biggest changes, asking a CEO to prognosticate where his company is headed might seem misguided at best. And yet, as Henry Ford once noted, "If you think you cannot go there, chances are you won't." So where does Mark Hurd see HP's future? One clue lies in a small monograph that he and Lars Nyberg, chairman of NCR Corporation, published just before Hurd was picked as HP's CEO. Titled *The Value Factor: How Global Leaders Use Information for Growth and Competitive Advantage,* the small book singles out the information infrastructure as a critical ingredient, coupled with a collaborative corporate culture. The authors cite leadership as a crucial element, "to enable a culture of proactive, solution-oriented employees" while building a company with "centralized goals and democratized decisions."[80] Sounding like a blend of Packard, Hewlett, Young, and Birnbaum's views, these words were penned two years before Hurd arrived at HP. By most accounts, Hurd is embodying these concepts in his leadership role at HP—a Herculean task to be sure.

Hurd wrote also that "Vision is the strategic underpinning of any success," but the "vision thing" keeps arising in critiques of his style, which note that he is operational (bringing to mind the pedestrian Platt, as well as the action-oriented Packard).[81] For a leader whose company has just burst in front of both IBM overall and Dell in PCs, the charge has to be irksome. It is disquieting that *BusinessWeek* continues the mantra, writing in December 2007 that IBM is one of only five thought-leaders for "the next new thing . . . Cloud Power,", alongside Google, Yahoo, Amazon, and Microsoft.[82] Meeting with a group of retired HP Labs executives in March 2008, Hurd boldly asserted that his task is to infuse "more R" into the "R&D" equation for HP.[83]

MAY 1, 2008, SAN FRANCISCO: Stan Williams, founding director of HP Labs' Information and Quantum Systems Lab, averred that HP had proved the existence of the memristor—a memory resistor element predicted thirty-seven years ago, one that joins capacitors, resistors, and inductors as fundamental electrical elements. This one could radically change memory systems for computing, although the timeframe to do so is long.[84] Even bigger discoveries and breakthroughs are rumored to be occurring in Williams's lab, fundamental work said to be of Nobel Prize–winning stature in quantum devices. Whether they understood the technologies or not, three separate CEOs—Platt, Fiorina, and Hurd—have strongly supported the heavy investment and continuation of this long-term effort.

Disquieting comments circulate in Silicon Valley, though. Much of the current innovation (including the excellent memristor work) is harvesting research begun and sustained in prior periods. Long-term HP Labs researcher Neerja Raman is concerned about HP Labs, and recently commented on prior management: "Carly loved to talk about HP Labs in public, but behind the scenes she was disinterested in the actual technical work being done there, and she was actively cutting budgets and staff."[85]

Critics view Mark Hurd's comments to retired HP Lab execs similarly—reflecting what they want to hear, rather than evidence of the new HP operationally embracing the R in R&D. It is just talk until proven otherwise.

The numbers support the concern. Under Lew Platt, the company shifted from a four-decade average annual 9.0 percent R&D investment to 6.0 percent by 1998. R&D expenditures then stayed constant at 6.0 until 2003; they have shrunk by a nearly uniform 0.5 percent per year ever since, reduced dramatically to a mere 3.0 percent in 2008. Actual expenditures peaked at $3.686 billion in 2003, versus $3.543 billion in 2008, while revenue climbed $45 billion to $118 billion. Meanwhile, IBM continued to hold its R&D investment steady at 6.0 percent for the entire seven years, while achieving increasingly positive profits (11.9 percent for 2008, up from 10.5 percent in 2007). HP profits were 7.0 percent for both 2007 and 2008, virtually the same as the Platt years.

But wait—*BusinessWeek* cited HP once again as one of the Top 50 Innovators in April, 2008, profiling Prith Banerjee's bold "Big Science" restructuring approach.[86] But Neil Jacobstein, CEO of Teknowledge Corporation and twenty-five-year veteran of Silicon Valley, observed,

> Unfortunately, the words reflect an operational spirit of cuts, consolidation, and business as usual. Overall, the "vibe" at HP Labs is not one that is technically talent-friendly, especially to the small nascent offbeat idea. Something fundamental seems missing—specifically, the leadership at the top needs to have a deep

understanding of science and technology, an appreciation for the critical and perishable role of brilliant technical talent, and the non-optional long-term view required to embrace the R in R&D.[87]

The concern in the Valley is that HP Labs is becoming "innovation hostile," in spite of continuing innovation there. Sour grapes from old-timers facing change at a crossroads or prescient observers sensing a sea-change?

Could HP Leave Palo Alto?

MARCH 20, 2008, SAN JOSE MERCURY-NEWS: The buried headline innocuously read "HP to Vacate 9 Buildings in Palo Alto and Cupertino,"[88] and those few folk who read it wondered, "What is this about?" Company spokesperson Ryan Donovan said, "A move out of either Palo Alto or Cupertino was never discussed with either city." Denial of a nonstory is puzzling, to say the least. What would it mean for HP to leave Palo Alto? Some speculated that the story was a cover for a strategy leaked prematurely, not sanguine for the local community. Is nothing sacred anymore? Doesn't HP have thirty-seven buildings in this bucolic residential town? Not to mention that 20 percent of Palo Alto residents are HP alumni or still work there. What will happen to the headquarters building on Hanover Street—a wonderfully understated complex far larger than can be appreciated from any outside vista except an airplane? Speculation was that the company will be moving to Cupertino—lock, stock, and barrel. Why? It somehow seemed unthinkable. Town leaders have not supported HP particularly well, but no one in the city's administration seemed to have considered that this iconic company of Palo Alto might pick up and leave.

Palo Alto has long been ambivalent about growth and industry, and about its evolution as a community. The social costs of the Oregon Expressway—condemning thirty-one houses in return for a mere five thousand jobs and an incredibly robust tax base—seemed inordinate to a clamorous committee in 1958. Roadway access, especially commuter traffic, is resented in Palo Alto to this day. Obstructive actions have been the continuing bane of any company seeking to operate in the community. Stanford University, with fifteen square miles of land, is not allowed to build parking lots because they'll bring cars through "our town." One of the world's great research universities, Stanford earns top ratings in more professional disciplines than any other American institution. Its campus offers the easiest potential access from interstate highways and airports, and compared to all of its competitors is the only one that isn't land-choked. Because of city and county land use restrictions, however, Stanford is unable to construct parking facilities on its own land that are even remotely commensurate with its needs. Analogously, Palo Alto blocked the logical extension of Sand Hill Road to El Camino Real for forty years; when it was finally allowed, the city required that the egress be diverted into neighboring Menlo Park rather than connecting into downtown Palo Alto.

The greatest indignity may be the city-mandated stop sign for Stanford Industrial Park commuters exiting southbound Interstate 280 at Page Mill Road. For over an hour every workday morning, the line snakes back a mile onto the freeway, creating an average fifteen-minute daily delay for several thousand workers. The productivity loss, figured at corporate rates, is $30 million of lost time per year—never mind the ragged nerves, higher accident rates, and psychological damage.

One might imagine that CEO Mark Hurd resolutely considered the options. Bill Sullivan, his counterpart at the far smaller Agilent Technologies, had summarily dismissed Palo Alto three years earlier. Even with a wholly owned, brand-new headquarters facility at 395 Page Mill Road, HP's original location in Palo Alto, Sullivan calculated that a bifurcated company divided by fifteen miles had high productivity loss compared to consolidating all operations on the company's Santa Clara site at Stevens Creek Boulevard and Lawrence Expressway, next to Interstate 280, six miles from the San Jose airport freeway exit. Agilent Technologies traced its heritage to Palo Alto even more than HP—Palo Alto had already chased Packard's team out by the time the computing initiative began.

On a long-owned, ninety-five-acre complex, bounded by North Wolfe Road and Tantau Avenue on the west and east sides, Pruneridge Avenue and Homestead Road on south and north sides, HP has plans to construct a series of eight-story buildings—hardly the stuff of high-rise New York City, but much higher than Palo Alto ordinances would ever allow, with site density that can accommodate HP's local thirty-thousand-person workforce. First reports suggest that HP's traditionally understated, disguised, low-profile style will be maintained—the twenty-two buildings on the site today are nearly invisible from any of the major streets, screened by tasteful berms and lush plantings. The new headquarters locale is 1.3 miles from Agilent Technologies' new headquarters, 7.7 miles from the San Jose airport exit, and 13.4 miles from the current HP Hanover Street headquarters. The two new company HQs are virtually the same distance apart as they were in Palo Alto, between 395 and 1501 Page Mill Road.

Towns sometimes take pride in driving out, or keeping out, industrial activities. For example, Santa Barbara, California, evicted Lockheed Aircraft, MGM Studios, and Kinko's as each developed past fledgling days. Boulder, Colorado, successfully kept at bay IBM, HP, and other high-tech firms who wanted synergy with the university. And companies do leave "company towns." Boeing forsook Seattle for Chicago, even though nearly all of its operations (and jobs) remained in its old locale.

One wonders—does Palo Alto really want HP to leave? Is traffic really that bad? Are the Stanford lease renewal terms that onerous? Is the sharp reduction in HP-sponsored research at Stanford since 2002 a precursor? Who decides who decides?

A week later, another insult to local communities occurred. Larry Ellison, reputed to be America's tenth-richest man at $14 billion in assets, sued the San Mateo County Assessor's office and won a reduction in his property taxes of a cool $3.06 million per year. He reasoned that the city was basing the tax assessment on the true cost of his home, $170 million, while the odds were that it wouldn't be resold for that amount.[89] Well, duh. The local papers, reflecting on the sizable losses for Portola Valley and Woodside school districts, lamented the decision.

Meanwhile at the Los Altos Museum, a six-month celebration of the lives of two residents—Lucile and David Packard—displayed some of their legacy, including gifts of the Stanford Children's Hospital and the 28,539-acre San Felipé ranch to the Nature Conservancy.[90] In sharp and poignant contrast to today's Silicon Valley leadership, which too often seems caricatured by greedy billionaires, stock option fraud, and pretexting, the Packards made a decision in 1963 to pay full residential property taxes on their new 33-acre Los Altos Hills property on Taaffe Road, even though the city had offered them the chance to file for an agricultural exemption.

In one of three letters on display, they stated, "We believe most of that tax money goes to local schools, and we want to pay our fair share."[91]

A Curious Leadership Style

As the 21st century unfolds, with global competition the norm and company managements besieged at every turn, Larry Ellison's egocentric style somehow seems much more consonant with American company leadership than that of the civic-minded Packard. Pundits have offered time and again the shopworn counsel that Packard's approach is anachronistic, unsuited to today's cutthroat climate, and indeed that the HP Way itself is an impediment to the company that would be better off discarded. And yet, HP's track record is really astonishing. The company morphed its leading product line six times, resulting in more renewal, more consistent and sizable growth, and more transformation than any other large company has ever displayed. With the EDS merger, HP is nearly 20 percent larger than IBM—hard to imagine—but it has managed to understate accomplishments, still focused more on results than publicity.

The myth says that prescient leadership by Hewlett and Packard guided the company, and the nimble, lithe company was able to take advantage of unrecognized market opportunity—thus building a remarkable growth engine unhampered by tradition or past success. Yet Packard, a curmudgeon, was often hard to persuade to undertake any new program; Hewlett, an enthusiast, usually had a short attention span. Neither was particularly product-strategic, accounting for some surprising omissions and short-sighted approaches—for example, oscilloscopes, personal computers, and software—and each had inordinate trust in the decentralized model, which proved costly and nearly fatal in the systems business. What they were was entrepreneurial, long before that word became popular in the business world. And it showed. They operated, rather than managed. They acted, listened, noticed, reacted, and acted again. Once the Objectives were written, they didn't write much else. They communicated, mostly in small ways—handing out steaks at the picnic, the occasional blowup, the focus on profits, the feature-set drive for leadership. And, as Packard did in the lobby in Beijing, they decided. They seldom revisited a decision; getting on with it was paramount.

Packard was very reluctant to enter the microwave test field, despite the entreaties of his mentor, Fred Terman. Hewlett, agnostic at best, never got involved directly in these products. It remains ironic that neither founder was excited by the oscilloscope opportunity or challenge. As Tektronix empowered an entire field of digital electronics, the founders dawdled. Goaded into action by their sales representatives, they mounted a tepid response. The oscilloscope, the largest single electronic instrumentation product of the twentieth century, lacked the effective presence of the largest electronic instrumentation manufacturer of the twentieth century.

The scientific instrumentation shift was also spasmodic. In buying Sanborn, neither Hewlett nor Packard did rigorous due diligence—they failed even to read the Harvard Business School case about the company. Most famously, both founders were resistant to entering the computer field. Packard insisted that the first machine be called an instrument controller. Hewlett would get excited about the desktop calculator, not the minicomputer. Both men were even more resistant to business computing. On the other hand, when Packard placed Ely in charge, he left no doubt that they were ready to commit HP to computing—a sharp about-face.

Eventually, Hewlett earned much praise from analysts and business school pundits for his boldness in bucking Packard, the executive committee, and a glum SRI market research report to launch the HP 35 handheld calculator. The device propelled HP into a new era, not just of computing, but of high-volume consumer product sales. Dave challenged everyone, though, saying "the only thing worse than a small shitty business is a large shitty business," but he let them continue.

Early on, Hewlett was also enthusiastic about the Laser printer business, but nine years later—after the second Watershed—he was absent for the LaserJet launch. Headquarters and the field sales teams showed antipathy just as with earlier transformative products. Ely drove the pricing decision; Hackborn, not Hewlett, defended both the unpopular OEM partnership agreement with Canon and the lack of support for HP computers. The founders practiced benign neglect; CEO Young on occasion campaigned against the laser printing business.

Leading from behind? A curious leadership style! Who decides who decides?

EPILOGUE

Where Now?

FEBRUARY 26, 2008, NEW YORK CITY: "HP Firing on All Cylinders in the Fiscal First Quarter." Somewhere, in the wintry confines of Westchester County, New York, there are a whole lot of executives at IBM who must be asking perplexing questions. Why did we get out of the printer business that is dominated by Hewlett-Packard and that gives the company so much profit? Why did we sell the PC business? Why didn't we buy Compaq to become the market leader in X86 and now X64 servers? How did HP get to be bigger than Big Blue in the IT space?

Such are the kinds of questions that it would be reasonable to ask as HP reported a fine opening to its fiscal 2008 financial year last week, with sales up 13 percent to $28.5 billion in the first quarter ended January 31. Even more significantly for HP, which has been challenged in years gone by to turn a profit from its Compaq acquisition, this no longer seems to be as much of a problem, with HP bringing $2.1 billion to the bottom line, up 38 percent from the year-ago quarter.[1]

By the end of second quarter 2008, Hewlett-Packard had achieved another milestone, passing the $1 trillion mark in cumulative products shipped and services provided in its history. With strong origins as a measurements company, it is remarkable how seldom HP talks about the revenue measures that compare its success to others. Catching IBM in equipment sales in 2002 and in overall sales in 2006 went unmentioned; becoming the first high-tech company to surpass the $100 billion revenue threshold in 2007 didn't merit a press release either.

Hewlett-Packard has grown more consistently than every rival it has ever faced, while maintaining a very high degree of employee loyalty and enthusiasm through a remarkable series of shifts in fundamental business direction. While events of the past decade have been tumultuous, every decade had its challenge; at no time was it clear that the path forward was simple or without peril. And yes, there have been costs—costs in specific jobs, costs to the ideal of employee compassion and concern, assaults even on the loyalty and fealty of alumni and employees alike on occasion. But as Packard often observed, without profits and without growth, nothing good can happen for the corporation, including its employees and customers. And that instinct for growth and for profit while remarkably still adhering to the ethics and ethos of the HP Way seems yet to characterize this company.

Disquieting Moments

Empowered mavericks and product contribution seemed far more often to make the difference than bold, prescient leadership from the top in terms of defining response to changing market conditions. The renewal factor, fundamental to revenue and profit growth over the years, was driven heavily by the decentralized autonomy built into the model. How will this "local initiative" work in a corporation of three hundred thousand employees with operations in 140 countries? Two examples from early 2009—a period of high uncertainty in national and international economics—give pause.

Citizenship in the Nation

Since John Young set up and chaired the National Council on Competitiveness in 1986, education—especially math and science education—has been a top priority for America. Following Young's leadership, chairmen and CEOs of IBM, Intel, Motorola, Dupont, BellSouth, Kodak, Qualcomm, GE, Merck, and Fedex among many other companies have volunteered much time and effort on this cause.

Cisco's chairman, John Morgridge, and CEO John Chambers, have been vocal on the national and international scene about improving education.

As Intel CEO, Craig Barrett carried the cudgel for the John Glenn Education Commission in Washington, D.C., and since—saying as chairman at the Intel Developer Forum in August 2008 that he has been to seventy-two countries in the past year, and the United States ranks at the very bottom for disinterest and lack of skill in mathematics and science achievement. He blames parents, company leadership, and government mismanagement as well as the school system for this national disgrace. More important, he vehemently asserts that it cannot help but injure if not kill American leadership in the technical world of tomorrow.

Dell Computer and Apple Computer have for years dominated the educational computing side of the K–12 and higher education tools for students, with both companies' chairmen—Michael Dell and Steve Jobs—on record repeatedly about the importance of the educational experience for students.

The founder and chairman of Microsoft, Bill Gates, has donated enormous sums from the Gates Foundation for improving education both locally and internationally. He and his CEO, Steve Ballmer, have made education one of their key issues for the past two years. Scott McNealy, chairman of Sun Microsystems, in 2008 funded the Curriki Foundation for open-source educational curricula, which by spring 2009 listed more than nine thousand courses available online for anyone with an Internet connection.

Sam Palmisano, CEO of IBM, vigorously campaigned in autumn and winter 2008 for infrastructure improvement as the surest way to deal with the depressed economy, with the educational opportunities as the content to ride on that backbone. Full-page advertisements and letters to the editor in leading newspapers and business magazines from Palmisano himself became almost routine.

American high-tech leaders were weighing in on the issues, the problems, and the opportunities.

On April 7, 2009, the *Wall Street Journal* featured a story describing the fruits of some of this effort. The Obama stimulus package includes large grant capabilities for improving infrastructure, equipment, and training materials. Cisco, Microsoft, Oracle, Apple, Dell, and Autodesk were featured in the article; Sun and IBM made headlines in the story above it.[2]

Given the historic Hewlett-Packard objective of citizenship, the legacy of scientific and engineering quality and excellence, and especially the large donation of executive time and money by the company for educational activities over decades, it seems curious that HP has no one visibly involved in this discussion. With the perceived crisis level in the country, one might hope that HP's new position as the largest high-tech company on the globe could be leveraged for societal advancement.

Unfortunately, there is scant evidence at the moment that HP's legacy of civic leadership is valued or even comprehended by the company's board of directors or the executive office—in sharp contrast to the leadership of nearly every other sizable high-tech firm in America. One wag offered that HP outsourced their seventh objective. Americans and the world community might hope that this is a temporary aberration.

Engineering Excellence

APRIL 14, 2009: Eighty-three people came together in the Pavilion Café in HP's Building 3 at 1501 Page Mill Road, Palo Alto, California, for the presentation of an IEEE Milestone in Electrical Engineering award by the outgoing president of IEEE, Dr. Lew Terman. Prith Banerjee, vice president of HP Laboratories, and Todd Bradley, executive vice president of the Personal Systems Group, welcomed the invitees, invoking the aura of the world's first electronic product that combined a microprocessor and a light-emitting-diode display—the HP 35 Scientific Calculator. Dave Cochran, the product manager for the HP 35, read the contribution and the name of each of the ten people on the design team who were represented in the room—developers of HP's most famous "game-changer" product. When it was announced, HP had sixteen hundred products in the catalog; none sold more than ten per day. Within weeks, the HP 35 was selling more than one thousand per day, changing HP processes and perspective irrevocably.

Tom Whitney's widow, Donna, accepted the award on his behalf, while his two coauthors of the seminal paper "The Powerful Pocketful," France Rodé and Chung Tung, walked forward along with legendary Tom Osborne, Rich Marconi, Ken Peterson, Dick Osgood, and Phil Missan, plus Chu Yen's son on his behalf. Their HP Labs manager, Paul Stoft, bedridden, sent his regards; Bill Hewlett's name was invoked again and again.[3]

Dave Cochran mentioned the irony and full-circle nature of Silicon Valley as he introduced Lew Terman to the group. Terman's father, of course, was the fabled Fred Terman, who befriended Bill Hewlett and Dave Packard seventy-five years earlier and nurtured them through their first forty years in business. Cochran couldn't resist telling the story about the elder Terman finding the first software bug in the HP 35 prototype, as well as the story about General Electric sending a Request for Quotation (RFQ) for twenty thousand units—presumably one for every engineer, to which Hewlett quipped, "no, they should borrow from one another."[4]

Whither the HP Way

On the one hand, it is tempting to conclude that HP's "local initiative" model is more aligned to the world of tomorrow than the command-and-control structures of most large corporations—and the tenets and precepts of the HP Way, when absorbed into the merged "family" of Compaq and EDS employees, will provide uncommonly powerful incentives and guidelines for handling the ambiguity of future market challenges. On the other hand, history would remind us that "the bigger they are, the harder they fall." In truth, success is never guaranteed in the future—and one might imagine two startlingly diverse scenarios for HP in the next thirty years.

And the Results Were . . . Scenario 1

OCTOBER 2038, PALO ALTO, CALIFORNIA: For the one-hundredth anniversary of HP and Agilent Technologies, the behemoth corporations founded as one company in this small town—once the center of the Valley of Heart's Delight—employees and alumni gathered at The Garage for a simple dedication. Odes were composed, orations offered, and memories invoked. Two names kept coming up with reverence and awe—Bill and Dave, the "H" and "P" of HP.

A few attendees recalled that others led at critical junctures—Barney Oliver and Joel Birnbaum in technology; Paul Ely and Dick Hackborn in group leadership; John Young, Lew Platt, and Mark Hurd as CEOs. Each made a fundamental contribution at a watershed moment. For their Warhol moment of fame, they got credit at the time, and their role is secure in posterity. Carly Fiorina, too, made a singular contribution, but she was recalled more somberly. Some charitably recalled her as a catalyst for necessary change—but the term *catalyst* was not precise. Three others were catalysts—the founders and Hackborn. Two were creatives—Birnbaum and Oliver. The CEOs—Hurd as much as Young and Platt—were immersed in activity and fundamental to major consolidation and managerial excellence.

Fiorina was all of the above, but, like Robespierre, she became a reactant, a cathartic sacrifice; by definition, catalysts are not consumed in the reaction they provoke, whereas reactants are. Carly saved HP from mediocrity as the Web 2.0 convulsive world unfolded. She was not unlike Paul Ely, who resolutely steered the company into uncharted waters as the computing world exploded all around the world's greatest instrumentation company. Each generated a torrent of press, a veritable flood of change, polarizing admiration or distaste. The saddest day for each, they independently reported, was their last day at HP—each left without fanfare or adulation.[5] Arguably, each was far and away the most important individual of his or her HP era, however brief. It is inconceivable that the Hewlett-Packard of Bill and Dave, sans computing, would have mattered in any significant way—never mind the HP 35, which was blunted relatively quickly by TI's predatory practices. Indeed, without Paul Ely's determined quest for computing leadership, the opportunity for HP to hire a Joel Birnbaum would never have arisen, and without Birnbaum, HP's history would look very different. It is equally inconceivable that the phlegmatic Hewlett-Packard at the end of the twentieth century would have rallied in short order to challenge IBM for supremacy on every front, let alone stare down Dell and rekindle momentum, without Fiorina's bold, aggressive leadership during the Compaq merger. Hurd's style, reminiscent of Packard's steady hand and focus on fundamentals, is not given to deft strategic surgery—in his own words, "We're just trying to run the fundamentals of a sound business."[6] Those from Agilent Technologies in the audience agreed that Ned Barnholt and Bill Sullivan at Agilent seemed of the same mold as Hurd—stolid and straightforward—and their fragmented company showed mixed results.

Somewhat inexplicably, but in full alignment with the HP Way and legacy, Hurd and his successors had been bold—redefining and providing IT services with an innate humane dignity that empowered local initiative and contribution in a very different manner from the slash-and-burn "outsourcing for efficiency at all costs" approach of most IT-services competitors. Not understood for a very long time by competitors, it proved to be a unique model for customer interaction that built loyalty and persistent partnership between HP and its clients, as well as within the client firms. In effect, they exported the HP Way to their clients.

The ceremony at the landmark garage, a mere twenty-two minutes, was understated and modest. Some in the audience asked, "Is this really the world's largest corporation?" Others murmured, "Yes, and it has always been a pretty special place. Here, the HP Way was pioneered."

And the Results Were . . . Scenario 2

OCTOBER 2038, PALO ALTO, CALIFORNIA: For the one-hundredth anniversary of the founding of HP and Agilent Technologies, alumni gathered at The Garage for a simple dedication. Odes were composed, orations offered, and memories invoked. Two names kept coming up with reverence and awe—Bill and Dave, the "H" and "P" of HP.

A few attendees recalled that others led at critical junctures—Carly Fiorina's term was cited as the turning point. She, according to many, signaled the end of the HP Way. No one could recall how she got there or why, but many seemed clear that she had somehow led HP into something it should never have become—focused on "brand," sans distinguishing engineering, a marketing company rather than a product leader and contributor. Some, unclear about the actual details, were sorry that she had gotten rid of Agilent Technologies, since it seemed now to be doing better than Hewlett-Packard. Perceptions that day were much stronger than facts—most would have been surprised to learn that Lew Platt, not Fiorina, divested HP instrumentation.

Everyone agreed that as the convulsive Web 2.0 world unfolded, Silicon Valley's innovative edge seemed somehow lost, and the consequent job loss for America was staggering. Some recalled that HP briefly exceeded $100 billion in revenues, but that was long ago; and aside from a few consolidators, HP and most American corporations had imploded with the rise of the e-trading companies centered primarily in the BRIC countries (Brazil, Russia, India, and China). Amazingly, Agilent Technologies, still about the same size that it was at the turn of the century, was not only as large as the savagely down-sized HP, it had a strong culture in which people loved the company and revered its leadership. HP, by contrast, was said to have lost that in the wake of two monumental acquisitions—one with Compaq, and one with EDS. Several ex-VPs wistfully said, "After that, there was nothing special about the place—the HP Way was dead, dead, dead."

The ceremony at the landmark garage, a mere twenty-two minutes, was understated and modest. Some in the audience said, "It must have been a pretty special place when they pioneered the HP Way." Others murmured, "Yes, I wonder why they let it go."

What Would Dave 'n' Bill Have Done?

How will the legacy—now with DNA planted firmly in two California-based corporations—evolve in the next century? Will the HP Way—intangible, hard to quantify, but real nonetheless for hundreds of thousands of employees and alumni—continue to animate the current and future employees and executives of Hewlett-Packard and Agilent Technologies, or will it ebb, to the point that these companies are relatively indistinguishable from their brethren?

Somehow, it feels important—important for the legacy, doubly important for the future, and maybe most of all, important for the world to know that decency, ethics, and concern for the individual on the one hand and for the community on the other can be combined with effective business practices and contribution in products, services, and process for customers, vendors, employees, and shareholders alike. Bill 'n' Dave would have been proud if that persists.

APPENDIX A

HP Transformations

FIGURE A.1. The 1st transformation—audio-video test → microwave test

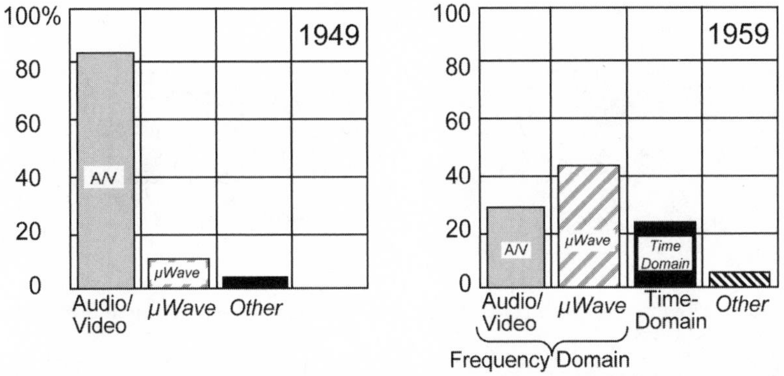

FIGURE A.2. The 2nd transformation—frequency domain test → scientific test

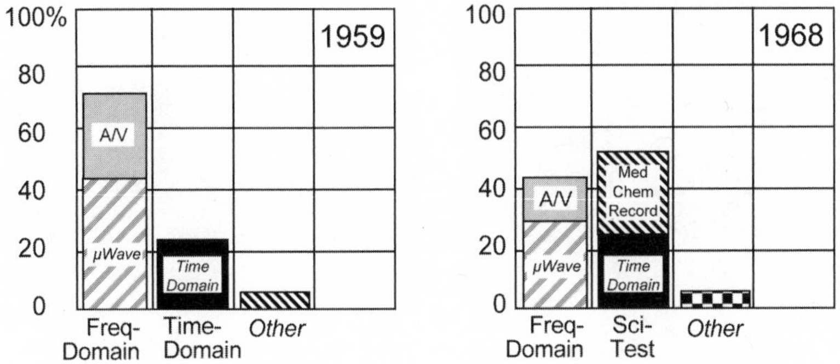

FIGURE A.3. The 3rd transformation—electrical engineering test → scientific systems

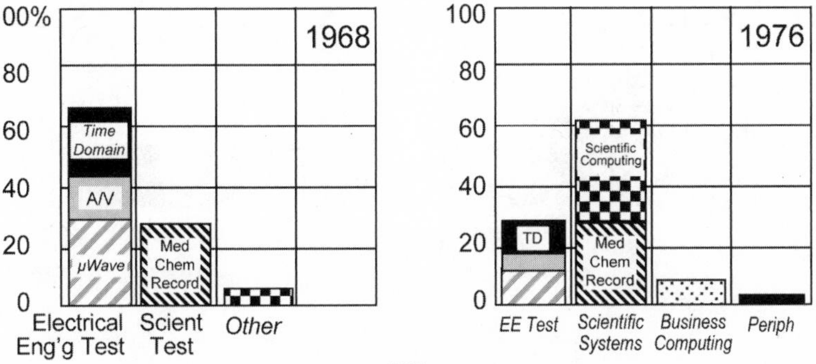

FIGURE A.4. The 4th transformation—scientific systems → business computing

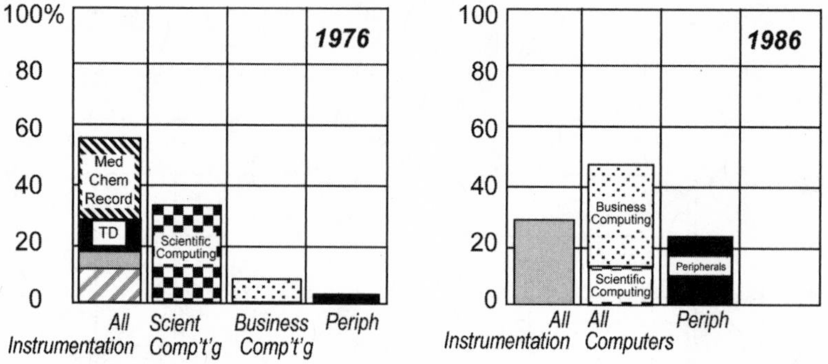

FIGURE A.5. The 5th transformation—computing → printing and imaging

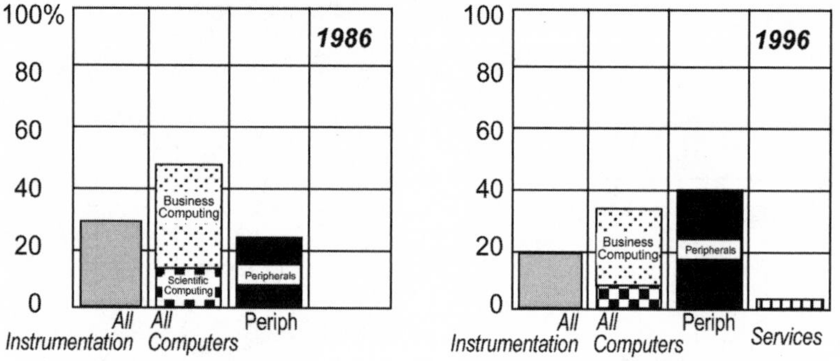

FIGURE A.6. The 6th transformation—enterprise → professional services

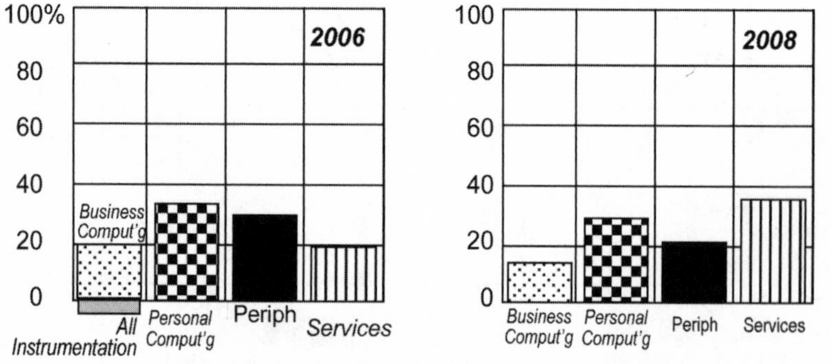

APPENDIX B

Packard's "Simple Rules"—aka "The Eleven Rules"

At the second management conference, in Sonoma in 1958, Packard felt it appropriate to address the management side. Packard's "Simple Rules,"[1] recorded by the new human resources director, Ray Wilbur, have been called "elegant" and "timeless" by many:

1. *Think first of the other fellow.* This is THE foundation—the first requisite—for getting along with others. And it is the one truly difficult accomplishment you must make. Gaining this, the rest will be "a breeze."
2. *Build up the other person's sense of importance.* When we make the other person seem less important, we frustrate one of his deepest urges. Allow him to feel equality or superiority, and we can easily get along with him.
3. *Respect the other man's personality rights.* Respect as something sacred the other fellow's right to be different from you. No two personalities are ever molded by precisely the same forces.
4. *Give sincere appreciation.* If we think someone has done a thing well, we should never hesitate to let him know it. Warning: This does not mean promiscuous use of obvious flattery. Flattery with most intelligent people gets exactly the reaction it deserves—contempt for the egotistical "phony" who stoops to it.
5. *Eliminate the negative.* Criticism seldom does what its user intends, for it invariably causes resentment. The tiniest bit of disapproval can sometimes cause a resentment which will rankle—to your disadvantage—for years.
6. *Avoid openly trying to reform people.* Every man knows he is imperfect, but he doesn't want someone else trying to correct his faults. If you want to improve a person, help him to embrace a higher working goal—a standard, an ideal—and he will do his own "making over" far more effectively than you can do it for him.

7. *Try to understand the other person.* How would you react to similar circumstances? When you begin to see the "whys" of him you can't help but get along better with him.
8. *Check first impressions.* We are especially prone to dislike some people on first sight because of some vague resemblance (of which we are usually unaware) to someone else whom we have had reason to dislike. Follow Abraham Lincoln's famous self-instruction: "I do not like that man; therefore I shall get to know him better."
9. *Take care with the little details.* Watch your smile; your tone of voice; how you use your eyes; the way you greet people; the use of nicknames; and remembering faces, names, and dates. Little things add polish to your skill in dealing with people. Constantly, deliberately think of them until they become a natural part of your personality.
10. *Develop genuine interest in people.* You cannot successfully apply the foregoing suggestions unless you have a sincere desire to like, respect, and be helpful to others. Conversely, you cannot build genuine interest in people until you have experienced the pleasure of working with them in an atmosphere characterized by mutual liking and respect.
11. *Keep it up.* That's all—just keep it up!

APPENDIX C

Memorable David Packard Speeches

Give 'em Hell[1]

We don't have to have every goddamn thing we're doing gold plated, and we can find places where we can save money, and we can get the job done just as well.

DAVE PACKARD

I heard about it first from a friend at Santa Clara Division—"Dave has gone off the deep end." Al Bagley confirmed that, but offered that the Computer Group "had it coming." He was glad that Pappy had stepped in as the mean one—said it was about time. Maybe a week later, Hal Edmondson called us all into one of the HP Colorado Springs conference rooms, and in strode Dave. He looked none too happy, I thought, with the unruly shock of nearly gray hair framing his gaunt face. The room was abuzz with chatter—I took it that most folk hadn't heard from the Bay Area just yet.

Hal quieted the crowd and announced our visitor. "Dave Packard is touring the company," he said, "to talk about our business performance." And with that, Hal stood aside and Packard, visibly older than I had remembered, began, with that familiar Colorado drawl, almost a slurred speech. Dave was never an orator, but on this day, he proved to be some speaker.

The opening was a dead giveaway:

Well, Gentlemen, I think it's a good thing for us to take a few minutes here this year and go back and remind ourselves of some of the things that we seem to have forgotten. I suppose each one of you was just as shocked as Bill and I were when we got the figures together and found out that the profits were such that they did not support as high a bonus this year as they did last year, and you know Bill got a little mad about it and I guess he got carried away over the PA, and he really didn't blame the right people, but in any case, I think it happened just because we were kind of soft about it, and there are a number of things that troubled us, but I guess one of the most serious was that we had known that there had been some problems during the year.

Wow, 122 words without pause in that sentence! I thought, boy, he is worked up.

We didn't realize that the problems were as bad as they were, and the fact that we didn't know until the last minute was a very troublesome thing. So I thought it might be helpful to take a few minutes and see if we can really define what some of our management objectives in this company should be and what I'm going to tell you today is not anything that you don't already know or shouldn't already know, but for some reason we've gotten a little bit off the track in the last couple of years. For some reason, we've got this talking about one of our objectives is to increase the share of the market, and I want to start right out by telling you that that is not a legitimate management objective of this company, that it leads you to the wrong kind of decisions, and that hereafter if I hear anybody talking about how big their share of the market is or what they're trying to do to increase their share, I'm going to personally see that a black mark gets put in their personnel folder, and I want you to understand that because that's extremely important.

Again, a run-on sentence of more than a hundred words, but this time his voice raised for the second half of the sentence, as he cast a baleful eye around the room. People averted their eyes as his gaze fell on them—no question, the old man is wrought up. We just didn't know the full extent of it yet. He continued,

Anybody can increase the share of the market by giving away their products, and that's exactly what we did in some cases in this company the last couple of years. This is not a subject that you people here were responsible for, but we have a rather significant share of the market in CATV amplifiers, and we'd be just a hell of a lot better off if we hadn't ever touched that business and if our share was zero. So, that's one of the reasons in my view that we've made some very bad mistakes in management, and that's the first lesson of this afternoon.

[Drucker] says that growth always requires that management of one man or a small handful of men be replaced by a genuine top management team. One way in which the chief executive of a small business that has growth ambitions can prepare himself for that day when the company will have outgrown management by one man is to build a top management team at the earliest possible moment.

Well, that of course is what Bill and I have been trying to do, and if our results in 1973 are any indication, we've not been very successful so far, so what I'm talking to you about is that we've got to somehow get this management team of ours so that it's on top of the job and this is going to determine the future success or failure of this company, and it's a very serious matter.

Somewhere about this point in the speech, we collectively realized something we maybe hadn't thought about quite this way before. Dave Packard was talking to us as though we're all the management team. He wasn't talking about John Young and some of the other Palo Alto managers—he was talking to us, and he saw this as our failing. After all, it's our company. This was the most powerful part of the talk:

Now if we go down and look at this (details in the new *Annual Report*) in terms of the various segments of the company, we found that Data Products looked very good. Indeed, their sales increased by 99 percent from 1972 to 1973, and their pre-tax earnings increased by 75 percent. Now this looks good, except that the one message that I want to get over today—I haven't gotten around to it yet, but I might as well tell you what it's going to be—is that management's primary requirement of the future is to get your pre-tax earnings to increase annually as fast as your sales, as fast as your shipments, so that by that measure, Data Products' performance, even though it was spectacular in terms of its overall magnitude, did not represent what I consider to be the kind of management that's going to keep this company on a sound footing in the future.

Packard was just standing in the front of the room, reading from the *Annual Report*. He analyzed each group, showing eventually that no one had done a worthy job—Instruments for example, grew 17 percent (the best showing in five years), but pre-tax earnings were only up 7 percent. He closed this section by noting that if APD (the new handheld calculators) and the desktop calculators had been excluded from the calculations, the rest of the company grew 23 percent, but pre-tax earnings shrank by 8 percent.

A little education was in order on balance sheets, information that appeared to be a bit arcane for most of the attendees in our room. He noticed as well, and practically roared at us:

Take accounts receivable . . . There is no justification for our accounts receivable to go up in one year any more than our sales went up percentage-wise. One of the difficulties here was that somehow you fellows didn't think this was a part of your responsibility, I guess, because you didn't do anything about it. . . .

Our inventories, finished goods, went up 49 percent. For the life of me, I don't understand why the hell we had finished goods inventories going up 49 percent when we had sales going up only 38 percent and when we had plenty of orders on hand to ship more. What the hell are we keeping all this goddamn stuff in finished inventory for? Now that's your job. . . . When you talk about raw materials, our raw material inventory went up 92 percent between 1972 and 1973. Now I understand that in running a manufacturing shop that it's a hell of a lot easier to run it if you've got three times as much raw materials on hand as you need, and that just makes it a very easy job, and if that's the way we're going to run this company, we don't need professional managers. We need a bunch of kindergarten kids, and so if you fellows who are responsible for running this manufacturing area can't keep your inventories in line, we're just going to find someone that can, and it's just as simple as that. . . . We had a lot of meetings during the year, and everybody had an excuse and a lot of rationalization, and all we want to do today is try to get the idea over, that we're not going to put up with this in the future, and I just want you all to understand that.

The old man was florid now, his hair even more askew and he uncharacteristically paced about. Usually when he read things, he would put his bifocals on and then take them off, repeatedly. It was a classic nervous tic. But this time was different—he was really on a roll, to be sure with a few notes and that *Annual Report,* but it was vintage Dave.

After a few more minutes of balance sheet education and Return on Equity discussion, Dave turned to some pet topics, things that he felt we could each take away:

I want to outline the specific management actions that are your responsibility and which, if done properly, will result in this end result we're talking about. The first responsibility you have is to control your profit as a percent of sales, and you have . . . three specific ways by which this can be done.

The first one is by pricing. . . . I was shocked to find some places in the company where we came out with a hell of a good product and where people had failed to price it in order to make a profit on a current basis. They got into the same goddamn trouble I used to have when I was on the board at Varian that they were always going to make a profit mañana, thinking they could get their costs down, and they never could, and they never did. I expect this pricing to be done so that it's going to pay off in the first year of that product and not when you think you're going to get your learning curve down, because you're never going to get your learning curve down where you think it'll go. I've seen this happen over and over again.

Moving to Perkins' Boston Consulting Group notions, Packard was having none of it. And he went on for some time on this topic before concluding that section of his talk with a pithy wrap-up: "I guess that really where I came out is that our management team failed in just about every count that I would call a measure of good management in 1973."

February 25, 1974

A Founder's Benediction[2]

The meeting was really upbeat. HP's fiftieth anniversary, our first $10 billion year, first $1 billion product, first $100 million customer, first $100 million dealer, and first one million units shipped of LaserJet—all significant milestones. And the year's first two months were off to a flying start, the best in five years—ahead by 31 percent, with Personal Computers, Peripherals, and yes, Workstations pacing the advance. One wag noted that it was the first time in five years that the sales force wasn't reorganized—he was quickly dismissed.

And, as significant as the gains were, the concerns were low—most notably the MPE woes that had plagued the HP-PA introduction for three years (and sorely tested the 3000 computer customer base) were reported to be behind us. The measure? MTBF (Mean-Time Between Failure) was up from five days in third quarter 1988 to thirty-five days in fourth quarter 1988. Vast, collective sigh of relief.

Equally important, we had gone back to our heritage—profit-based divisions—with the November reorganization. Rows and columns are a historic aberration. Thank gawd! So, unabashed confidence. Amid all this, by way of postscript, Dave Packard strode to the podium. As usual, he gave a short talk at the end. With the familiar slow slurred speech pattern, a product of his Colorado youth, with a goodly dose of "home-spun pragmatic" and the infectious sincere "Congratulations." We had all (many of us at least) heard him so much, came to know and trust and value his wisdom, come to know the stories, that as I glanced about the room it seemed somehow soporific. People weren't *not listening*, but they weren't *actively listening* either. It's sort of like singing the National Anthem or a Christmas Carol—you know it so well, it's so comfortable and so right, you become attuned to the point of unconscious consciousness.

And, realistically, Dave Packard was decoupled from the company that bears his name. Had been for years, but it hit me forcibly, at that moment. At HP's half-century mark, he observed that there's more opportunity now, for us, in the next period, than he and Bill ever faced in the beginning. And his sorrow in not being able to make the trip with us. Along with his and Bill's satisfaction that we were doing a great job—

things are in very good shape, how pleased they are, etc. A most familiar and reassuring theme.

He paused, softened his tone even more, observed that Bill was recovering from his heart attack and that he was sure he could speak for both of them, as indeed he has for this remarkable pair for fifty years. He could have then shifted to his basketball team story—we all knew it by heart, but we wanted to hear it again from the master. So comforting, so right to have your mentor, your coach, your idol, or your father intone the wisdom you cut your teeth on. But he didn't—no, he began with some concerns.

Yes, the meeting was upbeat. But he couldn't help concluding that many speakers believed their own stories, and he wondered aloud if the customers would be as sanguine. And he was deeply disturbed by the apparent interest and desire of all the corporate departments to "*help you boys out,*" and Dave opined that he doubted if we needed all that much help. Dave often slips into the "you boys" phrase just as I do about "the kids" doing the real work. It didn't come across as demeaning or sexist, at least to me, just another comfortable "and that's how he is" kind of recognition. Far less offensive to me than the significantly visible error of the Personnel department slide that lamented our 0.2 percent of women for the top 150 managers of HP. One wonders if Laura Cory, Nancy Anderson, and Carolyn Ticknor came to some agreement as to which of them served as the one-third of one person cited. Ah, those powers of ten that Charles and Ray Eames illustrated so well, that all engineers mastered, before Bill's HP 35 calculator changed the world's math skills irrevocably.

And then, a surprise, a real surprise. "*I think Bill Craven gave a very important talk.*" It had been a good talk, by the group manager for Components, the smallest real group of the company—some 2 percent of sales. And Craven, who'd seldom been billed as one of HP's premier speakers, had acquitted himself well.

Craven had described the newly enhanced aluminizing process for getting far more light output from our optoelectronic LEDs using gallium arsenide phosphide processing. His illustration—a very bright 1989 Ford Taurus taillight, manufactured with our LEDs. Dave began to weave a story about Bill Craven calling us "*a leading American vendor.*" Dave, who is among the least boastful business people I've ever known, started to say that we were a leading worldwide vendor, and then he switched, saying that we are *the* leading worldwide vendor. He then went on to note that he and Bill (Hewlett, not Craven) just felt in the early 1960s that any technology such as optoelectronics had to be fundamental because it coupled electronic precision with visual display using integrated circuit technology, which was reliable and very amenable to major cost reductions.

Warming to his topic now, he observed that he and Bill got "*lots of advice*" not to do it for years and years. "*HP couldn't develop critical mass.*" "*It wasn't consistent with or easily complementary to our other product lines.*" "*It wouldn't ever be profitable.*" He observed that it took a decade (and then only through the luck of the emerging high-volume pocket calculator market) to become profitable. It took fifteen years to become a leading company, and now, after twenty-five years we finally are the leaders. He softly added that it usually takes that long to come out "on top" in a formidable arena. He didn't add, but my guess is that we all heard to some degree, that he *expected* us to come out on top in each of our endeavors.

And then, he went down one of the side jaunts that I have always enjoyed so much: "*That reminds me—we were concerned about exploring the Monterey Trench the other day.*" Right. Totally disconnected, unrelated thought. Newer people in the audience, those who hadn't heard Dave or been around him too much, didn't have the value of history behind them to know how synergistically and pragmatically this man thinks.

"*We need good fiber-optics technology to be able to 'see' a mile deep in the ocean.*" Mercifully he omitted the digression about their goal being to find giant squid at that depth, and how hard it is to sneak up on them with a noisy motor-driven submersible on a mile-long tether:

Now, in the early seventies, Bill and I thought fiber optics would be a fundamental communications technology by the end of the century, so we started a program at the Labs. After ten years, we had made some good progress, and last year (some fifteen years in, now), I came to the Labs for help at the aquarium—and I found to my great surprise that we had largely let the program decline.

And, I don't know how you boys can expect to be leaders if you don't have control of your base technologies!

Arm pounding on the podium, the septuagenarian was florid. And the audience? Glassy stares, knowing nods, murmurs.

And then he said, "*And that reminds me of Spectrum.*" Ah, yes, *Spectrum.* The fabled RISC architecture. The program that when outlined in 1980–81 to Dave was described as the "one-line" unifying capability, suitable for rolling over all of HP's incompatible lines by 1984. He reputedly rejoined that it would take most of a decade. The reaction was of the form, "*It can't, we can't afford it.*" To which his answer ostensibly was, "*It will, and yes, we can't really afford it, but we can't afford not to either, if our goal is to be a major force in computing.*"

At the February 21, 1986, press event for Spectrum's introduction, Dave was quite a contrast to all others on the program—observing that we have a nice start, but a "*lot of work left*" to do. Trenchant! And now, an acknowledgment that we seemed to have mastered the initial learnings, and we can now begin—*begin*—to participate seriously in the computer business. And if we do our jobs diligently, we can indeed be *a,* if not *the,* world leader in computing equipments in just another fifteen years or so.

And now, to close, he said, "*That brings up an important matter also. The Berlin Wall will come down soon, I think even this year. And we need to think about that—you boys need to plan what you'll have to do as a result.*" I looked again around the room—and I mused about the new members in the audience—giant squid, number one in computing, the Berlin Wall? He closed with real emphasis, returning to his "back to basics" theme. Angry, riled—vintage Dave!

January 24, 1989

Management by Wandering Around (MBWA)[3]

The announcement came just forty minutes before the event. Dave Packard, seventy-eight, founder and chairman of the board, would be addressing the Northern Colorado division employees in the Fort Collins open-air pavilion. Bill Parzybok, EAG General Manager and HP's only vice president in Colorado, would moderate the meeting, with some four thousand attendees.

Many in the Software Engineering Systems Division (SESD), two miles up the road from the main Fort Collins site, weren't sure it was worth attending. Most of the eighty employees had seen Packard a year earlier, at the fiftieth anniversary party held at the U.S. Air Force Academy near Colorado Springs. Unfortunately—portentously perhaps—one of Colorado's fabled thunderstorms washed away that gala event just as Packard had started to speak to a crowd of nearly fifteen thousand. The division manager urged the employees to attend the return visit. His encouragement ran along the lines of "*This might be our last chance to hear from the founder and chairman,*" rather than any sense of impending big news.

Dave indeed was slow to warm up the crowd. Never an eloquent speaker, he thanked people for coming, and he said he had been in the area for his sixtieth high school reunion the previous Saturday night. Then, without notes, he said that he just wanted to "*get together and share a few thoughts.*" He said that really there were only three principles that he felt had guided the company all these years. First, that the company had always worked on fundamental contributions rather than "me-too" products; second, that the company had always worked as a team focused on its competitors rather than fighting about internal issues; and finally, that the company had been lucky to choose electronics as a field of endeavor because years ago there was a lot of room for contribution and it wasn't so hard to make a mark.

Just ten minutes had passed when the audience heard him say, "*In conclusion, Bill and I don't have much more time, and we just want to thank each of you for the choice you've made to work for our company. It won't mean much to us for very much longer, but twenty-five years from now, it will matter a lot to you what you've chosen to do for the company. Thank you for coming. I will now take a few questions.*"

The questions started slowly, and Packard answered patiently in his famous drawl. To a question about how the personal computer business was going, he opined that it didn't seem to him that folks had followed Rule Number 1—make a contribution, and thus it was hard to distinguish ourselves and certainly hard to make a profit. Another question, about the difficulty in making decisions for the Fort Collins Desktop Computing Division, evoked in answer that Packard felt maybe too many people from Corporate were "*trying to help you boys out.*" He expanded the value of having those closest to the problem make the decisions, and said he just didn't understand "*how all these committees help*"—Rule Number 2.

He parried a question about Software Products, something about how "*We can't be a leader in software if our software can only be sold on HP computers,*" noting that the Peripherals Group had concluded that printers should be sold with all computers, and "*it worked out pretty well.*" Packard observed in response to another question that one of the requirements in order to make a real contribution was that there be really big problems to solve (Rule Number 3), and he felt there were plenty of challenges in business arenas for which HP products could provide assistance. He again made the point that HP measures things, and whether it be physics questions or inventory control questions, the quantitative measurement is invaluable.

And then came the *coup de grâce*. Someone bluntly asked if company leadership was up to the challenge. Dave never changed expression as he began to extol John Young's virtues and achievements since he had become CEO. But then he said that this bureaucratic structure that had been created was going to be swept away, and that "*We'll get someone who can lead in this environment.*" People weren't sure that they heard him correctly. And a second question brought an answer that spoke volumes. He said this was very important for both Hewlett and him, and that they had decided to embark on "trips around the loop" to figure out what to do. "*In fact,*" he intoned, "*Bill is right now in Boise, talking to folk there about what to do.*" Yup, just out here for a high school reunion, with a chance to stop by and say hello to a few friends!

August 15, 1990

APPENDIX D

Managing Innovation: An Oxymoron?[1]

BY LEW PLATT

[Platt prefaced his speech with the opening anecdote about Thomas Edison and Bill Hewlett described in Chapter Thirteen. Then he continued. . . .] Let me start with some of the innovation HP has brought to market in more than a half-century:

Analytical Innovations

In 1965, HP entered the market for analytical instrumentation—that is, electronic instruments used for chemical analysis. Four years later, we introduced the first instrument with robotics for preparing the sample to be tested. This made it possible for people to run the systems unattended or overnight . . . greatly reducing the cost of chemical analysis. By 1974, we'd produced the industry's first instrument controlled by a microprocessor. That made it possible to make ten readings in 20 minutes . . . compared to hours for a single reading in previous models. It didn't require a Ph.D. in chemistry to operate . . . but, instead, could be used by laboratory technicians. The result was an even more dramatic reduction in the cost of analysis . . . which helped open up the market for environmental analysis.

Medical Innovations

In 1967, HP introduced the world's first non-invasive technology to monitor fetal heart-rates . . . which made it possible to evaluate a baby's condition during labor. [HP has built] another non-invasive approach to patient monitoring, a new family of reusable sensors that measure arterial oxygen. As you know, a human being cannot survive for more than 5 minutes without an oxygen supply to the brain. This device means that doctors no longer have to draw blood in order to gauge how things are going . . . but, instead, can monitor the situation continuously.

Information Innovations

Many innovations are what we call "killers" in that they render another industry obsolete. . . . Products that killed the slide-rule industry [are] the first programmable desktop calculator, introduced in 1968 [and] the pocket-sized version developed in response to Bill Hewlett's challenge to HP engineers, [introduced] in 1972. You probably can't imagine solving problems without it. A marketing study commissioned before we introduced this product showed that there wasn't much interest in it. I bet you're glad no one listened. And that brings up an interesting question: When do you listen to that kind of feedback, and when do you ignore it? John Doyle coined an expression that summarizes what's required . . . and that is "an imaginative understanding of customer needs."

Printing Innovations

Inkjet technology was born around the coffee pot at HP Labs, our central research facility, as a couple of engineers discussed the principle of vaporization that operates coffee percolators. That led to the development of small resistors, heated by an electric pulse, [creating] a vapor that ejects ink through a nozzle. That work began in the late 1970s—before the days of drip coffee makers or the rise of Starbucks, for that matter. We didn't come out with a product based on the technology until 1984. It was the HP ThinkJet. It sold for $495, and it bombed. Back to the drawing board. Four years later, we came out with another version that delivered laser-quality print for under $1,000. That was the first of the HP DeskJet . . . a product that has become the world's best-selling printer.

Inkjet printers today [produce] truly photographic-quality—so much so, even, that when we put Kodak prints next to our InkJet prints and asked Kodak executives to guess which was an actual photograph, some of them picked the InkJet print. We're already combining these capabilities with our scanners, CD-ROMs and PCs to produce home photography systems that allow people to feed a negative into the system, edit the image, and print their own family calendars, Christmas cards, whatever. Soon, you can expect to see those capabilities enhanced by the addition of digital cameras.

Illumination Innovations

In the 1960s, our central laboratory began working on the physics and chemistry involved in making light-emitting diodes, or LEDs, as they are called. No product division picked up the technology, but we continued to invest, nonetheless. That was a wise decision, because advances in LED technology helped make possible the pocket-sized calculator I spoke of earlier. By the mid-seventies, we'd produced yellow and green LEDs, but they weren't bright enough. We continued fundamental research and developed a process based on aluminum gallium arsenide technology, which produces very bright lights. As a result, LED technology is moving beyond the digital display of your calculator or alarm clock. They're being used in outdoor signage like you see here. Some cities have started using red, amber and green LEDs in their traffic signals. They offer lots of advantages, because they require only half as much electricity as incandescent bulbs . . . and they never need to be replaced. Looking forward, we've just perfected blue LEDs. And that means we can combine the colors to produce white light. Remember the advantages—energy efficiency and, essentially, no need for replacement. Will HP go into the light bulb business? Stay tuned.

Environment of Innovation

The factors at work fall into three categories—organization, management and culture. All are really interdependent and reinforce each other. [First] HP is a very decentralized organization. We push decision-making and accountability to the lowest possible level. We divide our activities—some are the same companywide. We wouldn't, for example, want to have different personnel policies in different businesses, because that would limit our ability to move people around the organization and leverage their learning. [Some] activities are unique to each business. They determine their own business strategy. Nobody waits around for orders from some omniscient team of senior managers telling them which hill to take. Instead, business strategy is set by the people closest to the customers, technologies and competitors. And, as you'll see from what else is on that list, the businesses control all the resources required to execute those strategies. They are empowered and, therefore, accountable. The businesses keep their eye on the ball in the arenas for which they are responsible. They're very focused on their strategic intent in that space, and their people have frequent and passionate discussions of what they're doing and what it takes to be great.

The Role of HP Labs

Hewlett-Packard Laboratories is a second organizational factor in HP's ability to innovate. HP Labs bridges the gap between the kind of pure research that universities like Yale perform and the product-development responsibility of HP divisions. They perform what we call applied research, working on many of the same challenges our businesses face . . . but with longer time horizons in mind. HP Labs has two roles. First, it explores areas of research that would move HP's current businesses forward. Secondly, its researchers are looking quite creatively across HP's breadth of expertise in measurement, computation and communications to identify ways we might combine them to create entirely new businesses.

An Environment of Innovation

Let me move on now to the subject of management, beginning with "the vision thing," as George Bush called it. I'll start by reading the minutes from the first meeting Dave Packard and Bill Hewlett had, back in 1938. They go like this. . . . "It seemed the general consensus of opinion that the work should be limited to manufacturing and merchandising our own manufactured goods entirely. The question of what to manufacture was postponed to a later date." How's that for vision? Blindly clear, right? And, as the HP historians have chronicled, Bill and Dave subsequently went on to design a notable number of failures. There was the automatic foot-fault finder for bowling alleys . . . an electronic toilet flusher for the dormitories at Stanford . . . and an electronic lettuce picker that destroyed a farmer's entire field and made them run for their lives. In studying visionary companies [for *Built to Last*], the authors concluded that Bill and Dave's uncertainty about what they would produce had a very positive effect—instead of concentrating on building a particular product, they concentrated on building a visionary company.

Two Approaches to Vision

In the first paradigm, vision is conceived of and driven by the top. A visionary leader aims at directing change. The top management articulates a vision, motivates others to implement it, and remains visible so everyone knows where to focus their efforts. In the second, top management creates the environment in which others' visions may emerge, and then provides the resources so that people may realize their visions. When attention is focused, it is at those in the organization who have done some pioneering work . . . and not on top management. In the paradigm on the left, a visionary leader emerges. In the one on the right, you have the makings for a visionary company. And, of course, HP's style more closely matches the second description.

Culture Highlighted

I'd like to move on now to culture, because I think it's perhaps the most important ingredient at work. The most important thing about HP's culture is the assumption it is built upon—namely, that people want to do a good job, a creative job, and will do so if given the right environment. That statement is Bill Hewlett's definition of the HP Way. It's central to everything we do. And, based on my visits to other organizations, I think the assumption is quite unique.

Combine that assumption with our stated reliance on people's creativity, and the result is the goal of making HP the employer of choice in our industry. We want to be able to attract the brightest people (especially new college graduates) from around the world . . . and then to earn their loyalty and enthusiastic commitment.

The HP Way

We also work hard at keeping our core values alive and using them as the basis for everything we do. In fact, I consider one of my most important roles at HP the stewardship of those values. They're real—not just something we put on a piece of paper. [Let me enumerate the five basic HP values]:

- We have trust and respect for individuals.
- We focus on a high level of achievement and contribution.
- We conduct our business with uncompromising integrity.
- We achieve our common objectives through teamwork.
- We encourage flexibility and innovation.

APPENDIX E

Stock Price Comparisons

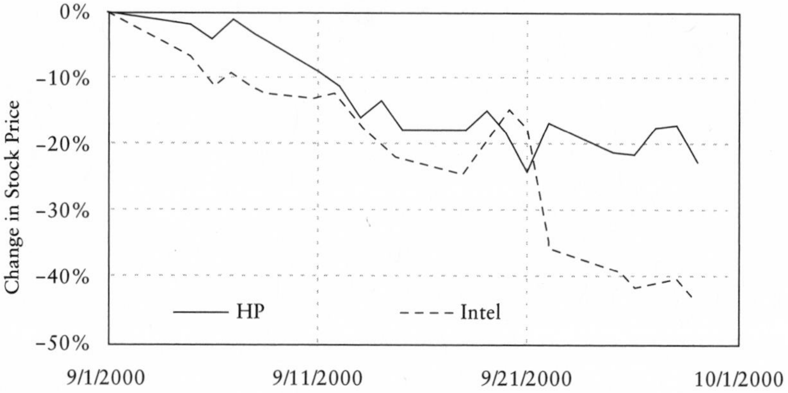

FIGURE E.1. Comparison stock prices for HP and Intel during September 2000

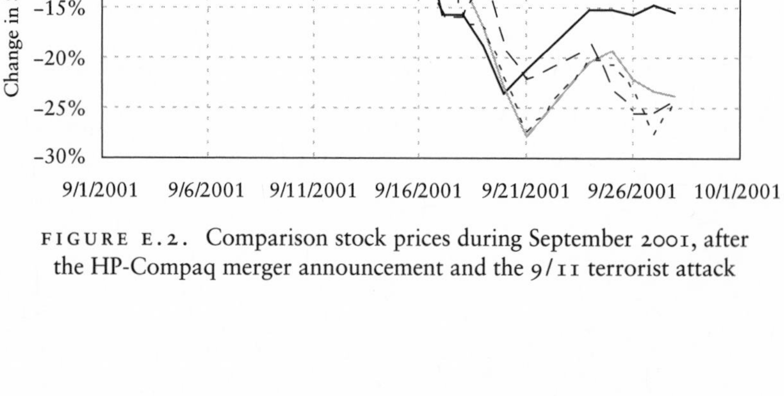

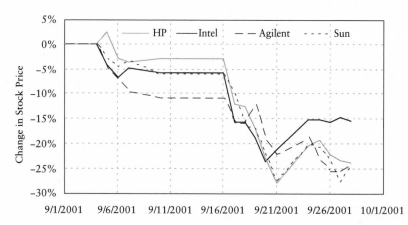

FIGURE E.2. Comparison stock prices during September 2001, after the HP-Compaq merger announcement and the 9/11 terrorist attack

Acknowledgments

Seated next to the Spartan offices of Dave Packard and Bill Hewlett in the old headquarters at 1501 Page Mill Road, and charged with the responsibility of nurturing and maintaining the HP culture of innovation for engineering, Chuck House had a unique vantage point for observing the topics presented herein. With an undergraduate degree in solid-state physics, plus advanced degrees in electrical engineering, history of science and technology, and business strategy, and nearly thirty years of service at Hewlett-Packard, he had breadth for the Corporate Engineering director role. House visited every HP engineering and manufacturing site around the globe (more than a hundred) several times over a five-year period, interviewing virtually every corporate officer and many executives about innovation, productivity, and business strategy. After executive positions at Informix Software, Veritas Software, Dialogic Corporation, and Intel, House has been a senior research scholar in Stanford's Human Sciences and Technologies (H*STAR) Institute, and executive director of Media X at Stanford since 2006.

Raymond Price completed a PhD in organizational behavior at Stanford in 1982, having studied HP with his advisor, Dr. William Ouchi (*Theory Z*) at the invitation of CEO John Young and VP of Human Resources John Doyle. He spent eight subsequent years at HP, serving in a variety of operational roles as well as in Corporate Training. Subsequently, he held executive Human Resource posts at both Boeing and Allergan Corporations before his appointment as the William H. Severns Professor of Human Behavior in the College of Engineering at the University of Illinois, Urbana-Champaign. Pioneering the Technology Entrepreneurship Center there in 1999, he later helped organize and lead the Illinois Leadership Center.

We were impressed with the unique Hewlett-Packard approach to innovation when we teamed in the early 1980s to write and teach a forty-hour project managers course within HP. Price's work with Ouchi studying HP culture and practices dovetailed with the perspective that House had just gained while designing and teaching a forty-hour video-based electronics course for GE engineers seeking mid-career redefinition for a digital world. The two experiences gave each of us an extraordinary view of the diversity and special strengths provided by a radically divided, semi-autonomous organization when combined with high encouragement of innovation and expectation of excellence.[1] Four years of working and traveling together reinforced these views.

Shortly thereafter, HP came to the notice of the business-author world, thanks to Bill Ouchi and colleagues at Stanford, who compared and contrasted HP with a small number of other companies. Bob Waterman and Tom Peters in particular cited HP heavily in their surprise best-seller, *In Search of Excellence.* Jim Collins would reemphasize the enduring strength of the HP Way in *Built to Last,* and though Richard Foster decried Collins's thesis in *Creative Destruction,* he too noted that HP's sustained growth rate and business creativity were remarkable.[2]

Over the years, we expected someone to write a definitive book about the company. But another characteristic about Bill 'n' Dave, as they preferred to be called within HP, was their modesty and desire for understatement. This carried deeply into the culture of HP. Packard's own autobiography near the end of his life was deceptively simple and direct. It seemed that the only readers who appreciated his writing were HP employees who knew the pair well enough to realize that this book was an eloquent statement about these men and how they operated.

Attending the sixtieth wedding anniversary party of HPite Art Fong and his wife, Mary, House was implored to write an HP history by his heroes and idols, many now stooped, graying, and even infirm. Both Hewlett and Packard had passed away. Two new books had just been published about HP by journalists—George Anders's *Perfect Enough,* and Peter Burrows's *Backfire.* The group was solemn. While many had been interviewed for the two books, all seemed dissatisfied with the results. Both books had a context-setting chapter about HP, but dealt primarily with the extraordinarily combative schism between Bill Hewlett's son Walter and new CEO Carly Fiorina over the proposed HP-Compaq merger.

House and Price met and concluded that there was plenty of room for another book; indeed it is remarkable that no history of the company had been published in seventy years. Other large companies—GE, IBM, Boeing, Microsoft, Intel, DEC, Ford, Sun Microsystems, Apple—have spawned many books. For all of the incredible history of HP, it seemed sad that the primary books about HP focused on one of the few blights in company history.

In our spare time, we assembled old notes and rummaged through collected arcana. Despite their misgivings from the journalistic books, CEO Carly Fiorina and marketing vice president Allison Johnson were supportive, allowing us access to the HP Archives, which contains irreplaceable records from early days. Twice in the past twenty years under archivist Karen Lewis's guidance, prescient HP old-timers have captured and transcribed oral memoirs from key players in HP's story. A third set is currently being compiled by HP archivist Anna Mancini. Via many HP alumni, we have been privileged to have access to many invaluable records chronicling the early years and operational style of the founders.

An early draft circulated to old colleagues quickly surfaced two problems. The first was personal pique at certain phrases, the bane of many writers. A long-time friend fired off an e-mail: "Your cute phrase is one popular among my MBA friends, but I was surprised to see you pick up on it. Being a sensitive old man, I have lost interest in your 'book.'"[3] The second problem is the historian's dilemma of verifying authenticity of recollections or accounts. None of us sees things in quite the same way; multiple observers of an event cannot report it cleanly at the time, let alone years later. We were admonished by seasoned authors that writing a book about individuals and a company has a particular set of risks. Joan Didion cautioned,

> It is one thing for me to write about them; you and I enjoy reading the sly innuendos about them. It is less fun when I write about us, and have you and I read about us. Where it gets difficult is when I write about you, and you read it. Almost by definition, that segment will be perceived as wrong—incomplete, misunderstood, distorted, pejorative.[4]

We radically shifted our approach, basing the book on a large set of interviews. The interviews became far more extensive than we anticipated, with each new interviewee filling in a key factoid or insight. Three years of interviewing yielded more than 120 in-depth interviews. More than five hundred individuals have provided stories, anecdotes, and materials for our consideration.[5] Candor and insight revealed in individual interviews is fundamental to understanding why something happened; groups of people are likewise vital to provide cross-referencing, to improve fortuitous memories. We were gratified by the willingness of so many to participate, including virtually every HP ex-officer. The achievements are those of the company, and the opportunity to learn about them and to acknowledge their creators has been our immense and distinct privilege. This is not the book we set out to write; it instead is a book about HP as told by hundreds of observers, woven together into a tapestry, buttressed by significant detail. It is a far better book because it is informed by those who made it happen.

With respect to early history, several people were particularly supportive. Carl Cottrell, Cort Van Rensselaer, Robert Grimm, Al Bagley, and Art Fong have devoted many hours to researching old records, re-creating events, locating files, and critiquing the manuscript many times along the way. Each was a significant contributor in multiple ways to the company, and each served HP for more than forty years. Their incredible dedication to this effort has been beyond anything we might have expected. Drafts were reviewed by more than fifty people. We are especially indebted to reviewers Bruce Abell, Ned Barnholt, Nina Bhatti, Joel Birnbaum, Zvonko Fazarinc, Bob Frankenberg, Robert Grady, Don Hammond, Neil Jacobstein, Judy Larsen, Steve Leibson, Webb McKinney, John Minck, and Dave Yewell for their thorough-going efforts. While many interviewees quoted have reviewed their contribution in the context of its citation, we are nevertheless responsible for all inaccuracies, misinterpretations, and omissions. We apologize in advance for inevitable errors and we welcome corrections and amendments for our website (www.innovascapes.com) and any subsequent printings.

Our goal has been to capture and codify the HP Way as seen from the change-agent side of HP. This is not the HP Way that has been written about so extensively. Our emphasis is effective product development for tangible specific business success—the HP Way of business creation rather than the HP Way of people interaction and culture. While inextricably linked, each by itself is insufficient.

Much HP material is in the public domain, including the *HP Journal* from its inception in September 1949; *HP Measure* (HP's worldwide employee newsletter) from July 1963 through its last edition, May-June 2000; *HP Annual Reports* from 1957 forward; hosts of articles in *Business Week, Fortune,* and *Forbes*; and many specific incidents, events, issues, and even chapters reported in hundreds of books.

We had access to HP's internal magazine, *Watt's Current* (for Palo Alto employees) from September 1943 through August 1971, and numerous other quasi-regular internal HP publications (such as *HP Network, HP Intercom, HP Manufacturing Forum,* and various divisional newsletters) are referenced in places. Financial results were primarily gleaned from HP and other company annual reports, plus correlated trade and analyst summaries (for example, Dataquest, Datamation, Electronics, and Frost and Sullivan annual analyses by product segment). Agendas, minutes, and materials from some annual general manager meetings, as well as specific histories, were selectively available from various attendees and participants.

We are indebted to many individuals and organizations for their valuable contributions to our effort. It is impossible to name them all, but we want to credit some of the most significant. Al Bagley was an early advocate for this book. He possesses a vast personal collection of memorabilia, and his work in instigating and developing the extensive HP Oral Histories housed at the Agilent and Hewlett-Packard archives provided an invaluable source of data, insight, and perspective. His singular contribution for House, besides persuading him to join HP in 1962, was to goad, persuade, and cajole him for years into doing this project. His critical and inimitable review at many steps along the way was remarkable for both its completeness and its accuracy.

Anna Mancini, HP's archivist, and Karen Lewis, her predecessor (and original Archives developer, who is now the Agilent Technologies Foundation director), were tremendously helpful at specific junctures to this process. Devon Dawson, archivist and public relations specialist at Agilent Technologies Archives, was invaluable in helping us finalize the manuscript and facilitating the permissions for archived interviews and photographs. David Kirby, HP's public relations officer for thirty years and the original Archives sponsor, has been a valued source of information, anecdotal material, and support. Kirby and Lewis brought Packard's autobiography to fruition; more recently, Lewis and Mancini were vital for a video documentary about the company, "Origins." Access to certain materials from both the Hewlett and Packard family archives is also gratefully acknowledged.

Six HP vice presidents—Susan Bowick, Debra Dunn, Allison Johnson, Dick Lampman, Webb McKinney, and Craig Samuel—were strong sponsors of the project within HP during 2003, when it was difficult to gain access to the Archives for various reasons. Similarly, the support of CEO Ned Barnholt and CTO Tom Saponas at Agilent Technologies is much appreciated. Most living ex-officers of the company were interviewed for this book, including Dick Alberding, Ned Barnholt, Rick Belluzzo, Alan Bickell, Joel Birnbaum, Bob Boniface, Doug Carnahan, Doug Chance, Ray Deméré, John Doyle, Debra Dunn, Paul Ely, Carly Fiorina, Bob Frankenberg, Dieter Hoehn, Dick Love, Ed McCracken, Webb McKinney, Dean Morton, Franz Nawratil, Wim Roelandts, Emery Rogers, Bill Terry, Ed van Bronkhorst, Bob Watson, Dick Watts, Dave Weindorf, Cyril Yansouni, and John Young. Each graciously contributed hours of interview time. Bob Wayman, acting HP CEO for an interim period, provided useful background information, and Dick Hackborn graciously agreed to allow access to his private archive interview. Board member Tom Perkins also granted an interview in spring 2006, when he chaired the board's Strategic Council.

As the book neared publication, HP formally requested that we state clearly that Hewlett-Packard is *not* a sponsor or supporter of the book.

House has copious notes from interactions with Bill Hewlett, David Packard, and Barney Oliver, as well as interview notes about Ralph Lee, Frank Cavier, Bruce Wholey, Ray Wilbur, and Dick Hackborn. In addition, the archives have materials providing rich information about each of these people except Wilbur. Early figures Noel Eldred and Noel Porter left no significant written histories; their premature deaths helped stimulate the decision to capture others' sagas. Several people important to HP's history have passed away more recently, including CEO Lew Platt. Fortunately, House had interview material from earlier meetings with Platt.

There are a number of self-volunteered resident historians of Hewlett-Packard lore and history, along with some invaluable websites for devotees of HP equipment, lore, and camaraderie. John Minck has written an insider's view of the essence of the HP Way. Roland Haitz has compiled a Components Group product timeline; Chuck Sieloff has a similar project concerning Corporate IT services. HP and Agilent Technologies have each assembled modest collections of HP equipment and products in addition to more traditional library artifacts. Their websites are increasingly rich in detail; curators will respond to serious inquiries. Neither company has a museum. The Computer History Museum (CHM) has a History of Calculators display that features HP products; CHM began life in Boston in the late 1970s; relocated to Mountain View, California, in the late 1990s, it has consistently been adding equipment from later eras.[6]

There is an outstanding website on HP handheld calculators, another on the desktop calculator evolution, and a third on HP business computers;[7] there are two HP equipment museums, each comprising both a website and physical museum.[8] Glenn Robb, an inveterate hobbyist, hosts a website with nearly a hundred thousand scanned pages of HP records, including nearly all *HP Measure* issues, product catalogs, and many product manuals.[9] Re: the early days of HP, see the Southwest Museum of Engineering, Communications and Computation, www.smecc.org.

Several surprises emerged. One was the extent to which HP's culture was continually renewing, usually without overt leadership at the top in terms of product direction, but through insistent guidance to "make a contribution" with whatever products were being developed. Mavericks were not just tolerated, or occasionally singled out—they were often prevalent.

Another surprise was how seldom HP people talk about their products or their departmental contribution. When probed, however, we found the depth of pride in their work contributions to be extraordinarily high. We conclude that this is an essential aspect of the secret of HP's commercial success that has been missed by outside observers. HP Museum websites exhibit this extraordinary product pride extremely well.

A third surprise was the discovery of curious omissions in other technical histories. For example, in Leslie Berlin's biographical tome about Robert Noyce there is no mention at all of the pivotal role that the Intellec I and

II played in the metamorphosis of Intel and the sudden switch of the industry to synchronous digital design, nor has the parallel role of HP Logic Analyzers been described for their role in that move, in DEC's VAX 780 ascension, or in the rise of Bangalore's software industry. Ernst Guillemin garners only two sentences in Stewart Gillmor's 642-page book about Fred Terman, and computing as a topic earns little more. Terman gets precious little coverage in Christophe Lécuyer's *Making Silicon Valley—1930-1970*, precisely Terman's most important career years. Computer histories often fail to mention HP at all, a singularly ironic omission given that HP is now the world's largest computer equipment supplier, with pioneering leadership in both scientific and personal computing.[10]

The Stanford University Press has been very supportive of this project, both in time and energy devoted to its success, and in patience with our schedules. Susan Harman was an important interlocutor, and Martha Cooley had faith in us early; their encouragement was vital. Geoffrey Burn provided the bulk of support, however, to bring the manuscript to fruition. The symbiotic relationship over the years between HP and Stanford makes it especially appropriate that this book be a Stanford University Press product. Our wonderful research assistant, Holli Burgon, was invaluable in tracking and finding references, providing valuable edits, and helping to complete the final production process. Vickie Bierman faithfully transcribed almost all the interviews we conducted and was instrumental in the early research efforts. Our independent editor, Kathleen Much, was an encouraging resource, with invaluable comments and a keen eye. Our Stanford Press editor David Horne kept a sharp focus on the constantly evolving HP division names, among myriad other details; Senior Production Editor Judith Hibbard was unparalleled for her support and effective coordination. Laura Koritz's indexing saved our sanity.

Finally, our families and our colleagues have been consistently tolerant, unfailingly good-humored, and enthusiastic on our behalf. We especially thank Jennifer Reese House and Stephanie Price for their forbearance and support.

April 20, 2009
Palo Alto, California; Urbana, Illinois

Notes

(ATA) indicates that the source is the Agilent Technologies Archives, located at Agilent Technologies Santa Clara, California, headquarters.

INTRODUCTION

1. Carol Loomis and Oliver Ryan, "Why Carly's Big Bet Is Failing," *Fortune* 151, 3 (February 7, 2005): 50–64; Ben Elgin, Steve Hamm, Spencer Ante, Robert D. Hof, Cliff Edwards, and Peter Burrows, "Can Anyone Save HP?" *BusinessWeek* 3921 (February 21, 2005): 28–35; Peter Burrows, *Backfire: Carly Fiorina's High-Stakes Battle for the Soul of HP* (New York: John Wiley & Sons, 2003); Carol Loomis and Oliver Ryan, "How the HP Board KO'd Carly," *Fortune* 151, 5 (March 7, 2005): 99–102.

2. Tom Perkins, interview by Charles H. House and Raymond L. Price, March 24, 2006.

3. Robert Levering, Milton Moskowitz, Feliciano Garcia, and Karen Vella-Zarb, "The 100 Best Companies to Work For," *Fortune* 141, 1 (January 10, 2000): 82–110.

4. Kate Bonamici and Christopher Tkaczyk, "The List of Industry Champs," *Fortune* 153, 4 (March 6, 2006): 79–81; "Where Companies Rank in Their Industries," *Fortune* 153, 4 (March 6, 2006): 82–86.

5. Louis V. Gerstner Jr., *Who Says Elephants Can't Dance?* (New York: Collins, 2002).

6. Rachel Konrad, "Hewlett-Packard May Have Ex-Chief to Thank for Success," Associated Press, August 18, 2006, run widely, including in the *San Francisco Chronicle*, the *San Jose Mercury-News*, and the *Rocky Mountain News*.

7. See Ellen Nakashima and Yuki Noguchi, "HP CEO Allowed 'Sting' of Reporter," *Washington Post*, September 21, 2006, A01; also Yuki Noguchi and Ellen Nakashima, "House Panel Digs Deep in HP Spy Case: Dunn, Hurd Shoulder Brunt of Tough Questioning at Hearing," *Washington Post*, September 29, 2006, D01.

8. The garage is in the backyard at 367 Addison Avenue. HP had only a very modest role with the silicon technologies that earned the nickname "Silicon Valley" for the region.

9. "Fortune 500," *Fortune* (April, 5, 2004): F-1. The #8 ranking omits nonmanufacturers Wal-Mart, CitiCorp, and American International. Three oil companies, two auto manufacturers, GE, and IBM were larger. For world rankings, see "Forbes 2000, Sales," *Forbes* (April 12, 2004): 147.

10. For months in 2004, Hewlett's picture sat askew in its frame—unnoticed, uncorrected, symbolic of the stress at HP?

11. Named to the National Academy of Engineering in 1966 for his HP role, Oliver was selected in 1973 for the National Academy of Science for establishing SETI (Search for Extra-Terrestrial Intelligence).

12. Hackborn was thinly disguised as Jack Wakefield in Michael Maccoby, *The Gamesman: The New Corporate Leaders* (New York: Simon & Schuster, 1977).

13. The McKinsey study from 1958–1998 was reported by Richard Foster (lecture, Entrepreneur Series, University of California, Santa Barbara, April 14, 2003) (*cf.* Richard Foster, *Creative Destruction: Why Companies That Are Built to Last Underperform the Market* (New York: Doubleday, 2001). Foster didn't include HP in his book because he didn't regard HP as a major growth company (as opposed to Apple, Microsoft, Intel, Sun, Dell, or Compaq), and HP was Jim Collins' *Built to Last* model company, the antithesis of Foster's work. Other companies grew faster during part of the period, but not over the full forty years.

CHAPTER 1

1. Don Hammond, interview by Alan Bagley, October 25, 1990, 14–15 (ATA).

2. Quentin Hardy, "The UnCarly," *Forbes* 179, 5 (March 12, 2007): 82–90.

3. Peter Burrows, "HP: Poised to Unseat IBM," *BusinessWeek*, November 17, 2006, http://www.businessweek.com/technology/content/nov2006/tc20061117_589560.htm?chan=search.

4. Hewlett earned a Stanford bachelor's degree in electrical engineering in 1934, a master's degree in electrical engineering at MIT in 1935, and an engineer's degree at Stanford in 1939. The patent application (three pages of text, one page of figures), filed July 11, 1939, was granted January 6, 1942. The application, award, and thesis are on file at HP Archives (ATA).

5. This is one of those Sherlock Holmes detective stories about which historians do battle. Every reference to the 200 oscillator history in *Watt's Current* issues for the first twenty-four years of the company (notably the fifth and tenth anniversary issues, August 5, 1944, and November 1949), cites nine units for the Disney order. Oddly, when *HP Measure* was launched in July 1963 as a worldwide employee newsletter, the "official number" shifted inexplicably to eight rather than nine (*cf.* the HP twenty-fifth anniversary issue, September-October 1964[3]). David Packard, *The HP Way: How Bill Hewlett and I Built Our Company* (New York: HarperCollins, 1995), Packard's autobiography, derived from the twenty-fifth anniversary article, cited eight units, each at a recollected price of $71.50. Subsequent biographers have inferred that Packard mispriced the original units, but quickly realized his error and astutely raised the price as soon as possible, from the original $54.50 to $71.50 each. The $71.50 price, however, wasn't established until December 1940.

Al Bagley, in composing the Los Altos Museum exhibit about Dave and Lucile Packard in January 2008, found Lucile Packard's original cash ledger, in which a big shipment to Disney accounts for a sale of $517.50 for nine units at $57.50 each. The first two units (standard HP 200A's) were sold at list price of $54.50 (to Caltech and the Radio-Television Company); Hewlett charged $3.00 more per unit to Disney and renumbered the units to the HP 200B to cover the changed capacitor and the rackmount front panel costs. The next unit, another HP 200A, was sold to MIT for $54.50.

In Dave Packard and Bill Hewlett, *History Documentation* (Palo Alto, CA: HP TV Network, A Hewlett Family Production, 1983), Hewlett recalled that the original price was $54.40, having associated the price with the longitude of the the old Oregon Territory–Canadian dispute; his recollection was erroneous by a dime. Packard couldn't recall the price or the association when asked.

The Southwest Museum of Engineering, Computing and Communication has long insisted that nine is the right number, citing both the original salesperson, William Stancil, and the Disney archives. See Ed Sharpe, "Hewlett-Packard: The Early Years," http://www.smecc

.org/hewlett-packard,_the_early_years.htm. William V. Stancil, who had introduced Norm Neely to Bill Hewlett and Dave Packard, sold the units to Bud Hawkins at Disney through Neely Enterprises. Stancil wrote a letter dated January 18, 1989, to Bill Hewlett (which is posted on the SMECC website) that cites the nine units twice. In the fiftieth anniversary *HP Measure* issue, Jean Burke Hoppe devoted a half page to Stancil's role, but omitted his reference to nine units. Hoppe, "What a Mickey Mouse Way to Start a Company" *HP Measure* (September-October 1989): 8–11.

6. Al Bagley, interview by Charles H. House, October 11, 2005.

7. Charles H. House, "A Founder's Benediction," essay shared in Upside's online encomium at Packard's death. This was also distributed at GBN Presents (March 18, 1996).

8. Dean Morton, personal communication with Charles H. House, January 1989.

9. Charles H. House, private correspondence to the Global Business Network (GBN), November 14, 1989.

10. David Packard, personal communication to Charles H. House, January 1990.

11. Alan Bagley, interview by Raymond L. Price, March 23, 2005, 6.

12. Carl Cottrell, interview by Raymond L. Price, October 6, 2004, 1.

13. "David Packard Memorial Service," March 29, 1996, comments by Lew Platt.

14. Michael S. Malone, *The Valley of Heart's Delight: A Silicon Valley Notebook, 1963–2001* (New York: John Wiley & Sons, 2002), 241.

15. Peter Burrows, *Backfire: Carly Fiorina's High-Stakes Battle for the Soul of HP* (New York: John Wiley & Sons, 2003), 59–60.

16. David Pierpont Gardner, "William Redington Hewlett," *Proceedings of the American Philosophical Society* 147, 2 (June 2003): 162–166).

17. Program, Hewlett Memorial Service, Stanford Memorial Church, January 20, 2001.

18. Howard A. Kelly and Walter L. Burrage, *Dictionary of American Medical Biography; Lives of Eminent Physicians* (New York: D. Appleton, 1928); *Who Was Who in America: A Companion Volume to Who's Who in America*, Volume 1, 1897–1942 (Chicago: A.N. Marquis, 1943), 558. For the California trip, see Packard, *The HP Way*, 20.

19. Carolyn E. Tajnai, "Fred Terman, The Father of Silicon Valley," NetValley, May 31, 1985, http://www.netvalley.com/archives/mirrors/terman.html.

20. Ibid.

21. *Who's Who in Finance and Industry*, 18th edition, 1974–1975 (Wilmette, IL: Marquis, 1974), 377. Ed's father, an Episcopal minister, married Bill and Flora, baptizing three of their five children.

22. Packard, *The HP Way*, 21–22.

23. Barney Oliver, interview by David Kirby, March 26, 1991, 8–9 (ATA).

24. Packard, *The HP Way*, 22.

25. Packard, *The HP Way*, 31–32.

26. Lucile Packard Scrapbook, "Lucile and David Packard: Valued Partners" exhibit, Los Altos History Museum, January-June 2008. Charles House led an evening remembrance of David with five HP oldtimers on March 28, 2008 under Museum auspices at the Los Altos High School.

27. David Woodley Packard at Hewlett's funeral service. It surprised many attendees to hear that Hewlett provided the goad to launch the company.

28. Lucile Packard Scrapbook.

29. Packard, *The HP Way*, 32–34.

30. Marion Meredith Reese, personal communication to Charles H. House, April 1986. Marion, daughter of a California Superior Court judge, was Flora's sorority sister.

31. Ed van Bronkhorst, interview by Alan Bagley, May 2, 1995, 11–12 (ATA).

32. The first sale was a diathermy machine for the Palo Alto Hospital (ATA). The duo built a thyratron drive to calibrate a large, machine-drive telescope, a radar oscilloscope, and an electric-shock-reducing machine among other things. "There was no attempt at specialty. . . . They would literally try anything." *HP Watt's Current* (February 13, 1948): 4.

33. The next-bench syndrome is in the notes from the first general manager meeting, June 14, 1957.

34. Stewart Gillmor, *Frederick Terman at Stanford: Building a Discipline, a University, and Silicon Valley* (Stanford, CA: Stanford University Press, 2004).

35. Ward Winslow and Joanna McClean, *Pages from a Palo Alto Editor's Scrapbook* (Palo Alto, CA: Ward Winslow Writing, 1994), 166. See the terse outline in Packard, *The HP Way*, 165–166.

36. Burrows, *Backfire*, 49–50.

37. Ralph Lee, interview by Al Bagley, December 7, 1990, 14–15.

38. Frank Cavier, interview by David Kirby, January 28, 1991, 2 (ATA).

39. Alan Bagley, interview by Robert Grimm, July 10, 1990, 7–8 (ATA).

40. Bruce Wholey, interview by Alan Bagley, August 15, 1990, 22 (ATA).

41. Wholey, interview, 25 (quoting Alan Bagley) (ATA).

42. Barney Oliver, interview by Arthur Norberg, August 9, 1985, 29–30, Charles Babbage Institute, University of Minnesota, Minneapolis.

43. Lee, interview, 23–24 (ATA).

44. Wholey, interview, 23 (ATA).

45. Hammond, interview, 21 (ATA).

46. Barney Oliver, interview by Arthur Norberg, April 14, 1986, 4, Charles Babbage Institute, University of Minnesota, Minneapolis.

47. Cavier, interview, 6 (ATA).

48. David Packard, "Growth from Performance" (lecture, IRE 7th Region Conference, April 24, 1957).

49. Ed van Bronkhorst, interview by Alan Bagley, May 18, 1995, augmented with Ed van Bronkhorst, interview by Charles H. House and Raymond L. Price, March 24, 2005 (ATA).

50. Wholey, interview, 13–14 (ATA).

51. Robert Grimm, interview by Al Bagley, November 13, 1991, 13 (ATA).

52. Packard, *The HP Way*, 77, shows the HP lineup of 373 products available in 1959.

53. Cort Van Rensselaer, interview by Alan Bagley, November 9, 1991, 32–33 (ATA).

54. Van Rensselaer, interview, 33, 38–39 (ATA).

55. Grimm, interview, 17–19 (ATA).

56. Wholey, interview, 17–18 (ATA).

57. Frank Cavier, interview by David Kirby, January 26, 1991, 60–61 (ATA).

58. Ed van Bronkhorst, interview by Alan Bagley, May 18, 1995, 24 (ATA).

59. Packard, *The HP Way*, 58.

60. Bagley, interview, 35 (ATA).

61. Packard, *The HP Way*, 100–101.

62. Alan Bagley, personal correspondence to Charles House, November 20, 2005.

63. Bill Terry, interview by Raymond L. Price, September 16, 2005, 21.

64. Terry, interview, 51.

65. Ed van Bronkhorst, interview by Alan Bagley, October 3, 1995, 5 (ATA).

66. John Doyle, interview by Raymond L. Price, March 23, 2005, 7.

67. Cort Van Rensselaer, interview by Alan Bagley, November 21, 1992, 1–2 (ATA).

68. Fred Terman, interview by Charles Susskind, 12 (transcript in Stanford archives).

69. Roger Heyns, personal communication to Charles H. House, February 1986.

70. Doyle, interview, 3.

71. Friedrich Wilhelm Schröder, "From Measurement to Information (Episodes and Observations), June 1991," self-published in Germany (provided by Carl J. Cottrell).

72. Frank Ura, "Electron Beam Lithography," *Hewlett-Packard Journal* 32, 5 (May 1981): 5.

73. Sam Lightman, "The Eight-Year Overnight Success Story," *HP Measure* (November-December, 1992): 8–10.

CHAPTER 2

1. Sir William Thomson (Lord Kelvin), *Popular Lectures and Addresses* (1891–1894, 3 volumes), attributed to a speech March 5, 1883. See http://zapatopi.net/kelvin/quotes/.

2. Russell Varian was a Stanford student with Hewlett and Packard. They were good friends.

3. C. Stewart Gillmor, *Frederick Terman at Stanford: Building a Discipline, a University, and Silicon Valley* (Palo Alto, CA: Stanford University Press, 2004).

4. Dave took pride in advising both Vollum and Fluke regarding their nascent companies. Hewlett and Packard were lifetime friends with Fluke and Vollum.

5. Hewlett's contribution: inserting an inexpensive tungsten filament bulb as the negative-resistance element. See John Minck, *Inside HP: A Narrative History of Hewlett-Packard from 1939–1990*, 63, http://www.home.agilent.com/upload/cmc_upload/secure/MinckHPNAR29.pdf.

6. "Our Efforts Should Be Concentrated on Electronic Instrumentation; Our Energies Toward Making Significant Contributions," *HP Measure* (September-October 1964): 2–4 (contains Fred Terman quote). Also Frederick Emmons Terman, interview by Art Norberg, Charles Süsskind, and Roger Hahn, 1975, Bancroft Oral History Project, History of Science and Technology.

7. "These significant contributions [in the HP 400A] are not as well known as Bill's stabilized oscillator, but are equally as great." Kenneth Kuhn, speech, HP Building 20A Auditorium, June 4, 2007. Packard always considered himself a design engineer, as exemplified by efforts at both his ranch and the Monterey Bay Aquarium. http://www.mbayaq.org/aa/timelineBrowser.asp?tf=3. Packard helped design and build the Kelp Forest exhibit and Sandy Shore Aviary wave machines. He personally cast the brass sea otter knobs on the macro-video exhibit, and the brass caps on the bollards lining the street in front of the aquarium. He helped formulate the cement recipes to withstand salt water, the engineering of the tidal pool wave generator, and the seven-inch-thick Plexiglas for the Kelp Forest exhibit.

Packard, limping when he hosted Queen Elizabeth II on an HP Cupertino plant tour, sheepishly told Computer Group VP Doug Chance that "I'd been molding impeller blades that morning for a home irrigation system and dropped a bucket of hot bronze on my foot." Upside online encomium in David Jacobson, "Founding Fathers," *Stanford Magazine* (July-August 1998).

8. Minck reported, "Standard instructions for preparing for a lab experiment called

for the experiment leader to come into the lab at dawn and turn on the HP 300A so that it could heat up for at least 4 to 5 hours before any measurements were made. The alignment procedure for the selectivity adjustments in the IF strip bandwidth, and LO were super-critical. The drift of the vacuum tubes would make all data useless if this alignment procedure weren't followed religiously" (Minck, *Inside HP*, p. 63).

9. For Bill Girdner's retirement, see "It Doesn't Seem That Long Ago," *HP Measure* (March 1975): 2–4.

10. "HP Revenue and Earnings by Year," *HP NOW* (January 6, 2004) (ATA).

11. Eldred, chair of the San Francisco IRE group in 1939, led the industry petition to nominate Fred Terman as the first West Coast IRE president. Gillmor, *Terman*, 173–174.

12. Minck, *Inside HP*, 5. This was the Model A signal generator, 500 megacycle to 1350 megacycle range, designed by several General Radio designers borrowed during wartime.

13. Frank Cavier, interview by David Kirby, January 28, 1991, 2 (ATA); see also David Packard, *The HP Way: How Bill Hewlett and I Built Our Company* (New York: HarperCollins, 1995), 56–58.

14. Cort Van Rensselaer, interview by Alan Bagley, November 9, 1991, 24–25 (ATA).

15. Ibid.

16. See ATT History of Television, http://www.att.com/history/television/milestone_1951.html. Truman first used television for a White House broadcast on October 5, 1947.

17. TV Land Shows, *I Love Lucy*, www.tvland.com/shows/lucy/.

18. "Television History—The First 75 Years," http://www.tvhistory.tv/Annual_TV_Sales_39-59.JPG. The *I Love Lucy* show was produced for seven years. Reruns haven't ceased.

19. A repeater is a communications device that takes a signal, attempts to remove any distortion and reconstructs the original signal, then amplifies it for further distribution.

20. In any repeater tower, there were twelve active microwave channels and two hot standby channels. This guaranteed reliable service.

21. "History of Innovation," Texas Instruments, http://www.ti.com/corp/docs/company/history/firsttrans.shtml. Morita founded Sony with Masaru Ibuka as Tokyo Tsushin Kogyo KK (Tokyo Telecommunications Engineering Corp.) in 1946 with twenty employees and ¥190,000; he renamed it Sony in 1958.

22. Lee and Fong did not know each other at the Labs. Lee started with MIT's Rad Lab and later transferred to the Research Construction Lab for 1944–45. Ralph Lee, interview by Alan Bagley, December 7, 1990, 7–9 (ATA); Arthur Fong, private correspondence with Charles H. House, December 24, 2005. Zeidler later joined Hew Crane's SRI team. Crane, inventor of the magnetic core memory at Sarnoff Labs (RCA), led the SRI team that invented the VISA card magnetic strip.

23. N. B. Schrock, "A New Amplifier for Milli-Microsecond Pulses," *Hewlett-Packard Journal* (hereafter *HP Journal*) 1, 1 (September 1949).

24. Packard, *The HP Way*, 64. A new building at 395 Page Mill Road was Agilent's corporate headquarters until it moved in early 2006 to Santa Clara.

25. Tom Perkins, a graduate student at Harvard, had a summer job in 1956 with General Radio, measuring HP specs; GR believed that HP was cheating. Perkins found that HP exceeded all published specifications by a 30 percent margin. Tom Perkins, interview by Charles H. House and Raymond L. Price, March 20, 2006.

26. Thus the wideband microwave amplifier that Schrock built during the war became a stepchild at HP, while sweepers became mainstays.

27. Bill Hewlett (comments, new engineer's dinner, January 1963).

28. Packard, *The HP Way*, 83–84.

29. Packard, *The HP Way*, 129.

30. Packard, *The HP Way*, 103–104.

31. Minck, *Inside HP*, 45, credited Fong's equipment with $200 million in sales for HP by 1980. See "616A Going to the Show!" *HP Watt's Current* (February 21, 1947): 3; and "The New 614A UHF Signal Generator," *HP Watt's Current* (May 1949): 2. See also Arthur Fong and W. D. Myers, "The HP Direct-Reading UHF Signal Generators," *HP Journal* 3, 9–10 (May-June 1952). See also Arthur Fong, "A New Signal Generator for the 7,000 to 11,000 MC Range," *HP Journal* 5, 5–6 (January-February 1954); Art Fong, "Special-Purpose Performance in a General-Purpose 50 KC-65 MC Signal Generator," *HP Journal* 10, 8 (April 1959); and "First Senior Engineers Honored," *HP Measure* (December 1964): 5.

32. Barney Oliver, interview by David Kirby, March 26, 1991, 13 (ATA). Oliver entered Caltech at age fifteen, and graduated from Stanford with a bachelor's degree at nineteen.

33. Bernard M. Oliver, *The Selected Papers of Bernard M. Oliver* (Palo Alto, CA: HP Press, 1997), vii (contains the contents of a letter from Bill Hewlett).

34. Barney Oliver, interview by Arthur Norberg, August 9, 1985, 26–27, Babbage Institute, University of Minnesota, Minneapolis; Barney Oliver, interview by David Kirby, March 26, 1991, 17–18 (ATA).

35. Frank Cavier, interview by David Kirby, January 28, 1991, 23 (ATA).

36. "Icon of Excellence, Reflections on Barney Oliver, Founding Director of HP Labs," *HP NOW* (June 28, 2002): 7 (ATA).

37. Barney Oliver, Norberg interview, 21–22, 27, 36.

38. Cavier, interview, 51. Packard, *The HP Way*, 36 (ATA).

39. "Hewlett-Packard Goes to College (Hewlett-Packard Wing of the New Electronics Research Laboratory on the Stanford Campus)," *HP Watt's Current* (January 1953): 3. Packard joined the School Board in 1948 (Packard, *The HP Way*, 167); he resigned eight years later ("Press of Executive Duties Force Packard's Retirement from School Board, Dr. Henry Gunn, Superintendent of Palo Alto School," *HP Watt's Current* (June 1956): 7). See also Packard, *The HP Way*, 56. For information about Hewlett's new role with IRE, see "Congratulations Bill! (Bill Hewlett Named President of the National Institute of Radio Engineers)," *HP Watt's Current* (December 1953): 1, and "William Hewlett Elected I.R.E. President," *HP Journal* 5, 5–6 (January-February 1954): 4. See also "Packard Elected Chairman of Stanford Board of Trustees," *HP Watt's Current* (June 1958): 7.

40. This remark, widely attributed to Thomas Watson Sr. in 1943, is debunked by his biographer, Kevin Maney, *The Maverick and His Machine: Thomas Watson, Sr., and the Making of IBM* (Hoboken, NJ: John Wiley & Sons, 2003), 355–356. IBM attributes the comment instead to Thomas Watson Jr. a decade later: "We believe the statement is a misunderstanding of remarks made at IBM's annual stockholders meeting on April 28, 1953. In referring specifically and only to the IBM 701 Electronic Data Processing Machine—which had been introduced the year before as the company's first production computer designed for scientific calculations—Thomas Watson, Jr., told stockholders that IBM had developed a paper plan for such a machine and took this paper plan across the country to some 20 concerns that we thought could use such a machine. The machine rents for between $12,000 and $18,000 a month, so it was not the type of thing that could be sold from place to place. But, as a result of our trip, on which we expected to get orders for five machines, we came home with orders for 18" (Peter Cavek, "Frequently Asked Questions," 26. Cavek, an IBM archivist, sent the document to the authors in March 2008).

41. Marshall M. Lee, *Winning with People: The First Forty Years of Tektronix* (Beaverton, OR: Tektronix, Inc., 1986): 100, 106–117, 128. For information about the role that Allen DuMont and DuMont Laboratories played in cathode ray tubes (CRT), see also Erik Barnouw, *Tube of Plenty: The Evolution of American Television* (New York: Oxford University Press, 1990). Packard, *The HP Way*, 78–79.

42. Packard, *The HP Way*, 60.

43. A. S. Bagley, "A 10 MC Scaler for Nuclear Counting and Frequency Measurement," *HP Journal* 2, 2 (October 1950); A. S. Bagley, "The High-Speed Frequency Counter; A New Solution to Old Problems," *HP Journal* 2, 5 (January 1951).

44. Lee, *Winning with People*, 98–100. Tektronix set up its first field office February 1, 1951; no manufacturer's representatives remained by the end of 1953.

45. Lee, *Winning with People*, 48. See also Marshall M. Lee, *A Passion for Quality: The First Fifty-Five Years of Electro Scientific Industries, 1944–1999* (Portland, OR: ESI, 2000).

46. Lee, *Winning with People*, 38.

47. Lee, *Winning with People*, 98–100.

48. Ernst Guillemin, *Introductory Circuit Theory* (New York: McGraw-Hill, 1953). From MIT Great Educators' biography: "Quantity alone does not portray adequately his greatness as an educator" (EECS Great Educators, "Ernst Adolph Guillemin," http://www.eecs.mit.edu/great-educators/guillemin.html).

49. Dick Reynolds and Duane Dunwoodie, "A New DC-300KC High-Sensitivity Oscilloscope with Triggered Sweep," *HP Journal* 7, 7 (March 1956).

50. The four follow-on models were 130B, 130BR, 120A, and 122A. Duane Dunwoodie, and Dick Reynolds, "A Rack-Mounting DC-300 KC Oscilloscope with Expandable Sweep," *HP Journal* 8, 12 (August 1957); Duane Dunwoodie, "Increased Operational Simplicity in a New DC-Several Hundred KC Oscilloscope," *HP Journal* 9, 6 (February 1958); John Strathman, "A Dual-Trace Automatic Base Line Oscilloscope for the DC-Several Hundred KC Range," *HP Journal* 10, 1–2 (September-October 1958).

51. Robert A. Grimm and Norman B. Schrock, "A New DC-10 MC Oscilloscope with Dual-Trace and High-Gain Preamplifiers," *HP Journal* 7, 8 (April 1956).

52. Lee, *Winning with People*, 240–241. Hewlett said, "'We agreed on a sum of money . . . that sounds like peanuts now . . . symbolic to cover past sins.' Vollum asked Packard for a donation to Reed College [Vollum's alma mater], saying, 'We'll forget the whole thing,' but Packard demurred, saying, 'Howard, I'll never make a donation to anyone but Stanford University. I'll give you the money and you give it to Reed College'".

53. George Rotsky, "A 25-Year Love Affair: Semiconductor Industry Pioneers Gerard and Lilo Leeds," *EE Times Chronicles* (October 30, 1997). See www.highbeam.com/library and also Nancy Konish and Richard Gawel, "Market Facts: Load Up! Semiconductors Moving Up in 1999," www.elecdesign.com/Globals/PlanetEE/Content/3116.html. In addition, Steve Scrupski, "40 Years Ago in Electronic Design: Pulse-Sampling Scope Reads Ultra-Fast Rise Times," *Electronic Design* (April 15, 1959): 42.

54. Lee, *Winning with People*, 16–17.

55. Barney Oliver, Kirby interview, 15 (ATA).

56. Lee, *Winning with People*, 100.

57. Vannevar Bush, "As We May Think," *Atlantic Monthly* 176, 1 (July 1945): 101–108. Bush's article was reprinted in James Nyce and Paul Kahn, *From Memex to Hypertext—Vannevar Bush and the Mind's Machine* (Boston: Academic Press, 1991),

85–107. See Martin Campbell-Kelly and William Asprey, *Computer: A History of the Information Machine* (New York: Basic Books, 1996), 286–288. See also *Life* magazine 19, 11 (November 19, 1945).

58. Thierry Bardini, *Bootstrapping: Douglas Engelbart, Coevolution and Origins of Personal Computing* (Stanford, CA: Stanford University Press, 2000); and Gary Wolf, "The Curse of Xanadu," *Wired* 3, 6 (June 1995).

59. Oliver learned these concepts at Bell Labs and taught them to HP engineers. Two *HP Journal* articles in November 1955 touted pulse generators and oscilloscopes as preferred methods: B. M. Oliver, "Square Wave and Pulse Testing of Linear Systems," *HP Journal* 7, 3 (November 1955); and B. M. Oliver, "Step Function Response of Typical Networks", *HP Journal* 7, 3 (November 1955).

60. In fact, it was not Thomas Watson Sr., as usually cited, but Thomas Watson Jr., a decade later, and the quote re: five machines was entirely out of context. See note 40 above.

61. Ken Olsen (keynote remarks, World Future Society Convention, Boston 1977). His biographer argues that this has been taken out of context: Edgar H. Schein, *DEC is Dead, Long Live DEC* (San Francisco: Berret-Koehler, 2003), 38–40.

62. The time away from HP took place primarily from late spring 1954 through early 1955. Bruce Wholey, Ed van Bronkhorst, Noel Porter, and Ralph Lee, personal communication with Charles H. House, May 29, 1986, on a company plane from Colorado Springs to San Jose after Norm Schrock's retirement party.

63. "Hewlett Completes Term as National I.R.E. Prexy," *HP Watt's Current* (February 1955): 1; "Bill and Flora Hewlett Sail on European Trip—Hewlett to Interview Prospective Sales Reps in Foreign Countries," *HP Watt's Current* (April 1955): 1; "Press of Executive Duties," 7.

64. Packard, *The HP Way*, 70.

65. Ibid.

66. Barney Oliver, interview by David Kirby, April 5, 1991, 36–37 (ATA). Oliver placed these meetings at 395 Page Mill Road circa mid-1955 to early 1956.

67. Ed van Bronkhorst, interview by David Kirby, May 18, 1995, 37 (ATA).

68. Dave Packard and Bill Hewlett, *History Documentation* (Palo Alto, CA: HP TV Network, A Hewlett Family Production, 1983).

CHAPTER 3

1. John Doyle, interview by Raymond L. Price, March 23, 2005, 1.

2. Frank Cavier, interview by David Kirby, January 28, 1991, 43 (ATA); Alan Bagley, interview by Robert Grimm, July 10, 1990 (ATA); Edwin van Bronkhorst, interview by David Kirby, May 18, 1995, 33–34 (ATA).

3. Cort Van Rensselaer, interview by Alan Bagley, November 9, 1991, 64–65 (ATA). The executive committee—Hewlett, Oliver, Cavier, Eldred, and Porter—participated on the draft. Attendees included designers Al Bagley, Bruce Wholey, John Cage, and Norm Schrock, plus Cort Van Rensselaer and Bill Doolittle on Eldred's staff; Ed van Bronkhorst and David Bates on Cavier's staff; Ralph Lee, Stan Selby, Gordon Eding, Bob Sundberg, Phil Towle, Ray Deméré, and Bill Myers on Porter's manufacturing team; and Harold Buttner.

4. See "Hewlett-Packard Statement of Corporate Objectives," *HP Measure* (July 1974): 7–10.

5. Doyle, interview. See also "The Test of Time," *HP Measure* (May-June 2000): 56–60.

6. Adapted from William G. Ouchi, *Theory Z: How American Business Can Meet the Japanese Challenge* (Menlo Park, CA: Addison-Wesley, 1981).

7. Albert Yuen, *Bill & Dave's Memos* (Palo Alto, CA: 2DaysofSummer Books, 2006), 249–251.

8. Official HP records for October 31 year-end numbers (ATA); David Packard, *The HP Way: How Bill Hewlett and I Built Our Company* (New York: HarperCollins, 1995), 70.

9. Larry Greiner, "Evolution and Revolution as Organizations Grow," *Harvard Business Review* 50 (1972): 37–46. Updated in HBR Classic Series, *Harvard Business Review* (May-June 1998): 55–64.

10. A logarithmic plot differs from a linear plot because it has a constantly shrinking dimensional axis. A constant percentage rate of increase is drawn as a straight line rather than curvilinear.

11. Dave Packard, "From Our President's Desk—Birth of Dynac, Inc.," *HP Watt's Current* (January 1956): 1 (ATA); Dave Packard, "From Our President's Desk—Dynac Stock Permit Issued," *HP Watt's Current* (March 1956): 1; and Jim Hobson, "Dynac in Gear—First Instrument Shipped," *HP Watt's Current* (May 1956): 6. See also Frank Bequaert, "The Inverted Circle—Dynac Ships First of Its Own Design," *HP Watt's Current* (February 1957): 12 (ATA); and Cort Van Rensselaer, "HP and Dynac Combine Forces for 12th Annual I.S.A. [Instrument Society of America] Show and Exhibit," *HP Watt's Current* (October 1957): 2 (ATA).

12. *Hewlett-Packard Annual Report* (1957): inside back cover. Personal income taxes were very regressive at this time, peaking at 91 percent. Taxed at these rates, Bill and Dave collectively netted $432,000 for themselves and gave away $885,000 to employees; the IRS netted $4.368M.

Such high taxes on personal income had impelled the duo to incorporate initially in 1947, but taking the company public yielded numerous other advantages. Dave Packard and Bill Hewlett, *History Documentation* (Palo Alto, CA: HP TV Network, A Hewlett Family Production, 1983).

13. Doyle, interview, 2.

14. "Hewlett-Packard Company Becomes Closed Corporation—Reasons and Effects of Change Set Forth by Hewlett," *HP Watt's Current* (August 12, 1947): 1 (ATA). Based upon a stock price of $121.50, and forty-eight shares per original share due to stock splits.

15. David Packard, "The Fourth Dimension of Management" (lecture, Paul Holden Management Luncheon, Los Angeles, April 6, 1966) (ATA).

16. David Packard, "Dave Packard of Hewlett-Packard Speaks on Choosing Tomorrow's Managers," *Electronic Design* (July 19, 1978): 92–96 (ATA).

17. Ibid.

18. Ibid.

19. William R. Hewlett (ed.), *Inventions of Opportunity: Matching Technology with Market Needs* (Palo Alto, CA: Hewlett-Packard, 1983), vii.

20. Packard and Hewlett, *History Documentation.*

21. Bagley, interview, 61 (quoting Packard) (ATA).

22. "New HP Research and Development Divisions," *Hewlett-Packard Journal* (hereafter *HP Journal*) 9, 6 (February 1958): 6.

23. Ed van Bronkhorst, interview by David Kirby, July 31, 1995, 43 (ATA).

24. "Complete Co-operation with Development Lab Highly Essential," *HP Watt's Current* (July 1953) (ATA); "Should We Break Picnic into Smaller Groups?" *HP Watt's Current* (July

1959); "We're Proud of Our New Affiliates," *HP Watt's Current* (December 1959); "HP's Progress Result of Teamwork," *HP Watt's Current* (December 1959); "HP's Program Requires Effective Communications at All Levels," *HP Watt's Current* (August 1960); "Interchange of Personnel—Vital to a Lively HP," *HP Watt's Current* (September 1961).

25. General George Marshall, chairman of the Joint Chiefs of Staff during World War II, was Truman's secretary of state.

26. This is remarkably under-reported in HP history. Hewlett's network from his Army days was robust and very well-connected to the scientific leadership of the day. This led, for example, to Luis Alvarez serving on HP's board. See "William Hewlett: An Interview Conducted by Michael McMahon, November 27, 1984, #046, 10, http://www.ieee.org/portal/cms_docs_iportals/iportals/aboutus/history_center/oral_history/pdfs/Hewlett046.pdf.

27. Packard and Hewlett, *History Documentation.*

28. Dick Alberding, interview by Charles H. House, September 19, 2006. Alberding, twenty-three, was picked because he could read and converse in German.

29. Carl Cottrell, interview by Raymond L. Price, October 28, 2005, 5.

30. Packard and Hewlett, *History Documentation.*

31. "Ray Deméré Off for Germany to Manage Stuttgart Plant," *HP Watt's Current* (September 1959): 3 (ATA); Bill Feeley, "Production Rolling at Boeblingen," *HP Watt's Current* (November 1959): 16.

32. Packard and Hewlett, *History Documentation.*

33. Bro Utall, "The Fortune Directory of the 500 Largest Industrial Corporations," *Fortune* (May 1975): 208–235.

34. Ward Winslow, *Palo Alto: A Centennial History* (Palo Alto, CA: Palo Alto Historical Association, 1993): 54.

35. Winslow, *Palo Alto.*

36. Ward Winslow and Joanna McClean, *Pages from a Palo Alto Editor's Scrapbook* (Palo Alto, CA: Ward Winslow Writing, 1994), 177.

37. Winslow and McClean, *Scrapbook*, 168.

38. Winslow and McClean, *Scrapbook*, 168.

39. *Hewlett-Packard Annual Report* (1959): 6.

40. The five main criteria for new plant sites: (1) an esthetic smaller town; (2) a good local university with a graduate engineering program; (3) a stable, sizable local manufacturing labor pool; (4) good airport access; and (5) a stable secular and political environment. Scoffers said new plant sites near corporate officers' natal homes or great skiing venues had an edge. See "Loveland Colorado Division Perspective," *HP Measure* (January 1965): 6–7.

41. Hewlett repeated this phrase frequently; *viz.* the R&D Manager's forum with 2100 attendees in April 1986, aired from the corporate TV studios.

42. For information about the new plant, see "Ultramodern Scope Plant for Colorado Springs," *HP Watt's Current* (April 1963): 4 (ATA); and "Ceremonies, Tours Mark Four New Plant Openings," *HP Measure* (November 1964): 9. See the profile "HP Perspectives: Colorado Springs Division," *HP Measure* (March 1966): 6–7. See also "New Oscilloscope Division Formed (H-P's Fifth New Division Will Be Located at 395 Page Mill Road)," *HP Watt's Current* (March 1961): 3.

43. "New HP Research and Development Divisions," *HP Journal* 9, 6 (February 1958).

44. See Alan Bagley and Dexter Hartke, "Counter Transfer Oscillator System for Microwave Frequency Measurements," *IEEE* (1956), www.ieee-uffc.org/main/publications/

fcs/proceed/1956/s5610496.pdf - 1982-07-01. See also "HP Perspective: Frequency and Time Division," *HP Measure* (May 1965): 6–7.

45. Data computed from Charles House source documents dated June 1, 1976, compiled from corporate records.

46. "HP Perspective: Loveland Colorado Division," *HP Measure* (January 1965): 6–7. See George Rotsky, "Gauging the Impact of DVMs," published in *Electronic Engineering Times* in 1997 as part of the publication's twenty-fifth anniversary celebration. The article is now located at www.eet.com/anniversary/designclassics/gauging.html. Ballantine Laboratories, in Boonton, New Jersey, provided test equipment for Radio Frequency Laboratories, one of the early radio companies. Ballantine spin-outs included Boonton Radio (acquired by HP in 1959).

47. Rod Carlson (sampling scope program) and John Blokker (pulse generator program) later became HP division managers. Dick Monnier (HP 140A program) became project leader for the HP 9100A desktop calculator; Kay Magleby, the principal sampling scope designer, transferred to HP Labs, initiating the HP 2116A instrumentation computer. Duane Dunwoodie joined Bill Jarvis in forming Wiltron Corporation.

48. "HP Announces Plans to Acquire New Building Site," *HP Measure* (July 1966): 8; "News in Brief," *HP Measure* (September 1968): 14; "News in Brief," *HP Measure* (June 1969): 14; "Looking at New Growth: Santa Clara, Formerly F&T, and Loveland," *HP Measure* (July 1969): 10–13; Leonard S. Cutler and Alan S. Bagley, "A New Performance of the 'Flying Clock' Experiment," *HP Journal* 15 (July 1964): 11; also Albert Benjaminson, "Precision Measurement of Ocean Temperatures," *HP Journal* 18 (April 1967): 8–12.

49. Doug Chance, interview by Raymond L. Price and Charles H. House, March 24, 2005, 11.

50. Chance, interview, 11–12.

51. Chance, interview, 12.

52. Many *HP Measure* stories attest to community involvement and receptivity.

53. While vintage charts were both ubiquitous and a crucial tool for management, their adoption and use was quite variable. It often took guidance from Bill or Dave for groups to actually study and understand the charts. For example, when Packard challenged Barney Oliver in 1953: "Are you going to give me a lot of excuses or are you going to get something done?" (Chapter 2).

54. Brunner later worked for Norm Neely in North Hollywood before returning to Palo Alto when HP bought the rep companies in 1963. He became the first Corporate Engineering director after a brief stint as Scope Division marketing manager for Cort Van Rensselaer.

55. Brunnergrams were used widely throughout the company for lab project management. See *Project Management Anthology, Volume 1: 1984–1988* (Palo Alto, CA: Hewlett-Packard Corporate Engineering, 1988), 1–101.

56. Cort Van Rensselaer, interview by Charles H. House, December 6, 2005.

57. Bill Hewlett, personal communication with Charles H. House, May 29, 1986 (on a plane ride to Norm Schrock's retirement party in Colorado Springs).

58. Walt Selsted, interview by Raymond L. Price, September 17, 2004, 5.

59. "The HP Express," *HP Measure* (September 1975): 2–7.

CHAPTER 4

1. Bill Hewlett, "From the President's Desk—Corporate Organizational Structure," *HP Measure* (May 1975): 2.

2. Michael Polayni, *Personal Knowledge: Towards a Post-Critical Philosophy* (Chicago: University of Chicago Press, [1958] 1974).

3. Bruce Wholey, interview by Alan Bagley, August 15, 1990, 25 (ATA).

4. Paul Ely, interview by Raymond L. Price, December 2005, 8.

5. Ibid.

6. Kenneth Jessen, *How It All Began, Hewlett-Packard's Loveland Facility* (Loveland, CO: J.V. Publications, 1999), nostalgically describes the first decentralized HP division.

7. James Pettit, "A DC-to-VHF Oscilloscope," *Hewlett-Packard Journal* (hereafter *HP Journal*) 21, 4 (January 1970): 2–8; David Chaffee, "A Fast-Writing, High-Frequency Cathode-Ray Tube," *HP Journal* 21, 4 (January 1970): 9–10; Alan J. DeVilbiss, "A Wideband Oscilloscope Amplifier," *HP Journal* 21, 4 (January 1970): 11–14.

8. In late 1982, the HP 1980 scope family was launched, with strong HPL support, doubling scope revenues by 1988 to $85 million. William B. Risley, "Oscilloscope Measurement System Is Programmable and Autoranging," *HP Journal* 33, 9 (September 1982): 3–4; William E. Watry, Monte R. Campbell, Russell J. Harding, John R. Wilson, and Wilhelm Taylor, "Designing the Oscilloscope Measurement System," *HP Journal* 33, 9 (September 1982): 5–13; William Duffy, John Meredith, and Mike McTigue, "Custom Microcircuits Make the 1980A/B Possible," *HP Journal* 33, 9 (September 1982): 7; Zvonko Fazarinc, "The Early History of the 1980A/B Oscilloscope Measurement System," *HP Journal* 33, 9 (September 1982): 14; William B. Risley, "The Design and Development of the 1980A/B at Colorado Springs," *HP Journal* 33, 9 (September 1982): 14; Robert M. Landgraf and Eddie A. Evel, "Digital Waveform Storage for the Oscilloscope Measurement System," *HP Journal* 33, 9 (September 1982): 15–20.

9. "News in Brief," *HP Measure* (November 1971): 14; "News in Brief," *HP Measure* (June 1972): 14.

10. Doug Chance, interview by Raymond L. Price and Charles H. House, March 24, 2005, 11–12.

11. H. Wolff, *How They Sell* (New York: Dow Jones and Company, 1965), 5 (includes a quote from Noel Eldred, HP marketing vice president).

12. Marshall M. Lee, *Winning with People: The First Forty Years of Tektronix* (Beaverton, OR: Tektronix, Inc., 1986), 99.

13. The Institute of Electrical and Electronic Engineers (IEEE) was a 1963 merger of two professional societies for electrical engineers, American Institute of Electrical Engineers (AIEE) and the Institute of Radio Engineers (IRE). IEEE managed a New York City trade show each March; the Western Electronic Manufacturer's Association (WEMA) (now American Electronics Association, or AEA) hosted WESCON (Western Electronics Conference) on the West Coast.

14. "Five Key Promotions in Sales Re-organization," *HP Watt's Current* (March 1963): 5 (ATA).

15. Dave Yewell, interview by Charles H. House, April 2006.

16. Harry J. Lang, "Meet Our Representatives: Bivins and Caldwell," *The Boonton Radio Notebook* 20 (Winter 1959): p. 7, http://hparchive.com/Boonton/BRC-The-Notebook-20.pdf.

17. *HP Watt's Current* covered various manufacturer's reps over the years. See Cort Van Rensselaer, "Yewell Associates' Open House—One of the Most Successful of All Time," *HP Watt's Current* (January 1956): 3; and Noel Eldred, "Our Reps Are Selling," *HP Watt's Current* (January 1956): 3; also see "Tenth Anniversary for Yewell Organization," *HP*

Watt's Current (January 1963): 6. Neely had its own newsletter, *La Prensa*, continued for years after acquisition by HP.

18. Neely Enterprises was the West Coast distributor for HP in the 1950s. Many HP leaders began their careers at Neely, including Bob Boniface, Al Oliverio, and Bob Brunner. For information about the Neely bus, see the photo "Norman B. Neely's Mobile Lab," *HP Watt's Current* (September 1953): 3 (ATA). See also emulators in other regions, especially "Earl Lipscomb's Fifty-Three Foot Travel-Lab, Interior/Exterior," *HP Watt's Current* (November 1953): 3; and "Crossley Associates' New Electro-Cruiser (30-Passenger Airport Bus Converted to Demo Vehicle)," *HP Watt's Current* (August 1961): 4.

19. "A Happy Wagon for Smooth Demonstrations," *HP Measure* (December 1964): 8.

20. Ibid.

21. David Packard, *The HP Way: How Bill Hewlett and I Built Our Company* (New York: HarperBusiness, 1995), 50.

22. Wolff, *How They Sell.* See also W. Noel Eldred, "Around the Circuit," *HP Measure* (December 1964): 10.

23. Wolff, *How They Sell*, 5, 7.

24. "Order Processing Streamlined," *HP Measure* (November 1963): 6–7.

25. Ibid.

26. Bud Eldon, private correspondence with Charles H. House, August 22, 2008.

27. John Doyle, *Hewlett-Packard Laboratories* [brochure] (1982): 2.

28. William R. Hewlett (ed.), *Inventions of Opportunity: Matching Technology with Market Needs* (Palo Alto, CA: Hewlett-Packard, 1983), viii.

29. Doyle, *Laboratories.*

30. B. M. Oliver, J. R. Pierce, and C. E. Shannon, "The Philosophy of PCM," *Proceedings of the I.R.E.* 36 (November 1948): 1324–1331).

31. Hewlett, *Inventions of Opportunity.*

32. Don Hammond, interview by Raymond L. Price, September 15, 2005, 4.

33. Bernard M. Oliver, *The Selected Papers of Bernard M. Oliver*, ed. Zvonko Favarinc, Thomas Hornak, and Leonard S. Cutler (Palo Alto, CA: HP Press, 1997) (includes 191 papers not previously published) (ATA). See also B. M. Oliver, "Square Wave and Pulse Testing of Linear Systems," *HP Journal* 7, 3 (November 1955): 1–6; B. M. Oliver, "Time-Domain Reflectometry," *HP Journal* 15, 6 (February 1964): 1–7; and Bernard M. Oliver and John M. Cage, *Electronic Measurements and Instrumentation* (New York: McGraw-Hill, Chapter 3).

34. Charles H. House, notes from eulogies and interviews, 1st Methodist Church, Palo Alto, California, November 20, 1995.

35. Notable contributions were made for scopes, including internal graticule capability to reduce parallax ambiguity for the user, a radial-field helical CRT, variable-persistence storage, and an extremely low-duty-cycle bright CRT for a TV signal monitor. Bertrand W. Squier Jr., "A New DC-450 KC Oscilloscope Using the Internal-Graticule CRT," *HP Journal* 12, 11–12 (July-August 1961); R. H. Kolar, "Variable Persistence Increases Oscilloscope's Versatility," *Electronics* (November 29, 1965): 66–70; Ralph R. Reiser and Richard E. Monnier, "A New TV Waveform Oscilloscope for Precision Measurements of Video Test Signals," *HP Journal* 17, 6 (February 1966): 2–6; John J. Dupre, John R. Page Jr., and Richard C. Keiter, "Advances in Spectrum Analysis," *HP Journal* 19, 6 (February 1968): 7–16.

36. "The Radial Field Cathode-Ray Tube," *HP Journal* 15, 1 (September 1963): 7, presaged the lead paragraph in the article by Richard E. Monnier, "A New Electronic Calculator (HP

Model 9100A) with Computerlike Capabilities," *HP Journal* (September 1969): 3, which describes the importance of the CRT display, but doesn't cite William Kruger's individual contribution. Milton E. Russell, "Factors in Designing a Large-Screen, Wideband CRT," *HP Journal* (December 1967): 10–11.

37. Ivan Sutherland, *Sketchpad: A Man-Machine Graphical Communication System* (New York: Garland, 1980). See also Proceedings of the ACM/IEEE 3rd SHARE Design Automation Workshop, New Orleans, May 1966; and G. J. Culler and B. D. Fried, "The TRW Two-Station, On-Line Scientific Computer: General Description," in Margo A. Sass and William D. Wilkinson (eds.), *Symposium on Computer Augmentation of Human Reasoning* (Washington, DC: Spartan Books, 1965): 66–67.

38. Ed Holland, interview by Raymond L. Price, December 7, 2004, 14.

39. Gifford Pinchot III, *Intrapreneuring: Why You Don't Have to Leave the Corporation to Become an Entrepreneur* (New York: Harper and Row, 1985), 28. See also *HP Origins* (March 2006), a video produced by HP for employees.

40. The *Hewlett-Packard Annual Report* (1967), 3, highlighted the CRT gun structure; and the *Hewlett-Packard Annual Report* (1968), 10–11, showed pictures of the HP 2116 with the HP 1300A in three photos along with the just-released HP 9100A with its integral CRT.

41. Douglas C. Engelbart et. al, demonstration, Joint Computer Conference, San Francisco, December 9, 1968. Engelbart and his seventeen researchers in the Augmentation Research Center at Stanford Research Institute in Menlo Park, California, gave a ninety-minute live public demonstration of the NLS online system they had been building since 1962. The session, attended by a thousand computer professionals, was the public debut of the computer mouse and many other innovations, including hypertext, object addressing, and dynamic file linking, as well as shared-screen collaboration involving two persons at different sites communicating over a network with audio and video interface. See the Engelbart Collection at Stanford University, http://sloan.stanford.edu/MouseSite/Archive.html.

42. The Flex Machine predated HP's 9100A desktop calculator introduction. Alan Kay, Art Museum interview, http://www.artmuseum.net/w2vr/archives/Kay/00_Flex.html.

43. Alan Kay, interview by Charles H. House, January 20, 2006. Faced with claims by Stewart Brand about a citation from 1974, and Alan Kay from 1972, *OED* etymologist and Yale Law School librarian Fred Shapiro did some digging and found the following HP ad: "The new Hewlett-Packard 9100A personal computer," the ad proclaims, is "ready, willing, and able . . . to relieve you of waiting to get on the big computer," (*Science*, advertisement, October 4, 1968, http://www.hp.com/hpinfo/abouthp/histnfacts/museum/personalsystems/0021/). See Aaron Clark, "The First PC," *Wired* 8, 12 (December 2000), http://www.wired.com/wired/archive/8.12/mustread.html?pg=11.

44. "Down to Earth Study of the Moon," *HP Measure* (May 1968): 16; "HP to the Moon," *HP Measure* (May 1969): 16; "The Giant Step," *HP Measure* (September 1969): 2–5. Denton Cooley's heart transplant was a national story that ran May 4, 1968, with an Associated Press wirephoto of the HP1308A Medical Monitor in use during surgery.

45. Pinchot, *Intrapreneuring*, 23–30; "Extraordinary People," *HP Measure* (September-October 1985): 8–9; Packard, *The HP Way*, 107–108; and *HP Origins*.

46. DEC's well-known VT-100 video display terminal was not offered for another decade; even the VT-52 didn't appear until 1975, http://en.wikipedia.org/wiki/VT100. The first use of large-screen displays and CRT-based data entry display capability is described in Kenneth Fox, Marc Pasturel, and Peter Showman, "A Human Interface for Automatic Measurement Systems," *HP Journal* 23, 8 (April 1972): 10–17; and John Riggen and Douglas

Fogg, "An Agile Graphic Display Device," *HP Journal* 23, 8 (April 1972): 18–24. Major cost reductions in magnetic TV display units changed the instrumentation display business in the 1980s away from HP's electrostatic CRTs.

47. LaThare N. Bodily, Ronald C. Hyatt, and Dexter Hartke, "World-Wide Time Synchronization, 1966," *HP Journal* 17, 12 (August 1966): 13–20. LaThare N. Bodily, "A Summary of Some Performance Characteristics of a Large Sample of Cesium-Beam Frequency Standards," *HP Journal* 18, 2 (October 1966): 16–19; and Darwin H. Throne, "A Rubidium-Vapor Frequency Standard for Systems Requiring Superior Frequency Stability," *HP Journal* 19, 11 (July 1968): 8–14.

48. Hammond, interview, 13.

49. The HP 3800 distance meter, introduced in 1970, was first cited at $3,550 in *HP Catalog* (1972): 79. Michael L. Bullock and Richard E. Warren, "Electronic Total Station Speeds Survey Operations," *HP Journal* 27, 8 (April 1976): 2–12.

50. See Don M. Cross, "High-Accuracy Laser-Interferometer Camera for IC Masks," *HP Journal* 18,12 (August 1967): 5–8. See also John N. Dukes and Gary B. Gordon, "A Two-Hundred-Foot Yardstick with Graduations Every Microinch," *HP Journal* 21, 12 (August 1970): 2–8; Glenn M. Burgwald and William Kruger, "An Instant-On Laser for Length Measurement," *HP Journal* 21, 12 (August 1970): 14–16; three other articles (by four HP authors) in the August 1970 issue are also devoted to the Model 5525A Laser Interferometer.

51. Don Hammond, interview by Raymond L. Price, September 15, 2005, 14.

52. The most difficult aspect of highly toxic three-five semiconductor processing was extreme susceptibility to surface contamination. This problem initiated Hammond's work in inks. See Egon Loebner, T. J. Diesel, and Cristy M. Schade, "ADAC—An Automatic System for Measuring Hall Effect in Semiconductors," *HP Journal* 18, 3 (November 1966): 9–14; and "A Study of Indium Arsenide Using ADAC Equipment," *HP Journal* 18, 3 (November 1966): 15–16.

53. Peter Coy, "Research Labs Get Real: It's About Time," *BusinessWeek* 3706 (November 6, 2000): 51, is sharply critical of XeroxPARC's approach and accomplishments. Nathan Myhrvold, who headed Microsoft Research for a decade, believed that "long-term basic research projects are being neglected in Corporate Research labs, which have moved toward customer-driven applied research. Invention just gets short shrift." Robert Weisman, "Inventing the Future," *Boston Globe* (April 3, 2006): E4, E5.

54. Jim Gibbons, interview by Charles H. House, September 14, 2006, 1–2; Kay, interview.

55. Tennenhouse, DARPA director of computing in the 1990's, joined Intel in 1999 as director of research, establishing multiple lablets at major universities. Bell, chief architect of many DEC computers, has been a senior researcher with Microsoft Research since 1997.

56. Hammond, interview, 14.

57. Hammond, interview, 15.

CHAPTER 5

1. David Packard, *The HP Way: How Bill Hewlett and I Built Our Company* (New York: HarperBusiness, 1995), 101.

2. http://www.darpa.mil/body/overtheyears.html.

3. Federal Communications Commission, "About the FCC," http://www.fcc.gov/aboutus.html. The Federal Communications Commission regulates interstate and international

communications by radio, television, wire, satellite, and cable. For the Echo satellite speech, see http://www.historychannel.com/speeches/archive/speech_440.html. For information regarding ARPA's impact on computing, see Martin Campbell-Kelly and William Asprey, *Computer: A History of the Information Machine* (New York: Basic Books, 1996), 212–213, 288–294.

4. Bernard M. Oliver and John Cage (eds.), *Electronic Measurements and Instrumentation* (New York: McGraw-Hill, 1971).

5. Janet Dale, editorial column, *Sanborn Monitor* 3, 2 (February-March 1982): 9.

6. "On November 3, 1958, the Company exchanged 30,000 shares of its capital stock for 3,120 shares of the capital stock of F. L. Moseley Co., which represents an 80% interest in that company. At October 31, 1958 the F. L. Moseley Co. capital stock had a book value of $72.39 a share." *Hewlett-Packard Annual Report* (1966): 11, footnote 5. Book value of the company thus was $282,321; the sale to HP was equivalent to a total company valuation of $2.0M since HP stock had risen by a 3.3 factor.

7. "Moseley Autograf, Model 7101B Strip Chart Recorder, 1965," HP Virtual Museum, http://www.hp.com/hpinfo/abouthp/histnfacts/museum/imagingprinting/0015/.

8. *Hewlett-Packard Annual Report* (1959): 10.

9. See Hewlett-Packard annual reports for the years 1958 through 1966. The numbers cited do not count sales companies that were acquired.

10. *Hewlett-Packard Annual Report* (1966): 5.

11. Peter Moseley, interview by Charles H. House, March 2003 (Peter is Francis Moseley's son); Peter Moseley, private correspondence with Charles H. House, December 2005.

12. William D. Loughlin invented the "Q-Meter", founding Boonton Radio in Boonton, New Jersey, in 1934 after working for years with Stuart Ballantine at the Navy Labs and the Radio Frequency Labs. When he died in 1950, his son Robert W. Loughlin Sr. took over, selling the company to HP in 1961. Robert Sr. served for years on the Princeton Institute for Advanced Study Board. See "In Memory of William D. Loughlin," *Princeton Institute for Advanced Study Attributions* 1 (2001): 3.

13. Frank Boff invented the Boff diode at HPA, known now as the step recovery diode. Overacker was at the MIT radiation lab during World War II.

14. John Minck, *Inside HP: A Narrative History of Hewlett-Packard from 1939–1990*, 33, http://www.home.agilent.com/upload/cmc_upload/secure/MinckHPNAR29.pdf.

15. "When there's merger in the air, both sides just love each other and they can't see the faults of each other. And if you tell them something negative about the other party, it's just like calling some guy's bride-to-be a hooker!" Frank Cavier, interview by David Kirby, January 28, 1991, 32–33 (ATA).

16. See Dave Packard, "From Our President's Desk: Sanborn Association Creates Challenging Opportunity," *HP Watt's Current* (October 1961): 2 (ATA).

17. Minck, *Inside HP*, 33.

18. The *Hewlett-Packard Annual Report* (1961) listed in detail total revenue for 1960 at $60,656,096 without Sanborn, $77,365,956 with—an incremental gain of $16,709,860.

19. Dave Packard and Bill Hewlett, *History Documentation* (Palo Alto, CA: HP TV Network, A Hewlett Family Production, 1983).

20. When Hewlett tired of M&A in 1966, Cage briefly managed Mechrolabs, then at HP Labs was editor for a McGraw-Hill opus: Bernard M. Oliver and John M. Cage, *Electronic Measurements and Instrumentation* (New York: McGraw-Hill, 1971).

21. F&M was named from founder Frank Martinez's initials. Martinez left HP shortly after the sale.

22. See "HP 4953A Protocol Analyzer," *Hewlett-Packard Journal* (hereafter *HP Journal*) 36, 7 (July 1985): cover (includes a photo).

23. Melchor left HP in 1968, starting a successful career in venture capital; Perkins did likewise in 1972. See Michael S. Malone, *The Valley of Heart's Delight* (New York: John Wiley & Sons, 2002), 243.

24. See Hewlett-Packard annual reports for the years 1958 through 1966. The numbers cited do not count sales companies that were acquired.

25. Packard and Hewlett, *History Documentation.*

26. Packard and Hewlett, *History Documentation.*

27. Packard and Hewlett, *History Documentation.*

28. Dave Packard, "From Our President's Desk," *HP Watt's Current* (July 1958): 2 (ATA).

29. Greenewalt, later to become president of DuPont, worked with University of Chicago physicists trying to obtain enough plutonium for the Manhattan project. This connected Vannevar Bush, Felix Bloch, and Luis Alvarez to Hewlett. See Crawford Greenewalt, *Manhattan Project Diary*, Hagley Library, Wilmington, Delaware. McCarthy ran the Freon lab, which identified the cause of the hole in the ozone and subsequent action to ban CFC manufacture.

30. Alan Bagley, interview by Robert Grimm, July 10, 1990, 34 (ATA).

31. Ibid.

32. Don Hammond, interview with Alan Bagley, October 25, 1990 (ATA).

33. Albert Benjaminson, "Precision Measurement of Ocean Temperatures," *HP Journal* 18, 9 (April 1967): 8–12.

34. Minck, *Inside HP*, 59–60.

35. Leonard S. Cutler and Alan S. Bagley, "A New Performance of the 'Flying Clock' Experiment," *HP Journal* 15, 11 (July 1964).

36. LaThare N. Bodily, "Correlating Time from Europe to Asia with Flying Clocks," *HP Journal* 16, 8 (April 1965). See also LaThare N. Bodily, Ronald C. Hyatt, and Dexter Hartke, "World-Wide Time Synchronization 1966," *HP Journal* 17, 12 (August 1966): 13–20.

37. Charlie Trimble, working for Al Bagley, purchased rights to the body of work, founding Trimble Navigation, which became a leading developer of GPS concepts. Ex-HPite Thomas Mitchell Coates pioneered Trimble's superior algorithms for the speed-of-light transmission along irregular coastlines.

38. Heinz Sommer, Walter Ruchsay, Peter Salfeld, and Erich Courtin, "A Versatile, Semiautomatic Fetal Monitor for Non-Technical Users," *HP Journal* 28, 5 (January 1977): 16–24.

39. Douglas H. Smith, "Model 5700A Gas Chromatograph: High Performance Flame-Ionization Detector System," *HP Journal* 24, 7 (March 1973): 2–10.

40. John N. Dukes and Gary B. Gordon, "Model 5525A Laser Interferometer: A Two-Hundred-Foot Yardstick with Graduations Every Microinch," *HP Journal* 21, 12 (August 1970): 2–8.

41. Michael L. Bullock and Richard E. Warren, "Electronic Total Station Speeds Survey Operations," *HP Journal* 27, 8 (April 1976): 2–12.

42. William F. Craven, "Protecting Hospitalized Patients from Electrical Hazards," *HP Journal* 21, 7 (March 1970): 11–17.

43. Thomas C. Horth, "Premonitory Heartbeat Patterns Recognized by Electronic Monitor," *HP Journal* 21, 2 (October 1969): 12–20.

44. The HP 1300A Graphical Display and HP 1308A Eight-Channel Medical Monitor were 12 percent of Colorado Springs Division's revenue, and 40 percent of profits; shifting the 1308A to Waltham was not popular in Colorado Springs. Deciding after the fact where a program ought to continue development was a common HP practice—instead of strategic planning up front, HP dealt with successes after the market developed.

45. "HP's Daring Young Products and Their Flying Machines," *HP Measure* (January-February 1977): 2–5. See also Ronald D. Gatzke and Sherry R. Grobstein, "A Battery-Powered ECG Monitor for Emergency and Operating Room Environments," *HP Journal* 29, 1 (September 1977): 26–32; Edwin Merrick and Thomas Hayes, "Continuous, Non-Invasive Measurements of Arterial Blood Oxygen Levels," *HP Journal* 28, 2 (October 1976): 2–9; Sommer, Ruchsay, Salfeld, and Courtin, "Versatile Fetal Monitor," 16–24.

46. Michael A. Kelly and Charles E. Tyler, "A Second-Generation ESCA Spectrometer," *HP Journal* 24, 11 (July 1973): 2–14.

47. Howard W. Harrington, John R. Hearn, and Roger F. Rauskolb, "Rotational Microwave Spectrometer," *HP Journal* (June 1971): 2–12.

48. An entire thirty-two-page issue of the *HP Journal* was devoted to the HP 8450A Spectrophotometer. See Barry G. Willis, "Design and Performance of a Highly Integrated Parallel Access Spectrophotometer," *HP Journal* 29, 6 (February 1980): 3–11; and Richard E. Monnier, "How the 8450A Was Developed," *HP Journal* 29, 6 (February 1980): 31–32.

49. Ben Johnson was caught in the Seoul, Korea, games by a new HP LC tester. His coach, even with advance warning, believed that the illegal ingestion was still undetectable. See David Anear, "Keeping the Olympics Drug Free: The Real Champion at Montreal May Be a Machine," *HP Measure* (June 1976): 6–7.

50. Jim Serum, interview by Raymond L. Price, November 2, 2004, 13.

51. Computer History Museum, private correspondence with Charles H. House, April 18, 2007.

52. Dave Weindorf, interview by Raymond L. Price, November 11, 2004.

53. Robert D. Hall and Stewart M. Krakauer, "Microwave Harmonic Generation and Nanosecond Pulse Generation with the Step-Recovery Diode," *HP Journal* 16, 4 (December 1964). See also Hans O. Sorensen, "Using the Hot Carrier Diode as a Detector," *HP Journal* 17, 4 (December 1965): 2–5; and Milton Crane, "Using the Hot Carrier Diode as a Microwave Mixer," *HP Journal* 17, 4 (December 1965): 6–8.

54. A Nixie tube was a multi-grid vacuum tube that displayed numerals from 0 to 9. HP used an estimated 60 percent of all Nixie tubes. Gerald P. Pighini and Howard C. Borden, "Solid-State Displays," *HP Journal* 20, 6 (February 1969): 2–12. See also A.M. Cowley, "Design and Application of Silicon IMPATT Diodes," *HP Journal* 21, 9 (May 1970): 2–13.

55. Weindorf, interview, 6.

56. Weindorf, interview, 10.

57. Weindorf, interview, 7–8.

58. Wolfgang E. Ohme, "Loudness Evaluation," *HP Journal* 19, 3 (November 1967): 2–11. See also Wisu T. Kapuskar and Christopher J. Balmforth, "Monitoring Airport Noise," *HP Journal* 20, 11 (July 1969) 11–15.

59. Katsumi Yoshimoto, "A New Universal Impedance Bridge with Simplified, Semi-Automatic Tuning," *HP Journal* 18,1 (September 1966): 2–5.

60. Charles H. House, presentation, HP Corporate Software Conference, Cupertino, California, April 22, 1988.

61. The Indian Institutes of Technology (nine campuses) are usually given credit for the

extraordinary rise of the Indian software industry, along with their adoption of standard practices (*e.g.*, Carnegie Mellon's CMM process models); *cf.* AnnaLee Saxenian, World Economic Forum Innovation 100, September 3, 2008. Texas Instruments commissioned a satellite in 1986 and is generally credited with the first America R&D lab in Bangalore. In fact, the origin of the Indian software design community traces back much further—to the mathematics department at IIS and its adoption of algorithmic methodologies, abetted by the HP seminars given by David Dack of HP South Queensferry in 1977 that taught ASM design with HP Logic State Analyzers, much as did Chris Clare within HP. These techniques yielded world leadership in telephone software, such as echo-cancellation and suppression algorithms that Bell Laboratories, AT&T, and Motorola found extremely valuable for import over the satellite connection in the late 1980s.

62. House, presentation, April 22, 1988.

63. Douglas K. Smith and Robert C. Alexander, *Fumbling the Future: How Xerox Invented, Then Ignored, the First Personal Computer* (New York: William Morrow, 1988); Michael A. Hiltzig, *Dealers of Lightning: XeroxPARC and the Dawn of the Computer Age* (New York: HarperCollins, 1999); and Henry Chesbrough, *Open Innovation* (Boston: Harvard BSP, 2003).

64. Steve Jobs, keynote address, Seybold Conference, San Jose, California, May 1988.

65. Steve Shepard, "A Talk with Scott McNealy," *BusinessWeek* (April 1, 2002): 66–68, www.businessweek.com/magazine/content/02_13/b3776087.htm (contains McNealy's remarks).

66. Regis McKenna, "Marketing Is Everything," *Harvard Business Review* (January-February 1991): 65–79; John Seely Brown, "Research That Re-invents the Corporation," *Harvard Business Review* (January-February 1991): 102–111; and Charles H. House and Raymond L. Price, "The Return Map: Tracking Product Teams," *Harvard Business Review* (January-February 1991): 92–100.

67. The meeting, on January 24, 1991, was hosted by *Harvard Business Review* editor-in-chief Rosabeth Moss Kanter; McKenna and Brown described their articles. Charles House was emcee.

68. The "Seven Dwarfs" were Burroughs, Control Data Corp (CDC), GE, Honeywell, NCR, RCA, and Univac. See Homer R. Oldfield, presentation, "King of the Seven Dwarfs: GE's Ambiguous Challenge to the Computer Industry," IEEE, New York, 1996).

69. See Barney Oliver, interview by David Kirby, April 5, 1991, 55 (includes Hewlett HP board remark) (ATA).

70. Oliver, interview, 55 (ATA).

71. Alan Kay, interview by Charles H. House, January 20, 2006. As discussed in Chapter 4, Kay was impressed by a 1968 HP advertisement for the 9100A calling it a "personal computer," the first such claim he saw.

72. Packard, *The HP Way*, 97.

73. George Rotsky, "Gauging the Impact of DVMs," *EE Times*, Anniversary Edition, http://www.eetimes.com/anniversary/designclassics/gauging.html.

74. R. A. Anderson, "A New Digital Voltmeter," *HP Journal* 13, 6 (February 1962): 2–4; Ed A. Hilton, "A Versatile Digital Recorder for BCD Data," *HP Journal* 13, 6 (February 1962): 5–6; Ed A. Hilton, "A Digital-to-Analog Converter with High Output Resolution," *HP Journal* 13, 6 (February 1962): 7–8.

75. Kay B. Magleby, "A New Scope Plug-In for Convenient Measuring of Fast Switching Times," *HP Journal* 13, 7 (March 1962): 1–3; Roderick Carlson, "The Kilomegacycle Sampling

Oscilloscope," *HP Journal* 13, 7 (March 1962): 4–5; and H. C. Stansch, "A Digital System for Automatic Measurements of Switching Times," *HP Journal* 13, 7 (March 1962): 6.

76. "The First Digital Voltmeters and the Birth of Test Automation," www.hp9825.com; Theodore C. Anderson and Noel Pace, "A New Digital DC Voltmeter with Automatic Range and Polarity Selection," *HP Journal* 10, 5 (January 1959). See also David S. Cochran and Charles W. Near, "A New Multi-Purpose Digital Voltmeter," *HP Journal* 15, 3 (November 1963).

77. Frank J. Burkhard, "Our Preparations at Hewlett-Packard for the Instrumentation of Tomorrow," *HP Journal* 16, 1 (September 1964).

78. John Markoff, *What the Dormouse Said* (New York: Viking Press, 2005), 10.

79. The Douglas Jones (University of Iowa) website hosted at Ohio State University is devoted to DEC PDP history: http://www.faqs.org/faqs/dec-faq/pdp8-models/section-1.html. DEC built 116 PDP-5 embedded controllers, plus 118 "true" computing machines (PDP-1, 3, and 6).

80. Packard, *The HP Way*, 102.

81. Rick Bensene, "Wang Laboratories: From Custom Systems to Computers," October 2001, http://www.oldcalculatormuseum.com/d-wangcustom.html; An Wang, *Lessons: An Autobiography* (Boston: Addison-Wesley, 1986).

82. George T. Gray and Ronald Q. Smith, "Before the B5000: Burroughs Computers, 1951–1963," *IEEE Annals of the History of Computing* 25, 2 (April 2003): 50–61.

83. Alfred D. Chandler Jr., *Inventing the Electronic Century: The Epic Story of the Consumer Electronics and Computer Industries* (New York: Free Press, 2001), 86–103.

84. Kay B. Magleby, "A Computer for Instrumentation Systems," *HP Journal* 18, 7 (March 1967): 2–10; see also "Successful Instrument-Computer Marriages," *HP Journal* 18, 7 (March 1967): 11–12.

85. "The article and other text followed Packard's desire, but the simple '2100A Computer' designation was arrived at after much discussion and debate, in line with the labeling of other HP products." Robert Grimm, private correspondence with Charles H. House, December 4, 2005.

86. Computers then were in low-contaminant, controlled-humidity rooms with a maximum temperature variation of 15°–35° C (59°–95° F). Standard HP instruments met Class B specs—temperatures of 0°–55° C (32°–127° F); Class A was −15° to +65° C (5°–145° F).

87. Fritz K. Weinert, "The RF Vector Voltmeter—An Important New Instrument for Amplitude and Phase Measurements from 1 MHz to 1000 MHz." *HP Journal* 17, 9 (May 1966): 2–9; Paul C. Ely Jr., "The Engineer, Automated Network Analysis, and the Computer—Signs of Things to Come," *HP Journal* 18, 6 (February 1967): 11–12.

88. "Hewlett-Packard Corporation: Computer Division," Case S-M-150R, Stanford Graduate School of Business, 1973.

89. Ibid.

90. David Ricci and Gerald Nelson, "A Practical Interface System for Electronic Instruments," *HP Journal* 24, 2 (October 1972): 2–7; Donald Loughry, "A Common Digital Interface for Programmable Instruments: The Evolution of a System," *HP Journal* 24, 2 (October 1972): 8–11.

91. Robert Grimm, private correspondence with the author, March 3, 2008.

92. David Packard, "The Fourth Dimension of Management," (lecture, Paul Holden Management Luncheon, Los Angeles, April 6, 1966) (ATA).

93. Tom Perkins, interview by Charles H. House and Raymond L. Price, March 24,

2006, 10–12. Ely, "The Engineer," had just been published. See also Tom Perkins, *Valley Boy: The Education of Tom Perkins* (New York: Gotham, 2007), 75.

94. Perkins, interview, 13–14.

95. Thomas C. Poulter Jr., "A Practical Time-Shared Computer System," *HP Journal* 37, 7 (July 1968): 2–7.

96. Perkins, interview, 17.

97. Carl Cottrell, interview by Raymond L. Price, November 17, 2004, 25.

98. Cottrell, interview, 10.

99. Perkins, interview, 17–22.

100. Bill Davidow, interview by Charles H. House and Raymond L. Price, November 18, 2005, 6–7.

101. Stanford, "Computer Division, Case S-M-150R."

102. Roy Clay, interview by Raymond L. Price, August 18, 2004, 6, 8.

CHAPTER 6

1. Cort Van Rensselaer, "Bill Hewlett Stories," private essay, 2, shared with Charles H. House November 29, 2005.

2. CDC manufactured only computers. IBM was already 75 percent computing. The six small entrants were divisions of much larger corporations: Honeywell ($113M/$700M), Burroughs ($104M/$457M), GE ($101M/$6.214B), RCA ($86M/$2.041B), National Cash Register ($86M/$737M), and Sperry-Univac ($360M/$1.26B).

3. Gerald E. Nelson and William R. Hewlett, "The Design and Development of a Family of Personal Computers for Engineers and Scientists," in Amar Gupta and Hoo-min D. Toong (eds.), *Insights into Personal Computers* (New York: IEEE Press, 1985), 38.

4. See "Tom Osborne's Story in His Own Words," www.hp9825.com.

5. Bernard M. Oliver, "How the Model 9100A was Developed," *Hewlett-Packard Journal* (hereafter *HP Journal*) 20, 1 (September 1968): 20.

6. Richard E. Monnier, "A New Electronic Calculator (HP 9100A) with Computerlike Capabilities," *HP Journal* 20, 1 (September 1968): 2–9; Thomas E. Osborne, "Hardware Design of the 9100A Calculator," *HP Journal* 20, 1 (September 1968): 10–13; David S. Cochran, "Internal Programming of the 9100A Calculator," *HP Journal* 20, 1 (September 1968): 14–16. See also Charles H. House, "Hewlett-Packard and Personal Computing Systems," in Adele Goldberg (ed.), *A History of Personal Workstations* (New York: ACM Press, 1985), 401–437.

7. An Wang, *Lessons: An Autobiography* (Palo Alto, CA: Addison-Wesley, 1986).

8. David Packard, *The HP Way: How Bill Hewlett and I Built Our Company* (New York: HarperBusiness, 1995), 175.

9. Ibid.

10. Al Bagley, interview by Raymond L. Price, March 23, 2005, 16.

11. The net distribution from the trust was $22.3 million, almost entirely from dividend earnings. The stock price varied by just pennies from when Packard left for Washington. Tom Perkins, interview by Charles H. House and Raymond L. Price, March 24, 2006, 18–19.

12. Carl Cottrell, interview with Raymond L. Price, October 6, 2004, 11–15.

13. Ibid.

14. Bill Hewlett, "From the President's Desk," *HP Measure* (August-September 1970): 15. See also Bill Hewlett, "From the President's Desk," *HP Measure* (November 1970): 15. The founders never envisioned "guaranteed employment"; see "Attrition Without Tears," *HP Measure* (April 1971): 16.

15. Packard, *The HP Way*, 104.

16. Perkins, interview, 18.

17. Cottrell, interview, 14.

18. David Packard, "From the President's Desk," *HP Measure* (October 1968): 15.

19. "The Group: A New Kind of Team, A Blueprint for Growth," *HP Measure* (November 1968): 6–7; "Open for Business," *HP Measure* (May 1969): 2–5.

20. Terry is taciturn about this career chapter, while Ely is voluble.

21. Bert Forbes, interview by Raymond L. Price, October 2004, 7.

22. Bill Terry, interview by Raymond L. Price, September 16, 2005, 7–8. Related products are discussed in the following: Fred F. Coury, "Price, Performance, Architecture, and the 2100A Computer," *HP Journal* (October 1971): 2–3; Richard D. Crawford and Gregory Justice, "A Bantam Power Supply for a Minicomputer," *HP Journal* (October 1971): 13–15.

23. Terry, interview, 8–9.

24. Ray Smelek, interview by Charles House and Raymond L. Price, October 19, 2004, 5, 7.

25. Smelek, interview, 8.

26. Roy Clay, interview by Raymond L. Price, August 16, 2004, 7.

27. "News in Brief," *HP Measure* (June 1973): 14.

28. Richard E. McIntire, "Powerful Data Base Management System for Small Computers," *HP Journal* 25, 11 (July 1974): 2–10.

29. Bert Forbes and Michael Green, "An Economical Full-Scale Multipurpose Computer System," *HP Journal* (January 1973): 2–6; William E. Foster, "Software for a Multilingual Computer," *HP Journal* (January 1973): 15–19; Thomas A. Blease and Alan Hewer, "Single Operating System Serves All HP 3000 Users," *HP Journal* (January 1973): 20–24.

30. Nancy Anderson, interview by Raymond L. Price, September 19, 2004, 1; Bob Frankenberg, interview by Charles H. House and Raymond L. Price, October 20, 2004, 12.

31. Bill Terry, interview by Charles H. House, September 28, 2006, 13.

32. Paul Ely, interview by Raymond L. Price, December 15, 2005, 19.

33. Ely, interview, 3, 20.

34. Ely, interview, 20.

35. Ely, interview, 21.

36. Ely, interview, 23.

37. Ely, interview, 30.

38. Ely, interview, 28, 31.

39. Ely, interview, 24.

40. Joe Schoendorf, interview by Raymond L. Price, August 13, 2004, 5.

41. "More Tumult for the Computer Industry," *BusinessWeek* (May 30, 1977): 58–66.

42. Welch's dictum was "#1 or #2, and if not, 'Fix, Close, or Sell.'" Jack Welch and John A. Byrne, *Jack: Straight from the Gut* (New York: Warner Business Books, 2003), 111.

43. Steve Wozniak and Gina Smith, *IWoz* (New York: Norton Press, 2006), 158.

44. Wozniak and Smith, *IWoz*, 124.

45. Robert Frankenberg, private correspondence with Charles H. House, July 2, 2008, described the origin of Siber, Inc., which built a Z-8-based personal computer that APD declined. The HP team—Greg Hansen, Earl Stutes, Dennis Silva, Jan Hofland, Jim Heaton, and Frankenberg—sold the prototype with HP permission. Frankenberg noted Wozniak's keen interest in the prototype's TV display.

46. House, "Hewlett-Packard and Personal Computing Systems," 433.

47. "Model 10: Now It's the World Series," *HP Measure* (October 1971): 10–13; "News in Brief," *HP Measure* (December 1972): 14. See also Robert Watson, "Development of the 9800 Series," *HP Journal* 24, 4 (December 1972): 27–28.

48. Henry Kohoutek, "9800 Processor Incorporates 8-MHz Microprocessor," *HP Journal* 24, 4 (December 1972): 19–22.

49. DRAMs, pronounced dee-rams, were dynamic random access memory designs. Their advantage was size and speed; using one transistor instead of six per cell, they dramatically increased the amount of storage per chip. Dynamic meant that the stored charge had to be refreshed periodically, so storage was lost when system power was turned off.

50. "New 'Desk Tops' Introduced: Calculator and Printer," *HP Measure* (October 1975): 14; "9815 Calculator," (December 1975): 5; "High-Powered New Desktopper," *HP Measure* (January 1976): 14; "HP's New Product Express: Coming Around the mountain," *HP Measure* (January 1978): 2–5. Description of HP's NMOS process is in J. E. DeWeese and T. R. Ligon, "An NMOS Process for High-Performance LSI Circuits," *HP Journal* 29, 3 (November 1977): 26–32. The BPC was not in the 9815, but debuted the same month (September 1975) in the 9871 printer. The BPC was the mainline processor in the 9825 (debuted January 1976), and later models. Donald E. Morris, Chris J. Christopher, Geoffrey W. Chance, and Dick B. Barney, "Third Generation Programmable Calculator Has Computer-Like Capabilities," *HP Journal* 26, 10 (June 1976): 2–14; William Eads and David S. Maitland, "High-Performance NMOS LSI Processor," *HP Journal* 26, 10 (June 1976): 15–18.

51. "New 'Desk Tops'," *HP Measure* (October 1975): 14; "New Product Parade," *HP Measure* (December 1975): 2–5; "HP News," *HP Measure* (January 1976): 14; "New Product Express," *HP Measure* (January 1978): 2–5.

52. Jack M. Walden and William D. Eads, "A Highly Integrated Desktop Computer System," *HP Journal* 29, 8 (April 1978): 2–11; there are another seventeen pages on Series 45.

53. "New Building Programs," *HP Measure* (April 1976): 14; "Ft. Collins' Third Building," *HP Measure* (December 1978): 14.

54. John B. Frost and William L. Hale, "Color Enhances Computer Graphics System," *HP Journal* 31, 12 (December 1980): 3–5.

55. Ken Olsen, interview by David Allison, September 28, 29, 1988. Digital Historical Collection Exhibit, Division of Information Technology & Society, National Museum of American History, Smithsonian Institution.

56. Bill Terry, interview for HP documentary film, *Origins*, November 2005.

57. Cort Van Rensselaer, comments at the Dave and Lucile memorial evening, April 9, 2008.

58. www.hp.com/calculators/articles/rpn.html. The Polish mathematician: Jan Lukasiewicz.

59. Edward T. Liljenthal, "Packaging the Pocket Calculator," *HP Journal* 23, 10 (June 1972): 12–13.

60. HPA had already created a specification and design to respond to a strikingly similar proposal from Unidynamics. When Unidynamics decided to stop the project, John Minck, HPA's marketing director, sent the project description to John Young, setting the stage for Hewlett's idea. John Minck, "Inside HP: A Narrative History of Hewlett-Packard from 1939–1990," 65–67, http://www.home.agilent.com/upload/cmc_upload/secure/MinckHPNAR29.pdf. Minck's letter was dated January 27, 1970, two years before the HP 35 debuted.

61. "It Takes a Lickin'," *HP Measure* (November-December 1988): 22.

62. "New Electronic Eyes for the Blind," *HP Measure* (December 1972): 12–13; "The Late Afternoon Balloon," *HP Measure* (November 1978): 16.

63. Bill Hewlett, "From the President's Desk," *HP Measure* (February 1973): 15.

64. William L. Crowley and Francé Rodé, "A Pocket-Sized Answer Machine for Business and Finance," *HP Journal* 24, 9 (May 1973): 2–9.

65. Thomas Whitney, Francé Rodé, and Chung Tung, "The 'Powerful Pocketful': An Electronic Calculator Challenges the Slide Rule," *HP Journal* 23, 10 (June 1972): 2–9; David Cochran, "Algorithms and Accuracy in the HP 35," *HP Journal* 23, 10 (June 1972): 10–11; Chung C. Tung, "The 'Personal Computer': A Fully Programmable Pocket Calculator," *HP Journal* (May 1974): 2–7; R. Kent Stockwell, "Programming the Personal Computer," *HP Journal* (May 1974): 8–14; Robert B. Taggart, "Designing a Tiny Magnetic Card Reader," *HP Journal* (May 1974): 15–17. See also "The Big Parade of New Products for 1972," *HP Measure* (January 1972), 2–7; and "A Superstar Is Born," *HP Measure* (June 1972): 6–8.

66. The HP delegation, led by Ron Griffin, included Bob Grimm, Dave Crockett, Chuck House, and Marco Negrete.

67. See Randall B. Neff and Lynn Tillman, "Three New Pocket Calculators: Smaller, Less Costly, More Powerful," *HP Journal* 27, 3 (November 1975): 2–7.

68. David R. Conklin, Bernard E. Musch, and John J. Wong, "Powerful Personal Calculator System Sets New Standards," *HP Journal* 31, 3 (March 1980): 3–12.

CHAPTER 7

1. David Packard, "High Technology, High Stakes" (lecture, Department of Commerce conference, "Public Policies for the 1980s," Shoreham Hotel, Washington, DC, February 2, 1983).

2. Peter Burrows, *Backfire: Carly Fiorina's High-Stakes Battle for the Soul of HP* (New York: John Wiley & Sons, 2003), 55. Cort Van Rensselaer, interview with Charles H. House, December 6, 2005, 26–27.

3. Burrows, *Backfire*, 55.

4. Paul Ely, interview with Raymond L. Price, December 15, 2005, 43–44.

5. Van Rensselaer, interview, 24–25, 27.

6. Colossus was the most improbable of these systems. Although it was created as a preferred parts sorting-index database by Mike Mercadante at the New Jersey Power Supply Division under Johan Blokker, Cort Van Rensselaer recognized it as a useful corporate manufacturing tool. Hosted on a new relational database from UNIX startup Informix, it was established corporation-wide by 1990.

7. Cort Van Rensselaer, interview with Raymond L. Price, November 17, 2004, 17.

8. Carl Cottrell, interview by Raymond L. Price, November 17, 2004, 22–24.

9. Dave Packard, comments, HP Management Meeting, Monterey, California, Jan 11, 1967, 1.

10. Packard, Monterey comments, 3.

11. This was long before Proxmire introduced the infamous Golden Fleece Awards.

12. David Packard, *The HP Way: How Bill Hewlett and I Built Our Company* (New York: HarperBusiness, 1995), 184–185.

13. John Doyle, interview by Raymond L. Price, March 23, 2005, 15.

14. Charles DeBenedetti, *An American Ordeal: The Anti-War Movement of the Vietnam Era* (Syracuse, NY: Syracuse University Press, 1990).

15. When Packard returned to HP, Hewlett wanted to stay on as CEO. Packard agreed, even though Bagley and van Bronkhorst implored Dave to assert himself. Ed van Bronkhorst, interview by Charles H. House and Raymond L. Price, March 24, 2005, 13. Packard ran Nixon's California reelection campaign, then established the family foundation.

16. There were five documented second guesses: (1) asking Roy Clay back in August 1972 to "get HP out of computing"; (2) installing Paul Ely in November 1972 to head the HP 3000; (3) squelching the Stanford business case that outlined the HP 2116 dilemma and the Boston Consulting Group thesis; (4) thwarting a bond issue in February 1974; and (5) taking the stump in March and April 1974 with his "Give 'em Hell" talk, which infused a new training focus for HP. It was a new experience for Packard to be available but not in charge. After this period of relatively active intercession, Packard relaxed and did not visibly confront Hewlett again.

17. Tom Perkins, interview by Charles H. House and Raymond L. Price, March 24, 2006, 18.

18. "Hewlett-Packard Corporation: Computer Division," Case S-M-150R, Stanford Graduate School of Business, 1973.

19. *Hewlett-Packard Annual Report* (1971), 8–9.

20. *Hewlett-Packard Annual Report* (1972), 1–2.

21. *Hewlett-Packard Annual Report* (1973), 2.

22. Ibid.

23. Ibid., 3.

24. Ed van Bronkhorst found medium-term money in Europe, far less expensive than the short-term borrowing that the company was using; van Bronkhorst, interview, 14; Dick Alberding, interview by Charles H. House, September 19, 2006, 31; plus Dave Packard and Bill Hewlett, *History Documentation* (Palo Alto, CA: HP TV Network, A Hewlett Family Production, 1983).

25. Van Rensselaer, interview, 7; the story is corroborated in Cottrell, interview; Bob Grimm, interview by Raymond L. Price, December 8, 2004; Al Bagley, interview by Raymond L. Price, March 23, 2005; and in Packard's own words in Packard, *The HP Way*, 86–87. The first of these speeches is cited in George Anders, *Perfect Enough: Carly Fiorina and the Reinvention of Hewlett-Packard* (New York: Penguin Group, 2003), 19.

26. van Bronkhorst, interview, 14–15.

27. Alberding, interview, 31.

28. David Packard, "Things We Need to Remember (Give 'em Hell)" (speech, EPG, February 11, 1974).

29. Van Rensselaer, interview, 7.

30. Richard T. Pascale, *Managing on the Edge: Companies That Use Conflict to Stay Ahead* (New York: Viking Penguin, 1990).

31. John Young, interview by Charles H. House and Raymond L. Price, November 17, 2005, 6–8. Re: price bombing, see Michael S. Malone, *Bill and Dave: How Hewlett and Packard Built the World's Greatest Company* (New York: Portfolio Books, Penguin Group, 2007), 325.

32. Packard, very concerned about the lack of managerial sophistication as revealed in his study, drove a very innovative program under Bill Nilsson's leadership.

33. William G. Ouchi, *Theory Z: How American Business Can Meet the Japanese Challenge* (Menlo Park, CA: Addison-Wesley, 1981); Robert H. Waterman Jr. and Thomas J. Peters, *In Search of Excellence: Lessons from America's Best-Run Companies* (New York:

HarperCollins, 1982); Thomas J. Peters and Nancy Austin, *A Passion for Excellence: The Leadership Difference* (New York: Warner Books, 1989).

34. Marv Patterson, interview by Charles H. House, December 1, 2006; Jim Serum, interview by Raymond L. Price, November 2, 2004, 4; Dieter Hoehn, interview by Raymond L. Price, November 5, 2004, 16. See also Marvin L. Patterson and Samuel Lightman, *Accelerating Innovation* (New York: Van Nostrand Reinhold, 1993); and Marvin L. Patterson, *Leading Product Innovation: Accelerating Growth in a Product-Based Business* (New York: John Wiley & Sons, 1999).

35. Doyle vehemently urged such an approach on Mark Hurd in the summer of 2005 as a cultural regalvanizing antidote to the Carly era, unsuccessfully. John Doyle, interview by Charles H. House, September 28, 2006, 7.

36. Malone, *Bill and Dave*, 261–262.

37. Malone, *Bill and Dave*, 325.

38. Caleb Pirtle III, *Engineering the World: Stories from the First 75 Years of Texas Instruments* (Dallas, TX: SMU Press, 2005), 129.

39. David Packard, General Managers' Meeting, January 1977.

40. John Young, private correspondence with the authors, January 20, 2006; Young, interview, 42.

41. "Celebrating Leaders," *Menlo College Magazine* (Fall-Winter 2002): 6–7.

42. Malone, *Bill and Dave*, 301.

43. Over one hundred companies entered the semiconductor watch business in one year's time; virtually all failed. TI, using aggressive pricing akin to calculators, was most successful; Intel famously failed with their Microma line. Cricket had three fundamental flaws—the keys, accessed via a sideboard stylus, were extremely small; the watch was too large and heavy to wear comfortably (a common joke was that you could tell who was wearing one by their lengthened left arm); and the price was excessive. Quote from Barney Oliver, personal communication with Charles H. House, April 1982, when Chuck was appointed Corporate Engineering director.

44. "The Multifaceted HP-01 Wrist Instrument" *Hewlett-Packard Journal* (hereafter *HP Journal*) 29, 4 (December 1977): cover; Andre F. Marion, Edward A. Heinsen, Robert Chin, and Bennie E. Helmso, "Wrist Instrument Opens New Dimension in Personal Information," *HP Journal* 29, 4 (December 1977): 2–10.

45. Marion, Heinsen, Chin, and Helmso, "Wrist Instrument," 7.

46. Bill Terry, interview by Raymond L. Price, September 16, 2005, 38–39. Michael L. Bullock and Richard E. Warren, "Electronic Total Station Speeds Survey Operations," *HP Journal* 27, 8 (April 1976): 2–12. For information about the BEAR, see David E. Smith, "Electronic Distance Measurement for Industrial and Scientific Applications," *HP Journal* 31, 6 (June 1980): 3–11; and David E. Smith and Troy L. Brown, "Industrial Distance Meter Applications," *HP Journal* 31, 6 (June 1980): 11–19.

47. Ely, interview, 54, 78–79.

48. Terry, interview, 25.

49. Perkins, interview, 38–39.

50. "The Xerox Alto Computer," FortuneCity, http://members.fortunecity.com/pcmuseum/alto.html. The Alto, conceived in 1972, was used at PARC after 1975. Fifty machines, valued at $32,000 each, were donated to Stanford, Carnegie Mellon, and MIT in 1978.

51. Couch's team would develop the first commercially successful GUI (Graphical User

Interface). He was the general manager for the Apple Lisa, which led to the Apple MacIntosh. Sieler, later co-founder of Allegro, was project lead for the Amigo OS.

52. http://en.wikipedia.org/wiki/HP_300; http://www.answers.com/topic/hp-300.

53. George R. Clark, "A Business Computer for the 1980s," *HP Journal* 30, 6 (June 1979): 3–6; Ronald E. Morgan, "World-Wide Regulatory Compliance," *HP Journal* 30, 6 (June 1979): 30. See also Arndt B. Bergh and Kenyon C. Y. Mei, "Cost-Effective Hardware for a Compact Integrated Business Computer," *HP Journal* 30, 7 (July 1979): 3–8; Alfred F. Knoll and Norman D. Marschke, "An Innovative Programming and Operating Console," *HP Journal* 30, 7 (July 1979): 13–17. Many other articles offer more HP 300 detail in the June and July 1979 *HP Journal* issues.

54. http://en.wikipedia.org/wiki/Xerox_Star.

55. A. Peter Hamilton, "A Human-Engineered Small-Business Computer," *HP Journal* 30, 4 (April 1979): 3–5. In the same issue, the cover and six other articles deal with the HP 250.

56. Robert Frankenberg, interview by Charles H. House and Raymond L. Price, October 20, 2004, 3.

57. Frankenberg, interview, 4–5.

58. Wim Roelandts, interview by Charles H. House and Raymond L. Price, November 18, 2005, 21, 24–25.

59. Jef Graham, interview by Raymond L. Price, October 6, 2004, 21–22.

60. Nancy Anderson, interview by Raymond L. Price, September 19, 2004, 1.

61. Ed McCracken, interview by Charles H. House, October 2, 2006.

62. Anderson, interview, 4; Arie Kurtzig was an HP Labs section manager when his wife Sandy formed ASK. Their initials formed the name. HP was ASK's first computer partner.

63. Letter to Frank Cavier from Doug Mecham, February 13, 1976. Displayed at Burt Grad (Chair) HP Minicomputer Software History meeting, Computer History Museum, Mountain View, California, June 5, 2008.

64. Letter to Doug Mecham from David Packard, February 25, 1976. Displayed at Burt Grad (Chair) HP Minicomputer Software History meeting, Computer History Museum, Mountain View, California, June 5, 2008.

65. From discussion at Burt Grad (Chair) HP Minicomputer Software History meeting, Computer History Museum, Mountain View, California, June 5, 2008.

66. Graham, interview, 28–29.

67. Joe Schoendorf, personal communication with Raymond L. Price, August 5, 2008.

CHAPTER 8

1. David Packard, "High Technology, High Stakes," lecture, Department of Commerce conference, "Public Policies for the 1980's," The Shoreham Hotel, Washington, DC, February 2, 1983.

2. The film *Standing in the Shadows of Motown* celebrates "the unheralded group of musicians [who] play on more Number One hits than the Beach Boys, the Rolling Stones, Elvis Presley, and The Beatles combined, making them the greatest hit machine in the history of popular music. But no one knows their names" (see http://www.standingintheshadowsofmotown.com/).

3. David Packard, "Dave Packard of Hewlett-Packard Speaks on Choosing Tomorrow's Managers," *Electronic Design* 15 (July 19, 1978): 92–96.

4. Ibid.

5. Packard, "High Technology, High Stakes."

6. As indicated earlier in this book, "MRP" initially stood for "material requirements planning," but as the systems became more sophisticated it came to stand for "manufacturing resource planning."

7. David Packard, comments, General Managers' Meeting, Pebble Beach, California, January 1983.

8. R. W. Anderson, "The Japanese Success Formula: Quality Equals the Competitive Edge," Seminar on Quality Control—Japan, Key to High Productivity, Washington, DC, March 25, 1980, 40.

9. T. R. Reid, "Meet Dr. Deming, Corporate America's Newest Guru," http://www.aliciapatterson.org/APF0605/Reid/Reid.rtf.

10. Ibid.

11. American Dr. W. Edwards Deming developed statistical quality control concepts and was a tireless teacher of quantitative improvement practices. The Japanese Union of Scientists and Engineers adopted his methods widely.

12. Charles H. House, notes from the meeting.

13. Claire Makin, "Ranking Corporate Reputations," *Fortune* (January 10, 1983): 34–44. Chuck House made the comment regarding Boeing quality.

14. Jeremy Main, *Quality Wars: The Triumphs and Defeats of American Business* (New York: The Free Press, 1994). For Six-Sigma, see Tom McCarty, "Six Sigma at Motorola," Motorola, September-October 2004, http://www.motorola.com/mot/doc/1/1736_MotDoc.pdf.

15. The demurring division manager was Chuck House. The Logic Systems Division HP 64000 integrated products and component sets from fourteen divisions; product quality varied by nearly two orders of magnitude. The weakest link—the disc—determined the system uptime. The HP 64000 was simultaneously the most reliable computer system in HP and the least reliable product in the Instrument Group.

16. "Order Processing Streamlined," *HP Measure* (November 1963): 6–7. Bud Eldon, personal communication with Charles H. House, August 18 and August 22, 2008.

17. BAEDP was the centralized IT or EDP facility for HP.

18. Dick Alberding, interview by Charles H. House, September 19, 2006, 12–13.

19. John Toppel, interview by Charles H. House, January 11, 2007; Rich Nielsen, interview by Charles H. House, February 22, 2007.

20. "Fast as a Speeding Electron . . . The Penny Post Rides Again," *HP Measure* (April 1974): 11–13.

21. "Comsys Goes to Market," *HP Measure* (June 1977): 7–9.

22. "The Information Network That Knows How, Where, and When," *HP Measure* (November 1977): 9–13; see also "Comsys' Big Savings," *HP Measure* (December 1978): 14.

23. Robert A. Adams, Kristy Ward Swenson, Rebecca A. Dahlberg, Amy Tada Mueller, and Luis Hurtado-Sanchez, "Implementing a Worldwide Electronic Mail System," *Hewlett-Packard Journal* (hereafter *HP Journal*) 37, 9 (September 1986): 30–48.

24. It was fitting that instrumentation would end strongly during Hewlett's leadership.

25. During the 2000 presidential race, a common engineering joke was that Al Gore invented algorithms, pronounced Al-Gore-rhythms, just prior to his invention of the Internet.

26. Chris Clare, interview by Raymond L. Price, August 21, 2004, 15.

27. Clare, interview, 17.

28. Clare, interview, 15–16.

29. At the seminar in Colorado Springs, Walt Fischer became very enthusiastic. He embedded the new micro-chip in the first micro-controlled, answer-calculating oscilloscope, the HP 1722A, which calculated rise time, fall time, and pulse width. See William B. Risley and Walter A. Fischer, "Improved Accuracy and Convenience in Oscilloscope Timing and Voltage Measurements," *HP Journal* 26, 4 (December 1974): 2–11.

30. The decade counter in the HP 3440A digital voltmeter's counter is described in Charles W. Near and David S. Cochran, "A New Multi-Purpose Digital Voltmeter," *HP Journal* 15, 3 (November 1963).

For Brooksby's work, see Merrill Brooksby and Richard D. Pering, "Monolithic Transistor Arrays for High-Frequency Applications," *HP Journal* 21, 5 (January 1970): 15–16; Merrill W. Brooksby and Patricia L. Castro, "University and Industrial Cooperation for VLSI," *HP Journal* 32, 6 (June 1981): 29–33; and Patricia L. Castro, Merrill W. Brooksby, and Fred L. Hanson, "Benefits of Quick-Turnaround Integrated Circuit Processing," *HP Journal* 32, 6 (June 1981): 33–35.

For Santa Clara Logic products, see Gary B. Gordon, "IC Logic Checkout Simplified," *HP Journal* 20, 10 (June 1969): 14–16; Robin Adler and Jan Hofland, "Logic Pulser and Probe: a New Digital Troubleshooting Team," *HP Journal* 24, 1 (September 1972): 2–7; and Mark Baker, Howard D. Marshall, and Robin Adler, "The Logic Analyzer: A New Instrument for Observing Logic Signals," *HP Journal* 25, 2 (October 1973): 2–16.

31. William A. Farnbach, "The Logic State Analyzer—Displaying Complex Digital Processes in Understandable Form," *HP Journal* 25, 5 (January 1974): 2–9.

32. "Engineering Hall of Fame," *Electronic Design* (October 21, 2002): 202–220, 232.

33. Bill Hewlett (comments, HP Instrument Group R&D Managers, Keystone, Colorado, May, 1973).

34. Bruce Nussbaum, "The Power of Design," *BusinessWeek* (May 17, 2004): 86–94. The Grid laptop is in the Museum of Modern Art in New York.

35. See Dave Packard, "H-P's New Cabinet Program—Hit of Show," *HP Measure* (April 1961): 2; Carl Clement, "New Multi-Purpose Modular Cabinet Concept and How It Was Conceived," *HP Measure* (May 1961): 10.

36. Carl Clement, private essay, "The History of the Xerox Alto," (March 19, 2002), on file at the Computer History Museum, Mountain View, California.

37. In fact, the payback for Xerox was extraordinary from the laser printer work originally begun in Rochester. Gary Starkweather invented this technology for an unappreciative audience in Rochester, and then transferred to the newly established PARC in 1971, where he pursued his dream of a "personal printer." His work spawned returns for Xerox that have totaled nearly a quarter of a trillion dollars to date, according to long-time lab director John Seely Brown, with profits exceeding a hundred times the total investment in PARC.

38. Michael A. Hiltzik, *Dealers of Lightning: XeroxPARC and the Dawn of the Computer Age* (New York: HarperCollins, 1999), 169–170.

39. See Douglas K. Smith and Robert C. Alexander, *Fumbling the Future: How Xerox Invented Then Ignored the First Personal Computer* (New York: William Morrow, 1988). Xerox, laden with profits from a wildly profitable copying business, sought new arenas. They bought Scientific Data Systems, a struggling minicomputer manufacturer in El Segundo, California, building a new Palo Alto research facility. They balked at Doug Engelbart's irascible personality, hiring Bob Taylor, J. C. Lickliter's right-hand man at DARPA. Taylor knew (and had funded) nearly every interesting new computer program in America's universities.

40. All had great careers, but none are listed in most anthologies about PARC's glory days. White would finish his career as ACM CEO and executive director from 2000 to the present; Hagstrom led the crucial optical diode development at PARC, served for years on the Nobel Prize selection committee in Stockholm, and is professor emeritus of materials science and engineering at Stanford; Thornburg, widely published, has been acknowledged as one of the twenty top pioneers in the field of educational technology. Suchman, a pioneer of human-computer interaction (HCI), is also widely published; Wynn, a linguistic anthropologist at Intel since 2000 and an early leader in ethnography for information systems, has edited *Information Technology & People* since 1985. Stuart Card, senior research fellow and manager of the user interface research group at PARC, led the "mouse" introduction by Xerox. His group has created a dozen Xerox products plus three spin-out software companies and many seminal articles. Mark Stefik earned much respect for his visionary observations about e-mail, networked groups, and the sociological impact of computing before his untimely death. Fame came to some: most computer buffs know Alan Kay as the inventor of the first personal computer as well as the Smalltalk language, Butler Lampson as the true architect of the Xerox PARC Alto, and Adele Goldberg as the fiery co-creator of Smalltalk plus several books and startup companies.

41. Peter Marks, COFES 2009, http://cofes.com/Events/COFES2009/tabid/457/Default.aspx.

42. Hiltzik, *Dealers of Lightning*, 29 (contains McColough's statement when he bought SDS).

43. The investment rate at XeroxPARC was $60 million per year, paltry compared to IBM's $2.514 billion in 1983 alone. See also "R&D Scoreboard 1983," *BusinessWeek* 2850 (July 1984): 65–77. Summing R&D for the top ten American computer companies, XeroxPARC averaged less than 2 percent of their investment for two decades, all the while transforming completely the user paradigm: Jim Gibbons, interview by Charles H. House, September 14, 2006, 2.

44. Carl Clement, interview by Charles H. House, February 28, 2007, 1.

45. Ibid.

46. Clement later established his own firm in Palo Alto, Clement Designlabs, a precursor to Frog Design and IDEO. With Robert McKim and James Adams, he helped establish a strong industrial design group at Stanford University that now is augmented by the Hasso Plattner Institute of Design at Stanford, infused with David Kelley's genius. At age eighty-six, Clement grinned when recalling conversations he'd had with Kelley; Clement said proudly, "We are of kindred philosophy" (Clement, interview, 2).

47. Chung C. Tung, "The 'Personal Computer': A Fully Programmable Pocket Calculator," *HP Journal* 26, 9 (May 1974): 2–7.

48. Allen F. Inhelder, "A New Instrument Enclosure with Greater Convenience, Better Accessibility, and High Attenuation of RF Interference," *HP Journal* 27, 1 (September 1975): 19–24.

49. This work was sophisticated, requiring an Apollo workstation and a Symbolics processor with BitStream software to generate a wide variety of fonts in various sizes, profiled for a multitude of dot-array structures. Stu Center, interview by Charles H. House, April 18, 2007.

50. Axel O. Deininger and Charles V. Fernandez, "Making Computer Behavior Consistent: The HP OSF/Motif Graphical User Interface," *HP Journal* 41, 3 (June 1990): 6–12.

51. The IP suit is described in Tom Hormby, "The Apple vs. Microsoft GUI Lawsuit," Low End Mac, August 25, 2006, http://lowendmac.com/orchard/06/apple-vs-microsoft

.html. For information about Motif, see Shiz Kobara, *Visual Design with OSF/Motif* (Reading, MA: Addison-Wesley, 1991). The human factors group included Robin Jeffries, Lisa Thorell, Anna Wachinsky, Wanda Smith, and Joyce Farrell. See Lisa G. Thorell and Wanda J. Smith, *Using Computer Color Effectively: An Illustrated Reference* (Upper Saddle River, NJ: Prentice-Hall, 1990).

52. Tom Saponas, personal communication with Charles H. House, September 30, 1999. The conversation occurred at the Computer History Museum fellows' dinner.

53. Gibbons, interview, 26.

54. Gibbons, interview, 29.

55. Gibbons, interview, 30–32.

56. Gibbons, interview, 31–32.

57. Gibbons, interview, 33–34.

58. Gibbons's work is described in John Seely Brown and Paul Duguid, *The Social Life of Information* (Cambridge, MA: Harvard Business School Press, 2002), 221–222. See also Jim Gibbons, Rob Pannoni, and Jay Orlin, "Tutored Video Instruction: A Distance Education Methodology that Improves Training Results," lecture, ASTD International Conference, Orlando, Florida, June 3, 1996.

59. Although this report was widely available for many years, and used extensively to coordinate divisional and sales operations, few copies are known to exist currently.

60. LinkedIn is one of several social networking software offerings circa 2008.

61. See "Project Prelude: Dawn of the Global Business Meeting—Where Everyone Stays Home!" *HP Measure* (August 1978): 12–13; "The 1,200 Mile Conference Table," *HP Measure* (January-February 1985): 10–11; and Starr Roxanne Hiltz and Murray Turoff, *The Network Nation: Human Communication via Computer* (New York: Addison-Wesley, 1981).

62. Charles H. House, "Education via Satellite Transmission—Experimental Results and Concerns," *Proceedings of the 1984 Frontiers in Education* (Philadelphia, PA: IEEE, 1984), 5.

63. The Monterey Bay Aquarium was being finished at this time, for a record $40 million of Packard Foundation funding.

64. Tony Fanning and Bert Raphael, "Computer Teleconferencing: Experience at Hewlett-Packard," in *Proceedings of the 1986 ACM Conference on Computer Supported Co-Operative Work* (New York: ACM, 1986), 291–306.

65. Bruce Wholey, interview by Alan Bagley, August 28, 1990, 57.

66. Wholey, interview, 63–64.

67. Joel Birnbaum, comments, R&D Managers' Meeting, Oakland, California, December 14–18, 1986.

68. Jim Serum, interview by Raymond L. Price, November 2, 2004, 3–4.

69. NIST (National Institute of Standards and Technology) is the U.S. government body for standards in all engineering and science fields.

70. Neerja Raman, interview by Charles H. House, September 14, 2006, 41, 43.

71. Raman, interview, 43.

72. David Packard, "Enterprise, the Vital Catalyst" (lecture, 7th International Forum, Scottish Council, Aviemore, Scotland, 1975).

CHAPTER 9

1. Edward Iwata, "A Look Back to When PC Power Took Off," *USA Today* (August 8, 2001): 3B.

2. "The Silicon Engine: A Timeline of Semiconductors in Computers," Computer History Museum, http://www.computerhistory.org/semiconductor/timeline.html#1950s.

3. James L. Buie, "Coupling Transistor Logic and Other Circuits," U.S. Patent 3,283,170 (Filed: September 1961. Issued: November 1, 1966); R. H. Beeson and H. W. Ruegg, "New Forms of All-Transistor Logic," lecture, ISSCC, University of Pennsylvania, Philadelphia, February 14, 1962, 10–11; T. A. Longo, I. Feinberg, and R. Bohn, "Universal High Level Logic Monolithic Circuits," *Electron Devices Meeting, 1963 International* 9 (1963): 66.

4. http://en.wikipedia.org/wiki/Magnetic_core_memory.

5. "The Silicon Engine: A Timeline of Semiconductors in Computers," Computer History Museum, http://www.computerhistory.org/semiconductor/timeline/1970-DRAM.html.

6. "Moore's Law: Made Real by Intel Innovation," Intel, http://www.intel.com/technology/mooreslaw/index.htm.

7. Charles H. House, "Viewpoints: Chuck House on the Ongoing Revolution in Digital Testing," *Hewlett-Packard Journal* (hereafter *HP Journal*) 29, 11 (February 1978): 11–13.

8. Chris Clare, interview by Raymond L. Price, August 21, 2004, 17–18.

9. Richard S. Tedlow, "The Education of Andy Grove," *Fortune* (December 12, 2005): 116–138.

10. David J. Bradley, "The Creation of the IBM PC," *BYTE* magazine 15, 9 (September 1990): 414–420.

11. "Personal Computer Announced by IBM," IBM Information Systems Division Product Release, http://www-03.ibm.com/ibm/history/exhibits/pc25/pc25_press.html.

12. Clayton Christiansen, *The Innovator's Dilemma: When New Technologies Cause Great Firms to Fail* (Boston: Harvard Business School Press, 1997).

13. John Doyle, interview by Raymond L. Price, March 23, 2005, 10.

14. Michael S. Malone, *Going Public: MIPS Computer and the Entrepreneurial Dream* (New York: HarperCollins, 1991).

15. John Cocke, "The Search for Performance in Scientific Processors: The Turing Award Lecture," *Communications of the ACM* 31, 3 (March 1988): 250–253; John Cocke and V. Markstein, "The Evolution of RISC Technology at IBM," *IBM Journal of Research and Development* 34, 1 (January 1990): 4–11.

16. Joel Birnbaum, interview by Raymond L. Price and Charles H. House, November 16, 2005, 11–14.

17. A four-quarter Stanford Synthesis class with Tuttle (1962) had a weekly oral defense. The first quarter had sixty-eight enrollees; the second thirty-seven; the third twenty-one; the final quarter nine.

18. Birnbaum, interview, 11.

19. Birnbaum, interview, 18.

20. Birnbaum, interview, 20.

21. Birnbaum, interview, 22–23.

22. Birnbaum, interview, 24.

23. Robert J.Frankenberg, interview by Charles H. House and Raymond L. Price, October 20, 2004, 11–13.

24. Ibid.

25. Joel Birnbaum, personal communication with Charles H. House, May 18, 2005.

26. Bill Terry, interview by Raymond L. Price, September 16, 2005, 31–32.

27. A program evaluation review technique (PERT) chart is a project management

tool for scheduling, organizing, and coordinating project tasks; the critical path method (CPM) is similar.

28. John Young, interview by Charles H. House and Raymond L. Price, November 17, 2005, 19.

29. Charles H. House, lecture, Accreditation Board for Engineering Technologies (ABET) Annual Meeting, San Antonio, Texas, December 1980.

30. Byron Anderson, interview by Raymond L. Price, November 11, 2004, 5–6.

31. 30 *mils* is a dimensional specification: 30 millionths of an inch = 0.00003" thickness.

32. Johnson gave a talk in HP Cupertino, reciprocated by House at DEC Maynard in 1986.

33. Western Behavioral Sciences Institute (WBSI), later merged with U.C. San Diego's Management School, was a virtual university based in La Jolla, California. Established by Richard Farson, it pioneered such topics as intellectual property, remote commuting, and early social networking tools. See Richard Farson, *Management of the Absurd: Paradoxes in Leadership* (New York: Simon & Schuster, 1996). "[WBSI in 1981] created its highly regarded School of Management and Strategic Studies, the first program ever to employ online distance education, thereby launching this now burgeoning field. This program brought together [via computer conferencing] senior executives from all sectors of the economy, and 26 countries. . . . The school demonstrated the power of this medium not only to serve educational goals, but to create a community, a network of leaders communicating in relevant, detailed, thoughtful, and personal ways" (http://www.wbsi.org/smss/index.htm).

34. Confer was created by Bob Parnes at the University of Michigan; EIES (Electronic Information Exchange System) was created by Murray Turoff at the New Jersey Institute of Technology. WBSI used EIES.

35. Charles R. Moore, "A New Distortion Analyzer with Automatic Nulling and Broadened Measurement Capability," *HP Journal* 17, 10 (April 1966): 2–7; see also Robert L. Dudley and Virgil L. Laing, "A Self-Contained, Hand-Held Digital Multimeter—A New Concept in Instrument Utility," *HP Journal* 25, 3 (November 1973): 2–9.

36. Doyle, interview, 12.

37. Charlie Elman, compiled notes from the HPC:MOTMOR Conference distributed in HP Corporate Engineering, April 1986.

38. Elman, MOTMOR, items 4, 8, and 27.

39. Paul Ely, interview by Raymond L. Price, December 2005, 69.

40. Ely, interview, 29.

41. All but Ely were recent college graduates. Hewlett, Packard, and Oliver asked each person to introduce themselves and share their goal at HP. Paul said, "Everybody had used up all the good goals when it got to me, so I said, 'My goal is to be sitting at the front table in ten years at one of these meetings'" (Ely, interview, 13–14).

42. Michael S. Malone, *Bill and Dave: How Hewlett and Packard Built the World's Greatest Company* (New York: Portfolio Books, Penguin Group, 2007), 289, 339 (contains quotes about Ely's personality).

43. Joel Birnbaum, interview by Raymond L. Price, December 15, 2005, 8, 17–18.

44. William S. Worley Jr. and Joel S. Birnbaum, "Beyond RISC: High-Precision Architecture," *HP Journal* 36, 8 (August 1985): 4–9. The extended capability logic analyzer card, designed by Dave Hood at the Logic Systems Division in Colorado Springs, was noted

in Joseph A. Lukes, "HP Precision Architecture Performance Analysis," *HP Journal* 37, 8 (August 1986): 30–39.

45. Nicholas Katzenbach, attorney general of the United States under Lyndon Johnson, was chief counsel for IBM; he personally conducted Birnbaum's exit interview and spelled out the non-compete terms. Katzenbach was IBM's lead counsel for the protracted thirteen-year antitrust suit brought by the U.S. Government against IBM.

46. Birnbaum, interview, December 15, 2005, 21–22.

47. Birnbaum, interview, December 15, 2005, 30.

48. Birnbaum, interview, December 15, 2005, 28–30.

49. Birnbaum, interview, December 15, 2005, 31–32.

50. Birnbaum, interview, November 16, 2005, 6–7.

51. Charles H. House, notes from July 1999 video session for HP Labs with Roseanne Wyleczuk.

52. Important devices included optoelectronic devices, giving HP a strong LED position; transducers, for very high-frequency signals that enabled extremely fast digital oscilloscopes; and microwave devices for the 20 GHz—40 GHz frequency spectrum.

53. Hewlett said, "Two out of five projects ought to succeed in their technology pursuit, and of those, divisions ought to adopt roughly two out of five" (Bill Hewlett, personal communication with Charles H. House, May 1986). If these ratios are followed, (2/5)*(2/5) = 4/25, or 16 percent successful economic transfers; the question becomes how to keep from demotivating the five researchers of every six whose work may be superb, but whose projects are not turned into economic successes. Using this line of reasoning, one of Silicon Valley's mainstays—using stock options to reward winning projects—is a disastrous policy for long-term research lab management. See Charles H. House, letter to the editor, *Fast Company* 3 (June-July 1996): 25, commenting on Mort Meyerson, "Everything I Thought I Knew About Leadership Is Wrong," *Fast Company* 2 (April 1996): 71.

CHAPTER 10

1. Jim Hall, interview by Raymond L. Price, September 8, 2006, 11. The product was actually introduced by HP in Palo Alto on Thursday, December 4, 1980; the story ran on page one of the Sunday business section of *The Idaho Statesman*, December 7, Pearl Harbor Day. This was an ironic date to announce the start of a joint relationship (between Canon and HP) that over the next twenty-five years would account for more than one hundred million machines, and $100 billion revenues for each company. Marilyn Chase, "Hewlett-Packard, with Its Laser Printer, Enters Market for the Automated Office," *Wall Street Journal*, December 5, 1980, 37.

2. James A. Hall, "Laser Printing System Provides Flexible, High-Quality, Cost-Effective Computer Output," *Hewlett-Packard Journal* (hereafter *HP Journal*) 33, 6 (June 1982): 3–8; James T. Langley, "Laser Printing System Architecture," *HP Journal* 33, 6 (June 1982): 8–10; and others, including Billie J. Robison, "The People Who Made the Product," *HP Journal* 33, 6 (June 1982): 36. Part of the next *HP Journal* issue was also devoted to the Model 2680 system.

3. Gary Starkweather, at XeroxPARC, is credited with inventing the laser printer in 1971. See Edward Webster, *Print Unchained: Fifty Years of Digital Printing, 1950–2000 and Beyond, a Saga of Invention and Enterprise* (Dover, VT: DRA of Vermont, 2001), 146; the XeroxPARC anthologies, Douglas K. Smith and Robert C. Alexander, *Fumbling the Future: How Xerox Invented Then Ignored the First Personal Computer* (New York:

William Morrow, 1988); and Michael A. Hiltzik, *Dealers of Lightning: XeroxPARC and the Dawn of the Computer Age* (New York: HarperCollins, 1999). At PARC, as at HP and nearly every computer company, the focus was on the CPU and software—peripherals were peripheral. See Charlene O'Hanlon, "Gary Starkweather: Laser Printer Inventor," *CRN*, November 13, 2002, http://www.crn.com/it-channel/18838549.

4. Kathleen Wiegner, "The One to Watch," *Forbes* (March 2, 1981): 60, said that the machine, offered at $121,000, was introduced on December 4, 1980, although the price was reduced within the first six months. The Computer History Museum in Australia notes on its website, http://www.hpmuseum.net/display_item.php?hw=442, that "The 2680A was HP's first laser printer, offered for $92,000. It was also the only laser printer entirely designed and built by HP. The 2680A had a print resolution of 180 dots per inch and a top speed of 45 pages per minute. It printed on A/A4-size fanfold paper rather than cut sheet paper. HP shipped 1500 units of the 2680A by the end of 1987." Thus the product averaged unit sales of eighteen per month for its sales lifetime.

5. Hall, interview, 13.

6. Hall, interview, 6.

7. Ray Smelek, interview by Raymond L. Price and Charles H. House, October 19, 2004, 17.

8. From public Executive Briefing documents used by Carly Fiorina and her staff in 2004, titled "Q1: Did You Know?" slide #6, titled IPG, noted that "In Q1 FY04, the Imaging and Printing Group shipped 14.4 million hardware units, or more than 1 million units a week. We now have shipped more than 300 million printers. Dell has shipped 2 million." On June 26, 2006, on the website and via a public relations release, HP announced a contest to find the hardest working LaserJet in the world, to commemorate reaching 100 million LaserJet units: "In May, HP announced the shipment of the 100 millionth LaserJet printer, a milestone representing HP's history of quality, reliability and innovation. HP pioneered personal laser printing with the introduction in 1984 of the first LaserJet printer." www.hp.com/go/itjustworks.

9. Michael S. Malone, *Bill and Dave: How Hewlett and Packard Built the World's Greatest Company* (New York: Portfolio Books, Penguin Group, 2007), 327. Ray Smelek, not Hackborn, managed the Boise Division; Hackborn came to Boise in 1976, four years after Smelek, to establish the Disc Memory Division next door, which he managed as GM until November 1980, when he became head of the new Peripherals Group—DMD, Boise, Greeley Division, and Vancouver Division ("The Hewlett-Packard Organization," *HP Measure* (September-October 1980): 11–14). After the 2680A failure, Hackborn's printing focus remained on InkJet technology rather than on laser technology. In mid-1983, InkJet responsibility shifted from Hackborn to Cyril Yansouni and the Personal Computer Group; San Diego Division printers and plotters were still in the Electronic Instrument Group under Bill Parzybok (see "Hewlett-Packard Corporate Organization, June 1983 *HP Measure* (July-August 1983): 12–13). Hackborn, with group responsibility for five network divisions as well as Boise and Greeley divisions, spent the bulk of his time on networking issues; he reportedly was not involved in the LaserJet decisions, including important pricing decisions, which Paul Ely carried to John Young. While many HP divisions did exhibit the "not invented here" (NIH) syndrome to which Malone refers, the Boise Division was exemplary for partnering.

10. Jerry Merryman, interview by Charles H. House, September 25, 2007. Merryman, of Texas Instruments, was interviewed at the Smithsonian Museum ceremony celebrating the fortieth anniversary of the first operational handheld calculator.

11. Wilton Woods, "Guide to the Global 500," *Fortune* 126, 2 (July 27, 1992): 175–232.

12. Andrew Pollack, "Hajime Mitarai, 56, President Of Canon, Electronics Giant," *New York Times*, September 1, 1995, D18.

13. "In making its selection for Man of the Year for 1982, TIME reasoned that: 'There are some occasions when the most significant force in a year's news is not a single individual but a process, and a widespread recognition that this process is changing the course of all other processes.' TIME's Man of the Year for 1982—the greatest influence for good or evil—is not a man at all. It is a machine: the computer" (*Time*, January 3, 1983, http://www.time.com/time/personoftheyear/2006/walkup/).

14. Hall, interview, 19–21.

15. "COMDEX, for those who don't know, is—or was—the major industry trade show for personal computers. It started as a 'Computer Dealers' Exposition' (hence the name) in Las Vegas in 1979 (computer dealers were just emerging). The 'Fall COMDEX' in Las Vegas was always the main event, but in the 1980s there were 'Spring COMDEX' shows, mostly in Atlanta. As newlyweds, Melody and I spent a day at 'COMDEX/Spring 1984' in the Los Angeles Convention Center. That was just before the IBM PC became the dominant personal computer—so there were plenty of Apples, Ataris, Kaypros, and oddballs. AT&T was displaying its new (and now forgotten) 3B2 systems in a room populated by salesmen in expensive suits who started by asking if I had 'signature authority' to buy computers for my institution" (Michael Covington, associate director of the Artificial Intelligence Center at the University of Georgia, June 28, 2004, http://www.covingtoninnovations.com/michael/blog/0406/index.html).

16. Hall, interview, 20–21. An unknown Bill Gates would give his first COMDEX speech, "Information @ Your Fingertips," at Fall COMDEX, Las Vegas, November 1984.

17. "It's Not Peripheral," *HP Measure* (November-December 1988): 7–11.

18. Hall, interview, 22.

19. Even within the Boise Division, the Personal LaserJet was held in some contempt. "When we were in two divisions, we had BLD (Boise LaserJet Division) which had the medium and big printers, and we had PLD (Personal LaserJet Division) which had the small printers. We said it stood for Big LaserJet Division and Piddly (or Peon) LaserJet Division" (Gary Stringham, e-mail to the HP Alumni Club, December 8, 2007).

20. Carly Fiorina, *Tough Choices: A Memoir* (New York: Portfolio, Penguin Group, 2006), 196, 198.

21. See the Ticknor biography at Inflexion Partners, http://www.inflexionvc.com/team/carolyn.html.

22. Kodak, http://www.envisionreports.com/EK/2008/13fe08011m/index.html.

23. Robert A. Sanderson, "Pressurized Ink Recording on Z-Fold Strip Charts" *HP Journal* 18, 11 (July 1967): 2–12; Dale R. Davis and Charles K. Michener, "Graphic Recorder Writing Systems," *HP Journal* 20, 2 (October 1968): 2–7; and Otto S. Talle Jr., "High Dynamic Performance X-Y Recorder," *HP Journal* 20, 4 (December 1968): 8–11.

24. "Isometric Projection of a Function Computed by the 9100A Computing Calculator and Plotted Simultaneously by the 9125A Plotter," *HP Journal* 21, 1 (September 1969): cover.

25. "News in Brief," *HP Measure* (March, 1975): 14; and "On the Road to 1976," *HP Measure* (December 1975): 5; James A. Doub, "Cost-Effective, Reliable CRT Terminal Is First of a Family," *HP Journal* 26, 10 (June 1975): 2–5. See also other chapters in the *HP Journal* 26, 10 (June 1975) issue.

26. Ampex is an acronym of the founder's initials, plus "*ex*cellence"; some averred

that the "ex" stood for "experimental." Ampex, founded in 1944 in San Carlos, California, invented the first video film recorder. See http://recordist.com/ampex/index.html and www.ampex.com.

27. Walter T. Selsted, "A New Instrumentation-Class Tape Transport of Simplified Design," *HP Journal* 16, 5 (January 1965). Gerald L. Ainsworth, "A New High-Performance 1.5 MHz Tape Recorder," *HP Journal* 18, 4 (December 1966): 2–7; "Magnetic Tape Recording and Reproducing," *HP Journal* 18, 4 (December 1966): 4; "Square Wave Response of The HP Model 3950 Magnetic Tape Recording System," *HP Journal* 18, 4 (December 1966): 6; and Arndt B. Bergh, "A Current Preamplifier for Magnetic Tape Playback Systems," *HP Journal* 18, 4 (December 1966): 8–9.

28. Walt Selsted, interview by Raymond L. Price, September 17, 2004, 10–11.

29. Myrt McCarthy, Stan's wife, was Lew Platt's personal secretary for many years.

30. No *HP Journal* or *HP Measure* article described these early tape drives.

31. Smelek, interview, 5.

32. Smelek, interview, 9–10.

33. Dick B. Barney and James R. Drehle, "A Quiet, Low-Cost, High-Speed Line Printer," *HP Journal* 24, 9 (May 1973): 18–24; Robert B. Bump and Gary R. Paulson, "Character Impact Printer Offers Maximum Printing Flexibility," *HP Journal* 27, 10 (June 1976): 19–23.

34. Peter Dickinson and William Egbert, "A Pair of Program-Compatible Personal Programmable Calculators," *HP Journal* 28, 3 (November 1976): 2–8; Bernard Musch and Robert Taggart, "Portable Scientific Calculator Has Built-In Printer," *HP Journal* 28, 3 (November 1976): 9–16.

35. James Herlinger and James Barnes, "A Faster, Tougher Disc Drive for Small Computer Systems," *HP Journal* 23, 9 (May 1972): 2–5. See also Herbert P. Stickel, "New 50-Megabyte Disc Drive: High Performance and Reliability from High-Technology Design," *HP Journal* 28, 12 (August 1977): 2–15.

36. "Disc Memory Division Formed—to Boise," *HP Measure* (October 1976): 14; "HP's Computer Business: Passing the 10-Year Mark," *HP Measure* (October 1976): 10–13.

37. Smelek, interview, 10–11.

38. Todd M. Woodcock, "Printer and Printing Terminal Gain Versatility and Mechanical Simplicity with Microprocessor Control," *HP Journal* 29, 15 (November 1978): 2–7; Robert Cort, "Mechanical Design of a Durable Dot-Matrix Printer," *HP Journal* 29, 15 (November 1978): 9; F. Duncan Terry, "Versatile 400-lpm Line Printer with a Friction-Free Mechanism That Assures Long Life," *HP Journal* 29, 15 (November 1978): 20–22; and several other stories in the same issue.

39. Duncan Terry, interview by Raymond L. Price, October 18, 2004, 14–15.

40. Richard L. Smith, "A Small, Low-Cost 12-Megabyte Fixed Disc Drive," *HP Journal* 30, 7 (July 1979): 11.

41. Emerson W. Pugh, *Building IBM: Shaping an Industry and Its Technology* (Cambridge, MA: MIT Press, 1995). This is the fourth of Pugh's books on early computing history and IBM's role in that evolution. See also Emerson W. Pugh, *Memories That Shaped an Industry: Decisions Leading to IBM System/360* (Cambridge, MA: MIT Press, 1984).

42. Robert W. Colpitts, Dan Allen, and Tom Vos, "Graphical Output for the Computing Calculator," *HP Journal* 21, 1 (September 1969): 5.

43. Terry, interview, 11.

44. Robert L. Dudley and Virgil L. Laing, "A Self-Contained, Hand-Held Digital Multimeter—A New Concept in Instrument Utility," *HP Journal* 25, 3 (November 1973): 2–9.

45. Lawrence G. Brunetti, "A New Family of Intelligent Multi-Color X-Y Plotters," *HP Journal* 29, 1 (September 1977): 2–5; Richard M. Kemplin, Robert D. Haselby, and Marvin L. Patterson, "Speed, Precision, and Smoothness Characterize Four-Color Plotter Pen Drive System," *HP Journal* 29, 1 (September 1977): 13–18; Richard M. Kemplin, Larry W. Hennessee, Leonard P. Balazer, and George W. Lynch, "Pen and Ink System Helps Assure Four-Color Plotter Line Quality," *HP Journal* 29, 1 (September 1977): 20–25; and other stories in the same issue.

46. Rick A. Warp, Majid Azmoon, and Jaime H. Bohorquez, "Desktop Plotter/Printer Does Both Vector Graphic Plotting and Fast Text Printing," *HP Journal* 29, 13 (September 1978): 24–30.

47. Terry R. Cobb, John A. Fenoglio, and Bessie W. C. Chin, "A High-Quality Digital X-Y Plotter Designed for Reliability, Flexibility and Low Cost," *HP Journal* 30, 2 (February 1979): 2–7; and other stories in the same issue.

48. Charles E. Tyler, Lawrence LaBarre, Wayne D. Baron, and Robert G. Younge, "Development of a High-Performance, Low-Mass, Low-Inertia Plotting Technology," *HP Journal* 32, 10 (October 1981) 3–7.

49. "To Market, To Market," *HP Measure* (September-October 1987): 8–9.

50. Donald L. Morris and Roger D. Quick, "Evolutionary Printer Provides Significantly Better Performance," *HP Journal* 31, 3 (March 1980): 15–19. This was the Corvallis HP 82143A.

51. Ronald W. Keil and Clement C. Lo, "A Compact Thermal Printer Designed for Integration into a Personal Computer," *HP Journal* 31, 7 (July 1980): 22–26.

52. Terry, interview, 11–12. See Sam Lightman, "The Eight-Year Overnight Success Story," *HP Measure* (November-December 1992): 8–10.

53. "HP in the Pacific Northwest," *HP Measure* (January-February 1982): 3–5.

54. Bill Bondurant, interview by Raymond L. Price, August 19, 2004, 4.

55. Bondurant, interview, 4–5.

56. Bondurant, interview, 5.

57. Lightman, "Overnight Success," 8.

58. Bondurant, interview, 5.

59. Bondurant, interview, 6–7.

60. Lee Fleming, "Finding the Organizational Sources of Technological Breakthroughs: The Story of Hewlett-Packard's Thermal Ink-Jet," *Industrial and Corporate Change* 11, 5 (2002): 1059–1084.

61. Fleming, "Technological Breakthroughs," 1063.

62. Fleming, "Technological Breakthroughs," 1059–1084.

63. Bondurant, interview, 9.

64. Dick Watts, interview by Raymond L. Price, November 8, 2004, 1–2.

65. Watts, interview, 2–3.

66. Watts, interview, 4.

67. Lightman, "Overnight Success," 8.

68. Webster, *Print Unchained*, 146.

69. Tekla S. Perry, "From Podfather to Palm's Pilot," *IEEE Spectrum* 45, 9 (September 2008). Steve Chorak and Jon Rubenstein, "9826A vs. 9836A," *HP Journal* 33, 6 (May 1982): 4.

70. John Stedman, private essay, "HP Observations, 1969–2000" (March 21, 2006): 4–6.

CHAPTER 11

1. Charles H. House was present at the Executive Committee Meeting, March 1980, where David Packard spoke.

2. http://en.wikipedia.org/wiki/Evans_&_Sutherland.

3. "Selling the Computer Revolution," Marketing Brochures in the Collection, Computer History Museum, Mountain View, California, http://www.computerhistory.org/brochures/companies.php?alpha=a-c&company=com-42b9d348110c2.

4. Computer Terminal Corporation in San Antonio built the HP 2600A; reliability issues sent McCracken to Beehive Medical Electronics.

5. Jonathan R. Cross, James A. Doub, and John M. Stedman, "On-Line Data Reduction for Nuclear Analyzers," *Hewlett-Packard Journal* (hereafter *HP Journal*) 22, 8 (April 1971): 2–10; James A. Doub, "Cost-Effective, Reliable CRT Terminal Is First of a Family," *HP Journal* 26, 10 (June 1975): 2–5; and other articles in the same issue.

6. Robert G. Nordman, Richard L. Smith, and Louis A. Witkin, "New CRT Terminal Has Magnetic Tape Storage for Expanded Capability," *HP Journal* 27, 9 (May 1976): 2–15.

7. Kenneth A. Van Bree, "CRT Terminal Provides Both APL and ASCII Operation," *HP Journal* 29, 11 (July 1977): 25–28.

8. "HP's New Product Express: Coming Around the Mountain," *HP Measure* (January 1978): 2–5. Peter D. Dickinson, "Versatile Low-Cost Graphics Terminal Is Designed for Ease of Use," *HP Journal* 30, 5 (January 1978): 2–5.

9. *HP Catalog* (1979): 631.

10. *HP Catalog* (1983): 604; Gary C. Stass, "New Display Station Offers Multiple Screen Windows and Dual Data Communications Ports," *HP Journal* 33, 3 (March 1981): 3–8; Gordon C. Graham, "Display Station's User Interface Is Designed for Increased Productivity," *HP Journal* 33, 3 (March 1981): 8–12; John D. Wiese and Srinivas Sukumar, "Hardware and Firmware Support for Four Virtual Terminals in One Display Station," *HP Journal* 33, 3 (March 1981): 13–15; Jean-Claude Roy, "A Silicon-on-Sapphire Integrated Video Controller," *HP Journal* 33, 3 (March 1981): 16–19. "The Hewlett-Packard Organization," *HP Measure* (September-October 1980): 11–14.

11. "The HP-85, HP's First Personal Computer," *HP Journal* 31, 7 (July 1980): cover; Todd R. Lynch, "A New World of Personal/Professional Computation," *HP Journal* 31, 7 (July 1980): 3–7; William Hewlett and Gerald Nelson, "The Design and Development of a Family of Personal Computers for Engineers and Scientists," in Amar Gupta and Hoo-min D. Toong (eds.), *Insights into Personal Computers* (New York: IEEE Press, 1985), 38.

12. Fred Gibbons, interview by Raymond L. Price, October 10, 2004, 6–7.

13. Ken Fox, interview by Raymond L. Price, November 11, 2004, 10.

14. Fox, interview, 11.

15. *HP Catalog* (1983): 602.

16. *HP Catalog* (1984): 599.

17. "Half a Million Terminals Later," *HP Measure* (January-February 1985): 19.

18. Steve Joseph, interview by Charles H. House, 1986. Dick Hackborn stood and strode to the podium, saying, "We will fix that issue."

19. Eileen Birkwood, the ex-quality assurance manager for GSD Cupertino, commissioned Sandy Sheehan and Sue Stetak for this Corporate Engineering study in 1983.

20. John Doyle, speech, Cupertino, California, November 1983.

21. Frederic C. Amerson, Mark S. Linsky, and Elio A. Toschi, "High-Performance Computing with Dual ALU Architecture and ECL Logic," *HP Journal* 33, 3 (March 1982):

3–12. The quote is from Richard P. Dolan, "1 MIP . . . Is a Very Creditable Number and a Real Bargain at the Series 64's Price," *HP Journal* 33, 3 (March 1982): 2.

22. Robert Frankenberg, interview by Charles H. House and Raymond L. Price, October 20, 2004, 25.

23. Dick Alberding, interview by Chuck House, September 19, 2006, 53–55.

24. Alberding, interview, 55–57.

25. "The Evolving HP Organization," *HP Measure* (July-August 1984): 12–13.

26. "The Macintosh Marketing Campaign," Technology and Culture in Silicon Valley, http://library.stanford.edu/mac/market.html. See also "1984—Lost Mac Introduction Video Recovered," http://myoldmac.net/FAQ/1984-mac-intro.htm.

27. Doug Chance, personal communication with Charles H. House, 1985. The conversation was at the General Manager's Meeting.

28. No firm data exist for who at HP had operated a Macintosh prior to the ad. Chuck House had done so two months earlier, due to friendship with ex-HP designers Tom Whitney and John Couch, both now executives at Apple. For a surreptitious Summerhill Partner Angel investing evening in November 1983, John Couch provided a Macintosh prototype. Charles Ying, the CEO who led Atex, hosted the event, which led Summerhill Partners to angel-fund Aldus Corporation. Paul Brainerd had been Ying's marketing manager at Atex Inc., when it was acquired by Eastman Kodak (see John Markoff, "Can Atex Keep Its Proprietary Place in the Newsroom?" *New York Times*, March 17, 1991, F4).

At HP, Bob Frankenberg knew of the Mac but had not seen it; ditto for Joel Birnbaum, Bill Worley, and Cyril Yansouni. Paul Ely wasn't concerned about the rumored machine, nor was Bill Terry. Ed McCracken, Doug Chance, and Dick Hackborn had seen the Lisa, but not the Macintosh.

29. "The Evolving HP Organization," *HP Measure* (July-August 1984): 12–13.

30. Lee A. Daniels, "Official at Hewlett Joins Convergent," *New York Times*, January 8, 1985, D2.

31. Sam Lightman, "Personal Computers: Past, Present, and Future," *HP Measure* (November-December 1985): 3–5.

32. Yansouni, a proud man, was crystal-clear: "In the computer group we did a lot of things right. Our dealer channel was great. The advertising was superb. Our marketing was solid. We broke new ground on convincing the company that we had to have a distribution system. We couldn't just take orders and tell people you're going to get your printer in six weeks. It was tough. Some of it was anti-cultural. We did a great job marketing the peripherals. You know, we (the PC Group) marketed the laser printer. Others get all the credit for laser printers, but we marketed it. Without us, it would have taken a lot longer." Cyril Yansouni, interview by Charles H. House and Raymond L. Price, November 16, 2005, 30, 35–36.

33. H. Kent Bowen, Kim B. Clark, Charles A. Holloway, and Steven C. Wheelwright, *The Perpetual Enterprise Machine: Seven Keys to Corporate Renewal Through Successful Product and Process Development* (New York: Oxford University Press, 1994), 413–418.

34. Ibid.

35. Srini Sukumar, personal communication with Charles H. House, January 1987.

36. This was discovered by local police in Portola Valley, California.

37. George Anders, *Perfect Enough: Carly Fiorina and the Reinvention of Hewlett-Packard* (New York: Penguin Group, 2003), 67.

38. D. A. Garvin, "Product Quality: An Important Strategic Weapon," *Business Horizons* (March-April 1984): 40–43.

39. Rit Keiter, "Ideas for Improving Engineering Productivity: Engineering Productivity Task Force Report," Hewlett-Packard report (January 1982).

40. Jean Burke, "McMinnville: Good Medicine for HP: Employees in Oregon's Small-but-Mighty McMinnville Division Open the Door to Their Corner of the Medical Products World," *HP Measure* (March-April 1986): 12–15.

41. Frankenberg, interview, 24–25.

42. Frankenberg, interview, 34.

43. A small company held the Spectrum name copyright, and wouldn't relinquish it. Joel Birnbaum, interview by Raymond L. Price, December 15, 2005, 28.

44. Nancy Anderson, interview by Raymond L. Price, August 19, 2004, 9–10.

45. Anderson, interview, 10–11.

46. Anderson, interview, 11–12.

47. *Business Planning for Competitive Advantage: The Ten Step Approach* (Palo Alto, CA: HP Press, 1990).

48. Michael Maccoby, *The Gamesman: The New Corporate Leaders* (New York: Simon & Schuster, 1977).

49. Doyle's desire to be number one was very strong, describing Fort Collins computing efforts once as a serious strategic mistake, since they forfeited leadership in voltmeters to chase the shibboleth of desktop calculators. John Doyle, personal communication with Charles H. House, April 1982.

50. Yansouni, interview, 34–36.

51. Dean Morton, interview by Charles H. House and Raymond L. Price, November 17, 2005, 6–7.

52. Bill Bondurant, interview by Raymond L. Price, August 19, 2004, 15.

53. Michael S. Malone, *Bill and Dave: How Hewlett and Packard Built the World's Greatest Company* (New York: Portfolio Books, Penguin Group, 2007), 339.

54. Alan Kay, interview by Charles H. House, January 20, 2006; John Couch, interview by Charles H. House, August 31, 2007; Frankenberg, interview.

55. Frankenberg, interview, 35–37.

56. Frankenberg, interview, 37.

57. HP-PA Introduction Manual, "Introduction to the HP 3000," http://www.docs.hp.com/en/32650-90421/ch01s01.html.

58. HP-PA Introduction Manual, "Introduction to the HP 3000." For Worley's career, see Joan Tharpe, "Bill Worley: Captaining the Next Generation," HP Labs website, Spring 2001, http://www.hpl.hp.com/news/2001/apr-jun/worley.html.

59. John Young, interview by Charles H. House and Raymond L. Price, November 17, 2005.

60. Carl Cottrell, interview by Raymond L. Price, October 6, 2004, 24.

61. Young, interview, 26–28.

62. Ironically, Robert Frankenberg had already negotiated an HP license for Apollo Domain. Frankenberg, interview, 53.

63. http://en.wikipedia.org/wiki/Apollo_Computer; Karen Southwick, *High Noon: The Inside Story of Scott McNealy and the Rise of Sun Microsystems* (New York: John Wiley & Sons, 1999); also http://www.old-computers.com/museum/computer.asp?c=141.

64. "Updated Version of HP Organization Chart," *HP Measure* (January-February 1986): 23.

65. Lightman, "Personal Computers," 3–5.

66. Sharon R. King, "Dow Climbs by 52.56 to Reach Its 6th Consecutive High," *New York Times*, February 19, 1988, D9.

67. "Compaq's Deskpro 386, priced at $12,499, produced the most revenue." Thomas C. Hayes, "Texas Instruments Net Down, Compaq's Up," *New York Times*, April 22, 1988, D5.

68. Joel Birnbaum, personal communication with Charles H. House, August 14, 2008.

69. Dean Morton, interview, 25–26. The stock-based purchase, $476 million when concluded, was down from $760 million at the announcement.

70. Michele Clarke, "HP Won't Abandon Apollo Users," *EDN*, May 4, 1989, http://www.highbeam.com/doc/1G1-7582701.html.

71. "Combination Forms Worldwide Leader in Fast-Growing Automated Software Quality Market. . . . Reed Hastings . . . will be president and CEO. . . . Paul H. Levine . . . will be chairman of the board." ("Atria Software and Pure Software Become Pure Atria with Shareholder Approval of Merger," *PRNewswire*, August 26, 1996, http://www.prnewswire.com/cgi-bin/stories.pl?ACCT=104&STORY=/www/story/26399&EDATE=). Pure-Atria was larger than the combined software offerings of the HP instrument and engineering computing groups.

72. "OSF. Open Software Foundation," *HP Measure* (July-August 1988): 12. "There are still many areas of leadership HP may choose to pursue—price/performance, networking, graphics, quality, support, and unique value-added functionality, to name just a few." Young, interview.

73. Phil Lemmons, *Personal Workstation Magazine* (March 1991).

74. Andrew Pollack, "Hewlett's Sprightly New Mood," *New York Times*, March 21, 1991

75. Rhea Feldman, "SSSSsnakes: HP Apollo 9000 Series 700 workstation family," *HP Measure* (May-June 1991): 3–8. The table on page 6 lists SPECmarks of DECStation 5000 = 18.5; SPARCstation 2 = 21; IBM Model 320H = 32.4; HP 9000/700 = 55; HP9000/730 = 72.2 SPECMarks.

CHAPTER 12

1. David Packard, speech, Fort Collins, Colorado, August 15, 1990.

2. "Up, Up and Away," *HP Measure* (January-February 1983): 18.

3. Young said, "Systems integration was the hardest cultural thing to break. . . . The rows and columns idea was really trying to demonstrate to people that it doesn't help to have a CPU with no networking, or if the operating system doesn't work. These things have to work together." John Young, interview by Raymond L. Price and Charles H. House, November 17, 2005, 29.

4. For the 1985 management council retreat at the tony Meadowood Country Club in St. Helena, California, John Young commissioned a facilitated DEC analysis for twenty-four HP executives. The opening perusal of DEC's 1984 annual report was followed by a question to each attendee of how many DEC officers or board members they knew personally, or had met and talked to in some depth. This was the first time in HP history that the leadership team analyzed one competitor in depth. It was shocking that, aside from the two R&D attendees, no one had ever met anyone on DEC's team; when DEC was just surpassing HP in total revenues, going head-to-head across virtually all of HP's computing product lines. The next day, *Fortune* and *Forbes* reporters canceled an annual HP financial briefing to attend

an impromptu Apple meeting. An upset COO Dean Morton reversed a decision to allow HP to be covered on Jane Pauley's *Today Show* for its part in Gifford Pinchot, *Intrapreneuring: Why You Don't Have to Leave the Corporation to Become an Entrepreneur* (New York: HarperCollins, 1986).

5. Charles H. House, notes taken during David Packard speech, Fort Collins, Colorado, August 15, 1990. The afternoon speech videotape is from Bill Tippett, Loveland Division GM. Also Tom Saponas, interview with Charles H. House, November 7, 2005, re: Packard's dinner two nights before in Colorado Springs.

6. George Anders, *Perfect Enough: Carly Fiorina and the Reinvention of Hewlett-Packard* (New York: Penguin Group, 2003), 25.

7. Charles House, with Corporate Engineering, hosted the SW Developer's meeting. The source of the rumors re: Young's resignation was the Palo Alto janitorial staff, who found his palatial CEO office empty on Saturday morning, and then filled again on Monday. The unconfirmed story would speak volumes about both men.

8. John Young, interview by Charles H. House and Raymond L. Price, November 17, 2005, 38.

9. Young, interview, 38.

10. Robert D. Hof, "Suddenly, Hewlett-Packard Is Doing Everything Right," *BusinessWeek* (March 23, 1992): 88–89. See also Eric Nee, "Dave and Bill's Last Adventure," *Upside* (June 1991): 40.

11. Joel Birnbaum, interview by Raymond L. Price, December 15, 2005, 63.

12. Michael S. Malone, *Bill and Dave: How Hewlett and Packard Built the World's Greatest Company* (New York: Portfolio Books, Penguin Group, 2007) (includes obituary column).

13. The Wang Corporation was dissolved in 1992. See An Wang, *Lessons: An Autobiography* (Palo Alto, CA: Addison-Wesley, 1986).

14. Birnbaum, interview, 34–35.

15. Birnbaum, interview, 35–36.

16. Birnbaum, interview, 35–36.

17. Birnbaum, interview, 36–38.

18. Birnbaum, interview, 38–40.

19. Birnbaum, interview, 41–42. Though relatively young, Bruce Campbell died suddenly; Clive Surfleet then managed the group for years.

20. Denny Georg, interview by Raymond L. Price, September 14, 2006, 8. Georg today is chairman of the board for Secure64, a Denver firm concentrating on Enterprise Security for 64-bit computing systems. Secure64 was co-founded by William Worley after he transferred HP's 64-bit team to Intel for the Itanium chipsets. Worley was an HP Fellow, Chief Scientist, and Distinguished Contributor before retiring in 2002.

21. Georg, interview, 9.

22. Georg, interview, 10.

23. Georg, interview, 11–12.

24. Georg, interview, 20.

25. Dana Blankenhorn, "IBM's Akers Should Resign," *Newsbytes News Network*, May 31, 1992. While the IBM PC was successful by everyone's standard, the R6000 RISC workstation inclusion in Blankenhorn's short list of successes was a surprising minority view.

26. Eric Nee, "Back to Basics at Hewlett-Packard" *Upside* (June 1991): 38–42, 68–77. The cover of the June 1991 issue of *Upside* carries the headline "Dave and Bill's Last Adventure:

Restoring the Oomph at HP." Richard T. Pascale, *Managing on the Edge: Companies That Use Conflict to Stay Ahead* (New York: Viking Penguin, 1990).

27. Anders, *Perfect Enough*, 31.

28. Bill Terry, interview by Charles H. House, September 28, 2006, 27.

29. John McCormick, "DEC and H-P Both Lose Heads," *Newsbytes News Network*, July 17, 1992, http://findarticles.com/p/articles/mi_moNEW/is_1992_July_17/ai_12617091.

30. Nee, "Back to Basics". See also Malone, *Bill and Dave*, 354.

31. Dave Barram, interview by Raymond L. Price, December 9, 2004, 17–18. Charles H. House attended the breakfast for Informix CEO Phillip E. White.

32. Barram, interview, 18.

33. Barram, interview, 19.

34. Barram, interview, 19–20.

35. David Packard, "Executives for Clinton Have Blundered," *San Jose Mercury-News*, September 17, 1992, 6B (letter to the editor).

36. Young, interview, 40–41. Two of Packard's three daughters made the list of the top one hundred political donors in California for the 2004 presidential campaign: "#60, Franklin and Susan Packard Orr, Stanford, $500,000, Hewlett Packard heir, Democratic donors; #66, Nancy Packard Burnett, $458,000, Hewlett Packard heir, Democratic donor." "Top 100 California Political Donors," *Orange County Register*, Sunday, July 24, 2005, http://www.ocregister.com/ocr/2005/07/24/sections/news/news/article_609800.php.

37. Calvin Sims, "Silicon Valley Takes a Partisan Leap of Faith," *New York Times*, October 29, 1992, D1, D24. See also http://query.nytimes.com/gst/fullpage.html?res=9E0CE6D8123BF93AA15753C1A964958260.

38. Barram, interview, 19, 21.

39. Jef Graham, interview by Raymond L. Price, October 6, 2004, 15–16.

40. Dick Alberding, interview by Chuck House, September 19, 2006, 63–64.

41. Julie Pitta, "It Had to Be Done, and We Did It," *Forbes* 151, 9 (April 26, 1993): 148–152.

42. Young, interview, 39.

43. Young, interview, 19–20, 22.

44. Peter Burrows, *Backfire: Carly Fiorina's High-Stakes Battle for the Soul of HP* (New York: John Wiley & Sons, 2003), 75–77, reports these events from the perspectives of John Young and Jay Keyworth, and includes a Lew Platt comment revealing a higher level of animosity between Hackborn and Platt than is generally reported. Anders, *Perfect Enough*, 23–27, reports some of these events as well, although the ordering is confused.

45. Two subsequent coaches with higher winning percentages than John Wooden have not been viewed as successful at UCLA—the irony is that it took Wooden sixteen years at UCLA to produce his first NCAA contender.

46. Doug Chance, interview by Raymond L. Price and Charles H. House, March 24, 2005, 2.

47. Chance, interview, 3–4. See "The HP Experience," *HP Measure* (August-September 1973): 2–31.

48. Doug Chance, slide provided to the authors.

49. Chance, interview, 5.

50. Chance, interview, 6.

51. Ibid.

52. "Workshop on Employees: How to Keep That Small Company Feeling," *HP Measure*

(July 1975): 11–12; Chance, interview; Chance produced a letter from Dick Hackborn dated May 29, 1975 with the slide redrawn in HP Draw.

53. Chance, interview, 9–10.

54. David Packard, *The HP Way: How Bill Hewlett and I Built Our Company* (New York: HarperCollins, 1995), 150.

55. Two books were rushed to print in the aftermath of the HP-Compaq merger fight—Anders, *Perfect Enough*, and Burrows, *Backfire*. Burrows has continued periodic coverage of HP with his *BusinessWeek* post, contributing solid analytical perspective to the present. Agilent Technologies, though, has not experienced such publicity, and the antecedents that built both companies have been incompletely covered.

56. Robert Grimm, interview by Alan Bagley, November 13, 1991, 68.

CHAPTER 13

1. Platt's first wife, a cancer victim at a young age, left him with two young daughters. After later marrying a widow with two daughters, raising the four girls gave Platt a vantage point for "fresh eyes."

2. Dick Lampman, personal communication with Charles H. House, May 18, 2005.

3. Wim Roelandts, interview by Charles H. House and Raymond L. Price, November 18, 2005, 12–14.

4. Mark Smotherman, "Understanding EPIC Architectures and Implementations," ACM Southeast Conference, 2002, http://www.cs.clemson.edu/~mark/epic.html.

5. Cheskin-Masten CEO Davis Masten, studying HP brand identity, found that computer-screen identity eluded HPites even as nearly every product human interface was a CRT.

6. Carly Fiorina, *Tough Choices: A Memoir* (New York: Portfolio Books, 2006): 199, 203.

7. Debra Dunn, interview by Charles H. House and Raymond L. Price, September 28, 2006, 51. SAP is the world's largest business software vendor, and the third largest software vendor overall. It began in 1972 as Systems Applications and Products for Data Processing; the headquarters are located in Germany, and the company today is just known as SAP.

8. Fiorina, *Tough Choices*. Also Carly Fiorina, interview by Charles H. House, June 6, 2007, 12.

9. Joel Birnbaum, interview by Raymond L. Price, December 15, 2005, 67–70.

10. John Young, interview by Raymond L. Price and Charles H. House, November 17, 2005, 22–23.

11. Birnbaum, interview, 72–74.

12. Birnbaum, interview, 67–72.

13. This internecine battle is described in Fiorina, *Tough Choices*, 186–187, 196, 198.

14. Hackborn joined the Microsoft board in August 1994. The "conflict of interest" charge arose periodically; *cf.* Peter Burrows, *Backfire: Carly Fiorina's High-Stakes Battle for the Soul of HP* (New York: John Wiley & Sons, 2003), 77, 79.

15. Shiz Kobara, *Visual Design with OSF/Motif* (Palo Alto, CA: HP Press, 1991).

16. See Lewis Gerstner, *Who Says Elephants Can't Dance: Leading a Great Enterprise Through Dramatic Change* (New York: HarperCollins, 2002).

17. Rick Belluzzo, personal communication with Raymond L. Price, August 28, 2008.

18. Roelandts, interview, 14.

19. Burrows, *Backfire*, 79.

20. Rick Belluzzo, interview by Charles H. House, October 2, 2006, 5–6.

21. Peter Burrows and Ben Elgin, "The Surprise Player Behind the Coup at HP," *BusinessWeek* (March 14, 2005): 36–37.

22. Dick Watts, interview by Raymond L. Price, November 8, 2004, 4.

23. Watts, interview, 4–5.

24. Ibid.

25. Bill Bondurant, interview by Raymond L. Price, August 19, 2004, 16–18.

26. Roelandts, interview, 28–29.

27. Birnbaum, interview, 67–74.

28. "Chaos Theory: A Brief Introduction," In My Humble Opinion, http://www.imho.com/grae/chaos/chaos.html.

29. Critics had a field day with the paucity of effect from the HP-Intel Itanium IA-64 partnership. On Slashdot, "The nuts and bolts for nerds," envisionary wrote on December 18, 2004, "Hewlett-Packard Co. and Intel Corp. have ended their partnership to co-develop the Itanium 64-bit processor line, according to a report from Reuters. The move follows disappointing sales for servers based on the processor, according to the report. Intel and HP developed the processor about 10 years,[*sic*] but the chip has been a flop due to delays, cost overruns and lackluster demand" ("HP, Intel Call It Quits on Itanium Partnership," Slashdot, http://hardware.slashdot.org/article.pl?sid=04/12/18/1428223&from=rss).

30. "Hewlett-Packard CEO to Deliver Sheffield Address at Yale," February 20, 1997, Yale University archives, http://www.eng.yale.edu/sheff/platt/announce.html.

31. Ibid.

32. Ibid.

33. Ibid.

34. Birnbaum, interview, 36.

35. Jagdish Rebello, quoted in "LED Market Lights Up," Philips Electronics Australia Ltd, May 5, 2005, Newsletter, http://www.ferret.com.au/c/Philips-Electronics-Australia/LED-market-lights-up-n698639. Nick Holonyak Jr. at GE was the developer of the first practical visible-spectrum LED in 1962; his former graduate student and long-time HP researcher, M. George Craford, invented the first yellow LED.

36. Nina Bhatti, interview by Charles H. House, September 12, 2006, 7.

37. Bhatti, interview, 8–9.

38. Bhatti, interview, 10–13.

39. Bhatti, interview, 11–13.

40. Jim Mackey, "The Curse of the Fortune 50," HP white paper, supported by KPMG (2003). Also see Jim Mackey and Liisa Välikangas, "The Myth of Unbounded Growth," *MIT Sloan Management Review* 45, 2 (Winter 2004): 89–92.

41. Polly Labarre, "The Industrialized Revolution," *Fast Company* (November 2003): 114.

42. Charles H. House, presentation, Product Development and Management Association (PDMA), Fourth Annual Front End of Innovation Conference, Boston, May 22–24, 2006. The comments were made during the question-and-answer portion of the presentation.

43. Ned Barnholt, interview by Raymond L. Price, December 15, 2005, 7–8.

44. Belluzzo, interview, 27–28.

45. Belluzzo, interview, 28.

46. Belluzzo, interview, 28–29.

47. Christine McDonald and Tim Clark, "HP Swipes VeriFone in Stock Deal," CNET News, April 23, 1997, http://news.cnet.com/HP-swipes-VeriFone-in-stock-deal/2100-1001_3-279131.html.

48. Rick Belluzzo, personal communication with Raymond L. Price, August 28, 2008.

49. Belluzzo, interview, 30–33.

50. John Sheets, personal communication with Charles H. House, November 20, 2005.

51. Lisa DiCarlo, "HP's Metamorphosis Continues," *Forbes*, July 25, 2001, http://www.forbes.com/2001/07/25/0725hp.html.

52. Belluzzo, interview, 34.

53. Watts, interview, 20.

CHAPTER 14

1. Paul Ely, interview by Raymond L. Price, December 15, 2005, 9.

2. Chad Fasca, "Shakeup at HP," *Electronic News*, January 26, 1998, http://findarticles.com/p/articles/mi_m0EKF/is_n2203_v44/ai_20201007. McCracken, joining Silicon Graphics from HP in 1984, built the company from $9 million in revenue to $4 billion in twelve years. Nonetheless, in a very short period, the company cratered; McCracken resigned in 1997. See Robert D. Hof, Ira Sager, and Linda Himelstein, "The Sad Saga of Silicon Graphics," *BusinessWeek* (August 4, 1997): 66–72. McCracken, disliked by founder Jim Clark, was portrayed unsympathetically in Michael Lewis, *The New, New Thing: A Silicon Valley Story* (New York: W. W. Norton, 2000).

3. Peter Burrows, *Backfire: Carly Fiorina's High-Stakes Battle for the Soul of HP* (New York: John Wiley & Sons, 2003), 84; George Anders, *Perfect Enough: Carly Fiorina and the Reinvention of Hewlett-Packard* (New York: Penguin Group, 2003), 38–39.

4. Rick Belluzzo, interview by Charles H. House, October 2, 2006, 26.

5. "Compaq CEO Pfeiffer Unveils Company Strategy; Synergy of Compaq-Digital-Tandem Laying Cornerstone for 'New World of Computing,'" *Business Wire*, June 12, 1998, http://findarticles.com/p/articles/mi_m0EIN/is_1998_June_12/ai_n27536307.

6. Carolyn Whelan, "Unix to Battle Windows NT," *Electronic News* 44, 2200 (January 5, 1998): 52, 54.

7. Lawrence M. Fisher, "Compaq Reports Loss Following Acquisition," *New York Times*, July 16, 1998, D4.

8. "Combined Issue: Compaq Makes $4.7bn Charge and Predicts Annual Losses," *Computergram International*, July 2, 1998, http://findarticles.com/p/articles/mi_m0CGN/is_n131/ai_20866922.

9. Burrows, *Backfire*, 120.

10. "Silicon Graphics Q4 Losses Larger Than Expected," *Computergram International*, July 24, 1998, http://findarticles.com/p/articles/mi_m0CGN/is_n147/ai_20944034.

11. Ned Barnholt, interview by Raymond L. Price, December 15, 2005, 23–24.

12. Barnholt, interview, 3–4.

13. Hewlett-Packard announced the split on March 2, 1999, *Agilent Technologies Annual Report* (1999): 1; the Agilent Technologies name was revealed on July 28, 1999. Public trading (NYSE:A) began November 18, 1999.

14. On March 31, 2000, Cisco hit $73.625 per share, with 7.84 billion shares, a market capitalization of $575 billion on revenues of $16 billion. Seven years later, on March 13, 2007, the company valuation was $157 billion on revenues of $28 billion—still heady! General Electric on March 31, 2000, closed at $51.875 per share, with 10.28 billion shares

outstanding, a market cap of $533 billion. GE set the all-time capitalization high at $615 billion on August 25, 2000; March 13, 2007, it was valued at $353 billion on revenues of $163 billion.

15. Encyclopedia of Company Histories, http://www.answers.com/topic/lucent-technologies-old-company.

16. Y2K was the acronym for the "Year 2000" software bug—a legacy of Fortran programs wherein the date field was only two digits, not four (done in the early 1950s—no one thought fifty years ahead). The fear was that computers, especially in banking and commerce fields, would abort as they tried to decide between 1900 and 2000 for date fields on January 1, 2000. Much IT effort, reprogramming, and updating processes before January 2000 added fuel to the boom.

17. Amey Stone, "Crawling from the Dot-Com Wreckage," *BusinessWeek*, December 19, 2000, http://www.businessweek.com/bwdaily/dnflash/dec2000/nf20001219_800.htm; see also http://en.wikipedia.org/wiki/Dot-com_bubble.

18. Mike Bush, *Tulipomania: The Story of the World's Most Coveted Flower and the Extraordinary Passions That It Aroused* (New York: Three Rivers Press, 2001).

19. Barnholt, interview.

20. "Agilent Posts 28% Increase in Net Revenue for 3Q," *ElectronicsWeekly*, August 21, 2000, http://www.electronicsweekly.com/Articles/2000/08/21/17366/agilent-posts-28-increase-in-net-revenue-for-3q.htm.

21. Ibid.

22. "Agilent Offers to Buy OSI for $665 Million," *Sacramento Business Journal*, November 27, 2000, http://sacramento.bizjournals.com/sacramento/stories/2000/11/27/daily1.html. The relative acquisition price vis-à-vis Agilent's revenue was roughly analogous to HP's purchase of Apollo Computer in 1988.

23. Tom Saponas, interview by Charles H. House, November 7, 2005, 33.

24. Jean Burke Hoppe, "Extraordinary People," *HP Measure* (July-August 1987): 8–11.

25. Saponas, interview, 34–37.

26. zaywa.com.

27. Dean Morton, interview by Charles H. House and Raymond L. Price, November 17, 2005, 14–16.

28. Ned Barnholt, personal communication with Charles H. House, January 30, 2007.

29. www.icadmed.com.

30. Michelle Barkley was the TICU/MICU nurse manager at Christus Santa Rosa Medical Center in Houston at the time. "Marquette Medical Systems Inc., a company co-founded in Milwaukee 33 years ago by flamboyant entrepreneur Michael J. Cudahy, is being sold to General Electric Co. in an $810 million stock deal. Cudahy and his partner built Marquette Medical from a one-person shop into a world leader in cardiac diagnostic and monitoring equipment." Joe Manning, "Marquette Medical Sale Announced," *Milwaukee Journal Sentinel*, September 22, 1998, 1.

31. Bill Terry, interview by Charles H. House, September 28, 2006, 72–73.

32. Barnholt, personal communication.

33. "Agilent to Layoff 4,000 as It Downsizes for Slow Recovery," *Microwave Engineering Online*, August 21, 2001, http://www.mwee.com/mwee_news/showArticle.jhtml?articleID=10809031.

34. Trish Saywell, "Tough Times, Tough Choices," *Singapore Times*, http://unpan1.un.org/intradoc/groups/public/documents/APCITY/UNPAN001745.pdf.

35. Agilent Technologies Press Release (June 11, 2003).

36. Daniel Roth, "How to Cut Pay, Lay Off 8,000 People, and Still Have Workers Who Love You: It's Easy, Just Follow the Agilent Way, *Fortune* (February 4, 2002): 62–68.

37. See, for example, http://www.answers.com/topic/ned-barnholt.

38. Agilent Technologies Press Release (June 24, 2005).

39. Ibid.

40. Ibid.

41. Roland Haitz, interview by Charles H. House, February 27, 2006, 25–26.

42. Ned Barnholt, personal communications with Charles H. House, January 18, 2007, and January 30, 2007.

43. "Agilent Confirms Sale of Semiconductor Unit," http://compoundsemiconductor.net/cws/article/news/22877.

44. Sweta Singh, "Verigy Shares Soar on Strong Results, Outlook," *Reuters*, February 23, 2007, http://uk.reuters.com/article/hotStocksNewsUS/idUKBNG6615120070223.

45. *Agilent Technologies Annual Report* (1999): 3–4.

46. *Agilent Technologies Annual Report* (2006): 1.

47. In 2000, revenue from continuing operations was $7.2 billion; *Agilent Technologies Annual Report* (2000).

48. Singapore (#1), Korea (#3), Australia (#5), and India (#6) were cited in the *Agilent Technologies Annual Report* (2002).

49. *Agilent Technologies Annual Report* (2002): 3; *Agilent Technologies Annual Report* (2003): 8.

50. *Agilent Technologies Annual Report* (2004): 4.

51. "Agilent Technologies Names Patrick Byrne as Senior Vice President, President of Electronic Products and Solutions Group," http://www.thefreelibrary.com/Agilent+Technologies+Names+Patrick+Byrne+as+Senior+Vice+President%2c...-a0128216962.

52. Loralee Stevens, "Agilent Plans Unaffected by Byrne Exit," *North Bay Business Journal* (April 2, 2007): 1, 6.

53. Agilent Technologies Press Release (February 1, 2007).

54. "Agilent Technologies Named Instrument Business Outlook's 2006 Company of the Year," Agilent Technologies, February 1, 2007, http://www.agilent.com/about/newsroom/presrel/2007/01feb-ca07005.html.

55. Ely, interview, 9.

CHAPTER 15

1. Dave Packard and Bill Hewlett, *History Documentation* (Palo Alto, CA: HP TV Network, A Hewlett Family Production, 1983).

2. August 28, 1995, was Platt's reorganization announcement; September 5, 2006, was the SEC filing that revealed the pretexting incursion.

3. Paul Ely, interview by Raymond L. Price, December 15, 2005, 4.

4. Ely, interview, 5.

5. Rick Belluzzo, interview by Charles H. House, October 2, 2006, 4, 42.

6. Rick Belluzzo, personal communication with Raymond L. Price, August 29, 2008.

7. David Packard, speech, Fort Collins, Colorado, August 15, 1990; see Appendix C.

8. George Anders, *Perfect Enough: Carly Fiorina and the Reinvention of Hewlett-Packard*

(New York: Penguin Group, 2003), 43; Peter Burrows, *Backfire: Carly Fiorina's High-Stakes Battle for the Soul of HP* (New York: John Wiley & Sons, 2003), 120.

9. Martha Stewart had not yet been indicted for stock fraud, for which she went to jail.

10. Ned Barnholt, interview by Raymond L. Price, December 15, 2005, 21–22.

11. Michael Kanellos and David Becker, "PC Shipments Shrink; Dell Keeps Growing," news.cnet.com, reported growth rates of Dell for 2001 up +24 percent, while others had shrunk (Compaq by 9 percent , HP 5 percent, IBM 7 percent, NEC 12 percent). Worldwide shares for the year were Dell 13.3 percent, Compaq 11.1 percent, HP 7.2 percent, IBM 6.4 percent, NEC 3.8 percent.

12. "Dell bumped off Compaq in US market share by soaring 53% in unit sales to steal 16.8% of the overall US market to eclipse Compaq's 16.1%. Hewlett Packard showed even faster unit sales growth at 64% then [*sic]* Dell, increasing their market share from 7.3% in 1998 to 10.2% last year in US sales. For the whole planet: Compaq, still rules the earth in over-all sales but their lead is slipping, from 15.1% in 1998 to 13.7% market share in 1999. Dell [was] number two with a 10.5% market share, while IBM hung on to 8.2% for third place. Hewlett Packard holds fourth place with 6.7%." (Wes George, "The Mac Tide Is Rising, Threatening to Swamp IBM and Gateway Market Share," *The Mac Observer*, January 25, 2000, http://www.macobserver.com/news/00/january/000125/pcdata.shtml).

13. Debra Dunn, interview by Charles H. House and Raymond L. Price, September 28, 2006, 37, 46–47.

14. Bojana Fazarinc, personal communication with Charles H. House, August 20, 2007.

15. Fiorina noted that six female executives left not long after she did, "and no one thought the pattern was worth commenting on" (Carly Fiorina, *Tough Choices: A Memoir* (New York: Portfolio Books, 203): 222).

16. Dunn, interview, 50–51.

17. Lydia Lee and Mark Boslet, "The Honeymoon's Over for Carly," *The Industry Standard*, November 27, 2000, http://findarticles.com/p/articles/mi_m0HWW/is_49_3/ai_67502029.

18. Anders, *Perfect Enough*, 94; Burrows, *Backfire*, 168.

19. Anders, *Perfect Enough*, 119–120.

20. Stephen Shankland, "IBM Takes Over PwC Consulting," CNET News, July 31, 2002, http://news.zdnet.co.uk/itmanagement/0,1000000308,2120076,00.htm, quotes Jonathan Eunice; the stock swap calculations are based on HP closing prices of $62.63 and $13.57 on September 1, 2000, and July 17, 2002, respectively, the dates of the closed meeting agreements that PwC reached with each company. The IBM deal was 72 percent cash, but the HP deal was expected to be mostly stock.

21. "HP Re-iterates Guidance," http://money.cnn.com/2000/12/06/technology/hp/index.htm.

22. "Agilent Technologies Reports Q3 EPS of 33 Cents," Agilent Technologies, August 17, 2000, http://www.agilent.com/about/newsroom/presrel/2000/17aug2000a.html.

23. Burrows, *Backfire*, 171.

24. John Markoff, "Cisco Results Come In Short of Forecast," *New York Times*, February 7, 2001, C1, C4.

25. Victoria Shannon, "Rebound Not Near, Fiorina Says—A Bleak Outlook from HP Chief," *International Herald Tribune*, March 22, 2001, http://www.iht.com/articles/2001/03/22/

cebit_ed3_.php. For Specker's remarks, see Stephen Shankland, CNET News, June 7, 2001, "HP Gets Ready for Hard Times," http://news.zdnet.co.uk/itmanagement/0,1000000308,2088406,00.htm.

26. Jessica Hall, "Sun's McNealy Calls 2002 View Rough Estimate," *VAR Business*, May 10, 2001, http://www.crn.com/it-channel/18814729.

27. Elizabeth Montalbano, "Sun Meets Lowered 3Q Earnings Expectations: Executives Confident Despite Economic Slowdown," *CRN Business*, April 19, 2001, http://www.crn.com/it-channel/18823088.

28. William C. Taylor and Alan M. Webber, "Our Forecast: Pragmatic Optimism," *Fast Company* 48 (June 2001): 22.

29. Lew "sent a company plane to New Jersey and flew me to San Jose's airport, where [we] met in the hanger that housed the company fleet." Fiorina, *Tough Choices*, 151.

30. See separate accounts re: the luncheon with Hewlett in Anders, *Perfect Enough*, 71–72; Burrows, *Backfire*, 150, 156; and Fiorina, *Tough Choices*, 208–209.

31. Dunn, interview, 8.

32. Jocelyn Dong, "The Rise and Fall of the HP Way," *Palo Alto Weekly*, April 10, 2002, http://www.paloaltoonline.com/weekly/morgue/2002/2002_04_10.hpway10.html.

33. The old guard struggled with the new headquarters when Young constructed it. See passages in Michael S. Malone, *Bill and Dave: How Hewlett and Packard Built the World's Greatest Company* (New York: Portfolio Books, Penguin Group, 2007), 336–338.

34. According to some, there was a strong feeling that, over time, much progress could be made in printing and imaging, in that 95 percent of the world's printing is done in large-scale presses (*e.g.*, newspapers, *et al.*) that are unapproachable with the kinds of products that HP produced. But this was not a business held by one or two firms, but rather a very fragmented, piecemeal kind of industry that might take years to find the right solutions; Joel Birnbaum, personal communication with Charles H. House, August 14, 2008.

35. "Compaq Confident of Meeting Earnings Forecast," *Electronics Times*, January 29, 2001, http://findarticles.com/p/articles/mi_m0WVI/is_2001_Jan_29/ai_69841884.

36. Fiorina, *Tough Choices*, 240.

37. Andrew Grove, *Only the Paranoid Survive: How to Exploit the Crisis Points That Challenge Every Company* (New York: Doubleday, 1999); T. J. Rodgers, *No-Excuses Management: Proven Systems for Starting Fast, Growing Quickly, and Surviving Hard Times* (New York: Doubleday Business, 1993); Jack Welch and John A. Byrne, *Jack: Straight from the Gut* (New York: Business Plus, 2003); Larry Bossidy, Ram Charan, and Charles Burck, *Execution: The Discipline of Getting Things Done* (New York: Crown Business, 2002).

38. Pamela Mendels, "Downsizing Pay, Not People," *BusinessWeek*, April 18, 2001, http://www.businessweek.com/careers/content/apr2001/ca20010418_060.htm.

39. Rachel Konrad, "Layoffs Erode Support for the 'HP Way,'" CNET News, July 27, 2001, http://news.zdnet.co.uk/itmanagement/0,1000000308,2092078,00.htm.

40. Fiorina, *Tough Choices*, 237.

41. Innovation Awards 2003 citation from the Great Places to Work Institute: http://www.greatplacetowork.com/education/innovate/honoree-2003-agilent.php.

42. Webb McKinney, private correspondence with Charles H. House, June 3, 2008.

43. John Toppel, interview by Charles H. House, September 15, 2007.

44. Vicky Ward, "The Battle for Hewlett-Packard," *Vanity Fair* (June 2002): 180–185, 234–239.

45. Louis Lavelle, Frederick F. Jespersen, and Michael Arndt, "Executive Pay,"

BusinessWeek (April 15, 2002): 80–100, includes the fifty-second annual *BusinessWeek* Executive Compensation Scoreboard, compiled with Standard & Poor's EXECUCOMP.

46. Toppel, interview.

47. Sarah Lacy and Robert Mullins, "What Is the HP Way?" *Silicon Valley/San Jose Business Journal*, March 15, 2002, http://www.bizjournals.com/sanjose/stories/2002/03/18/story1.html.

48. This is treated in various books differently. Fiorina, *Tough Choices*, 240, says 23 percent; Anders, *Perfect Enough*, 137, says 19 percent; and Burrows, *Backfire*, 189, says 18 percent. The calculation using end-of-day numbers for August 31 and September 4, 2001 is 18.7 percent, from $23.21 on end of day Friday to $18.87 at end of day Tuesday (Monday was a holiday).

49. Burrows, *Backfire*, 137, 139.

50. Dunn, interview, 8.

51. Rosen took over briefly in 1991 and fired Rod Canion; he stepped in again in April 1999 when he fired Pfeiffer.

52. Ian Fried, "HP-Compaq Merger—Communication Is Key," CNET News, September 3, 2002, http://news.zdnet.co.uk/itmanagement/0,1000000308,2121654,00.htm.

53. It is worth comparing the two books rushed to print in the aftermath of the "food fight"—Anders (*Perfect Enough*) was sanctioned by HP and abetted by numerous interviews, whereas Burrows (*Backfire*) was barred from internal management interviews.

54. The ad labeled Hewlett "an academic and a musician." Put together by Allison Johnson and ad executive Steve Simpson, it "looked Carly." See Burrows, *Backfire*, 221.

55. Burrows, *Backfire*, 189–210; Anders, *Perfect Enough*, 158–159; and Fiorina, *Tough Choices*, 252–254.

56. Burrows, *Backfire*, 220.

57. Stanley Holmes and Mike France, "Boeing's Secret," *BusinessWeek* (May 20, 2002): 110–120, was an in-depth, cover-feature story about the travails at Boeing Aircraft.

58. Boeing placed a full-page ad extolling Platt's service and virtues, "Lew Platt: 1941–2005," *Wall Street Journal*, September 15, 2005, A17. HP ran a small press release that described Lew's service in one paragraph, and HP product offerings in the next three paragraphs. The SETI board was more generous, http://www.seti.org/page.aspx?pid=498.

59. Ward, "Battle for Hewlett-Packard," 180–185, 234–239.

60. Bill Terry, interview by Raymond L. Price, September 16, 2005, 10.

61. Ian Fried, "HP Declares Victory in Compaq Merger," CNET News, March 19, 2002, http://news.cnet.com/2100-1001-863432.html.

62. William Shiebler, personal communication with Charles H. House. See also Burrows, *Backfire*, 20–21, 232–237; and Anders, *Perfect Enough*, 183–186, 193–195. From March 18, 2002, until January 2007, Shiebler was CEO and later advisory vice chairman of Deutsche Asset Management Americas.

63. "The Securities and Exchange Commission today charged Deutsche Asset Management, Inc. (DeAM), the investment advisory unit of Deutsche Bank AG, for failing to disclose a material conflict of interest in its voting of client proxies for the 2002 merger between Hewlett-Packard Company (HP) and Compaq Computer Corporation. . . . The Commission's Order censures DeAM, directs it to cease and desist from further violations, and imposes a civil penalty of $750,000." *SEC News Digest*, http://www.sec.gov/news/digest/dig081903.txt.

64. Barnholt, personal communication with Charles H. House, January 30, 2007.

65. Tom Perkins, interview by Charles H. House and Raymond L. Price, March 24, 2006, 23.

66. Dick Alberding, interview by Charles H. House, September 19, 2006, 73. Ely, interview, 4. Bill Terry, interview by Charles H. House, September 28, 2006, 79. John Doyle, interview by Charles H. House, September 28, 2006, 47. Dean Morton, interview by Charles H. House and Raymond L. Price, November 17, 2005, 14–16.

67. John Young, interview by Raymond L. Price and Charles H. House, November 17, 2005.

68. Craig Samuel, interview by Charles H. House, September 13, 2006, 18–20.

69. Eric Hoffer, *The True Believer: Thoughts on the Nature of Mass Movements* (New York: Harper Modern Classics, 2002).

70. Mike Cassidy, "HP Messes Up by Unloading Worker Retreat," *San Jose Mercury News*, June 1, 2007, B1.

71. Packard was notoriously decisive. See Chapter 16, "Who Decides Who Decides?"

72. Barnholt, personal communication with Charles H. House, January 30, 2007.

73. Lacy and Mullins, "What Is the HP Way?"

74. www.top500.org.

CHAPTER 16

1. Title is from Donald N. Michael, "Who Decides Who Decides: Some Dilemmas and Other Hopes," Committee on Science and Technology, U.S. House of Representatives, March 1977, #24, US6PO, 803–831. Reprinted as an excerpt in *The Hastings Center Report* 7, 2 (1977): 23.

2. Alan Bickell, interview by Charles H. House, December 13, 2007. Bickell helped arrange the trip. In fact, just one board member took umbrage—about the size of the suite rather than bath facilities. The executive team had larger suites in order to conduct important state protocol business. Young was unable to placate the board member, and Packard took the offended man aside.

3. It is likely that Packard helped persuade Hewlett to retire, which would mean the board has changed the last four CEOs. Three of the four left in "normal retirement" circumstances.

4. Paul Ely, interview by Raymond L. Price, December 15, 2005, 26.

5. Carly Fiorina, *Tough Choices: A Memoir* (New York: Portfolio Books, 203), 153.

6. "HP-Compaq Merger—Communication Is Key," cnet.news.com.

7. "Before joining Compaq, Napier was the CIO for a number of other organisations, including . . . Lucent Technologies, where he first worked with Fiorina." Ian Fried, CNET News, "CIO Who Merged HP and Compaq Dies," http://news.zdnet.co.uk/itmanagement/0,1000000308,39117162,00.htm

8. Fiorina, *Tough Choices*, 264.

9. Even though the HP-Compaq deal was the largest in the computing sector, it was small compared to the ten largest mergers or acquisitions between 2000 and 2007.

10. Carly Fiorina, "Corporate Governance" (lecture, Kellogg School of Management, Northwestern University, Chicago, April 30, 2007, 9).

11. "Update 2-HP's PC Market Lead Grows; Dell Back to Growth-IDC," *Reuters*, October 17, 2007, http://www.reuters.com/article/marketsNews/idUKN1720967820071017?rpc=44.

12. Craig Samuel, interview by Charles H. House, September 13, 2006, 17–18.

13. Franz Nawratil, interview by Charles H. House, September 6, 2006, 1–2.

14. Rick Belluzzo, interview by Charles H. House, October 2, 2006, 3–6.

15. Samuel, interview, 29.

16. Nawratil, interview, 43–44; 46–47.

17. Tom Krazit, "FAQ: The HP 'Pretexting' Scandal," ZDNet News, September 6, 2006, http://news.zdnet.com/2100-9595_22-149452.html

18. Fred Vogelstein, "Carly Fiorina Tells Her Story," *Wired*, October 9, 2006, http://www.wired.com/science/discoveries/news/2006/10/71926.

19. Two Harvard classes of Francis Flynn (male) were given the Roizen case, written by Kathleen McGinn. See https://alumni.gsb.stanford.edu/women/issues/networking.html.

20. Chris O'Brien, "Was Sexism 'A Factor' in Firing of VMWare CEO?" *San Jose Mercury-News*, July 23, 2008, C1; Steve Johnson, "Chip Maker AMD's 10th Loss in a Row," *San Jose Mercury News*, April 22, 2009, C1.

21. Marguerite Wilbur, in Chris O'Brien blog, "Readers React: Was Sexism a Factor in Firing of VMware CEO?" SiliconBeat, July 28, 2008, http://blogs.mercurynews.com/obrien/2008/07/28/readers-react-was-sexism-a-factor-in-firing-of-vmware-ceo/#more-149.

22. "David Yermack, an associate professor at New York University's Stern School of Business, is credited with the earliest research on option-grant timing. A second study, by Professor Erik Lie at the University of Iowa and Randall Heron of Indiana University's business school, showed the patterns all but ceased after August 2002, when rules put in place by the Sarbanes-Oxley corporate-reform law [passed in 2002].

"Mercury [Interactive Corp] said it found 49 instances of misdating. Since 1996, insiders have sold about $250 million in stock. . . . The executives argued that 'they didn't focus on the fact that the practices . . . were improper'." Mark Maremont, "Authorities Probe Improper Backdating of Options," *Wall Street Journal*, November 11, 2005): A1, A4.

The Pulitzer Prize award is cited in James Shapiro, "Two Alums Win Pulitzer Prizes," *Brown Daily Herald*, April 7, 2007, http://media.www.browndailyherald.com/media/storage/paper472/news/2007/04/17/CampusNews/Two-Alums.Win.Pulitzer.Prizes-2846010.shtml.

"Reporters aren't known for writing algorithms, but one that The *Wall Street Journal*'s Charles Forelle devised helped trigger federal investigations of nearly 140 companies for massive and long-hidden fraud. Forelle, working with *Journal* colleagues James Bandler, Mark Maremont, and Steve Stecklow, used the statistical-modeling technique to find likely perpetrators of stock-options abuses. The *Journal* showed that options were often rigged, providing billions in extra pay for executives. In one case, the *Journal* determined that the odds of a chief executive's stock-option grants always being dated just before a rise in the stock price were one in 300 billion. As a result of the *Journal*'s inquiry, at least 70 top business executive lost their jobs." Charles Forelle and James Bandler, "The Perfect Payday—Some CEOs Reap Millions by Landing Stock Options When They Are Most Valuable: Luck—or Something Else?" *Wall Street Journal*, March 18, 2006, A1, A5.

23. Justin Scheck, "Options Morass Deepens at Wilson Sonsini," *The Recorder*, March 29, 2007, http://www.law.com/jsp/article.jsp?id=1175072645397.

24. Carly Fiorina, interview by Charles H. House, June 5, 2007; "Mercury Interactive (HP) to Pay $28 Million to Settle Stock Option Backdating—4 Former Execs Still Dangling However," June 24, 2007, Ethisphere, http://ethisphere.com/mercury-interactive-hp-to-pay-28-million-to-settle-stock-option-backdating-4-former-execs-still-dangling-however; Clint Boulton, "SEC Settles Backdating Cases with Mercury, Brocade," May 31, 2007, internetnews.com, http://www.internetnews.com/bus-news/article.php/3680771.

25. Sandy Kurtzig, *CEO: Building a $400 Million Company from the Ground Up* (Boston: Harvard Business Press, 1994).

26. Ken Fox, interview by Raymond L. Price, November 11, 2004, 10–11.

27. Sally Dudley, interview with Raymond L. Price, September 14, 2005, 14.

28. Ashlee Vance, "HP's Hurd Lets Us Pretend Compaq Never Happened," *The Register*, March 30, 2005, http://www.theregister.co.uk/2005/03/30/hp_hurd_first.

29. Lauren McSherry, "Impact of HP Layoffs on Area's Workers Unclear," *Los Altos Town Crier*, August 3, 2005, https://latc.com/2005/08/03/news/news5.print.html.

30. Quentin Hardy, "The UnCarly," *Forbes* 79, 5 (March 12, 2007): 82–90.

31. Hardy, "The UnCarly," 88 (cites Robert Samson, sales VP at IBM Corporate Hardware).

32. Neoview was developed at HP as an answer to Teradata's successful high-performance data warehousing capability, which Hurd ran for years; Therese Poletti, "HP's Neoview Debuts Today," *San Jose Mercury News*, April 24, 2007, 2C; Chris Mellor, "HP's Neoview Stealth Data Warehouse," Techworld, March 26, 2007, http://www.techworld.com/storage/news/index.cfm?newsID=8367.

33. Anne Fisher, "America's Most Admired Companies," *Fortune* 155, 5 (March 19, 2007): 88–94, 115–122. See also the detail in www.fortune.com/mostadmired. IBM was 1st in 1983–1986, 7th in 1987, and 10th in 2004.

34. Pancorbo "provided technical support to large corporations who bought the high end of the HP 9000 product line (K-class, V-class, XP disc arrays)." Fernando Gomez Pancorbo, private correspondence with the authors, September 19, 2007.

35. Cindy Hosszu, post to the HP Alumni Association, September 19, 2007, in response to a similar lament by Mary Szvetecz.

36. "Open Line," *HP Measure* (March-April 1981).

37. Lew Platt, "Letter from Lew Platt," *HP Measure* (March-April 1993): 26–27.

38. Paul Ely, interview with Raymond L. Price, December 15, 2005, 11.

39. Reported in George Anders, *Perfect Enough: Carly Fiorina and the Reinvention of Hewlett-Packard* (New York: Portfolio Books, Penguin Group, 2003), 80–82.

40. Thomas Friedman, *The World Is Flat: A Brief History of the Twenty-First Century* (New York: Farrar, Straus and Giroux, 2005), 166, 188. See also Katherine M. Chudoba, Eleanor Wynn, Mei Lu, and Mary B. Watson-Manheim, "How Virtual Are We? Measuring Virtuality and Understanding Its Impact in a Global Organization," *Information Systems Journal* 15 (October 4, 2005): 279–306.

41. Friedman, *The World Is Flat*, 166–167.

42. Dean Takahashi, "Technology Closes Gaps to Talk Better Face to Faces," *San Jose Mercury News*, September 17, 2007, C1.

43. Bruce Piasecki, *World Inc.* (Naperville, IL: Sourcebooks, 2007), 140.

44. Piasecki, *World Inc.*, 127.

45. "Pollution," *HP Measure* (February 1967): 8–9. A report led by researcher Lidia Morawska, "at the Queensland University of Technology in Australia [using Agilent Technologies equipment], classified 17 out of 62 printers as 'high particle emitters' because of the amount of toner released in the air. . . . The study, published last week online in the American Chemical Society's Environmental Science and Technology [said] the inhalation of ultra-fine particles can affect human health depending on the material inhaled and the quantity." "Particle Emissions from Laser Printers Might Pose Health Concern," August 2, 2007, http://www.sciencedaily.com /releases/2007/07/070731103629.htm. HP and Morawska

agreed that more research was needed, especially on factors that affected levels, such as printer or cartridge model and age.

46. "The Inner Space Invaders," *HP Measure* (November 1967): 11–13.

47. The air pollution and emphysema issues, plotted on an HP 9100A, were reported by Charles H. House (report, Colorado Air Pollution Control Commission, Federal hearings Durango, Colorado, January 1972). Graphs that enabled the pinpointing of colon cancer from an unusual buildup of iodine (from shrimp) and strontium (from cattle grazing on northern grasses) were developed by Eric Carlson (ex-CEO of ASK Computer, now at Science/Technology and Society Program at University of Santa Clara) and others under NIH grants; published in Edward Tufte, *The Visual Display of Quantitative Data*, 2nd edition (Cheshire, CT: Graphics Press, 2001), 17–19.

48. "Golden Treasure of the Trash Barrel," *HP Measure* (January 1975): 2–5.

49. Kevin O'Connor, "HP and the Environment: A User's Guide," *HP Measure* (March-April 1990), 13–20.

50. Charles H. House (and the R&D team), personal communication, May 1987, at Waldbronn Division. This was the same tool that caught Ben Johnson in the 1988 Olympics; see Chapter 4.

51. http://en.wikipedia.org/wiki/Philip_Don_Estridge; http://en.wikipedia.org/wiki/Microburst.

52. Bill Hewlett, "From the President's Desk," *HP Measure* (January 1974): 15; see also "2001—The New Ice Age?" *HP Measure* (January 1974): 2–6.

53. Charles (Bud) Eldon (1985), along with Barney Oliver (1965), served as IEEE president. Bill Hewlett (1954) and Dean Fred Terman (1941) had served as IRE presidents prior to the IEEE formation from IRE and AIEE. John Meredith, Agilent Technologies, served as IEEE-USA president (2007). Charles House served as ACM president 1996–1998. Today, Agilent Technologies and HP together have only two members in the much larger National Academies.

54. Mary A. Easley, "It All Started with a $5 Donation," *HP Measure* (November-December 1990): 13–17.

55. Michael S. Malone, *Bill and Dave: How Hewlett and Packard Built the World's Greatest Company* (New York: Portfolio Books, Penguin Group, 2007), 293.

56. Debra Dunn and Keith Yamashita, "Microcapitalism and the Megacorporation," *Harvard Business Review* (August 1, 2003): 46–57.

57. Friedman, *The World Is Flat.* See also Jeremy Moon, Andrew Crane, and Dirk Matten, "Can Corporations Be Citizens? Corporate Citizenship as a Metaphor for Business Participation in Society (2nd Edition)," *Business Ethics Quarterly* 15, 3 (July 2005): 429–453. See also Vidhi A. Chaudhri, "Organising Global CSR: A Case Study of Hewlett-Packard's e-inclusion Initiative," *JCC Journal* (Autumn 2006): 39–51.

58. Malone, *Bill and Dave*, 364.

59. Carly Fiorina, keynote address, 2003 ITU Telecom World, Geneva, Switzerland, October 12, 2003,. See http://www.hp.com/hpinfo/execteam/speeches/fiorina/telecom2003.html.

60. Joel Birnbaum, interview by Raymond L. Price, December 15, 2005, 74–75.

61. "This isn't the first time that H-P has licensed its inkjet technology for medical uses—its technology also is used for inhalers and for applying coatings for medical implants. If H-P's idea holds up, 1-inch-square patches containing hundreds of microneedles controlled by a microprocessor could . . . painlessly deliver doses of insulin to diabetics or cocktails

of multiple drugs to heart patients or AIDS sufferers." Bob Keefe, "HP Techology to Help Deliver Medications," Cox News, September 12, 2007, coxnews.com.

62. P&G, a major participant at the Imperial College Virtual Cave (London), described their activities in a variety of collaboration and innovation seminars during 2006.

63. Paula Musich, "HP, Proctor and Gamble Sign $3 Billion Deal," eWeek.com, April 11, 2003, http://www.eweek.com/article2/0,1895,1654530,00.asp.

64. "HP Finalizes $3 Billion Outsourcing Agreement to Manage Procter & Gamble's IT Infrastructure," HP Press Release, May 6, 2003, http://www.hp.com/hpinfo/newsroom/press/2003/030506d.html.

65. Nina Bhatti, interview by Charles H. House, September 12, 2006, 14–18.

66. Exemplars are women who have already been evaluated to calibrate the system.

67. Bhatti, interview, 22–25.

68. Shane Robison, interview by Robert Burgelman and Webb McKinney, December 2006, described to the authors on December 11, 2006, and February 21, 2007. See also Shane Robison, keynote lecture, Software 2005, Santa Clara, California, April 27, 2005.

69. "HP Names Dean of University of Illinois at Chicago, Prith Banerjee, as Director of HP Labs. Banerjee will report to Shane Robison, executive vice president and chief strategy and technology officer. He replaces Richard H. Lampman, who is retiring after 35 years at HP, including 25 years in HP Labs." *HP Press Release*, May 2, 2007.

70. Aaron Ricadela, "HP Labs' Latest Experiment: Itself," *BusinessWeek* (April 17, 2008): 72.

71. Stacy Cowley, "HP CEO: We Have More Cutting to Do," ChannelWeb, December 12, 2006, http://www.crn.com/sections/breakingnews/dailyarchives.jhtml?articleId=196603340.

72. This coincidentally was the same day that Mark Hurd and Pattie Dunn met with Congress for information about the pretexting issue. See also multiple articles in the *Wall Street Journal*, September 29, 2006, B1-2, B6.

73. Anil Desai, personal communication with Charles H. House, January 5, 2007.

74. http://www.voodoopc.com/#/history. Subsumed into HP historical archives one year after purchase.

75. Paul Campbell, interview by Charles H. House, January 5, 2007.

76. HP Real Life Technologies, http://h50016.www5.hp.com/reallife_adaptive.asp.

77. In 2008, Kitson is vice president of applications research at Motorola after a twenty-year career at HP Labs. See http://www.motorola.com/content.jsp?globalObjectId=6661-9277.

78. Leslie Katz, "EDS Chief Executive Ron Rittenmeyer to retire," *Business Tech*, CNET News, December 6, 2008.

79. ACM '97 Text and Videos available at http://research.microsoft.com/ACM97/. Charles House was ACM president from July 1996 through June 1998.

80. Mark Hurd and Lars Nyberg, *The Value Factor: How Global Leaders Use Information for Growth and Competitive Advantage* (Princeton, NJ: Bloomberg Press, 2004), 25, 28.

81. Hardy, "The UnCarly," 82–90.

82. Stephen Baker, "Google and the Wisdom of Clouds," *BusinessWeek* (December 24, 2007): 48–55; Nicholas Carr, "Rains on Cloud Computing," *Wired* (January 2008): 42.

83. Zvonko Fazarinc, "Secret Sauce of Innovation," lecture, Stanford University, April 9, 2008.

84. Deborah Gage, "Particle Could Revolutionize Computers," *San Francisco Chronicle*, May 1, 2008, C1.

85. Neerja Raman, private correspondence with Neil Jacobstein, May 4, 2008.

86. Jena McGregor, "The World's Most Innovative Companies," *BusinessWeek* (April 28, 2008): 60–63.

87. Neil Jacobstein, personal communication with Charles H. House, July 9, 2008.

88. Matt Nauman, "HP to Vacate 9 Buildings in Palo Alto and Cupertino," *San Jose Mercury News*, March 20, 2008, 2C.

89. Marjorie Mader, "Ellison Wins Lower Taxes on Woodside Estate," *The Almanac* 43, 30 (March 26, 2008): 5, 8. The insult to community continued: *The San Jose Mercury News* reported on August 21, 2008, that Ellison's 2008 paycheck was a whopping $84.6 million in direct wages, plus $544 million more in stock option exercises—and an estimated $25 billion net worth. The tax saving of $3.04 million per year that he garnered on local property taxes occurred as California became the fiftieth-ranked state in America for funding per school child; Michele Liedtke, "Ellison's Payday: $84.6 million," *San Jose Mercury-News*, August 21, 2008, 3C.

90. Paul Rogers, "Massive Ranch Will Be Preserved," *San Jose Mercury News*, January 20, 2008, 1A, 8A.

91. Three letters in Lucile's Scrapbook, Los Altos Museum exhibit, January-June 2008.

EPILOGUE

1. Timothy Prickett Morgan, editor, "HP Firing on All Cylinders in the Fiscal First Quarter," *Linux Beacon*, February 26, 2008, http://www.itjungle.com/tlb/tlb022608-story04.html.

2. Ben Worthen, "Tech Giants Help Clients Tap Stimulus Funds," *Wall Street Journal*, April 7, 2009, B1.

3. Thomas Whitney, Francé Rodé, and Chung Tung, "The Powerful Pocketful," *HP Journal* 23, 10 (July 1972): 2–9.

4. Notes by attendee Chuck House.

5. Paul Ely, interview by Raymond L. Price, December 15, 2005, 73; Carly Fiorina, *Tough Choices: A Memoir* (New York: Portfolio Books, 203), 305.

6. Adam Lashinsky, "The Hurd Way," *Fortune* 153, 7 (April 17, 2006): 92–102.

APPENDIX B

1. Cort Van Rensselaer, private correspondence with Charles H. House, December 6, 2004. Van Rensselaer is one of four living attendees.

APPENDIX C

1. Charles H. House, notes from meeting, Santa Clara, California, February 11, 1974, and presentation, Colorado Springs, Colorado, February 25, 1974.

2. Charles H. House, notes from General Managers' Meeting, Monterey, California, January 24, 1989. Shared at the *Global Business Network Forum*, March 28, 1996, and with the website re: Packard Encomium for *Upside Magazine*, March 28, 1996.

3. Charles H. House, notes from speech, Fort Collins, Colorado, August 15, 1990. No official record or written transcript of this speech exists. A videotape of a subsequent (much more circumspect) speech at HP Loveland the same afternoon has been provided by GM Bill Tippett to the authors.

APPENDIX D

1. From Lewis E. Platt, Sheffield Fellowship Lecture, "Managing Innovation: An Oxymoron?" Yale University, February 28, 1997, http://www.eng.yale.edu/sheff/platt/platt-remarks.html.

ACKNOWLEDGMENTS

1. William G. Ouchi, *Theory Z: How American Business Can Meet the Japanese Challenge* (Menlo Park, CA: Addison-Wesley, 1981). HP and GE maintained a knowledge-sharing arrangement for many years.

2. Thomas J. Peters and Robert H. Waterman, *In Search of Excellence: Lessons from America's Best-run Companies* (London: HarperCollins, 1995); James C. Collins and Jerry I. Porras, *Built to Last: Successful Habits of Visionary Companies* (New York: HarperCollins, 1994); and Richard Foster and Sarah Kaplan, *Creative Destruction: Why Companies That Are Built to Last Underperform the Market—and How to Successfully Transform Them* (New York: Broadway Business, 2001).

3. Al Bagley, private correspondence with Charles H. House, October 9, 2003.

4. Joan Didion, personal communication with Charles H. House, May 2004.

5. We gathered far more material than we were able to use; selection has been difficult and often arbitrary. We apologize to all who find that their efforts are not adequately reflected herein; many times the mutually reinforcing aspects of several interviewees were critical to be able to include the segment, even though it was impractical to name all who contributed insight to each topic. In places the parallel path of a competitor is traced for a period because of the importance of that segment to HP's evolution. Inclusions for other companies have been corroborated through annual reports and corporate histories.

6. www.computerhistory.org.

7. In addition to David G. Hicks's Museum of HP Calculators, www.hpmuseum.org, see Steve Leibson's site, www.hp9825.com, and the Australian-based HP Computer Museum (1966–1991) at www.hpmuseum.net, created by Jon Johnston. See also Stefan Graef, The Museum of T&M Instruments, www.messmuseum.de.

8. Long-term HPite Marc Mislanghe, who resides near Biarritz, France, has collected and restored more than five hundred pieces of equipment, plus countless documents, pictures, and other artifacts. Fervent engineer Kenneth Kuhn, in Birmingham, Alabama, has also rescued and refurbished several hundred pieces of equipment. See www.kennethkuhn.com/hpmuseum/ for the American hobbyist; the French collector's website is www.hpmemory.org.

9. Robb's invaluable archival trove is at http://www.hparchive.com/about_glenn_robb.htm. None of these sites are official HP or Agilent sites; all have working agreements with HP and Agilent archivists.

10. Leslie Berlin, *The Man Behind the Microchip: Robert Noyce and the Invention of Silicon Valley* (London: Oxford Press, 2005); C. Stewart Gillmor, *Fred Terman at Stanford: Building a Discipline, a University, and Silicon Valley* (Palo Alto, CA: Stanford University Press, 2004); Christophe Lécuyer, Making Silicon Valley: Innovation and the Growth of High Tech, 1930–1970 (Cambridge, MA: MIT Press, 2007). Perhaps most surprising is that the fine history by Martin Campbell-Kelly and William Aspray, *Computer: A History of the Information Machine* (New York: Basic Books, 1999), fails to cite HP contributions at all.

HP/Agilent Name Index

This index includes employees of HP and/or Agilent, including those who have done work elsewhere if described herein, and members of the Board of Directors and founders/CEOs of acquired companies. Photographs are indicated by italicized page numbers.

HP/Agilent Specific Topics Index

Includes acquired companies and products, if bought directly (for example, Compaq is included here, but DEC and Tandem are found in the general index because they were competitors throughout their independent corporation history). Products that are pictured are indicated by *italicized* page numbers.

HP PRODUCTS BY NUMBER

HP HANDHELD CALCULATORS

HP DESKTOP CALCULATORS AND COMPUTERS

HP COMPUTERS

HP INSTRUMENTS

HP PERIPHERALS

General Index

Photographs are indicated by italicized page numbers.